WELCOME TO NORMANDY

Main Author :
GÉRARD ROGER
In collaboration with
VÉRONIQUE SIEPKA, SERGE SOCHON and JEAN-LUC GAZAN

Translation :
K.R.T. CONSEIL
F-61250 - Saint-Cénéri-le-Gérei

Proof-Reading :
DANIELLE BORRETT
St. Johns Hill
Wareham, Dorset
amberwood@aic.co.uk

ALAIN GUICHARD

Cover photo :
PHOTO GILLES BEAUGRAND
"OBJECTIF PHOTO"
Vimoutiers/Saint-Pierre-sur-Dives

Publisher :
ÉDITIONS BERTOUT
"LA MÉMOIRE NORMANDE"
BP 7 - 76810 Luneray - France

THANKS

The Editions Bertout would like to thank the following for their helpful assistance :

- The Regional Council of Lower Normandy
- The 'Conseil Général de l'Orne'
- The Regional Committee of Tourism of Normandy
- The Committee of Tourism of Manche
- The Tourist Offices of Normandy
- The Regional Federation of the 'Logis de France' of Normandy
- The I.R.Q.U.A. of Normandy
- Brittany Ferries
- Daniel Goulet and Michel Greusard.
- Olivier Guichard
- The 'Cité de la Mer'

ISBN 2-86743-479-3

© Gérard ROGER
© Editions BERTOUT, "La Mémoire Normande"
6, rue Gutenberg - 76810 Luneray - France
www.editionsbertout.com
SIRET 418 961 298 00019

INDEX

IV - NORMAN ART

V - TRADITIONAL NORMANDY

VI - AGRICULTURE, CRAFTSMANSHIP AND INDUSTRY

VII - MARITIME TRADITION

VIII - NORMAN GASTRONOMY

IX - THE UNUSUAL AND SECRET NORMANDY

X - NORMANDY AND THE HORSE

XI - HAVE FUN IN NORMANDY

XII - SPORT AND LEISURE IN NORMANDY

XIII - SHOPPING IN NORMANDY

XIV - GITES AND ACCOMMODATION

PREFACE

Open towards both the British and Nordic worlds and to Southern Europe, Normandy is at the heart of the Atlantic Arc, going from Scotland to Spain linking together those regions of the west side of our continent.

To reinforce this vocation of European crossroads, the 'Calais-Bayonne Axis' was created in 1969.

This project had a triple objective :

*- **Inter-regional** to regroup regions linked together historically and economically.*

*- **National** in order to ease the North-South traffic by avoiding Paris.*

*- **International** linking together Northern and Southern Europe, giving it the name as always of 'The English road'.*

When the association was created in 1970, its Founder President Louis Terrenoire had anticipated History imagining that before the end of the century :

- Spain and Portugal would become democracies and would join the European concert.

- Great Britain would join the Common 'Market'.

- The Tunnel under the Channel would be built.

Today, one can see how right his predictions were.

For the last 30 years the association of the 'Calais-Bayonne Axis' made up of members of parliament, Regional Councils, General

Councils, towns, Chambers of Commerce, Chambers of Agriculture, from the territories crossed by it, have fought for the realisation of a motorway linking the Belgian frontier to that of Spain.

To this day the only breaks in this axis are made up by the 120 km of 'Trou Normand' situated between Rouen and Alençon and by the section 'Ecommoy-Tours'.

The association together with very wide popular support is waiting for the beginning of the construction and the opening in 2005.

The opening of the tunnel under the Channel and the integration of Spain and Portugal into the CEE have contributed from the 1980's in increasing the European function of the Calais-Bayonne Axis and very naturally asked the question about its extension North and South.

With the collaboration of the 'Fédération Routière Internationale' in Geneva, the association organised a large seminar in 1989 in Bordeaux intended to define the contents of a great transcontinental axis. : because of the North-South Atlantic axis going from Oslo to Gibraltar, the rôle of 'backbone' for the Calais-Bayonne axis was thus strengthened.

As in the XIIth century, at a time, at the heart of the Plantagenet Empire, it was closely associated under the same crown with England, the Loire country, Aquitaine. I am convinced that Normandy will find once more, in the European crossroads, the radiance and influence which it has had over the centuries.

DANIEL GOULET

Senator of Orne
First vice-President of the Regional Council of Lower Normandy
President of the 'Calais-Bayonne Axis'

I - THE NORMANDY
OF OUR ANCESTORS

1 - Normandy before the Duchy

Do you know, dear visitors from Great Britain, that we have known each other for more than two millenia ? We have in reality the same origins and come from the same Nordic stock.

Our story begins even before the arrival on your island of the **Angles** and **Saxons**.

Thus more than two thousand years ago the inhabitants of what would become England, the **Bretons**, traded with *'those opposite'*, the future **Neustriens,** who established themselves in the region that would become Normandy.

They bought tin from Cornwall to make bronze pots, utensils, weapons.

The arrival of the Angles and Saxons simply changed the individuals but not the commercial flow…

These *'commercial relationships'* continued to the time of the Gauls. The different tribes peopling the future Normandy, the **'Calettes'** (who gave their name to the 'Pays de Caux'), the **Aulerques**, **Eburosices**, **Lexoviens**, the **Véliocrasses**, the **Viducasses** and others **Bajocasses**, **Esuviens** and **Unelles** kept these contacts whilst not being able to work with you to hold back the invading Romans, whose presence, on the positive side, improved the organisation of the territory of Gaul. It would be more difficult for them to apply the same authority to you ! Nevertheless this civilisation has left traces on both sides of the Channel, more important, however, on this side with the administrative system, the development of transport links (Roman roads) and the creation of large, essentially agricultural, centres (villae).

From the 3rd century, the Roman Empire suffered the shock of repeated invasions. On the Channel, commercial ships appeared with small groups wanting to establish themselves on our shores : these were the **Frisians** and **Saxons**.

In England, but also in the region of *Bayeux* in Neustrie and in Gaul, invaders came in successive waves. The **Francs** imposed their political system, in fact that meant conserving the gallo-roman system, they installed courageous leaders as heads of the 'villae'. After three centuries of rule the royal family of the merovingian grew weaker and gave way to a new family from 'Maires du Palais'', the Carolingians. They undertook the construction of a veritable empire stretching from the Atlantic coasts to the *Elbe* in the east and from *Denmark* in the north to the borders of *Spain* in the south, stopping completely the advance of the Arabs. Curiously, the Emperor **Charlemagne** did not interest himself with England, preferring above all to consolidate his *'continental empire'*. In spite of this he caused concern with his successive pushes worrying the neighbours to the north, the **Scandinavians.** Many of

9

them knew the Caroligian Empire through various exchanges and business. They could see the strengths but also the weaknesses. The Empire had a redoubtable army but for interior peace the administration had '*demilitarised*'. The society composed three groups : the clergy, the nobility and the peasants. The region is scattered with towns and villages where one finds many monasteries, veritable economic centres of the period.

5 June 793 ! A bolt from the blue !

Places to visit...

AREA OF MANCHE

Anneville-en-Saire : **A foundry of Celtic objects**, discovered in 1821.

Le Grand-Celland : **Megalithic remains** at 'La Pilière'.

Isigny-le-Buat : **Oak mistletoe carrier** (very rare).

Le Petit-Celland : **Menhir** of the devil's rock.

Montchaton : **Caesar's camp.**

Montebourg : **'Mont Castre' Oppidum roman** - 'La Musaresse' - Superb view of the Cotentin, height 118 metres.

Mortain : **Irish eucharistic casket** from the 7th century with runic inscriptions.

Port-Bail : **Gallo roman baptistry** from the 4th century (hexagonal). The harbour was, since ancient times, a stop on the **'Pewter or Tin Route'**.

Saint-James : **Megalithic polishing stone of Saint-Benoît** dating from 4000 B.C. It lies in the remains of an ancient gallic camp called Beuvron.

Gallic camp and megalithic stone. At the entrance to Saint-James, when coming from Avranches, is found, at Saint-Benoît, the vestiges of an ancient gallic camp called 'Beuvron'. One can see an exceptional megalithic stone (a polishing stone).

Saint-Mère-Eglise : **'Miliare' marker stone** in the church square, vestiges of the Roman era. The markers point out the route to 'Alauna' (Valognes) at 'Crociana-tum' (Saint-Côme-du-Mont). The 'miliares' were placed every thousand paces and indicated the distance from Rome.

Viereville : **Neolithic tumulus** : cemetery from before the merovingian era. Mound with dolmen (parcelle A 114). Habitation structures dating from the 3rd millenium B.C.

AREA OF CALVADOS

Caen : **'Two billion years in Normandy'.**

Under the category of tourist visits 'to discover the environment', the company 'Lithosphère', proposes to plunge you back into an era when Normandy was populated by dinosaurs.

Contact : SARL Lithosphère, 7, rue Alfred-Kastler, 14000 Caen.

Tel (33) 2 31 93 25 95.

Lion-sur-Mer : House of fossils.

2, place des Victimes du 2 juillet 1944, (opposite the church).
Tel (33) 2 31 96 88 00.
Open to the public : In May and October every day except Tuesday from 2-6 pm.
From June to September every day except Tuesday from 10 am-12 noon and 2-6 pm. Out of season open weekends and school holidays from 14h to 18h except Tuesdays.
Important collection of fossils from Normandy and the main sites in Calvados (150 square metres of exhibition). Under sea Normandy from the Jurassic to the Cretaceous period. Instructional documents, shop and library.

Lisieux : Archeological remains.

During the construction of the boiler room for Lisieux General Hospital in 1962 they fortuitously discovered vestiges of an ancient gallo-roman quarter from the ancient Noviomagus Lexoviorum. The excavations, undertaken from 1978 to 1984, have brought to light some of the most beautiful wall paintings from the whole of northern Gaul, which include a head of Christ and an interesting design of fish done at the end of the 1st century A.D.
Called the 'Square des Thermes' the site has been developed by the town of Lisieux. The paintings have been restored and are now displayed in the 'Musée du Vieux Lisieux'.
An important Roman Way has also been opened up in the centre of Lisieux, the rue Pont-Mortain.

Saint-Aubin-sur-Mer : A gallo-roman statue.

A gallo-roman statue representing the Holy Mother was found in 1943 by a German officer studying architecture. He also discovered a gallo-roman villa and a well. A copy of the statue can be found in the Tourist office.

Saint-Germain-de-Tallevende : Dolmen of Mount Savarin.

In the place called 'La Lande Vaumont' you can see a dolmen in 'Bleu de Vire' which displays originality and stands on only three of its four supports.
A fifth stone situated in front of the hall certainly came from the same site. You can reach this dolmen by the regional road RD 577 and then by the RD 282 in the direction of 'La Lande Vaumont'.

Vieux : Vestiges of the Roman era.

In this little community to the south of Caen you will find the archaeological garden of Bas de Vieux which includes numerous remains from the Roman era including a house dating from the second half of the 2nd century.
For information Tel (33) 2 31 71 10 20.
Open to the public from January to June from 9 am to 5 pm (the saturday = from 10 am to 8 pm,) Entry 3s,

Ver-sur-Mer : The beach where Saint Gerbold, coming from England, disembarked in the 7th century. He would become Bishop of Bayeux.

Archaeological sites with traces of habitation from various eras, including neolithic, chalcolithique and gallo roman.

Villers-sur-Mer : Association of Paleontology (Free entry).
8, rue Boulard - Tel (33) 2 31 87 19 00.

AREA OF ORNE

L'Aigle : **'Musée d'Archéologie'.**
Place Fulbert de Beina.
Regional prehistoric objects.
Free entry. Tel (33) 2 33 24 12 40, Fax (33) 2 33 34 23 77.
Open all year from Monday to Saturday from 9.30 am-12 noon and 2-6 pm.
Closed Sundays and public holidays.

Antoigny : (in the Forest of Andaine).
Remains of Roman baths.

Bailleul : (near Argentan).
Menhir : 'La pierre au pas de bœuf'.

Bellême : **Gallo/Roman Fountain of the portcullis.**
Beside the road which crosses the forest and leads to Mortagne.
Bellême takes its name from 'Belisama', gallic goddess whose name means the most beautiful. The place of the portcullis is a mythical site in Perche. It was developed around a ferruginous spring known since ancient times. Rediscovered in 1770, the real fountain is made up of 6 stones, two of which carry Latin inscriptions which can be traced to Roman gods and goddesses : Venus, Mercury, Mars and Aphrodite. Numerous legends are linked to this site.

Boissy-Maugis : **'La Grosse Pierre'.**
Dolmen of the neolithic period in the woods of Saint-Laurent.

Céaucé : **Menhir** in the place called **'The Great Stone'.**

Chennedouit : **Dolmen** called the **'Fairies table'** which dates from 3,500 years B.C.

Craménil : **Menhir - Roman bridges** including the **'Pont de La Motte'.**

Echauffour : **Three menhirs** called **'Les Crouttes'**, in the hamlet of Fumecon.

Exmes : **Ancient Roman Camp.**
In the 'Gallic Wars' Julius Caesar makes mention of a tribe of Gauls, called the Esuviens, living in this place. Once the 'pax romana' was imposed on the region, the Romans installed themselves on the site and created an important military and administrative post. Exmes controlled the communications of the major part of Armorica and the north and east of Gaul. It is difficult to imagine today that this little town was an important cross roads. One can still see the last remnants of the powerful fortress on the highest point of the city.

La Ferté-Fresnel : **Dolmen** at the place called **'Le Bocage'.**

Fontaine-les-Basset : **Dolmen** of the **'Pierre aux Verres'.**
The name of this village is taken from the presence of an ancient fountain whose water had magic powers. The Gauls of the region gathered around the fountain. A dolmen called the 'Pierre aux Verres' was put up near the fountain (a small

rectangular megalith resting on a block of sandstone). The Romans would build at this site an important city of which remains can still be found.

Giel-Courteilles : **Menhir of 'la longue Roche'.**

Near the river, a block of sandstone 3 metres high. About a hundred metres from the bridge.

Glos-la-Ferrière : **Menhir** at the place called **'Le Boulay'.**

Habloville : **'Dolmen des Bignes'.**

Neolithic site. A vast granite table about 3 metres long supported by 6 stones. This dolmen was part of a group of 3 mounds forming a triangle. The third is still visible.

Joué-du-Bois : **Dolmen** called 'La Pierre aux Loups'.

Juvigny-sous-Andaines : **Megalith** at the place called **'La Ligne de faite'.**

La Cambe : **Ancient Roman camp called 'De César'.**

La Carneille : **Small menhir 'christianised'.**

La Lande-de-Goult : **Vestiges of a Roman camp.**

La Lande-Patry : **Thousand year old yew trees.**

In the parish cemetery of this community, close to Flers, are found two very ancient yews. The first dates from the 5th century and has a circumference of 10.8 metres. The 'younger' would have been planted in the 8th century and has a circumference of 8.6 metres. It is said that the hollow trunk of the older tree was used in the 19th century as a barbers shop. This service was offered before mass. These trees were perhaps witnesses to the coming of Harold of England to the parish in 1064 when he was welcomed by William Patry.

La Lande-Saint-Simon : **Menhir called 'Pierre à la Demoiselle'.**

Loré : **Roman ford.**

Méri : **Celtic camp of 'Bierre' (9th century B.C.).**

The camp of Bierre, also called Caesar's Camp, is one of the rare primitive defensive camps in western France and has still not given up all its secrets. It is situated on a natural promontory of sandstone and surrounded by deep ditches. It overlooks the Valley of the 'Dives'. One can find in the 'poultry yard' varieties of plants unique in Normandy.

Montabard : **Ancient Roman camp called 'de César'.**

Passais-la-Conception : **Menhir du Perron.**

Raised stone situated near to the village of the 'oak of the fairies' and a covered walkway of the 'Table au Diable'.

Rânes : **Prehistoric museum** (in the castle). Tel (33) 2 33 39 72 94.

Lithic material - Jean-Jacques **Rivard**, retired teacher, President of the Friends of Prehistory in Orne has gathered in this place a rich collection of utensils dating from the early to middle Palaeolithic period. (Between 50,000 and 200,000 years B.C.) The majority were discovered in Rânes during drainage work in 1968. This exceptional collection (scrapers, knives, bifaces) helps to prove that the site at

Rânes was, long before our time, populated by an organised and industrious community, who, using the materials offered to them by their surroundings, created in this place the first form of industry in western Normandy ; possibly supplying the nearby communities with utensils.

Avernes-Saint-Gourgon : **The oldest church in Normandy !**
Here for a long time, the parish of Saint-Cyr-d'Estrancourt, was attached to that of Avernes. There remains, in the middle of a field, a primitive church which shows the first signs of Christianity in Normandy.

Saint-Céronne-la-Mortagne : **Ancient Gallo-Roman city.**

Sainte-Eugénie : **Ancient Roman Camp called 'de César'.**

Saint-Evroult-Notre-Dame-du-Bois : **Ancient Roman camp.**

Le Sap : **Ancient centre of Druidic culture.**
The druids venerated the pine in this place, a rare tree in the huge forest of Auge, although it covers much of the country otherwise. On the edge of the road leading to *Monnai :* a **'Pierre aux Sacrifices' (very rare !).**

Saint-Cyr-la-Rosière : **'La Pierre Procureuse'.**
Dolmen from the neolithic period with an explanatory panel.

Saint-Jean-des-Bois : **Gallic bridge over the Egrenne.**

Saint-Sulpice-sur-Risle : **'Dolmen du Jarrie'.**

Silly-en-Gouffern : **Menhir of the 'Pierre levée' or 'Pierre aux Fées'.**
Situated on the road to Alménêches, in a clearing, there stands a sandstone rock 5.4 metres tall. The tallest menhir in Orne.

Les Tourailles : **Roman bridge over the 'Rouvre'.**

Tournai-sur-Dives : **Menhir** in sandstone, some 3.5 metres tall with a rounded top. In a pasture.

Tourouvre : **Ancient Roman camp** at the place called 'Saint Gilles'.
Ancient Gallo-Roman city. In the little village of Mézières. Ancient paved roads, potteries, arms, coins and medals have been discovered.

Trun : **Gallic city.** The church was built on an ancient druidic site. One can still make out the immense dolmen which served as the base for the bell tower.

Vimoutiers : **Ancient Roman road.**
Côte de la Bergerie (near the Gendarmerie).
A road which linked the plain of Argentan with that of Orbec.

AREA OF EURE

Berthouville : **Silver treasure of the Gallo-Roman period.**
In 1830, a peasant, working in his field, discovered in the place called 'Le Villeret', the most beautiful treasure of silverware dating from the Gallo-Roman period (3rd century). It makes up a treasure of more than 70 objects in solid silver, vases and perfectly preserved figurines.

Nearby to where these objects were unearthed excavations were undertaken in 1861 and brought to light two temples dedicated to Mercury and Maïa. Two other temples were later discovered as well as baths and an ancient theatre for 5000 people. (In Berthouville head to the left towards *Saint-Cyr-de-Salerne*).

Conches-en-Ouche : **'Musée de Conches'**. (Route de Sainte-Marguerite).
Collection of prehistoric stones, fossils and utensils. Tel (33) 2 32 30 90 41.

Evreux : **Numerous remains of the ancient Gallo-Roman city.**
At the 'Musée Municipal', rue Charles-Corbeau (ancient bishop's palace).
Underground room where one of the walls is made from part of the raised ramparts from the 3rd century and which contains among other prehistoric treasures, Gallo-Roman and Merovingian remains which testify to the first inhabitants of Eure.

Hardencourt-Cocherel : **Grave of Houlbec-Cocherel.**
In 1685, having ordered important excavational work on his property to facilitate navigation on the Eure, the Lord of Cocherel unearthed a neolithic grave which is considered to be the most ancient 'prehistoric excavation' known in France.

AREA OF SEINE-MARITIME

Caudebec-en-Caux : **'Musée Bichet-Bréchat', 'Maison des Templiers'.**
Gallic objects found at Mont Calidu which remind us that Caudebec was the capital of the important tribe of 'the Calètes'.

Elbeuf : **'Musée d'Histoire naturelle, d'Histoire et de Préhistoire'.**

Eu : **Store of archaeological excavations.**
The ancient 'logis' of the community of hospital sisters shelters a collection of Gallo-Roman findings from excavations.
Site of the 'Bois de l'Abbé'. Dating from the Gallo-Roman era.

Gruchet-le-Valasse : Numerous **fossils** as well as **primitive flint instruments** have been found.

Le Havre : **'Musée d'Histoire naturelle'.**
Place du Vieux-Marché - Tel (33) 2 35 41 37 28.

Le Mesnil-sous-Lillebonne : **Museum and church.**
In the church of Sainte-Anne (12th-16th century) an important exhibition of minerals, fossils, religious art, paleontology and minerology.
Open from 1st May to 30th October from 2.30-6.30 pm.

Lillebonne : **Roman theatre-amphitheatre** built in the 2nd and 3rd centuries.
It is the biggest Gallo-Roman monument of its kind north of the Loire. (Historic monument) Entrance is free, or get the key from the Municipal Museum or from the café of the Hôtel de Ville. Tel (33) 2 35 98 55 10.
Roman baths.

Rouen : **'Musée des Antiquités'.**
198, rue Beauvoisine - Tel (33) 2 35 98 55 10.

2 - The Norman invasions

Montesquieu wrote : *'We know only four great changes in Europe since the establishment of the Greek and Phoenician colonies : the first caused by the Roman conquests, the second by the barbarian invasions which destroyed the same Romans, the third the victories of Charlemagne and the last by the Norman invasions...'.*

In the north of England a fleet of Scandinavian ships landed on *Lindisfarne*. A horde of seasoned warriors pillaged the monastery and killed the monks.

The news spread quickly in the Empire to *Aix-la-Chapelle*, the capital of the Francs, where the dignitaries received it with incomprehension, even incredulity.

THEY WERE GOING TO UNDERSTAND !

This attack was a prelude to more than a century of raids, hand to hand fighting, battles, and skirmishes between the Scandinavian warriors and the Francs, whose heavily equipped army was at times handicapped when faced with the tactic of lightning strikes from the Vikings.

In the northern countries the name 'Vikings' came to mean the men whose warrior operations always came from the sea.

These 'sons of the sea' on board their 'drakes', known as such because of the dragon's head which decorated the prow, had been redoubtable sailors and fantastic explorers. It was indeed they who, four centuries before Columbus, had crossed the north Atlantic ocean in the year 1000 A.D. under the leadership of **Leif l'Heureux** before establishing themselves on the north-east coast of America and creating a colony called *'Vinland'*.

It was also they who to the east had established a vast domain with *Novogorod* as the capital. From there, their expeditions continued towards Kiev, then the Black Sea, establishing trading relations with Byzantium while others via the Volga and the Caspian Sea reached *Baghdad*.

They struck as much in England, Ireland and Scotland as in the Franc Empire. No western region was soon spared.

The estuaries were often chosen by the **Vikings** who could penetrate far up the rivers with their **'esnèques'** thanks to the incomparable nautical quality of these flat bottomed boats. But these ships were equally capable of confronting the high seas being driven either by sail or by oars.

After a first phase of pillaging, fighting and other skirmishes, the **Vikings** would profit from their superiority by *'exploiting'* the invaded territories with frequent ransom demands notably in the east of England, in the region of *York* where *'Danelaw'* a form of colonisation was applied.

When there was nothing left to plunder they established themselves and developed settlements in more hospitable areas than the harsh landscape and climate of Scandinavia. It suited many of the rough warriors to settle permanently at the mouth of the **Seine**, the **Loire**, the **Garonne**, around the **Humber** in Great Britain and also in *Ireland* and *Scotland*.

The routes of penetration are obvious especially for the Carolingian empire : passing from the North Sea or the direct route via 'Pas-de-Calais' and the Channel. At this start of the 10th century, the Carolingian kings, like the Saxon kings in England, weakened by divisions, not even counting on their 'faithful supporters', made more or less lasting treaties.

We know of one wonderful example. Suffice it to say that in 911 at **Saint-Clair-sur-Epte** in eastern Normandy, **King Charles III, called The Simple**, and the **Viking chief Rollon, called The Walker**, concluded an agreement which conceded a vast territory and the estuary of the Seine (corresponding roughly to today's departments of *Seine-Maritime*, *Eure* and part of *Calvados*). This shy norwegian warrior was a prince, son of **Roguald The Rich**. One must note, however, that if at this moment the confrontations continued between Francs, Angles, Scots and Irish and the Scandinavians and the momentary agreements came and went... commerce continued !

Places to visit...

AREA OF MANCHE

Sainte-Marie-du-Mont : **'Chapelle de la Madeleine' :** this building was constructed on the remains of a primitive site by **Vieul Aux Espaulles.** Caught in a storm, this Viking chief vowed to be baptised if his ship escaped shipwreck and to construct a chapel at the place where he landed. Of this sanctuary only a baptismal font remains (situated at the entrance to the cemetery) which, according to legend, is that in which Vieul Aux Espaulles was baptised. Some of the cornice are carved with Nordic motifs which recall the design of the rigging of the 'drakes'. These Viking decorations are rare in Normandy. They exist only at this sanctuary and at **Saint-Côme-du-Mont,** near **Carentan.** Rebuilt as a votive offering by British sailors also miraculously saved from danger at sea, this little church was badly damaged during the June 1944 bombardments and then admirably restored.

Sainte-Mère-Eglise : **Feudal mound :** 'site of the proud' on the edge of *Merderet*. It has a huge and very ancient enclosure, in a semicircle, built on the edge of the marshes of the valley of *Merderet*, protecting a ford which still exists beside the current bridge. This enormous mound of earth, surrounded by a large, deep ditch has a diameter of almost three hundred metres, but undoubtedly, at the beginning of the Middle Ages a second small enclosure was built to the south, against the larger one which had probably become impossible to defend without sufficient means. A section of the larger enclosure was separated from the rest at its southern extremity by a small perpendicular ditch; this isolated section, enlarged with additional earth, thus became a true feudal mound which was therefore practically in the centre of the smaller enclosure. An ancient mill, a manor, various outbuildings and a disused chapel were built on the flat centre of the entrenched semicircle.

AREA OF CALVADOS

Grimbosq (forest of) : **Castral Mound of Olivet.**
A wooden fortress was built on this earth mound in the 11th century. Situated in the forest of Grimbosq (16 kilometres south of Caen) the mound was attached to a spur formed by the convergence of two small narrow valleys where tributaries of the Orne flow.
This fortification, home of a Viking lord, is surrounded by two yards. In the centre a wooden tower was built which served as a lookout post. The northern yard held living accommodation with a communal living room, a kitchen (isolated for fear of fire) and a chapel. In the southern yard was an enclosure for animals, a stable and a small forge.
There are information panels on the site.

La Pommeraye : **'Château Gannes' - Feudal mound.**

Saint-Germain-de-Montgommery : **Feudal mound of 'Montgomeri' (10th century)** the best preserved in Normandy. Private property - birthplace of the celebrated Anglo-Norman family of Montgomery.

Le Plessis-Grimoult : **Feudal mound.**

AREA OF EURE

Saint-Clair-sur Epte : On the edge of the Epte to the left of the bridge :
a plaque erected in 1911 during the millennium celebrations of Normandy.
In the choir of the old **church** : the place where the treaty between **Rollon and Charles the Simple** was finalised.

At *Château-sur-Epte : (1 kilometre from Saint-Clair).*
Remains of the fortress built at the end of the 11th century by Guillaume Le Roux called **'Château Neuf'** it defended the Norman border. Circular keep on a feudal mound.

AREA OF SEINE-MARITIME

Moulineaux : Ruins of the castle of Robert the Devil - Viking museum.
Paying visits - full scale model of a 'drake' - wax tableaux evoking the history of the Vikings and the Dukes of Normandy.
Rue Pierre-Gosselin - Tel (33) 2 35 18 02 36 - Fax (33) 2 35 18 11 73.
Open to the public from 1st March to 15th September every day from 9 am-7 pm and from 15th November to 1st March on Sundays only. (Closed in January).

3 - The Duchy of Normandy

On a part of the ancient territory of *Neustrie*, **Rollon**, renamed Robert 1ˢᵗ, **First Duke of Normandy** succeeded in a rare 'tour de force' in establishing himself with the King of France, the latter understanding, that with him in place, his possessions in the north would be protected from other invasions.

The Duke also knew how to retain the respect of his followers by entrusting them with important military posts. Equally he excelled in reaching a compromise with the Church which retained his organisation and even accepted him for baptism ! Better still he succeeded in having his son accepted as his successor !

It is to him that the Normans owe the declaration of **'Haro'**, which allows to each person the right to appeal directly to the rule of the Duke.

When he died in 932 his territory, which he had divided into counties, extended from the *Bresle* and the *Epte* in the east up to the *Vire* in the west and to the south as far as *Alençon*.

His son, **William 'Longue Epée'**, who had succeeded him in 927 enlarged Normandy roughly to today's limits with the acquisition of *Cotentin*, in fighting the Bretons and the *'Normans of the West'* stayed true to the Viking traditions. A fervent Christian, he reconstructed the **Abbey of Jumièges**, built three centuries earlier.

But the new Duke was assassinated in 942 at the instigation of the Count of Flanders… backed by the King of France. He was succeeded by his son **Richard 1ˢᵗ 'Without Fear'** who consolidated the ducal heritage building or restoring the **Cathedral of Rouen** and the **Abbeys of Mont-Saint-Michel and Fécamp**.

He died in 996. His son **Richard 2ⁿᵈ 'The Good or The Intrepid'** continued his work. To help confirm his power against his dangerous neighbours he called on the Nordic fleet commanded by **Olaf 'The Large'** who would be baptised in the cathedral of Rouen and become in his country **Saint Olaf**. At this time **Knut the Dane** married **Emma** sister of **Duke Richard** and widow of the **Anglo-Saxon King Ethelred. King of Denmark, Norway and England** he thus laid the foundations of a Norman Empire which would take **Tancred of Hauteville** to Sicily, Calabria and Apulia and **Bohémond** to Antioch. Richard accorded great privileges to the Church and backed the building of monasteries.

Richard 3ʳᵈ succeeded him in 1027 but died some months later on his return to *Falaise*… poisoned by his younger brother, the **Count of Hiemes**, who thus became Duke under the name of **Robert 'The Magnificent'**,

Here the romantic episode of his meeting with young **Arlette of Falaise** intervenes...

****

The meeting of Robert and Arlette

*As he returned to his castle in Falaise after a hunting party, the young Duke noticed at the spring of the **Ante**, the river which runs past the castle, in the middle of a group of young women 'wringing' the laundry, a 'magnificent creature'. He fell in love with her there and then and led her 'in full array' to the castle and married her 'in the style of the Danes'.*

A chronicler reported : 'The first night of their acquaintance, Arlette who was asleep, trembling, gave a loud cry. The Duke asked the reason, she replied that she had dreamt that there was a large tree coming from his stomach which extended branches so long and so high that they put all of Normandy in the shade... Being huge she thought his entrails would extend throughout the whole of Normandy and England'.

This young woman which legend calls Arlette Fulbert was in fact named Herlève Herbert. Her father was a citizen of Falaise, a furrier of Flemish origin.

*At the end of December 1027 a happy event was celebrated in the castle of Falaise : **Arlette** brought into the world a strong child who was called **William**.*

Seeing the baby pull towards him the straw of the mattress on which she had placed him, the wise woman, cried out 'By my faith ! This child starts acquiring and amassing young !'

*The child was raised alongside his father up to the day when the latter, wanting to atone for the crime that he had previously committed, decided, against the advice of his barons to leave on a pilgrimage to **Jerusalem**.*

*Before his departure he had his young bastard son accepted as his successor. He also made one of his faithful supporters, **Eudes de Conteville**, promise to marry Arlette if anything happened to him on the journey.*

****

In *Constantinople as in Jerusalem*, **Robert the Magnificent** did not go unnoticed with his impressive Norman knights and his expensive entourage. He showed off the power of the Duchy of Normandy.

Alas, on his return journey, in Asia Minor, he contracted the plague.

Before dying, he charged a Norman pilgrim to announce his demise to his people. His last words being *'Tell them I go to heaven carried by four black devils !'*.

Once the the news became known in Normandy, there was a period of depression and then shortly afterwards, forgetting their promises and their oaths, a group of Norman knights *(at the head of which - as always, the 'Normans of Cotentin' who wanted to return to the scandinavian traditions)* began a rebellion refusing to accept that the young William succeed his father under the pretext that he is a **'bastard'**. The child would never forget this terrible insult. Keeping his promise **Eudes de Conteville** married **Arlette** who gave him two sons : **Odon,** future bishop of Bayeux and **Robert of Mortain**.

William took refuge with his father in law to forget for a moment... Without ever forgetting.

In 1042, **Edward 'the Confessor'**, uncle of William, became King of England.

In 1047, after having already two years earlier escaped a plot led by Guy of Brionne who wanted to get rid of him and put in his place Guy of Burgundy[1], the

---

(1) When the young William had been hunting in the south Cotentin and staying in **Valognes**, he learned from the Court 'fool' that he had overheard a conversation between conspirators that they wanted to take him prisoner. He decided to flee alone on horseback towards **Falaise**. Without stopping he rode all day and all night passing the Vire at the ford of Saint-Clement then crossing the Bessin beside the sea and arriving in the morning in **Ryes**. There a faithful baron gave him his horse and ordered his three sons to accompany him. The knights rejoined the valley of the Orne crossing the river at the ford of **Foupendant** and arrived exhausted in **Falaise**.

young William, powerful with the support of a large part of Norman nobility, regained his title. Thus he confronted the rebel barons.

William, already a strong strategist, sought the help of his overlord, the King of France, **Henry 1st** (1031-1060).

The meeting took place to the south-east of Caen at *Val'-ès-Dunes* on the 5th of August 1047.

Before the battle, William, who had established his camp on the banks of the Muance, attended Mass in the church of Valmeray.

The rebels charged to the cry of the Viking ancestors **'Thor Aie !'** (Thor help us !) whereas William's troops, to the cry of **'Dex Aie'** (God help us !) won a brilliant victory. Shortly afterwards, the young Duke put down the remaining active rebels.

Henceforth, he was indisputably Duke of Normandy and he set about reinforcing and organising his domain. He made *Caen* the second capital of his Duchy to keep a closer eye on his barons.

He gave important posts to his closest acquaintances and cultivated useful relations with the clergy. In 1049 he gave his half brother **Odon** the Diocese of Bayeux and a year later he gave the County of Mortain to his other half brother Robert.

In 1050, in spite of a ban on the marriage to his cousin by Pope Léon IX at the Council of Reims, he married **Princess Mathilde**, 23 years old, daughter of Beaudoin V, **Count of Flanders** and grand-daughter of the King of France, Robert II The Pious. The ceremony took place at *Eu* in strict privacy.

Being aware of his appetite for power and conquest, the neighbours of the young Duke, the **Bretons**, the **Angevins** kept a close watch on the borders of Normandy. The King of France, who had helped William to seize power, was concerned to see such a strong and attractive Duchy close to Paris.

In 1053, the siege of Arques took place and in 1054 William defeated at *Mortemer* a Franco/Angevine coalition.

Three years later, at *Varaville*, near *Dives* he gained a second victory against the same Franco/Angevines. The royal troops and the Angevines, coming from Angers, entered Normandy by the Hiesmois. The King of France, who was commanding the armies stopped at the Abbey of *Saint-Pierre-sur-Dives* before reaching the Caen plain.

Therefore, as they crossed the Orne, William left *Falaise* and set out at the head of his cavalry for the bridge at *Varaville* where the Franco-Angevins had to cross the the **Dives**.

With clever strategy and the help of the peasants who joined him along the way, William, coming from Bavent, attacked the army of Henry 1st from behind pushing the majority of the troops towards the bridge which collapsed. Almost all the soldiers died in a river with a level increased by the high tide. But William had a larger view of his destiny, more global than the norm in the years around 1060 !

He was kept regularly informed of everything that happened at the Court in *London,* where '*his relative*' the king, **Edward the Confessor** reigned. The latter was the son of **Emma**, the widow of the King of England, **Ethelred**. **William** was, therefore, the cousin of **Edward** who in his youth had been elevated to the Court of Normandy. Having returned to reign in England in 1044 he had around him numerous Norman advisers such that the Anglo-saxons said that Edward had a

'**Norman section**' in the Court of London. Edward was married to a Saxon princess, Edith Godwinson, but no successor was born to the marriage. In 1051 he had offered the succession to William 2nd of Normandy.

At the beginning of the year 1060 William had his eyes firmly fixed on the 'Grand Ile'. He knew that Edward the Confessor would die.

In 1063, he conquered Maine.

In 1064, the son of the head of the Anglo-Saxon part of the Court of London, **Harold Godwinson**, was charged with a mission to the Duke of Normandy. He made a hazardous crossing and landed on the beaches of **Ponthieu**. Taken prisoner, he was 'bought back' by William who brought him to Normandy. Harold was given a warm welcome and joined with the Duke in several 'rides' notably in Brittany. Harold carried a message from Edward confirming to William the promise that he had made. At William's request, Harold, before his return to England, swore on the ancient relics of the **Château de Bonneville-sur-Touques** that he would accept to be his servant.

Places to visit…

Tourist routes

Historic route of the Dukes of Normandy

Ten centuries of history.

Stopping points : **Caen-Bénouville** (castle) - **Canapville** (Manoir des Evêques - Manor of the Bishops) - **Pont-l'Evêque - Saint-Germain-de-Livet** (castle) - **Crévecœur** (castle) - **Canon** (Park and gardens of the castle) - **Saint-Pierre-sur-Dives - Vendeuvre** (castle, museum and garden) - **Falaise**.

Office : Château de Crévecœur, Tel (33) 2 31 63 02 45 - Fax (33) 2 31 63 05 96. E.Mail : musee.schlumberger@wanadoo.fr

Historic route of William the Conqueror

Information and free guide from the Tourist Office in Caen. Tel (33) 2 31 27 14 14 - Fax (33) 2 31 27 14 18.

This tour of discovery allows you delve into the heart of the ducal city and to enter into the most secret and special places whilst admiring the architectural beauty of the many monuments.

AREA OF CALVADOS

Caen :

'Abbaye aux Hommes - Abbatiale Saint-Etienne' :

(11th, 13th and 17th centuries). Tel (33) 2 31 30 42 81 - Fax (33) 2 31 86 02 38.

'L'Abbaye aux Hommes' is made up of the Abbey Saint-Etienne sheltering the tomb of William the Conqueror, the conventual buildings (18th century), the current 'Hôtel de Ville' and the 'Salle des Gardes' (14th century) ancient ceremonial room and current meeting place of the Municipal Council. The windows of the first floor of the 'Hôtel de Ville' give a view on to the Cloister. (currently being restored).

The abbey church, 'Eglise Saint-Etienne', remains one of the most remarkable roman religious buildings in Normandy. Organ 'Cavaillé' from the 19th century. Open to the public from 8.15 am-12 noon and from 2-7.30 pm (visits are stopped during religious services).

The monastic buildings which housed the municipal services of the city of Caen since 1965, were reconstructed in the 18th century at the instigation of William de la Tremblaye.

Guided visits every day except 1st January, 1st May and 25th December at 9.30 am, 11 am, 2.30 pm and 4.00 pm. Visits last between one and a quarter and one and a half hours. Departures from the hall of the 'Hôtel de Ville'.

Information : Tel (33) 2 31 30 42 81 - Fax (33) 2 31 86 02 38.

'Abbaye aux Dames' :

Main work of Roman art (11th century)

Open from 9 am-6 pm. Information Tel (33) 2 31 06 98 98.

Founded by Queen Mathilde, the Church of the Trinity is a major work of Roman Norman art. Do visit : The crypt from the 11th century, under the choir resting on 16 fine columns, the tomb of Mathilde.

Magnificently restored the buildings conventual of the 18th century sheltered a Benedictine abbey up to the Revolution.

Having become a hospital and then a hospice they are today the office of the Regional Council for Lower Normandy.

Visits every day at 2.30 pm and 4 pm except 1st January, 1st May and 25th December. Entry is free. Information : Tel (33) 2 31 06 98 98.

Do visit the cloister and the grand staircase.

The Castle :

Founded by William the conqueror and completed by Henry 1st Beauclerc, it was a powerful castle destroyed during the Revolution.

Free exterior visits every day - Plan from the Tourist Office. Tel (33) 2 31 86 06 21 - Fax (33) 2 31 85 27 94.

Built around 1060 as the principal residential palace, the castle of Caen is one of the largest fortified enclosures in Europe. It was above all a fortress and barracks and today a cultural cross-roads still rich with numerous monuments from the Middle Ages and especially the Room of the Exchequer of Normandy, (12th century).

Exhibitions are held here as well as in Saint George's church, (12th to 15th).

Museum of Normandy :

Within the walls of the castle 'Logis des Gouverneurs'.

The museum illustrates through its archaeological and ethnographic collections, the cultural evolution of man over the whole region of ancient Normandy, from the beginning of our times. The three main themes are : the habitat, techniques and beliefs.

Reconstructions with virtual imagery, models, archaeological exhibits, coins, engravings, texts and ancient plans.

Open every day except Tuesday from 9.30 am-6,00 pm,

Entry =1s55 (0,70s for students)

Free for everyone on Sunday.
Guided visits available (Sunday at 3,00 pm). Free parking.
Information Tel (33) 2 31 30 47 60 - Fax (33) 2 31 30 47 69.
http://www.ville-caen.fr/mdn - mdn@ville-caen.fr

Falaise : Castle where William the Conqueror was born.
Place Guillaume-le-Conquérant, 14700 Falaise.
Tel (33) 2 31 41 61 44 - Fax (33) 2 31 90 25 55.
Internet : château@ville-falaise.fr
Free exterior visits all the year except January,
Guided visits, Audio-visual system,
Even if William was born in this castle, we should realise that it owes much of its actual look to his sons and grandsons. Two keeps were built in typical Anglo/Norman style while the third, the round tower, was built on the orders of Philippe Auguste. Its restoration in the 1980's has been variously appreciated and criticised.
Visits are available with a British guide who is enthralled by the history of this château and the 'bastard' who was born there.
At the 'Mairie' : List of the principal companions of William.

Val-ès-Dunes à Bellengreville : Monument commemorating the battle which took place on this plain in 1047 and set William against the Norman barons who were conspiring against him. (On the edge of the RN13 after Bellengreville on the right in the direction of Lisieux and on the D41).

Varaville : **Stele of William the Conqueror.**
Commemorating the battle of Varaville in 1057.

DEPARTMENT OF ORNE

Rémalard : Feudal Mounds of the Chatelier, of the Butte and Beauregard.

4 - William becomes King of England

On the 5th January 1066, **Edward the Confessor** died in London, without descendants…

Forgetting his promises and his oath, **Harold** had himself crowned as King of England by the Bishop **Stigan** on the 6th in Westminster. Informed of this perjury and sensing treason William protested and tried to negotiate but in vain…!

Assuring himself of the agreement of his supporters, not without some reticence on their part, the Duke gathered together in the Roads of *Dives* an immense flotilla of more than **900 drakes** and an army of **40,000 men** and **14,000 horses** to help him recover 'his' kingdom.

The Pope, who reproached the Court of England for not paying him regularly the 'denier of Saint Peter', sent to protect him the Standard of Saint Peter, a white flag with a red cross on it.

On the 25th August 1066, William, aboard his admiral's ship : the **'Mora'** (built in **Barfleur**), on the mast of which flew the banner of the sovereign pontiff, gave the order to weigh anchor and assemble at *Saint-Valéry-sur-Somme*. There to await favourable winds.

In fact William, whose intelligence services functioned perfectly, knew that another pretender to the throne of England had just landed on the shores of Eastern England. It was the King of Norway **Harald Hardrada**.

The latter successfully entered the mouth of the *Humber*. **Harold Godwinson** mobilised his troops and, profiting from the imprudence of King Harald, beat his men at the **Battle of Stamford.** The Norwegian king was killed during the fighting.

However, as he prepared to take his place on the throne, Harold learned in amazement the news of the embarkation of William on the morning of 26 September and that he was half way across the Channel.

Fifty miles from the English coasts William, stopped his ships in order to regroup.

On the morning of 29 September they landed at *Pevensey* on the *Sussex* coast. No one was there to rebuff them ! He was able to disembark knights, then materials, in complete calm, install themselves and create fortifications.

The last to disembark, William slipped and fell with his head in the sand. The soldiers considered this fall as a bad omen but the Duke recovered the situation by shouting : *'By the splendour of God ! I hold earth in my hands and as my companions, it is yours !'*.

William, as a good Norman, did not 'burn his boats' which returned to Normandy to transport new troops.

Exhausted after an 11 day forced march, Harold, who had sent back a part of his troops and ships, headed south.

Towards 10 October, he arrived in **Hastings** and 'dug in' on *Senlac* hill.

William left for the confrontation and in the morning of 14 October 1066 after a long night where the two armies were a few hundred metres apart, a fearsome battle was ready.

Three corps made up William's army, on each side of the Norman knights were the soldiers of the Counts of Boulogne and Ponthieu and the conscripts from Maine, Brittany and Poitou.

The Duke, mounted on a powerful charger, was at the head of his troops. To the cry of **'Diex Aïe !'** standing in his stirrups, he launched the battle, the troops advanced singing the **'Chanson de Roland'**.

It took three assaults by William to beat the troops of Harold supported at the foot of the hill. William was everywhere, sword in hand. Suddenly an arrow hit Harold, mortally wounding him. William had won the battle.

His first gesture was to pay homage to the 15,000 warriors from his army that had been killed. At the top of the hill he had an abbey built in their memory, **'Battle Abbey'**. Then resolute, the Duke went on to London via the coast, fortifying *Dover* on the way. The Norman troops crossed the *Thames at Wallingford*.

On 25 December 1066, the coronation took place in Westminster. While William was at the foot of the alter the Archbishop of York asked the English and the Bishop of Coutances the Normans, if they agreed to recognise William as their legitimate sovereign. The ovation of the English was so loud that the Normans remained outside fearing a last minute treason.

By his reign on the 'Grande Île' William founded a new overseas dynasty with the wish to unite the two people under the same law.

The Norman barons were recompensed with numerous fiefdoms confiscated from the nobles who had supported Harold. They became the stock of the new English aristocracy : Montgomery, Chawford, Rokely …Hugues 'the wolf', Viscount of *Avranches*, became Count of Chester. But to combat the abuses, William imposed, twenty years after his accession to the throne, the **'Domesday'** in which were listed all the possessions and benefits in England since 1066.

Up to his death, he had castles built to spread his net across England but he also introduced a number of important social, administrative and religious reforms : numerous abbeys and monasteries being restored or built with white stones which were brought from Normandy.

Two beautiful examples can be cited : the use of the **'stone of Caen'** brought by ship from the Norman quarries to *London* to rebuild **Westminster Abbey** on the plan of the **Abbey of Jumièges** on the banks of the Seine in eastern Normandy and the **Tower of London**, the **White Tower**, typical tower of feudal Normandy which shows strange similarities to the castle of *Ivry-la-Bataille*.

In 1070, he named **Lanfranc**, Abbot of Saint-Etienne in Caen as Archbishop of Canterbury and Primate of England, and little by little Norman priests replaced Saxon priests.

Born in Pavie around 1010, Lanfranc taught in Avranches before becoming a monk and then Abbot of Bec where he would manage to give to his community an intellectual level never attained before. He became in time the friend and close adviser of William. After Lanfranc was nominated, in Saint-Etienne another Italian succeeded him as Abbot of Bec-Hellouin, he was Saint-Anselm who would also become Primate of England in 1093.

This great theologian left celebrated works and also helped to reinforce the cultural influence of Normandy.

Henceforth given the titles of Duke of Normandy and King of England, William would live partly in Normandy and partly in England.

He introduced Norman customs to the island.

Historians have reproached the Normans for having lacked modesty in their success such that the English forged on their side a tenacious resentment. They also say that the Battle of Hastings raised between the two people a 'bronze wall'.

It is true that the relations between the Saxons and the Normans became so difficult that the later imposed their own 'institutions' beginning with the law against hunting *(Only the King had the right to hunt and no one could kill an animal even if on his own land without the permission of the sovereign. Death was the penalty for those who disobeyed)*. The Normans also imposed their language to the detriment of the Saxon language. We see, however, the development of this language, full of Norman vocabulary would become the English tongue.

For many years the *'Norman French'* (which is still spoken in Jersey and Guernsey) would be the official language of the Court of the *'great'* of England.

At Easter 1066, the 'bastard' become 'Conqueror' was received in Rouen, capital of Normandy, with extraordinary pomp. He later had his wife **Mathilde** crowned in Westminster as Queen of England, true homage to she to whom he had entrusted the Regency of Normandy during his stay in England.

1st July 1067, saw the consecration of the Abbey of Notre-Dame de Jumièges.

In 1068, the people of Yorkshire rose up against the authority of William and a year later it was on the continent that things deteriorated with the freeing of Maine from the Norman tutelage.

In 1072, William led an expedition to Scotland and in 1073 the Normans reconquered Maine.

In 1075, the counties of Hereford and Norfolk revolted.

1077, saw the consecration of the 'Abbaye aux Hommes' in Caen and the Cathedral of Bayeux.

The same year a disagreement put the Duke-King against his son Robert Courtheuse who left Normandy.

In 1079, William was wounded at the siege of Gerberoy.

In 1082, he imprisoned Odon, Bishop of Bayeux and Duke of Kent.

On the first of November 1083 his faithful wife died.

In 1086, in Salisbury, William received the oaths of allegiance from the assembled English Counts and Barons. His kingdom was thus a model modern state, far in advance of his neighbours, the kingdom of France in particular and the German states.

Injured in a fall from his horse in *Mantes* as he directed his troops towards *Paris,* **William** died in ***Rouen*** on 10 September 1087.

If the French underestimate him, or almost, the English consider him as the founder of their country. *'For the Normans'* has written one of the great historians of the region, *'William lived without doubt as a great enigma. It is he who left them succeeding, however, without doubt in implanting the Norman spirit overseas... For the English, William is a fact, a sort of 'Father of the Country' whose reality continues to today in the single presence of their sovereign, his distant heiress'.*

William has been criticised for having helped England at the cost of Normandy, having taken too important a contribution from the human capital of Normandy at the risk of weakening its power towards the King of France, as his successors have been criticised for being more English than Norman such that it would assist the annexing of Normandy to France some years later. It is true that William lived more in his new kingdom than in Normandy where he would rarely return after 1066, leaving the Regency of the Duchy to his wife, Queen Mathilde, but one must underline that from the 11th century Normandy had known an exceptional economic development tied to an important increase in the population. It is notably in the area of agriculture that this expansion is visible with clearance of immense forests, which covered the basic Norman soil, and the development for cultivation. We should note that since the Middle Ages the horse had been used in Normandy to work the fields. But the economy of Normandy was also at this time one of exchange with England but also with the countries of Northern Europe. Cloth, stone and wine were sold... At the same time an impulse without precedent was given to the intellectual and artistic work of the Abbeys.

A visionary, William was convinced that, in spite of their differences, the people of England and Normandy were linked and that it was in the interests of the two nations, both 'daughters of the sea', to become closer when faced with the continental bloc.

Without the Anglo-Norman episode the Norman history would not be so glorious.

We should recall that at that time *London* was the nearest capital to **Rouen** after *Paris*, that maritime and commercial relations between England and Normandy had always existed *(the ships from Rouen delivering the wines of France to London were excused taxes)*, that already in the time of Edward the Norman, literary leaders maintained close contacts with those in England *(They spoke of the 'Norman' at the Court of Edward who had been educated in Normandy)*, that the English and Norman clergy worked closely to 'christianise' the two people and that in 1051 a Norman cleric, in the person of Robert Champart, Abbot of Jumièges, became Archbishop of Canterbury. Business people, ship owners..., the Normans were solidly established in England since the 10th century and would offer William their support.

When in January 1087, William arrived in his palace in Rouen to march on Paris to obtain through the King of France, Philippe 1st, the return of the french Vexin to the bosom of the Norman family, the Anglo-Norman sovereign, who was 60 years old, was tired. He was stout and his character had become gloomy since the death of Mathilde.

Nonetheless courageous, he mounted and headed for Paris. At Mantes as he raised the town to the ground, the Duke-King took a bad fall from his horse and the pommel of the saddle perforated his abdomen. He was taken to Rouen, to the **Priory of Saint-Gervais** and, after a long period in agony, the sovereign died on 10 September 1087 in complete solitude.

What would have happened if, at the head of his troops, he had entered Paris ?

William, on his death bed, had time to share out his kingdom : to the eldest **Robert 'Court-Heuze'** he gave Normandy, to the second son, **William Le Roux**, or **Rufus**, England and to the third, **Henry**, an important sum of money.

But there was soon discord between the three brothers. The eldest, Robert, intrepid and extravagant, left on a pilgrimage to the Holy Land in 1096 where he covered himself in glory. He left Normandy, partially secured, drifting, to William Le Roux, who had a difficult and disagreeable character. The latter was killed in 1100 during a hunt in the **'New Forest'**...

Finally it was the last son, **Henry**, surnamed **'Beauclerc'**, who chroniclers present as a barbaric and egocentric person with a touch of cupidity, who collected all the benefits and restored the Anglo-Norman kingdom. He had a slightly magesterial manner not tolerating any drifting.

On his return from Jerusalem, 'Courte-Heuse' tried in 1101 to invade England where Henry had declared himself king. The affair ended with an agreement between the two brothers. Henry returned to Robert his authority over the Duchy of Normandy with the exception of ***Domfront*** over which he swore to remain lord.

In 1105, faced with disastrous reports sent to him on the running of the Duchy, Henry decided, with the blessing of the Pope, to invade Normandy to liberate it from the power of the incapable Robert. On 28 September 1106 a battle took place at

Tinchebray between the two sons of the Conqueror. Robert was taken prisoner and transported to England. He remained locked up in Cardiff for 28 years. He learnt the Welsh language and wrote poetry.

****

The Battle of Tinchebray

In the month of September 1106, Henry Beauclerc lay siege to the castle of Tinchebray, held by the supporters of his brother Robert. As they cannot agree on the military strategy used, nor on the numbers of troops or even on the number of dead in battle, historians cannot today identify for certain where the battle took place but they believe that it was to the west and north of the fortress. This battle is interesting for several reasons :

- It is a model of military tactics from the Middle Ages, notably for the large proportion of foot soldiers used.

- It is of great importance historically as it allowed Henry to reform the Anglo-Norman kingdom which his father had created.

The battles have left traces on the local plan in the place names : 'le champ Henriet' (currently a market field), the crosses (built on the graves of three knights killed in the combat), 'la prise' (the place where Robert was taken prisoner), La ruisseau du traite (by which Robert de Bellême escaped)...

****

During his reign, Henry had to resist an attempted annexation by the King of France, **Louis VI 'le Gros',** who entered Normandy by the *Vexin* before being defeated on the *Plain of Brémule* between *Grainville* and *Ecouis*. The king succeeded in escaping by the 'skin of his teeth'.

Henry 1st would be a great Anglo-Norman sovereign but above all an eminent King of England. It was in this country, where he was born, that he felt really at home. He gave his people a 'Magna Carta' and took various measures, among which :

- The fixing of measures of cloth by the 'yardstick' or 'rod' calculated on the length of a man's arm.

- The confirmation to the City of London of the principal communal rights

****

The wreck of the Blanche Nef

In 1120, Henry 1st Beauclerc, who was then aged 52 and felt his powers diminishing, after having passed four years in Normandy to re-establish peace in the Duchy, decided, in November, to return to England with all his Court.

He went to Barfleur and some time before his departure on the royal ship, he received a visit from a sailor presenting himself as the son of Etienne who took his father to England in 1066. He commanded a ship called the 'Blanche-Nef' and asked to be allowed to take the royal family to Southampton. Henry said that he would make the crossing on his own ship but to be friendly, he agreed to entrust to him as passengers, his sons William and Richard and a part of the Court.

On the departure on 25 November, in dull weather, the 'Blanche-Nef' followed the Esnecca Regis at a short distance, then she moved away from the route and struck, at the exit from the port, the reef of Quilleboeuf which is situated at the end of Garreville, about one and a half kilometres from Barfleur and eight hundred metres from the coast. Badly damaged, the ship sank rapidly. All of some three hundred passengers perished in the waves with the exception of a butcher from Rouen called 'Bérold'. He recounted how the night before, the Captain and his crew had celebrated the crossing by drinking far too much and were incapable of sailing the ship.

They searched for several days for the bodies of those lost. They eventually found, scattered on the neighbouring beaches, some 200 corpses.

The royal ship had continued her voyage to England being unaware of any problem. On arrival in Portsmouth the king waited in vain for the arrival of the 'Blanche Nef'.

The death of his two sons was a terrible tragedy for the sovereign and for the Anglo-Norman kingdom. It changed the course of history for the two nations. Chroniclers report that from that day on, the king never smiled again.

In spite of the drama, Barfleur remained for two centuries, the principal port for the exchanges between Normandy and Great Britain.

****

On Henry's death in 1135, lacking any male heir, his daughter **Mathilde** called **'The Empress''**, young widow of the **Emperor of Germany** was designated to succeed him.

****

The Norman conquests at the end of the 11th century

Although William called 'the Conqueror' had just died, the Normans continued to conquer the world and in 1090, the Count Roger 'Le Puîné (the Younger) defeated the Arabs who controlled the Mediterranean and took control of the Island of Malta which completed his possessions in that area. He was master of Sicily in 1091. His father, Tancrède de Hauteville and seven of his fourteen brothers, descendants of an old, noble family from Cotentin carved out for themselves important domains in southern Italy.

In Italy, other Norman families conquered land at the expense of the byzantines and the arabs. They included Rainolf, des Moulins, from Moulins-de-la-Marche in Orne (they would give their name to a region of Italy : 'Molise').

We should also remember the unusual destiny of Robert de Grandmesnil, Abbot of Saint-Evroult who hunted by William 1st, against whom he had plotted, took refuge in Calabria.

The Normans held numerous points on the north coast of Africa. These conquests opened for Christians the route to Jerusalem allowing for the different crusades.

During the first crusade, in 1099, Bohémond, son of Robert Guiscard - himself son of Tancrède de Hauteville - appropriated a strategic region around Antioch. The family ruled there for two centuries.

Equally the Normans made invasions into Spain. We know from the monk, Ordéric Vital that the Count of Perche Rotrou established areas on Iberian soil in the 12th century and that one of his associates, Robert Bordet, became Prince of Tarragona.

****

Places to visit…

AREA OF MANCHE

Barfleur : At the entry to the port a plaque fixed to a rock that recalls that it was a man from Barfleur, Etienne, who commanded the ship of Duke William, 'La Mora', on the crossing to England in 1066. The port of Barfleur was well known in the Middle Ages. It was the embarkation port for Anglo Norman sovereigns. It was some distance up the coast that the 'Blanche-Nef' was wrecked in 1120.

Mortain : Vestiges of the feudal castle of Robert de Mortain, half brother of William of Normandy, who participated in the epic period of Hastings.

AREA OF CALVADOS

Bayeux : **Museum of the Bayeux Tapestry**
Centre Guillaume-le-Conquérant - 13 bis, rue Nesmond.
Tel (33) 2 31 51 25 50 - Fax (33) 2 31 51 25 59.
E.Mail : bayeux-tourisme@mail.cpod.fr
Internet site : http://www.cpod.com/monoweb/bayeux-tourisme
Tapestry of coloured wool on linen 70 metres long by 50 centimetres high telling in 58 scenes, the preparation for the invasion of England, the landing and the Battle of Hastings. A major work of the 11th century. Open every day all the year.

Caen : In the church of **Saint-Etienne**, ancient church of the Abbaye aux Hommes : **the tomb of William of Normandy**. The grave was desecrated by the protestants in 1562 and then by the Revolutionaries in 1793.
In the **'Abbaye aux Dames'**, which she had founded in 1059 : in the **Abbey Church** : **the tomb of Mathilde**, Queen of England, Duchess of Normandy, who died 3rd November 1083.

Dives-sur-Mer : **Embarkation port** for the Norman troops to England in 1066 commanded by William.
'La liste des Compagnons de Guillaume'. Containing the names of all those who accompanied William to England in 1066, this list is engraved on the western wall of the nave of the church of Dives, inside, above the entry door. You may perhaps find here, when looking at it, the name of one of your Norman ancestors.

Asnelles-la-Belle-Plage : **'Sente au bâtard'**. The name of a road where William passed.

Argentan : Remains of the **castle** from the 12th century built by Henry 1st. *Beauclerc.* **Tour Marguerite** (12th century) ancient 'Tour au Febvre' which was part of the urban enclosure built by Henry 1st.

Domfront : Ruins of the **castle** of Henry 1st Beauclerc and the ramparts built under Jean sans Terre. **Castle** where Aliénor of Castille was born, daughter of Aliénor of Aquitaine and Henry 2nd Plantagenêt and... grandmother of Saint Louis.

Tinchebray : **Battlefield** where the sons of the 'Conqueror', Robert and Henry, fought in 1106.

AREA OF SEINE-MARITIME

Lillebonne : Remains of the **castle** where Duke William gathered his trusted advisers before deciding on the expedition to England. The Duke-King stayed here on many occasions.

Neufchâtel-en-Bray : The remnants of the **castle** built in 1106 by the son of William the Conqueror. It was destroyed on 1595. In 1150 Henry 2nd of England gave Neufchatel, then called Drincourt, to Louis VII, King of France.

Saint-Denis-le-Thiboult near *Ry :* Ruins of a **fortress** where Henry 1st, Duke of Normandy, King of England, died in 1135.

5 - The Plantagenêt Empire

From 1135 to 1144, **Mathilde**, Countess of *Argentan* was called Duchess of Normandy and Queen of England but **Etienne de Blois**, nephew of Henry 1st had himself proclaimed Duke of Normandy at the Castle of 'le Neubourg' and crowned King of England with the backing of the Anglo-Norman barons.

Geoffroy le Bel Plantagenêt, Count of Anjou and husband of Mathilde, in whom she had entrusted the reins of power, fought him and having won was crowned in Rouen on 19th January 1144. He would reign until 1151 founding a great dynasty.

In 1143 he unified the Anglo-Norman kingdom by introducing a single currency and confirming that the Duke of Normandy should be accepted as a king and that the King of England must be honoured as Duke of Normandy.

There were several children born from his union with Mathilde and **Henry 2nd Plantagenêt** succeeded his parents in 1148 and was crowned King of England in 1154.

The King of France **Louis VII** had just renounced his wife, **Aliénor of Aquitaine**, Henry 2nd married her... on 18 May 1152 in the Cathedral of *Lisieux* !

She brought with her as a dowry *Acquitaine* and *Poitou* making **Henry 2nd 'Court Mantel'** the most powerful ruler in Europe.

The **Anglo-Norman kingdom** became the **'Plantagenêt Empire'**.

The possessions of Henry 2nd extended from the lowlands of *Scotland* to the *Pyrenees*.

The Duke-King administered his vast domain remarkably and one can notice that slowly the *'centre of gravity'* of this empire became England, Normandy being henceforth a state among the others.

****

The tragic end of Saint Thomas Becket

If Thomas Becket remains in the history of the United Kingdom as one of the most celebrated Archbishops of Canterbury, this great man of the church was also known for his stormy relationship with his 'childhood friend' and sovereign Henry 2nd who in 1170 decided to have him assassinated.

Originating from Normandy, (his family being called Becquet) He fought all his life against the power of the Anglo-Norman sovereign to have the spiritual power of the church respected, which Henry did very little.

In 1164, to weaken the church, the king publicly delcared the Constitutions of Clarendon which guaranteed the 'dignity of the crown'.

Weary of fighting the prelate, who had excommunicated the higher members of the English clergy, Henry accused him of misconduct which obliged him to flee to France in 1164. Negotiations between the official representatives of Pope Alexander III - who supported the Archbishop - took place at the Castle of Domfront, in Bayeux and finally at the Manoir Ducal de Bur and ended in stalemate. After seven years in exile, Thomas Becket finally returned to Canterbury but the king, not appreciating the triumphal welcome reserved for him by his subjects, sent four Norman 'gentlemen' from Argentan who assassinated him in the choir of the cathedral on 29t[h] December 1170.

Thomas Becket was canonised on 21 February 1173 and the Pope obliged Henry to repent publicly of his crime. The cult of Thomas Beckett has been very durable in Normandy which keeps numerous souvenirs of the saint but also in England where the ancient archbishop has become a figure in the theatre.

****

Henry 2nd was succeeded in 1189 by his son the famous **Richard the Lionheart** *'troubadour commander in chief'* who was to have a glorious life.

After having paid homage on behalf of Normandy to **Philippe Auguste**, his relations with the King of France deteriorated and after his return from the third crusade, they fought. He profited from a truce, imposed by the church, to build *Castle Gaillard*, in 14 months, *'key to Normandy'*, on the banks of the *Seine*, thus cutting the road to Rouen. The battle recommenced to the advantage of Richard. The King of France, beaten at *Courcelles* near *Gisors,* narrowly escaped death when falling in the river *Epte*. Richard stupidly wounded himself at *Chalus* in Limousin on 26th March 1199. He died the following 6th April.

Without an heir from his wife **Bérengère,** it was his brother **Jean sans Terre**, *Shakespearian character,* who succeeded him in 1199. *(He was crowned in Rouen on 25th April and in London on 27th May).*

At worst he is considered as *'the most loathsome of the Dukes of Normandy"*. Underhand and ferocious, the real person was close to that of fiction created by the author of *'Robin Hood'* known equally by the young British as by the young French [1].

Contrary to his brother, this man did not have the stature to fight against his redoubtable adversary, the King of France **Philippe-Auguste**. He shamefully abandoned his Norman possessions, leaving **Roger de Lascy** and his valiant knights who were on a mission to defend Castle Gaillard to die without help. Beseiged by 6000 men since August 1203, the castle finally fell into the hands of the King of France on 6th March 1204.

Philippe Auguste could then annexe Normandy which then ceased to be a free nation.

Symbolically, already in 1188, the king had decided to destroy the old elm which was between Gisors and Triel-sur-Seine under which successive Dukes of Normandy had regularly held their conferences with the kings of France.

In 1215, retaining his English throne, King Jean signed, under duress, the famous 'Grande Charte' of English freedoms.

Places to visit...

AREA OF MANCHE

Avranches : Stèle at the place where Henry 2nd Plantagenêt came in 1172 to make honourable amends before the official representatives of the Pope at the door of the cathedral in reparation for the death of Saint-Thomas Becket.

Coutances : **Stained glass window of the Cathedral** representing various moments in the life of **Saint-Thomas Becket**.

Omonville-la-Rogue : Wall painting in the church depicting the death of **Thomas Becket**.

AREA OF CALVADOS

Balleroy : **Statue of Saint-Thomas Becket** at Montfiquet.

Caumont-l'Eventé : **Stained glass window** depicting the death of Thomas Becket. In the church of Parfouru-l'Eclin.

Lisieux : Situated in the heart of Normandy, the city of Lexovi became one of the major towns of the Anglo-Norman kingdom. An important place for exchanges, Lisieux was placed under the authority of a Bishop-Count who was nominated directly by the sovereign. The Bishop Arnoul (1141-1182) was builder of the cathedral and a friend of **Thomas Becket**. The vestments belonging to the latter are conserved in the General Hospital of Lisieux.

---

(1) Everyone in Normandy and France knows of Walter Scott, Robin Hood, Richard the Lionheart and the infamous Jean sans Terre, Ivanhoe…

AREA OF ORNE

Argentan : **Remains of the Church of Saint-Thomas Becket.**

A vestige of the glorious era during which Argentan figured among the capitals of the Anglo-Norman kingdom, the church of Saint-Thomas Becket was built in 1177 on the site of the current general hospital, rue Aristide-Briand, part of the ancient Hôtel-Dieu. Abandoned after the French Revolution and turned into a quarry under the Empire it was one of the jewels of the local architectural heritage.

Nothing remains of the building today except 19 cornices in 'Caen stone' major works of Roman art, magnificently sculpted, with designs of vegetation and animals inspired for the most part by Viking motifs. They are displayed in a gallery on the ground floor of the hospital where they can be freely admired.

Entry though the main accueil (Reception) of the building.

Neuville-sur-Touques : **'La Bove des Chevaliers'.**

This mysterious place is situated in a pasture in the hollow of a small valley between the hamlets of 'La Jaunière' and 'La Haute Jaunière'. One enters it by a narrow slit in the chalky rock of little more than a metre in width and fifty centimetres in height. After 3 metres of alleyway one arrives in the first vestibule with a width of 2 metres, a height of 1 metre and a depth of 1.25 metres. The work to excavate the solid rock is incredible. The Room of Pillars which one goes into next is a circular room with seven carved alcoves all around and a table in the centre of monolithic stone. It undoubtedly served as a meeting room. The third and last room appears to be some sort of sanctuary. The overall length of this underground establishment is 18.60 metres and the width 12.60 metres. The historians and esoterists have argued over the centuries as to the significance and use of this strange place. It is generally thought that it was a primitive type of monastery from the time of the first hermits who came to preach the Gospel in the heart of the Auge forest. Some are certain that it was a meeting place founded by the Templars to hold council in secret. Various places indicate their presence in the region. The mystery has never been solved.

Sées : **Comb of Saint-Thomas Becket coming from *Argentan*.**

AREA OF EURE

Gisors : **Mediaeval Castle.**

Tel (33) 2 32 27 60 63 - (33) 2 32 55 59 36

The castle can be visited throughout the year except in December and January. From 1st April to 30th September : Every day except Tuesday from 10 am-12 noon and from 2-6 pm. From 1st October to 30th November and from 1st February to 31st March it is open at weekends from 10 am-12 noon and 2-4 pm. A remarkably conserved group of Norman military architecture from the 12th century.

Guided visits at 10,30 am, 2,30 pm and 4 pm (during the summer = 10 am, 11 am, 2 pm, 15,30 pm, and 5 pm),

Entry = 5€ (students = 3€)

It is made up of a central castle built on an artificial mound, in the middle of an interior court which is now converted to a public garden. The group is surrounded by ramparts reinforced by 12 towers of which the most celebrated 'Tour du prisonnier' possesses, almost intact, its ribbed vaulted rooms and its prison where the prisoners have left inscriptions on the walls. Started by Guillaume-le-Roux, the construction of the castle was continued by Henry 1st and Henry 2nd.

The Templars stood guard there from 1158 to 1161.

Le Neubourg : It was in the **'Vieux Château'** that Etienne de Blois was proclaimed Duke of Normandy and King of England in 1135. In the same place in 1160 that Marguerite of France, daughter of Louis VII, married Henry 'Le Jeune', son of Henry 2nd of England.

Vernon : **Glove of Thomas Backet.**

AREA OF SEINE-MARITIME

Gruchet-le-Valasse : **Abbey of Valasse** : destroyed by the English in 1437, it had been founded in 1150 by Waleran de Meulan and Empress Mathilde, granddaughter of William the Conqueror. Notre-Dame-du-Vœu keeps its mediaeval origins of beautiful rooms in Roman, Norman and Ancient Gothic style.

Rouen : At the church of Saint-Ouen : **Stained glass window** depicting **Saint-Thomas Becket.**

36

List of the companions of William 1ˢᵗ having established themselves in England after 1066
It has been drawn up by Léopold Delisle from the Cotentin

Achard
Achard d'Ivri
Aioul
Aitard de Vaux
Alain le Roux
Amauri de Dreux
Anquetil de Cherbourg
Anquetil de Grai
Anquetil de Ros
Anscoul de Picquigni
Ansfroi de Cormeilles
Ansfroi de Vaubadon
Ansger de Montaigu
Ansger de Sénarpont
Ansgot
Ansgot de Ros
Arnoul d'Ardre
Arnoul de Perci
Arnoul de Hesdin
Aubert Greslet
Aubri de Couci
Aubri de Ver
Auvrai le Breton
Auvrai d'Espagne
Auvrai de Merleberge
Auvrai de Tanle
Azor
Baudoin de Colombières
Baudoin le Flamand
Baudoin de Meules
Bérenger Giffard
Bérenger de Toeni
Bernard d'Alençon
Bernard du Neufmarché
Bernard Pancevolt
Bernard de Saint Ouen
Bertran de Verdun
Beuselin de Dive
Bigot de Loges
Carbonnel
David d'Argentan
Dreu de la Beuvrière
Dreu de Montaigu
Durand Malet
Ecouland
Engenouf de l'Aigle
Enguerrand de

Raimbeaucourt
Erneis de Buron
Etienne de Fontenai
Eude, Comte de
Champagne
Eude, Evêque de Bayeux
Eude, cul de loup
Eude le flamand
Eude de Fourneaux
Eude le Sénéchal
Eustache, Comte de
Boulogne
Foucher de Paris
Fouque de Lisors
Fouque d'Appeville
Fouque le Bourguignon
Fouque de caen
Fouque de Claville
Fouque de Douai
Fouque Giffard
Gautier de Grancourt
Gautier Hachet
Gautier Heusé
Gautier d'Incourt
Gautier de Laci
Gautier de Mucedent
Gautier d'Omontville
Gautier de Risbou
Gautier de Saint Valéri
Gautier Tirel
Gautier de Vernon
Geoffroi Alselin
Geoffroy Bainard
Geoffroy du Bec
Geoffroy de Cambrai
Geoffroy de la Guierche
Geoffroy le Maréchal
Geoffroy de Mandeville
Geoffroy Martel
Geoffroy Maurouard
Geoffroy de Montbrai
Geoffroy comte du Perche
Geoffroy de Pierrepont
Geoffroy de Ros
Geoffroy de Runeville
Geoffroy Talbot
Geoffroy de Tournai

Geoffroy de Trelli
Gerboud le flamand
Gilbert le blond
Gilbert de Blosseville
Gilbert de Bretteville
Gilbert de Budi
Gilbert de Colleville
Gilbert de Gand
Gilbert Gibard
Gilbert Malet
Gilbert Maminot
Gilbert Tison
Gilbert de Venables
Gilbert de Wissant
Girard
Gonfroi de Cioches
Gonfroi Mauduit
Goscelin de Cormeilles
Goscelin de Douai
Goscelin de la Rivière
Goubert d'Aufai
Goubert de Beauvais
Guernon de Pois
Gui de Craon
Gui de Raimbeaucourt
Gui de Rainecourt
Guillaume Alis
Guillaume d'Ansleville
Guillaume l'Archer
Guillaume d'Arques
Guillaume d'Audrieu
Guillaume de l'Aune
Guillaume Basset
Guillaume Belet
Guillaume de Beaufou
Guillaume Bertran
Guillaume de Biville
Guillaume le Blond
Guillaume Bonvalet
Guillaume du Bosc
Guillaume du Bosc Road
Guillaume de Bourneville
Guillaume de Brai
Guillaume de Briouse
Guillaume de Bursigni
Guillaume de Cahaignes
Guillaume de Cailli

Guillaume de Cairon
Guillaume Cardon
Guillaume de Carnet
Guillaume de Castillon
Guillaume de Céaucé
Guillaume la chèvre
Guillaume de Colleville
Guillaume Corbon
Guillaume de Daumerai
Guillaume le Despensier
Guillaume de Durville
Guillaume d'Ecouis
Guillaume Espec
Guillaume d'Eu
Guillaume, Comte d'Evreux
Guillaume de Falaise
Guillaume de Fécamp
Guillaume Folet
Guillaume de la Forêt
Guillaume de Fougères
Guillaume Froissart
Guillaume Goulaffre
Guillaume de Lêtre
Guillaume de Loucelles
Guillaume Louvet
Guillaume Malet
Guillaume de Malleville
Guillaume de la Mare
Guillaume Maubenc
Guillaume Mauduit
Guillaume de Moion
Guillaume des Monceaux
Guillaume de Noyers
Guillaume fils d'Osberne
Guillaume Pantoul
Guillaume de Parthenai
Guillaume Péché
Guillaume de Perci
Guillaume Levrel
Guillaume de Picquiogni
Guillaume Poignant
Guillaume de Poillei
Guillaume le Poitevin
Guillaume de Pont de
l'Arche
Guillaume Quesnel
Guillaume de Reviers
Guillaume de Sept Meules
Guillaume Taillebois
Guillaume de Toeni
Guillaume de Vatteville
Guillaume de Vauville
Guillaume de Ver

Guillaume de Vesli
Guillaume de Warenne
Guimond de Blangi
Guimond de Tessel
Guibenoud de Balon
Guinemar le flamand
Hamelin de Balon
Hamon le Sénéchal
Hardouin d'Ecalles
Hascouf Musard
Henri de Beaumont
Henri de Ferrières
Herman de Dreux
Hervé le Berruier
Hervé d'Espagne
Hervé d'Hélion
Honfroi d'Ansleville
Honfroi de Biville
Honfroi de Bohon
Honfroi de Carteret
Honfroi de culai
Honfroi de l'Ile
Honfroi du Tilleul
Honfroi Vis de loup
Huard de Vernon
Hubert de Mont Canisi
Hubert de Port
Hugue l'Ane
Hugue d'Avranches
Hugue de Beauchamps
Hugue de Bernières
Huge de Bois Hébert
Hugue de Bolbec
Hugue Bourdet
Hugue de Brebeuf
Hugue de Corbon
Hugue de Dol
Hugue le flamand
Hugue de Gournai
Hugue de Grentemesnil
Hugue de Hodenc
Hugue de Hotot
Hugue d'Ivri
Hugue de Laci
Hugue de Maci
Hugue Maminot
Hugue de Manneville
Hugue de la Mare
Hugue Mautravers
Hugue de Mobec
Hugue de Montfort
Hugue de Montgomeri
Hugue Musard

Hugue de Port
Hugue de Rennes
Hugue de Saint Quentin
Hugue Silvestre
Hugue de Vesli
Hugue de Viville
Ibert de Laci
Ibert de Toeni
Ive Taillebois
Ive de Vesci
Josce le flamand
Juhel de Toeni
Landri
Lanfranc
Mathieu de Mortagne
Mauger de Carteret
Maurin de Caen
Mile Crespin
Murdac
Néel d'Aubigny
Néel de Berville
Néel Fossard
Néel de Gournai
Néel de Muneville
Normand d'Adréci
Osberne d'Arques
Osberne du Breuil
Osberne d'Eu
Osberne Giffard
Osberne Pastioreire
Osberne du Quesnay
Osberne de Saussai
Osberne de Wanci
Osmond
Osmond de Vaubadon
Ours d'Abbetot
Ours de Berchères
Picot
Pierre de Valognes
Rabier d'Avre
Raoul d'Aunou
Raoul Baignard
Raoul de Bans
Raoul de Bapaumes
Raoul Basset
Raoul de Beaufou
Raoul de Bernai
Raoul Blouet
Raoul Botin
Raoul de la Rivière
Raoul de Languetot
Raoul de Limési
Raoul de Marci

Raoul de Mortemer
Raoul de Noron
Raoul d'Ouilli
Raoul Painel
Raoul Pinel
Raoul Pipin
Raoul de la Pommeraie
Raoul du Quesnai
Raoul de Saint Sanson
Raoul de Saussai
Raoul de Savigni
Raoul Taillebois
Raoul du Theil
Raoul de Toeni
Raoul de Tourlaville
Raoul de Tourneville
Raoul Tranchard
Raoul fils d'Unspac
Raoul Vis de Loup
Raoul de la Bruière
Raoul de Chartres
Raoul de Colombières
Raoul de Conteville
Raoul de Courbépine
Raoul l'Estourmi
Raoul de Fougères
Raoul Framan
Raoul de Gael
Raoul de Hauville
Raoul du l'Ile
Ravenot
Renaud de Bailleul
Renaud Croc
Renaud de Pierrepont
Renaud de Sainte Hélène
Renaud de Torteval
Renier de Brimou
Renouf de Colombelles
Renouf Flambard
Renouf Pévrel
Renouf de Saint Waleri
Renouf de Vaubadon
Richard Basset
Richard de Beaumais
Richard de Bienfaite
Richard de Bondeville
Richard de Courci
Richard d'Engagne
Richard l'Estourmi
Richard Fresle
Richard de Méri
Richard de Neuville

Richard Poignant
Richard de Reviers
Richard de Sacquenville
Richard de Saint Clair
Richard de Sourdeval
Richard Talbot
Richard de Vatteville
Richard de Vernon
Richer d'Andeli
Robert d'Armentières
Robert d'Auberville
Robert d'Aumale
Robert de Barbes
Robert le Bastard
Robert de Beaumont
Robert le Blond
Robert Blouet
Robert Bourdet
Robert de Brix
Robert de Buci
Robert de Chandos
Robert Corbet
Robert de Courçon
Robert Cruel
Robert le Despensier
Robert Comte d'Eu
Robert Fromentin
Robert fils de Géroud
Robert de Glanville
Robert Guernon
Robert de Harcourt
Robert de Lorz
Robert Malet
Robert, Comte de Meulan
Robert de Montbrai
Robert de Montfort
Robert, Comte de Mortain
Robert des Moutiers
Robert Murdac
Robert d'Ouilli
Robert de Pierrepont
Robert de Pontchardon
Robert de Rhuddlan
Robert de Romenel
Robert de Saint Légier
Robert de Thaon
Robert de Toeni
Robert de Vatteville
Robert des Vaux
Robert de Veci
Robert de Vesli
Robert de Villon

Robert de Vitot
Roger d'Abernon
Roger Arundel
Roger d'Auberville
Roger de Beaumont
Roger Bigot
Roger Boissel
Roger de Bosc Normand
Roger de Bosc Roard
Roger de Breteuil
Roger de Bulli
Roger de Carteret
Roger de Chandos
Roger Corbet
Roger de Courcelles
Roger d'Evreux
Roger d'Ivry
Roger de Laci
Roger de Magni
Roger de Meules
Roger de Montgommeri
Roger de Moyaux
Roger de Mussegros
Roger de Ouistreham
Roger d'Orbec
Roger Picot
Roger de Pistres
Roger le Poitevin
Roger de Rames
Roger de Saint Germain
Roger de Sommeri
Ruaud d'Adoubé
Sanson
Seri d'Auberville
Serion de Burci
Serlon de Ros
Sigar de Cioches
Simon de Senlis
Thierri Pointel
Tihel de Hérion
Toustain
Toustain de Guéron
Toustain de Sainte Hélène
Toustain fils de Rou
Toustain Mantel
Toustain Tinel
Turold
Turold de Grenteville
Turold de Papelion
Vauquelin de Rosai
Vital
Wadard

6 - The Hundred Years War
Normandy in the Kingdom of France

The Plantagenêt Empire at that time, was being constantly reduced under the attacks of the Kings of France. For Philippe-Auguste the conquest of Normandy was primordial : it opened for him the access to the sea and he 'broke' this menacing empire.

One of his first decisions was to force the Norman nobility to choose between their possessions in Normandy and those in England, which resulted in the emigration overseas of a large number of nobles. The period of peace, which would last more than a century, allowed the Normans to develop their traditional activities, notably fishing and agriculture.

The successors to Philippe-Auguste, the Kings **Louis VIII, Philippe III** and **Philippe IV le Bel** continued to hunt the possessions of the English.

Philippe IV had three sons who succeeded him without leaving an heir. The crown of France thus passed to the cousins, the **Valois.** But the daughter of **Philippe IV, Isabelle of France,** who was married to **Edward 2ⁿᵈ of England,** claimed with her son **Edward 3ʳᵈ,** the succession of his father on the throne of France.

In 1337, a conflict broke out, the **Hundred Years War !**

Normandy then became one of the principal theatres of operation in this long war. An important stake for the two kingdoms. In Normandy there existed three groups : the pro-English, the pro-Norman and the pro-French.

Several Kings of England disembarked at **La Hougue, Barfleur, Touques**, 'natural doorways' to Normandy at that time, while King Philippe, in 1340, attempted a landing on the English shores and mobilised to this end, 9 ships and 700 men who left from Barfleur on a disastrous expedition.

On 13 July 1346, the King of England, **Edward 3ʳᵈ** disembarked at *Saint-Vaast-la-Hougue* where he established a bridgehead with support of the unfortunate **Geoffroy d'Harcourt,** Lord of *Saint-Sauveur-le-Vicomte*. Edward 3ʳᵈ devastated **Barfleur**, besieged **Valognes** and arrived on 20 July in front of Carentan not without, on the way, having ravaged and pillaged *Montebourg* and then *Sainte-Mère-Eglise*.

This turbulent period was equally marked by epidemics and natural catastrophes which caused an unprecedented demographic fall in Normandy. In the Cotentin, famine and the plague would wipe out almost half of the population.

At the place called 'La vallée de misère' at *Sainte-Mère-Eglise* there was a village whose inhabitants were either massacred by the English or decimated by the plague.

In 1355, this same region, was subjected to the occupation of the **fort du Houlme** and the quagmires of *Chef-du-Pont* by **Charles de Navarre** who, allied to the King of England and put in charge of Cotentin, arrived in *Cherbourg* with 10,000 men. In 1388, the English troops under the command of the Count of Arundel, left their garrison in Cherbourg and devastated Cotentin again.

After the defeat at **Azincourt** in 1415, Normandy lived again 'à l'heure anglaise'.

In 1417, several hundred English ships landed at today's **Trouville** beach.

In 1419, Honfleur, which Charles V had fortified, was taken by the English who occupied it until 1450. The construction of the church of Saint-Etienne was finished in 1432, during this 'occupation'.

In 1450, Charles VII liberated the town and some years later, a reprisal raid was made on England and the town of Sandwich (today twinned with Honfleur) was attacked and ramsacked.

At the end of the 15th century, the chapel of Sainte-Catherine, destroyed during the seige of 1450, was replaced by a wooden church, the work of marine carpenters.

During this time the Kings of England, notably **Henry 5th** and the regent **Duke of Bedford**, wanting Normandy to be attached permanently, created commercial and administrative institutions and even the University of Caen in 1432. But little by little the English troops were pushed back under pressure from the French troops. The Hundred Years War in Cotentin would end at *Grand-Vey* : **Thomas Kyriel** was in the process of crossing the Bay of Veys, the French took up position in the middle of a ford and held the position with the tide rising. The next morning the English forced a passage, the survivors were pushed back towards Veys with the tide rising. The majority were drowned. Those who escaped were met on the bank by peasants stirred by the sound of the alarm. The English would be crushed at *Formigny* in April 1450. The last English combatants re-embarked in *Cherbourg*.

****
550 years ago : Formigny

550 years ago, on 5th April 1450, at Formigny, near to Bayeux, the French, thanks to the indispensable power of the Bretons, inflicted a heavy defeat on the English army, thus putting an end to the Hundred Years War. The troops of Henry 6th of England were erased from Norman soil by the troops of Charles VII placed under the command of the Count of Clermont.

The cost of this decisive battle, which put Normandy definitively on the French side, was very heavy : 4,000 dead on the English side and 1,000 on the French.

In the year 2000, as in Hastings, a reconstruction of the battle took place with more than 400 taking part... including around fifty English !
****

The King of France had to accept the victory against the English, due greatly to the 'messianic' intervention of a well-off young country girl from the East of France : **Joan of Arc** who ended her dazzling life in *Rouen* : taken prisoner by Jean de Luxembourg at Compiègne, she was tried by a Burgundian and 'Sorbonnicard' (people who had studied at the Sorbonne) tribunal in Rouen. The 126 judges of the Sorbonne came from Paris, which was still in the hands of the Burgundians, - they declared her to be a witch and condemned her to be burned alive in the centre of the Norman capital, *Place du Vieux-Marché* on 29th May 1431. Contrary to that which continues to be told and written on the subject, the English were not directly responsible for this sentence or torture.

After her death, and in order not to make the young woman a martyr, the ecclesiastical tribunal demanded from the executioners, that nothing should remain of the body but in spite of the sulphur, the oil and the coal used to ensure that the incineration was complete, it is recorded that the heart, intestines and teeth were not destroyed. Thus they speeded up the fire by throwing all the cinders of the stake on the remains and putting everything into a sack and throwing it into the Seine.

It is said that in 1891 remains were found in the sludge and sand where they were thrown.

Although **Charles VII** confirmed to the Normans their institutions and liberties, his successor Louis XI, suppressed the Duchy of Normandy to end all possibility of sedition and broke the ducal ring, the premier symbol of Norman power, in 1469.

A new lengthy period of peace allowed Normandy to repopulate and to find again its prosperity by re-launching, notably, its maritime and business activities.

This period would be from time to time troubled by the skirmishes between the English and French fleets like the Battle of Barfleur in 1692.

On 29 May of that year, the ships of the Norman admiral of Tourville were tied up alongside in the port of Barfleur when suddenly he was informed that the Anglo-Dutch fleet, twice as large as that which he commanded, had been seen coming from the North-east.

Faced with 100 ships heading towards the Norman coast, Tourville had no other solution than to hoist the flag for action stations.

It was a Dutch ship which around 10 o'clock opened hostilities by firing broadside at the ships of the King of France. The huge battle was relentless and lasted until evening and ended by the defeat of the aggressor without any loss of a ship being reported on the French side.

The next day, the victory changed sides following a strategic error on the part of the French and the ships of the 'Royale' (the French navy) were all destroyed.

****

Le Havre-Harfleur in the Hundred Years War

In 1356, the troops of the Duke of Lancaster attempted a landing in the port of Leure. Three years later the port was destroyed by the English.

On 14 August 1415, Henry V, King of England, landed and set up in the Priory of Graville. His brother, Clarence, besieged Harfleur which remained at that time the principal port of Normandy.

He gave to Duke Jehan de Wychefort the lands of Vitavant dominated by a humble fortress. The Duke demolished this castle and built, a little lower, a Manor which one can still see today.

22 August 1415, Harfleur is bombarded, the English besiege the port.

On 19 September, the inhabitants asked for a four day truce then on 22 September they gave in. Some of the people of Harfleur tried to resist taking refuge in their towers. The English forced the people to leave the town, 'without baggage or carts'.

During the following thirty years, Le Havre would be under the domination of the English.

On 4 November 1435, a group of 'cauchois' revolted, led by Le Carnier and Jehan de Grouchy, helped by around a hundred people of Harfleur liberated the port of Harfleur.

In April 1440, the English again besieged Harfleur which was defended by Jehan d'Estouteville Dunois. The Count of Eu offered to lend a forceful hand but he arrived too late and Harfleur had to give in.

On 8 December 1449, Charles VII, King of France, in turn besieged the port. The English finally gave in on 24 December.

****

The 17th century would be marked by the religious wars which cast a shadow over the land of the Province.

Places to visit...

AREA OF MANCHE

La Haye-du-Puits : The **keep** (10th-11th century) is apparently the oldest in the area of Manche. It was occupied by the English from 1418 to 1450 who restored and fortified it. It is still standing on a mound but the rest of the castle has been destroyed.

Pontorson : Fortified under the Dukes Robert and William, the town situated on the borders of Brittany, experienced the friction between Catholics and Protestants during the Hundred Years War. Under English domination until 1449, the fortress was destroyed and rebuilt several times. It was defended by the Counts of Montgomery and also Du Guesclin.

Sainte-Marie-du-Mont : Relic of the Hundred Years War, a field still bears the name **'Field of the English'**; English gold coins have been found there.

In the area of Saint-Mère-Eglise : The **Bastille de Beuzeville** built in the 14th century to defend the marshes and the plain against English interference. It was demolished in 1925.

The **Manor-farms**, typical of architecture on the plain, they were built in the period of the Hundred Years War for protection against the English invader.

Saint-James : The community of Saint-James, at the extreme south of the Cotentin was orginally called after Saint-Jacques-de-Beuvron and had been created by William the Conqueror (There remains from this period the Priory of Saint-Jacques, the ramparts, the ancient hospital 'maison Dieu' and the 'maladrerie'). It was the English who named it 'Saint-James' during their occupation in the Hundred Years War.

Sourdeval : A field, in the village of la 'Pesentière', on the land of the community of Vengeons carries the name of 'Battlefield' or 'Cemetery of the English'. Here the English and French fought in 1449.

Mont-Saint-Michel : At the entrance to the Mount : **English bombards** recovered in 1434.
Logis de Bertrand Du Guesclin who fought against the English for the King of France.

Pontorson : In this little village close to Mont-Saint-Michel the **fortified castle** of the celebrated **Du Guesclin** was built, it is now destroyed.

Régneville-sur-Mer : The **feudal castle** was twice taken by the English and twice retaken by the French troops.

AREA OF CALVADOS

Formigny *:* Beside the town-hall : **Monument commemorating the battle of Formigny.** One can see the Count of Clermont and his faithful Breton ally.

Orbec-en-Auge *:* The town holds many memories of the Hundred Years War, beginning with the defensive tower built by the English at the beginning of the 15th century which now makes up the bell tower of Notre-Dame church, rebuilt after the war. The development of Orbec was encouraged by the Dukes of Normandy. Their cousins, the Lords of Orbec, descendants of Duke Richard 1st and better known under the name the Counts of Clare and Pembroke, participated actively in the Anglo-Norman government.

AREA OF ORNE

Aunou-le-Faucon (near Argentan) *:* **'Fort aux Anglais'.**

Alençon *:* The **'Place du Champ du Roi'** recalls that the King of England, Henry V, besieged Alençon on 2nd October1417 before taking the town which was then retaken by the French on 23rd September 1449.

Ceaucé *:* **Oratory of Saint-Radegonde.**
Built in the 15th century to mark the end of the Hundred Years War.

La Perrière *:* **Castle of Monthinet** : It was built between 1429 and 1450 by the English after the destruction of the fortress built in the 11th century by the Counts of Bellême. In the ducal period, La Perrière was one of the principal strong points in Perche.

Ecouché *:* In the majority of the villages in the region of Ecouché, community adjoining Argentan, there existed the 'maisons des anglais' which attested to the presence of British troops in the area.
Charles VII stayed in the town from where he visited his 'honourable' friend Harcourt. He signed (after the English had done it themselves !) the Charter for the foundation of the University of Caen.

Fresnay-le-Samson in the Canton of ***Vimoutiers*** *:* In the valley, close to ***Roiville***, can be found the **'Fort aux anglais'** a very old fortified dwelling which was besieged by Du Guesclin.

Saint-Martin-du-Vieux-Bellême *:* **Site of the 'Croix feue Reine'.**
After the annexation of France, the region of Bellême was entrusted under Royal authority to Pierre de Breux but the latter, being allied to the King of England, soon refused to submit to the authority of the Regent of France, Blanche de Castille. She had a siege set at the Castle of Bellême and came in person to take part in the defeat of her perfidious vassal in 1229. At the place where the regent stood, with her young son at her side, the future Saint Louis, a white cross has been built.

Tinchebray *:* **Chapel of Saint-Remy** (11th century).
It was fortified during the Hundred Years War as well as the castle, occupied by the English it was destroyed by the French.

AREA OF EURE

Hardencourt-Cocherel : In 1364, at Hardencourt, Du Guesclin defeated the troops of the King of England and of Charles le Mauvais.

Verneuil-sur-Avre : Situated at a strategic point on the border between the Duchy and France, Verneuil was founded in 1120 by Henry 1st Beauclerc. The fortified town was the theatre for one of the bloodiest battles of the Hundred Years War.

AREA OF SEINE-MARITIME

Caudebec-en-Caux : **'Les Tours d'Harfleur et des Fascines'** are the only vestiges of the fortifications built by the English during the Hundred Years War.

Rouen : **'Place du Vieux-Marché' :** A cross marks the place of the pyre where **Joan of Arc was burned** at the stake.

Musée Jeanne d'Arc. 33, place du Vieux-Marché - Tel (33) 2 35 88 02 70.

At the place where Joan of Arc was executed there has been for some forty years a museum dedicated to her. In a vaulted Roman-style cellar there have been collected models, engravings, books, the reconstruction of the armour and standard of Jeanne La Lorraine.

The waxworks gallery contains images of around fifty of the great people of the time who bring to life the story of this out-of-the-ordinary, historic person.

Open to the public : From 15th April to 1st October from 9.30 am-7 pm. From 1st October to 14th April from 10 am-12 noon and 2-6.30 pm. Closed 25th December and 1st January.

Entry = 4€ (Student and children = 2€).

7 - The Great Discoveries
of the Renaissance and the end of the Old Regime

A new period opened with the Renaissance, that of the 'Great discoveries".

Everywhere in France, buildings went up. Castles were built, feudal castles were transformed by opening the windows, etc. On the intellectual front, there was an explosion, a thirst for knowledge. Printing enlarged and spread knowledge. Normandy excelled in this domain with religious thinkers, men of the law, and philosophers such as **Nicolas Oresmes** or **Malherbe**…

In terms of discoveries, it was the great sailors that Normandy sent in all directions.

In 1357 or 1364, the ships from Dieppe sailed along the coast of Africa as far as Guinée (now Sierra Leone) where the Normans founded 'Little Dieppe'.

In 1402, **Jean de Béthencourt** left the Alabaster coast to discover the Canaries, of which he became King, but he had to give up this new territory to the King of Castille.

Jean Cousin, a man from Dieppe, discovered Brasil in 1488 after having spotted the American coasts.

In 1503, aboard the ship 'L'Espoir', **Paulmier de Gonneville**, a captain from Honfleur, landed in Brazil.

The *Saint-Lawrence* was discovered by the pilot **Jean Denis or Denys** (originating from *Honfleur*) in 1503. It should be noted that the crews of **Jacques Cartier**, who explored the banks of the great river, following information furnished by Denis, were in large part made up of Normans.

In 1524, his expedition being financed by the ship owner **Jehan Ango**, the Florentine **Verrazano**, leading pilot of François 1st, left Dieppe on the caravelle 'La Dauphine' to discover the 'New France' which he called Arcadia and then the place that would become New York which he called 'New Angoulême'.

Equally financed by the patron of the arts, Jehan Ango, **Parmentier**, a great Norman explorer, invented the crazy ceremony for crossing the equator.

In 1551, **Guillaume Le Testu** (1509-1572) pilot and cosmographer from Le Havre, explored the Brazilian coasts and signalled to Henry II the discovery of the magnificent bay of Rio de Janeiro.

In 1555, **Admiral de Villegaignon** established a colony of Huguenots from the Le Havre region in that same bay.

In 1563, **René de la Laudonnière** succeeded with a similar operation, with the Protestant people from Le Havre and Dieppe, in Florida. They founded the fort of Carolina but the Spanish massacred all of them.

In 1579, **Jacques Devaux** from Le Havre, visited the region of the Amazon, from 1585 to 1587, he travelled along the American coast from Brazil to Newfoundland.

In 1608, the *saitongeois* **Samuel de Champlain**, ship owner from Dieppe, left from *Honfleur* with numerous ships and colonists. He began to take possession of New France and founded *Québec.*

In 1635, **Pierre 'Le Dieppois'**, with his real name of Belain d'Esnanbuc, took possession of Martinique in the name of France before discovering Guadaloupe.

René Robert Cavelier de la Salle (1643-1687), originating from Rouen, some years later, looking for a passage to reach the Pacific visited the lakes of Ontario, Erie, Michigan and Huron, discovering the site of Chicago and then descending the Mississippi to the Gulf of Mexico. He was the first to see Louisiana to which he gave it's name.

In 1662, **Pierre Boucher** left in his turn, his town of *Mortagne,* in Perche, for New France, where he created the town of *'Boucherville'* in the area of Montreal.

A captain of a frigate from Le Havre, **Michel Dubocage** (1676-1728) undertook a voyage to the Far East. He discovered numerous islands.

In the course of the first third of that century, the bulk of the colonists came from Normandy. Soon the rivalry, then the conflicts, with England multiplied in America. The Normans were also the front line in the latent battle between the two kingdoms : departure ports, ship's crews, colonists of New France.

****

Norman emigration to Canada.

A great number of Normans and especially the people from Perche emigrated in the 17*th* century to North America to help found the 'New France'. In the church of Saint-Aubin in Tourouvre, a stained glass window evokes the departure for Canada in 1640, of 80 families from Perche. Among these men and women was Julien Mercier, whose family would later play a leading role in the developments across the Atlantic. On departure, their parents called out : 'Don't forget either God or France !'. A second window commemorates the official visit of his Honour Mercier, head of the Canadian Government to Tourouvre in 1891. He declared 'We have not forgotten either God or France !'. Still in the church are plaques attached to the walls in memory of Robert Guiguère and the three brothers Gagnon, who left around 1640 in the company of their cousin Robert de la Ventrouze. They founded a new Gagnon family which numbers today some 50,000 members in Canada and the United States ! On another plaque are inscribed the names of inhabitants of the region who left afterwards for Canada having been baptised in the church of Tourouvre between 1589 and 1713. In addition to the Gagnons and the Diguères, the Juchereaus, the Pelletiers (one of the descendents of whom would become Ambassador for Canada in Paris), Jean Guyon who made the staircase to the bell tower of the church in 1616, Louis Guimont, martyr, Pierre Tremblay de Randonnai, Madame de la Pelletrie and Bivilliers who founded the Ursuline Convent in Quebec, Robert Giffard, who became Lord of Beaufort, near the Saint Lawrence.

Mortagne-au-Perche is the native town of Pierre Boucher (1622-1717) 'patriarch of French Canada' who founded 'Boucherville', a town in the suburbs of Montreal which numbers today more than 30,000 inhabitants. Arriving very young in Canada, Pierre Boucher was quickly noticed by the Governor who sent him to meet the Indians whose language he spoke, to try to subdue them and to give up the 'strong arm' methods used on occasions. In the battle which remains noted in Canadian history, he repulsed the Iroquois and saved the new town of Trois Rivières thus assuring the survival of all the population. In October 1653, he was nominated as Governor of this place. Also leaving from Mortagne for the New World were the Trudel and Drouin families.

****

Finally it was the English who took the new continent, being more motivated than the French who, generally, had little desire for the distant colonies in America. It is true that public opinion was made to believe that there was little more than 'acres of snow' (Voltaire dixit).

In addition, the French Canadian population remained static while the inhabitants of the English colonies multiplied regularly.

And then it is said that the heirs of **Hugues Capet**, who reigned in France, contrary to the Norman leaders, 'sons of the sea', had never had ambitions 'overseas'. The 'Capétiens' were the continentals, more at ease engaging in the interminable European conflicts where their sole aim was to consolidate the frontier to the East of the Kingdom.

The great administrators like **Richelieu** or **Colbert** (*who organised in Le Havre the office of the East India Company*) had clearly seen the stakes with maritime expansion in building fleets capable of rivalling the English but often their efforts were exhausted after a few years.

We must recognise that England and the States of Holland have certainly known and benefited from our weaknesses.

Finally, in 1768, with the **Treaty of Paris**, we lost all the archipelago of Saint-Pierre-et-Miquelon… for cod fishing !

Some years later, ships left Norman ports to go to the aid of the 'insurgent' Americans rebelling against England.

At the end of the 'Old regime', the Norman ports had considerably developed their exchanges with the colonial ports but the **Treaty of Paris**, signed in 1763, put a large part of the Norman fleet at a disadvantage, losing France the business openings in India.

Some time later, Louis XVI dealt a new blow to Normandy with the business treaty that he signed with the English which would have a detrimental consequence and create a serious crisis in the textile industry.

To close this part on the explorers, we can cite Admiral Dumont-D'Urville, of Condé-sur-Noireau (1790-1841) who directed several expeditions to the Antarctic.

Places to visit...

AREA OF MANCHE

Céaux : It was in this village that the revolt of the 'Nu-pieds' began under Louis XIII.
Ile de Tatihou : **'Musée Maritime'**.
This museum brings to life the Battle of La Hougue in 1692.

AREA OF ORNE

Dame-Marie : (near Bellême) '**Borne de Généralité**'.
Marks the limits of the 'généralités' of Alençon and Le Mans (administrative divisions of the old regime). It is a pyramidal pillar which was erected in the 18th century on the orders of the 'Intendant de la Généralité d'Alençon'. It is sited on the D938 which was in other times a 'royal' route leading from Paris to Le Mans. It was enlarged in 1734. One can note along this route, small pillars in sandstone engraved with the fleur de lys and carrying in figures the distance from each of them to Paris.

Tourouvre : **Museum of the history of the Perche emigration to Canada**
Reconstruction of the room of the 'Hôtel du Cheval Blanc' where the people of Perche signed their commitment to leave for New France in the 17th century.
'Obligatory' place of pilgrimage for Ambassadors of Canada in France.
Information : Tel (33) 2 33 25 74 55 - Fax (33) 2 33 25 43 46.
Entry = 2€

8 - Normandy and the Revolution

The **Revolution** which broke out in 1789 began a long conflict which would last until 1815 and would have disastrous consequences on relations between England and Normandy, ruining the commercial relations between the two nations otherwise allied.

Normandy was a border with England, presenting badly defended coasts : no military port (!) on the Channel to shelter the country from strikes by the English navy.

It should be recognised during this period the support both moral and financial, of the British Cabinet for the 'emigrants' from France in general and Normandy in particular.

England accommodated those who were against the Revolution and gave it's help to the landing of **Puisage, Cadoudal** and the head of Norman 'Chouannerie', (Royalist insurgents from western France) : **Count-General de Frotté**.

During the dramatic years at the end of the 18th century, Normandy lost her liberties and privileges but also her unity, the Province being split up into five areas.

Places to visit...

AREA OF MANCHE

Le Petit-Celland : **Les 'Trois Croix'.**
Top place of the Norman Chouannerie where royalists and republicans clashed.

Sainte-Mère-Eglise : **Manor of Roueur** *(Fauville)* : the royalist insurgents of the region would gather there.

Chef-du-Pont : **Castle 'Le Val'** (18th century) : It is here that 'Monsieur de Bricqueville', Lieutenant of Frotté, head of the Norman royalists, was arrested by the republicans in 1797. He was then summarily tried and shot at **Coutances**.

Liesville-sur-Douve (near to Saint-Mère-Eglise) : **'L'arbre de la Liberté'** (the tree of freedom) : a cedar - planted in 1791 by the local revolutionaries still stands. It carries on its trunk a notice which states that it is 'protected by law'.

AREA OF ORNE

Colonard-Corubert : **Church of Notre-Dame de Courthioust** (11th - 12th century). This church, which was modified in the Renaissance, had been sold as 'truly national' under the French Revolution. So that it was not destroyed and should serve its purpose, the 'peasants and inhabitants of Courthioust' decided to buy it. It is therefore still the property of the 47 families who lived in the parish at the end of the 18th century.

Couterne : **Castle of the Count of Frotté**, Head of the Norman royalists. It is today still the property of his family. (Private property).

Flers : **The castle**, today Mairie and Museum, ancient headquarters of Frotté and the Norman royalists.

9 - Birth of the 'Entente Cordiale'

After the Revolution, the Empire and the Restoration, renewed 'English style' Franco-British relations and on the way those between England and Normandy. It was thus that on his territory, at the castle of **Eu**, in eastern Normandy that the 'bourgeois' **King Louis-Philippe 1st** received **Queen Victoria** - First British sovereign to officially set foot in continental Normandy since **Edward 7th** - to cement the **'Entente Cordiale'.** This spectacular 'getting together' was the occasion for sumptuous festivities but it was also however measured.

****

'Saturday 2 September 1843, 5 o'clock in the evening. The sun set on the Channel as a cortege of carriages and knights rattled out of the Château d'Eu...

Louis-Philippe, King of France, accompanied by his wife Marie-Amelie, and Louise, Queen of the Belgians, set off to meet Queen Victoria and her husband Prince Albert, whose yacht dropped anchor off Tréport. A boat manœuvred by 24 oarsmen dressed in white, brought Victoria ashore, blonde with blue eyes wearing a small yellow hat topped with a white feather.

For five days, the town of Eu cemented, happily, the famous 'Entente Cordiale'...

****

In spite of the normalisation of relations between the two countries there came little by little a 'controlled' rivalry because of the colonial expansion.

But Franco-British friendship continued to increase, thanks notably to the influence of powerful people such as **King Edward 7**[th] , close friend of France who strengthened the 'Entente Cordiale' at the end of the 19th century.

The Normans, for themselves, were delighted with the new links which came into place allowing them to restart the exchanges with their neighbours. Captured by the 'chic' of **Queen Victoria**, the Normans decided even to swap their traditional 'coiffes' for the little hats, imitating those worn by the sovereign.

Add to this the effect that produced the development of transatlantic transport between Europe and America.

The ports such as *Le Havre, Cherbourg* and *Southampton* specialised in transatlantic transport taking to the distant Americas a substantial number of emigrants but also a well-off clientele on the liners which were ever more luxurious and efficient.

Also the voyage to *New York* was seen as the height of fashion and 'l'art de vivre', and of great prestige, adding to the image of England and Normandy who, rich with their maritime past, their traditions, invited the new aristocracy to the journey of their dreams.

Places to visit...

AREA OF SEINE-MARITIME

Eu : **Museum 'Louis-Philippe'**. Castle of Eu -
Tel (33) 2 35 86 44 00.
Internet E,mail = chateau.eu@wanadoo.fr

10 - The 20th century

But the skies of Europe suddenly darkened. The **First World War** broke out. This conflict involving the whole of Europe would cost Normandy dear, who although far from the front, was mobilised everywhere. Large numbers of buildings: hotels, public and private buildings were used as places of rest, convalescence and hospitals for the allied troops.

Traffic between the Norman and English ports was intense in spite of the danger presented by the German submarines.

11th November 1918 at the end of four years of merciless conflict, marked the end of the slaughter of which above all the young had been the victims : 1.5 million killed throughout France! Like other provinces, Normandy paid a heavy price in this war with the remarkable conduct of the Norman regiments. The courage and determination of the Norman soldiers, as with their neighbours the Bretons, has many times been hailed by **General Foch**, Commander in Chief of the allied forces.

This slaughter was going, for a while, to put in danger the renewal of the population.

Between the two wars Normandy developed seaside tourismr. Hotels and other attractive villas appeared all along the Norman coast : *Le Tréport, Eu, Dieppe,*

Etretat, Le Havre on the *Alabaster and Opal Coasts* ; *Deauville, Trouville, Cabourg*, on the *Floral Coast* ; *Ouistreham* on the *Mother of Pearl Coast* without forgetting *Granville,* were all frequented by a continental clientele but also an English one giving a special style to the seaside resorts with the development of hotels, racecourses and casinos…

It was the **'Belle Epoque'** !

Again, however, the European skies were covered by menacing clouds.! Come back our 'Epoque', 20 years have quickly passed!

1918-1938! The rise of nazism in Germany, the lack of resolution from the democracies generated a **Second World War,** which this time was really going to be that. During four years it covered Europe, Asia and Africa.

All seemed well when at last the democracies realised the danger ! But Germany, after several months of '**phoney war'**', subdued France and her continental allies.

Only England resisted! Germany attacked Russia in June 1941, then Japan attacked the United States in December of the same year. The USA entered the war alongside the allies and became the **'Arsenal'**.

Little by little, after the **Battle of Stalingrad**, the ejection from Africa of the German-Italian troops, the allies opened a second front.

In the plan envisaged for the liberation of Europe, Normandy gradually became identified and was chosen at the **Conference of Québec** as the place for the landings.

Since 1940, the Normans, after a short exodus from the cities in 1940, lived under the boot of the German troops who occupied even the smallest villages and brought about martial law.

Secret places were established for parachute drops from small English transport planes to the Norman resistance.

A feat of arms too, often forgotten, should be stressed : 19 August 1942, Anglo-Canadian forces landed at *Dieppe*. This operation ended in disaster and cost the Canadians dearly but it allowed nevertheless, a test of the equipment and the solidarity of the **'Atlantic Wall'**, defences that the Germans had put in place all along the Norman coast.

For ten months allied bombardment was concentrated on Normandy and the Atlantic Wall fortifications.

With minute attention to detail, a faultless preparation in the choice of materials and equipment but also in the elite troops, the allies, placed under the supreme command of **General Eisenhower** landed on the beaches of Normandy on the morning of 6th June 1944…

Places to visit…

AREA OF EURE

Les Andelys : **Musée Normandie Niémen.** Tel (33) 2 32 54 49 76.
rue Raymond Philip,
Open all days of the year (except Thuesday) from June to September = from 10 am at 12 am and 2 pm to 6 pm,
http//:normandie.niemen.free.fr

Dieppe : Landing beach from 19 August 1942 and commemorative monument.

11 - The Battle of Normandy

On the allied side, the operation **'Overlord'** assembled the British and American forces under the command of which were placed troops of the Free French with notably the legendary 2nd French battalion who, under the command of **General Leclerc de Hautecloque**[(1)], distinguished themselves on many battlefields and, joined the strength of those commanded by **General Montgomery**, the Canadian troops, those from the Empire and the Polish volunteers of **General Maczek**, the Belgians of **General Piron**, the French of the **Commando unit Kieffer**…

The Americans landed in the sectors known as : **'Utah beach'** and **'Omaha beach'**, which run from *Saint-Laurent-sur Mer* to *Sainte-Mère-Eglise* whereas the Anglo-Canadian forces landed on the beaches **'Gold'**, **'Juno'** and **'Sword'** in the region of Calvados to the north of *Caen*.

On the night preceding, parachute commandos commanded respectively by Generals **Taylor** and **Gale**, had been dropped from the American side on *Sainte-Mère-Eglise* (82nd and 101st Airborne) and from the British side (6th Division) on *Bénouville* close to the famous **'Pegasus Bridge'**, a bridge situated on the Orne between *Caen* and *Ouistreham* and the no less celebrated **'Café Gondrée'**, today still a place of pilgrimage for the old soldiers of Britain.

The landings took place in the early morning and unfolded at enormous cost **(11,000 killed during the first day).**

---

(1) The family of whom still live in Normandy some kilometres from Lisieux at the Castle of **Mesnil-Guillaume**.

****

When the ancestors of Montgomery, Patton and Rommel
lived peacefully in Normandy

The American **General Omar Bradley**, *commanding the allied forces in Normandy,* **General George S. Patton**, *commander of the 3rd American army and the British* **General Montgomery**, *under the orders of Commander in Chief* **Dwight D. Eisenhower**, *would show their great military skill.*

On the German side, charged by the high command with the defense of the Norman coasts, **Field Marshal Rommel** *would equally be one of the great strategists of this battle.*

It is worrying to realise that three of these players in the Battle of Normandy were, if one believes the assertions of certain historians, the descendants of Norman country squires established for centuries on the land of the Vikings.

Field Marshal Montgomery had as ancestor **Roger de Montgommery**, *powerful lord of the fortress built in the 11th century close to **Vimoutiers**[(1)] on the hill called **'Mont Gomeri'**. He was close to Duke William who gave him land and honours in Great Britain after 1066.*

*The **Patton** family was, under a slightly different name, **(Pâton)** originally from the region of **Trun**[(2)]. The first **George Patton** landed in the United States in the second part of the 18th century became wealthy before giving birth to a military dynasty which continues today.*

*To complete this picture, it is claimed equally that the ancestors of **Erwin Rommel** lived in the area of **Exmes**[(3)] and being protestant were forced to leave Normandy and take refuge over the Rhine because of the religious wars which shook France...*

---

(1) (2) (3) - The communities of **Vimoutiers, Trun and Exmes** are all in the region of Argentan on the battlefield of the 'Falaise Gap'.

****

The Battle of Normandy was going to last for three months until 22nd August 1944 : a **'terrible battle of the hedgerows'** in the divided landscape of the hedged farmland of Normandy where the enemy troops fought each other mercilessly.

****

The Battle of the Falaise-Argentan-Trun-Chambois Pocket.

*On 19th August 1944, two and a half months after the beginning of the Battle of Normandy, at the border of the **Plain of Argentan** and the **Pays d'Auge**, at the end of unremitting and decisive fighting which will remain in history as the **'Battle of the Falaise Gap'** what was left of the powerful German 7th army was encircled and then, defeated, fled in disorder...*

*In rags with haggard faces, uniforms dirty and in tatters, as if they had escaped from an inferno, the 'lions' of the Führer who four years before paraded in our towns proving an insolent hegemony were, on this beautiful summer's day, a sorry sight. With a mixture of powerful tigers and horse-drawn vehicles which slowed the continuous tide, they were 20,000, although 40,000 had escaped the massacre, they pulled back to the East after following the **'corridor of death'** and crossed in a straggling order the **'Gué de Moissy'**.*

The picture is 'Dantesque'. All the roads and lanes of the region were strewn with the bodies of horses and men swollen by the heat and of abandoned materials.

*This battle that the German soldiers who had fought on the Eastern front compared to the terrible **Battle of Stalingrad**, in that the exchanges were so severe, undoubtedly marked a turning point in the course of the Second World War and shortened its duration as from this day on the German army in the West were totally in retreat first towards the **Seine** and then to the **Rhine**, even if certain final efforts intervened, notably in the Ardennes.*

The impact was made ten days earlier on the Normandy plain...

On 8 August, **General Omar Bradley** who commanded the allied forces controlling from then on the West of Normandy, holding **Avranches** and preparing to enter **Brittany**, decided to adopt another strategy and gave the order to his troops to move towards the east, choosing immediate confrontation with the Germans in the hope of pushing them finally out of Normandy.

The main 'players' in this offensive were the **Generals Patton and Montgomery**.

Patton, who commanded the 3rd American army and was at Avranches, received the order to head towards **Le Mans** and then to move towards **Alençon and Argentan** in order to join up with the Anglo-Canadian forces who were still in the outskirts of **Caen** and who were to be sent towards the South via **Falaise**, in order to concentrate and isolate the 7th German army and the elite troops (SS divisions) who were combined under the command of **Obergrüppenführer Paul Hausser**.

The encircling manœuvre was to operate without the Germans being aware or escaping.

On the American side :

After liberating **Le Mans** on 8th August, the American forces, reinforced on their right flank by the 2nd Battalion of **General Leclerc**, changed direction and headed for **Alençon** which was liberated by the French on 12th August. The next objective was **Argentan**. In the **Forest of Ecouves**, the French tanks experienced serious clashes with the tanks of the **9th Panzer Division**.

A part of the forces pushed on towards **Argentan** while a handful of men went towards **Ecouché** to cut off any German retreat.

While Leclerc established his base at **Fleuré**, at the entry to **Argentan**, the Americans 'dug in' in the woods of **Silly-en-Gouffern** and put in place powerful artillery. Under this pressure, the German troops, cut off to North, West and South and regrouped on the banks of the **River Dives** and endeavoured to keep open an escape route to the East preventing notably the Americans from taking control of the village of **Bourg-Saint-Léonard** in the direction of **L'Aigle**.

Paul Hausser was totally aware of the scenario that was unfolding, he knew that retreat was the only possibility left to him in order to save his 7th army, but the order did not come... By the 15 August **Patton** was in position and waiting for the Anglo-Canadian forces to close the pocket, the Shermans of **Montgomery** had come up against a division of German tanks on the **Plain of Falaise**.

On the British side :

On the 8th August the troops of '**Monty**' were being given a rough ride by the German artillery. The men of General Simons to the south of **Caen** were taking heavy losses due to an attack on the 12th SS Panzer. The next morning a regiment of British tanks was all but wiped out by the elite German troops, from the SS, for the most part fanatical and determined.

For more than a week it was practically a battle for position where the English, Canadians and Poles suffered heavy casualties.

After the difficult conquest of **Caen**, the battle around **Falaise** was fierce. The birthplace of **King William** was almost totally destroyed, only being liberated on 16 August.

It was to the acclaim of a relieved and jubilant people that the Canadian troops entered.

*The Polish volunteers of **General Maczek**, whose names would go into legend for the acts of heroism that they would achieve, received the order to regroup to the south and take up position on the high ground of **Montormel** which marked the first foothills of the **Pays d'Auge** and from where one could easily monitor the movements on the plain where the Germans were and where they had been repulsed.*

*The Poles overcame the obstacle of the **Dives** and deployed on the high ground although the Germans seemed to ignore for the moment all danger on the ground, too occupied in saving themselves from massive attacks from the allied airforces. Opposite them the Poles could see the forest of **Gouffern** where the Americans were established. To the northwest the men of the 2ⁿᵈ **British Army** headed towards **Flers** and connected up in this zone with the American troops at **Briouze**.*

The Germans caught in a trap :

When the chief of the 7ᵗʰ German Army at last received the order to retreat, on 16 August, he knew that it was already too late and that he would not be able to save all his men. The allies increased the pressure continuously in a pincer movement.

*On **Montormel**, the Poles realised little by little the precariousness of their situation. They represented only a minor obstacle when faced with the thousands of German soldiers ready for anything to flee the moments of horror that they would face in the 'cauldron' of the allies, bounded by the **Dives**. In this territory of some square kilometres, where thousands of shells landed, the Germans 'shared' with the civilian population hours of intense gravity.*

*To the north-west, the Canadians took up position at **Trun**, liberated on 18 August, then headed towards **Saint-Lambert-sur-Dives**, a strategic point to hold the Germans.*

*The Americans regrouped along the RN 24 while **Argentan**, in ruins, was still in the hands of the enemy.*

*On the morning of 19 August, The Germans beaten and always in retreat massed together on the width of the single and narrow way of evacuation which led to **Saint-Lambert-sur-Dives**. It is said that the night before a large number of officers of the Wehrmacht fled, leaving their men.*

*At the heart of the operation, while in the cellars of the white stone houses men, women and children took cover united in the same fear of being subjected to the madness of the SS, the village of **Tournai-sur-Dives** was an inferno. It was then that **Abbé Launay**, priest of the parish tried to walk to the American forces in order to convince them that the Germans were ready to surrender and that it was pointless to continue the shelling. The allies, having the same day been victims of suicide attacks from SS commandos coming towards them with a white flag, wanted to believe him and sent some men on reconnaissance.*

*At the sight of a single Canadian soldier entering the village some 2000 Germans threw down their arms and were taken prisoner in the yard of a farm situated near the church and which would be called the '**Cour de la Capitulation**'.*

On the evening of 19 August, the Poles who had been subjected to repeated assaults from the Germans but had not given an inch, at last joined up with the

*Americans coming from **Chambois**. In early evening, the pocket was closed or almost !*

The attacks would last several more days and several thousand Germans among them a large majority of the SS managed to slip through the narrow gap which existed but the German High Command had admitted defeat, the loss of a considerable number of fighters and materials. All the world knew, even in Berlin, with the exception of Hitler, that the final countdown had begun.

*Thus on 23 August the allied troops again took up their offensive to the east, on the battlefield of **Falaise-Argentan**, soldiers and civilians began to care for wounds both human and material.*

*Flying over the sector some days later, **General Eisenhower**, supreme commander of the allied forces, took in the dimension of the tragedy which had been played out there.*

He said to his officers that the odour of putrefying animal and human bodies was at times so strong that the pilot of the plane was forced to go higher.

The people of the encircled communities collected their dead and repaired the damage caused but the farmers for more than fifty years and still today avoid burning the dead wood in the hedgerows and do not trust unknown objects that the ploughshares may turn up from the soil. Many tons of explosives were abandoned there by the routed German army.

The toll :

*During the '**Battle of the Pocket of Falaise-Argentan-Trun-Chambois**' there were huge losses both human and material.*

*More than **200,000 men** were killed or wounded as well as the destruction of **1,000 tanks and 3,000 pieces of artillery.***

*The beautiful monument which glorifies the bravery of the Polish soldiers engaged in the battle was built in the 60's on the way to the hill on the initiative of a local association made up of some of the elected people and some residents of the communities of **Montormel** and **Coudehard**. The land having been donated by the owner.*

****

At the end of August 1944, the vanquished German cohort, fleeing in disarray, had recrossed the *Seine* and then the *Rhine*… At last, on 8th May 1945, nazi Germany capitulated unconditionally.

Normandy had suffered the worst disaster in its history. The first six months of 1944 had been for the old province a terrible test during which 50,000 Norman men and women died or disappeared. Whole towns and villages had been wiped from the map and with them immense architectural and artistic works such as in *Lisieux, Caen, Falaise, Rouen, Le Havre, Argentan, Vimoutiers, Saint-Lô*… Its industry, agriculture, ports and economy all laid waste.

The reconstruction would be long, very long.

It started as soon as the war was over to finish in the 60's. The development of tourism which is today the prime source of revenue for Normandy attracts an ever more numerous clientele. Great Britain represents one of the special targets for the

Norman tourist trade : a long common history of some six centuries between the two sister nations makes us believe that we have still much more to say to each other !

On the initiative of the Normandy Day Association, there officially came into being in 2001, the 'Normandy Day", which will henceforth be celebrated each year throughout Normandy on 6th June. This institution is destined to promote the image of Normandy outside its boundaries and to promote its heritage.

****

Visitors to Normandy - especiallly those intending to visit some of the many British and Commonweulth War Graves in Normandy - may like to know that there is a branch of the Royal British Legion in the area Its offices are in the Town Hall (Mairie) of Ranville, near Ouistreham, just over the road from the church where the first British fatality of D. Day, Lt Denny Brotheridge, is buried, and close to the excellent new museum 'Memorial Pegasus'. At Ranvillel-Bénouville it explains the action in June, July and August 1944 to capture and hold the vital eastern flank of the Allied Assault into France. There is also a major Commonwealth War Graves Commission cemetery in Ranville. The Normandy Calvados Branch of the Royal British Legion is available to give whatever help it can to those visiting the area, but especially to ex-Servicemen and their dependants and to those on a pilgrimage of remembrance to Normandy. Poppy wreaths and crosses are available at the branch's offices in Ranville, as is information of the War Graves cemeteries in Normandy, but we would welcome a telephone call in advance if possible, since our offices are not permanently manned. Our telephone number is (33) 2 31 78 36 40.

****

Places to visit...

AREA OF MANCHE

Avranches : **Patton Monument.** In homage to the liberator of the town.

Azeville : **The batteries of Azeville and Crisbecq.**
Les Cruttes - Tel (33) 2 33 05 98 83 - Fax (33) 2 33 05 98 16.
Open all the days from June to September from 11,00 am to 7 pm,
Vestiges of the Atlantic Wall.

Cherbourg-Octeville : **'Musée de la Montée des Résistants ou de la Libération'.**
'Fort du Roule' : This recently created museum retraces the history of the Second World War seen from Cherbourg. The landings of 6th June 1944 are of course featured. One discovers also the role played by the port of Cherbourg in the Battle of Normandy through documents and objects such as an historic American film : 'Cherbourg, porte de la France'. Tel (33) 2 33 20 24 12,

Denneville : (near *Port-Bail*) **British graves** in the parish cemetery.
These are the graves of British soldiers killed on 18th June 1940 as a result of the German invasion. They were in a lorry that hit a mine in the station of Denneville.

Foucarville : (near to *Sainte-Mère-Eglise*) **Stele** marking the site a camp for German prisoners : **'Continental Central Enclosure n° 19'.**

Granville : **Souvenirs of the landing... German on 8th March 1945 !**

On 31 July 1944, the third American army commanded by General Patton liberated the town of Granville without a fight.

Granville, due to the good fortune of being in a 'cul de sac' had not represented a strategic objective. The people of Granville believed they had been liberated once and for all from the German yoke and life returned to normal after four years of occupation. But the respite only lasted six months as during the night of 8/9 March 1945, numerous German army commandos, coming from **Jersey**, landed at Granville and launched an attack on the port and the town. The few French and American soldiers charged with the defense of the site were taken by surprise and the Germans struck them, equally with the civilian population, and there were serious losses and destruction in the port from bombardment with shells. The soldiers of the 3rd Reich departed with American prisoners and a cargo containing more than three hundred tons of coal.

Hiesville : **'Ferme de Franqueville'.**

It was in this property that the distribution of food supplies took place during the war. General Maxwell Don Taylor, commander of the 101st Airborne established there the first command post of the American troops on 6th June 1944. There is a **commemorative plaque.**

Huisne-sur-Mer : **German Mausoleum.**

On the 'Mont-de-Huisne' is sited the only German Mausoleum in France, on a promontory some 30 metres high. Since the beginning of the 60's, 11,956 dead from the Battle of Normandy, rest here.

Quinéville : **'Musée de la Liberté'.**

Daily Norman life under the occupation is recalled.

18, avenue de la Plage-Rens. Tel (33) 2 33 21 40 44 - Fax (33) 2 33 21 52 20,

Open all the days from march to November,

Numerous photographic documents, propaganda posters, dioramas and videos - reconstruction of a street under the occupation.

Saint-James : **American Military Cemetery.** *(Montjoie-Saint-Martin) :* 4,410 Gaves - Tel (33) 2 33 89 24 90 - Fax (33) 2 33 89 24 91

Sainte-Marie-du-Mont : **Museum of the landings at Utah Beach.**

The museum is open from June to September from 9.30 am-7 pm. In April, May and October open from 10 am-12 noon and 2-6 pm. From November to March the museum is open Saturdays, Sundays, National Holidays and school holidays from 10 am-12.30 pm and from 2-5 pm. Information : Tel (33) 2 33 71 53 35 or (33) 2 33 71 58 00. Internet Site : www.utah.beach.com

A remarkable collection, landing barges, elements from the German defences. In a stained glass window : a reconstruction of the fighting at Pointe du Hoc.

Sainte-Mère-Eglise : **Airborne Museum.**

14, rue Eisenhower. Open every day from 1st February to 31st March and from 1st October to 30th November from 9.30 am-12 noon and from 2-5 pm. From 1st April to 30th April from 9 am-12 noon and from 2-6.45 pm. From 1st May to 30th September from 9 am-6.45 pm. Closed 1st December to 31st January.

Information : Tel (33) 2 33 41 41 35 - Fax (33) 2 33 41 78 87.
Http:/www.musée.airborne.asso.fr - E-mail : musée airborne@wanadoo fr
Situated in the centre of the village, the museum, which takes the form of an immense parachute, displays an American glider of the Waco type, arms, uniforms, photographs, newspapers of the period, flags and maps of the parachute zones. A second building houses a Douglas aircraft.

Le Val-Saint-Père : **Museum of the Second World War.**
2, Le Moulinet - Tel (33) 2 33 68 35 83 - Fax (33) 2 33 68 75 55. Open every day from 15th April to 11th November.
Important material is exhibited (armaments, motorcycles, communications systems), models displaying uniforms.

AREA OF CALVADOS

Arromanches :
Arromanches 360°.
Circular cinema that is unique in the region. Shows of the film 'Le prix de la liberté' on the 6th June 1944 landings.
Open all year except January from 9,40 am to 6,40 pm (summer),
B.P.9, 14117 Arromanches. Tel (33) 2 31 22 30 30 - Fax (33) 2 31 22 33 55.

Museum of the Landings
Permanent exhibition - Place du 6 Juin. Tel (33) 2 31 22 34 31.
Internet site : www.normandie1944.fr
Presentation of the different phases of the allied landings from the conception of the artificial port Winston to the liberation of the coast.
Open all year except January.

Asnelles : **Funeral Monument of Maurice Schumann** in the new cemetery. He, who was 'the voice of Free France' at the BBC from 1940 to 1944 before becoming one of the Ministers of the Vth Republic close to General de Gaulle, landed at Asnelle with the British troops in June 1944. Loving this seaside town where he returned many times, he wanted to be buried there. The main street of the town bears his name.

Asnelles-la-Belle-Plage : **Pontoons of the jetty and artificial port** built by the allies.

Bayeux :
Musée Memorial 1944, Battle of Normandy.
Boulevard Fabien-Ware - Parking and picnic space.
Visiting days and hours : from 1st May to 17th September from 9.30 am-6.30 pm uninterrupted and from 18th September to 30th April from 10 am-12.30 pm and from 2-6 pm. Closed 25th December, 1st January and from 15th to 31st January.
Tel (33) 2 31 51 46 90 - Fax (33) 2 31 51 46 91.
Site Internet = www.mairie-bayeux.fr.
Entry = 5,50 (students = 3,60 - children = free), Free for veterans,
In the first French town to be liberated on 6th June 1944, this museum retraces the

military and human history of the battle of Normandy. How did 1,500,000 allied soldiers come together against nazism and bring down 740,000 defenders of the Third Reich in 77 days of continuous fighting on Norman soil? It is this question that the Museum of Bayeux tries to answer in a space of 2,300 square matres. Authentic documents - materials of war - models - diorama - cinema.

Musée Memorial de Gaulle
10, rue Bourbesneur - Tel (33) 2 31 92 45 55.

Photographic documents, texts and personal mementos of General de Gaulle who made in Bayeux on 16th June 1944 an historic address launching the outlines of the future constitution of the Vth Republic.

Open every day from February to December from 9.30 am-12.30 pm and from 2-6.30 pm. Internet site : www.normandie1944.fr

Bénerville : The batteries of Mont Canisy

Situated at Bénerville-sur-Mer, this natural site protected by Mont Canisy, overlooks the sea from the height of 110 metres. From 1935 to 1940 the French Navy installed two batteries to ensure the security of the estuary and the port of Le Havre. From 1942, the site became an important element in the 'Atlantic Wall' conceived by Rommel.

Various remains (bunkers, storage rooms, fortified spaces connected by a gallery some 260 metres long). Free guided visits.

Caen : 'Mémorial pour la Paix'

'Three hours of journey to the heart of the Battle of Normandy and the history of the 20th century'.

A 'muséographique' site unique in Europe. Le Memorial is an astonishing place on the history of the Second World War, its origins and its consequences.

Open every day from 9 am - 6 pm (7 pm from February to July and from Closed 25th December. Information : www.memorial-caen-fr

Esplanade Eisenhower - 14066 Caen Cedex - Tel (33) 2 31 31 06 44 - Fax (33) 2 31 06 01 66 - E.mail = contact@memorial-caen.fr

* **A'muséographique' journey (1918-1945).**
* **Audiovisual spaces (1944-1994).**
* **The gallery of the Nobel Peace Prize.**
* **The international park for the liberation of Europe.**

Guided visits of the landing beaches. Every day except 25 December and the first 15 days of the year. Tel (33) 2 31 06 06 44 - Fax (33) 2 31 06 06 70. From 8th November to 17th December from 9 am-6 pm. From 6th February to 9th July, from 23rd August to 7th November and from 18th to 31st December from 9 am-7 pm. From 10th July to 22nd August from 9 am-8 pm.

La Cambe : German military cemetery.

At the side of RN 13. The graves of more than 21,000 German soldiers. Open every day of the year from April to September from 8 am-7.30 pm or 8 pm, from October to March from 8 am - 6 pm. Information : Tel (33) 2 31 22 70 76.

Chouains : (Between Bayeux and Tilly-sur-Seulles).
Small military cemetery of some forty graves.

Colleville-Montgomery : Site fortifié Hillman.

Situated on the southern edge of the community towards Beuville-Biéville, it is made up of a site of 24 hectares containing 12 underground bunkers constructed by the Germans between 1942 and 1944 to shelter the base of the commander of the defences on the Côte de Nacre. (The mother of pearl coast).

See the monument to the 1st Battalion of the Suffolk Regiment which seized the post on 6th June 1944. (free visits throughout the year).

The association 'the friends of the Suffolk Regiment' undertook the restoration of this site. Gatherings take place on the first Saturday of the month.

Information : Tel (33) 2 31 97 12 61 or (33) 2 31 37 39 11.

Colleville-sur-Mer : American Military Cemetery.

Overlooking the Omaha beach, more than 9,000 white marble crosses set in 20 hectares of lawn recall the immense sacrifice made by young Americans for the liberty of France.

Memorial dedicated to the young of America and a chapel. Information : Tel (33) 2 31 51 62 00. Open from 1st October to 15th April from 9 am-5 pm and from 16th April to 30th September from 9 am-6 pm. Free visiting.

****

The Flowers of Remembrance

The American cemeteries of Colleville-sur-Mer in Calvados and Saint-James in La Manche, number 13,886 graves of American soldiers killed, for the most part in the flower of youth, during the Battle of Normandy. To honour their sacrifice and their memory by putting flowers on the graves in the place of the families and the veterans who can no longer travel because of their great age, an Association was born. It is called : 'Les Fleurs de la Mémoire' and its mission is to put flowers regularly on the graves. It has been established by Norman volunteers and its headquarters have been established in the community of Saint-Jean-Daye.

****

Courseulles-sur-Mer : 'Croix de Lorraine'.

18 metres high, a cross of Lorraine, emblem of the Free French Forces, set facing the sea, commemorates the return to French soil of General de Gaulle, 14th June 1944.

Creully : 'Musée du Matérial radio'.

In June 1944, journalists, allied war correspondents, installed themselves in the square tower of Creully (15th century) which today houses the museum open in July and August, (See Chapter 2).

Douvres-la-Délivrande : 'Musée du Radar'.

Route de Basly - Tel (33) 2 31 06 06 45 or (33) 2 31 37 74 43. Route de Caen, Open from 15th February to 31th August,

Cross of an English regiment in the church of Saint-Rémi.

Falaise : Museum of August 1944.

This private museum, situated near the ducal castle in an ancient dairy is the work of an enthusiast of the period and of military material : Michel Leloup.

It retraces the battle of Falaise Gap and has as historic adviser the writer Eddy

Florentin author of the book 'The Battle of Falaise Gap' and undisputed specialist on this battle. **It offers a selection of material unique in Normandy and merits a visit in this capacity.**
Chemin de Roches. Tel (33) 2 31 90 37 19 - Fax (33) 2 31 90 07 26.
Open from April to November. Crom 10 am-12 noon and 2-6 pm. Closed on Tuesdays in June, July and August.

Grandcamp-Maisy : **Museum of the Rangers.**
30, quai Crampon - Tel (33) 2 31 92 33 51.
This museum retraces the assault on the 'Pointe du Hoc' by the 'rangers' of Colonel Rudder.
Open in June, July and August every day from 10 am-7 pm except Monday morning. In April, May, September and October every day except Monday from 10 am-1 pm and 3-6 pm.

Hermanville-sur-Mer : **Sword historic exhibition.**
In season.

Longues-sur-Mer : **Battery of Longues.**
Situated between the beaches of the British and American sectors, this battery is made up of 4 bunkers and a command post. It is the only one of the Atlantic Wall to have preserved it guns.

Merville-Franceville : **'Musée de la Batterie'.**
4 blockhaus - avenue de la Batterie de Merville. Tel (33) 2 31 24 21 83.
Open every day from 10 am-6 pm from 1st April to 30th September,

Ouistreham : **'Musée du Débarquement - no. 4 commando'**
Place Alfred-Thomas - in front of the casino. Tel (33) 2 31 96 63 10.
Museum retracing the saga of the commando landings on Sword beach.
Open from 1st April to 30th September every day from 10.30 am-6 pm.

Museum of the Atlantic Wall 'The Bunker''.
Avenue du 6 Juin - Tel (33) 2 31 97 28 69 - Fax (33) 2 31 96 66 05.
Old gun command post from the Atlantic Wall overlooking the estuary of the Orne. Open from February to 15 November from 10 am to 6 pm,. From 1st April to 30th September from 9 am-7 pm uninterrupted.

Port-en-Bessin-Hupin : **Museum of the underwater wrecks of the landings.**
Hameau Escures - Route de Bayeux - 14520 Commes. Tel (33) 2 31 21 17 06.
Open to the public week-ends and national holidays in May and from 1st June to 30th September from 10 am-12 noon and from 2-6 pm every day.
Numerous wrecks (tanks, remains of planes…), or objects and documents coming from these wrecks taken from the sea depths.

Ranville : **Memorial Museum of Pegasus Bridge.**
Open from 1st May to 30th September from 9.30 am-6.30 pm every day, from 1st October to 30th November and from 1st February to 30th April from 10 am-1 pm and from 2-5 pm. Closed from 16th December to the end of January.
Avenue du Major Howard. Information : Mairie Tel (33) 2 31 78 76 08 - Fax (33) 2 31 78 00 52 - Guided visits - Entry = 5€ ; children 3,50€
E.mail : memorial.pegasus@wanadoo.fr

MEM RIAL PEGASUS

Relive the dawn of June 6th 1944 !

This new historical site is dedicated to the men of the British 6th Airborne, first of the liberators landing in Normandy during the night of June 5th to the 6th 1944. Situated in a park of 12.000m² the Memorial associates a modern museum exhibiting an exceptional collection and the original Pegasus Bridge.

Open every day except December and January. Open all through the day in summer.

Guided visit and screening of filmed archives.

Entrance fee : Individuals 5 € per person. Groups 3,5 € per person.

Tel (33) 2 31 78 19 44 - Fax (33) 2 31 78 19 42
Avenue du Major Howard - 14860 RANVILLE
E-mail : memorial.pegasus@wanadoo.fr

Museum of the D-Day Landing in Arromanches

The permanent landing exhibition is situated opposite the remains of the extraordinary artificial port, real life souvenirs, relief plans, animated models, diorama, and filmed archives from the British Admiralty.

Open every day. The visit of 1h15 is commented by a guide.

The price is modest : 5 € per person (group tariff), 6 € per person (individual tariff).

Tel (33) 2 31 22 34 31 - Fax (33) 2 31 92 68 83 - 14117 ARROMANCHES
Internet : http://www.normandy1944.com

This new museum, opened in June 2000 by the Prince of Wales is dedicated to the men of General Gale (who commanded the 6th Airborne) and were the first to liberate Norman soil on 6th June 1944.

Put into retirement since 1993 and replaced, on the canal from Caen to the sea by an identical (practically) structure, the famous 'Pegasus Bridge' is for the old British combatants a 'monument' of their history.

The Museum which from now on is close to Ranville, very near to the historic site, displays more than 100 original photos, more than 1,000 objects including the famous bagpipes of Bill Millin to the sound of which he crossed the bridge under the hail of bullets, the cap of Major Howard, who commanded the Division, a jeep transported aboard a glider, a diversionary parachutist figure and other objects entrusted by the veterans.

Saint-Aubin-sur-Mer : **Commemorative monument to D. Day.**
A community liberated by the British troops.

Saint-Charles-de-Percy : **British Military Cemetery** (800 graves).

Saint-Laurent-sur-Mer : **6th June 1944 Omaha Museum.**
On one of the highest points of the landings. A collection of military vehicles, armaments, clothes,… Themed panoramas.
Rue de la Mer - Tel (33) 2 31 21 97 44. Open to the public from 15th February to 15th March and from 1st October to 20th November from 9.30 am-6.30 pm ; from 16th May to 30th September from 9.30 am-7 pm - in July and August from 9.30 am-7.30 pm.

Saint-Martin-des-Besaces : '**Musée de la Percée du Bocage**'.
Mementos and documents, 60 models in diorama, mannequins, 300 panoramic photos relating to the liberation of the region.
RN 175 - Tel (33) 2 31 67 52 78. Open every weekend and national holidays in May from 10 am-12 noon and from 2-6 pm. From 1st June to 15th September open every day except Tuesday from 10 am-12 noon and from 2-6 pm.

Thury-Harcourt : **Monument to the memory English soldiers of the 59th Division Staffordshire Regiment who liberated Thury in 1944.**

'Blockhouse' which was stormed by the British troops.

Tilly-sur-Seulles :
British Military Cemetery (1224 graves).
Museum of the battle of Tilly.
Set in the interior of the canonial chapel of Notre Dame du Val (12th century).
Information : Tel (33) 2 31 80 92 10 or (33) 2 31 80 30 26.
Open to the public on weekends and national holidays in May from 10 am-12 noon and from 2-5 pm. In June every day from 10 am-12 noon and from 2-6.30 pm. In July and August every day from 9 am-12 noon and from 2-6.30 pm. In September from Monday to Friday from 2-5 pm and at weekends from 10 am-12 noon and from 2-5 pm.

Troarn : Numerous reminders of the liberation of the town by British troops on 17 August 1944 remain, steles, graves in the parish cemetery and the names of roads.

A copy of the monument to the deado of Trevieres in the U.S.A.

The little town of Trévières, in Calvados, like the majority of French communities, possesses, opposite the Mairie, a commemorative monument to the 'Great War' with a proud "Marianne" of the First World War in bronze. The Americans wanted at one point to buy it to place it in front of the Memorial to the Landings of 6th June 1944 which will be dedicated in the State of Virginia but the Mayor refused. So the Americans have asked if they can make a copy and will shortly send a sculptor to take the dimensions of the monument.

Vierville-sur-Mer : **Museum 'D. Day Omaha'.**
Route de Grandcamp-Maisy - Tel/Fax (33) 2 31 21 71 80.
Site internet = www,vierville-sur-mer,htm
This community paid a heavy tribute to the liberation of Norman soil. Living museum, educational aids designed to transmit the memories to future generations.
Open to the public from 1st April to 1th May from 10 am-12.30 pm and from 2-6 pm ; from 1st June to 30th September from 9.30 am-7.30 pm and from 1st October to 11th November from 10.30 am-12.30 pm and from 2-6 pm. Entry = 4,57€

Ver-sur-Mer :
Museum of America Gold Beach.
2, place Admiral Byrd - Tel/Fax (33) 2 31 22 58 58.
Open to the public every day except Tuesday from 1st May to 1st October from 10.30 am-1.30 pm and from 2.30-5.30 pm. Open every day in July and August.
The museum possesses souvenirs of the events that took place on the beach at Ver, bridgehead of the British landings 6th June 1944.

2 educational panels explain the action of the 50th British Infantry Division :
* the first Place Byrd.
* the second Place Winston-Churchill.

2 British Memorials : The first for the 2nd Hertfordshire Regiment. The second for the 86th Royal Field Regiment.
Commemorative plaque to the memory of the numerous civilian victims (western façade of the museum).

Vierville-sur-Mer : **Museum 'D. Day Omaha'.**
Route de Grandcamp. Tel (33) 2 31 21 71 80. Internet Site : www.vierville-sur-mer.htm, Open from 1st April to 31th May from 10 am to 12,30 am and from 2 pm to 6 pm ; from 1st June to 30th September from 9.30 am to 7.30 pm and from 1st October to 11th November from 10,30 and to 12,30 am and from 2 pm to 6 pm,

Vire : **Graves of British airmen** in the parish cemetery.
Memorial to June 44 (Inside the Porte Horloge).

AREA OF ORNE

AREA OF ORNE

L'Aigle : **Museum of June 1944.**
Place Fulbert de Beina - Tel (33) 2 33 24 19 44 - Fax (33) 2 33 84 94 94.
Museum created after the war by Roland Boudet, previously Deputy Mayor.
Scenes of the Battle of Normandy and of the Second World War. Wax museum with authentic voices of the principal 'actors' in the conflict.
Open from April to 11th November every day except Monday from 9 am-12 noon and 2-6 pm. Free for veterans.

Alençon : **Museum of General Leclerc.**
31-33, rue du Pont-Neuf beside the Leclerc monument. Tel (33) 2 33 26 27 26.
In the ancient 'Quartier Général' of the prestigious head of the 2nd French Armoured Battalion, (12 and 13 August 1944).
Homage from the town of Alençon to its liberator.
Open every day of the year except Sundays and national holidays from 10 am-11.30 am and from 2-5.30 pm. Guided visits.

Chambois : **Stele and relief mural of the battle of Falaise Gap.**
Place du Donjon.

Ecouché : **Char 'Massoua'.**
Souvenir of the liberation of the town, 13th August 1944, the Sherman tank 'Massoua' of the 2nd French Armoured division took part in the fightuing of the Battle of Normandy before coming to a halt at this point hit by a German shell.

Fleuré : (near to Argentan). **Command Post of Général Leclerc.**
A memorial monument has been built on the plain at the point where General Leclerc, head of the 2nd French Armoured Division, established his command post. It was there that he received on 22nd August 1944, the order to march on Paris.

Habloville : **Memorial of the 1st World War**, made from pieces of German artillery recovered after the Battle of Normandy.

Montormel : **Memorial of Montormel-Coudehard.**
The last Battle of Normandy. On the heights of the famous hill held by the celebrated 1st Polish Armoured Division, the Memorial and the Museographic collection commemorate the end of the Battle of Falaise Gap. Commentaries in English - Les Hayettes. Tel (33) 2 33 67 38 61 - Fax (33) 2 33 67 38 72.
Open from 1st May to 30th September every day from 9 am-6 pm, From 1st October to 30th April only Wednesday, Saturday aund Sunday from 10 am to 5 pm,

Saint-Lambert-sur-Dives : **Gué de Moissy and 'The Corridor of Death'.**
Only way across the Dives in the last hours of the Battle of Falaise Gap, thousands of German soldiers perished there.
Stele to the Canadian liberators.

Tinchebray : **The operational reports** of the Royal Northumberland Fusiliers (32nd Reconnaissance Regiment) Royal Armoured Corps are conserved in this town.

Tournai-sur-Dives : **Cour de la Capitulation** (Beside the church).

It was in the courtyard of this farm that the Germans, weary of fighting, surrendered in the evening of the Battle of Falaise Gap by laying down their arms at the feet of a single Canadian soldier, who had entered the village.

Vimoutiers : **The place where Field Marshal Rommel was wounded.**

At the place called 'La Gosselinaie' at the entrance to Vimoutiers when coming from Livarot opposite the old Laniel Laundry exactly on the border between Calvados and Orne, one can find the little bridge where on 14 July 1944 as he carried out an inspection visit to the front, his car was machine gunned.

The last 'Tiger' in Normandy.

On the road to Gacé, coming out of the town towards Alençon, a German 'Tiger' tank recalls the hard battles that unfolded in the region in August 1944. Saved from destruction by the town of Vimoutiers at the intervention of historian Eddy Florentin, this tank is today classed as an historic monument.

AREA OF EURE

Beaumont-le-Roger : In the **parish cemetery** are a number of graves of British airmen whose aircraft were shot down by the Germans.

Bernay : Space kept for the graves of Canadian soldiers in the cemetery of **Notre-Dame-de-la-Couture.**

Tosny : **Museum of the Second World War.**

****

**The Norman Association of the aerial memory of 1939-1945,
extracting from the land the aircraft shot down during
the last war of Normandy.**

During the four years that the German occupation of Normandy lasted and notably during the period from June to August 1944, aerial activity was maintained over the province and the losses in materials but above all in men, were very heavy.

Recently, a group of enthusiasts have created an association to try to save a maximum of the elements of aviation history in Normandy from the Second World War.

Concerned to pay homage to the airmen who died in the liberation of their land, the members of the association, have as their aim, to extract from the land the remains of the planes still resting where they crashed. They have launched an appeal for help to veterans and eyewitnesses.

The association works to respect the memory of old combatants and are committed to not undertaking any commercial activity.

For information write to : L'A.N.S.A., Rue des 3 Cornets, 27190 Ormes or on the internet http://webhome.infonie.fr/ansa:index.htm

****

THE VAL-YGOT V 1 SITE AND ITS MEMORIAL AT ARDOUVAL

Ph. C. Féron, G. Bertout

Target... London !

This re-laying-out of a V1 site dedicated to the memory of the victims of secret weapons is a must for historians and tourists alike. It is, for the time-being, the only one in Normandy or elsewhere.

ARDOUVAL - FORÊT D'EAWY
SEINE-MARITIME - FRANCE

AREA OF SEINE-MARITIME

Ardouval : **Launch base of the V 1.**
In the Forets of Eawy, in the Val Ygot, the place chosen by the Germans to construct their launch pad for the V 1 in 1943. There remain the shelters, the workshops and the launch ramp.
Free access to the site, explanatory panels - Guided visits on request.
Information : Tel (33) 2 35 83 90 66 or (33) 2 35 93 15 04.

Auffay : It was in this small community that Michel Hollard, **'The man who saved London'** discovered the first V1 put in place by the Germans. The Place de la Gare carries his name.

Dieppe :

Monuments to the memory of Canadian and American troops who landed in Dieppe 19th August 1942.

Memorial 19th August 1942, Petit Théâtre, place Camille-Saint-Saëns. Open every day from June to September. Tel (33) 2 35 06 60 00.

Forges-les-Eaux : **Museum of the Resistance and of the Deportation.**
Open every day from 2-6 pm, from 1st March to 31th October.
Tel (33) 2 35 90 64 07.

The most
relaxing...

Aaaaãhhh

...or the fastest way
to Normandy

Woooosh

POOLE PORTSMOUTH
CHERBOURG
CAEN

Ease across to Cherbourg or Caen and take full advantage
of our award winning service. Or tear across to Cherbourg
in just over 2 hours, and start your holiday sooner.
And all for less than you'd expect.

Reservations & Information **0870 908 9699**

Brittany Ferries

www.**brittanyferries**.com

II - THE NORMAN HERITAGE

An exceptional wealth !

The tourist posters from between the wars gave Normandy the heavenly image of a land of cockaigne with its thatched half-timbered cottages at the foot of green hills, its rich pastures where lived, in the shade of the apple blossom, the peaceful ruminants and the blonde, red cheeked peasants wearing the shawl and bonnet of traditional lace…

If Normandy was and remains still that, in certain places, like the Pays d'Auge, this is not the image of the whole Province which offers to its visitors a huge variety of attractions and regions with strong identities and traditions which have generated so many types of houses where the stone, natural white or granite, in the hedged farmland gives way little by little to houses of wood or brick.

Normandy, such a puzzle, offers an exceptional wealth of nature and architecture which places it, in heritage terms, immediately after the Parisian region.

But how best to visit Normandy ?

It all depends on what you want to see ! The time that you have ! There are so many things to see that each visit the visitor has to select.

As an arbitrary choice we shall use the **'department'** as geographic regions to visit.

Normandy was divided into 5 departments after the Révolution : from west to east : **la Manche, le Calvados, l'Orne, l'Eure and la Seine-Maritime.** These areas gather together 3,234 communes of which the majority account for less than 200 inhabitants.

The departmental tourist committees, the information offices and the tourist offices provide good documents to help and advise on visits. You can find a list of the principal points at the end of this guide.

LA MANCHE

La Manche is almost an island, *'a finger pointing over the sea in the direction of England',* the **'end of France'** and the **'Cape of Europe'**. It is a formidable barrier which cuts the Cotentin perpendicularly on its main axis over half its width. The battle between sea and coast is here of total significance.

Geologically, la Manche is attached to the Armoricain massif. The area is made up of three great topographic and hydrographic basins : **la Presqu'île du Cotentin - le Saint-Lois et le Coutançais - l'Avranchin et le Mortanais.**

Of the 600 kilometres of Norman coastline, La Manche accounts for more than half. Presenting a variety of beaches, bays and cliffs, it is without argument the region most appreciated by British tourists who, every year more numerous, continue to 'drop anchor' there.

From the left bank of the river *Vire*, stretches a low coastline, place of repose and habitat of birds, characterised by kilometres of sandy beaches bordered by dunes as far as *Saint-Vaast-la-Hougue.*

One finds there the historic beaches of **Utah Beach** around *Varaville-sur-Mer.* Places such as *Sainte-Mère-Eglise* recalling the audacity of the allied troops, the tenacity of the fighting during the landings which were almost interrupted by the terrible storm of 6th June 1944.

Stop at the church which 'The Longest Day' made famous. The oldest part of which dates from 11th century (transept crossing).

Nearby, the belltower of the church of *Brucheville* is one of the most beautiful in Roman style of the region, (12th century).

One can equally find in the region three beautiful 'Manor farms' typical of local architecture.

The village of *Carquebut* offers numerous attractions beginning with the astonishing narrow alleyways bordered by tall buildings, several wash houses and two houses of particular interest :

* The **'Château de Courcy'** : beautiful dwelling with very old outbuildings. In the middle of the main courtyard one can see a curious isolated niche for a dog. It seems probable that this château was built on a 'Gallo-Romain' site of which traces have been found by chance during farming work.

* The **'Manoir de Franquetôt'** : property of the ancient and noble Norman family of Lécuyer. It is an immense dwelling with a beautiful tower from the 15th century on the external corner in the form of an 'L' The double door customarily surmounted by fantasy crenellations open now on to a vast meadow.

Liesville-sur-Douve can be found the remains of the oldest windmill in the western world. It is situated some hundreds of metres from the church.

Then the coast, after the soft banks of the valley of the Saire, gives way to the Cherbourg foothills becoming rocky with dangerous reefs off *Gatteville* (on which foundered the 'Blanche Nef'). The bay, one of the most sumptuous in Europe, opens on to a wild countryside, regulated by the winds, the tides and the legends.

Make a stop at *Barfleur*, the ancient great Anglo-Norman port, today officially recognised as 'One of the most beautiful villages of France'. The uniqueness of this community is in being the smallest in the Area of La Manche. It is unusally made up of houses which encircle the port. Over the centuries the sea has nibbled away at much of Barfleur and that which the Hundred Years War did not destroy, the Channel has. The majority of the mediaeval town has been submerged, and the ancient port where the Anglo-Norman sovereigns embarked has become unusable. The promontory on which the church of Barfleur is built was in bygone days in the centre of the town.

Cherbourg-Octeville, which for many of you is the 'landing' point in Normandy, is a transatlantic port where the Titanic called in April 1912 before her first and last crossing towards New York. The town retains a slightly old world charm, in spite of the terrible destruction that was inflicted on it at the end of the Second World War.

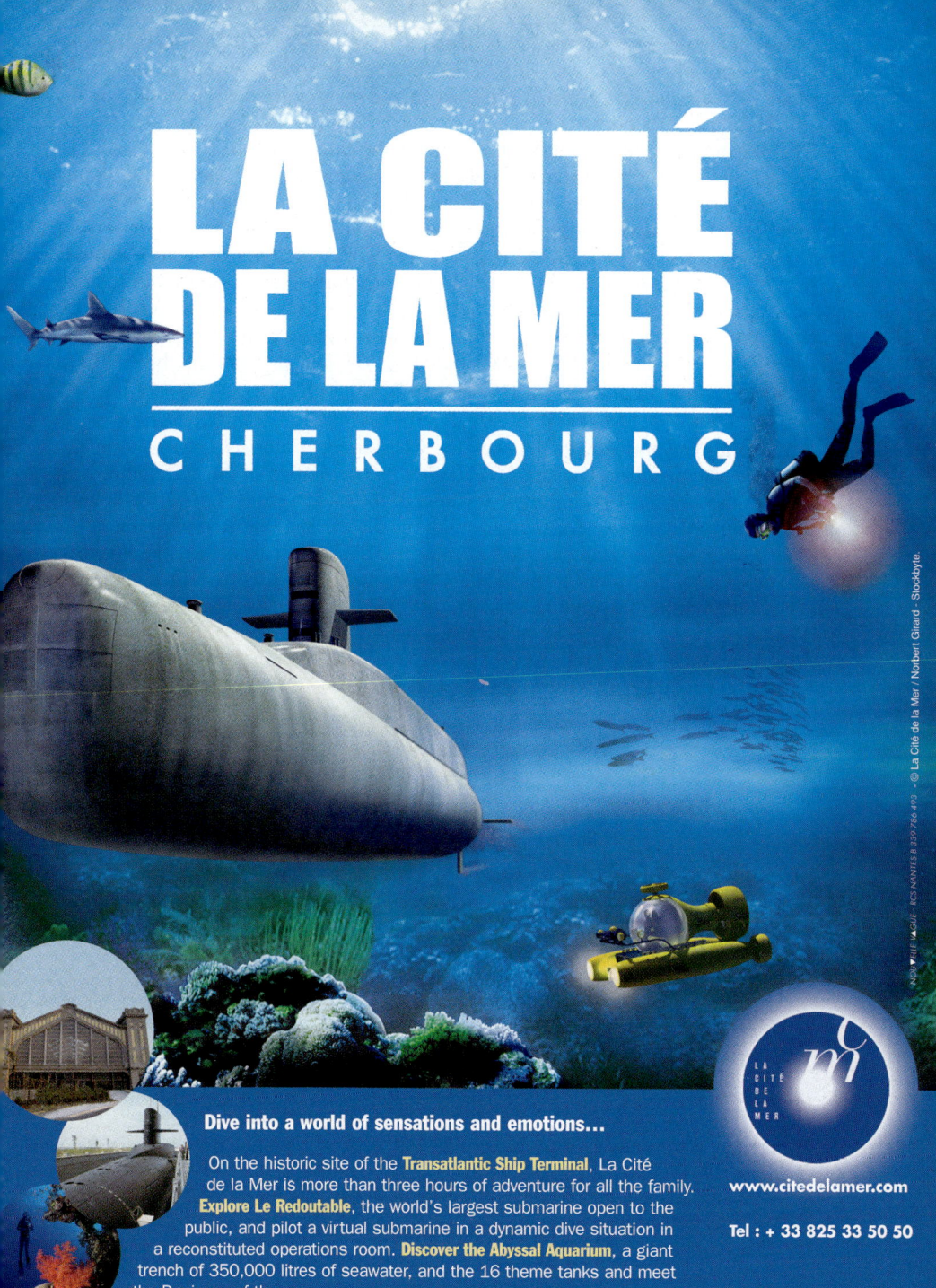

LA CITÉ DE LA MER

CHERBOURG

Dive into a world of sensations and emotions...

On the historic site of the **Transatlantic Ship Terminal**, La Cité de la Mer is more than three hours of adventure for all the family. **Explore Le Redoutable**, the world's largest submarine open to the public, and pilot a virtual submarine in a dynamic dive situation in a reconstituted operations room. **Discover the Abyssal Aquarium**, a giant trench of 350,000 litres of seawater, and the 16 theme tanks and meet the Denizens of the sea.
The whole extent of underwater conquest awaits you.

www.citedelamer.com

Tel : + 33 825 33 50 50

La Cité de la Mer, subaquatic sensation.

INOUI ▼ THE HAGUE - RCS NANTES B 339 786 493 - © La Cité de la Mer / Norbert Girard - Stockbyte.

'Town of atmosphere' Cherbourg is in one *'City at the end of the world where one does not come by chance, full of history, strategically unique and to which the murmurs give an outdated aspect'*. Here are mixed the dream, the noises, the smells and the ambiance of a port.

The Italian theatre, the monumental fountain, the exotic gardens which should not be missed under any circumstances and the picturesque gardens such as the public garden of the Avenue de Paris, the park Emmanuel Liais, the garden of the Maritime Hospital and the garden of arboriculture and acclimatisation should be part of your visit. Topping the harbour wall, the largest in the world, the **Fort du Roule** reminds us, as with the statue of Napoléon Bonaparte pointing his finger… towards England, of the military past of this fortified harbour which lives today as a commercial port, a fishing port and a port for pleasure craft and which reserves a warm welcome for English visitors. On the heights above Cherbourg you can also find the little village of *La Glacerie* and its interesting museum of A.T.P. From the garden you have an exceptional panorama of Cherbourg and its port.

At *Urville-Nacqueville*, to the west of Cherbourg, a stop is called for at the 'Château de Nacqueville'. The latter was built at the beginning of the 16th century and added to in the 18th and 19th centuries. It is one of the most beautiful private buildings of the Cotentin. On the façade, an inscription recalls the last English incursion in the region : *'Les anglais ont descendu le 7 d''aouest' 1758'*. The romantic park, designed in the 16th century, looks out to the sea and gives to the nostrils of visitors pleasant scents coming from the plantations of tall trees and the numerous groves of rhododendrons.

(Open to the public from Easter to the end of September every day except Tuesdays and Fridays unless these are national holidays - Information : Tel (33) 2 33 03 21 12.

****

Le Tourp at Omonville-la-Rogue
Or when nature meets history

On the extreme point of Cotentin, the 'almost island' of La Hague is a picturesque region which has a rich natural and cultural heritage. To the north, on a steep hillside, on the side of a valley and overlooking the sea, one can find the Manor of Le Tourp.

From the ancient Scandinavian 'Thorp', which means 'village', and which is applied in Normandy to rural establishments, such as the farms created outside villages, the Manor has inherited its name : 'Le Tourp'.

From past centuries, the manor farm of Le Tourp has kept its noble characteristics and those linked to its farming activity, which today give its identity.

A fortified farm from the 15th and 16th centuries (traces of bartizan, arrow slits…) Le Tourp grew in stature from the beginning of the 17th century (lord's house, pigeon loft, chapel, bakery).

Le Tourp is today a cultural and museographic space of international dimension which has the will to become a true place of exchanges and of the expression of a heritage common to the European oceanic peninsulas. Around the paths of the Hague, Le Tourp is confirmed as a place of activity and of cultural meetings.

To cater for its new function, the restoration of the site has been carried out respecting its authenticity : roofs in schist of the area, openings as originally...

We invite you to discover it...

For information : Tel (33) 2 33 01 85 89. LeTourp@Wanadoo.fr

****

In **Tourlaville**, neighbouring community to Cherbourg, there is still present, the memory of a criminal affair, which was the talk of the town in the chronicles of the 16th century.

The primitive dwelling of the lord, which then was only a wooden manor having been built in the 8th century then replaced by a strong castle and finally by a picturesque building in the 16th century.

Continuing along the coast by *'Port Racine'*, considered to be 'the smallest port in France', to Saint-Germain-des-Vaux, one discovers the grandiose countryside of **Cap de la Hague**, la **Baie d'Ecalgrain**, le **Nez de Jobourg** which invite the daydreamer.

The north coast of Cotentin presents alternately beaches and cliffs from east to west as far as **Cap de la Hague**, 'rocky lookout posts facing the raging of the sea'. From there one can reach the **Nez de Jobourg** and its 128 metre high cliffs. It is in this place, it is said, that one finds the oldest rocks in Europe, more than two billion years old.

Stop if you have the time at the bird reserve at **Mare de Vauville**.

The presence of fuchsias, mimosas and palm trees in this region demonstrates, if one needs it, the mildness of the prevailing climate.

****

Voyage in the stars with Ludiver !
Observatory-planetarium of the Cap de la Hague

This site of scientific culture wants above all to be recreational and attractive to the general public. It is a place of discovery of astronomy across three different but complimentary spaces and offers visitors two hours of travel in the stars : a 100 seat planetarium, an exhibition describing space adventure and the solar system and sessions of observation, a station giving the weather directly. Everything is translated into English !

Children can follow an itinerary adapted to their age.

A shop offers educational products and souvenirs. Free entry.

For information : Ludiver, Flottemanville-Hague (route du Haras) - Tonneville, 1700, rue de la Libération.

Postal address : BP 217 - 50442 Beaumont-Hague cedex.

Tel (33) 2 33 78 13 80 - Fax (33) 2 33 78 13 89.

E mail : ludiver@wanadoo.fr Internet site : ludiver.lahague.org

****

La Hague, at Cotentin
The Land, the Sea and the Stars

At the extreme point of Cotentin, La Hague peninsula is a wild and natural area that possesses a rich natural and cultural heritage.

Land of contrast and light, La Hague is a paradise for artists, painters and writers. Taking advantage of the abundant and preserved natural environment resulting from its temperate climat, the parks and gardens unveil their beauty.

The Sea - The calm after the storm, the wind from the high seas, the storm which blows from nowhere and everywhere, leave their chaos on the landscape of the Blanchard straight. The strength of the wind, the tumultuous elements are a spectacle that will take your breath away.

The Stars - Due to the excellent quality of the air and the preservation of its natural surroundings. La Hague has become a tourist site of discovery for astronormers. The LUDIVER, observatory/planetarium at Cap de La Hague has installed its high tech equipment at a site closest to the stars on one of the highest points of Cotentin.

L'observatoire-planétarium du Cap de La Hague
www.ludiver.com
Information contact (33) 2 33 78 13 80

Office du Tourisme de La Hague
www.lahague.org
Tel (33) 2 33 52 74 94

The west coast is characterised by 'havres' After the **'coast if islands'**, a cordon of regular dunes runs as far as *Granville*.

Note, in the tiny port of Goury, the lifeboat station which is original with its two boat launching ramps. Then there are the ports of *Portbail* and *Barneville-Carteret*, fitted out as ports for pleasure boats much appreciated by our cousins from the *Iles Normandes*, (the Channel Islands).

'Barneville-Plage' could be the oldest seaside town in France.

The *Cap de Carteret*, in part recovered by the dunes, is a place for a pleasant and picturesque walk looking out to the islands.

At *Port Bail* a visit to the 11ᵗʰ century church is a must. This building welcomes, during the high season, concerts and exhibitions.

Nature lovers should note the *'dunes Lindberg'* and the *'Havre de Portbail'*.

Granville, *'the Monaco of the north'*, thus named because of the rocky promontory on which the town is built, with its old *'upper town'*, surrounded by ramparts from the 16ᵗʰ century and its eventful past, it now offers itself for your visits. The harbour is both a pleasure and a fishing port.

The **Pointe du Roc** which crowns the town is an exceptional site.

In the town there remain mementos of **Christian Dior**, the great couturier, *'enfant du pays'* owner of the **'Villa Les Rhumbs'** which is going to be changed little by little into a museum. There is also a statue of Corsair **'Pleville le Pelley'**. Granville is proud to be the birthplace of sailor **Christophe Auguin**, single handed yachtsman, twice winner of the BOC Challenge and leader in the Vendée Globe Challenge. His boat 'Geodis' was built by the JMV shipyard in Cherbourg.

The casino and the thalassotherapy centre were created in 1911.

Beautiful fine sandy beaches, such as *Jullouville* and *Carolles*, continue the coastline as far as the immense Bay of Mont-Saint-Michel and the prestigious rock, prodigy of Norman religious art which our Breton neighbours don't hesitate to appropriate in their tourist brochures.

Here one can observe the largest tides in Europe.

On **Mont-Saint-Michel**, note that **Duke Richard 1st** began the construction of the impregnable abbey and his successors continued the developments in order to receive there little by little pilgrims from all over the world to pay homage to **Archangel Saint Michael** whose statue in gold, crowns the top of the abbey.

Quickly the atmosphere invites one to meditate, to *'take the time that it needs'*...

Premier historic and tourist site in France, Mont-Saint-Michel and its bay were classified in 1972 by U.N.E.S.C.O. as 'WORLD CULTURAL HERITAGE OF HUMANITY'.

The chief attractions of the Mount are the Abbey (11th-16th century) and the mediaeval military village with its surrounding ramparts.

The little village, which today numbers only about forty inhabitants, is 'hung' from the side of the rock. It is one of the most picturesque in France and has kept through the centuries its legendary tradition of welcome and hospitality.

Mont-Saint-Michel has always been the great centre of pilgrimage of the western Christian. Since almost a century ago the tourists, in their millions, have replaced the pilgrims. They come from all corners of the globe to admire its architecture, its history and its site, unique in the world.

The perimeter of the Mount is one kilometre. Its surface of 397 hectares, (36 sq. metres) is made up of three poles : the rock, the village of 'the barracks' and the polders.

The 'Order of the Knights of Saint-Michael' became, from the 15th century, the first 'Military Order of the Kingdom of France'.

Places to visit...

The abbey.

The village and its parish church dedicated to Saint Peter, Patron saint of fishermen, which shelters a statue of **Archangel Saint Michael**, crowned and lamé in silver.

The museums : Maritime Museum (Information : Tel (33) 2 33 60 14 09, the Historical Museum : Tel (33) 2 33 60 14 09 and the Archéoscope : Tel (33) 2 33 48 09 37.

The Bay of Mont-Saint-Michel occupies between the headlands of Granville and Cancale, a depression of about 500 square kilometres or 25,000 hectares of sand and silt.

Each year a million cubic metres of sediment is deposited by the sea. This 'tangue' forms vast salt marshes with a special vegetation on almost 4,000 hectares. On the 'salty fields' graze around 7,000 sheep which produce a particularly well flavoured meat.

In the south of the bay, towards Brittany, 300 kilometres of oak posts along the shore, produce each year nearly 10,000 tons of mussels.

In the bay one can register tides of an exceptional range of close to 15 metres at times of the spring tides. The size of these tides is the biggest in Europe.

The gigantic work of dredging around the Mount as well as the demolition of the sea wall are going to be undertaken shortly in order to give back to the rock its maritime character. The hydraulic works have as their object, to stop the advance of vegetation, by modifying the currents and the current deposit of sediment.

After having admired the savage beauty of the bay of *Mont-Saint-Michel* (Polders, grasslands, marshes, the Valley of Couesnon,...) we invite you to make a stop at *Pontorson* to discover the house, from the Roman period, of **Guischard de la Médardière**, an ancient protestant preacher of the 15th and 16th centuries and the **home of the Montgomery's** in the 17th and 18th centuries. *Pontorson* owes its name, it is said, to Captain Orson, faithful captain of **Chevalier du Guesclin**, who constructed a bridge over the Couesnon in order to enter Brittany.

In *Ducey*, a charming little flowered village on the banks of the Sélune, one can find the Castle of **Gabriel de Montgomery** who lives in history for having accidentally killed King Henry II in a tournament in 1559, his lance having broken the skull of the poor monarch. Returned to *Ducey*, he became chief Huguenot. Captured by Matignon at *Domfront* he was beheaded in Place de Grève in 1574. Built in 1625 the current **'château de Montgomery'** is a massive building made of brick and stone. The old bridge over the Sélune, which dates from 1613, is one of the crossing points on the salt and fish route which links *Granville* to Paris.

The little community of *Ceaux*, nearby, has the originality to possess a public barometer (near the Mairie). On the *'route du Mont-Saint-Michel'*, in the heart of the Mortagne countryside, *Saint-Hilaire-du-Harcouët*, town of tradition, built in the 11th century between the valleys of the Sélune and the Airon. Fortified under William the Conqueror, its military role ended in the 15th century. Town of gastronomy and meeting place it possesses an exceptional heritage of which we draw to your attention : the **Chapel Saint-Yves** (from the end of the 14th century) and the **Tower of the Old Church.**

At *Brécey*, 'station verte de vacances' situated some 25 kilometres from Mont-Saint-Michel, known for its sheep market, runs the Sée, a first category river for trout and salmon fishing. It is the birthplace of the **Vassy family** who distinguished themselves at the side of William 1st in England.

The interior of the La Manche area offers many possibilities for visits with numerous castle-farms and manors... Towns such as *Valognes, Bricquebec, Montebourg, Saint-Sauveur-le-Vicomte,* conserve the individual character of this astonishing region which remains attached more than others to the Viking past of Normandy. The names of the places and the families are there to remind us.

Rich with numerous sumptuous hotels, the town of *Valognes* has usurped nothing with its title of the **'Little Versailles of Normandy'.**

The **Abbey of Montebourg** was built by an Italian monk. The latter, came, it is said, from Monte Cassino in Italy and having been shipwrecked on the coast of Normandy had a vision and heard a voice commanding him to build a sanctuary.

Close to Saint-Sauveur there stretches a forest of 235 hectares in which are offered a variety of activities such as walking and horse-riding routes, cross country biking, educational tours, an arboretum...

In *Montebourg* stories recount that **'Roger the Hermit'**, who came from the Savoie, after having seen in a dream a star fall into the valley and heard a voice coming from heaven telling him of the wish of the Virgin to have a sanctuary in this place, built a chapel that would become the **'Abbaye Notre-Dame-de-l'Etoile'**.

The centre of the Cotentin offers a more open countryside, with towns such as *Coutances* and its **'Cathédrale de Fierté'** (11th-13th century), a miracle of construction, which offers an admirable synthesis of the Norman Gothic art later exported to England. Take the time to pass a few minutes in the magnificent **'Jardin des Plantes'**, 'enchanted' place designed in 1853. The garden extends the Museum of the **'Hôtel Le Poupinel'** and contains rare trees and huge flower beds all integrating magnificently the most diverse styles. (Open to the public all year - Information : Tel (33) 2 33 45 17 79 - Fax (33) 2 33 45 25 42.

In the region of Countance, make a call at *Régneville-sur-Mer* where you can visit the ancient lime kilns and the museum.

Places to see...

The harbour of Régneville, the marshes where the lambs, known for the quality and fineness of their meat, feed in the salt meadows.

The classified site of the Bay of Sienne. On the edge of the coastline, at *Annoville* the sand dunes make up one of the best natural classified sites in France.

The Museum of Tancrède de Hauteville at *Hauteville-la-Guichard.* 'Ancien Presbytère - le Bourg'

This village, nestling in the Countance countryside, is the birthplace of the Norman kings of Sicily. It was from here that in 1036 the sons of a modest lord, Tancrède de Hauteville, left for the south of Italy. In Sicily, they founded a powerful kingdom and were the creators of one of the most brilliant civilisations of the mediaeval period. Installed in the ancient presbytery, the exhibition 'Tancrède de Hauteville' presents the adventure of these valiant Normans in Italy and in all the Mediterranean basin as well as aspects of Norman art in Sicily.

Open every day except Mondays from 15th June to 15th September from 2-6.30 pm. Open also Saturday and Sunday mornings from 10 am-12 noon. Information : Tel (33) 2 33 47 88 86.

Les 5 'chaussemiches' de la plage. Chalets dating 1900.

The Castle of Pirou. Restored in recent years by a priest who felt called to do this work - who also restored the Abbey of the Lucerne near Granville - the Castle of Pirou, constructed on a Viking site, is an authentic fortress of the 12th century. It is considered to be 'the oldest castle in Normandy'. We are told that a knight from Pirou participated in the conquest of England and received from William a domain in Somerset where he founded Stoke-Pero. The castle was besieged and destroyed during the Hundred Years War then restored during the 15th, 17th and 18th centuries

The fortress is built on an island in the middle of a lake. It retains ramparts from the 12th century.

Open from February to the end of December every day from 10 am-12 noon and from 2-6.30 pm. (5.30 pm from November to Easter except Tuesdays. Information : Tel (33) 2 33 46 34 71.

The panoramic view of Montmartin-sur-Mer : Overlooking Régneville, Cancale and the Islands of Chasey and Jersey. Montmartin is a regional centre for climbing.

Baptismal fonts from the 11th century in the Church of Contrières.

Church from 11th century at Hérenguerville.

At *Sainte-Marie-du-Mont*, go to the Mairie to discover 76 panels in carved wood done in 1875 by Isidore Le Goupils, Mayor of the community. These carvings show all the successive governments since Pharamond in 420 A.D. up to Maréchal de MacMahon in 1873. Each of the pieces feature, in a medallion, the bust of the ruler of the time and recall some of the historic deeds and customs which characterised the man and the era.

The community of *Sébeville* has one of the smallest **'Mairies in France'**.

****

The regional natural park of the marshes of Cotentin and Bessin

Formerly known under the name of 'the Marshes of Carentan', the Marshes of Cotentin and Bessin, were formed welding nature and man, and contain many undreamed of treasures. A large part, (25,000 hectares in total!), is in the canton of **Saint-Mère-Eglise**. *It was there that in 1991 the 'Parc Naturel Régional des Marais du Cotentin et du Bessin' was created. The area has wet zones, vast meadows that can flood in winter, and traditional hedged farmland, making up an ecological collection of major interest. The marshes of Cotentin give to the Park its originality and its value. Here, everything is peculiar : the marshes with their 'limes', real aquatic hedges extend the banks and the hedges while the water, the land and the sand are covered with rare and varied species of vegetation where a rich and precious fauna lives.*

In the 142 communities of the park, a tourism of discovery offers tours on foot, horseback and on the water.

In the marshes, the variation between the wet and dry seasons explains in part the originality of the flora and fauna. In addition, the position of the park on the migratory axis of birds between northern Europe and the winter habitats of the African continent make the area ideal for bird watching. You can see numerous species : lapwings, harriers, moorhens as well as the white swan which will repay the efforts of the attentive watcher.

Nearer to the sea, the Bay of Veys, an ornithologists paradise, shelters numerous birds living with the rhythm of the marshes : seagulls, gulls, woodcocks, cormorants, grebes, crested (harles)…

There are numerous viewpoints to discover the great expanses of the marshes, notably at **Liesville-sur-Douve, Beuzeville-la-Bastille, Chef-du-Pont** *and* **Picauville.**

For more information : Parc Naturel régional des Marais, 3 Village de Ponts-Douve, 50500 Saint-Côme-du-Mont.

Tel (33) 2 33 71 65 30 - Fax (33) 2 33 71 65 31.

****

Avranches, built on a mound between two small coastal rivers : the Sée and the Sélune, is known and appreciated for its panoramas - a unique view of *Mont-Saint-Michel* (classified site) - it has an **excellent botanical garden** - you should stop there to discover this beautiful place where the most varied and exotic species grow - and its rich historic past with the most ancient traces dating from the 9th century B.C. The most beautiful elements of its heritage are made up of the **'Manuscripts of Mont-Saint-Michel'** *(14,000 books and 200 manuscripts coming from the library of the monks and preserved in the Town Hall)* and its ancient quarter. The memory of **Aubert, Bishop of Avranches**, who was behind the foundation of the oratory on **Mont-Tombe**, first name of Mont-Saint-Michel, is always present in the ancient episcopal city. A strong English colony lived in Avranches in the 19th century. An **'English quarter'** which dates from 1880 still exists in the municipal cemetery. The abbeys such as *Hambye, La Lucerne d'Outremer, Lessay,* recall the prestigious religious past of this land.

The Abbey of Hambye was founded in 1145 by William Paisnel, lord of the area. The mediaeval conventual group is today the most complete in Normandy after Mont-Saint-Michel.

The Abbey of La Lucerne d'Outremer, about 15 kilometres from Avranches, is a 'must' to visit. It shows, in certain aspects, an inexplicable architecture. Situated near to the Abbey of Hambye, it was founded in 1143 by two devout monks from the mother Abbey of Ardenne near Caen. At the church there was a **Roman 'lavatorium'** added which is unique in Normandy, with four beautiful small arcades as well as a dovecote, an imposing round tower pierced by 1,500 openings. Tel (33) 2 33 48 83 56, Open all the days from 10 am to 12 am and from 2 pm to 6.30 pm,

La Haye-du-Puits has a remarkable heritage, notably : Its **Keep from the 11th century** and its Renaissance castle. You will also see the tomb of **Arthur de Magneville**, founder of the castle who died in 1553. Make a stop at the **Abbey of Blanchelande,** built in 1155 by Richard de la Haye du Puits and Mathilde de Vernon. Its last owners were British but today it is for sale…Visit the countryside of moors, the hedged farmland, the admirable places of interest in this region which is part of the 'Parc Natural Régional des Marais du Cotentin et du Bessin'.

To the south, La Manche offers a farming countryside continuing to the *'Bocage Virois'*. The places and the habitat tell us that we are in the *armorican massif* and that Brittany is not far away…

At *Saint-James*, in the extreme south of La Manche there remains a part of the rampart built by Duke William in 1066 to protect against the risk of Breton invasions. The Normans having previously built a 'wall of earth'. Sited behind this natural defence, on a rocky spur, the now vanished castle had previously a strategic place facing the Valley of Beuvron. The ramparts and ditches were built following the topography of the rocky platform. The traces of ancient roads correspond to the defensive lines. This 'city' was a staging post on the 'montois' roads. In the 18th century this community made the paper lanterns for the torch-light processions of the national festival on 14th July for the patronal festivals.

'**City of Copper**', '*Villedieu-les-Poêles et les Caudrons*' has acquired its renown thanks to its copper craftsmen. The little village in the valley of the Sienne, was originally called 'Siennêtre' It developed thanks to the installation of a command post for the Knights of Saint John of Jerusalem, founded in 1130 by Henry 1st Beauclerc. The latter offered the 'Hospitaliers de Saint-Jean de Jérusalem' the territory of **Sault-Chevreuil** of which Siennêtre was part. On receiving this land, the order constructed a hospital and established there its first 'Commanderie de la Langue de France". Siennêtre took the name of the hospital : house of God in latin : Villa dei which became *Villedieu*.

Following this donation the town changed its jurisdiction. The Order of Malta had its own costumes and rules which the town inherited. The town thus escaped the numerous taxes which hit neighbouring parishes. Even if one cannot speak of a 'tax paradise', Villedieu benefited from numerous privileges which had the effect of considerably enlarging the population.

Space was limited - about 1 kilometre - there was built therefore a compact, tight place with shafts of air and in spite of the fires that occurred over the centuries, this difficult construction gave Villedieu the configuration that we know today. With its bell tower which emerges from this labyrinth of roads, roofs, courtyards and gardens, Villedieu is a town which cannot be confused with any other. The 'city" lost its privileges during the Revolution.

Experience our short breaks packages :

A week-end in Cherbourg and the Hague peninsula

S. Fauré - CDT Manche

With Direct Ferry links from Poole and Portsmouth, Cherbourg is right on your doorstep ! For a relaxing week-end, come and explore the country lanes of the Hague peninsula at your leisure. You will stay in a charming hotel at the Manoir du Tourp and will visit La Cité de la Mer, Cherbourg's new attraction which will take you on a journey in the depths of the ocean.

This special offer is for two people sharing a room and includes accommodation at the Manoir du Tourp, a 3 course dinner, breakfast, admission to a Pottery workshop and La Cité de la Mer.
Offer valid all year 2003.

We have many other week-ends and short breaks suggestions for you to get away from it all :

Parks and Gardens
Gastronomy and cooking courses
D-Day landing beaches
Norman architecture
Golf
Water sports
...or just relaxing breaks in charming hotels
and Bed & Breakfast

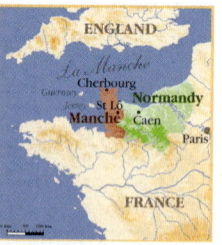

For further information contact :
Services du Tourisme de la Manche
Maison du Département - 50008 SAINT-LO cedex

Freephone from the UK :
N° Vert 0800 028 6572

Freephone from France :
N° Vert 0 800 06 50 50

www.manchetourisme.com • e-mail : manchetourisme@cg50.fr

La Manche,
it's just across the water !

From Cherbourg
to Mont Saint-Michel,
for those who take the time to explore,
this little corner of Normandy
has many hidden delights...

Création : Garrot Communication 02.33.71.74.92 - Crédit photo : P. Bernard / Mayenne Culture

  **NORMANDY**

LA MANCHE
Nos points de vue sont uniques

* The numerous workshops where items in copper are made and sold and notably the famous **'câne à lait'** of the Cotentin which makes up one of the principal attractions of the town. The choice is wide and the prices reasonable.

* **La Commanderie.**

The courtyards :

'La Cour de la Lucerne' : at its centre it has a well at which the 'Sourdins' came to nourish themselves with its drinking water.

'La Cour des Hauts Bois' : it is linked to the places called by the same name and situated on the road to Granville. People remark on its tower with its sculptured 'modillon' in Egyptian or oriental style.

'La Cour de la Bataille et de l'Enfer' : it is also called 'd'enfer' This place takes its name from the 'noise of hell' made by the hammers which resounded on the anvils of the numerous workshops found there.

'La Cour aux Moines' : from the name of William Le Moyne, grammarian, author of a French-Latin dictionary, author of around five hundred works, who lived there.

'La Cour du Foyer' : it should be pronounced 'fouiller". This courtyard has a peculiarity. A house of the mediaeval period carries on the top of its chimney an iron cross which was the sign of the Knights of Malta and of benefiting from privileges of exemption. One should note that these courtyards, for the most part, are intercommunicating as the ancient 'entries', closed today, testify. They were also closed by doors and some still retain their hinges.

'La Cour de Lys' : it has the peculiarity of possessing many façades of houses carrying arms with the fleur de lys, insignia of the French monarchy.

'La Cour des 3 rois' : in this courtyard, with its door and its double 'voussoir' one can find the Inn of the 3 kings, from which it takes its name. It is in the Cotentin that the British, in the 1980's bought a large number of rural houses to make them into second homes.

Towards the east of the area, *Saint-Lô*, Prefecture of La Manche, destroyed to such a degree in the bombardments of 1944 that it was renamed 'the Capital of Ruins", offers superb views from its promontory.

'Cité du Cheval', the town was founded in the 6th century by Laud, a monk who had come from Wales to evangelise the Cotentin. The town has developed today with the **National Stud** which is set in a political and tourist development based on the theme of the horse, notably aimed at Great Britain.

In 1946, the Irish Red Cross installed a field hospital in the ruined town. **Samuel Beckett** came there voluntarily and undertook the job as an administrative officer, shopkeeper, interpreter and driver. This Nobel winner made four trips to Saint-Lô and his name is today engraved at the entrance to the Musée des Beaux-Arts.

The **'Château de Canisy'** is one of the 'marvels' of La Manche. Built in the 16th century, it formed an important house.

The **castle of Torigni-sur-Vire** (it can be visited in July and August) was built as a fortress on the site of an ancient feudal mound by the Count of Gloucester, or Baron 'de Thorigny'. One of his descendants having married Jean-Sans-Terre, Torigni became the prerogative of the King of England.

The castle was bought back in 1370 by the first cousin and companion at arms of Bertrand du Guesclin. His daughter would marry **Sire de Matignon**. For several centuries the castle belonged to the celebrated family of Matignon who built in Paris the palace which bears his name and which is now the residence of the French Prime Minister.

In 1715, the Count of Thorigny, Jacques IV of Matignon, married the eldest daughter of the Prince of Monaco, **Louise Grimaldi**. He became **Sovereign Prince of Monaco** in 1731 under the name of **Jacques 1ˢᵗ**. The town owes to him the high wall (12 metres) built along the length of the great lake in order to protect his wife from the easterly winds which she could not bear !

Seated in the middle of vast marshes, *Carentan* remains connected to the sea and still has a port for pleasure boats. Carentan is situated in the Marshes of the Cotentin, *'low wet zone in the centre of an expanse without relief"*.

In *Mortain* there is always present the memory of Robert, half-brother of Duke William. You must see l'**Abbaye Blanche** (12ᵗʰᵗ century) and the Roman door from the Anglo-Roman period (11ᵗʰ century) at the Collegiale (Irish eucharistic casket from the 7ᵗʰ century bearing runic inscriptions). There are numerous wonderful panoramas for the visitor in the area around Mortain as well as the beautiful waterfalls on the tributaries of the Sélune (see the Grande Cascade with its fall of 20 metres).

The original attraction of *Sourdeval* is the **monumental chimney** built in the public garden next door to the Mairie. It was discovered in the village of Fourberie in *Vengeons* in the ruins of a manor dating from the English occupation(14ᵗʰ century). It was the property of two old families from Sourdeval who decided to give it to the community.

It was in *Sourdeval* in 1948 that **Guy Degrenne** founded on 700 square metres a company making steel place settings of the design of the period with a huge distribution. Then in 1958 he started the production of stainless steel plates. In 1968, he set up a new unit at *Vire* for the mass production of modern articles. In 1977 the success of the little Norman of *Brouains* was such that his company was quoted on the Paris Stock Exchange at the second step.

At **Chaulieu**, not far from there is the highest point of La Manche (368 metres) with a viewing tower and a 'table d'orientation'.

La Manche remains the Norman region which is most attached to its history, its traditions and its identity.

****

The Island Cotentin

*'**Les Iles Saint-Marcouf'** - Situated off the Utah Beach some 7 kilometres from the coast, the islands are named after a hermit who found shelter there in the 6ᵗʰ century. They have been colonised by thousands of seabirds, notably the 'Great Cormorant". The off shore island is the largest and is distinguished by a fort of the Vauban type. These islands were occupied by the English from 1795 to 1802. They also served to hide the chiefs of the royalist insurgents during the Revolution.*

'*L'Ile de Tatihou*' - Special domain of seabirds, Tatihou is situated opposite Saint-Vaast-la-Hougue on the east coast of the Cotentin. One comes here for its maritime museum, its maritime garden, its centre of scientific culture and its accommodation centre. Tourism has developed here since it was opened to the public in 1992 by the owner, the 'Conservatoire du Littoral'.

The museum, like the Vauban fort, evokes the battle of Hougue which took place in 1692 and in the course of which the fleet of Admiral de Tourville was decimated by the English off Saint-Vaast. Two years after this bitter defeat, the towers of the Hougue and Tatihou were constructed by Vauban on the orders of King Louis XIV. For three centuries the fort aged on this jewel of Norman heritage.

A workshop of naval carpentry completes the richness of these magic islands and makes the boats of another time live again. One reaches Tatihou by boat from Saint-Vaast. Departures from the Quai Vauban Tel (33) 2 33 23 19 92.

'*Les Iles Chausey*' - The Chausey islands make up an archipelago of 53 islands and 300 rocks which appear as the sea recedes. On the ebb tide, 5,000 hectares of shore are revealed. 'La Grande île' situated some 16 kilometres from Granville, measures 2 kilometres in length by between 200 and 700 metres wide and remains the only inhabited island. The lighthouse, built on the southern point of the island, watches from its height of 47 metres over a 45 kilometre circumference.

The fort, originally constructed to defend the island against attacks from the English, is today inhabited by the fishermen. The 'château Renault' was built in 1928 on the ruins of the first château by Louis Renault, the car builder. The village of Blanvillais is made up of low houses with gardens surrounded by dry stone walls.

It is possible to stay on Chausey where new gîtes have recently been converted in the old farm. For information : Tel (33) 2 33 90 90 53.

'*Les Iles Normandes*' (*the Channel Islands*). - When William of Normandy became King of England, the 'Iles Normandes' or the Channel Islands became an integral part of the Duchy of Normandy. They blended in with the new Anglo-Norman grouping to be part of the whole. That lasted until 1204.

When in that year the infamous Duke-King John lost practically all his Norman possessions, the inhabitants of the islands decided to remain loyal to their Duke. They were not obliged but made the choice. This is an important point; Since that time their position has never changed.

Over the years, the successive Kings of England confirmed by charter the total independence of the Norman islands in logical return for the allegiance of the islanders to the Duchy of Normandy and to the legitimate heirs of the ducal crown who would become the kings and queens of England.

It should be noted that this recognition is not that of the English government but solely an allegiance to the sovereign.

This subordination to the English crown started then and continues to this day. Her Majesty the Queen of England, Elizabeth II, is recognised as Duchess of Normandy and is held in the highest esteem throughout the islands.

On the coins of Jersey and Guernsey, the sovereign wears the ducal crown or sometimes the combined crown of Normandy and England and it is thus evident to the Crown of Normandy that the islanders are tied by their loyalty.

After the debacle of Jean-Sans-Terre in 1204, when continental Normandy was lost and reattached to the Kingdom of France, the islands were separated from the Duchy and assured of their own constitution. There exist in the archives of the islands the original charters granting specific privileges to the inhabitants of the islands such as that which says that they cannot be called upon to bear arms outside the islands except if it is to help the sovereign 'kidnapped by enemies' or 'to conquer England again"...!

It is probably because they are so small that the islands put such tenacity into protecting their constitutions and their rights. They have their own institutions, inspired by those of the ancient Duchy, for eight centuries and this historical situation could not be challenged.

Members of the Commonwealth, the islands are part of the European Community, they govern themselves and possess their own traditions and customs, their independence.

As an old Norman from Jersey said - they are becoming more and more rare ! - "We are proud to fly the Union Jack on our island... but only to remind us that England is our oldest conquest ".

If each year, more and more, the inhabitants of the Norman islands speak English, the Norman 'patois' remains the language of these unsubdued territories. It is still used by the fishermen and particularly on the island of Sark. It was tradition, for the members of the ruling elite, to teach their children 'la langue des aïeux" (the language of their ancestors) by sending them to study for a period in the colleges, schools or universities of Normandy... or France.

French was still, not so long ago, the official language of the courts of Jersey and Guernsey. It remains indispensable today for a solicitor or lawyer on the islands to speak fluent French and to study Norman law for some months at the University of Caen.

Aurigny-Alderney- 'This island, at the time of ebb and flow, castigates the Channel like the stem of a ship. It is often that the swirling, crested, foaming sea, is as if we are at the heart of the 'Raz Blanchard'. Six kilometres long by three wide, Aurigny is an island with a human dimension where time counts for nothing, where walking and cycling become the means of discovery and of seeing slowly. The multiple forts, sentinels of the circumference, testify to the history shared between France and England. At Sainte-Anne, only capital of the islands sited inland, one must wander in the roads from the Middle Ages of Huret and Marais and visit the little museum which retraces the history of the island. On the way out of the town, the Bay of Braye shelters a sea wall which dates from the Victorian era. On taking the very energetic zig-zag path, which leads to Trois Vaux Bay you will be offered swimming in Longis Bay which is always protected. The setting sun will allow you to admire Fort Cloncque, remains of Aurigny's fortifications.

Connections by air from Cherbourg. (Text from CDT of La Manche).

Herm - The island is two and a half kilometres by 900 metres. It combines a rich natural heritage with a measured tourist development. 'This island is the reflection of serenity born of the symbiosis of man and nature...'.

Guernsey - *The memory of Victor Hugo still hovers over Guernsey. Having to flee from France with the rise of Napoleon who he had described as 'Napoleon the Small', Victor Hugo settled in Jersey then banished from this island he moved to Saint-Peter where he bought 'Hauteville House'. He stayed there 15 years, giving himself to reading, walking and spiritualistic seances.*

With its 62 square kilometres and 70 kilometres of coastline, Guernsey makes up one of the two bailiwicks of the Channel Islands which also includes Alderney, Sark, Herm and Jethou.

Visit in Saint-Peter-Port : Cornet Castle on its little island between the port and Havelet Bay where remains the window of eight centuries of the history of the island begun in 1206 under King John.

Sark - *'Divided, a path over the sea links Great Sark with Little Sark. One must go to the beautiful beach of Dixcart which a natural arch splits in two. Derrible Bay is pitted with grottoes of which the most famous is Derrible Creux ...The impression of being in another age when one lands in Sark is one that dominates. If one visits the island on a foggy day, it seems sterile and like a true natural fortress which the cliffs defend and of which the tops seem inaccessible. On Robert Point the lighthouse stands out, the Maseline Bay or Creux Harbour, one lands, not a vehicle, a tunnel leads us... Sark, the island outside time welcomes you...*

(Text from CDT of La Manche).

Jersey - *The 'green island' is the biggest of the Channel Islands. It offers a face of contrasts from the north (wild coastline) to the south (sandy beaches) passing through a centre which is full of green valleys.*

The people of Jersey have abandoned little by little their traditional activities linked to the sea and to agriculture to devote themselves to finance.

Places to visit...

The castle of Grosnez (14th century).
The pinnacle (a rock 65 metres high).
The lighthouse at Corbière.
The Chapel of fishermen (12th century).
The farm of Hamptonne.
The castle of Mont Orgueil, built by Jean-Sans-Terre.
The port of Jersey, 'Saint-Helier''.

****

To also see in La Manche...

Natural Heritage :

With the 'Conservatoire du Littoral' the General Council of La Manche practises an intelligent and ecological policy for the coastline and is one of the départements to have purchased more coastal spaces to preserve them from random and unplanned development. More than 3,000 hectares are now protected.

****

THE BAY OF VEYS, JEWEL OF NATURAL HERITAGE OF LA MANCHE

The Bay of Veys is the marine continuation of the 'Col du Cotentin' between the flat areas of the Plain and the Bessin. It forms a deep gulf of 37 square kilometres where the fresh water outlets and the salt water of a basin of 3,500 square kilometres meet and mix, a mixture which makes for a great biological wealth. Also it is a sedimentary zone as its name indicates, a version of 'gué' (ford) which recalls that it was possible to cross on horseback between the 'Grand Vey' and Saint-Clément before the channelling of the principal waterways. In the ancient titles of the parish, this bay between the Cotentin and the Bessin, is always called 'le Grande Vey'. Before the construction of the bridge of 'Petit Vey' it was a frequently used crossing which linked the western and eastern parts of Normandy. Several Roman roads, or 'grandes voies', which in local dialect become 'vaies' - from which we have the name 'grand vey' - lead to this place.

The grasslands grow continually on the mud-flats. From 1856 to 1972, more than 2,000 hectares of polders have become agricultural land behind the sea walls which limit the horizon of this flat landscape of pastures scattered with occasional farms. On the western side, the coastal current builds up the bank of La Madeleine with sand which thickens and raises the strand in front of Sainte-Marie-du Mont. It was on these mud-flats that in 1906 the 'Spartine de Townsend' was identified before it invaded the shores of the continent.

The shell fish, cockles, clams, oysters and mussels are sufficiently numerous to give a living to around a hundred professional 'foot fishermen'. The fish find here a place to multiply.

Since 1991, marine seals come here to reproduce. But the variety of these biotypes above all explains the important international collection of birds. More than 20,000 frequent this place either as a stopping place like the 'bernache cravant' or as a wintering site like the silver plover, the oyster catcher, the ringed plover, the grey curlew, the russet godwit, the redshank. The ornithological reserve of Beauguillot offers a protected haven. 150 land hectares, of meadows protected by dunes, of ancient 'schorres' won from the sea, and 350 hectares of maritime domain. The vocation of Beauguillot is to welcome the seabirds that stop there or those that winter there and ensure the monitoring of the marine mammals in order to maintain and develop the populations. In winter, when the water levels are very high, the reserve receives between 30 and 40,000 birds on the land and marine habitats.

For information : Tel (33) 2 33 71 56 99.

****

Exceptional natural sites from north to south :

* **Coast and countryside of La Hague.**
* **The dunes of Héauville at *Vauville*.**
* **The botanical garden of the castle of Vauville at *Beaumont-Hague*.** Created in 1947, this garden shelters more than 500 species from the southern hemisphere and

is recognised as a unique and exceptional collection. Open to the public from 1st May to 1st October.

* **The capes and marshes behind the coastline from *Barfleur* to *Cap Lévi*.**
* **The western coasts of the Cotentin from *Saint-Germain-sur-Ay* to *Rozel*.**
* **The harbour of *Saint-Germain-sur-Ay* and the moors of *Lessay*..**
* **The west coast of the Cotentin from *Bréhal* to *Pirou*.**
* **The Valley of the Sée.**
* **The basin of the Erou.**
* **The great waterfall of Mortain.** Considered to be the most important of the waterfalls in western France, the fall formed by the Cance reaches a height of 20 metres.

  (Also see ; around Mortain, the small waterfall, le rocher brulé, the panoramic view of the little chapel and the view from Chaulieu).

****

Norman granite

The granite of western Normandy was in the past extracted from the rocky outcrops to make stones for building :

> *Houses and buildings*
> *Piles to enclose the fields*
> *Crucifixes*
> *Troughs and drinking places for the livestock*

Religious buildings

The two quarries which remain in the region cut cobbles for the roads and slabs for funeral monuments.

The Museum of granite at Saint-Michel-de-Montjoie - 'Le Bourg'

In the heart of the granite massif which extends from Carolles to Vire and constitutes the last foothills of the armorican massif, Saint-Michel-de-Monjoie remains the most active centre of quarrying of the granite basin of the south Manche known under the name of 'Bleu de Vire'.

The great era of these quarries dates back to 1930's when one hundred establishments were working.

The Museum of Granite wants to be the guardian of the history of granite working and of the old knowledge of this work. A large part of the visit is in the open air.

Open from 1st April to 15th June : Sundays and national holidays from 2-5 pm and from 16th June to 15th September every day from 2-7 pm. For information : Tel (33) 2 33 59 02 22.

****

ARCHITECTURAL HERITAGE :

* **The Abbey of Cerisy at *Cerisy-la-Forêt*.**
* **The Castle of Martinvast and its English park.**

The wet areas which encircle the castle were transformed at the beginning of the 19th century into a park inspired by the English countryside and made up of meadows, forests, lakes and waterfalls not forgetting a magnificent collection of exotic conifers. Seven routes allow one to discover the park. Open every day to the public from 5th April to 1st November (except Saturdays in April and October). For information : Tel (33) 2 33 52 02 23 - Fax (33) 2 33 52 03 01.

LE CALVADOS

Calvados is the best known Norman region outside the boundaries of the province.

Close to the image of Epinal that the 'foreigners' see as Normandy, the 'parisians' and other 'horsain' ("outsiders' norman word), in the 1970's, came in large numbers to buy and restore weekend houses notably in the north of the *Pays d'Auge* near to *Deauville* considered since then by many, as the '21st arrondissement of Paris'.

According to legend, it owes its name to a ship of the **'Invincible Armada'** armed by Philip II of Spain, the **'San Salvador'** or **'El Salvador'** which was wrecked on the *Côte de Nacre* (the Mother of Pearl Coast) in 1588 as it sailed towards England.

The name is gallicized to *Calvados* and has been attributed for a long time to the dangerous rocks which are found just above the waterline of *Bernières.*

If in 1762, the single guard on watch at the port, Michel Cabieu, succeeded in stopping a landing of English troops, today the times have changed and it is with warmth and conviviality that the whole population welcomes its British visitors when they arrive in the port of **Ouistreham** on the comfortable ships of Brittany Ferries. Created by the Vikings, this thousand year old town of which the coastal part is called **Riva-Bella** offers numerous attractions and notably :

* **A Roman church from the 11th and 12th centuries.**
* **A vast 'grange aux dîmes' (15th - 16th century).**
* **Some interesting areas of old fishermen's houses.**
* **A lively fishing port.**
* **A huge beach of fine sand.**
* **An historic canal, inaugurated by Napoleon III, which links the port with that of Caen.**
* **A protected natural site called 'pointe du siège'.**

The Department of Calvados offers a wide range of visits and discoveries.

To the west of Ouistreham the family beaches of the Côte de Nacre extend :

'Iodized' beaches, they have always been recommended for the health of children. Their names recall that it was in these places that the first Vikings landed and settled in the 9th century but equally evoke memories of the fighting of 6th June 1944 in the British sector : **Lion-sur-Mer, Luc-sur-Mer, Saint-Aubin-sur-Mer, Bernières, Courseulles, Ver-sur-Mer** and **Arromanches** where the coast begins to rise. This beach, like those of the American sector at **Saint-Laurent-sur-Mer, la Pointe-du-Hoc**, are places of intense emotion linked to the Battle of Normandy.

At **Saint-Pierre-du-Mont**, discover in the spring, the thousands of sea birds in the natural niche of the kittiwakes.

At **Ver-sur-Mer** (where on 1st July 1927 there occurred the first water landing of the 'America' which marked the first air mail link between America and France - see Museum). One can see a beautiful tithe barn from the 16th century, a church with a Roman bell tower from the 11th century and the surrounding wall of the 'Ferme de la Jurée' from the 14th century.

The bell tower of the church of Ver is *'one of the most significant in Normandy with its elevation, divided into five levels and its roof...'* this building expresses *'the remarkable success of Norman architects in the matter of towers...'*.

Note, in terms of natural heritage, that the marshes of Ver-sur-Mer (Opposite Paisty-vert) is to become a natural reserve for the preservation of the local flora and fauna. The marshes 'behind the coast' at Bassin Ver-sur-Mer / Meuvaines are already a protected site.

It was in the little port of **Courseulles-sur-Mer** that General de Gaulle, on 14th June 1944, set foot again on French soil. A 'cross of Lorraine' 18 metres tall, set facing the sea commemorates the return of the Head of the Free French. The castle, rebuilt in the 16th century, was occupied by the English during the Hundred Years War.

Bernières is one of the oldest towns on the Côte de Nacre as the numerous Celtic remains that have been discovered there testify.

An important 'Roman Camp' was built to the east of the town which had in earlier times been a major port. This port had a large traffic, specialising particularly in the transport of 'Caen stone' to England - with which the Normans constructed many buildings on the big island, starting with the famous **'Tower of London'**.

Visit the *Park of Barthélemy* which is a preserved natural space of coastal dunes.

Saint-Aubin-sur-Mer, the *'Queen of Iodine'* is not only a beach much enjoyed for family holidays but also numerous personalities of the last century liked to come there to recharge their batteries, people such as Malot, Massenet and even the great Pasteur - who with his wife stayed there in 1891, 1893 and 1894. Emile Zola also came there to spend several weeks with close friends in 1874. Saint-Aubin conceals many natural and architectural treasures.

One finds there the smallest natural reserve in France called : **'falaise du Cap romain'** with its fossilised sponges. This deposit is a rare reference point for the Jurassic period. Each day, in July and August, a geology student offers free visits to the site in co-operation with the tourist office where one can also find a window display and an explanatory panel. The sea wall of Saint-Aubin is typical with villas from the 'Belle Epoque' furrowed by the spray and the little perpendicular roads called 'venelles' which lead to the houses of the fishermen.

Langrune-sur-Mer has been classed as a health resort since 1926. It is called 'the beach of the children' as it presents no dangers for little ones.

The town was liberated by the 48th Royal Marine Commandos.

Visit the fountain of the three graces in the public garden around the Mairie.

Hermanville-sur-Mer benefits from an 1800 metre beach of fine sand. It is also a major point from D-Day. The well of Saint Pierre helped to provide fresh water to the British troops after the battle.

At *Douvres-la-Délivrande*, between Caen and the sea, there remains a souvenir of the **'Maison de Douvres'** (the House of Dover) It was founded by Osbern and his wife, contemporaries of William of Normandy, creator of the Barony of Dover. The family would provide two archbishops of York, a bishop of Worcester and one of Bayeux (Baudoin of Reviers, Count of Bessin and Baron of Dover who became Count of Devon and of the Isle of Wight and founded the Abbey of Quarr where he is buried).

This is also the oldest pilgrimage place in Normandy. In the neo-gothic basilica one prays to a Black Madonna who each year is dressed in magnificent vestments.

'Baronnie de Douvres' : ancient stronghold of the Barons of Dover - gate and buildings from the 15th century.

Many other seaside towns are also active fishing ports where one can find fresh fish, crustaceans and shellfish !

Along the coast, to the east there flow the superb beaches which edge the seaside towns of the **Côte Fleurie**. (the floral coast) which are to Normandy what Cannes, Nice and Menton are to the Midi of France.

You can discover by travelling along the coast in this direction *Franceville, Cabourg, Dives, Villers, Blonville, Deauville, Trouville and Honfleur.*

A zone 'sauvage' preserved between the tourist resorts, the estuary of the Orne, between *Ouistreham* and *Merville-Franceville* is made up of several hundred hectares of natural protected space where one can see the remains of numerous 'gabions' (hides cut into the marsh) used for duck hunting. See also the 'Redoute de Merville", building constructed in 1779 on the plans of Vauban to protect the mouth of the Orne.

The little community of **Sallenelles** owes its name to the sale of salt which was in earlier times made in this area. Note in passing that the author of the celebrated operetta 'Les Cloches de Corneville', M. Planquette, was born in this place.

At **Villers-sur-Mer**, in the soil of the cliffs called 'Vaches Noires' numerous fossils can be found, notably ammonites, sometimes pyrites, 'trigonies', terebratula and many other interesting remains. The lacertilia, which disappeared thousands of years ago and the remains of Ichthyosaurs have been discovered on the blockfield and deserted sites around **Auberville.**

If **Cabourg**, with its magnificent beach, its sea wall promenade, its legendary palace, its casino and its neo-norman villas, dear to the heart of Proust and the romantics in general - who had henceforth their festival there - remains the preferred resort of the authentic Norman bourgeoisie, who prefer it to **Deauville** which has become too 'parisian' for their taste.

Dives, the neighbouring resort, remains attached to the memory of Duke William who built his armada there (696 ships) and assembled it in the port in 1066 before embarking on his new destiny. The church of Dives (11th, 14th and 15th centuries) was built on the orders of William.

Dives was, in the 11th century, one of the major ports of the Duchy of Normandy. It was the natural 'maritime port' of the vast plain which extends up to Falaise, cradle of the 'Modern Normandy'. It was also the port of the 'Hiesmois', of Séez and of the County of Alençon. The Duke was able to convince his faithful lieutenants of the importance that the 'Butte de Caumont' constituted as it overlooks Dives and from the top of which one can see 15 leagues around. He told them 'We shall meet again on this hill at the foot of which my fleet will be reunited'.

To visit, without fail, in this historic town :

* **'Les Halles' from the 14th and 15th centuries in the heart of the town (beautiful carpentry and a roof in the brown tiles of the region).**

* **The village of 'William the Conqueror' from the 17th century, ancient relay station.**

* **The 'Lieutenance' from the 17th century.**

The activity of the port of Dives continued to grow over the centuries. In 1676, Colbert, Minister of Louis XIV undertook important work there, drying the marshes and altering the course of the Dives. The military dimension of the port was confirmed over the years, notably in the differences between England and France.

On 29th May 1798, the port of Dives was the setting of a naval battle. The frigate 'La Confiante' and the corvette 'La Vésuve' which had left Le Havre en route for Cherbourg were attacked by three English ships and tried to take shelter in the port of Dives. To stop them, the English opened continuous fire and after five hours of fighting the 'Confiante', the hull, completely shattered by the fire from the enemy guns, was wrecked on the point of Beuzeval before catching fire.

Honfleur, *'town of art and history'* was, with Rouen, in the time of William, one of the main transit ports for merchandise to England. The town has been built around the **'vieux bassin'** from which have left so many celebrated and courageous sailors. It is a true architectural jewel. Its monuments like the **church of Sainte-Catherine** (15th and 16th centuries) of which the nave was built by marine carpenters, its **bell tower** from the 17th century, the **'Lieutenance'** (16th and 17th centuries), quay Saint-Etienne, ancient home of the Lieutenant of the King, are remarkable. An in-depth visit of the town is essential, with its little narrow alleyways and the houses of ship owners or the humble houses of the fishermen, salt stores, built in the 1670 by the 'Ferme de la Gabelle', with the authorisation of Colbert. Colour is present everywhere as in the windows of the numerous art galleries which recall the pictorial past of the town. Also visit the **'Musée de la Marine'** and some kilometres from the town the **'Pont de Normandie'** which now links Upper and Lower Normandy at the mouth of the Seine.

On the heights above Honfleur, is the little church of Notre-Dame-de-Grâce (17th century) where the Normans, leaving to colonise the New France, went to pray. Until the 1980's there was held here the 'Fête aux Normands' which was created under William. From the esplanade around the chapel there opens up a majestic panorama of the estuary of the Seine, Le Havre and the Pont de Normandie. From Mont Joli, not far from there, one also has a superb view over the old town and the bridge.

Because of its strategic position, Honfleur was during the Hundred Years War, a defensive bastion against the English. During this period Charles V carried out enormous fortification works. During this era the port served as the departure point for many military expeditions towards England.

On the picturesque little road which runs along the coast in the direction of *Villerville* admire in passing the church of *Cricqueboeuf* (12th century) and the site of Barneville-la-Bertrand.

Trouville and above all *Deauville*, on the Floral Coast, are the most 'chic' places in Normandy with their old palaces, casinos, race-courses and the beautiful villas which evoke the aristocratic clientele of the second Empire and the **'Belle Epoque'** when the princes and the 'highnesses', from all of Europe and the industrial magnates, came after or before *Monte Carlo* to 'set alight' Deauville, while their companions went to take in the sea air along the famous **'planches'** which avoided them getting the bottoms of their long dresses wet. The 'creators' of *Deauville* were in 1860, **Morny**, half brother of Napoleon III, the architect Breney and Doctor Oliffe, who was the doctor at the British Embassy in Paris. From 1844, they came to *Trouville* where they built the first 'belles villas' in an eclectic style.

The great annual event in the life of the people of Deauville is now, in September, the **'Festival of American Film'** which brings together the stars of Hollywood in the resort. *Deauville* is also the world capital of the horse and equestrian events which take place each summer and autumn.

Places to see, in Deauville, the **'Villa Strassburger'**, historic house built at the beginning of the 20th century for the Baron Henri de Rothschild and acquired in 1924 by the American millionaire Strassburger then bequeathed by his son to the town. (visits in July and August).

Above the town are the ancient presbytery and the old school which are remains of the history of Deauville, but also **Mont Canisy**, today a holiday place which offers an immense panorama over the bay of the Seine. The Germans set up a strong battery there during the last war.

Trouville is the 'Siamese twin' of Deauville and likewise has gained celebrity status thanks to the fashion of sea bathing in the middle of the 19th century but it proudly claims its priority over the latter. The 'Queen of the Beaches' has carried for over a thousand years the name of a warrior Viking : 'Thorilfr' which, in the course of successive distortions has become Trouville. Its principal attractions remain :

* **Its 1200 metre long beach of fine sand with its promenande of 'planches' dating from 1867.**
* **The fish market on the quay.**
* **The casino built in 1912 and the picturesque fishermen's houses from the 19th century.**

In *Touques* neighbouring town to Trouville, admire the **Church of Saint Peter** from the 10th century, a real architectural jewel from the Roman era.

In the **Church of Saint-Thomas**, from the 12th century, it is said that **Thomas Becket** came to pray before embarking for England.

A few kilometres from Deauville, visit the 'safeguarded village' of *Beaumont-en-Auge* from the heights of which you can still discover a magnificent panorama over the valley of the Touques.

In the interior of this region, in the immense *Plain of Lower Normandy* which goes beyond the limits of Calvados and stretches from the *Bessin* in the west up to *Ouistreham* in the east and *Argentan* in the south, one cannot quietly pass by *Bayeux, Caen* and *Falaise* which possess the fundamental historical wealth of the rich past of the **Duchy of Normandy**.

Bayeux, 'the most English of all Norman towns' with its cathedral, its celebrated **'Tapestry of Queen Mathilde''**, its **Academy of Lace**, its **Memorial Museum of the Battle of Normandy**, its **Baron Gérard Museum**, its **de Gaulle Memorial**, its townhouses (17th-18th century), its **old roads**, its **art and craft workshops**, merits an extended stay for British visitors who will live 'like a lord' from the 'tasty morsels' in this town which knows so well how to welcome them.

The **cathedral** is a superb monument. Items from the Roman era remain in the crypt, the front towers and the lower parts of the nave are from the gothic period, one can admire the choir, the capitulary room, the chapels of the nave and the façade with five gates. (The cathedral is open for visits from 1st September to 30th June from 9 am-7 pm, from 1st July to 31st August, from 9 am-7 pm. Visits are not permitted during services. Mass is celebrated on Sunday at 11 am).

****

THE BAYEUX TAPESTRY OR 'THE STORY OF THE CONQUEST'

*The **Bayeux tapestry**, this immense 'designed strip' called the **'Tapestry of Queen Mathilde'** is one of the major attractions of Normandy. It draws to **Bayeux** each year thousands of visitors, the majority British. This decoration was previously part of the Treasure of the Cathedral of Bayeux. It is embroidery in wool* *on linen cloth, around 70 metres long, and 50 centimetres wide, made in the 11th century, it tells the saga of Duke William in England across 58 scenes grouped into three acts.*

This tapestry has revealed to historians hundreds of details of the greatest interest on the life, the customs and the art of war in the 11th century.

Guided visits in English in six parts - Exhibition hall and audio-visuals.
Contact : Centre Guillaume-le-Conquérant, rue de Nesmond.
Tel (33) 2 31 51 25 50 - Fax (33) 2 31 51 25 59.

Visits from 15th March to 30th April and from 1st September to 15th October from 9 am-6.30 pm continuously ; from 16th October to 14th March from 9.30 am-12.30 pm and from 2-6 pm and from 1st May to 31st August from 9 am-7 pm continuously.

****

Bayeux is the capital of the Bessin, a natural region which extends from east to west from **Courseulles-sur-Mer** to **Isigny** *and from north to south from the sea to* **Caumont-l'Eventé**. Continuation of the huge plain of Caen, the Bessin offers varied and different countryside, permanent meadows dotted with characteristic 'manor farms' with their lovely porches and by the sea the majestic steep cliffs. At **Lantheuil**, near to **Creully**, one can find the **'Château de Manneville'** which still belongs to the Turgot family, the celebrated minister of Louis XVI.

You can visit it by appointment from 15th April to 15th October from 2-6 pm (Tel/Fax (33) 2 31 80 11 12).

Other places to discover in the Bessin :

= The **Feudal Castle of Creully** : ancient stronghold built in the 11th century then modernised in the 15th century. It is one of the rare testimonies to civil Roman/Norman architecture. See the ramparts and the vaulted rooms from the 12th century.
For information : Tel/Fax (33) 2 31 80 18 65. Visit in July and August only from 10 am-12 noon and from 3-6 pm. (Tuesdays, Thursdays and Fridays).

= The **Castle of Balleroy** : magnificent home of Louis XIII built between 1626 and 1636 on the plans of François Mansart (1598-1666), it was his major work. This property was bought by the American millionaire **Malcolm Forbes** in 1975. This patron of the arts has improved the castle by furnishing it magnificently and by installing an important collection of works by great artists. Malcolm Forbes has organised international gatherings of balloonists here and created the **Museum of Balloons** which retraces the history of balloons from the Montgolfier brothers up to the modern day.
Open to the public from 15th March to 30th June and from 1st September to 15th October from 9 am-12 noon and from 2-6 pm. (closed Tuesdays). - From 1st July to 31st August open from 10 am-6 pm. For information : Tel (33) 2 31 21 60 61 - Fax (33) 2 31 21 51 77.
E mail : forbes.inc@wanadoo.fr - Internet site : www.château-balleroy.com

= Castle of Fontaine-Henry.
Jewel of the Renaissance, this beautiful home, furnished and inhabited is open to the public for guided visits. For information : Tel/Fax (33) 2 31 80 00 42.

The typical village of *Crépon* with its **fortified manor-farms (La Rançonnière, La Grande Ferme, Mathan, Le Pavillion Lérondel and le Clos Mandeville...**

The city of *Caen* has for several years refocused its promotion around the Duke-King William and his huge castle, one of the largest feudal dwellings in France within which is the prestigious **Museum of Normandy.**

You cannot leave Caen without visiting l'**'Abbaye aux Hommes'** and l'**'Abbaye aux Femmes'** - especially the abbey churches - major works of Roman art (which historians have for a long time classified simply as... Norman). In the choirs of these two buildings are buried respectively **William and Mathilde de Normandy.**

These two remarkable monuments were built by the Duke and Duchess to 'compensate for their faults". Their union had in fact been invalidated by the Church which criticised their 'blood relationship'. If the bombardments of 1944 destroyed almost entirely the town of Caen, there remain some vestiges of the rich architectural heritage of the ducal city, such as :

= The **'Hôtel d'Escoville'** (16th century), place Saint-Pierre.

= The **'Maison des Quatrans'** near the castle.

= The churches of **Saint-Peter and Saint-John** (with its leaning bell tower which reminds us that Caen was built on the marshes), **Saint-Michel-de-Vaucelles, Notre-Dame-de-la-Gloriette, Saint-Nicolas, Saint-Sauveur...**

= The old quarters : le Vaugueux, la rue Froide, le rue Ecuyère, la place Saint-Sauveur, la rue Caponière, la place Malherbe...

Note specially the monuments of the city of Caen which are illuminated each evening.

****

CAEN, GREEN CITY

= *'Le Jardin des Plantes'* - *5 Place Blot - Tel (33) 2 31 86 28 80 - Fax (33) 2 31 86 33 04 - Open all year from 8 am (10 am on Saturday and Sunday).*

Birthplace of the Botanical Garden of Caen, this garden created in 1736 as a university garden of medicine and pharmacy has represented on more than three hectares, since the French Revolution, a true museum of vegetation showing Norman flowers, medicinal flowers, rock plants, exotic species and a complete 'palette' of horticulture.

= *'Le Parc floral de la Colline aux Oiseaux'* - *Avenue de l'Amiral Mountbatten (Near the Mémorial). - Tel (33) 2 31 86 28 80 Fax (33) 2 31 86 33 04. - Open all year from 10 am. Free entry. Annual closure after the main season.*

17 hectare landscaped and floral site created in 1994 for the 50th anniversary of the Battle of Normandy. All the gardens of the park are dedicated to Peace. Visit the superb rose garden with 15,000 plants.

= *'Parc Michel d'Ornano'* - *Abbaye aux Dames - Tel (33) 2 31 86 28 80 - Fax (33) 2 31 86 33 04. - Open all year from 8 am (10 am at weekends and national holidays). Free entry. Annual closure after the main season.*

French garden in the style of the 18th century. The old Parc Saint-Louis, with an area of more than 5 hectares, forming part of the Abbaye aux Dames. It offers flower beds in a French style, alleys of old lime trees, a cedar of Lebanon and a maze on a mound.

****

Visit, to the west of Caen, the **church of Norrey-en-Bessin** at ***Saint-Manvieu-Norrey.*** It is one of the most beautiful jewels in the Norman-Gothic style of the 13th century. (To visit it ask for the key at the neighbouring bar).

Falaise, following the example of Bayeux, is one of the Norman towns **most visited** by **the British.**

They come to visit *(guided by an enthusiastic compatriot)* **the feudal castle,** recently restored *(that was not done without arousing cries of concern among the Normans… and even among the British)* where Duke William was born.

The visitors also like to go to the little fountain at the foot of the ramparts where, according strong spoken tradition, the beautiful **Arlette,** daughter of a citizen of Falaise, was doing her laundry when **Robert** noticed her as he was returning from hunting. On top of the keep flies the red flag with the yellow cross of **Saint-Olaf**, emblem of the Norman nation.

A visit of the town on foot is a must to discover the main elements of the rich heritage of this ducal city.

= **The mediaeval castle which was built and enlarged by the dukes up to Jean sans Terre.**

= **The castle of Fresnaye (17th century) place of exhibitions.**

= **The venerable townhouses.**

= **The old quarters (Guibray and Saint-Laurent).**

= **The four churches : Saint-Gervais, Notre-Dame-de-la-Trinité, Notre-Dame-de-Guibray, and Saint-Laurent as well as the chapel Saint-Vigor…** restored by a Japanese artist.

= **'L'Hôtel-Dieu'.**

= **The old washing place.**

= **The fortified enclosure with the doors, especially the door of the Cordeliers.**

= **The statue of William on horseback at the entry to the castle and those of the first dukes.**

At the 'Mairie' : the list of the principal companions of William at Hastings.

'L'Hôtel de Souza'. Dwelling from the 17th and 18th centuries in the town : 26 rue du Camp fermé. Possibility of guided visits by the owner.

Tel/Fax (33) 2 31 40 84 25.

To also visit outside the town :

= **The remains of the 'Abbaye aux Dames'** of *Villers Canivet*

So that God would pardon him for having chased the girls in his household, Roger de Montbray, Anglo-Norman lord, founded in 1127 at 'Villers-le-Quennyvet' a priory for women.

This humble house was raised to the rank of 'Abbaye Royale' in the 17th century and the buildings were reconstructed to welcome Cistercian nuns. The most remarkable building is that of the entry to the Abbey. This structure from the 14th century, with passages for pedestrians and carts is today the only mediaeval Cistercian doorway which remains practically in its original state in France. It is also the only one among the 'abbayes de femmes'.

Guided visit with diaporama - Possibility to order a Norman 'snack'.

Tel (33) 2 31 90 81 80. E mail : abv.canivet@wanadoo.fr

= **'Les Monts d'Eraines' and the natural reserve of Mesnil-Soleil,** 6 kilometres away.

= **The site of the 'Devil's breach' - 'Le Mont Joly'.**

Rocky promontory overlooking the gorges of Laizon, one of the most beautiful natural sites of the region.

= **The Roman Church** of *Norrey-en-Auge* and its painted frescoes from the 11th century.

= **The Church** of *Aubigny* which possesses a unique collection of six statues of the lords of Aubigny aligned in chronological order.

= **The Plain of Caen,** which makes up a large part of the **plain of lower Normandy** is an immense expanse given over to the growing of cereals.

The habitat is grouped into little towns, villages with major farms built in white stone and surrounded by high walls with magnificent porch openings which give a great nobleness to these buildings.

To the south west of the area, the **hedged Virois farmland,** country of *'bonne vie'* and of *'bonne chair',* known for ciders, calvados and other gastronomic specialities is especially appreciated by British visitors. It is a countryside made up of parcels of land enclosed by impenetrable hedges where the royalists took refuge during the Revolution.

Vire, constructed on a rocky spur, was built and fortified at the beginning of the 12th century on the orders of Henry 1st. Very badly damaged during the last war, the town, harmoniously reconstructed, is an unbeatable stop for the gourmet. Stop there to admire **the Keep** (12th century) of the ancient feudal castle, beautiful example of a square Norman keep and the celebrated **Clock Doorway** (13th-15th centuries) a fortified entrance flanked with two towers and surmounted by a belfry with a little steeple (open to the public every day in summer except Sundays and national holidays from 2.30-6.30 pm).

See also in Vire **'le Cotin'**, old hotel from the 18th century situated in the rue du Cotin, where King Charles X stopped on the road from exile, spending the night of 11th August 1830. Also the **Chapel Saint Louis** inside the hospital which retains three

beautiful sculptured stalls and a superb high altar. Visit by appointment.
3Tel (33) 2 31 43 52 56.

Nature lovers should visit the **'Lac de la Dathée'** and the **'Gorges de la Vire'**. The bird reserve of 10 hectares which is close to the lake of 43 hectares, at Saint-Manvieu-Bocage and ***Saint-Germain-de-Tallevende,*** is managed by the Groupe Ornithologique Normand. Some 86 species of bird live there (Duck, coot, grebe…). Bird watching expeditions are organised. For information : Tel (33) 2 31 43 52 56.

****

Le Bocage (Hedged farmland)

The word 'Bocage' comes from the Norman 'bosc' meaning 'bois' (wood).

It has been taken to designate a particular type of farming countryside to the west of Normandy in the regions of La Manche, to the west of Calvados and the south west of Orne. It is a collection of enclosures which are often set in open countryside. Characterised by a multitude of fences, formed by dense living hedges, the whole forming a veritable network that was used by the royalists to hide (during the Revolution).

****

To the south, Calvados is continued by the **'Suisse Normande',** a chaotic countryside of narrow valleys, of cliffs which present a totally unexpected landscape : ***Clécy*** is the capital of this unusual region of Normandy with the astonishing **'Roche d'Oëtre'** and, close to there, the highest point of Calvados : the **'Mont Pinson'**, 365 metres high ! The 'Suisse Normande', where one also finds numerous British residents, is a favoured place for relaxation and long walks.

Near to ***Condé-sur-Noireau*** is the **'Château de Pontécoulant'**, a beautiful dwelling from the 16th century enlarged in the 18th century. (Castle, pavilions, dovecote, country park, farm, wood and land). Magnificently furnished the castle, which is today the property of the 'Conseil Général of Calvados', evokes the history and the style of life of a family from the aristocracy of the 19th century : the 'Doulcet de Pontécoulant'.

Open to the public - For information : Tel (33) 2 31 69 62 54.

****

The Harcourt family

At Thury-Harcourt the memories of one of the oldest and most noble Norman families endures : the feudal house of Harcourt. It goes back to Rollon, first Duke of Normandy and a branch was established in Great Britain.

The history of the Anglo-Norman kingdom and that of the Harcourt family are truly inseparable. We know that Philippe d'Harcourt was bishop of Salisbury and Bayeux and that he built the cathedral - where he was buried - in 1145.

Jean IV, first Count of Harcourt, fighting on the French side, was killed at the battle of Crecy in 1346. His brother Godefroy, Marshal of England, who was commanding the British troops, when he learned that Jean was dead went into the

****

For lovers of walking and the open air note the surroundings of ***Thury-Harcourt:*** The **'Boucle du Hom'** at ***Thury.***

The **'Route des crêtes'** at ***Saint-Omer***.

The **'Pain de sucre'**, the **'Rochers des Parcs'**, the **'Rochers de la Houle'**, the **'Site de la Favère'**, the **'Eminence'**, around ***Clécy,*** the **Forest of Grimbosq**.

To the south west of Bessin, after Bayeux, there stretches a countryside of semi-open 'bocages' with farms. Pastures for the raising of cattle and the production of milk are essential to this area.

Situated close to the sea, on the border between Calvados and La Manche is ***Isigny*** where they make the celebrated products recognised as the **'1ˢᵗ cru laitier de Normandie'.**

This is also the original homeland of **Walt Disney,** true descendent of the lord **Raoul d'Isigny,** whose family, after spending a long time in England, emigrated to the USA.

We shall finish this presentation of Calvados with the *'Figure of the prow of the Norman Drake'* : The **'Pays d'Auge'** which perhaps alone corresponds to the traditional image that the 'horsains' have of Normandy.

The *'Pays d'Auge'* extends over three areas (Calvados, Eure and Orne) between ***Dives*** in the west and ***Touques*** in the east and ***Exmes*** in the south and the ***Floral Coast*** in the north, but principally in Calvados where its most beautiful jewels, apart from the coast, are the towns of ***Pont-l'Evêque, Lisieux, Orbec, Saint-Pierre-sur-Dives, Crévecœur, Cambremer, Troarn, Mézidon, Beaumont-en-Auge, Beuvron*** (protected village) and ***Livarot*** which between them hold more than half the architectural treasures of Normandy with a multitude of monuments such as churches, chapels and priories of which many date from the 11ᵗʰ century, but also numerous castles and manors which are often difficult to find as they are buried in the heart of the countryside of hedges and hills which have given renown to this country of Cockaigne.

On the edge of the plain of Caen and the Pays d'Auge, make a call at the ***'Château de Mezidon-Canon'***. In a marvellous park (permanent exhibition dedicated to gardens), you will discover a veritable jewel, a joining together of French and English styles in an ornate décor of statues and romantic 'fabrications'.

This collection from the end of the 18ᵗʰ century was built by the lawyer Elie de Beaumont. Tel (33) 2 31 20 05 07 - Fax (33) 2 31 78 04 39.

Also situated on the frontier of the two natural regions, the town of *Saint-Pierre-sur-Dives* possesses an impressive architectural heritage especially the **Abbey church.**

A Norman monastic collection of very great quality, it is made up of the Benedictine church of 13ᵗʰ, 14ᵗʰ and 15ᵗʰ centuries and the Capitular room which possesses a remarkable enamelled terracotta paving from the 13ᵗʰ century. The **'Halles'** of Saint-Pierre-sur-Dives also date from the 13ᵗʰ century and are made up of three naves in wood ending on two gables of masonry. Every Monday morning they hold an important and picturesque market and on the first Sunday of the month an antiques market of repute.

In the **'Jardin conservatoire'**, rue Saint-Benoist, you can find flowers and vegetables of the Pays d'Auge : astonishing diversity of plants from the garden. Free or guided visits. Seasonal exhibitions ; exchange markets, conferences…

A contemporary Norman author, Jacques Viquesnel, imitator of Alphonse Allais, does not hesitate to confirm that the Pays d'Auge stretches over land that was the origin of time… earthly paradise ! Everything is still united there : luxuriant nature, the apple tree, not to mention souvenirs of the presence of Adam and Eve.

Lisieux is the capital of this divine land. The bombardments of 1944 have unfortunately laid waste the main parts of the architectural treasures of this city which included a considerable number of old and beautiful houses in sculptured wood from the 15ᵗʰ and 16ᵗʰ centuries. Lisieux is also the **2ⁿᵈ town for pilgrimages in France.** One comes there to pray to **'Sainte-Thérèse-de-l'Enfant Jésus'**, Doctor of the Church, Patron of Missions, who lived and died at the **'Carmel'** de Lisieux.

On the 15ᵗʰ August, the last Sunday in September and the 30ᵗʰ September, anniversary day of the death of Sainte-Thérèse, great religious ceremonies take place in Lisieux (the 'fêtes thérésiennes").

Begun in 1929, the **Basilica** was officially consecrated on 11ᵗʰ July 1954. With a surface area of 4,500 square metres it is topped with a dome 93 metres high which makes it one of the biggest churches built in the 20ᵗʰ century.

See in the basement the crypt with three ornate mosaic aisles.

More than 50,000 faithful took part in the transfer of the body of the young saint from the cemetery of Lisieux to the **Chapel of Carmel** in the years before the war.

The **'Maison des Buissonnets'**, an elegant house of the 19ᵗʰ century, situated at 22 Rue des Buissonnets, where Thérèse Martin lived up to the age of 15, can be visited. Conserved there are the family furniture and personal effects of the saint. Her relics are exhibited in a glass reliquary called the 'Reliquary of Brasil' as it was given by generous Brasilians.

The **'Diorama Thérèse Martin'**, a wax museum, retrace the life of the saint through figures animated by sound and light.

The magnificent **Cathedral of Saint-Peter,** begun in the 11ᵗʰ century and completed in the middle of the 15ᵗʰ century, saw the marriage of **'Duc Henri' and**

Aliénor of Aquitaine. You can also see the tomb of **Bishop Pierre Cauchon** (1432-1442), President of the ecclesiastical tribunal which condemned **Joan of Arc** to the stake. Although at that time he was in charge of the diocese of Beauvais, he directed the prosecution during the trial of the 'Maid of Orleans'. In 1432, he was named Bishop of Lisieux and ordered the building of an expiatory altar to the virgin in Saint Peter's cathedral also having rebuilt the central chapel of this beautiful building, which resembles in many facets Notre-Dame-de-Paris.

It was in this sanctuary that Thérèse Martin had the revelation of her vocation.

Bishop Arnoult (1141-1181), intellectual and diplomat, friend of Thomas Becket and associate of Henry 2nd, undertook the construction of this cathedral on the site where a Roman building had stood a century before.

« *The works started with the narthex around 1160-1170 ; the raising of the nave followed in the most modern style : for the first time in Normandy they used the flying buttress originating from Ile de France. Lisieux was thus an experimental construction. Between 1230 and 1250, the transept, the ambulatory and the choir were achieved just after the typically Norman lantern tower, the doors and the two towers of the western façade had been put into place. A buttress pierced with arrow slits, hiding a staircase inside, reinforces the Norman character of the cathedral… ».*

Neighbour of the cathedral, the current **'Palais de Justice'** is the ancient residence of the Count-Bishops and dates from the 17th century.

2 minutes from Lisieux, on the Livarot road
Domaine de
St Hippolyte
A 16th century domain...
An authentic manor house and estate from ancient times.
...rediscover the feeling of a Normandy farm from a bygone era
Three areas of agricultural interest encompassing products made from Norman soil
Wine and cider tasting available from original presses.
Make Normandy soil your destination
Open every day from 1st May - 30th September 10 am - 6 pm. Tel (33) 2 31 31 30 68

Lisieux, cœur de Normandie
Lisieux, town of pilgrimage, discovery of the unusual story of the little Thérèse.
Lisieux, town of history, where the architectural beauty of timber framed houses, of the castle of Saint Germain de Livet, of the manors are united with the beauty of the scenery.
Lisieux, town of taste, where cheese, cider, calvados, perry express the flavour of the Norman soil.
Lisieux, heart of Normandy, to discover a Normandy whose charm has no longer any need to be proven.
Office de Tourisme - B.P. 17197
14107 Lisieux cedex - FRANCE
Tel : (33) 2 31 48 18 10
Lisieux
CAPITALE DU PAYS D'AUGE

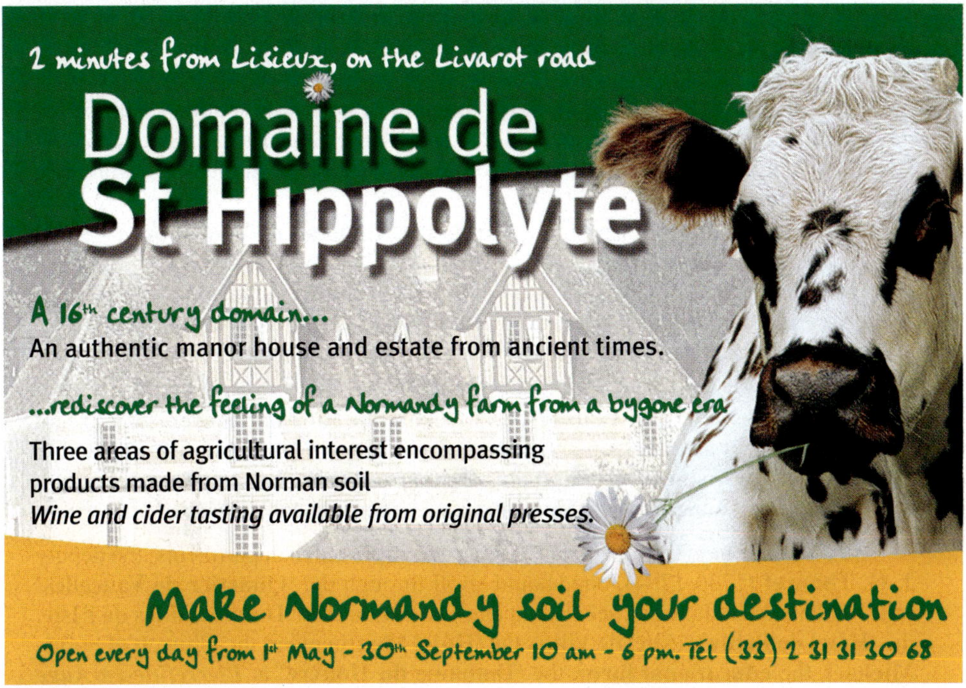

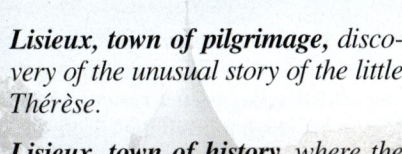

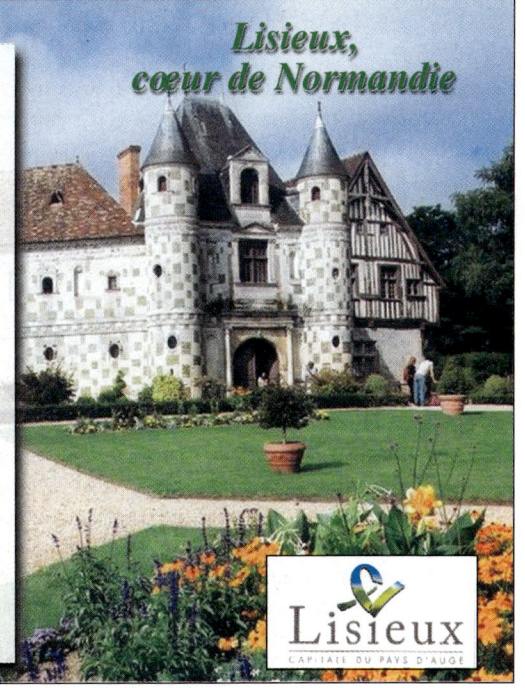

To the rear you, look at the **French gardens of the diocese** and the splendid **'Hôtel du Haut Doyenné'** from the 18th century which houses the Academy of Music.

Discover also the **Church of Saint-Jacques,** flamboyant gothic construction which has become a place for exhibitions ; the **'Hôtel de Ville'** (18th century) the **Italian style municipal theatre** dating from 1885 and also the numerous townhouses from the 19th century…

A few kilometres from Lisieux, a visit to the **'Château de Tournebu'** (15th and 16th centuries) at *Saint-Germain-de-Livet* is very worthwhile. 'Jewel of the Pays d'Auge' from the Renaissance era, 'castle of ivory spangled with emeralds' said Jean de la Varende. Inside there is beautiful furniture from the 17th and 19th centuries, paintings from the 19th century, souvenirs of Eugene Delacroix and Alphonse Daudet.

Property of the town of Lisieux - For information : Tel (33) 2 31 31 00 03.

Visiting times : Guided visits from 1st October to 30th March, every day except Tuesdays from 10 am-12 noon and from 2-5 pm. From 1st April to 30th September every day except Tuesdays from 10 am-12 noon and from 2-7 pm. Annual closure from 1st to 15th October, from 1st December to 1st February and 1st May.

At *Pont-l'Evêque,* birthplace of the creator of the French departments, the deputy **J.-G. Thouret** (1746-1794), one should stroll through the **'Quartier de Vaucelles'** (old wood panelled houses), see the ancient **Convent of the 'Dominicaines de l'Isle,** the **'Hôtel de Brilly'** (Hôtel de Ville), the **'Hôtel Montpensier,** the **Church of Saint-Michael,** the **educational farm,** the **'Domaine du Houvre'** at *Pierrefitte-en-Auge* and the **Priory of Saint Hymer** six kilometres from the town through which runs the *Touques.* The town has given its name to the famous cheese still made in the Pays d'Auge.

Country of cider and calvados, the **'Pays de Cambremer'** possesses an exceptional number of noble wood panelled dwellings from *Beuvron*, **'protected village'** which is one of the **'hundred most beautiful villages in France'** and can pride itself on its numerous half timbered buildings of which the **'vieilles halles'** and the **15th century manor** are the jewels. They are sited in the centre of the village. A visit is recommended to this place held back in its 'flavour' of the 19th century. From the **Chapel of Clermont,** on the heights above the town, one can benefit from an extensive view over the marshes of the Vie and the Dives.

In terms of its natural heritage, the canton of Cambremer offers two sides :

* To the west the **marshes of the Dives,** which make up vast meadows where cattle and sheep live peacefully, on lands that are completely flat apart from the occasional 'island' and 'causeway' which emerge.

* To the east heading towards the 'cuesta' one comes up against the last foothills of the Parisian basin. This area offers superb panoramas.

Several types of countryside succeed each other, going from east to west : in a partly hedged Pays d'Auge with its closed fields, its orchards planted with apple trees, the houses are made in a special **half timbered style** with a great variety and richness of architecture and, in all cases, precise rules of construction. The habitat is dispersed and split up by the hedges.

It is the country of grand and prestigious stud farms for thoroughbreds, but also those of more modest livestock, the trotters. The Pays d'Auge, which was originally only an immense sombre forest is the homeland par excellence of 'her majesty the Norman Cow' and of fat cheeses that the people from here have created from its milk (Pont l'Evêque, Livarot, Camembert), the region of the 'grands crus' of ciders and calvados, a land where the apple, as everywhere here, has been and remains the origin of pleasure…

****

THE MOST BEAUTIFUL WOOD PANELLED MANORS OF THE PAYS D'AUGE

Authentic jewels, in settings of greenery, the wood panelled manors are one of the riches of the Pays d'Auge. Built from the 16th century in the hollows of large valleys in a 'U' or on the side of a hill, they are found for the most part along the Touques and its tributaries.

The best are without doubt :

*The '***Mesnil de Roiville'*** *(16th century) near to* ***Vimoutiers.***

*The '***Manoir de Coupesarte'*** *(16th century) near to* ***Saint-Julien-le-Faucon.***

*The '***Manoir de Bellou'*** *(15th and 16th centuries)* (1) *and of* ***Chriffretôt*** *(16th century) near to* ***Livarot.***

*The '***Manoir des Evêques'*** *at* ***Canapville****, ancient residence of the Bishops of Lisieux, near to* ***Deauville*** (2)*.*

*The '***Manoir du Bais'*** *built in the second half of the 15th century. It offers the most beautiful architectural collection of* ***Cambremer****. It can be seen from the D85.*

*The '***Manoir du Champ Versant'*** *(can be visited) built to the north of the village of* ***Bonnebosq****. It has conserved the typical buildings of agricultural development of earlier times. Notably you can see the barn, the stable and the sheep barn. Inside there are three beautiful monumental fireplaces.*(3)

(1) Open to the public from mid July to mid August every day from 3-7 pm.

(2) Open to the public from 2-6 pm. Every day except Tuesday from 15th June to 31st August. Saturdays, Sundays and national holidays from 1st April to 14th June and from 1st September to 1st November ; Tel/Fax (33) 2 31 65 24 75.

(3) Visiting days and times : from the Easter weekend to 30th September every afternoon from 2.30-6 pm except Mondays and Tuesdays (closed Mondays in July and August).

****

Also See in calvados…

NATURAL HERITAGE :

Caen : **'Maison de la Nature'.**

Villers-sur-Mer : **'Les Vaches Noires'.**

Saint-Rémy-sur-Orne : **'Les Fosses d'Enfer".** Maison des Ressources Géologiques de Normandie 14570 Saint-Rémy-sur-Orne - Tel (33) 2 31 69 67 77 - Fax (33) 2 31 69 70 39. Open from March to September from 10 am-12 noon and from 2-6 pm. October to December, open at weekends, national holidays and school holidays from 2-5.30 pm. Closed Tuesdays except in July and August. Shop and tourist information point. In the Suisse Normande, the rocks the countryside and the people have secrets to reveal. On the site of the ancient mine of Saint-Rémy, la Maison des Ressources Géologiques de Normandie opens to you a huge book of the earth. 650 million years, Normandy was not born yesterday ! Ancestors of man, primitive mammals, dinosaurs and fossilised fish wait for you. Mountain chains, invasions of the sea, our peaceful Normandy has seen everything in the course of the geological ages : an impressive spectacle to see on a big screen.

On the 'Sienne' : **'Lac du Gast' : Dam and ornithological reserve.** It is above all a reservoir of 65 hectares holding drinking water put into operation in 1987 to regulate the course of the Sienne. In the reserve, operated by the Groupe Ornithologique Normand, live diverse species of birds linked to wet zones, nesting there regularly : grebes, 'huppés' ducks, mallard, water fowl, coot... The zone also serves as a stop for migratory birds. For information : Tel (33) 2 31 43 52 56.

Caumont-l'Eventé : **'Souterroscope des Ardoisières'.** An invitation to discover an underground world in this astonishing site. 'Thanks to technology in the vanguard, an initiatory journey under the earth to discover an extraordinary and little known world. 3.5 hectares in area, open space, parking, souvenir shops... A visit of 1 hour 15 minutes, Access for the disabled. Temperature underground : 12°. Exhibition 'Les dents de la terre' giant crystals, extraordinary stones. Address and information : Route de Saint Lô - Tel (33) 2 31 71 15 15 - Fax (33) 2 31 71 15 16. Open all year from 10 am-5 pm. (In July and August from 10 am-6 pm) closed Mondays from October to April. Annual closure from 15th December to 10th February.

Honfleur : **'Le Naturospace'.** Opposite the lighthouse of l'Hôpital towards Villerville Tel (33) 2 31 81 77 00. E.Mail : damico@naturospace.com. Open to the public from 1st February to 30th November (from 1st February to 31th March : from 10 am to 1 pm and from 2-5.30 pm all the days. From 1st April to 30th September : from 10 am to 7 pm all the days; From 1st October to 30th November from 10 am to 1 pm and from 2-5 pm all the days). 'Le Naturospace' proposes a journey to the heart of a tropical country of 800 square metres. The temperature remains at 28° allowing the discovery of a luxuriant flora coming from distant lands. Visitors follow 200 metres of paths caressed by the wings of hundreds of butterflies which fly around them.

Merville-Franceville : **Ornithological reserve of the 'Gros Banc'.** 330 hectares of terrain transformed for the protection of aquatic birds. Signposted discovery path with explanatory panels. For information : Tel (33) 2 31 78 71 06.

Saint-Denis-de-Meré : **'Arboretum de la Royauté'** 150 species to discover in 7000 square metres.

Saint-Julien-de-Mailloc : **Natural farm of the 'Dame Blanche'** 'La Quentinière' Tel/Fax (33) 2 31 63 91 70. Conservation of domestic animals and rare species in danger of extinction. 35 types to discover in their natural habitat... Botanical paths with hedges, trees and groves. Natural space for the environment. Open to the public every day from 1ˢᵗ April to 30ᵗʰ September from 10 am-7 pm and every day except Monday from 1ˢᵗ October to 30ᵗʰ March from 10am - 5 pm. Annual closure from 1ˢᵗ December to 31ˢᵗ January.

Saint-Pierre-du-Mont : (1 kilometre from the parking at Pointe du Hoc). **Sea bird reserve.** More than 600 nests of gulls, a hundred fulmars on 600 metres of cliffs.

Sallenelles : **'Maison de la Nature et de l'Estuaire'** Permanent exhibition on the life of an estuary, its flora and fauna and the human activities which develop there. Sales shop, network of pedestrian and cycling paths. For information : Tel (33) 2 31 78 71 06. Open to the public from 15ᵗʰ June to 31ˢᵗ August : every day from 2-6 pm ; from Easter to the end of October (out of season) Sunday 2-6 pm ; a week during the spring and autumn half-term school holidays. Free visits.

Ussy : **'Arboretum d'Ussy'.** Numerous specimens of young trees coming from the whole of Europe, America and Asia.

Exceptional natural sites from north to south.

* **The Marshes inland from the coast of the Bessin.** The Bessin is in part, made up of diverse natural spaces where the interest in ecological terms is preserved. These natural environments are inhabited by a rich and diverse fauna at the heart of which one finds very rare species which are protected and under careful surveillance such as the stork. Constructed paths allow discovery of this preserved space. Contact the Association 'Le Fayard', Tel (33) 2 33 05 68 04.

* **The Marshes of the Valley of the Aure at Saint-Germain-du-Pert**. Along a path of around 5 kilometres punctuated with 15 commentary points, discover a superb countryside.

* **The estuary of the Seine.**

* **The alkaline marshes** of *Chicheboville-Bellengreville.*

* **The waterfalls of Pont-ès-Retours** at *Roullours/Maisoncelles-la-Jourdan.*

  Classified site 'area of natural ecological interest for flora and fauna'.

  Valley of the Orne and its tributaries.

* **The Basin of the Souleuvre.**

* **The Basin upstream of the Druance**

TOURIST ROUTES

* **'La Route des Douets' :** The little tributary streams of the Touques are called in the Pays d'Auges, 'douets''. Situated inland from the Floral Coast, around Pont-l'Eveque, this tour will help you to discover one of the most astonishing regions of the Pays d'Auges. Free leaflet available from Tourist Offices in Calvados.

* **'La Route des Gorges de la Vire' :** Signposted car tour, kept to 35 kilometres. One joins it from the major roads RN175 (Caen-Villedieu-les-Poèles - Le Mont-Saint-Michel) and the D577 (Caen-Vire). This itinerary which does not follow entirely the course of the Vire and which leads the visitor successively to *Campeaux,*

Mont-Bertrand, Saint-Martin-Don, Sainte-Marie-Outre-l'Eau, Pont-Bellanger, Malloué... will help you to discover a very charming region, full of poetry : le Bocage.

* **'La Route des Marais'** : Tour situated to the south of Cabourg between Troarn and Dozulé. The marshes of the Dives are criss-crossed by numerous, small, twisting and picturesque routes and many canals separating the rich pastures and connecting the watercourses crossing the marshes of the 'little Holland". Ideal on foot or by cycle. Free leaflet available from Tourist Offices in Calvados.

* **'La Route de la Suisse Normande'** : This tour allows you to discover the marvellous countryside : (rocky escarpments, above the route of the Orne, meanders on the plain, hills and valleys of the Bocage) and the superb buildings. A region equally favourable for sporting activities. Brochure on request from the Tourist Offices.

L'ORNE

Like la Manche, l'**Orne**, takes its name from the river which has its source there and which flows into the sea at *Ouistreham* after running through *Caen.* It is a land of traditions, or even reactionary some would say.

Orne presents a countryside connected to its neighbouring areas of Manche, Calvados and Eure. To the west : *Flers,* one of the principal commercial and industrial centres of the area, an ancient town of the royalists with its castle which sheltered the headquarters of **General Count Frotté,** leader of the counter revolutionaries in Normandy who was assassinated in a cowardly way on the orders of Napoléon Bonaparte. A few kilometres, towards la Manche, *Tinchebray*, whose name reminds us of its Gallic origins. French capital of hardware from where **Guy Degrenne** originated, creator of various lines of place settings and dishes.

In the little village of **Saint-Jean-des-Bois,** on the border with la Manche, they previously made knives and mother of pearl buttons.

Domfront, capital of a countryside of 'Bocage' where farming attitudes remain strong, is the top place for a 'cru' of cider and calvados of repute, but the town, on the edges of the *Maine* and strategically placed, remembers also, a glorious past which is recalled by the ruins of its Keep built by **Henry 1ˢᵗ.**

The city was founded in the 6ᵗʰ century by a hermit named 'Front". In the surrounding forest **Arthurian legend** was born which tells the adventures of the **Knights of the Round Table.** This legend was written down in the 13ᵗʰ century by William of Troyes.

Equally one can enjoy in Domfront the church of **'Notre-Dame-sur-l'Eau'** (11ᵗʰ-13ᵗʰ centuries), one of the most beautiful Roman buildings in Normandy beside the river *'Varenne'*. You can admire the Roman paintings. Situated on the *'chemin de Mont-Saint-Michel'*, a multitude of great men have come there to pray, among them William of Normandy, Richard the Lionheart, Philippe Auguste, Louis XI, Aliénor of Aquitaine... Thomas Becket celebrated mass there in 1166.

It was saved from destruction (when they built the route of Mont-Saint-Michel) by Prosper Mérimée who was profoundly moved by its sad lot.

In the direction of Argentan, in the heart of the forest of **Andaine,** a massive thousand year old forest, known to mushroom lovers, which owes its name to a good fairy, the town of **Ferté-Macé,** stopping point for lovers of good food, which has experienced considerable tourist development thanks to the proximity of the spa town of **Bagnoles-de-l'Orne,** charming city, with a slightly old world charm, set in the heart of the forest, of which the water, even if it has cared for more than four centuries for illnesses of the circulatory system, possesses other virtues... (see the chapter on legends).

Oasis of water in the middle of a 7000 hectare ocean of greenery, Bagnoles is an hospitable town which offers pretty walks to the heart of a luxuriant nature and on the banks of the lake.

Visit the roads of the 'Belle Epoque' (set out in 1886 in the forest and scattered with numerous second homes of which a free guided tour is offered every Wednesday from April to October - Leaflet from the Tourist Office).

The thermal spa, which has been entirely renovated in recent years, has welcomed many international celebrities. It treats illnesses linked to vascular problems and rheumatology.

In the plain, continuation of the great 'open Norman countryside' previously described, **Argentan, Sées** and **Alençon** are towns possessing remarkable stories of a flourishing architectural heritage but also of intense activity.

It was in this last town that Thérèse Martin, called **'Sainte-Thérèse-de-l'Enfant-Jésus'** was born, (1873-1897), visit the house where she was born in rue Saint-Blaise. This dwelling is situated opposite to the **'Hôtel de Guise'** which has been for more than two centuries the residence of the State representative in the area. It is considered to be *'the most beautiful 'Préfecture' in France''*.

Much esteemed by the English visitors, the town of Alençon has numerous charms :

Places to see...

* **The Church of Notre-Dame (nave from the 15th century - flamboyant (gothic) doors from the beginning of the 16th century).**

* **'La Halle au Blé'. (The market hall for wheat).**

* **The 'Château des Ducs' (14th century) today a prison, within an extension the Courts and the Hôtel de Ville.**

* **The ancient town centre with its pedestrianised areas.**

Lifting your head you will also see the hundreds of cast iron balcony rails which decorate the facades of the old houses in the centre of the town.

Around Alençon a stroll in the forests of Ecouves and Perseigne will enable you to discover enchanted places.

If Alençon guards the memories of its more prestigious lords **Roger de Montgommery** and his wife, **Mabile de Bellême,** who ruled over a territory practically the same as the current region of Orne, from *Perche to Vimoutiers, Sées,* centre of the diocese (where the producer Besson filmed his 'Joan of Arc') shows today, to all who care to look, its inestimable jewels in terms of buildings and religious art.

Sées possesses a precious architectural jewel. You should visit the cathedral from the 13th century, a pure marvel of Norman gothic art which has acoustics unique in France. (Guided visits), stroll through the old roads and alleys and stop for a moment before the remains of the Abbey of Saint-Martin founded in the 11th century.

Argentan, of which the '**Empress**' was the Countess, remembers having been from **Henry 1**[st] to **Jean-sans-Terre** the **privileged holiday town** of the **Anglo-Norman kings.** One recalls still today the stays made by **Thomas Becket** at the castle. It was from Argentan, in 1170, that four Norman 'gentlemen' left to go to assassinate the latter, then Archbishop of Canterbury. It was also in the castle of Argentan, in 1172, that Henry 2nd, King of England, Duke of Normandy, gathered all his counts and barons to seek with them a means to conquer Ireland which he wanted to add to his possessions.

In 1189, **Aliénor of Aquitaine** made her home there and received frequent visits from her son **Richard the Lionheart.** The public retirement homes of the general hospital of Argentan were named in 1999 'Thomas Becket' and 'Aliénor of Aquitaine' in memory of the privileged links of the 'ornaise' city with the Anglo-Norman sovereigns.

Remember also that in 1199, 5 years before the annexation of Normandy by France, Jeans sans Terre held a full court in Argentan before the Christmas festivities.

This ancient railway town (Argentan, the regional centre for the repair of steam locomotives) was almost entirely destroyed during the last war. Argentan, floral town, has lifted itself courageously from the ruins and its dynamism has allowed it to double its population.

Places to see in Argentan...

* **The castle** (now the law courts) and the **Chapel of Saint-Nicolas** (Tourist Office) (14th century).

* **The Keep** - remains of the ancient mediaeval stronghold.

* The '**Maison des Fossés Tanares**' (wood panelled from the 14th century).

* A collection of **28 townhouses from the 17**[th] **and 18**[th] **centuries.**

* The **church of Saint-Martin** from the 16th century which is said to possess the 'most beautiful stained glass windows of Normandy'.

* The **church of Saint-Germain** constructed from the 15th to the 17th centuries (Guided visits).

In the little neighbouring community of *Bailleul* there remains engraved the mark of **Jacques de Bailleul** who founded the celebrated '**college of Bailleul**' in England.

In the heart of the field of battle at the Falaise Gap is the little community of *Chambois* with its Keep from the 15th century which reminds us of the military buildings of the Normans in England. It is from this community that **Etienne de Lessard** originated (1623-1703) before leaving for Québec. He would start there the Canadian branch of the Lessards which today numbers several hundred thousand members !

In Orne, the livestock farming of the horse, present everywhere in Normandy, assumes here a major significance with its numerous 'haras' (studs) of which the *National Stud of Pin* at *Pin-au-Haras*, is considered as the *temple of the horse in France*.

ARGENTAN

Holiday resort of the Anglo-Norman sovereigns

Tourist Office : (33)2 33 67 12 48

Municipal Campsite, Noë lake : (33)2 33 35 05 69

Further on towards *L'Aigle*, one crosses the *Pays du Merlerault*, where the climate, the land and the grass which it produces are said to be the best in the world for the raising of horses.

To the east of *Argentan* begins the Pays d'Auge of Orne whose capital is **Vimoutiers, 'City of cheese, ciders and calvados'**, which conceals heavenly places such as *Crouttes* - see the **Priory of the Benedictines, *Les Champeaux-en-Auge***, where Charlotte Corday was born, **'l'Ange de l'assassinat'**, *Le Renouard, Mardilly, the Valley of the Touques, Le Sap and Gacé* which like Vimoutiers was in the 18ᵗʰ century a famous centre of agriculture where important fairs were held.

****

The gardens of the Priory of Saint-Michel at Croutles

President Mitterrand loved this place with its warm atmosphere, in the real heart of the Pays d'Auge. The gardens, created in 1984 by Madame Chahine, are organised in enclosed arbours and include a collection of roses, iris, plants from the vegetable garden, perennials and an orchard. The ancient Priory, makes an admirable collection with its 'dîmière' barn, its chapel, the Priory and its community.

Open to the public all the days from April to 30ᵗʰ October from 2-6 pm (except Tuesday), For information : Mr and Mrs ULRICH - Tel (33) 2 33 39 15 15 - Fax (33) 2 33 36 15 16.

****

But the uncontested treasure of the Ornais Pays d'Auge is the little community of 180 inhabitants, situated at the doors of Vimoutiers, whose name is universally known, **Camembert** where, at the end of the 18th century, they *invented* **'the King of Cheeses'**. A farm cheese maker continues the tradition of the making of camembert in a local setting. One can also visit in the village, the 'Maison du Camembert', created on the initiative of the municipality and the Syndicat d'Initiative. Another place of interest for the British in Camembert is the shop of Rosemary Rudland, one of your compatriots, who in spite of her wrangles with the local town councillors still offers, against wind and tide, cheeses, products and local souvenirs to the visitors.

On the hill which overlooks the village one can see - and even visit : - a superb wood panelled building from the 16th century which is none other than the **'Manoir de Beaumoncel'** where the farmer Marie Harel, around 1791, invented camembert (possibility of visiting the interior and the buildings - Tel (33) 2 33 39 27 01).

Gastronomic Capital of Normandy, City of Cheeses, **Vimoutiers** has for a long time been the centre of the production and marketing of Norman products of quality, ciders, 'pommeaux', calvados, milk, butter (In the 1960's, the Halle received the biggest butter market in Normandy) and meat. See on site the statue of 'Ratisfaite' built in homage to the Norman bovine race opposite to the statue of Marie Harel, 'Creator of Camembert Cheese' who spent the last years of her life in Vimoutiers.

To the east of the region, neighbour of the Pays d'Auge, stretches the **Pays d'Ouche** with its economic capital, **L'Aigle.**

This very beautiful town with a flourishing industrial past possesses a remarkable architectural heritage and interesting museums but also and above all, Tuesday morning, an important market (**the third most important in France**) which takes place in the streets of the centre of the town for the movable businesses and on the 'foirail', on the road to Argentan, for the animals.

Some kilometres in the direction of Argentan is the community of **Aube** where one finds an old forge that can be visited and the **'château des Nouettes'** where the **Countess of Ségur** resided. See also the castle of **Villers-en-Ouche** and its gardens in the direction of Vimoutiers. Built on the site of a Roman villa, the château from the 17th century is surrounded by a park of twenty hectares made up of two styles of garden. One part is organised as in the 17th century with a great avenue of beeches, a court of honour and flowerbeds enclosed by walls which open in a half-moon shape on to the second part in 'English' style. Laid out in the 18th century, the garden is enlivened with fabrics, a temple, statues, large lakes and a vegetable 'rond à danser'.

In the forest of **Saint-Evroult-Notre-Dame-du-Bois,** which covers 668 hectares between L'Aigle and Gacé, see the ruins of the **'Abbaye de Saint-Evroult'** which was founded in the 6th century and where lived the monk-historian Ordéric Vital (1075-1150) from whom we owe much precious information on the lives of the first Dukes. One can walk freely among the ruins.

Near to l'Aigle also, it is worth stopping in the town of **Saint-Ouen-sur-Iton.** The old lord of the manor/mayor of this rich and individual country, had the majority of the houses in the village built with **twisted chimneys.** The mayors who have succeeded him have continued to impose the same type of chimney.

At *Vitrai-sous-l'Aigle* the little parish church possesses round altars. They were in fact ancient granite wheels used previously to crush apples.

Further to the south following on from the Pays d'Ouche you have the **'Perche Normand'**, a region nearer to Paris and loved by artists, which offers dreamy countryside and possibilities for a relaxing stay.

Mortagne-au-Perche is the capital.

Gastronomic stopping point, built on high ground, you really must visit the ancient town with its marvellous houses so unusual in their pastel colours. The **'Porte Saint-Denis'** (13th century), which is part of the Fort Toussaint, the townhouses from the 17th, 18th and 19th centuries, the ramparts and the remains of the ancient fortified city merit a stop, as do the 24 sundials which decorate the fronts of the old houses and make up one of the curiosities of the town.

****

The 'Manoirs du Perche'

The Perche countryside waking in the mist of spring or autumn, allowing to suddenly appear in the distance the silhouette of a majestic manor with creamy white facades and a tiled salmon coloured roof is one of the most beautiful sights that Normandy presents for your admiration.

Built after the Hundred Years War, these manors were the 'mirror of a country nobility' who led a rustic existence there. Among the jewels of this inheritance we should cite:

'Le Verger'', 'Boiscordes'', 'Vaujours'', 'Brigemont''...

A leaflet on the 'Manoirs du Perche' is available from Tourist Offices.

****

Longny-au-Perche, town situated on the ancient Roman road, between Maletable and Saint-Jacques-de-Compostelle was called : 'La Mauvaise étape'.

This small, very dynamic town contains around its old 'halles' numerous riches beginning with the home of the Jumeau family, making the 'Jumeau' dolls.

****

The Jumeau brothers

Georges Jumeau (1841-1873) invented the sprung joint system for the heads of dolls and his brother Emile (1843-1910), father of 'baby Jumeau', commercially developed the famous dolls from 1879.

****

In the same vein, stop and visit on foot the little town of *Bellême*, which owes its name to the famous Gallic goddess. Equally you should enjoy the pleasure of a walk into the heart of a neighbouring forest, loved by mushroom enthusiasts who gather there every autumn. Built in part on the site of the ancient feudal castle, Bellême was one of the keystones in the defence of the Norman boundaries.

La Perrière is one of the most well off places of the Perche 'ornais'. There are numerous dwellings of great architectural interest :

ÉCOMUSÉE DU PERCHE

The living museum of the Perche is situated in a Benedictine Priory founded in the XIth century. It maintains simultaneously both remarkable architecture and the testimony of peasant culture.

It is possible to visit the Priory during weekends and school holidays. Nearby, paths for ramblers.

Open every day from 14h to 18h except Tuesdays. Shop, bookshop, light drinks, sweets. Bicycle park, enclosure for horses, picnic area.

ÉCOMUSÉE DU PERCHE
Prieuré de Sainte-Gauburge
61130 SAINT-CYR-LA-ROSIÈRE
Tel (33) 2 33 73 48 06

* The **'Logis de l'Evêque'** (the bishops house) (13th century).
* The **'Château de Monthiret'** (15th century).
* The **'Manor of Soizay'** (16th century).
* The **'Manors of Vauvineux and Blanou',** and numerous natural sites which merit a visit :
* The **'Site de l'Eperon'** which overlooks a vast panorama offering to the dazzled eyes of the tourist a countryside where one can make out 17 bell towers, farms, forests and woods.
* The **'Chêne de l'Ecole'** three hundred year old tree in the heart of the forest of Bellême.
* The **'Bûte de Montgaudry'** : the town tops a high point from which it takes its name. This village was used from 1067 as a strategic position to defend Perche from the west.

At the heart of the magnificent, dense thousand year old *forest of Perche (one of the most beautiful in France where the marine carpenters came to choose the trees which would serve in the construction of masts for their ships)* one finds treasures like the little town of *Tourouvre* from where many of the colonists of the New France left in the 17th century and where there is now a **Museum of Emigration from Perche** and also **'l'Abbaye de la Grande Trappe'** a great place of spirituality but also of monastic work - it is possible to take part in religious services on request - Magasin de la Trappe (Books, crafts, food products produced by the monks).

Note that at **Courtomer,** not far from there, a house carries the name of a native of the region, born in 1881 and died in 1947, who created the celebrated make of car **'AMILCAR'.**

A route to follow in Perche is the 'Circuit des Manoirs and Traditions du Perche' which, leaving from *Nocé,* allows you to admire some of the most beautiful jewels of Perche architecture (Distance of the tour : 87 kilometres).

****

The Regional Natural Park of Perche

Between the fertile plains of the Beauce and the rich Norman hedged farmland (bocage), between Tourouvre and la Ferté-Vidame to the north, Authon-du-Perche to the south, Bellême and La Loupe from east to west, in a natural region where forests and hedged farmland alternate, stretches an enchanted country in human dimensions, La Perche.

At the heart of this country of traditions and legends is the Parc Regionale which extends over 182,000 hectares. Signed by the participating bodies, the Charter of the park founds its aims on 4 constituents :

* A dynamic approach to Perche heritage which foresees the protection, the management and the promotion of the overall natural, countryside, building and cultural heritage.

* The management of the evolution of the region and particularly the urban environment.

* A contribution to a durable economic development, in order to promote local resources.

* A development of activities and communication to inform, to make aware and to make responsible the participants, the inhabitants and the visitors and to ensure a high quality welcome.

The Park of Perche extends, from south to north from La Chapelle-Guillaume in Eure et Loir to Bresolettes in Orne and from west to east from Montgaudry in Orne to La Loupe in Sarthe.

For information : BP 23 - 61110 Rémalard. Tel (33) 2 33 85 36 36 - Fax (33) 2 33 85 36 37.

****

For Orne, let us not forget, is the country par excellence for vast dense forests.

Near to the forests of Ecouves and Perseigne, already mentioned, on the border with Sarthe, near to *Alençon*, you can visit the **'Mont des Avaloirs'** and the **'Signal des Avaloirs',** highest point in Normandy at 417 metres in the massif of the Alpes Mancelles. One cannot ignore in this region the charming village of *Saint-Cénéri-le-Gérei* in the loops of the Sarthe with its magnificent Roman church on a rocky promontory. Featuring among the **'Plus beaux villages de France',** *Saint Cénéri* is a meeting place for artists and walkers.

Another reason to visit Saint-Cénéri, the mayor is one of your compatriots, Ken Tatham !

It was in this region, today called the Pays d'Alençon where, thousands of years ago, the Parisian basin and the Armoricain massif collided. It is there that the waters divide, some, like those of the Sarthe, heading towards the Atlantic and others joining the Channel.

Mêle-sur-Sarthe, as in many other places in Normandy, an activity centre has been developed with a lake offering diverse activities but the community is equally known for its great annual competition for 'poulains'.

Not far from the massive forests are four magnificent castles to be discovered :

* **The 'Château d'O'** *at Mortrée* **(15th-17th centuries),** jewel of the Renaissance which after having been the property of the intendant **Henry III, François d'O,** was restored by **French Academician Jacques de Lacretelle** and his wife and today welcomes visitors and gatherings of French and British vintage car collectors. The d'O family was of Saxon origin.

* **The 'Château de Sassy'** **(18th century),** at *Saint-Christophe-le-Jajolet* property of the **d'Audiffret-Pasquier family** which each year welcomes visitors. On several occasions the **Duc d'Audiffret,** a great breeder of horses, who died in 2000, received and accommodated **Queen Elizabeth II of England.** The classic garden was created around 1925 replacing the ancient kitchen garden. Made up of five flower beds enhanced by the walkways of pink sand, it looks majestic when viewed from the terraces. Visit the gardens and the château from Easter to All Saints every day from 3-6 pm. For information : Tel (33) 2 33 35 36 90.

* **The 'Château de Carrouges',** built in the Renaissance (from 14th to 17th centuries) was constructed on the site of an ancient fortress.

For information : Tel (33) 2 33 27 20 32.

Moats, terraces, elegant castle like entrance to the gardens with ancient doors and grills. Visit the apartments (beautiful furniture) with a new presentation of the 'salons'. Chapter Chapel, accommodation from the 15th century.

Concerts, exhibitions, hunting festival...

Open to the public every day of the year except 1st January, 1st May, 1st November, 11th November and 25th December. From 1st April to 15th June and from 1st to 30th September : from 10 am-12 noon and from 2-6 pm. From 16th June to 31st August :

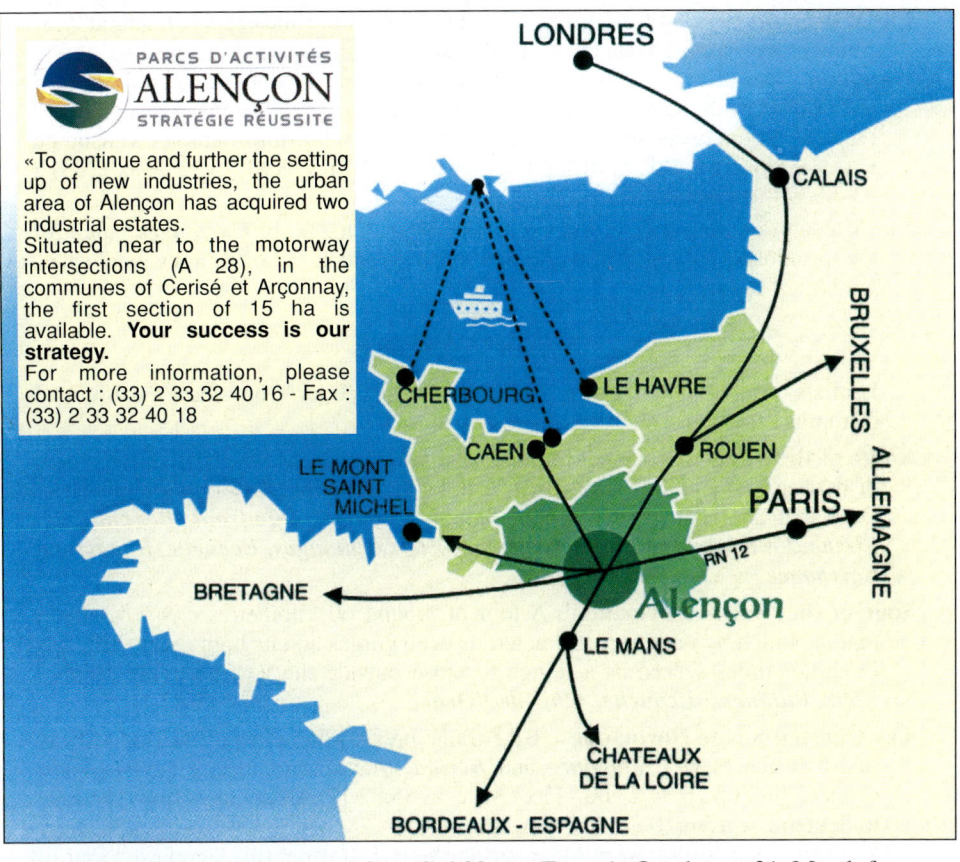

from 9.30 am-12 noon and from 2-6.30 pm. From 1st October to 31st March from 10 am-12 noon and from 2-5 pm. Guided visits (45')

* The 'Château of Médavy' (15th-18th century).
On the edge of the Forest of Ecouves - private inhabited property.
Two towers topped with lantern domes (15th century) - Furniture from the period - Grand salon with parquet flooring of a unique design - Chapel - Three arched bridge - French style gardens - Walkways of ancient Douves lime trees - Ecuries. Famous gardens in terraces and borders in 'broderie'.
Visits to the castle and the park from 14th July to 14th September from 10 am-12 noon and from 2-6.30 pm - Visit to the park is free. For information : Tel (33) 2 33 35 34 54.

The Regional Natural Park of Normandy-Maine

On the borders of Normandy and Maine, into which it makes an incursion of several kilometres, the territory of the Regional Natural Park of Normandy-Maine covers more than 234,000 hectares. Situated on the foothills of the Armoricain massif, this park offers enchanting countryside.

La **'Maison du Parc'** at **Carrouges.** The buildings of the ancient 'chanoinerie' (15th century) have been arranged as the Maison du Parc to welcome visitors and to inform them of the special things offered by the establishment, natural heritage and culture, walking tours, various events, temporary exhibitions of art, craft and regional products during summer and in December. For information : Maison du Parc, Le Chapitre, B.P. 5, 61320 Carrouges. Tel (33) 2 33 81 75 75 - Fax : (33) 2 33 28 59 80.

La **'Maison des Métiers'.** In the Collegiate of the Chapter of **Carrouges** : area for the promotion of artisan work and food products : exhibitions and sales, temporary events.

TOURIST TOURS

Leaflets available in the Tourist Offices of Orne or from the Departmental Committee for tourism.

Route of the Studs and castles, cultural and tourist tour. Made up of various tours of between 50 and 185 kilometres. It links the principal historic monuments of Orne that are open to the public. Stopping points : **Domfront, Bagnoles-de-l'Orne, La Ferté-Macé, Sées, Argentan, Flers, Putanges, Ecouché, Rânes,** and **Carrouges,**

Tour of the 'Suisse Normande'. A tour of around 60 kilometres criss-crossing a region, which by its savage character, its deep gorges and its high rocky cliffs has in earlier times served as a refuge to those outside the law. Stopping points : **Flers, Putanges, Ecouché, Athis-de-l'Orne.**

The Unusual Suisse Normande. 'Bike-trails' on six kilometres of disused railway line between **Pont Erambourg** and **Berjou.** Maximum capacity : 64 persons. Contact : Tel 06 16 54 23 60 - Fax (33) 2 33 35 82 12. All the days from 15th June to September from 10 am to 7 pm,

The route of 3 forests from Mêle-sur-Sarthe to Domfront this signposted tour of 85 kilometres allows the discovery of three magnificent state-owned forests and of cultural and historic places.

Stopping points : **Sées, Carrouges, La Ferté-Macé, Bagnoles-de-l'Orne,** and **Domfront.** Leaflet available in the tourist offices of the towns shown as stopping points.

Historic route of the parks and gardens of Normandy.

This tour allows the discovery of some enchanting places rarely open to the public. Information and leaflet from : 'Le Prieuré Saint-Michel' - 61120 Crouttes.

Tour of the Forests and Abbeys of Perche.

Departing from Mortagne, this itinerary pieces together the area of the old great forest of Perche linking the massif of Réno-Valdieu to that of Perche-Trappe.

Towns to stop at : **Mortagne, La Chapelle-Montligeon, Tourouvre, Soligny-la-Trappe.**

The quiet roads of Perche. Nine tours of discovery of the Perche heritage identity. Sign-posted itineraries - brochure available in the tourist offices of the stopping points : **Bellême, Brou, Longny-au-Perche, Mortagne-au-Perche, Nocé.**

The 'Dame aux Camélias' tour.

This tour allows you to follow the itinerary of Alphonse Plessis, immortalised by the novel which Alexandre Dumas dedicated to him : La Dame aux Camélias.

Stopping points : *Gacé, Nonant-le-Pin, Le Bourg-Saint-Léonard.*

Tour of the Orchid country.

The side of the hill at *Courménil* shelters a very individual flora. The queens of this place are the orchids. On fine days, the butterflies, and notably the 'Blue Argus", come to invade this flowery sweet smelling paradise.

Also to See in Orne…

NATURAL HERITAGE :

Exceptional natural sites from North to South :

'Marais du Grand Hazé'. Guided visits possible - Tel (33) 2 33 81 75 75. (Parc Normandie-Maine) This fortunate place offers a great variety of natural environments : peat bogs, roselières, peaty woods… You can see the horses of the Camargue and Scottish highland cattle which clean the marshy areas and feed on the willows, rushes and brambles. You can reach there from Briouze - Guided visits in English from June to September

'Maison de la Rivière et du Paysage - Le Moulin de Ségrie' at *Ségrie-Fontaine* (Close to Flers). Ancient mill situated on one of the most beautiful rivers of the Suisse Normande : la Rouvre. A permanent exhibition : 'The river from pre-history to the present day' - Video space and library - counting of migrating fish (demonstrations in season) - Guided walks to discover the Suisse Normande. For Information : Tel (33) 2 33 62 80 70 or (33) 33 96 79 70 - Fax (33) 2 33 62 80 71

'Landes du Tertre Bizet et Fosse-Arthour'.

'L'étang de Morette', to the west of *Mantilly*, receives, depending on the season, visits from a varied fauna : Herons, cormorants, marsh harriers, woodcocks, geese, ducks, souchets, mallard, kingfishers, coot…

'La tourbière de la Lande-de-Goult'. The peat bog of Petits Riaux at La Lande-de-Goult presents very special plants : les droseras et les grassettes, small carnivorous plants, the spagnum which forms a veritable sponge carpet. For Information : Tel (33) 2 33 81 75 75.

Upper valley of the Orne.

The lakes, forests and peat bogs of upper Perche.

The woods and hillsides to the west of *Mortagne-au-Perche*.

The basin of the Andainette.

The upper valley of the Sarthe.

The quarry of *Loisail*.

The woods and chalky hillsides below *Bellême*.

The quarry of the Mansonnière in Perche.

Floral towns and villages : *Saint-Fraimbault* : **4 flowers - Grand Prix National Blooms - International Trophy of l'Entente floral**. *Argentan, Moussonvilliers, Saint-Victor-de-Réno, Alençon, Flers, La Chapelle-Montligeon, La Sauvagère, Domfront, La Ferté-Fresnel.*

Arboretum of the Château de Tessé la Madeleine and ornithological tour. In a superb 18 hectare park, very lovely botanical collection of more than149 species. Contact : Centre d'animation de Bagnoles-Tessé : Tel (33) 2 33 30 72 70,

Arboretum of the Etoile d'Andaines. In the heart of the Andaines forest, on the road going from *La Ferté-Macé to Domfront*. Forest and ornamental species. Contact : Office National des Forêts - Tel (33) 2 33 82 55 00 - Fax (33) 2 33 32 20 69.

L'EURE

Between Seine-Maritime and Calvados with Orne to the south west, Eure, let us make no mistake, is a coastal area even if it only benefits from a narrow 'window' on the sea at *Berville-sur-Mer* which possesses **the smallest beach in France (150 metres)**.

Berville has today abandoned fishing which was important in former times, the town having been a reputed port. The last fishing boat enthroned, like an ancient relic, at the sea's edge.

Eure presents, like its neighbouring regions an astonishing diversity of landscapes. The *Seine* crosses it separating it from *Seine-Maritime*. The valley of the great river is a series of enchanting places.

This area, one of the 'youngest and most dynamic' in France, is the country of 'the water courses which sing'.

Evreux, 'the pretty city', brightened with numerous green spaces and dominated by its beautiful cathedral has a restored old quarter traversed by the peaceful course of the *Iton*.

Places to see...

* **The Episcopal church**, cathedral of Notre-Dame, built from the 10th century with multiple architectural styles of which diverse elements remain. It has in fact been modified over the centuries following wars, fires… It shelters one of the most beautiful collections of stained glass windows from the 14th century on which one can see the 'yellow of Evreux' a unique colour which was later used by the Master glassmakers of Chartres, Rouen and Beauvais. (Guided visit on request from the Tourist Office).

* **'Le Palais de l'Evêché'**, (the Palace of the Diocese), adjacent to the cathedral showing gothic architecture of great beauty.

* **The church of Saint-Taurin** built on the site of the tomb of Saint-Taurin, evangelist and first Bishop of Evreux, it contains the reliquary of Saint-Patron, major work of the goldsmith's art from the 13th century given by **King Saint Louis**. Conceived as a miniature gothic church, it is one of the most beautiful pieces of goldsmith's work from the 13th century.

ÉVREUX
town of tradition and history

Contact :
(33) 2 32 31 82 60

* **The Belfry or 'clock tower'** dates from the 15th century. It is one of the remains of the ancient fortifications of the city. Its role was to allow surveillance over the road from Rouen.

* ***The Valley of the Risle*** is pleasant and offers up to the sea a pretty verdant countryside. In the hollows of this green setting nestle inestimable jewels such as the superb **Benedictine Abbey of Bec-Hellouin** built of stones filled with history and culture which must be visited.

****

L'Abbaye Notre-Dame du Bec

A striking story of the intellectual and religious influence of mediaeval Normandy, the Abbey of Notre-Dame of Bec-Hellouin was founded in 1034 by Father Herluin 'For the education of the monks' and its construction was continued by Lanfranc (1042) and Anselme (1059). It was one of the most prestigious Norman abbeys under the Dukes and counted among its monks numerous dignitaries from the Anglo-Norman church. It was a major place of western thinking.

The group is dominated by the high tower of Saint-Nicolas which dates from 1467.

The abbey has been twinned for almost a thousand years with that of Canterbury.

Used as a quarry under the Empire, there remains no more today than rare ruins on the ground of the abbey church. The tower remains, the remains of the Capitular room (14th century) and the cloisters and the three classic conventual buildings of the 17th century.

In the years following the Second World War, the Benedictine monks have returned to Bec and perpetuate their tradition there.

In the 1980's, the State restored to them all the buildings of the ancient abbey.

Guided visits - Shop (Sales of ceramics made by the monks and candles made by the nuns of the neighbouring abbey of Saint-Martin du Parc). Services are sung in Gregorian and French.

For information : Tel (33) 2 32 43 72 60 - Fax (33) 2 32 44 96 69.

****

LES ANDELYS
On the banks of the Seine
With its famous castle
'Château Gaillard'
'The key to Normandy'

Tourist Office : (33) 2 32 54 41 93 - Mairie : (33) 2 32 54 04 16
www.ville-andelys.fr

Brionne is a welcoming and historic town of which one of the remains is the **Keep** of the old castle. One gets there by the 'Road of the Canadians' and the 'Sente du Vieux Château' (footpath of the old castle). This Keep was constructed in Caen stone at the end of the 11th century by Robert de Meulan following a fire in the primitive fortress in 1090. Besieged on many occasions, the new building was in its turn burnt and restored. It is one of the rare square Norman keeps still existing and recalls the Norman military constructions in Great Britain in the 11th and 12th centuries. This keep was dismantled in 1735 by the Dukes of Lorraine, Counts of Brionne, and its materials used for the construction of mills. It has been the property of the community since 1869 and has been the subject of three consolidation campaigns.

Pont-Audemer, the *'Norman Venice"*, ancient river port on the Risle, possesses an excellent heritage of old Norman houses along the arms of the *Risle.* To stroll along its canals and picturesque alleyways is a real delight. On the vast plateau bordered by the estuary of the Seine and the valleys of the Risle, the Morelle and the Corbie, nestled in the heart of Normandy, stretches the canton of *Beuzeville*. In terms of typical villages and wood panelled houses, you should know that the village of *Vieux-Pont*, a stop on the 'Route des chaumières' (the route of thatched cottages) possesses an exceptional heritage. William who was still only 'the bastard' spent his first years at the castle of *Conteville*. Of this great period, there remains only a ruined pillar in the centre of the **Abbey of Grestain**, founded in 1050 at *Fatouville* at **Herluin de Conteville** which Duke Robert gave to Arlette on their marriage.

Thierville, near to *Montfort-sur-Risle*, is a community 'blessed by the gods'. Unlike all the other Norman communities, you will not find there a Monument in memory of the dead for the simple reason that its population went through the wars of 1870, 1914-1918 and 1939-1945 without losing a single one of its sons ! And now we come to the *Marais Vernier*, an immense marshland of more than **2000 hectares** where cattle grow fat in the meadows. It is without doubt one of the most picturesque sites of Normandy, at the centre of an ancient meander of the Seine, a very unusual countryside between *Pont-Audemer* and the *Pont de Tancarville*.

Le Marais Vernier

The draining of the vernier marsh is the work of the Dutch who in the time of Henry IV constructed a sea wall marking out an 'amphitheatre' of green with the surrounding hills, also protecting the land which was cultivated from incursions by the sea. The vernier marsh constitutes today the premier French peat bog because of its size and wet zone it is classed as of economic European interest, endowed with a habitat made up principally of thatched houses. One also finds there, the local speciality : 'la pomme de rêve' and a number of ancient traditions. One can admire the most beautiful farms and rural houses of the region. The marsh also shelters the natural reserve of Mannevilles which receives some 15 protected species and the hunting reserve. One comes across Highland cattle and Camargue horses. Visits are organised, Tel, Comité du tourisme de l'Eure (33) 2 32 62 04 27 - Fax (33) 2 32 31 05 98,

A union administers this territory : each year the parcels of land are allocated to a collection of farmers. You can go on foot or by cycle to see the unusual fauna and flora. The Valleys of the Charentonne, of the Eure and of the Iton present equally verdant countryside. From the towns and villages, monuments chime out along these well stocked fishing waterways : **Broglie**, town of the Princes of Broglie who were eminent servants of the King and the Republic, **Montfort-sur-Risle, Ivry-la-Bataille, Pacy-sur-Eure, Louviers, Pont-de-l'Arche sur l'Eure, Conches-en-Ouche, Evreux-sur-l'Iton…**

See at **Pont-de-L'Arche**, the **Abbey of Bonport** which was built at the beginning of the 13th century at the wish of Richard the Lionheart. It belongs to the order of 'Citeaux'. The monastic buildings are perfectly preserved as well as the monk's kitchen and the extraordinary vaulted refectory looking out over the valley of the Seine. For information : Tel (33) 2 35 02 19 42.

At **Hardencourt-Cocherel**, it is said that Aristide Briand who had got lost from a hunting party found himself by chance in the village of Cocherel. He was so seduced by the beauty and serenity of the place that he moved there and continued to live there.

Watered by the Charentonne, **Bernay** is undoubtedly one of the most beautiful and liveliest of the towns of Eure. Its architectural heritage is particularly abundant and of great quality.

Places to see...

* **The Abbey Church of Notre-Dame** - treasure of Roman art from the 11th century, it is at the origin of this architecture in Normandy. Built at the request of Judith de Bretagne, grand-mother of William the Conqueror.

* **The Churches of Sainte-Croix and Notre-Dame-de-la-Couture** (13th and 16th centuries).

* **'Hôtel de la Gabelle'** (18th century).

* **Abbey and museum** (18th century).

* Ancient quarters (numerous wood panelled houses from the 16th and 17th centuries).

* Ancient laundry places,...

At **Beaumesnil** in the Pays de la Risle-Charentonne, there existed a splendid castle built for one of the companions of William the Conqueror of which the Keep remains. The new castle is considered to be one of the jewels of the architecture of the 17th century. Also see the gardens.

The charming little town of **Beaumont-le-Roger** retains the memory of the confrontations which took place in the 14th century when the King of France Charles V opposed Charles the Bad, King of Navarre and Count of Evreux. Bertrand Duguesclin seized the castle of Beaumont in 1378 and ordered it to be dismantled.

Places to see...

* Remains of **the Priory** from the 13th century.

* The forest of Beaumont.

* The Valley of the Risle.

The Priory of the Sainte Trinité was founded in the 11th century. William should have taken part in its dedication when he was killed in 1087.

The stalls from the ancient church of Harcourt, some five or six kilometres away, have been transferred to the little church of **Goupillères**. Among them all connoisseurs of enigmatic symbols must see the *chair of the Prior* in sculptured wood.

We shall talk about the valley of the Seine in the chapter given over to the Seine-Maritime.

There still hangs over **Louviers** the memory of a famous affair of witchcraft called **'The Affair of the possessed of Louviers'** it unfolded in 17th century at the **Convent of Saint-Catherine.**

Vernon still possesses pretty quarters and a French cylindrical keep erected by King **Philippe-Auguste** after the conquest of Normandy. See the **Collegiale Notre-Dame** the construction of which was begun in the 11th century to be completed in the 16th. The Choir from the 15th century is surrounded by a diagonal rib vaulted ambulatory, considered as one of the oldest of this style in Normandy.

The **'Château de Bizy'** is one of the curiosities of the town. It was built in the 18th century and welcomed King Louis XV. It has belonged to the Duke of Penthièvre and to King Louis-Philippe. English park with terraces. (Guided visit).

One can see on the right bank of the Seine beautiful remains like those of the **Abbey of Fontaine-Guérard, the castle of Gaillon**, the **fortresses and castle of Neaufles, Epte, Gisors** of which the restoration offers a magnificent example of a Keep on a mound. (It was constructed on the orders of Guillaume Le Roux, King of England), **'Château Gaillard'**, *'the key to Normandy''*, model of mediaeval military architecture erected by **Richard the Lionheart** in 1196 to survey the road from Rouen or still from the castle of **Robert Le Diable** at *Moulineaux* beside the A13 autoroute.

We should say that at Gisors there remain the vestiges of the expiatory chapel built by Henry 2nd Plantagenêt to the memory of his famous victim **Thomas Beckett.**

We shall not forget the charming site at *Giverny* where, for more than forty years, the great painter **Claude Monet** stayed : see **his incomparable garden, his property** where one can view some of his major works. This property is the object of continual visits, a veritable cult… merited !

On the old 'frontier' between Normandy and France, *Verneuil-sur-Avre*, has kept its military structure and the majority of its fortifications. In the heart of the old town, along roads crossed by streams one can still see magnificent wood panelled dwellings as well as magnificent houses from the Renaissance era.

The Tourist Office will give you a marked plan that will allow you to discover the innumerable riches of this town.

Places to also see…

Acquigny : **The park of the castle of Acquigny.** The gardens of the castle, built for one of the ladies in waiting of Catherine de Medici, composed of exotic trees, oriental plane trees and giant pines, they were planted in the 18th century. Open to the public every day in summer (weekends and national holidays during Autumn). Tel (33) 2 32 50 23 31 - Fax (33) 2 32 40 46 68.

Saint-Germain-de-Pasquier : **The smallest 'Mairie' in France : 3 metres by 2.7 metres !**

Beaumesnil : castle of Beaumesnil (17th century). 'The Norman Versailles'. Furstenberg Foundation - castle, park, gardens, museum of bookbinding and gilding. Designed by a pupil of Le Notre, the park offers a palette of exceptional lights and colours thanks to the presence of many ornamental lakes in which the château is reflected. Open : in July and August every day except Tuesday from 10 am-12 noon and from 2-6 pm. In April, May, June and September from Friday to Monday from 2-6 pm. For information : Tel/Fax (33) 2 32 44 40 09.

Le Neubourg : **'Château et Jardins du Champ de Bataille'.** For information : (33) 2 32 34 84 34 - Fax (33) 2 32 35 18 38 Open to the public from 1st March to 30th November. Weekends and national holidays from 2-6 pm. From 1st May to 15th September : every day from 10-12 am (reservation) and from 2-6 pm. Astonishing private dwelling, richly furnished. 7 hectare park made up of flower beds with boulingrins, Italian statues, mazes, fabriques, forest park…

Harcourt : **'Le Domaine d'Harcourt'.** Public welcome : Domaine open from the beginning of March to 15th November. Every day except Tuesday from 1st March to 15th June and from 15th September to 15th November from 2-6 pm. Every day of the week from 15th June to 15th September from 10.30 am-6.30 pm. For information : Tel (33) 2 32 46 29 70 - Fax (33) 2 32 46 53 38.
The castle from the 12th-14th centuries, which had replaced a wooden fortress from the 10th century, on a domain given by Rollon to his companion Bernard le

Danois, is one of the best preserved in Normandy. It was the ancestral birthplace of the powerful Harcourt family. It allows us to trace the evolution of military architecture up to the invention of artillery.

'L'arboretum' : unique collection of a thousand trees, broad-leaved and conifers coming from all over the world including some immense sequoias. Created in 1802 with the goal of naturalising exotic plants, it is a real treasure of vegetation which puts it among the most important in France. Sign-posted itinerary.

La 'Forêt Mosaïque' - This forest offers 95 hectares of great variety. It constitutes a résumé of the larger European forests of educational value but at the same time a pleasure. This example striking associations between indigenous species and exotic trees is a privileged place of botanical discovery in a vast area for walking.

Lisors : **'Abbaye de Mortemer'**. First Norman Abbey to rally the Cistercian order in 1137. Only the vestiges are left today haunted by the ghost of Mathilde, daughter of Henry 1st Beauclerc, in the heart of the Forest of Lyons. (Guided visit on request).

Lyons la Forêt : **The classified site of Lyons**. In the heart of the most beautiful beech wood in France, the village was built on the site of a fortress constructed in the 12th century by Henry 1st Beauclerc. See 'les halles' from the 15th century and the beautiful wood panelled houses from the 16th century.

Broglie : **'Le Jardin aquatique'**. Contemporary garden inaugurated in 1993, on the edge of the Charentenne. Open each day from 1st april to 30th September from 8.30 am to 8 pm and from 1st October to 31st March from 9 am to 5.30 pm - free entry. For information : Tel (33) 2 32 44 60 58 or (33) 2 32 46 27 52.

Le Mesnil-de-Courbépine (near to Bernay) : **'Le Labyrinthe de l'Eure'. Vegetable mazes (rape seed and maize)** To lose yourself… or find yourself in nature.

Vegetable garden The advantages of the vegetable garden without the inconveniences.

Shop of farm produce Traditional and regional ! Tasting of farm products - country snacks - picnics - fruit picking - cultural events. Opening hours : Fruit picking : 9.30 am-12 noon and 2.30-7 pm, from May to October from Wednesday to Sunday midday. Shop : 9.30 am-12 noon and 2.30-7 pm, all year from Wednesday to Sunday midday. Rape seed maze : from 15th May to 1st July. Maize maze : from 1st July to 15th September.

****

The Valleys of the Eure

The area of Eure includes numerous valleys which offer great enchantment, and we invite you to visit :

* The Valley of the Oison : From Saint-Amand-des-Hautes country with a succession of little villages ever more picturesque.

* The Valley of the Risle : Its countryside resembles the image of the 'Epinal' of Normandy. It was in earlier times a place of intense industry.

* The Valley of the Charentonne : Wild and melancholic, paradise for fishermen and walkers who can follow its sinuous course.

* The Valley of the Eure : From Saint-Georges-Motel to Louviers, men have since ancient times sought to domesticate the course of the river which has long been used for commercial navigation.

* The Valley of the Avre : Born in the lakes of Perche, the Avre runs into the Eure after having watered Verneuil and crossed superb countryside.

One finds on its banks numerous mills as well as wash places. Crossed by pretty bridges it invites you to relax on its flowery, mossy banks.

****

TOURIST ROUTES

= **Tour to discover Evreux and its surrounding country**. Tours proposed by the Tourist Office.

= **'La Route des Chaumières' (The route of thatched houses).** For a long time 'shelters of poverty', become little by little rural dwellings, made of clay, stone and wood, the thatched cottages heirs of a long Norman tradition, raise their sloping roofs topped with thatch, surmounted with a crest of iris, concealed behind their holly hedge and apple trees. An enjoyable walk in Spring - in May - when the apple trees are in flower - around fifty kilometres stretching between the Seine and the forests of Sainte-Opportune-la-Mare to the confines of the Marais Vernier. Free leaflet from the Maison du Parc de Brotonne.

= **The valley of the Eure by railway**. Tourist railway which runs along the valley of the Eure. Rue des Poilus - Place de la Gare - 27120 Pacy-sur-Eure. Open from 2-6.30 pm from Easter to 1st October Sundays and national holidays. From 1st July to 31st August, Wednesdays, Saturdays, Sundays and national holidays.

= **Historic route of Normandy-Vexin**. Folder available from Tourist Offices.

= **Tourist and cultural itinerary on the marches of Normandy**. Between Paris and Rouen, 200 kilometres of tour where the great river reveals its greatest riches : *Castle of Vascœuil, Abbeys of Mortemer and of Fontaine-Guérard, the classified site of Lyons-la-Forêt, the castle of Gisors, castle Gaillard at Andelys, castle of Gaillon, Vernon, Giverny and Monet's garden*, Folder available from the Comité du Tourisme de l'Eure - Tel (33) 2 32 62 04 27.

LA SEINE-MARITIME

Formed from a vast plain ending in the impressive cliffs to the north, limited by the meanders of the Seine to the south and to the east by the ***Bresle*** and the ***Epte***, Seine-Maritime also possesses remarkable countryside, historic sites of great interest and numerous places of relaxation and activity.

133

The coast is essentially formed of cliffs, sometimes 100 metres high, which resemble the coasts of southern England. The coastal rivers have eroded the valleys and it is in the chalk, of the 'valleuses', where one finds, for the most part, the ports such as *Dieppe, Fécamp, Yport, Veules, Etretat,...* Sometimes, these curious 'valleuses' stop dead in the middle of the cliff ! The coast, we have said, is made up largely of escarpments made from alternating beds of flint and white chalk which have given its name to the *'Côte d'Albâtre'* (the Alabaster coast). 130 kilometres long, it constitutes the largest line of cliffs in France. At their feet, the beaches, most frequently are made of white pebbles which some like and some dislike.

From the east of the west, take the time to visit *Le Tréport* at the mouth of the *Bresle*, at the foot of the highest cliffs in Europe.

The maritime tradition of *Le Tréport* dates from the Middle Ages. King Louis Philippe had a 'villa' built there where he received Queen Victoria.

On the right bank is the beach of *Mers-les-Bains*. The beach 'nearest to Paris', it knew at the end of the 19th century its time of glory as the villas of the 'Belle Epoque' as its sea-front affirms. From the **'calvaire des terrasses'**, situated on the cliff top one can take in a magnificent countryside. The church of Saint-Jacques is a remarkable monument from the Renaissance.

Eu, which benefits from the label 'Les plus beaux détours de France' indeed merits a stop, with its castle built from 1578 by the protestant family of Guise and embellished by the 'Grande Demoiselle', cousin of Louis XIV, who acquired it in 1660. Exiled from Paris by her cousin for political reasons she lived there for a large part of her life. By the chance of inheritance, it came again in the 19th century to the family of Orléans, more precisely to one of the most illustrious representatives, Louis-Philippe (to whom the museum is dedicated). The 'Roi-bourgeois' restored it. It is here that celebrated meetings took place between King Louis-Philippe 1st and the young and beautiful Queen Victoria. The castle served as a refuge for the last emperor of Brasil : Pedro II. One of the pavilions still shelters today the home of the Countess of Paris, descendent of Louis-Philippe and widow of Henry, pretender to the royal crown of France.

In the crypt of the 'collégiale Notre-Dame et Saint-Laurent' (12th and 13th centuries) characteristic of pre-gothic Franco-Norman art, rests Saint Laurent O'Toole.

Saint Laurent O'Toole, had left Ireland following a disagreement which put Rory O'Connor, top King of Connaught against Henry 2nd Plantagenêt on the subject of the annual taxes to be paid by the Irish to the Anglo-Norman sovereign. Laurent O'Toole, archbishop of Dublin, had been chosen as mediator by O'Connor. He thus went to plead the cause of the King in London where Henry 2nd received him with little consideration to the support which had been accorded to him by the Pope.

The King forbade him to return to Ireland. Some weeks later, the archbishop wanted to again ask the sovereign for permission to return but the latter had gone back to Rouen. He therefore embarked for Normandy. After an exhausting journey, he arrived in Eu on 10th November 1180. His state of health, not allowing him to continue his journey, he was taken to the monastery of the monks of Saint Victor where he succumbed four days later.

See also the Chapel of the Ancient College of Jesuits, a building constructed in 1624 of which the Louis XIII façade is remarkable. In the Choir, two mausoleums were built in marble in homage to Catherine of Cleves and Henry de Guise called 'le Balafré'.

The *forest of Eu* is made up of three beautiful beech woods.

Yport is remarkable for its architectural and artistic riches :
= **Fisherman's houses, houses in brick and flint with roofs of slate with skylights.**
= **Villas.**
= **Manor of the painter J.-Paul Laurens**, where Jeff Friboulet, painter of international renown, actually lived.
= **The Moorish villa.**
= **The 'Chemin de Croix'** (the way of the cross) in the church, painted by Jeff Friboulet.
= **The wooded valleuse.**
= **The beach of preserved pebbles.**
= **'Platier' uncovering** at low tide a line of 80 metre high cliffs from the point of chicard at Yport up to Fécamp.
= **Walking trails.** Almost the whole of the village is ancient (a classified site) and traversed by little alleyways which lead successively to fisherman's houses and

magnificent villas. On the beach little boats in vibrant colours wait for the tide to leave for the fishing.

Dieppe, historic port of departure for pirates and corsairs but also for the colonists for New France is a much frequented seaside resort, notably by the English who appreciate its 'so British' charm with its long promenade and green lawns which border the beach.

The **Castle of Dieppe** is a remarkable feudal collection modified many times which houses an interesting museum. You can find there sculptures made from the ivory which passed through the port of Dieppe since the Renaissance. There are several steles and monuments commemorating **Operation Jubilee**, the Anglo-Canadian landing of 19th August 1942, and the sacrifice of the soldiers massacred on the beach. Not far from Dieppe, one can see the *'Castle of Miromesnil'*, where Guy de Maupassant was born and the powerful **'château fort'** of *Arques-la-Bataille*, perfect illustration of that which was the Norman military architecture in the Middle Ages and of which impressive ruins remain.

Among the monuments which present an enigma in Dieppe, we can cite the **church of Saint-Jacques** too often 'forgotten' by the visitors. By its plan and conception, it can without risk be dated from the 13th century yet it seems much closer to 'French gothic' than the Norman architecture of the period.

These later contributions evoke in large number, similarities with a no less mysterious monument : the tower of Saint-Jacques in Paris.

On the door of the sepulchre one can note three styles, one presents the starry insignia carried by two lovers, the other shows birds facing each other before a vase filled with fruit and on the last, one sees eagles and fighters of different sex.

Against the side sections, there are centaurs and winged quadrupeds, together with angels carrying incense above a chalice and the host. Look out also for the strange scenery which surrounds the edge of the Chapel of treasure. Featured there are Indians, Brazilians and an exotic fauna.

Close to Dieppe a stop should be planned in the charming little town of *Luneray*, ancient headquarters of an important protestant enclave in eastern Normandy.

One must continue along the coast to visit *Varengeville* and the **Manor of Jehan Ango**, pearl of Renaissance architecture in Normandy, with its remarkable dovecote. The church and its picturesque marine cemetery attached to the cliff are a moving sight. It was constructed at the beginning of the 16th century by the powerful Jehan Ango, Governor of Dieppe, maritime adviser to François 1st and enlightened patron of the arts.

See the **Parc des Moustiers** conceived on the plan of English parks of the 18th century and the **lighthouse of Ailly** which offfers a magnificent view point.

Peopled over the centuries by humble fishermen and weavers, the village of *Veules-les-Roses* is without argument one of the most beautiful and picturesque in Normandy. This charming seaside town which offers numerous pedestrian promenades seduced 'Parisian' clientele in the 19th century.

Saint-Valery-en-Caux rebuilt, as it was almost totally laid to waste on 11th June 1940, is a pleasant family place with its beach and its sea-wall/promenade… It is the most important seaside town of 'Caux Maritime'. See the **house of Henry IV** behind which you will find the **Cloister of the Penitents**, founded in the 17th century, the buildings of which are today occupied by the hospital.

On the cliff, a monument recalls the memory of the heroic fighters of the **51st Scottish Division** and of the **2nd French Cavalry Regiment** who were defeated in this place in 1940.

Veulettes-sur-Mer, at the mouth of the Durdent, possesses the longest seafront of the Alabaster coast. If your feet don't like the pebbles, go to *Saint-Aubin-sur-Mer* which has the largest beach of fine sand on the Alabaster coast.

For lovers of magical and genuine places, we suggest a visit to *Sotteville-sur-Mer* where you can discover an unusual site on condition that you are good 'climbers' as one must undertake a staircase of 231 steps to get down to the beach... then go up again to the parking place, but the spectacle merits this particular effort.

Ancient port of the **Norman Newfoundlanders**, *Fécamp* is both a large fishing port and a pleasant seaside town with its long beach of pebbles bordered by the **boulevard des Belges**, but it was also the official residence of the first Dukes of Normandy and **the most important sacred place of the Province** before the development of the pilgrimage to Mont-Saint-Michel.

Each year the famous relic of **the precious blood** was put on show there to which, on the Tuesday and the Thursday following the Festival of the Trinity, numerous pilgrims came to ask for help and protection. It rests in the white marble tabernacle of a chapel of the **Church or Abbey of the Trinity**, striking in its architecture and imposing dimensions. It testifies to the past prestige of the town (Part Roman dating from 1106, gothic nave and lantern tower from the 12th and 13th centuries, Roman reliquary, tombs of the Dukes of Normandy...).

According to spoken tradition, the sanctuary was consecrated in the 10th century by a pilgrim-angel who in 943 had ordered the building dedicated to the *'Invisible Trinity'*. The angel disappeared in a shining cloud leaving the imprint of his foot on a stone which has been preserved in the chapel of the Dormition.

One can also see at n° 12 Rue de l'Aumône a fountain built on the place where, carried by the tides, there landed the trunk of a fig tree in which a lead box contained drops of blood from Jesus Christ, collected at his death by one of the disciples. The mystery of the precious blood is part of the cycle of the **Grail.**

During a visit to *Fécamp*, one should certainly not forget to visit the **distillery and museum of Bénédictine** in the outrageous neo-gothic building constructed by **'Alexandre Legrand'** *(sic)*.

At the Trinity rest two Dukes of Normandy : **Richard 1st** and his son **Richard 2nd** who richly endowed this abbey.

Some years ago they discovered nearby the ruins of the **first Ducal Palace of Normandy**. Its simple architecture, recreated, gives the appearance of a palace of Nordic origin.

The marine village of *Yport* is huddled facing the sea, shut in by high white cliffs. Today as yesterday the town is much appreciated by painters.

Etretat ! The *'Falaises d'Aval"*, the *'Manne porte d'amont'*, the *'Aiguille'*, the

'**Valleuse du Curé**'... Everything has been admired and expressed, be it by the great impressionist painters, or still by the greatest authors. At the end of the 19th century, *Etretat* was for the Parisians the beach 'à la mode'.

The site is grandiose and romantic ! The pebble beach is bordered by a sea-front promenade, 'La Terrasse'. In the town, the reconstructed old style 'halles' are remarkable as is the **Castle of Agues**, ancient summer residence in the 19th century of the Kings of Spain with furniture and reminders of the Iberian sovereigns. On the plateau, **Notre-Dame-de-la-Garde** pays homage to sailors lost at sea. A little further on, a monument and museum recalls the passage, aboard their plane '**Le Point d'Interrogation**' (the question mark), of the aviators **Nungesser and Coli** on their attempt to cross the Atlantic which ended tragically with the death of the two men off Newfoundland.

After the '**Cap d'Antifer**', at *Bruneval*, a monument commemorates the successful action of British parachute commandos who destroyed a German radar post. From there one can also see the **petroleum port of Havre-Antifer** designed to accept super-tankers of 500,000 tonnes.

The *Cap de la Hève* is, also, impressive with a lighthouse having a range of 50 kilometres ! At Sainte Adresse a School for the Merchant Marine was established some years ago. With a strong reputation it has trained several generations of Norman captains through its courses. Set some hundreds of metres back from the place where, in 1370, the village of *Saint-Denis-Chef-de-Caux* was swallowed up during a terrible storm, *Saint-Adresse*, the 'Nice of Le Havre', has known great repute thanks to Alphonse Karr, Director of the newspaper 'Le Figaro' who fell under the charm of the site and bought a house there in 1841 and invited his friends the writers Eugène Sue, the son of Alexandre Dumas, the actress Sarah Bernhardt, the musician Gabriel Fauré, even the painters Claude Monet and Raoul Dufy, to come there.

There are pretty villas bordering the roads of Sainte-Adresse which also offers as a curiosity its '*sugar loaf*'. During the First World War, the north east side of the town-port of Havre was the **Capital of invaded Belgium**. The King of the Belgians and the government stayed there. The '*free*' Belgian post was stamped there. There remains a post box to remind us of this episode ! From the lighthouse of Sainte-Adresse a magnificent panorama of the Floral coast opens up.

Le Havre is a town well known to the English. The port, first oceanic port of France, was built at the beginning of the 16th century to succeed that of Honfleur, on '*the other side of the water' (Norman expression)* as it was silting up.

Originally, on the site of present day Havre, there was a sailor's village with at the centre, a humble chapel dedicated - as on the other side of the estuary in Honfleur - to Notre-Dame-de-Grace protecting Saint of sailors and fishermen.

From 1509, Louis XII planned to replace the old port of *Harfleur*, which had become obsolete, with a new 'havre'.

François 1st entrusted the conception to an Italian architect called **Belarmato** and to the great Admiral **Bounivet**. The principal of setting out like a draughtboard adopted by Belarmato was copied by the architects charged with reconstructing the town after the last war.

The King wanted to associate his name and the symbol of his power, the Salamander, with the new city. He proposed that it be called *'Franciscopolis'* or *'Françoiseville'* but the names were not to the taste of the population who, very tied to the Virgin Mary, preferred the name *'Havre de Grâce'*, recalling the devotion of their ancestors to *l'Etoile de la Mer (Stella Maris), the star of the sea*.

Thus, desirous of overcoming this difference, François 1st imposed the name of *'Ville Françoise de Grâce'* but this name still did not please the fishermen who gave back to the city when they were given the chance, the name of *Havre de Grâce* before it became *Le Havre-Marat* under the Revolution and finally *'Le Havre'*.

'De Grâce', name which one finds on the other side of the estuary, in **Honfleur**, is a deformation of the Normand' grasse' which means : 'wet land, marsh'. One finds this word again in the English vocabulary as 'grass'. 'Le Havre de Grâce' can thus be translated by 'the shelter in the heart of the marsh'.

The port activity of Havre would take some centuries to become one of the most important in France and then in Europe but from the era of Louis XIV it saw major activity, the India Company fitting out its ships there. In the 18th century, an important traffic was set up with the New World, thanks to the American War of Independence supported by France.

Under Charles X, the town was encircled by a triple ditch and ramparts. To enter on land, one had to use one of the existing five great gateways equipped with a drawbridge. The port benefited from nine quays and three basins separated from the outer port by four locks. On the south jetty, a large lock, 'La Floride', prevented the sea from entering the port and served to free the entrance.

The chief monuments which catch the eye of those arriving are : the **'Tour François 1st'** (21 metres high and surmounted by an optical telegraph), the **Church of Notre-Dame** and the **Church of Saint-François**. Where today is the **'Bassin de la Citadelle'** there stood a fortress constructed under Cardinal Richelieu.

The development and enlargement of the port of Havre since 1838 was done on the model of English ports, the latter being more advanced because of the Industrial Revolution.

The Second World War laid waste Le Havre at the beginning of the month of September 1944. The Germans had destroyed the port, the allies reduced the town to rubble and killed many civilians.

The reconstruction of the town with the **'Porte Océane'** would be slow. The maritime traffic had changed character. Le Havre was always a dynamic city**, premier oceanic port of France** and if the local, political and economic personalities really want it, its *'container'* traffic, activity of the future, can be considerably developed. The town of Le Havre is twinned with that of Southampton.

With the withdrawal from service of the liner 'France' in the 1970's, Le Havre certainly lost a part of its soul.

The principal elements of Le Havre heritage are : **'La Maison de l'Armateur'** (18th century)**, 'Le Manoir de Vitanval'** (14th century) which unfortunately cannot be visited, **'La Cathédrale Notre-Dame'** (16th century), **'Le Musée de l'Ancien Havre'** (17th-19th century).

The **Priory of Graville** is of great architectural interest with the **Church of Saint-Honorine**, ancient abbey from the 11th and 13th centuries and conventual buildings in the Anglo-Norman gothic style. One can view here an important collection of religious art.

From Le Havre go back up the right bank of the Seine. These are chalky cliffs bordering the meanders of the River 'Séquanien' that we are following. This place is a protected natural zone.

Stop at the foot of the '**Pont de Normandie**', where there is an immense work of girders, spanning 856 metres. The bridge was anchored across the estuary of the great river. Inaugurated in 1995, it is a veritable feat of technology and a major work of contemporary architecture, which leaves the important industrial zone of Le Havre.

Harfleur, one of the 'most beautiful villages of France', presents a lovely collection of granite houses and the mediaeval remains of the court of Sainte-Catherine.

Then we meet the '**Pont de Tancarville**' (609 metres span) original in its time (1959) which seems to survey the ruins of the ancient feudal castle of the **Tancarville**, faithful servants of Duke William. Proudly standing on a rocky spur, it overlooks the river with its ramparts and towers.

At **Port Jérôme** you wait for the ferry towards *Quillebeuf*, so typical with its '**Hôtel de la Marine**' and its old houses.

Then follow the **Pont de Brotonne**, work of girders with a span of 320 metres, slender, elegant, close to the dense thousand year old **forest of Brotonne** which borders the left bank opposite *Caudebec-en-Caux*, ancient capital of the 'Calètes', tourist town on the banks of the Seine which has a rich heritage. You must visit the church of Notre Dame with its flamboyant gothic style (15th century), 'the most beautiful chapel of the kingdom', King Henry IV said of this building. A stop at the **Museum of the 'marine de la Seine'** is a must afterwards. This 'museographic' space beautifully laid out on the banks of the river, brings to life, across thirteen rooms, the history of navigation on the Seine. Equally it evokes the life along the river over the ages, the tidal bore, the story of the little ferries and the bridges. The last 'gribane' of the Seine is exhibited there.

People used to meet in earlier times at Caudebec to watch, depending on the high tides, the unwinding of the tidal bore ; a fast high wave which returns up the Seine from the estuary, flooding its banks.

At the Chapel 'La Barre-y-Va', one can see numerous offerings, tokens of gratitude from sailors in an era when navigation on the river offered certain dangers.

The banks of the Seine are a privileged place to walk and to discover with their orchards, the stone houses and thatched cottages.

From Caudebec, head for *Yvetot*, capital of the 'Pays de Caux' which retains its traditions such as a picturesque market on Wednesday mornings.

'LE PAYS DE CAUX'

One reaches it through Yvetot, its capital, in the heart of this fertile land celebrated by Maupassant, which conceals an architectural heritage of great diversity with its wood panelled buildings, cob walls, bricks, sandstone and flint and an incalculable number of marvellous sites : Villequier, village squeezed between the cliff and the Seine, where Victor Hugo stayed, as the museum created on the edge of the Seine recalls (his family is buried in the little parish cemetery), the thousand year old oak of Allouville, Barentin and its '1000' statues, Clères, where it is said, Léon Deboutteville and Léon Malandin in 1884 invented the car propelled by the internal combustion engine, above all known for its ornithological reserve created in 1919 by Jean Delacour, beautifully placed in the park of the castle (15th century) destroyed by the English in 1418. The reserve, which one has been able to visit since 1930 is today placed under the authority of the Museum of Natural History of Paris. It covers 13 hectares of the 65 of the park and shelters 230 species of birds and 200 mammals in semi-freedom (wallabies, antelopes, gibbons…). The routes for walking abound in this area where the natural setting is particularly pleasant, notably along the River 'La Clairette' crossed by charming little flowery bridges. In 1472, the community and 17 neighbouring villages were burnt by Charles le Téméraire in vengeance on the population who had put up a resistance against his troops. Do see : la 'Cohue' (ancient court of justice near the castle) and the wooden 'halles' from the 18th century which have replaced the primitive 'halles'. We know that from the end of the 12th century there takes place in Clères every Tuesday a market created with the authorisation of Richard the Lionheart. On the edge of the Seine stop at Duclair, 'city of ducks', which prides itself in having every Tuesday one of the oldest markets in the region - It was actually founded by Richard the Lionheart on 7th June 1198 - it has an admirable church in white stone dating from the 11th and 12th centuries. In the foundations are Roman-Gallic columns. One of the principal curiosities of Duclair remains its ferry to Bourg-Achard.

One can discover in the neighbourhood two jewels filled with history : the Benedictine abbey of Saint-Wandrille (13th-16th centuries) (previously the Abbey of Fontenelle), founded in 688, still consecrated, and of which the life is governed by the rhythm of the services sung in gregorian. For information on guided visits : Tel (33) 2 35 96 23 11 - Fax (33) 2 35 96 49 08, and the exceptional ruins of the Abbey of Jumièges which was a light of knowledge from the 11th to the 16th century.

Built under the direction of Robert Champart from 1040 to 1067 on the site of the primitive monastery from 654, built by Saint-Philibert, in the typical white stone from the cliffs on the banks of the Seine, it was consecrated on 1st July 1067 by the Archbishop of Rouen in the presence of Duke William and his court. Its majestic towers (46 metres) still overlook the site but, like the majority of other Norman abbeys, Jumièges was dismantled and sold stone by stone under Napoléon 1st. In defence of the Emperor, we should realise that there was at that time a serious crisis of 'vocation' and the abbeys were practically deserted.

In this respect, one always queries the lot of the cloister of the abbey. We know that it was taken down on the orders of Stewart of Rothesay, who was then Ambassador of Great Britain in Paris, to be transported to England (or Scotland !) but we don't know where it was reconstructed. It is claimed that a treasure - which could be the gold statue of Saint-Philibert - could have been buried around the yew in the cloister during the Revolution. (Guided visits of the ruins and the park, splendid in Autumn with its hundred year old trees).

Backing on to its abbey, the village of Jumièges is made up of country houses built in part with the stones coming from the abbey church and its adjoining buildings.

The typical farms of the Pays de Caux, are called 'Cours-masures' (literally hovel courts). They are surrounded by ditches and banks generally planted with beech trees with multiple functions : wind breaks, defining the boundaries...

* **The dovecotes of the Pays de Caux**

The dovecotes of Seine-Maritime and more especially of the Pays de Caux are part of the architectural curiosities of this country of Cockaigne. It is generally in the farmyard or close to the Manors and Castles that one finds them. Reserved solely for aristocrats up to the French Revolution, the 'droit de colombier' allowed the construction of memorable buildings, most frequently cylindrical covered with a pepper pot roof and encircled half way up by a dripstone to prevent access to rodents.

Among the most picturesque we can cite those of the Farm of Plessis at Bosc-Guérard-Saint-Adrien, Claville-de-Bois-Guilbert, Bois-Héroult and of course the 'Château de Martainville'.

At the Manor of Auffay (15th-16th centuries), one of the most beautiful Manors of the Pays de Caux with its rich and varied 'polychrome' décor, at Oberville, you can visit the Museum of Colombiers (dovecotes). For information : Tel (33) 2 35 97 69 69.

****

Places to see...

Gruchet-le-Valasse :

= **The Abbey of Valasse :** ancient Cistercian establishment with rooms from the beginning of the Gothic period and its very lovely restored chapel. Classical façade from the 1800's.

= **The temple of Lintot.**

= **The temple of Mont Criquet** founded following the Edict of Saint-Germain in 1562.

= **The great door of the 'Rue Thiers'** with a pediment decorated with bricks from the 16th century.

= **The 'Circuit des Ruelles'** (the tour of the narrow alleyways).

Lillebonne :

Numerous remains of an important Roman presence (Theatre, spas).

Some kilometres from Jumièges, at *Yainville*, the church, built in the 11th century is a replica of that in Newhaven.

In the direction of Duclair, at *Mesnil-sous-Jumièges* you can visit the **Manor of Agnes Sorel**. (14th century). The **'Dame de Beauté',** favourite of King Charles VII, died in childbirth in this place on 9th February 1450.

In the Pays de Caux, one should head for *Cany-Barville* to admire **the castle** built between 1640 and 1646. Its plans were drawn up by a member of the **Mansard family** *(visits possible in summer - beautiful furniture of the period).*

In the chapel of *Barville*, built in local sandstone in 1527 and renovated in 1993, one can see the very beautiful statues and coats of arms of the Grimaldi family, Princes of Monaco. See also the **'Salle de Baillage de Caux'** (the room of the Bailiwick of Caux) which dates from the end of the 18th century and was a court room during the Revolution.

Further towards *ROUEN,* protected by the cliffs, is *La Bouille* with its narrow alleyways bordered by wood panelled houses, its salt loft, its gastronomic restaurants which make it the most charming *'tourist place'* on the river. At *Saint-Martin-de-Boscherville*, about ten kilometres from Rouen, in the valley of the Seine, the ancient **Abbey of Saint-Georges** from the 11th and 12th centuries, displays a collection of ruins of which the ancient abbey church stands out having been saved from demolition during the Revolution by becoming the parish church. It is a major work of Roman-Norman architecture, of harmony and luminosity. It is also typical of the decoration which is so particular to the Norman abbey churches. See the Capitular room from the end of the 12th century remarkable for its historiated cornices and the conventual building from the 17th century. The previous minister of Valéry Giscard d'Estaing, Mayor of Rouen and President of the 'Conseil Général', **Jean Lecanuet**, who was renamed the *'Duke of Normandy'*, was buried there at the beginning of the 1990's.

At *Moulineaux,* on the outskirts of Rouen, is the stronghold castle of **Robert the Devil** - *who should not be confused with the Duke Robert* - whose ruins still stand as a lookout on a promontory above the Seine. One can see there a reproduction of a *Viking 'drake'.*

From the old village of *Canteleu*, where **Gustave Flaubert**, creator of the novel, lived, on the heights, the view offered of Rouen and the river is exceptional. A surprising place to visit in Canteleu is the **Troglodyte Convent of Sainte-Barbe** where, since the 15th century, in the ancient quarries cut into the cliff has lived a community of penitents.

Rouen, chosen in the 10th century by Rollon as the 'Capital of Normandy', has presided during almost three centuries over the destiny of the province.

After the creation of the Anglo-Norman kingdom, Rouen was the holiday town of the Court and the greatest nobles. It has, over the centuries, marked its difference by preferring to welcome the English rather than the French.

It is said that horror reigned in the town at the announcement of the annexation of Normandy by the King of France in 1204. Under the the command of their mayor, Rouen decided to resist the French and the siege began... It would end by the recognition for the town by Philippe-Auguste of special rights and privileges and the obtaining of a truce before the honourable surrender of the town on 12 June 1204. Philippe-Auguste, who suddenly claimed to be descended from William on his mother's side, made his entry into Rouen in his role as 'Duke of Normandy' Thanks to the resistance of the people of Rouen, Normandy kept its laws, its customs and its institutions.

The town, after the terrible bombardments of 1944, which damaged so many of the architectural treasures not least the cathedral, has finally lifted itself from the ruins. *'The historical town'* or still *'The most beautiful town of France'* or *'The town of a hundred bell towers'* was founded in the Roman era *(Rotomagus)* in a meander of the Seine forming a natural amphitheatre surrounded by hills. Long time rival of Paris, situated some 100 kilometres upstream, the town has been blessed over the centuries with superb monuments the majority of which have been regrouped around the **sumptuous cathedral** whose restoration has just been completed.

Major work of Norman art, the cathedral of Rouen is closely tied to the history of the town. Charlemagne came to kneel there, Rollon was baptised there in 912 and then... buried. Olaf the King of Norway, who had come to lend a hand to the Normans received his baptism there before later becoming Saint-Olaf, emblematic figure of the Scandinavians (Normandy, like all the other nordic nations, has since adopted his cross as an emblem). Also there came to this cathedral Saint-Bernard, King Henry 2nd and Jean sans Terre.

One can follow through its construction which extended over several centuries the succession of different periods of gothic style : The Tower of Saint-Romain from the 12th century, the Gateway of the Booksellers and the Gateway of the Calends from the 14th century, the western façade and the 'tour de beurre' from the 15th and 16th centuries, and the 152 metre high cast iron spire from the 19th century.

One finds there the **Church of Saint-Maclou** (dedicated to this man saint who stayed in Normandy before moving on to Brittany where he would be venerated under the name 'Saint-Malo'), a major work of flamboyant gothic, the **'Aître Saint-Maclou'** (now the **School of Fine Arts),** the ancient parish cemetery with its curious ossuary, the **Abbey of Saint-Ouen**, built from the 14th to the 16th century, with beautiful examples of 'Gothic art, radiant with slender and imposing proportions', the **'Hôtel de Bourgtheroulde'**, a gothic edifice from the 15th century with a Renaissance gallery (One can admire a representation of the meeting of the 'drap d'or' between Henry 8th and François 1st), the **Parliament or Exchequer of Normandy,** in our time still the 'Palais de Justice', a marvel of civil architecture in the flamboyant gothic style (It is made up of a main building begun in 1509, and two wings at right angles) where the barrister **Pierre Corneille**, native of Rouen, pleaded, the ancient **'Hôtel-Dieu'** (which has become the Prefecture), the ancient **'Hôtel des Finances'** (today the Tourist Office opposite the cathedral), the **Jewish monument** (built at the end of the 11th century)...

Rouen also possesses an important number of old wood panelled dwellings with corbels in the narrow roads like the **'Rue du Gros Horloge'**, principal artery of the old town, which runs from the Cathedral to the **'Place du Vieux Marché'** where **Joan of Arc** was burned. A modern church dedicated to **Joan of Arc** recalls the torture of the young woman. The **'Gros Horloge'** and belfry is one of the principal attractions of the Norman capital. It is a stone arch in Renaissance style which spans the road. From each side one can admire a richly decorated polychrome clock face. It is flanked by the belfry.

One finds, in the centre of the town, a large number of manufacturers of **Rouen porcelain** which is much sought after.

Before the Revolution, Rouen was one of the three foremost towns of the Kingdom of France.

Visit without fail the Keep or **'Tower of Joan of Arc'** which is a remnant of the castle of Philippe-Auguste (13th century). In this vaulted room Joan of Arc was threatened with torture.

At *Elbeuf*, an industrial town situated not far from Rouen, the past cloth industry is omni-present. The histories recall that the presence of a beehive on the coat of arms of the city came from a visit that Napoléon Bonaparte, then First Consul, made to Elbeuf on 3 November 1802. In fact the latter declared after having visited the town : 'This town is a beehive, every one is working there'.

One can admire the traces of the rich past of Elbeuf from the pretty bourgeois houses with small courtyards, the 'cirque-théâtre' (one of six permanent existing in France), the architectural grandeur of the Chamber of Commerce and Industry and the majestic 'Hôtel de Ville'.

In terms of the natural heritage we should note that the **'Rochers d'Orival'** on which grow wild orchids and numerous other species is a haven for botanists. Elbeuf is blessed with a museum of natural history, of history and of pre-history (numerous collections).

At **Ry**, which holds on to the memory of the great Flaubert, see the church from the 12th century but also and above all the magnificent Renaissance Porch sculpted in wood.

The 'Syndicat d'Initiative' of the 'three valleys' invites the walker to follow a path 'to the country of Emma Bovary' across countryside of great beauty, close to the Forest of Lyons.

Moving away from Rouen to the east, there are certainly places that merit a detour : the **Basilica of Bonsecours**, the **castle of Martainville**, **Lyons** with its beautiful beech wood, the **Abbey of Mortemer**, first Cistercian abbey of Normandy, **Forges-les-Eaux**, reputed spa town in the past, built in a verdant setting with its casino.

Among the celebrities who have come to 'take the water' we can mention, King Louis XIII who was accompanied by Anne of Austria and Richelieu. During the First World War, the town was transformed into *'a hospital town'* by the allies.

Places to see...

= **'Porte de Gisors'** (17th century).
= **'Maisons à Colombages'** (18th century) (half timbered houses).
= **'Granges'** (18th century) (Barns).
= **The park of the 'Hôtel de Ville'.**
= **The wood and lake of Epinay, the lake of Andelle.**

145

The **Pays de Bray**, renowned for its horses but also for its top quality regional products such as the cheese of Neufchâtel and its ciders.

At **Neufchâtel-en-Bray**, visit the **Museum of Mathon-Durand** and the **church of Notre-Dame**.

In **Gournay-en-Bray**, *'city of the horse'* in Upper Normandy, the **church of Saint-Hildevert** has a nave from the 12th century where one can see interesting Roman arcades and gothic vaults. The cornices of the columns present geometric 'rinceaux' and *grimacing masks*.

Auffay, cider capital of Upper Normandy, has magnificent 'Halles' built in 1775.

To end the visit we should mention, the valleys of the coastal rivers such as the **Arques** (a union of three rivers : the **Béthune**, the **Eaulne** and the **Varenne**), the *valley of the Durdent*, of the **Veules**, the **Saâne**...

TOURIST ROUTES

Free leaflets from the Tourist Offices of Seine-Maritime.

= **Route of the Abbeys of the Seine Valley**. The exceptional countryside of the majestic valley of the Seine offers a grandiose setting to this tour around the Norman abbeys which have made the history of Normandy but also the history of the world : Abbey of Saint-Ouen in Rouen, Abbey of Saint-Georges at Saint-Martin-de-Boscherville, Abbey of Jumièges, Abbey of Saint-Wandrille, Abbey of Bec Hellouin, Abbey of Valasse, Abbey Saint-Sauveur in Montivilliers... Information and free brochure : Tel (33) 2 32 62 04 27.

= **Tour of Sandstone**. In the building of farms, thatched cottages, manors, châteaux and churches one generally finds sandstone as the principal material used in the basements and around the openings. It is often associated with other local materials producing beautiful examples of 'polychromie'.
Sandstone was also used in the production of finely carved calvaries.
The 'Tour of Sandstone' (80 kilometres), from village to village, leads you along picturesque small roads to the discovery of the heritage of the Pays de Caux.
Information panels advise you from time to time. A free leaflet is available in the tourist offices.
Principal stops : *Saint-Aubin-sur-Mer, Le Bourg-Dun, Fontaine-le-Dun, Doudeville, Gueutteville-les-Grés...*
= **Tour of the Valley of the Durdent.**
= **Route of the Dovecotes of the Pays de Caux.**
Close to the Alabaster Coast, the Route of the Dovecotes of the Pays de Caux runs along the Valley of the Durdent, and those of Valmont and Ganzeville and winds all the time through the Pays de Caux. In the slightly undulating plain, the curtains of trees planted on their 'ditches' indicate a hamlet, and the beautiful avenues of beech announce a castle or manor. It is often in the centre of the courtyard, called here the 'cour-masure' (the hovel court !) that proudly stands the dovecote. It has this place of honour under feudal right, in force in Normandy in

bygone days. The dovecote symbolised the authority of the lord, the noble land and the territory.

= **The route of Normandy-Vexin (see under Department of Eure).**

= **The route of the thatched cottages.**

To also see in Seine-Maritime…

= **The Valley of the Seine.**

****

The Valley of the Seine :
A natural setting for flora and fauna.

The Seine flows majestically, having hollowed out its bed in the chalky plateau leaving wonderful cliffs on its left bank and fertile meadows on its right.

The life of the great river is punctuated by the passage of cargo vessels which are going to or coming from Rouen. In this natural setting unique species of vegetation grow : orchids, horse fennel, euphorbia of the marshes, insects like the large green grasshopper, hundreds of species of bird proliferate flying over the banks : reed bunting, reed warblers. The marshes are bordered with pollarded willows.

****

= **The semi-troglodyte Church** of *Orival* from the 15th and 18th centuries built into the side of a hill.

= The **castle Taillis** at *Duclair*. Home from the 16th and 17th centuries in an Italian Renaissance style. 4 hectare park of three hundred year old trees.

= **'Château de la Rivière Bourdet'** at *Quevillon*. On the edge of the forest, close to the Seine, building from the 17th century in stone from the Pays de Caux. Beautiful dovecote of the 17th century.

Pays de Caux :

= **'Collégiale' of Auffay.** Building from the 11th and 12th centuries celebrated for its 'Tour des Jacquemarts', unique in this region.

= **Abbey of Montivilliers.** Entirely restored, it has just reopened its doors to the public.

= **Abbey of Notre-Dame-du-Pré** in *Valmont*. Centre from the Renaissance and conventual buildings from the 17th century.

= **Viaduct** of *Barentin*. Important construction built in brick by the English in 1845-46 then rebuilt in 1945.

= **Manor of Vitanval** at *Saint-Adresse*. Jean de Wichfort, Captain of King Henry V had this manor constructed in 1417 in the purest Norman style with stones, flint and wood panels as materials. The British influence is present everywhere : the monumental chimney, sculptured thistle cornices…

= **'Château des Ifs'** at *Tourville-les-Ifs*. In the style of Louis XIII.

= **Feudal castle** of *Valmont.* One of the oldest existing Keeps in Normandy. The exterior and the park are open to the public.

147

= **Museum of Nature** at *Allouville-Bellefosse* (near Yvetot). Dioramas and settings presenting the flora and fauna of Normandy. Room given over to marine mammals. Centre for the protection of wild fauna. Open from 15th March to 15th October every day from 9 am-12 noon and from 2-7 pm ; from 16th October to 14th March Wednesdays, week-ends and national holidays from 9 am-12 noon and from 2-6 pm.

= **Residential study centre for nature and the environment** at *Allouville-Bellefosse* - Hamlet of Bouillot - Tel (33) 2 35 96 06 54.

= **Route and botanical garden** of *Mesnil-Durdent* : Trees and wild flora of the Pays de Caux. Botanical route in the smallest community of Seine-Maritime. The plants are marked as you encounter them. There are 300 weeds or local herbs presented around the Mairie. An information and documentation room complete the visit. (Open weekends and national holidays and in summer).

= **'Le Village des Epouvantails'** (the village of scarecrows). *Blosseville-sur-Mer* offers numerous activities throughout the summer and notably the Le Village des Epouvantails. The streets are filled with strange personages. An exhibition of the Harvest is also held in the church.

Pays de Bray - Vallée de la Bresle :

= **'Collégiale' of Saint-Hildevert** at *Gournay-en-Bray*. Remarkable building from the 11th and 12th centuries.

= **Castle of Merval** at *Brémontier-Merval*. Dwelling from the 17th century Ancient park - Dovecote - Produce.

= **Castle of** *Mesnière-en-Bray*. Beautiful Renaissance property flanked with two strong towers. Park and gardens. Open to the public from April to November.

= **Manor of Randillon** at *Rouvray-Catillon*. This dwelling from the 16th century is the centre of the Memory and Identity of the Pays de Bray. (Conferences and exhibitions) - Open by appointment

= **Fortified farm of the Valouine** at *Mesnil-Follemprise*.

= **Tower of Mailly** at *Saint-Léger-aux-Bois*. Circular tower from the 16th century.

= **'Marais de Fresques'**. Guided visits of this place of great interest in terms of flora and fauna are organised. Natural environment protected by a biotope decree, on the banks of the Eaulne. For information contact the Tourist Office of Neufchâtel-en-Bray.

PARKS AND GARDENS - accessible to the public

= **Gardens of** *Bois-Guilbert*. A 'hymn to nature' in 7 hectares.

= **Park of the castle of Bosmelet** at *Auffay*. Belonging to the same family since 1632, the castle and the park, occupied by the Germans during the last war, were restored in the 1950's. The kitchen garden of almost a hectare has been remodelled in 1996 by the landscaper Louis Bénech who ordered plants and vegetables for the 'potager' following the colours of the rainbow. 'Monsieur de Bosmelet', a staunch anglophile, rents his castle for ceremonies. Open from June to September (the week-end) and all the days from July to August from 1-7 pm. Tel (33) 2 35 32 81 07 - Fax (33) 2 35 32 84 62.

= **Garden of Valérianes** at *Bosc-Roger-sur-Buchy*. In the hamlet of Ennecuit : 1,000 largely perennial plants.

= **'Le Clos du Coudray'** at *Etaimpuis*. This 15,000 square metre park, containing 22 gardens with 6,000 species of plant, a river bank garden, a rockery, an exotic garden and a beautiful rose garden, was started in 1976. It benefits from a favourable micro-climate for the development of exotic plants. Open all the days from 1ˢᵗ April to 30ᵗʰ October from 10 am to 6 pm. For information : Tel (33) 2 35 34 96 85 - Fax (33) 2 35 34 52 57.

= **Park of the castle of Orcher** at *Gonfreville-l'Orcher*.

= **Gardens of Agapanthus** at *Grigneuville*. 'Garden of ideas and of research allying mineral and vegetable…'

* **Gardens of Angélique** at *Montmain*. Charming garden of roses and perennials, it was created in the 1990's in memory of Angélique, daughter of the owners. It has more than 2,000 varities of rose both ancient and modern. Open every day from 1ˢᵗ May to 15ᵗʰ October except Tuesdays. For information : Tel (33) 2 35 79 08 12.

= **Municipal Park** of *Oissel*. A combination of botanical interest and architectural richness.

= **Garden of the Museum Pierre-Corneille** at *Petit-Couronne*. Kitchen garden where they cultivate vegetables and herbs as in the 17ᵗʰ century.

= **Plant Garden of** *Rouen*. Created in 1832, it extends over 8 hectares. Botanical reference collections : medicinal plants, rose garden, gardens of iris and rockeries, orangery, tropical area where grows the 'Victoria amazonica' : giant water-lily of the Amazon. Open every day from 8 am to nightfall. Free entry.

= **Garden of 'Les Forrières du Bosc'** at *Saint-Jean-du-Cardonnay*. Close to Rouen, this garden is planted around a beautiful house of the 17ᵗʰ and 19ᵗʰ centuries. The wooded park of 2 hectares, conceived at the end of the 19ᵗʰ century, contains more than 2,000 species of vegetation including a national collection of perennial geraniums. For information : Tel (33) 2 35 33 47 06.

= **Gardens of Bellevue** at *Beaumont-le-Hareng*. Facing the Forest of Eawy, 6 hectares of flowers and walks : Christmas roses from Turkey, peonies from China, blue poppies from the Himalayas, hydrangeas from China, Japan and America. National collection of 'hellébores and méconopsis'.

For information : Tel (33) 2 35 33 31 37 - Fax (33) 2 35 33 29 44.

= **Garden of the Mesnil** at *Monterolier*. English style garden structured by yew hedges and arbours. Collection of maples coming from all over the world… 3,000 species in 2 hectares for the pleasure of all the senses.

= **Floral Park of William-Farcy** at *Offranville*. Around the body of a farm from the 18ᵗʰ century, in a park of more than 2 hectares, this garden, started in 1993, offers a succession of compositions on a floral theme from April to October : 2,000 species of roses, perennials, bulbs, trees and shrubs… Nearby there is mini-golf, riding and camping. Open to the public from April to September (weekends and national days). May and June : all the days except Tuesday from 10 am to 8 pm. July and August : all the days from 10 am to 8 pm. For information : Tel (33) 2 35 85 40 42.

= **Park of the Wood of Moutiers** at *Varengeville-sur-Mer*. Remarkable park created in 1898 by Edwin Lutyens and Gertrude de Jekyll as the extension of the house which is inspired by the 'Arts and Crafts' movement. Its principal attraction is made up of the English garden which extends across undulating countryside up to the sea. Enjoy the colours and the subtle scents of azaleas, magnolias, spectacular rhododendrons, roses, hydrangeas and Japanese maples.

Open every day from 15th March to 15th November from 10 am-12 noon and from 2-6 pm. For information : Tel (33) 2 35 85 10 02.

= **Park of the castle of Bailleul** at *Angerville-Bailleul*. Around a vast, beautiful Renaissance dwelling in which you can discover an aromatic and medicinal herb garden as well as a maze of arbours. Open every day in summer. Tel (33) 2 35 27 77 87.

= **Garden of Annabele** at *Beauval-en-Caux*. Cul-de-Sac of Bennetot - Tel (33) 2 35 32 85 59. This garden of a typical house of the Pays de Caux marries the French style in the lay out of the beds and the English style in the freedom given to the plants. Open to the public from 1st May to 30th September.

= **Gardens of Cotelle** at *Derchigny-Graincourt*. Avenue Gabriel-de Clieu - Tel (33) 2 35 83 61 38. Superb English style garden close to the castle of Derchigny. Gabriel de Clieu, who lived in this place had the first coffee tree planted in Martinique in the 18th century. Open to the public from the end of April to the 1st November. Communal garden of Amouhoques at Le Mesnil-Durdent.

In one of the smallest communities of Seine-Maritime they present wild flowers of the Pays de Caux in a botanical garden (315 species in beds) but also on the embankments of the village 142 species are spread out. Open and free visits from the end of April to the end of October.

Note : There exists in Upper Normandy a club of Parks and Gardens which gathers together around fifteen of the exceptional sites in Seine Maritime and Eure. Information from the Regional Committee of Tourism.

****

The Forest, the green lungs of Normandy

Marvellously set out by **President Herriot** *in his book* **'The Normandy Forest'** *there is here, one of the essential elements of natural Norman heritage. Since the first human inhabitants in this land, the forest is one of the principal riches and one of the major attractions of the old Province.*

In the depths of its plantations of tall trees were born the legends, the pagan rites were developed there until the first hermits, at the dawn of our time, came to take refuge there and to spread the Christian faith, helping the establishment of churches and monasteries. It has influenced the character of the populace, it gave them the indispensable material as a base for the construction of their houses, the fruits, its game to feed them, its wood to warm them... it has thus helped and developed the growth of the first industries.

150

Of the immense forest which previously covered almost all the countryside, there remains important large sections which today still occupy several tens of thousands of hectares. The most important major forest areas are governed by the O.N.F. (Office National des Forêts).

They are, for the most part open to walkers. Outside the hunting season, one can walk, cycle or horse-ride. In the Autumn, enthusiasts come often from far afield to find and pick mushrooms.

The storm of December 1999 dealt a rude blow to the Norman forests which will take tens of years to heal the wounds.

****

THE PRINCIPAL FORESTS OF NORMANDY

In Orne :

= **The Forest of Ecouves (8,161 hectares).** Near **Alençon,** it is one of the biggest forest areas in western France.

To see...

= **La Sapaie 'Pichon' :** magnificent collection of pines that are hundreds of years old.

= **The Forest of Andaine (5,312 hectares).** Place of mysteries and legends where numerous historians place the origin of the **Legend of Arthur.** It is said that it conceals numerous treasures. Surrounding the' thermal spa of Bagnoles-de-l'Orne, one finds there, large numbers of oaks, beeches, Scots pines, spruces... The Forest of Andaine was seriously damaged by the storm of December 1999.

To see...

At **'L'Etoile d'Andaine'** (between *La Ferté-Macé* and *Domfront*).

The Arboretum of 'l'Etoile d'Andaine'.

At **Antoigny,** in the heart of the forest, not far from **Bagnoles-de-l'Orne :** The **'Gorges du Villiers' :** traces of ancient Roman thermal baths. A hot gassy water flows out there.

= **Forest of Perche-Trappe (3,201 hectares).** It was in former times part of the Abbaye de la Trappe in **Soligny.**

= **Forest of Bellême (2,400 hectares).** Situated in the Perche of Orne, the ancient forest of **Bellême** is principally planted with majestic oaks and beeches. It is considered as **'one of the best forests of France'.** It was there that in the 17th century they chose the long trunks necessary in the construction of the biggest French war ships. This superb forest invites you to walk and to discover its ancient trees and its legends.

= **Forest of Réno-Valdieu (1,596 hectares).** Also situated in Perche, this forest has a number of impressive centuries-old trees. In 1669, Colbert sent commissioners to Normandy to draw up an inventory of the massive forests capable of producing the lengths of marine wood used by the Royal Navy to construct ships capable of facing the English vessels. Only the forests of Perche could then reply to this need. In the old forest of tall trees on the Route de la

Gautrie proudly stand old oaks more than three hundred years old. With trunks over 40 metres high in a single stem, these venerable ancestors have names such as : **Oxford, Aberdeen...** Homage rendered by numerous British visitors who have come to look at them.

Guided visits of the forests of Bellême and Réno

For information and bookings : Office National des Forêts 36, rue Saint-Blaise - 61000 Alençon - Tel (33) 2 33 82 55 00 - Fax (33) 2 33 32 20 69 - Paid visits.

= **Forest of Saint-Evroult (2,200 hectares).** In walking the numerous marked trails, one cannot stop thinking of the heroes of the Varende who rode in this superb forest where oaks rub shoulders with larches. In its heart is the source of the Charentonne.

In Calvados :

= **'Forêt domainiale de Balleroy-Cerisy'.** 2,130 hectares on both sides of the main road from Bayeux to Saint-Lô. Huge forest essentially made up of groves of tall beeches (80%), oaks (18%), birches, chestnuts, maples... It shelters does, stags, roe deer, wild boar, badgers, hares, rabbits, foxes, woodcock, buzzards, cuckoos, falcons, hobby falcons... An arboretum, situated near to the Carrefour de l'Embranchement allow discovery of the different species. Do visit the 'Forest House' called 'Belle Loge' which is a centre of Introduction to the Environment with exhibitions and walks of discovery. (Off the RD 572 - Tel (33) 2 33 05 68 04). The 'Route de la Forêt des Biards' is a tour of approximately 40 kilometres between Bayeux and Saint-Lô which allows an excellent approach to the 'forêt domaniale' and a discovery of the activities of the region and its heritage. Free leaflet available from Calvados Tourist Offices.

= **'Forêt domaniale de Valcongrain'** in the 'pre-bocage'. 375 hectares of broad leafed trees (65%) : oaks, birches, and conifers : Scots pine... Free circulation (except motorised vehicles) on the forest roads.

= **Forest of Gatien at** *Saint-Gatien-des-Bois*. Pleasant walks on the long paths of this 2,800 hectare forest of which only a small part is open to the public.

= **'Forêt domaniale de** *Saint-Sever'*. 1,552 hectares of broad leafed trees (beech and oak) and conifers (pectin and douglas pines) growing from a granite based soil. The forest is controlled by the Office National des Forêts. Wood production site.

= **Wood of the castle of Gavrus** *(near to Evrecy)*. An area of 80 hectares open to the public - 8 kilometres of footpaths under the trees in the valley of the Odon.

= **Forest of Grimbosq** *(near to Caen)*. It makes up the western part of the Forest of Cinglais. Its 475 hectares have been acquired by the town of Caen who have made it into a place of walks and discovery. 15 kilometres south of Caen towards Thury-Harcourt, this site offers an animal park of more than 8 hectares, two arboretum (including one with a giant sequoia), a botanical path, sign-posted pedestrian paths and even a sporting circuit. A cemetery for small animal pets was set out in 1982.

= **The Wood of Breuil at** *Honfleur-Pennedepie*. Forest collection in 120 hectares - Great variety of species (oak, beech, maple, wild cherry, birch, ash, hornbeam…).

In Eure :

= **Forest of Lyons (10,695 hectares).** The forest of Lyons which stretches across the departments of Eure and Seine-Maritime, is a huge extended, very divided area constituted chiefly of beech trees. It makes up the **most beautiful beech wood in France.** In the Middle Ages, it was devoted to hunting. Up to the 19th century, it furnished the prime material to a large number of craftsmen : layetiers (makers of chests); charcoal burners and clog makers. It was made famous by Gustave Flaubert who set in Ry, a charming village on the edge of the forest, his famous novel 'Emma Bovary'.

= **Forest of Brotonne (6,750 hectares)** You can find more than 90 species of tree there, broad leafed and conifer stand shoulder to shoulder (beech, oak, cherry, Scots pine…). Guided visits are organised by the O.N.F. Tel (33) 2 35 12 24 24.

= **Forest of Evreux.** It offers the public 545 managed hectares for walking, from the deer ponds to the ancient quarries. Plan available from the Tourist Office of Evreux.

In Seine-Maritime :

= **Forest of Trait-Maulévrier (3,000 hectares).** On the right bank of the Seine, it is controlled by the Office National des Forêts. It offers a diversity of terrain which bring out the different species contained therein : (oak, beech and pine).

= **Forest of Eawy (7,220 hectares)** around **Saint-Saëns.** This huge forest area covers the uneven region defined by the valleys of the Varenne and the Béthune. The **'allée des Limousins'** in the heart of the tall beech trees is astonishing.

= **Forest of Eu (9,293 hectares).** Property of the State and the department of Seine-Maritime, it extends between the valley of the Bresle and that of the Yères and is divided into three great 'massifs' : Le triage d'Eu, and the upper and lower forests of Eu.

= **Forest of Arques** - Near to Dieppe. 1,000 hectares for rest and relaxation!

Discovering Normandy by water

Area of La Manche

Discover the Natural Regional Park of the Marshes and the 'Bessin'.

Leaving from **Port Jourdan** - **Saint-Come-du-Mont** *(near* **Carentan***)* : *On board the* **'Barbey d'Aurivilly II'** *(Capacity 68 places)* : *half-day or full day trips with commentary on the Douve. (9.30 am-6 pm) - from 1ˢᵗ May to 30ᵗʰ September by reservation. For information and bookings : Tel (33) 2 33 71 55 81 - Fax (33) 2 33 71 12 52.*

Leaving from **Saint-Hilaire-Petitville** *(near* **Carentan***)* : *On board* **'La Rosée du Soleil'** *(Capacity 50 places)* : *journey to the rhythm of the history of 'La Taute' and discover the fauna and flora of the Cotentin marshes. By reservation every day from May to September.*

Area of Calvados

*Leaving from **Caen** or **Ouistreham** : **Voyage on the canal from Caen to the sea.** On board 'l'Hastings' (80 places) discover peacefully during a two and half hour mini-cruise the banks of the canal from Caen up to the sea (as far as Ouistreham) and the monuments which border them. Possibility to eat on board (60 places). Leaving from the Bassin Saint-Pierre in **Caen** or from **Ouistreham** (one way trips are possible) - Departures from April to October. During the season there are four departures per day : 9 am (by reservation) 12.15 pm, 3.15 pm, 7 pm or 7.30 pm (by reservation). Information and Reservations : 'L'Hastings' quai de Vendeuvre - BP 3052 - 14018 Caen Cedex 02 - Tel (33) 2 31 34 00 00 - Fax (33) 2 31 72 52 00.*

*Leaving from **Honfleur** : **Discovery of the Pont de Normandie** : Aboard the launches 'Stephanie' (32 places) and 'Alphée' (62 places). Information and Reservations : 42, Rue des Bucailles and the Quai des Passagers in **Honfleur** from the Easter weekend to 11th November every day from 11.30 am-4.30 pm (6.30 pm in summer) : Duration 50 minutes. Tel (33) 2 31 89 21 10.*

Journey on the estuary of the Seine *: On board the launch 'l'Evasion' : Quay for passengers in **Honfleur** from Easter to 1st June : week-ends and national holidays ; from 1st June to 11th November : every day - Duration 25 minutes. For information : Tel (33) 2 31 89 41 80.*

*On board the launch **'Jolie France'** : Waiting jetty in **Honfleur** from 1st April to 30th September - Duration 1h30. For information : (33) 2 31 89 05 83.*

*Aboard the launch **'le Calypso'** : Quay at la Planchette in **Honfleur** - (Capacity 68 places) : visit of the port from 1st April to 30th September - Duration 30 minutes. For information : Tel (33) 2 31 89 20 93.*

Area of Orne :

*Leaving from **Putanges** : **Cruises on the Orne.***

*Cruises on board the **'Val d'Orne'** (170 people 'en promenade') to discover on leaving **Putanges,** during a trip of 14 kilometres, the charms of the Lac de **Rabondanges** and the wild sites of the **Suisse Normande.** Air conditioned salon - Possibility of lunch or dinner cruises (by reservation). At 4 pm lasting 1hr 15 minutes (2hrs 15 minutes with a meal) from March to December. Information and Reservations : Tel (33) 2 33 39 30 30 - Fax (33) 2 33 39 76 34.*

Area of Eure :

***Cruises on the Seine** : Leaving from **Vernon** : Journey on the Seine on board 'La Belle Gabrielle'* *from 1st June to 15th September, every day. In May : weekends and national holidays by appointment. Capacity : 60 persons. Tel 01 34 79 71 23 - Fax (33) 234 79 71 58.*

*Aboard the **'Guillaume le Conquérant'**, with a capacity of 140 places (120 for meals) : cruise on the Seine with stops at **Poses** and **Andelys** all year except January and February. Day trips, seminars. For information and reservations : Rives de la Seine croisière : Tel (33) 2 35 78 31 70.*

Area of Seine-Maritime :

Cruises on the Seine : *Leaving from* **Le Havre** *: On board '**La Salamandre**' (150 places - 78 for meals) Different possibilities are offered : cruises on the Seine with stops at* **Honfleur, Villequier, Caudebec, Duclair, La Bouille, Rouen**. *Visit to the port of* **Le Havre** *or cruises with meals. - Only in summer. For information and reservations : Tel (33) 2 35 42 01 31. Quai de la Marine - BP 1086, 76062 Le Havre cedex.*

Leaving from **Rouen** *: Visit of the port on board the '**Cavelier de la Salle**". For information and reservations : Office de Tourisme Rouen, Tel (33) 2 32 08 32 40.* **Cruises :** *On board the ship '**Le Châteaubriand**' (280 persons), gastronomic cruises on the Seine from October to May. Duration 3 to 4 hours. Departures from* **Rouen** *with stops at* **Caudebec-en-Caux, Villequier and Honfleur**. *Gala evenings, marriages, seminars... For information and reservations : Société Harbour - Quai Bois-Guilbert - Hangar n° 5, Tel (33) 2 35 15 21 31 or (33) 2 99 16 35 32.*

Cruises on the Seine leaving from Paris :

*Prestigious hotel ship the '**M/S Normandie**' offers from mid-April to the end of October, one week cruises on the Seine between* **Paris** *and* **Honfleur** *with stops at* **Rouen, Caudebec-en-Caux...** *Good ambiance, piano bar, gala dinners... Cabins and gastronomic restaurant - capacity 104 passengers - 54 cabins - 104 beds - Available for Company trips or seminars. For information and reservations : Aqua Viva Croisières - Port de Grenelle - 75015 Paris. Tel (33) 1 45 75 52 60.*

*On board the '**Winner**", restaurant ship which travels all year between Paris and Rouen (Capacity 95 persons). 100 square metre salon, bar, sound equipment, breakfasts, lunches, snacks and dinner cruises, (90 places). For information : Compagnie normande de tourisme fluvial. Tel (33) 6 80 10 34 84 - Fax (33) 2 32 59 43 43.*

*Aboard the ship '**La Douce France**', hotel-ship with 74 double cabins - cruises of 5 to 7 days on the Seine between* **Paris** *and* **Honfleur**. *For information and reservations : Croisèreurope - 12, rue de la Division Leclerc, 67000 Strasbourg. Tel (33) 3 88 76 40 66.*

III - THE NORMAN REPUTATION

1 - Literature and the writers of Normandy

There is a tendency in France to state that a region not possessing its own language cannot claim a true culture, the language being the special expression of the culture. That is hardly the case in the contribution of Normandy to that which we today call the French language. Indeed there are numerous Norman writers who over the centuries have made an essential contribution to the enrichment of French, even to its foundations.

The 'Norman French' also participated greatly to the enrichment of the English language (the opposite is equally true) *and to the French that they still speak in New-France.*

Among those authors who embody the **'Norman Reputation'***, we can cite in chronological order :*

Dudon de Saint-Quentin (10th-11th century) - His principal work (of which there remain today no more than ten copies in the world) was entitled : **'De Moribus seu Actis primorum Normanniae Ducum'** and recounts the saga of Duke Rollon and his successors up to Richard 1st. His work was continued by the historian William of Jumièges who related the reigns of Richard 2nd, Richard 3rd, Robert the Magnificent and William the Conqueror.

Ordéric Vital (11th-12th century) - Born in England in 1075, the monk-historian from the Abbey of Saint-Evroult is today recognised as the greatest specialist on Ducal Normandy. His **'Historia Ecclesiastica'** began in 1174 and remains the reference for all histories of Normandy. He founded some 15 monastic establishments and notably the Priory of' La Cochère', the Abbeys of Alménêches and Saint-Martin of Sées. He gave his name to the Abbey of Saint-Evroult where he was buried. His grave was desecrated and his body stolen by the men of the Duke of Orléans who took it to Orléans. The road followed by the profaners is punctuated with places of 'ébruffiens' worship : églises de Champs, Favières, 'Le Favril', Orrouer, 'Pré Saint-Evroult'… In Orléans, his remains were dispersed to Angers and Rebais, in the diocese of Meaux. The worship of Saint-Evroult is still important to this day in those two cities. He is normally represented as a Benedictine monk with, at his feet, a small kneeling figure, hands bound by chains. In the abbey church of Boscherville, which is linked to the abbey of Ouche, the imagery is inspired by a legend representing a mysterious horse carrying bread to the monks of Saint-Evroult to repay the charity of the Saint-Abbot.

François de Malherbe (1555-1628) - **'At last came Malherbe...'** it is said of he who is considered as **the precursor of classic French poetry.**

A good number of places and 'institutions', beginning with the local football club who carry the name 'stade Malherbe', recall this great writer in his native town of Caen.

Marie de Medicis introduced him to King Henry IV who made him an 'ordinary gentleman of the King's chamber' before he became one of the favourite poets of the court and the confidant of the sovereign. He shared with him an excessive taste for the ladies...

Places to see...

In *Caen* :

= **The house of the writer** situated in rue Saint-Pierre in the centre of the town.

Pierre Corneille (1606-1684) - Born in *Rouen*, **Pierre Corneille** was one of the two greatest dramatic French poets. Lawyer at The Bar in Rouen, he wrote his first verses in 1625. **Cardinal Richelieu** had him come to work with him in 1633 and he entered the **'Académie Française'** in 1647. If he started by writing comedies, his master works remain his tragedies such as **'Le Cid', Horace, Cinna, Polyeucte ...**

Places to see...

Ecorches : in Orne :

= The **Manor** where his daughter Marie lived.

Petit-Couronne - 8 km from Rouen, at 502, rue Pierre-Corneille, Tel (33) 2 35 71 78 78 or (33) 2 35 68 13 89 :

= **La Maison des Champs de la famille Corneille or the 'Musée Corneille'.** Pierre Corneille had inherited this humble, wood-pannelled house of the 16th century from his father. The current furniture is not from the period. It is there simply to recreate the atmosphere of this family village place much appreciated by the tragedian. One finds there, documents recalling Corneille and his family, sculptures, paintings, engravings, medals, rare original autographed editions...

The orchard, the bread oven, the kitchen garden from the 17th century give the property a very convivial rural character.

The house is open to the public from 1st April to 30th September every day except Tuesday from 10 am-12.30 pm and from 2-6 pm. From 1st October to 31st March from 10 am-12.30 pm and from 2-5 pm. Sundays from 2-5.30 pm (winter) and from 2-6.30 pm in summer.

Rouen

= **Musée Corneille :** In his native house, 4, rue de la Pie, Tel (33) 2 35 71 63 92. Reconstruction of his work place, furniture, paintings from the 17th century and a model of the 'Place du Vieux Marché' of that period. With prior authorisation, access is possible to the library dedicated to the works of the tragedian and to their presentation. Open from 10 am-12 noon and from 2-6 pm every day except Monday, Tuesday and Wednesday morning.

= **'Le Palais de Justice, Parlement de Normandy'** Where he pleaded.

His statue beside the Seine, on the forecourt of the Theatre.

Henri Bernardin de Saint Pierre (1734-1814) The author of the celebrated romantic novel **'Paul and Virginie'** (1788) was born in Le Havre. A great traveller he spent several months on Mauritius where he found the inspiration for this major work which made him known throughout the world. Napoléon 1st, himself a great lover of the exotic, put him into the 'Académie Française' in 1803.

François Guizot (1787-1874) A historian, Guizot also interested himself in politics. He played an important role in the taking of power by Louis-Philippe and was his Minister of Public Education before being named as head of the Government. He favoured the strengthening of the alliance with England and supported the 'Entente Cordiale'.

Places to see...

Le Val Richer :

= **The castle**, acquired in 1836, where in a totally exceptional undulating site, Guizot lived.

Jules Michelet (1798-1874) -This great historian - but also a poet - was charged by King **Louis-Philippe** with the education of his daughter **Clémentine**. Head of the historical section of the National Archives, academic, Professor at the 'Collège de France', it was at the **Castle of Vascœuil** in Eure that he wrote a good number of his works numbering among them a voluminous **'Histoire de France'** which is still used as a reference today and a **'Histoire de la Révolution française'** in seven volumes. Disciple of sea bathing, which helped him to forget his stomach pains, he stayed for the latter part of his life in *Dieppe* and in *Granville*.

Places to see...

Perriers-sur-Andelle in *Eure* :

Castle of Vascœuil (14th-16th centuries. ISMH - classified site) where Michelet lived, 8, rue Jules-Michelet - Tel (33) 2 35 23 62 35 (Private property).

After having been restored, this **Regional Centre for Art and Culture** presents important exhibitions of contemporary artists and constitutes the only **Musée Michelet** existing in France.

At the top of the tower from the 12th century, his work place has been recreated. The environment is exceptional : Dovecote with a remarkable turning ladder system - Park with a garden 'à la française', sculptures and mosaics of great contemporary artists.

Open to the public : from the beginning of March to 1st April : Saturday, Sunday and Monday from 2.30-5.30. From 1st April to 21st April : from 2.30-6.30 pm all the days. From 26th April to 14th June : from 2.30-6.30 pm all the days. From 15th June to 14th July and from 17th July to 31st August : from 11 am to 7 pm all the days. From 1st September to 19th October : from 2.30-6.30 pm all ths days. From 20th October to 16th November : from 2.30-5.30 pm all the days.

Honoré de Balzac (1799-1850) - Verbose writer, author of **'La Comédie Humaine'** stayed in *Alençon* which he chose as the setting for three of his novels.

Sophie Rostopchine, Countess of Ségur (1799-1874) - Born in Saint-Petersbourg, she was the daughter of **Russian Prince Rostopchine**, *governor of Moscow,* who burnt the town at the approach of the troops of **Napoléon 1st**. Arriving in France at the age of 18, she married the Count of Ségur and lived for more than fifty years in the **'Château des Nouettes'** in *Aube* which was given to her by her father. 'Abandoned' there by her husband with eight children - he preferred Parisian life - she wrote there the majority of her works for children, such as **'Les Petites Filles Modèles'** or **'Les Malheurs de Sophie'**.

> *Places to see...*

Aube in *Orne* :

= **'Château des Nouettes'** (visits not permitted).

= **The Museum of the Countess of Ségur** in the town in the old presbytery. Rue de l'Abbé Roger-Derry - Tel (33) 2 33 24 60 09.

Portraits, documents, toys and souvenirs.

Open from 21st June to 28th September, all the days, except Tuesday, from 2-6 pm.

= **Museum of the Forge of Aube** (In the town). The Countess was inspired by the life of the master craftsman of the forge of the era to write **'La Fortune de Gaspard"**. Rue de la Vieille Forge - Tel (33) 2 33 34 14 93.

Charles-Alexis Clérel, Count of Tocqueville (1805-1859) - Coming from a noble family of *Tocqueville*, in the Valley of the Saire, the grand-son of the defender of Louis XVI is known as a political writer being interested above all in the evolution of democracy in the history of the world. After a stay in the United States and Canada in 1832 where he had been sent on a mission as magistrate of the Tribunal of Versailles, followed by a trip to England, he published a work considered as essential reading entitled **'De la Démocratie en Amérique'**. Having married for love, a young English woman, called Mary Mottley, he became Deputy of *Valognes*, in Manche under the July Monarchy and positioned himself as 'liberal'.

Minister of Foreign Affairs in the Second Republic, French Academician, he withdrew from public life under the Second empire and undertook, at *Tocqueville*, the production of his second great work : **'De l'ancien Régime à la Révolution'** which analyses the causes of the French Revolution and contains prophetic pages on the evolution of society.

Defender of the liberty of the Press which constituted in his eyes one of the principal oppositions, he is today recognised, throughout the world, and notably by the anglo-saxons, as an enlightened political scientist.

His successor at the Bourbon palace, **Pierre Godefroy**, created in 1978 the *'Prix Alexis de Tocqueville'* which rewards political writers every two years. The first Lauriat was Raymond Aron. The prize is presented inside the castle in the presence of numerous personalities of the world of politics and the arts.

Tocqueville in the north of the region of La Manche : **Castle birthplace** of Tocqueville.

Victor Hugo (1802-1885) - Born in Besançon Victor Hugo, son of a general of the Empire, 'monument' of French literature, inspirer of the Romantic Movement, was not truly Norman but he stayed frequently in our Province which he was particularly fond of, notably *Villequier*, on the banks of the Seine where the parents of his son-in-law, Vacquerie lived. It was there that, powerless, he witnessed the death of his daughter Léopoldine, victim of the 'mascaret'[1] in 1843 during a trip on the river when she was still not twenty years old.

Exiled by Napoléon III in 1852, he wrote some of his most beautiful pieces of work - and notably **'Les Misérables'** in *Jersey* and then in *Guernsey* where he lived until 1870.

Places to see...

Villequier, on the banks of the Seine :

= **The 'Musée départemental Victor Hugo'** - quai Victor-Hugo. Tel (33) 2 35 56 78 31 - Fax (33) 2 35 56 91 86 (Property of the department of Seine-Maritime). Open from April to 30th September from 10 am-12.30 pm and from 2-6 pm, (Closed Tuesdays) and from October to 31st March open from 10 am-12.30 pm and from 2-5 pm (closed Tuesdays). Sundays from 2-5.30 pm in winter and 2-6.30 pm in summer.

In this 'bourgeois' house from the 19th century, situated beside the Seine, ancient property of the Vacquerie family, where the writer and his family lived and where remain always the memories of the poor **Léopoldine**, his 'darling daughter' who drowned in 1843, are exhibited mementos of the great author and his family (paintings, designs of Victor Hugo, signed letters, furniture of the period and photographs).

= **The parish cemetery** around the charming church where **Madame Hugo and his children** are buried, **the writer** rests in the **Pantheon** in *Paris*.

Jules Barbey d'Aurevilly (1808-1889). Born in the region of La Manche, this great writer was the author of short stories and novels. Fiercely attached to his native land he was nick-named *'The Supreme Commander of Letters'* or even *'The Bailiff of Cotentin'*. Saying *'Norman before being French'*, he was at the base of the autonomist feeling in Normandy. A number of his novels are inspired by the Cotentin countryside, by the stories heard in his childhood, by the legends and the popular beliefs of his country.

Places to see...

Saint-Sauveur-le-Vicomte, in La Manche where the writer was born and lived. **Musée Barbey d'Aurevilly**. 64, rue Bottin-Desylles - Tel (33) 2 33 41 65 18.

---

(1) The mascaret was an enormous wave produced by the meeting of the waters of the natural current of the Seine with those pushed back in the estuary by the high tides.

Gustave Flaubert (1821-1880) - Son of a chief surgeon of the **'Hôtel-Dieu de Rouen'** (which today houses the buildings of the **'Préfecture de la Seine-Maritime'**) Gustave Flaubert is today recognised as one of the 'monuments' of French literature.

Frenzied worker, he consecrated all his life to his work and only to his work. He wrote 'under sufferance' in that he imposed on himself a great rigour in his literary work and documentation in the style of a journalistic investigation. **'Creator of the modern novel'** his major work was entitled **'Madame Bovary'** (1857). He was also the author of **'Salammbô'**, **'L'Education Sentimentale'** and he died before finishing **'Bouvard et Pécuchet'**. In terms of the second cycle, he is one of the most read Norman writers, even today.

Places to see...

Canteleu (9 km from Rouen in the direction of Duclair) :

= **'Pavillon Flaubert'** (classified historic monument - 18, quai Gustave-Flaubert at Dieppedalle - Croisset Tel (33) 2 35 36 43 91 - Property of the City of Rouen) open every day (except Tuesdays and Wednesday mornings and national holidays) from 10 am-12 noon and from 2-6 pm.

Doctor Flaubert acquired 'Croisset' in 1844. The house was sold after the death of the writer. Only the pavilion of the Louis XIII garden remains. The property was repurchased at the beginning of the century by the association of the 'Amis de Flaubert' which gave it to the town of Rouen in 1906. Some reminders of the writer and his work are collected there : writing objects, portraits, engravings and views of Croisset at that period.

= The **'Mairie'** of *Canteleu* : **The Flaubert Library** with its 1,300 books.

Rouen :

= **'Musée Flaubert' et 'Histoire de la Médecine'.**

51, rue de Lecat - Tel (33) 2 35 15 59 95. You can visit in this typical dwelling of the 18th century, the working accommodation of the surgeon father of the writer and the room in which Flaubert was born. Open every day of the year from 10 am-12 noon and from 2-6 pm except Sundays, Mondays and national holidays, from 10 am-6 pm Tuesdays.

Ry :

= **'Galerie Bovary'** : Place Flaubert - Tel/Fax (33) 2 35 23 61 44. From a personal sentimental adventure, Gustave Flaubert drew the personage of his celebrated novel 'Emma Bovary'.

= **'Musée d'automates'**. In a pressing shed from the 18th century, 500 automaton of which 300 relive the principal scenes of the novel 'Madame Bovary'. Document room on the 'Delamare-Bovary' and a reconstruction of the pharmacy of the village from around 1850. Tourist tour called the 'circuit Bovary' (brochure in English). Open from Easter to the end of October Saturdays, Sundays and Mondays and national holidays from 11 am-12 noon and 2-7 pm. In July and August : all the other days from 3-6 pm.

***Trouville-sur-Mer* :** Each summer, Gustave, his sister Caroline and his brother Achille spent the summer holidays of their youth in the company of their mother, who was born at *Pont-l'Evêque*, sea bathing at Trouville.

This was the theatre for his first amorous adventures. He would remain attached all his life to this village of fishermen which he described in these terms : *'The village was charming with its houses crammed one against the other, black, grey, red and white, facing in all directions without alignment or symmetry. Some years ago, nobody came there, in spite of its grand half-league beach and its charming position... Thus all is simple and wild, there was almost only the artists and the people of the region...'*

Hector Mallot (1830-1907) - Born at *La Bouille*, one of the most beautiful villages of Normandy, on the banks of the Seine, where his father was a lawyer, Hector Mallot owes his literary renown to his seminal work **'Sans Famille'** (1878) written for children. This work recounts the miserable life and the vicissitudes of youth of Rémi, a poor orphan.

Places to see...

La Bouille on the banks of the Seine :

= The old house where Hector Mallot was born and his father was lawyer and Mayor.

Octave Mirbeau (1848-1917) - Born in *Trévières*, journalist, romantic writer, author of the **'Journal d'une femme de chambre'** adapted for the cinema by **Bunüel**, the writer spent his childhood at *Rémalard* in Orne.

Guy de Maupassant (1850-1893) - Born at the castle of *Miromesnil* in 1850, Guy de Maupassant is a witness of his times, an attentive observer of life in western Normandy in the 19th century, a talented story teller who produced more than 300 short stories of which a number have been adapted for the cinema and television, with roles played by great actors. Denouncing the foibles of the small peasantry and of the little Norman middle class, he is at times biting. Under the protection of Flaubert, a friend of the family, he had a brilliant career but unfortunately too short since the author of **'Boule de Suif'** and of **'Contes de la Bécasse',** would die half mad in 1893, ravaged by drugs, tobacco and women... He claimed to have 'known' between two and three hundred...

Places to see...

***Auffay* :**

= **The Manor of Auffay, international centre for Guy de Maupassant.**

***Etretat* :**

= **The villa** which he had built. It was there that he met the English poet Swinburn who invited him to participate in the merry parties that he organised.

***Fécamp* :**

= **The 'Chemins des Falaises'** where Maupassant loved to walk.

Gisors :
 = **The old quarters** which inspired him to write the story of the **'Rosier de Madame Husson'.**

Gonneville-la-Mallet :
 = **'Auberge des Vieux Plats'** which Maupassant frequented regularly and which has kept its decor of yesteryear.

Grainville-Ymauville :
 = **'Château Blanc'**, beautiful residence belonging to the family of the writer.

Rouen :
 = **The 'Lycée Corneille'** which the young Maupassant frequented.

Tôtes :
 = **The 'Auberge du Cygne'** where Maupassant set a chapter of 'Boule de suif'.

Tourville-sur-Arques, near to *Dieppe :*
 = **Castle of Miromesnil.** In the heart of a delicious 10 hectare plantation of tall beeches stands the Château from the 17th century. The huge 'salons' on the ground floor conserve the memory of the Marquis of Miromesnil but also the memory of Guy de Maupassant born there on 5th August 1850. A two hundred year old cedar of Lebanon dominates the park where there stands a bust of the celebrated writer. Open to the public from 1st May to 15th October every day except Tuesday from 2-6 pm. For information : Tel (33) 2 35 85 02 80.

Yvetot : It was in the **capital of the Pays de Caux**, in the small **seminary of Yvetot** that **Maupassant** spent his first years of study.
 = **The countryside of the Pays de Caux,** setting for his novels and stories.

Alphonse Allais (1854-1905) - Born in *Honfleur* on 20th October 1854 of a 'papa' chemist who despaired of his son, who preferred the 'bons mots' and hoaxes, to the teaching of his good masters, Alphonse Allais finally settled into a career as a humorist and song writer rather than succeeding his father.

He began his career in the capital by publishing his texts - he wrote more than 1500 ! - in the Parisian press who soon scrambled for his collaboration. Thoughts, 'combles', crazy stories, where the things that Allais wrote appearing very much like that which we call in France *'English Humour'*. Forgotten for many years, he was rediscovered in France at the end of the 70's.

Among his turns of phrase we can cite /
'AGE : Impossible to tell you my age, it changes all the time !'
'English : I don't under stand the English ! Whereas in France we name our roads after famous victories : Wagram, Austerlitz,... over there they put up the names of defeats : Trafalgar Square, Waterloo place...'.
or even : *'England is an ancient Norman colony gone wrong !'.*

Places to see...

Honfleur : At n° 10, place Hamelin near the **famous 'Lieutenance' : the pharmacy of M. Allais Senior. There is a commemorative plaque.**

Paul Harel (1854-1927) - Innkeeper at *Echauffour* in Orne, This Norman who celebrated his Viking ancestry and the Norman spirit composed numerous poems and pieces for the theatre of which the most celebrated is called **'l'herbager'**, (the pastureland).

Paul Duval called Jean Lorrain (1855-1906) - This romantic story teller and poet, born in *Fécamp*, dedicated a great part of his work to the saga of the Vikings.

Charles-Théophile Féret (1859-1928) - Born at *Quillebeuf*, on the estuary of the Seine, 'fanatically attached' to Normandy, 'Norman autonomist', this great writer, considered as the 'first of the Norman poets'', became known through a very committed work in which he proclaims his unshakeable faith in his country, claiming to follow his Nordic origins. He was the Founding President of the Society of Norman Writers.

Maurice Leblanc (1864-1941) - Figuring among the greatest authors of French police novels, Maurice Leblanc was born in Rouen in the second empire to a ship-owning father. Considered as the *'French Conan Doyle'* [1] He was the creator of the personality **Arsène Lupin,** the *'Gentleman burglar'*, who inspired film makers and the writers of popular songs. He wrote him into his adventures in over 50 works of which a certain number are set in Normandy such as in **'l'Aiguille creuse'** where the intrigue takes place in *Etretat*.

Places to see...

Dieppe :

= **Castle of Gueures** where the writer lived.

Etretat :

= **The famous 'aiguille'** where Maurice Leblanc fixed the reference point of Arsène Lupin.

The **'Clos Lupin'** his secondary residence where his grand-daughter Florence Leblanc still lives. 15, rue Guy-de Maupassant - Tel (33) 2 35 10 59 53.

The dwelling has been transformed into a landmark of the 'gentleman burglar', 'soldier of the old guard', faithful accomplice of Arsène Lupin watchman on their 'jobs'. He receives you and presents indispensable material for the discovery of a great game with the prince of thieves. There are eight stages to follow in an atmosphere which plunges you back to the beginning of the century and into the imagination of Maurice Leblanc.

Open to the public from 2nd January to 31st March and from 1st October to 30th December, Fridays, Saturdays, Sundays and Mondays and school holidays from 11 am-5 pm. From 1st April to 30th September : every day from 10 am-6 pm. Shop accessible without entry to the exhibition.

---

(1) In several novels his heroes find themselves confronted by an English detective... *'Herlock Sholmes'*. *'Vélocipédiste émérite'* he loved to roam from Rouen to the coast, taking the little winding roads of Upper Normandy.

Jumièges :

= The large house where the adolescent writer spent his holidays. This dwelling is situated opposite the abbey and today houses the Syndicat d'Initiatve and the Post Office.

Emile Chartier called 'Alain' (1868-1951)[1] - He said *'I meditate as a peasant of Normandy, not as a city dweller...'* A Professor of Philosophy, he inspired by his ideas, a humanism, drawing heavily from the Ancient Greek, a whole generation of thinkers and men of politics (Radicals). Young holder of the aggregation, he was appointed to *Avranches*. His career moved to *Rouen* to the prestigious 'Lycée Corneille' and then to the Lycée Henri IV in *Paris* where he taught for more than twenty years. *Mortagne-au-Perche*, his native town, where his father worked as a veterinarian, organises each year a literary event in his honour.

Places to see...

Mortagne :

= **'Musée Alain'** - The office of the philosopher has been reconstructed there. Maison des Comtes de Perche, 8, rue du Portail Saint-Denis, Tel (33) 2 33 25 25 87. Free entry.

Gaston Leroux (1868-1927) - The creator of **'Rouletabille'** claimed to be a direct descendent of... William of Normandy. After having spent his youth in *Le Tréport* and spent time at the desks of the College of *Eu*, he passed a degree in law in *Paris* and became a lawyer. Very quickly he abandoned the Bar to become a journalist in the major Parisian journals and then a judicial commentator. He became a 'great reporter' and inspired by his experience he wrote his first novels and notably **'Le Mystère de la Chambre Jaune'** which remains his major work He created there the character of **Rouletabille**, a sort of *'Tintin'* of the period before creating that of **Chéri-Bibi.**

Louis Beuve (1869-1949) **called 'Maît'Louis'** - Born at *Quetreville-sur-Sienne*, this bookseller poet nursed an unbounded passion for Normandy and became one of the leading Norman militants. Creator of the journal 'l'Unité Normande' and the revue 'Le Bouais-Jan', author of a 'hymn to Normandy', he celebrated there the 'Northmen' its founders. His dialect was that of Lessay. Several pieces that he wrote to the glory of our dear province count among the major works of our dialectal literature and reflect a rich sensitivity. An unfinished autobiographical novel : 'La Lettre à la morte' shows in him a man of great dreams whose ambition was to 'renormanise' Normandy.

Places to see...

Lessay :

= **A monument** recalling the memory of this great Norman poet.

André Gide (1869-1951) - The celebrated author of the **'Immoraliste'**, the **'Nourritures terrestres'** (1897) and **'Les Caves du Vatican'** (1914) lived in the Pays d'Auge where there remain numerous reminders of him.

---

(1) He took his pseudonym of *'Alain'* from Alain Chartier, originally from Bayeux, poet to the court of Charles VI.

Formentin :

= **Castle :** which was immortalised by Gide under the name of 'Quartefouche". One can see, beside the road, a small building in stone and brick called the 'Pavillon d'Isabelle' which sheltered, according to the work of Gide, the clandestine romances of Louise de Saint-Alban with a gentleman from the neighbourhood.

La Roque-Baignard :

= **Castle :** it was bought by the grand-father of André Gide in 1846. Gide lived there up to the beginning of the 20th century. He pictured La Roque under the name of 'La Morinière' in the book 'L'Immoraliste' and in 'Feuillets d'Automne". La Morinière is in fact the name of a manor in the area. André Gide was Mayor of this community from 1896 to 1900.

Marcel Proust (1871-1922) - This idle society dandy came to Cabourg for the first time in 1891. He fell in love with the town and liked to stay there to recharge his batteries. From 1907 to 1914, he spent every summer in Cabourg which he pictured in his works under the name of 'Balbec'. He stayed at the 'Grand Hôtel'. In 1913 he published **'Du côté de chez Swann'** which marked the beginning of a series entitled : **'A la recherche du temps perdu'** (In search of lost time).

Cabourg :

= **The 'Grand Hôtel',** magnificent palace where the memory of Marcel Proust still lingers. **The sea-wall promenade :** along which the writer loved to walk.

Edouard Herriot (1872-1957) - French man of politics but also a man of letters and a writer, the **'Président Herriot'** was fiercely attached to the region of Lyon - he was **Mayor of Lyon** for 50 years ! - and we would not try to pass him off as a 'pure-bred' Norman but we allow ourselves to cite the admirable pages that he gives over to Lower Normandy in his work : **'Dans la Forêt Normande'**. Previous president of the Council, president of the Chamber of Deputies, several times a minister under the III and IV Republics, he wrote this work in 1925 after a health 'cure' at *Bagnoles-de-l'Orne*. Falling visibly 'in love' with this corner of 'bocage' he made a magnificent description.

Bagnoles-de-l'Orne, La Ferté-Macé and Domfront, in Orne. Walk in the Andaine forest in the footsteps of Edouard Herriot.

Lucie Delarue-Mardrus (1880-1945) - Daughter of a lawyer, this great 'poetess' was born in Honfleur. A 'liberated woman' before her time, she went to Paris and celebrated Normandy there with passion. The 'Norman George Sand' was the author of the exquisite verse 'L'odeur de mon pays était dans une pomme'.

Honfleur :

= **A commemorative plaque in rue des Capucins.**

<u>André Maurois</u> (1885-1967) - Elected last year as **'Norman writer of the century'** by the readers of the great regional daily paper **'Paris Normandie'**, Emile Herzog was born in *Elbeuf*, industrial neighbouring town of Rouen where his father directed a textile factory.

Influenced by 'Alain' of whom he was a pupil at the Lycée Corneille in Rouen, he chose, initially, at one and the same time to follow his father as the head of the family enterprise and literature. He published in 1918 under the pseudonym of André Maurois his first book : **'Les Silences du Colonel Bramble'**. This work was inspired by his experiences as an interpreter among the British armed forces during the First World War. A French Academician he would publish a great number of works of different types : biographies, novels, essays, historical studies (he was the author of a **'History of England'**), news and an anthology of memories.

Elbeuf :

The industrial zones where the author observed the worlds of the employers and the Norman working class.

<u>Jean Mallard, 'Vicomte de la Varende'</u> (1887-1959) - Was it for his monarchist tendencies, nostalgia for a world gone by, or even his attitude, that some judged 'equivocal'', during the last war with regard to the German occupation ? Always the work of one of our greatest writers, voice of the *Pays d'Ouche*, his work is still today victim of an unacceptable censorship, practically absent from library shelves and school schedules.

Inheritor of a great line of Norman nobility the origins of which are lost with those of the Duchy, **'Jean Balthazar Malard, Baron Agis de Saint-Denis, Comte de la Varende'** was born at the **Castle of Bonneville** in the community of *Chamblac* in **Eure**.

He spent all his life there in 'seclusion' giving himself over to his writing but also to his 'dear' ship models that he built to relax and to dream. For more than sixty years he declared his monarchist ideas and carried the flame for the Norman autonomists, for the defense of the identity of the Norman nation and its culture.

Historian and story teller he expressed his passion for the Pays d'Ouche, in which he showed its least known corners in several works which were among his major works and notably **'Nez de Cuir', 'Pays d'Ouche',** and **'L'homme aux gants de toile'.** Having fallen literally under the charm of 'Marie-Anne Charlotte de Corday d'Armont', better known by the name of 'Charlotte Corday', born at Champeaux-en-Auge, who assassinated Marat and was guillotined in 1793, he dedicated to her, who he considered as the 'Norman Joan of Arc', an astonishing work in 1936 and organised the same year in Vimoutiers, on a really popular front a 'Congrès Charlotte Corday'.

'Guillaume le Bâtard' is one of his best historical works as also, in tourist terms, his guide to Normandy called : 'A l'ombre des Pommiers en fleurs' is totally remarkable.

Places to see...

Le Chamblac in Eure near to **Broglie :**

= **The Castle of Bonneville** which is still the property of his family. (Visits only in groups and by request to Madame de la Varende).

= **The little parish church,** where 'Monsieur le Vicomte' took part in the mass, has been the talk of the town for many years. It was in effect the refuge of traditionalists from when an elderly Anglican priest of Norman origin : **'l'abbé Montgomery-Wright'** became the incumbent.

Jacques de Lacretelle (1888-1996) - French Academician, author of **'Silberman'** lived in **'Château d'O'**, near to **Mortrée,** beautiful renaissance property having belonged to François d'O, which he restored with his wife.

Places to see...

Mortrée :

= **'Château d'O' :** (private property).

André Breton (1896-1966) - The 'eulogist' of surrealism was born here.

Tinchebray :

Poet, storyteller, enthusiast of psychoanalysis, he was with **Aragon** one of the founders of the Review 'Littérature'. In 1924 he published his **'Manifeste du surréalisme'.**

Armand Salacrou (1899-1989) - Born in **Rouen,** Armand Salacrou died in Le Havre at the age of 90 in his famous **'Villa Maritime',** sited facing the sea. Prolific author of plays for the theatre, Goncourt academician, he was also the most inventive advertising person of his era. He remains the French dramatist most often performed in the theatres around the whole world. He wrote two plays linked to Le Havre : **'Les Fiancés du Havre'** in 1944 and **'Boulevard Durand'** in 1961.

Places to see...

Rouen, rue Grand-Pont : The birthplace of Salacrou.

Le Havre :

= **The 'Villa Maritime'** where Armand Salacrou ended his fascinating life in deep despair after having 'skimmed through' the century.

Jacques Prévert (1900-1977) - A poet and author of numerous popular songs (with notably the musician Joseph Kosma). A script-writer, he collaborated with Carné, Renoir, Gremillon on films which are today among the major works of French cinema sich as **'Drôle de Drame'** (1937) or **'Les Visiteurs du Soir'** a film made in 1942 under the occupation.

Prévert discovered La Hague in the 1930's and decided to live there permanenetly in 1970. He is buried close to the village church with his wife and daughter. His humble house became the property of the region of La Manche in 1993. His wife had made the wish that it should become a meeting place.

Places to see...

Omonville-la-Petite :
Community where the writer died and is buried. 'Maison - Musée Jacques Prévert'. 'Le Val' - Tel (33) 2 33 52 72 38.
Open to the public : School holidays : every day from 1-6 pm. March : Sundays from 1-6 pm. April to the end of May and October : every day from 1-6 pm. June to the end of September : every day from 11 am-7 pm.

Raymond Queneau (1903-1976) - A writer born in Le Havre, member of the Goncourt Academy, Director of the prestigious Pleiad Encyclopedia, he had a great success with **'Zazie dans le Métro'**. 'Virtuoso alchemist of laughter and gravity, keeping himself resolutely outside all literary movements, this disruptive child of pleasant words and verbal invention…'.

Georges Simenon (1903-1989) - This great writer of detective stories, creator of the character of **'Commissaire Maigret'**, who was also the author of plays for the theatre, of narratives and news stories, stayed in *Ouistreham* where he wrote **'Port des Brumes'**.

Marguerite Duras (1914-1996) - French author and film writer marked by her childhood in Indochina, she was the author of numerous novels and plays for the theatre. In the 1960's she discovered Trouville-sur-Mer and fell under the charm of this Norman seaside town. She came to stay there regularly in her apartment in Roches Noires, bought in 1963. She made it one of her favourite places for writing. She wrote : *'It is in Trouville that I have looked at the sea until there was nothing… When I move away from Trouville, I have the feeling of losing the light ! Not only the true light of full sunshine but also that sooty light of the storm…'*

André Castelot - *'Napoléon of letters'*, journalist, writer, dramatist, man of radio and television, André Castelot is one of the most prolific French historians. He has been chosen for his skills to put in place numerous 'son et lumière' spectacles across the world.
Founding President of the Society for Authors and Creative Artists of Normandy, he lives in Eure, in the region of Vernon, not far from the Seine.
His writing includes more than fifty historical works without speaking of the collections and other publications. He is, with **Alain Decaux,** the author of the **'Dictionnaire de l'Histoire de France'** (1979). He is also the craftsman behind a series of biographies on the Bonaparte family and notably one of **'Napoléon Bonaparte'** in ten volumes.

Gilles Perrault - Gilles Perrault has lived at *Sainte-Marie-du-Mont* since 1961. Previous student of the Institute of Political Studies and a graduate in law, he spent five years as a lawyer at the Bar in Paris before turning to writing with **'Les Parachutistes'** (1961). In 1964, **'Le Secret du Jour J'** awarded a prize by the Comité d'action de la Résistance, became an international best-seller. Other works have been a success and will be adapted to the screen such as **'Le Pull-**

over rouge'. In **'Les Gens d'ici'**, Gilles Perrault has re-orchestrated the collective saga of the inhabitants of *Sainte-Marie-du-Mont*.

Didier Decoin - Romantic story teller, script-writer, one of his works was rewarded in 1977 with the Prix Goncourt. He owns a house where he stays frequently in *Auderville* in North Cotentin.

To know more :

= **La 'Route des Maisons d'Ecrivains'** (The tour of writers houses) tourist tour. Leaflet available in Tourist Offices.

= **Literary walks in Trouville.** For information : guided visits in English - Tel (33) 2 31 14 60 70.

= **The Society of Norman writers** : President : Claude Le Roy, 1, rue des Marettes, 14760 Bretteville-sur-Odon.

= **The Society of Authors and Creative Artists of Normandy** : President : Jean-Philppe Deflorène, Espace des Prés, rue des Prés, 27950 Saint-Marcel.

These two societies organise or participate in numerous book fairs in Normandy.

2 - The Normandy of painters

If Normandy has given birth to a great number of painters, whose talent has not always, unfortunately, been recognised for its true value, it has also from west to east and from north to south, accommodated a great number of renowned artists who have come to the area to grasp the bright colours and contrasting countryside, the places of interest, the outline of a variety and wealth of incredible monuments but also to catch the astonishing light, the nuances, so special to Normandy, the greens which come from the heart of the hedged farmland, the forests and the changing blues of the sea and the sky which have attracted virtually all the masters of impressionism to the region.

= **The estuary of the Seine**[1] and **the beaches of the Floral Coast** were especially, in the years around 1830-1840 the privileged places where they loved to be, the little port of *Honfleur* being able to consider itself during this era as **the capital of the impressionists**. More generally Normandy has played a primordial role in French painting of the 19th century. It also welcomed the majority of English 'romantic' painters.

In the 20th century, Normandy, with painters such as **Dufy** or **Léger** has participated greatly in the search for and discovery of new forms of pictorial expression. Among these painters, we can cite :

Nicolas Poussin (1594-1665) - Born in **the hamlet of Villers** in the **Andelys**, he passed a great part of his life in Rome where he died. Embodying in himself the 'French classicism' he was greatly inspired in his works by the holy writings and by antiquity. His paintings are exhibited in the Louvre, in Lille and in Dijon but also in the British Museum and at Windsor.

---

(1) Provence and the estuary of the Seine are without doubt the two places in France most captured by painters.

Les Andelys : in Eure, where he was born :

= **Musée Nicolas Poussin.** The canvas 'Le coriolan' is exhibited there. Rue Sainte-Clotilde - Tel (33) 2 32 54 31 78.

William Turner (1775-1851) - Draughtsman and watercolour artist then painter, William Turner was born in Covent Garden, in England. From his manner of painting nature he can be considered as the father of Impressionism. The light, whatever the subject painted, is always the essential element of his paintings. It is said that he produced more than 20,000 canvasses ! In Normandy he painted in *Dieppe* and *Rouen*. Monet was influenced by him.

Fifty years before Impressionism, Turner was inspired by the atmosphere and the spectacle of the Seine Valley. Six journeys, made between 1802 and 1832 allowed him to discover the most hidden places. The majority of the paintings done in Normandy are exhibited in the Tate Gallery in London.

Théodore Gericault (1791-1824) - The author of the celebrated and immense canvas **'Le Radeau de la Méduse'** which one can see in the Palais du Louvre was originally from the area of *Mortain.*

Jean-Baptiste Camille Corot (1796-1875) - Famous talented colourist and landscape artist, Corot came often to *Vimoutiers* in Orne to paint the countryside of the Pays d'Auge. He also set up his easel in the area of *Mortain* where he stayed with his friends Deblain in Bourberouge.

Corot also lived, on several occasions, in the years from 1833 to 1866, at *Saint-Lô*. He painted the town and the surrounding countryside. The major part of his paintings are today exhibited in the Louvre but two among them are presented at the 'Musée des Beaux Arts'.

Jean-François Millet (1814-1875) - Son of a peasant, Jean-François Millet was born in the North Cotentin at *Gréville-Hague*. The works which have made him world famous are 'L'Angelus' and 'les Glaneuses'. We also owe to him some magnificent works dedicated to la Hague and la Manche. Millet was much influenced by Vincent Van Gogh. He was the only Master that he recognised.

Places to see...

Gréville-Hague :

= **'La Maison de Jean-François Millet'.** 'The feet on the land, the view of the sea. Jean-François Millet evoked his native village as a sensitive and beautiful place'. 'One has at a glance, in front of you, the great marine view and a horizon without limits'. You are at *Gruchy*, native country of the celebrated painter. Behind Gréville-Hague, two steps from the rocks and the open sea, is his house today restored on the initiative of the 'Conseil Général de la Manche'. Jean-François Millet was born there on 4th October 1814. 'At the sources of sensitivity', he took from there a great part of his inspiration. The visit to this house is not like a visit to a Museum. It is for the visitor to discover a place of memories and thus to take in the ambiance of the places, of the family context and of this region at one time harsh and exceptionally beautiful to better understand how la Hague and its inhabitants so strongly inspired this genius painter throughout his existence. In the course of the visit of about 45 minutes, a video presentation retraces the life and work of the artist followed by a visit to the house of his birth. Tel (33) 2 33 01 81 91. Fax (33) 2 33 01 81 94. E.Mail : musee.greville@wanadoo.fr

Gustave Courbet (1819-1877) - In opposition to the **'romanticism'**, he was at the head of the **'realist'** movement. His works and his social opinions offended a good number of his contemporaries. He loved to paint the sea, the cliffs and the pebbles of *Etretat* but also the hedged farmlands of the Bocage at *Mortain*. He enjoyed meeting again his painter friends in Normandy. A deep friendship united him with Maupassant.

Eugène Boudin (1824-1898) - The most Norman of the great painters was born in Honfleur at 33, rue Bourdet, with a father who was a naval officer. Painting as nobody else the country-sides, precursor of the impressionists, he always remained faithful to Normandy and painted principally the country and the sea. Close friend of Millet, Courbet and Corot, who called him 'the king of the skies", he was the first to set up his easel in the open air. He transmitted this new pleasure to Monet, whom he had met in *Le Havre*. His first exhibition took place in this town in 1850. He liked, in the latter years of his life, to paint scenes of the worldly and bourgeois life which had developed in *Trouville* and *Deauville*.

Places to see…

Saint-Lô :
= **Works exhibited in the Municipal Museum.**

Vimoutiers :
= **'La Cour des Miracles'**, at the place called 'La Hunière' where the artist, many times, set up his easel, conquered by the site.

Le Havre :
= **'Le Musée des Beaux-Arts'** where some of his works are exhibited. In the surroundings of *Le Havre :* **'La Vallée de Rouelles'**, where the artist loved to paint. He trained the young Monet there.

Honfleur :
= **'Le Musée Eugène Boudin'**, place Erick Satie, where many of the artists works are presented. Tel (33) 2 31 89 54 00.
= **The commemorative plaque,** rue Bourdet.
= **The Saint-Siméon farm :** this was a privileged meeting place for artists. This ancient inn has become a very 'high-class' restaurant.

Camille Pissarro (1830-1884) - Influenced by Corot, he was one of the masters of the impressionist group. His talent was not recognised until after his death. *Rouen* was for him a source of great inspiration. He considered the Norman capital as 'as beautiful as Venice'.

Places to see...

Gisors :
= **The ancient centre** where Pissarro set up his easel to paint market scenes.

Le Havre :
= **The works of the artist** are exhibited in the '**Musée des Beaux-Arts'**.

Rouen :
= **'Le Quai de la Bourse'** where the artist lived and the **'Hôtel d'Angleterre'** where he painted the Seine and its commercial port.

<u>**Jean-Théodore Fantin-Latour**</u> (1836-1904) - This great painter and lithographist was established in *Bures* in Orne where he died.

<u>**Alfred Sisley**</u> (1839-1899) - English painter of the French school, he was one of the masters of impressionist countryside. He lived for a long time in France and especially in Normandy, loving to paint beside the rivers. His art, having not been recognised while he was alive, he lived and died in poverty.

Places to see...

Rouen :
= **The 'Le Musée des Beaux-Arts'** : which exhibits at least one of his works.

<u>**Claude Monet**</u> (1840-1926). **Claude Oscar**, better known under the name of **Claude Monet** spent his childhood in *Le Havre* where his parents lived from 1845. He sold his first drawings in an art shop in the town where they were noticed by a certain Eugène Boudin who encouraged the young artist to continue and to work with nature. In Normandy, he refined his talent in working notably with **Jongkind**, at whom he marvelled. After having experienced the pangs of the 'bohemian life' in Paris, he became little by little the leader of **the impressionists**. Seeking to express 'light and its effects by colour' he loved especially to paint water and the sea in all its facets. Returning to live in *Le Havre* in 1866, he lived thanks to the generosity of his aunt, his friends and the family **Gaudibert** and did not really know success until the end of his life.

During the war of 1870, he took refuge in London where he developed his friendship with Pissarro and discovered Turner. He painted London and the Thames. After having shared his life, for thirty years, between the Paris region and Normandy in 1883 he fell in love with the little village of *Giverny*, in Eure and decided to settle there. Thanks to his first major gains, he rented a property irrigated by two watercourses, the Epte and the Ru. It took him many years to cultivate there an **'extraordinary garden'** in the heart of which he came each day to set up his easel. He created the famous **'basin aux nymphéas'** principle source of his inspiration (**he produced over 200 canvasses there !).** Henceforth he did not stop painting, leaving his garden only for the cathedral of *Rouen* to which he devoted a passion without limits and to which he dedicated an important series of canvasses. At *Giverny,* he received his friends **Renoir, Sisley and Pissarro** as well as his neighbour **Clemenceau,** the 'father of victory'. Artists came from all over Europe, and even from as far away as America, to set up in

Giverny, near to the **Master**. The Americans discovered him and lit a flame which has still not been extinguished. As a business man, he showed himself to be a generous man to his painter friends in need.

Places to see…

Caen :
= **His works exhibited in the 'Musée des Beaux-Arts'.**

Honfleur :
= **The quays** where the artist loved to set up to paint the port and the estuary.
= **The farm of Saint-Siméon** where he lunched frequently with his friends.
= **The 'Auberge du Cheval-Blanc'**, near to the Lieutenance, where he lived.

Trouville :
= **The beach** which inspired the artist towards the end of the second Empire. He stayed frequently in a little hotel in the **'Rue des Bains'** but also at the **'Hôtel des Roches Noires'**, a magnificent building, today divided into apartments.

Giverny in *Eure :*
= **The Monet Gardens.** In 1883, Monet went to live at Giverny and make there the cradle of Impressionism. In 1890 he acquired the 'pink house with the green shutters' where he set up his workshop and created his gardens. Close to the Seine, the **'Musée Monet'** is one of the most visited places in Normandy, notably by overseas visitors among whom the Anglo-Saxons are in the first rank. The house has been entirely restored as it was in the time of Monet and the garden has retained all its magic.
= **'Musée d'Art américain de Giverny'.** 99, rue Claude Monet - Tel (33) 2 32 51 94 67 - Fax (33) 2 32 51 94 67. www.fondation-monet.com
Privileged place of American art in France. Its collection gathers together paintings produced by American impressionists in France and especially at Giverny from the time of Monet.
The museum also presents exhibitions of American art from all eras. Numerous cultural events are also offered.
= **'Fondation Claude-Monet'.** His house and garden. 84, rue Claude-Monet - Tel (33) 2 32 51 28 21. The house and gardens are normally open from 1st April to 31st October from 9.30 am-6 pm. Closed on Mondays - Special opening on public holidays on a Monday. It is not a guided visit and correct dress is required. Animals are not accepted.

Etretat :
= **The Beach** where the artist came frequently to set up and paint and where he passed some time with his wife and son Jean.
= **The Upper Normandy countryside of** *Fécamp, Dieppe, Pourville* (he stayed at the **'Hôtel du Casino'**) and *Varengeville* inspired Monet.

Rouen :
= **The cathedral** to which he dedicated several exceptional canvasses. He set himself up over several months in various apartments opposite the building to paint it in different lights and from differing facets.

= **'Musée des Beaux-Arts'.** Some works of the artist are exhibited there.

Sainte-Adresse, facing the sea :

= **The house of his aunt** which assured him of board and lodging. She had the appropriate name of : Madame Lecadre. (Le cadre - the frame).

Albert Lebourg (1849-1928) - Born at *Montfort-sur-Risle*, in Eure and died in Le Havre, this artist, influenced by the impressionists, painted numerous canvasses on the banks of the Seine. He was the leading light of the **'Ecole Rouennaise',** created by a group of young students from the Ecole des Beaux-Arts of Rouen.

Jacques-Emile Blanche (1861-1942) - 'Everything in the work of Blanche breathes the Norman countryside' wrote one of the most fervent admirers of his painting. He was much inspired by *Offranville* and *Dieppe* where he lived for more than forty years. He remains one of the great masters of Norman impressionism.

Places to see…

Offranville :

= **'Musée J.-E. Blanche'.** Maison du Parc du Colombier. Open from Easter to the end of September, Sundays and national holidays from 2.30-6 pm. Other days of the year by appointment. Tel (33) 2 35 85 40 42.

Rouen :

= **'Musée des Beaux-Arts',** several works exhibited.

Charles Léandre (1862-1934) - A truly Norman artist born in the heart of the Andaine forest. Painter of the 'Norman spirit', Léandre is principally known for his caricatures in the Parisian journals of the 'Belle Epoque' but he was also a 'realist' painter of great talent and his works are dispersed in various museums and Town Halls in the region of Orne. *(Flers, La Ferté-Macé, Alençon, Domfront...)*, and the area of Calvados *(Condé-sur-Noireau)*.

Paul Signac (1863-1935) - This neo-impressionist painter stayed in *Barfleur* from 1930 to 1935.

Places to see…

Barfleur :

= **Plaque on the artist's house.**

Raoul Dufy (1877-1953) - Born in *Le Havre*, this painter, engraver and designer today internationally known and recognised, was initially influenced by impressionism then turning successively towards fauvism and then cubism before finding his own style. Illustrator of the books of Guillaume Apollinaire, he was also a designer of clothes. His seascapes and notably his scenes of races and regattas, figure among his greatest works.

Places to see…

One can admire some of his 'Norman' works in the **Museum of Dieppe,** the **Museum of Caen** and the **'Musée des Beaux-Arts'** of **Rouen.**

Othon Friesz (1877-1953) - Born in *Le Havre*, this painter and engraver, former pupil of the school of Fine Arts of Le Havre, was one of the founding artists of fauvism. His mastery of line is particularly strong.

Pablo Picasso (1881-1973) - At *Gisors*, in the département of Eure, at the place called 'Le Boisgeloup', is a property of the great painters family called 'Le Château de Picasso'. The artist stayed there from 1930 to 1936, a period during which he concentrated principally on sculptures.

Fernand Léger (1881-1955) - Fernand Léger was born in *Argentan*, in Orne, in a bourgeois house which the town has acquired with the intention of opening it to the public. His first period was influenced by Cézanne then he moved closer to the cubists before finding a very personal style which has made him a celebrity in world terms. He painted pictures but also made stained glass windows and immense ceramic works.

Places to see...

Saint-Lô in *Manche :*

= **The mosaic of the French United States Memorial Hospital.** Built in the 1950's thanks to donations from the United States, this general hospital benefits from a functional and aesthetic architecture. A huge mosaic by Fernand Léger on one of the façades pays homage to Franco-American friendship.

Lisores in *Calvados :*

= **'Ferme Fernand Léger'** : country house of the artist transformed into a museum: stained glass, ceramics.

Argentan in *Orne :*

= **House where the artist was born**. At the **General Hospital**, rue Aristide-Briand, which has been recently renovated, the colours of the façades, walls and interior doors, the bed covers, the uniforms of the nurses have been, on the initiative of the Director, Michel Renaut, inspired by the primary colours used by the artist and one of his ceramic works adorns a wall in the entrance hall.

Georges Braque (1882-1963) - Arriving at the age of eight in *Le Havre*, where his family settled, he would pass all his childhood in this town to which he remained attached throughout his life. Student of the School of Fine Arts in Le Havre, he moved to Paris at the turn of the century where he started to paint...

He was one of the first 'fauvists' then giving himself over to cubism, painting principally still-life.

Places to see...

Dieppe :

= **In the museum :** works by the artist.

Varengeville, *maritime cemetery :*

= **Funeral monument.**

Jean Dubuffet (1901-1985) - Painter, sculptor, writer, prophet of 'natural art' born in *Le Havre*. After having been a wine salesman, he carried out a considerable work, illustrating his refusal of all cultural institutions.

Raymond Savignac (1907-2002) - This genius of the poster left Paris more than a quarter of a century ago to set up his 'atelier' at *Trouville-sur-Mer* where after having worked for the major brands he still agrees to do some designs for the promotion of the seaside town.

André Lemaître (1909-1998) - This teacher born in *Falaise* became aware of his passion for painting when he discovered the work of Cézanne.

With a very individual style, he set to painting with a frenetic pleasure. His preferred themes are Normandy... and the Normans.

Places to see...

Falaise : '**Musée André Lemaître**' (open since May 2000).

Michel Ciry - Engraver, designer, figurative artist, composer and writer, Michel Ciry was born in *La Baule* in 1919. He studied at the School of Applied Arts in Paris and engraved his first copper work at the age of 16. A great part of his engravings were dedicated to the illustration of literary texts. The relationship between the written word and graphic work interested Michel Ciry from 1942 with 'La Reine morte' of Henry de Montherlant, it would be followed by the illustration of numerous works where the thoughts of the artist were married to that of the writer.

And of sculptors...

In the region of *Argentan*, *in Orne* :

Jean Goujon (1510-1564) - This great artist was picked out by François 1st when he lived with his sister in the castle of *Argentan*. He had him come to Paris where Goujon became one of the great sculptors of his time. His art was influenced by Italy and antiquity. He made the fountain of the Innocents in Paris.

Arthur le Duc (1848-1918) - Animal sculptor of great renown, friend of Millet.

Torigni-sur-Vire : a museum in the castle is dedicated to him.

****

Honfleur/Town of painters

The English landscape painters had 'landed' in Honfleur at the beginning of the 19th century. Bonington and Turner were there alongside Corot, Paul Huet and Isabey with whom they shared this pleasure of painting 'in the open air'.

Thus they criss-crossed Normandy, their sketch pads under their arms, the sights, and the colours offered by the old province, enchanting them. The Barbizon school had imitators who came to enlarge the ranks of the artists holidaying in Honfleur.

From 1855, under the influence of Boudin, a 'raw' painter of the new school (Ecole de Saint Siméon) was created in Honfleur. It would have a decisive influence over the evolution of 19th century painting.

In Honfleur the painters gathered together to work but also to spend good times together. Up to the war of 1870 many painters came to work there including Charles Daubigny, Duprés, Courbet, Diaz, Bazille, Sisley, Whistler, Harpignies...

The revolution happened around Boudin, Jongkind and Monet. It is especially the study of the sky, its reflections, its colours, that the three painters devoted themselves in Honfleur, beginning with Boudin, the 'King of the heavens'. This school later inspired the 'pointillism' and then 'fauvism'.

****

Museums that cannot be missed

AREA OF MANCHE

Cherbourg-Octeville :

= **'Musée des Beaux-Arts Thomas Henry'**. Rue Vastel - Tel (33) 2 33 23 39 30. This museum, created in 1830, contains treasures of great quality which go back to the origins of the great contemporary painters. Its main interest remains in the collection of works of **Jean-François Millet**, born in **Cherbourg**, 'painter of the humble'.

Coutances :

= **'Musée'**. 2, rue Quesnel-Morinière - Tel (33) 2 33 45 11 92. Paintings from the 17th and 20th centuries - Sculptures from the mediaeval era, and from the 19th and 20th centuries.

Saint-Lô :

= **'Musée des Beaux-Arts'**. Place du Champ de Mars - Tel (33) 2 33 72 52 55. Founded in 1835, the 'Musée des Beaux-Arts de Saint-Lô' was entirely destroyed during the Second World War. Only some paintings and tapestries put in shelter ,were preserved. The new museum, opened in 1989 inside the 'Centre Culturel Jean Lurçat' allows henceforth, in a surrounding of modern architecture to honour rich collections : the wall hangings of the loves Gombault and Macée made up of eight tapestries dating from 1600, great tapestries from the 18th and 20th centuries of which six are by **Jean Lurçat,** paintings of the great masters from the 19th century : **Corot,** (*'Homère et les Bergers'* from 1845, *'l'Etang'* from 1868), **Boudin** (*'Coucher de Soleil'* from 1884), **Millet** (*'Académie'* from 1836, Gustave Moreau (*'La mort de Sapho'* from 1871)... In the graphic arts section : works by **Géricault, Gustave Doré**...

AREA OF CALVADOS

Bayeux :

= **'Musée Baron Gérard'**. Place de la Liberté - Tel (33) 2 31 92 14 21 - Fax (33) 2 31 51 60 51. Open every day except 25th December and 1st January. From 1st June to 15th September from 9 am-7 pm. From 16th September to 31st May from

10 am-12.30 pm and from 2-6 pm. From Italian and Dutch 'primitives' to impressionism, the works of **Philippe de Champaigne, Boucher, David, Gros, Gérard, Corot, Boudin, Caillebotte and Cross** punctuate strongly the prestigious collection of paintings of the museum with which one must associate the names of great art lovers, among those of the Baron Gérard.

Caen :
 = **'Musée des Beaux-Arts'**. Within the Ducal Castle. This beautiful museum - **one of the most important in France** - displays paintings and ancient engravings. A very rich collection of paintings from the 15th to the 20th century. The most beautiful works exhibited are : *'La Tentation de saint Antoine'* of **Véronèse**, *'Abraham et Melchisédech'* of **Rubens**, *'La mort d'Adonis'* of **Nicolas Poussin**... Destroyed during the Battle of Normandy when it was in the 'Hôtel de Ville', the Caen Museum of Fine Arts reopened its doors in 1970 in the ramparts of the Ducal castle. 'In 1994, the rehabilitation of the place honours light and monumentality. The museum today offers a multiple structure which gives successively places of meditation and enjoyment, of study and culture, of relaxation and conviviality'.

The museum has one of the richest collections of paintings of the provincial museums for the 16th and 17th centuries, Italian, French, Flemish and Dutch **(Cosimo Tura, Le Pérugin, Véronèse, Tintoretto, Le Guerchin, Giordano, Poussin, Philippe de Champaigne, Rubens...)** presenting several major works of world painting.

The 18th century is represented there through the French and Italian portrait and landscape artists **(Rigaud, Tournières, Boucher, Lancret, Tiepolo)** while the 19th century unfolds around the romantic painters such as **Géricault, Chasseriau, Courbet, Isabey and again Corot and the landscape artists of Barbizon.**

Normandy as a place of inspiration is equally present through the works of **Monet, Boudin, Lebourg** then through the impressionism of **Vuilard, Bonnard, Marquet, Dufy.**

The 20th century stands out with a beautiful collection from the French cubists **(Gleizes, Villon, Metzinger)** and, for the contemporary period, by the presence of **Joan Mitchell, Vieira da Silva, Tobey, Soulages, Frydman, Debré, Pincemin,** around the major themes which are allegory, space and light.

Alongside the prestigious collections of paintings are gathered some 600 pictures, the print room holds the remarkable Mancel collection which gathers together more than 50,000 engravings, presented in thematic or one-man exhibitions.

Finally, the museum possesses a very lovely collection of 'objets d'art' made up of pottery from Rouen, Nevers, Delft and Strasbourg, pieces of the goldsmith's art and French furniture from the 17th and 18th centuries.

The museum organises three temporary exhibitions each year. For information : Castle de Caen - Tel (33) 2 31 30 47 70 - Fax (33) 2 31 30 47 80. Open every day from 9.30 am-6 pm. - Closed Tuesdays and national holidays. Free for under 18's and for everyone each Sunday. Conference visits - Public Library of the History of Art - RMN Library shop - Auditorium - Meeting room - exhibition gallery - space for cocktail receptions.

Clécy :

= **'Musée Hardy'.** Place du Tripot - Tel (33) 2 31 69 79 95. For opening hours please ask at the Tourist Office. More than 100 pictures exhibited among which are the works of impressionist painter André Hardy (1887-1986) on Norman topics : the countryside of the Suisse Normande, scenes of life from former years, portraits and posters...

Honfleur :

= **'Musée Eugène Boudin de Honfleur'.** Place Erik-Satie - Rue de l'Homme de Bois - Tel (33) 2 31 89 54 00. Opening days and hours : from 15th March to 30th September every day (except Tuesdays) from 10 am-12 noon and from 2-6 pm. From 1st October to 15th March : every afternoon, except Tuesdays, from 2.30-5 pm and Saturdays and Sundays from 10 am-12 noon and from 2.30-5 pm.

Annual closure from 1st January to 8th February and 1st May, 14th July, 25th December and Tuesdays.

Founded in 1868 by Dubourg and Boudin, the Municipal Museum of Honfleur principally dedicated to 'painters of the estuary' and to that of the Saint Simeon School, was transferred in 1924 to the chapel of the ancient Convent of Augustine Sisters. It was enlarged in the 1970's thanks to the help of the patron of the arts : Madame Schlumbeger. The museum has eleven rooms. One can admire on the first floor, the works of four painters from Honfleur : **de Saint-Delis, J. Driès, P.-E. Gernez** and **F. Herbo.**

One room is given over to old paintings from 16th and 18th centuries **Jordaens, Quellin, Van Dyck,** and great canvasses from the 19th century.

On the third level, on a base of living canvass are grouped the works of contemporary painters linked to Honfleur : **Marais, Dufy, Friesz...**

On the ground floor the canvasses of artists from 19th century are presented : **Corot, Isabey, Huet** and of course, above all, **Boudin** who bequeathed a great number of his works to his native town. One also finds there, works of **Cals, Jongkind, Pecrus, Gernez.**

Lisieux :

= **'Eglise Saint-Jacques'.** Temporary exhibitions - Information from the Tourist Office or the Municipal cultural service.

Trouville :

= **'Musée Montebello'.** 64, rue du Général Leclerc. Tel (33) 2 31 88 16 26. Open to the public from mid-April to September, every day except Tuesday from 2-6 pm. Installed in a sumptuous villa from the Second Empire, the Museum Montebello pays homage to the landscape painter **Charles Mozin,** the contemporary painter **André Hambourg** and to the poster painter **Ramond Savignac.** Works of **Isabey, Raoul Dufy, Van Dingen, Honoré Daumier** (Cartoonist), a collection 'bains de mer', contemporary art.

Vire :
 = **'Musée Municipal'.** Ancien Hôtel-Dieu. Tableaux of **Charles Léandre** - Works of the brothers **Delavante**, painters from the region from the 18th century.

AREA OF ORNE

Alençon :
 = **'Musée des Beaux-Arts' :** Cour Carrée de la Dentelle, 12, rue Charles-Aveline.

Flers :
 = **'Musée des Beaux-Arts' :** In the castle - Open from April to October, every day from 10 am-12 noon and from 2-6 pm (except 1st May). Tel (33) 2 33 64 66 49. E.Mail : musee.flers@wordline.fr Free and guided visits - visits for the young - temporary exhibitions.

The Beaux-Arts section of the museum holds works from the 16th to the 20th century. The 19th century is particularly well represented with the Barbizon School (Corot, Daubigny), the impressionists (Boudin, Caillbotte, Lépine) as well as Norman artists such as Charles Léandres. The painter Jean-Victor Schnetz, whose family owned the château in the 19th century and who was Director of the Villa Médicis, is particularly honoured. Finally contemporary works such as the engravings of Chaudeurge, the ceramics of Cocteau complete the collections.

AREA OF EURE

Bernay :
 = **'Musée Municipal'.** Installed in the Abbey accommodation, a visit is a marvellous moment for any art lover. The museum presents rich collections of Rouen pottery from the 16th to the 19th century, pictorials of the French, Italian, Flemish and Dutch schools as well as furniture from the 17th and 18th centuries. The first floor has retained its original décor and its museology. It constitutes one of the last vestiges of a 'museography' in France. Place Guillaume de Volpiano. Tel (33) 2 32 46 63 23 - Fax (33) 2 32 44 13 99. Open from the first weekend of June to the beginning of September and during the Easter holidays every day except Tuesday from 10 am-12 noon and from 2-7.30 pm. From September to May, open every day except Tuesday from 10 am-12 noon and from 2-5.30 pm, Sundays from 3-5.30 pm.

Evreux :
 = **'Musée'.** 6, rue Charles-Corbeau. Tel (33) 2 32 31 81 92 - Fax (33) 2 32 62 66 86. Laid out in the old bishop's palace, this museum possesses some pieces of architecture and elements of mediaeval statuary art, paintings and furniture from the 17th and 18th centuries, a beautiful collection of paintings from the 19th century (Boudin, Lebourg, Géricault...) as well as a contemporary section uniting artists from surrealism to the abstract of the years 1950-1960. - Painters of the Rouen School. Open from Tuesday to Saturday from 10 am-12 noon and from 2-6 pm - Guided visit on request to the Tourist Office.(Tel (33) 2 32 24 04 43).

Giverny :

= **'Musée d'Art américain'**. *'Founded by Daniel J. Terra, a great lover of impressionist painting, the American Museum of Giverny proposes a cross-view between the works of American painters of the 19ᵗʰ and the beginning of the 20ᵗʰ centuries who came to work at Giverny and largely inspired by Monet and the works of French painters. The museum also proposes a discovery of American art in all its forms from the middle of 19ᵗʰ century to the modern day. These temporary exhibitions are the occasion to present new artistic horizons and young creative artists'*. Free visits from April to October, every day except Monday. Accessible for the disabled. For information. Tel (33) 2 32 51 39 31.

Louviers :

= **'Musée des Beaux-Arts'**. one finds here settings and costumes from the cinema.

Vernon :

= **'Musée Municipal Alphonse-Georges Poulain'** set out in a magnificent townhouse from the 16ᵗʰ century, this museum gathers together the very lovely collection of **Alphonse-Georges Poulain**, archaeologist and local historian. This museum is based on three themes : 'Animal art' of great originality in this place which has over 300 works on this theme. 'The artists of Giverny with numerous impressionist and post-impressionist works including several by **Monet**. A 'Cabinet de dessin' which offers notably the paintings and designs of **Théophile-Alexandre Steinlen**. Free visits throughout the year - For information : Tel (33) 2 32 21 28 09 - Fax (33) 2 32 51 11 17. Accessible for the disabled.

AREA OF SEINE-MARITIME

Dieppe :

= **'Château-Musée'**. Castle - Rue de Chastes. Tel (33) 2 35 84 19 76. In a building from the mediaeval era, paintings, engravings, regional archaeology, folklore from the Pays de Caux and Dieppe region, traditional furniture... Dutch paintings from the 16ᵗʰ and 17ᵗʰ centuries - French paintings from the 19ᵗʰ and 20ᵗʰ centuries including a collection of lithographs of **Georges Braque** - Collection of **Camille Saint-Saëns** -Works by **Gonzales, Lebourg, Boudin and Renoir**. Admire **'L'Avant-port de Dieppe'** of **Camille Pissarro**. Open every day from 1ˢᵗ June to 30ᵗʰ September from 10 am-12 noon and from 2-6 pm. From 1ˢᵗ October to 31ˢᵗ May every day except Tuesday from 10 am-12 noon and from 2-5 pm (6 pm on Sunday). Closed 1ˢᵗ January, 1ˢᵗ May, 1ˢᵗ November and 25ᵗʰ December.

Elbeuf :

= **'Musée'**. Place Aristide-Briand.

Fécamp :

= **'Musée des Arts et de l'Enfance'**, 21, rue Alexandre Legros - Tel (33) 2 35 28 31 99. See 'Rochers à Yport' by Schuffenecker (1851-1934).

Le Havre :

= **'Musée des Beaux-Arts André Malraux'.** 2, boulevard Clemenceau. Tel (33) 2 35 19 62 62 - Fax (33) 2 35 19 93 01. Open from Monday to Friday from 11 am-6 pm and Saturday and Sunday from 11 am 7 pm. Closed Tuesday. Visits with commentary - conferences - educational activities - Studios of artistic practice. The canvasses are marvellously lit. One can admire the 'classic' works of **Boudin, Corot, Manet, Dufy, Millet, Géricault, Courbet, Pissaro, Sisley, Degas, Fragonard, Fantin-Latour**, but also the contemporary works of **Léger**...

Rouen :

= **'Musée des Beaux-Arts'.** Square Verdrel - Tel (33) 2 35 71 28 40. Entirely renovated in recent years, it has become **one of the most beautiful museums of France**. The impressionist collection is reputed to be the most important outside Paris. This is thanks to a generous Rouen industrialist, François Depeaux, who bequeathed 53 canvasses of the master impressionists to the museum in 1909. You can admire one of the **'cathedrals'** of **Monet**. Decorative arts from the 15th to the 20th century - Works by **Clouet, Caravage, Velasquez, Poussin, Géricault...** Open every day from 10 am-6 pm except Tuesday and national holidays.

****

Impressionist itineraries in Normandy

To discover during a weekend the setting of an artistic movement which revolutionised painting at the end of the 19th century, six impressionist itineraries are suggested to the public in Seine-Maritime and in Eure. Guided by travel documents and above all by the reading of material reproducing the celebrated paintings inset opposite the countryside which inspired them, the visitor can feel the sentiments of the artist.

Tourist journey : Leaflets available from Tourist Offices or the Tourism Committees of Eure and Seine-Maritime.

****

'LES SALONS DE PEINTURE'

Numerous 'salons' of professional and amateur painters are organised throughout the year in Normandy. To obtain a list and the dates contact the Departmental Committees and Tourist Offices of Normandy.

GALLERIES

Also ask at the Tourist Offices of Normandy for a list with addresses.

The towns of **Granville, Caen, Honfleur, Alençon, Rouen** and **Le Havre** are richly endowed in this area.

IV - NORMAN ART

1 - Furniture

If each Norman 'pays' presents, from the **Bocage** to the **Plain of the Pays de Caux** and from the **Pays d'Auge** to **Perche,** there are notable differences in terms of habitat but also in the style of living. The majority of Normans, as far as the fitting out of the house, with the exception of the aristocrats (and yet!), have always leant towards regional habits and traditions by using furniture and objects made in the area. The cost of the materials, the artistic qualities of the work were thus dependent on the natural riches of the land or the wealth of the families.

In the image of the Province the Norman furniture maker is rich and prosperous.

If in the bourgeois setting, after the Revolution, there were comfortable houses, with several floors, in the country, quite the contrary, all the life of the family revolved around a single central room with the fireplace as its principal element.

Among the different pieces of furniture that one finds inside Norman houses, there are the essentials such as : the **Chest**, the **Cupboard**, the **Sideboard**, the **Table** with its **benches** and **chairs** and the **Bed.** They are fashioned from the species that one finds readily in Normandy : oak, beech, cherry, elm, walnut, ash, apple, pear…

The Chest : It is without question the oldest piece of furniture used in our province since the first centuries. During the Ducal era, it was the primordial element of Norman furniture. They called it 'la huche' during the Anglo-Norman period and it had many uses. Its success lasted until the 18th century. From very simple origins, it was subjected over the centuries to improvements and embellishments. Very early on the craftsmen proved their exceptional knowledge through remarkable carvings. The nails, the metal fittings, the angle irons and locks were made in the east and the west of Normandy, notably in the region of *Tinchebray*, close to the places where iron was extracted and to the forges. There also existed **bench-chests** that is with a back and arm-rests. Wedding furniture par excellence up to the 18th century, the Norman carpenters constructed thousands on which the decoration was often inspired by works from the Middle Ages.

The Cupboard : Made generally from oak (present everywhere, in multiple varieties, in Normandy), the cupboard more practical in use, little by little dethroned the chest as the **'meuble de mariage'** until replacing it at the beginning of the 19th century and becoming the imposing piece of furniture that we know. Given as a dowry by the parents of the bride, it was a sign of the wealth of the family. They would call on a local craftsman or 'huchier' to make it. On the day of the wedding, in order for everyone to admire it, it would be transported on a cart from the home of the parents to that of the newlyweds not always necessarily taking the shortest route. Often simple in conception, but always personalised and finely carved, its principal characteristics are generally the 'drape' above two doors, the doves (which symbolise marriage) or the bunch of grapes (which recall the vine, ancient wealth of the region), or even the basket of fruit (which is evidence of opulence) in the rosette under the moulding, or in the medallions on the doors, the three strap hinges which support each door. Often very tall, when the interiors of peasant houses rarely exceeded two metres of usable height from floor to ceiling, many of them have been mutilated by their successive owners (feet cut off) and the superb mouldings have often been removed and lost. The most beautiful cupboards, made in light oak, have been, it is said, made in the 19th century in the Pays d'Auge in the region of *Lisieux.*

The Sideboard : It is towards the 15th century that the sideboard began to appear. As opposed to the older 'dresser' the Sideboard, which, like its predecessor, served to store dishes and cutlery, is a piece of furniture which is much more decorated. But the Norman sideboard that we identify today dates from the 19th century. The 'low' sideboard which in two ways, by its shape and its carvings, often recalls the cupboard of the same era. On the 'lower dresser' there was often placed a dresser on which were set out pewter items, pottery plates and glassware. In the Pays de Caux, the sideboard was made in 'pitch pine' with a moulding where the motif generally represented at the top, the sun, and a crescent moon below.

The Table : The table has hardly evolved over the centuries. Often made in oak, it was tall, solid, on fixed or moveable trestles.

The Chair : Ancestor of the armchair, it was often provided with armrests and reserved for the Master, at the head of the table.

The Bench : Provided with a backrest, a footrest, sometimes finely wrought, covered with cushions or material in the homes of the aristocrats and the 'bourgeois', the bench, narrow, light and lacking in decoration, was present in the countryside since ancient times.

The Bed : In the middle Ages, it was only a collection of 'tablettes' designed to take the bedding. This bedding in the 15th century consisted of a straw or horsehair mattress on which were placed hemp or linen sheets, made in the region, and then a counterpane. Under the head or the shoulders (one slept thus practically sitting) you put the bolsters or cushions. Obviously, the comfort of the beds depended, as always, on the financial state of the users, the peasants sleeping generally on simple straw mattresses. The closed bed (alcove bed) was in use in the Cotentin. The décor of the wooden bed and the 'tables de nuit' were sometimes matched to the cupboard.

The Clock : Norman clocks offer a great variety of models. In it's carved case, it is often a complementary element of décor to the furniture that we have just discussed. Obviously one finds it only in the homes of the bourgeois and the wealthy farmers. Assembled by local clockmakers who called on the best cabinet makers in their turn to make the case, they carried on the face, the name of the clockmaker and the town where it was sold. Among the best we can cite, in Upper Normandy, the 'clock of the Pays de Caux', square or violin shaped and robust, the 'clock of Saint-Nicolas', 'with its top of a flowery basket which largely overwhelms its svelte body'... and an exceptional carving, the clock called 'de Beaubec' in wood of the region, coming from the most beautiful light oaks of the Pays de Bray, marvellous pieces and not well-known.

Beautiful collections of antique Furniture

Places to see...

AREA OF MANCHE

Coutances :
= **'Musée Municipal'.** 2, rue Quesnel-Morinière - Tel (33) 2 33 45 11 92.

Villedieu-les-Poêles :
= **'Musée du Meuble Normand'.** Open every day except Tuesday morning, from Easter to mid-november from 10 am-12 noon and from 2-6.30 pm. Possibility of a joint ticket with the 'Musée de la Dentelle et de la Poeslerie'. Address and information : Rue du Reculé - Tel/Fax (33) 2 33 61 11 78. The Museum of Norman Furniture presents a collection of traditional regional furniture which is unique in Normandy for the number and diversity of the pieces shown : 150 typical ancient pieces of furniture coming from the four corners of Normandy.
= **'Musée Royaume de l'Horloge'.** 50, rue Carnot - Tel (33) 2 33 90 95 38. This regional clock museum presents four centuries of large clocks and watches. In its workshop, clocks are restored in front of you: pendulums and clocks.

Saint-Lô :
= **Beautiful collection of old chests** in the 'Hôtel du Département'.

AREA OF CALVADOS

Bayeux :
= **'Musée Baron Gérard'.** Ancient Episcopal Palace - For timings : see Musées des Beaux-Arts - rich collection of furniture from the 15th to the 19th century.

Fontaine-Henry :
= **'Château de Fontaine Henry'.** This superb dwelling built in the Renaissance has always passed on its heritage. The rooms of the ground floor contain a magnificent collection of old furniture and tables. Guided visits - Tel (33) 2 31 80 00 42. From Easter to 15th June and 15th September to November : Saturdays, Sundays and Mondays from 2.30-6.30 pm. From 15th June to 15th September all the days except Tuesday from 2.30-6.30.

Vendeuvre (near Saint-Pierre-sur-Dives) :
= **'Musée du Mobilier Miniature'** - **'Musée Guy de Vendeuvre'** In the outbuildings of the castle - Tel (33) 2 31 40 93 83 - Fax (33) 2 31 40 11 11.

E-mail : château@vendeuvre.com Internet site : http://www.vendeuvre.com
Open to the public in March, April, October and November every Sunday and
national holidays from 2-6 pm + the Easter and All Saints holidays, every day
from 2-6 pm. From 1ˢᵗ May to 30ᵗʰ September : every day from 10 am-6 pm.
Leading world collection : 600 small pieces of furniture and more than a thousand
miniature objects from the 16ᵗʰ to the beginning of the 20ᵗʰ century. You can also
visit the château, a beautiful dwelling from the 18ᵗʰ century. Very lovely furniture
and objects from daily life in the last centuries. Working automatons. Presentation
by an automated cook of the history of the kitchen and the wash room.
'Surprising' water gardens : Spread among the rare trees and fantasy
constructions, water games enliven the passage of visitors.

Vire :
= **'Musée Municipal'**. Old 'Hôtel-Dieu' - presentation of Norman furniture.

AREA OF ORNE

Flers :
= **'Musée Municipal'**. Castle of Flers - Antique furniture.

AREA OF EURE

Bernay :
= **A Norman furniture factory** is open for visits. Contact the Tourist Office.

Louviers :
= **'Musée Municipal'**. Beautiful collection of Norman furniture from the 16ᵗʰ and
17ᵗʰ centuries. Free visits every day, except Tuesday, from 2-6 pm. Accessible for
the disabled - Tel (33) 2 32 09 58 55.

AREA OF SEINE-MARITIME

Aumale :
= **'L'Horlogeur'**. One of the great specialists in Norman clocks. 20, rue de
l'Abbaye d'Auchy. Tel (33) 2 35 94 06 27.

Fécamp :
= **'Musée Centre des Arts'**. 21, rue Alexandre-Legros. Tel (33) 2 35 28 31 99.

Le Havre-Graville :
= **'Musée du Prieuré'**. rue Elisée Redus. Tel (33) 2 35 47 14 01

Martainville (to the west of Ry, on the road for Rouen) :
= **At the Castle** (16ᵗʰ century) : **'Musée Départemental'**. Superb permanent
exhibition of furniture from Upper Normandy. 'Le Bourg' - RN 30 - Tel (33) 2 35
23 44 70

Rouen :
= **'Musée des Antiquités'**.

= **'Musée de l'Horlogerie Aliermontaise - Château'.** 323, rue Edouard-Cannevel - Tel (33) 2 35 04 53 98. Open Thursday morning from 9 am-12 noon, Friday from 2-6 pm and by appointment. The history of Norman clock-making since 1725 through a local example.

Norman Furniture, Stars of the Antique shows in Seine-Maritime

= 'Puces Rouennaises' in Rouen in January.

= The Salon of Yerville in February.

= The Salon of Bacqueville-en-Caux in March.

= The Salon of Tôtes in April.

= The Salon of Aumale in October.

= The Salon of Criquetôt-l'Esneval in October.

= The Salon of Eu in November.

2 - Pottery and Ceramics

The Norman household used containers made on the spot which almost always linked practicality with aesthetics. This tradition dates back to the Gallo-Roman era. The potters used the excellent soils that can be found in the region, notably in the Pays d'Auge where the clay is of excellent quality and led to the 'birth' of the precious **'Pré d'Auge'**, sold principally in the market of *Lisieux*. Certain potters, like the **maison Vattier**, gave their produce a quality and an artistic character which is unequalled. In the Bessin, the village of *Norron-la-Poterie* perpetuates the knowledge of ancient Norman potters with several workshops which make and sell stoneware on the spot in bulk or retail. The **porcelain of Bayeux** was renowned for its fineness and patterns.

Places to see...

AREA OF MANCHE

Coutances :

= **'Musée Municipal'.** 2, rue Quesnel-Morinière **Beautiful collection of Norman ceramics. Ancient pottery.**

Ger :

= **'Musée regional de la Poterie Bas Normande'.** Le Placître - 3, rue du Musée - Tel (33) 2 33 79 35 36 - Fax (33) 2 33 79 35 45.
E.Mail : musee.ger@wanadoo.fr Opening hours : School holidays : from 2-6 pm (except Christmas holidays). April and May : from 2-6 pm. June and September : from 11 am to 6 pm. July and August : from 11 am to 7 pm. The regional pottery museum is set on the site of an authentic pottery dating back many centuries. In the 19th century more than 700 potters worked there. More than 2,000 pieces of

Ger pottery, but also some from other centres of pottery in the region, make up a magnificent collection. Videos and interactive panels create an interesting visit. A potter offers for sale material produced on site in a workshop/shop adjoining the museum.

Saint-Pair-sur-Mer :
 = **'Pottery of the Bay of Mont-Saint-Michel'.** 325, rue du golf. Tel (33) 2 33 50 61 58.

Saussey :
 = **'Musée du Manoir de Saussey'.** 3 kilometres from Coutances towards Villedieu. Tel (33) 2 33 45 19 65. Crèches and glassware from the 17th and 18th centuries - Pottery of Forges from the 19th century. Open to the public from 1st March to 30th September.

Portbail (Denneville) : = **Craftsman pottery.**

Saint-Pair-sur-Mer : = **Pottery.**

Vindefontaine : = **Ancient potteries.**

AREA OF CALVADOS

Bayeux :
 = **'Musée Baron Gérard'.** Ancient Episcopal Palace - for timings see 'Musée des Beaux-Arts'. Porcelain also makes up one of the industries which has profoundly affected the history of Bayeux. Since the beginning of manufacture in 1812, up to the closure in 1951, the museum chronicles a century and a half of creativity thanks to an exceptional collection.
 = **Ateliers du Bessin.** 9, place aux Pommes - Tel (33) 2 31 21 98 00. Studio of painting and decoration on porcelain ('bayeux' patterns both ancient and contemporary), ceramics, modelling, casting, visit to the studio by appointment. Open to the public from Monday to Saturday from 10 am to 7 pm. Friday : from 9 am to 12 noon and from 2-7 pm.

Colleville-Montgomery :
 = **'D'ici et là'.** Pottery. 8, bis, rue des Ecoles. Tel (33) 2 31 97 39 14.

Lisieux :
 = **'Musée du Vieux Lisieux'.** Boulevard Pasteur - Tel (33) 2 31 62 07 70.- Fax (33) 2 31 62 42 85. Beautiful collection of 'Pré d'Auge'.

****

'Les épis de faîtage du Pays d'Auge' (The finials of the Pays d'Auge)

True works of art made in terracotta, the finials that one saw flourish at the end of the 19th century on the roofs of bourgeois houses and the rich rural dwellings of the Pays d'Auge were originally utilitarian to protect the top of the roof from inclement weather but they became marks of wealth.

They were born in the Renaissance and were in some ways the 'major works' of the potters of the Pré d'Auge and of Manerbe near Lisieux.

They had their golden age in the 16th and 17th centuries and abandoned their green colour to adopt more lively tints.

Covered with a varnish, the finials were often made up of several layers fitting together one on the other. They were threaded on to a metal spike which held them together. The finial can sometimes be considered as being symbolic.

Victim of time, bad weather, thefts, the finials in terracotta are more and more rare. One can see magnificent examples in the Musée du Vieux Lisieux, the Museums of Caen, Orbec, Honfleur, Bernay, Rouen...

At Mesnil de Bavent, between Caen and Bavent, a pottery studio has reborn this tradition.

****

Montpinçon :

= **'Foyer Rural du Billot'** : (open in the summer) Art and popular traditions of the Pays d'Auge - Beautiful collection of stoneware and 'Pré d'Auge' - 'Musée de l'Ecole Rurale'.

Noron-la-Poterie :

= **Normandie poteries** and **'Poterie des Vieux Fossés'.** Route de Saint-Lô. Production of pottery stoneware 'Au Sel de Noron'. Visit to the workshop and turning demonstration every day from February to December, except Saturday and Sunday from 9.30 am-12 noon and from 2-5 pm. Call the day before to visit the studio - Tel (33) 2 31 92 56 29 - (33) 2 31 21 33 80 - Fax (33) 2 31 92 22 61.

= **Potteries of Noron stoneware.** Turgis ceramic studio. Tel (33) 2 31 92 57 03 - Fax (33) 2 31 92 68 15. Visits from Monday to Friday midday - Sales.

****

The Potteries of Noron

*At Noron-la-Poterie, between **Saint-Lô** and **Bayeux**, the potters perpetuate the tradition of only stoneware pottery which dates back to the 11th century. Formerly used in the conservation of foodstuffs, notably butter and cheese but also cider and calvados, these potteries are today turned more to decorative items. They use for this, work clay, from local deposits.*

Exhibitions and sales all along the main road of the town.

****

Trévières :

= **'Poterie d'Art'.** 2, rue du Calvaire. Production of pottery in blue enamelled stoneware. Visit to the studio and turning demonstration, by appointment. Shop open every day except Sunday afternoon. Tel/Fax (33) 2 31 22 56 73.

AREA OF ORNE

Crouttes :

= **A.D.L.A.A.** (Association pour le Développement des Loisirs Artisanaux et Agricoles). Pottery courses. Le Haut-Bourg - Tel (33) 2 33 39 22 16.

Moulins-la-Marche :

= **'Fête des Potiers'.** Demonstrations, exhibitions, sales, workshops for children. The last Sunday of July.

Sées :

= **Craftsman pottery.** Boisville - Tel (33) 2 33 28 19 76. Fabrication of traditional hand-painted pottery. Public welcome by appointment. Demonstrations, sales.

AREA OF EURE

Le Bec-Hellouin :

= **'Ateliers du Bec'.** Tel (33) 2 32 43 72 60 - Fax (33) 2 32 44 96 69.
E. Mail : ateliers@abbayedubec.com Benedictine Abbey of Bec-Hellouin.
Internet sites : http://www.ateliersdubec.fr or http://www.abbayedubec.com
Since the return of the monks to the abbey in 1948, the community has developed a craft pottery production. The 'Ateliers du Bec' was founded in 1957.
The Benedictines carried out on site, all the stages in the production of ceramics from the initial creation to the final firing. Principally centred around the arts of the table, the production is marketed in the Abbey shop and through the internet site. The monks can produce personalised or missing patterns to order. The monks take care of the dispatch.

Bernay :

= **'Musée Municipal'.** Place Guillaume-de Volpiano - Tel (33) 2 32 46 63 23.
Open : from the last weekend of June to the first week of September as well as the easter holidays from 10 am-12 noon and from 2-7.30 pm. Outside these dates : from 10 am-12 noon and from 2-5.30 pm. National holidays and Sundays : 3-5.30 pm. Closed Tuesday. Collection of ceramics coming principally from the Rouen region. It is the original reason for the creation of the museum and contains some 5,000 pieces on display or preserved in storerooms of the ancient 'Logis' of the abbey which became a museum in the last century. It is one of the most important French collections of pottery. Its base is in large part made up of pieces from Rouen.

Evreux :

= **'Céramique en Fête'.** Exhibition, sales, demonstrations, (pottery, porcelain, varnished terracotta, stoneware…). Workshop for children.The last weekend of May, in the Place de la Mairie.

Louviers :

= **'Faïencerie d'Art'.** 9, rue Victor-Hugo. Tel (33) 2 32 40 61 73 - Fax (33) 2 32 40 61 73. Studio for production, for decoration and restoration of pottery in the style of the potters of Rouen in the 18th century. Guided visits - Open from

Tuesday to Friday from 10 am-12 noon and from 2-7 pm. Weekends by appointment.

= **'Musée Municipal'.** Founded in 1972, this museum has assembled rich collections of pottery from Rouen, Nevers and Delft. Visit every day except Tuesday from 2-6 pm. Accessible to the disabled. Tel (33) 2 32 09 58 55.

Lyons-la-Forêt :

= **Honoured pottery of Hogues.** Open every day except Wednesday from 9 am-7 pm - Tel (33) 2 32 48 19 55. Known and recognised, the honoured pottery of Hogues has made a name and a reputation which goes far beyond the limits of Eure. More than 2000 reference products and items made to order.

Parville :

= **'Atelier de Poterie' - Association 'Terre'.** 26, rue de Beaumont - Tel/Fax (33) 2 32 39 18 00. Pottery, ceramics, courses in turning for adults and young people, courses in sculpture, modelling and decoration for children. Open all year by appointment.

AREA OF SEINE-MARITIME

Forges-les-Eaux :

= **Ancient pottery (19th century). Museum of the pottery of 'Old Forges'.** Visits by appointment through the Tourist Office - Tel (33) 2 35 90 52 10. Collection of popular pottery from the 19th century - more than 200 pieces exhibited. The pottery industry was born in Forges under the Roman occupation. Over the centuries they made basic objects in clay, then pipes. The clays, said to be white, from Forges, where much appreciated by the great potteries of the 18th century : Douai and Boulogne took their supplies from there. In 1797, Georges Wood, of British origin, set up in Forges with his family and founded the first pottery. He put into practice the production procedures of the counties of Staffordshire and Northumberland. Later other makers set up in Forges.

The characteristics of Forges pottery :

Delicate pottery. This is made with the white clay, a creamy white colour called 'pipe clay". This clay was used to make pipes. It was not enamelled but simply varnished. Other than the production of serving dishes, they produced shaped pieces, (soup tureens and salad bowls...). These pieces were made in a mould and decorated with a paintbrush and a sponge. The edges were often encircled with a black line of manganese. The sponge was used in the decoration on the 'marlis' or to imitate the foliage of trees. This decoration with a sponge, is one of the specialities of Forges. The motifs are diverse, inspired by classical models and the current day.

Heavy pottery.

- **the 'Culs Noirs' :** this pottery was made from a greyish white clay, generally crackled : they were called 'culs noirs' (black bottoms) as the underneath of the pieces was covered with a dark brown enamel, which was obtained by using an oxide of manganese employed for its robustness and the lowness of its price. This was heavy pottery, a little basic, destined for daily use by a 'modest' clientele. The decoration often carried naïve motifs.

- the 'Culs Bruns' : in the last third of the 19th century, the rules of fabrication were changed, thus the decoration by sponge of the 'marlis' were restricted, the colours lost their brightness and the quality of the enamel used for the underneath of the dishes was not such a beautiful deep violet brown...

= **'Les deux Gouttes d'Eau'.** Place de l'Ancienne Gare Thermale. Tel (33) 2 35 09 61 53. Production of pottery.

Lillebonne :

= **'Poteries. Martincamp-Bully' : Pottery of Martincamp.** Since the 19th century, they have made on this site, 'rustic' pottery : country dishes whose use is virtually reserved to the farms of the region. The more beautiful pottery, decorated with multicoloured animal designs such as the cockerel, were sold in the wealthy neighbouring area of Caux.

Rouen :

= **The Museum of Ceramics.** 1, rue Faucon - Tel (33) 2 35 07 31 74.

Laid out in an old luxurious town house of the 17th century, the museum is essentially dedicated to the pottery of Rouen and its history from the 16th to the 18th centuries. Numerous pieces are displayed there as well as others coming from the principal centres of production both in France and abroad. Exhibition of porcelain. Open every day of the year from 10 am-1 pm and from 2-6 pm except Tuesdays and public holidays.

****

'THE OLD ROUEN'
Rouen is the oldest site of faïence production in France.

Born in the 16th century, The faïence of Rouen saw a prodigious development a century later thanks to the faïence. E. Poterat who, the sole holder of the exclusive privilege of producing marked pieces, established on the outskirts of the earthenware works Norman capital at Saint-Sever, on the left bank of the Seine. His wife also and afterwards his son continued the tradition, founding a second production point in 1679. 'Rouen refined its style and set the sophisticated décor called 'au lambrequin' and its motifs such as the horn of plenty. The red mixes with the blue then, soon, the nielloed ochre, superb, makes its appearance in the 18th century. The privilege having lapsed, numerous earthenware works were created.

Up to the Revolution the works of the Rouen earthenware makers were renowned and much sought after for their quality.

For a long time benefiting from the clay extracted from the banks of the Seine, from the proximity to Paris and by the use of the river for transportation of the products, Rouen went into decline at the beginning of the 19th century, the clay began to run out and competition from England became too strong. In addition, the production places of Rouen which had made prestige earthenware works for the nobility, did not know how or could not adapt to the changes of the time.

****

= **'Conservation des Musées des Beaux-Arts, de la Ferronnerie et et de la Céramique'.** Square Verdrel - Esplanade Marcel Duchamps. Tel (33) 2 35 71 28 40 - Fax (33) 2 35 15 43 23

= **'Musée des Antiquités'.** 198, rue Beauvoisine. Tel (33) 2 35 98 55 10 - Fax (33) 2 35 70 25 16.

3 - Pewter

The use of pewter in Normandy goes back to the beginning of time. Originally destined to be made as pieces for the church (pewter was the third metal recognised by the church after gold and silver), it became the 'silverware of the poor' from the 13th century.

In the 14th century, coming for the most part from **Rouen,** the sometimes bizarre types and forms of pewter spread throughout Normandy, becoming the 'Norman vessel'. But there remain very few pieces from these periods as each generation was in the habit of melting down its utensils to make new ones better adapted to the fashion of the day.

There existed in Normandy, numerous renowned pewter workshops whose production of jugs, pots, bowls, venison dishes, drinking fountains, water pots, salt pots and measures were used nearby by the mistresses of the house. Each town, even each workshop, benefited from a controlled hallmark.

The most renowned 'factories' were to be found in **Rouen, Coutances, Lisieux...**

Places to see...

AREA OF MANCHE

Villedieu-les-Poêles :

= **'La Maison de l'Etain'.** Come here to discover the history of this noble metal through the workshop-foundry which operates throughout the year with guided and demonstration visits. See the prestigious Jules Brateau collection - unique in France ! A magnificent exhibition and a laser-video presentation which will allow you to understand all the secrets of this metal and of the craft of the 'pewter potter'.Open all year from Tuesday to Saturday from 9 am-12 noon and from 1.30-5.30 pm. Open Sunday in high season from 10 am-12 noon and from 2.30-5.30 pm. Address and information : 15, rue du Général Huard - Tel (33) 2 33 51 05 08.

AREA OF CALVADOS

Sannerville :

= **Copperware and pewter of Sannerville.** Repoussé work on metal, polishing. Sales on site. Z.A. Route de Liroze - Tel (33) 2 31 23 30 51.

AREA OF EURE

Les Barils :

= **Creative foundry of lead soldiers.** Presentation of historic scenes (Imperial Museum of the Miniature) - Free visits throughout the year, every day except

Mondays and Fridays from 10.30 am-12.30 pm and from 2-6 pm - 3, route de Gournay - Tel (33) 2 32 37 64 70.

4 - Artistic ironwork

Customary activity, notably on Orne and more precisely in the Bocage around *Tinchebray* and in the Pays d'Ouche in the region of *L'Aigle*.

Places to see...

AREA OF CALVADOS

Livarot :
= **Museum of the workshops of art in iron.** '100 years of craftsmanship' In the old Fromagerie Bisson. 66, rue Marcel-Gambier - Tel (33) 2 31 63 06 01.

Le Molay-Littry :
= **'La Forge de Cantepie'.** Ironwork and forge. Z.A. Les Planquettes - Route de Balleroy - Tel (33) 2 31 22 98 79.

Vire :
= **Art in ironwork.** Patrick Roger. Route des Vaux - Tel (33) 2 31 67 39 64.

AREA OF ORNE

There exists in this département a 'tour of iron'.

Alençon :
= **Balconies in wrought iron.** (See panel below).

Bagnoles-de-l'Orne :
= **Ancient quarter of artisans in wire and iron.** The area can still be visited but the artisans are no longer there.

Bazoches-sur-Hoëne :
= **'Aux Fers de Bazoches'** Artwork in iron - 5, rue du Presbytère - Tel (33) 2 33 73 48 76.

Flers :
= **Castle of Flers :** in the cellars. Beautiful collection of locks made in the area of *Tinchebray* and *Flers*.

Tinchebray :
= **Museum of the old prison :** Presentation of numerous objects in wrought iron.

****

The wrought iron balconies of old Alençon

*If you wander along the Grande-Rue in **Alençon**, we invite you to raise your eyes and admire the impressive series of balconies in wrought iron from the 18th century which adorn the facades of the buildings. The pharmacy alone offers a remarkable collection. You will be equally amazed by those of the Rue du Jeudi and the Rue des Grandes Poteries et du Plénitre.*

Between the two wars, the chronicler Boisseau counted 170 balconies in Louis XIV style and 74 in the style of Louis XVI, this lead Georges Massiot to produce under the title 'The Balconies of the old dwellings of Alençon', a study published in 1958. These balconies have undeniably a link with the existence in the area of iron mines and forges.

On a number of these balconies is a pattern of three figures on the house itself of a Master of Forging at 33, rue des Grandes-Poteries. A number of these balconies adorn the magnificent town houses from the 18th century.

****

AREA OF EURE

Conches :
= **'Le Saint-Jacques'.** 12, rue Sainte-Foy - Tel (33) 2 32 30 20 50. In an ancient wood panelled town house from the 15th century, site of the provosty in the 12th century, situated in the heart of the town, in the main road close to the church, M. Martin, blacksmith and farrier forges, following the tradition of the old makers of finely wrought staircase railings or gates but also works of art exhibited in the superb vaulted cellars. Free visits throughout the year, every day except Mondays and Tuesdays from 9 am-12 noon and from 2.30-6.30 pm.

Le Neubourg :
= **'Musée du Charron-Forgeron'.** 54, avenue de la Libération - Tel (33) 2 32 35 93 95.

AREA OF SEINE-MARITIME

Rouen :
= **'Musée de la Ferronnerie Le Secq des Tournelles'.** 2, rue Jacques-Villon - Tel (33) 2 35 88 42 92. In a disused church from the 16th century is assembled a unique collection of more than 5,000 pieces of ironwork dating from antiquity up to the beginning of the 20th century. One can find there signs, locks, various utensils, implements, elements from architecture… Open every day of the year from 10 am-1 pm and from 2-6 pm except Tuesdays and public holidays.

5 - Of Lace

**The tradition of lace-making in Normandy has been,
over the centuries, part of the renown of the Province.
In 1997, on the initiative of the town of *Argentan*, in Orne, there was created
the 'Route des Dentelles normandes' which has two objectives :
'to join together local initiatives in the area of lace and to offer a tourist circuit linking
all the towns of western Normandy that have decided to reactivate their lace making potential'.**

Places to see...

Villedieu-les-Poêles : Lace was already made and sold in Villedieu in the 17th century. While their husbands and fathers worked in copper, the women and children of the community and surrounding area, made lace from a white thread called 'chevron'. Others, more expert, made Cluny or Chantilly lace. This lace embellished sheets, collars, handkerchiefs, baby clothes... One finds almost always the same motifs : clover, roses and daisies.

In 1895, the lace makers of Villedieu created the 'hair lace' made with long black, chestnut or blonde hairs. Some tens of years ago they still made a much valued lace in Villedieu.

= **'Musée de la Poeslerie et de la Dentelle'** - 'La Cour du Foyer' - 50800 Villedieu-les-Poêles. Tel (33) 2 33 90 20 92 - Fax (33) 2 33 61 11 78. You will discover in this museum the ancient crafts of the lace makers, their lace bobbins or 'bloquets', their artistic work, and traces of their daily life. Video presentation and demonstrations. Exhibition of traditional lace in an authentic domestic setting. Open every day during the school holidays at Christmas and in February from 2-6 pm. In July and August, open from 10 am-6.30 pm. The rest of the year : open from 10 am-12 noon and from 2-6.30 pm except Tuesday mornings.

AREA OF CALVADOS

Caen : Since the beginning of the 17th century, the Ursulines of Caen taught lace-making to the orphans whose education was their responsibility.

This lace was in black or white flax thread. The first private manufacture was started in 1730. In 1745 they launched the making of the 'blonde', lace made from a natural coloured silk called 'jaune nankin'. To compensate for the progressive disappearance of the lace-makers at the beginning of the 20th century, a school to teach the techniques of Caen lace was created in 1900 but this activity did not survive after the second world war.

= **'Musée de Normandie'.** Castle - 'Logis du Gouverneur' - 14000 Caen. Tel (33) 2 31 30 47 60. E.Mail : mdn@ville-caen.fr - Web : http://www.ville-caen.fr/mdn - Open every day except Tuesday, from 1st October to 31st March from 9.30 am-12.30 pm and from 2.30-6 pm. From 1st April to 30th September, from Wednesday to Friday from 10 am-12.30 pm and from 1.30-6 pm, from Saturday to Monday and public holidays from 9.30 am-12.30 pm and from 2-6 pm. Closed 1st January,

Easter Sunday, 1st May, Thursday of Ascension, 1st November and 25th December. Easy parking in the Château car park - Guided visits - Beautiful specimens of 'blonde' lace in the 'Blonde' of Caen.

Beaumont-en-Auge : Ancient lace-making town.

Bayeux : From the 17th century, 'la Gueuse', 'la Bisette' and 'la Mignonette', all three fine lace in flax thread, were taught and made in Bayeux by the lace maker 'du Petit Bureau' directed by the Sisters of Providence. A great proportion of the works made at that time were exported to England. A second manufacturing site was created in the 18th century and a century later one could count twenty makers of lace in Bayeux. The activity prospered up to the first world war.

= **'Conservatoire de la Dentelle de Bayeux'.** 'Maison d'Adam et Eve', rue du Bienvenu - opposite the Cathedral, 6, rue Lambert-Leforestier, 14400 Bayeux. Tel (33) 2 31 92 73 80. Permanent and temporary exhibitions - courses - training Open all the year from 10 am to 0.30 pm and from 1-6 pm (Sunday and national days closed).

= **'Musée Baron Gérard'.** Hôtel du Doyen - 14400 Bayeux. Tel (33) 2 31 92 14 21 - Fax (33) 2 31 51 60 51. One room is reserved for the heritage of the lace maker of the town with a display of some beautiful specimens of Bayeux lace. Open every day except 1st January and 25th December from 10 am to 0.30 pm and from 1-6 pm (7 pm in August).

= **'Les Fils Croisés'.** School of lace, woven tapestry, painting on silk and porcelain, embroidery, bobbin- lace. Exhibition and sales throughout the year. 2, Rue de la Poissonnerie - Tel (33) 2 31 08 18 95. Days and times for visits : open Wednesday and Saturday morning and from 16th June to 14th September from 10 am-12 noon and from 1.30-6.30 pm (closed Sundays and public holidays) and from 15th September to 15th June from 10 am-12 noon and from 2-6 pm (closed Sundays, Mondays and public holidays). Free entry.

Courseulles : At the beginning of the 19th century, a private maker made lace in cashmere wool and in black silk. This establishment was the first in France to make bobbin appliqué flowers on a base of tulle, which explains their name of 'application'. At the end of the 19th century, this maker employed 1,200 workers. The black lace called Chantilly had a major international success up to the 1920's.

= **Musée de Vieux Courseulles** : 17, rue Amiral-Robert - 14470 Courseulles-sur-Mer. Tel (33) 2 31 37 70 00. Open from Easter to 30th September, from Wednesday to Sunday from 2.30-6 pm From 1st October to Easter, Saturdays and Sundays from 2.30-5 pm.

In this ATP museum has been gathered together, everything that could be saved from the bombardments of 1944 : coloured lace, gold or silver lace, 'blondes', chantilly but also large designs for shawls and the whole environment of lace making.

Douvres-la-Délivrande : Ancient lace-making town.

AREA OF ORNE

Alençon : One can safely say that the **'point of Alençon'** called 'point coupé' has been made for a very long time since it's production was already renowned in the 17th century. Over the years, this technique became needle lace and it's practice spread under the name of 'velin'. Colbert gave Alençon lace a nobility by creating a Royal Make in the town. Very quickly the **'point of France'** gained an international reputation surpassing that of Venice. At the end of the 19th century, the 'point' of Alençon received the title of **'Lace of Queens, Queen of Lace'**. The secret of the making of this lace was taught for many years by the nuns up to the point in 1874 when a Municipal School of lace-making was created in Alençon which has today become a National Establishment.

= **'Atelier national du Point d'Alençon'.** 13, rue Jullien, 61003 Alençon - Tel (33) 2 33 26 33 60.

= **'Musée des Beaux Arts et de la Dentelle'.** Cour carrée de la Dentelle (close to the Place Foch). Tel (33) 2 33 32 40 07 - Fax (33) 2 33 26 51 66. Presentation of Alençon lace and other lace from the 17th to 20th centuries. Open from Tuesday to Sunday from 10 am-12 noon and from 2-6 pm except 1st January, 1st May and Christmas Day. Open every day in July and August. Guided visits and lace-making demonstrations in July and August (Tuesday and Friday afternoon).

= **'Musée de la Dentelle et du Point d'Alençon'.** 33, rue du Pont-Neuf, 61003 Alençon. Tel (33) 2 33 26 27 26. Private museum which possesses very beautiful examples of lace in Alençon point. Needle lace from France and elsewhere in Europe, spindle and mechanical. Open from Monday to Saturday from 10 am-12 noon and from 2-6 pm. Audio visual presentation in English. Guided visits. Sale of lace.

Argentan : Argentan is one of the oldest and most important centres of lace making in Normandy. The **'Point de France'** (needle lace) was invented in Argentan around 1671 under the state monopoly imposed by Colbert, Minister of Louis XIV. In the 18th century, Argentan had four manufacturers of royal lace who made the 'Point royal de France'. The Benedictines of Argentan are today still the heirs of this ancestral knowledge. On the initiative of François Doubin, Mayor of Argentan, previous Minister of Commerce and Craftsmanship, lace-making, which was no longer taught since the disappearance of the School of Lace-making, has been re-established in Argentan with the creation of the House of Lace and Point d'Argentan and the centre for training in Arts and Crafts which offers several types of training in lace work.

= **'La Maison des Dentelles et du Point d'Argentan'.** 14, rue de la Noë, 61200 Argentan. Tel (33) 2 33 67 40 56 - Fax (33) 2 33 67 34 47.

In a magnificent dwelling in the centre of a floral park, the Museum presents prestigious collections on two levels : point lace from Venice, Point de France, Point from Sedan, Alençon, Argentan... from 16th century to modern times.

Exhibition of lace dresses from Calais. The models change every six months. Training and courses in needle lace are organised throughout the year. Guided visits on request. Sale of material and technical books. Actually closed !

= **Benedictine Abbey of Notre Dame - Lace workshops in Point of Argentan.**
2, rue de l'Abbaye, 61200 Argentan. Tel (33) 2 33 67 12 01 - Fax (33) 2 33 35 67
55. Open every day except Sunday and national holidays from 2.30-4 pm only by
appointment. In addition to their many activities the Sisters continue the lace
tradition of Argentan - the secret being passed on from nun to nun.
Video on the history of Argentan lace. Demonstrations - Sale of lace in the shop
along with other products of the Abbey - icons and works of calligraphy.

La Perrière : Although having essentially served in hunting and fishing, net had been
used since ancient Egyptian times as a cover for the body or as decoration on
clothing. It was in the middle of the 19th century that La Perrière developed the
making of net. There were soon 3,000 women in Perche to work for the
merchants of gloves, mittens and other net. Just before the last war, embroidered
net had an uninterrupted popularity. The speciality of La Perrière was the pearled
net for fashion or embroidered for bed covers or curtains. High fashion was
involved there in the 1920's which produced work for the three manufacturers set
up in the community.
= **'Atelier du filet'.** La Grande Place - 61360 La Perrière. Tel (33) 2 33 25 59 48
- Fax : Thirty years after the creation of the 'Maison du Filet', the municipality
undertook the creation of this workshop to organise training courses and
educational visits. Exhibition of pearled and embroidered net - Guided visits and
net-making demonstrations.

6 - Glass-making tradition

Glass-making traditions in Normandy go back, one can be sure, to antiquity but,
the real success of the Norman glass makers dates only from the 15th century.

This activity benefited from the abundance, on the spot, of primary materials
which were indispensable : sand, which was abundant in the quarries of the region;
kelp, present on the coasts, or the bracken, which grew in profusion in the forests and
from which they extracted the soda, and wood for burning.

The craft of the glass-maker was one of the rare openings for the nobility to
exercise 'without losing their dignity''. There were thus aristocrats who made
Normandy a great region for glass. The first glass works were created in western
Normandy towards the 14th century by the Brossard and Messange families. It was
above all in the 18th and 19th centuries, that this industry prospered with the growing
and ever more varied use of glass in houses.

Still today it is felt that the 'essential industrial knowledge on this planet when it
concerns the production of perfume bottles is situated in the valley of the Bresle
between *Aumale, Blangy, Eu* and *Le Tréport.*

Glassmaking activity still flourishes with notably a bottle making factory (No. 1
in the world). In Orne, at *Ecouché*, the Verrieres de l'Orne which is part of the Saint-
Gobain group, also perpetuate this ancient knowledge.

AREA OF CALVADOS

Canapville : **'Atelier Beautile'**. Decoration of glass by sandblasting. Ferme des Chartrains - Tel (33) 2 31 64 27 15.

Vieux-Pont-en-Auge : **Verrerie 'Atelier signalétik & Néon'**. Le Godet - Tel (33) 2 31 20 08 01.

AREA OF ORNE

Saint-Evroult - Notre-Dame-du-Bois : Important glassmaking centre. One finds there the vestiges of an ancient glass industry created in 1837 by Grégoire Gassot which operated up to 1935. There remains, on the route de L'Aigle, a major part of the works.

AREA OF EURE

Conches-en-Ouche : **'Musée de la Pierre et du Verre'**. Route de Sainte-Marguerite. Exhibition of the works of the master glassmaker François Décorchemont, child of the country born in 1880 who had a great success with his glassmaking alongside Lalique and Daum, applying to the art of stained glass, a special technique which allowed him to obtain shades and camaîeu of colours in the same piece. Also exhibited are the works of his grand-sons Etienne and Antoine Leperlier. Open to the public from 1st July to 15th September, from Wednesday to Saturday from 10 am-12 noon and from 2-6 pm Sundays from 10 am-12 noon. Tel (33) 2 32 30 90 41.

AREA OF SEINE-MARITIME

Blangy-sur-Bresle :

= **'Musée de la Verrie - Manoir de Fontaine'.** In this 15th century building, on the banks of the Bresle, is presented a magnificent collection of perfume bottles coming from all over the world. Workshop of hot glass with demonstrations of glass blowing of 'objets d'art'. Museum of models and moulds (upstream from the glassmaking). Ovens, machines and utensils allow the visitor to completely understand all the process manual and automatic production of glass, from raw sand to decorated bottle. Open every day from 1st March to 30th November except Tuesday and Sunday morning : from 10 am-12 noon and from 2-6 pm.
For information : Tel (33) 2 35 94 44 79.

= **'Atelier de Gino dei Rossi'**, glassmaking craftsman. He makes, entirely by hand, standard lamps in decorative sintered glass and decorative objects : ashtrays, vases and candlesticks in coloured glass. By appointment, in the mornings, it is possible to see the work in his workshop situated at 23, route d'Eu. His works are displayed in an exhibition room. Contact : Tel (33) 2 35 93 57 01.

Eu : **'Musée des traditions verrières'.** 140, Chaussée de Picardie - rue Sénirchon - 'Ancienne Caserne Militaire Morris'. Open from Easter to 1ˢᵗ November from 2.30-6 pm (Tuesday, Saturday and Sunday). Wednesday afternoon in July and August. Information from the Tourist Office of Eu. Tel (33) 2 35 86 04 68. Here they are brought to life : The history of glass and particularly that of bottle making from its origins to the present day. A presentation of the evolution of glass making techniques. The utensils : the blowing tube and the hand equipment, the semi automatic machines from the end of the 19ᵗʰ century, the current automatic machines. From concept to production : the route of a bottle. The completion : decoration - sand blasting - size. The great names of French perfumery : presentation of bottles made in the glass works of the region. The making of perfume.

Activities carried out by old glass makers.

Illustrations and video explanations.
Visit to the glass factory of Saint-Gobain-Desjonquières.
Prior registration at the Tourist Office.
Tourist route of glass in the Valley of Bresle.
Leaflet available from the Tourist Offices of Seine-Maritime.

7 - Windows and Mirrors

The charming little village of **La Glacerie,** on the heights above **Cherbourg** retains the memory of a very ancient activity which developed there a little by chance, but also because the sea offered the craftsmen the sand and the soda necessary in the making of the glass, which is said to adorn the most beautiful houses in France beginning with the famous 'Galerie des Glaces' in the castle of Versailles.

Places to see...

= **'Musée de la Glacerie'.** Village de l'Eglise - Hamlet of Luce. Open from 2.30-6 pm Sundays and public holidays from Easter to 30ᵗʰ June and every day except Tuesday from 1ˢᵗ July to 15ᵗʰ September. Tel (33) 2 33 22 27 15. Set up in the centre of an old farm from the 19ᵗʰ century, from the courtyard of which you can find a superb view over the harbour of Cherbourg, the museum offers its visitors the chance to rediscover the history of Norman life from an earlier time and particularly rural life, a collection of unique Norman headdresses and the history of the **Manufacture of Windows.** The glass works of Louis-Lucas de Néhou, Master glass maker in Tourlaville, because of the quality of it's production became a Royal Maker in 1668. Numerous objects and documents coming from this factory as well as a model of the factory and the village of La Glacerie in the 17ᵗʰ century are on view. See also an interesting exhibition of materials and decorative elements for roofing : blue 'shistes', wheat thatch, ridge tiles, end pieces, 'épis'...

8 - The sculptured Ivory of Dieppe

For five centuries, the craftsmen of Dieppe produced ivory sculptures.
A thousand pieces, the oldest dating from the 15th century, are presented in the Castle-Museum but this tradition continues and two 'Ivoiriers' have their workshop in Dieppe. Decorative objects are today favoured by the public while in earlier times they made principally utilitarian objects.

Places to see...

Atelier d'Ivoire. Annick Colette - 3, rue Ango. Tel (33) 2 35 82 73 74

Atelier d'Ivoire. Philippe. Ragault - 2, rue Ango. Tel (33) 2 35 82 10 50

'The Ivory and Spice route'

Tourist route - Leaflets available from the tourist offices of Seine-Maritime.

Yvetot : **'Musée Municipal des Ivoires'.** Stopping point on the 'Ivory and Spice Route", Yvetot offers, in the tourist office, an exhibition of 200 pieces in ivory, ceramic and terracotta set out in four windows (Statuettes, shells, cases, vases, 'diatyques and triptyques"). Open during Tourist Office hours throughout the year.

9 - Norman jewellery

The 'Norman cross' generally worn around the neck on a velvet ribbon was the jewel most frequently worn by women of the Province in earlier times.
This 'latin' cross came from the 'croix jeanette', a small jewel in gold which young girls received at the time of the Saint-Jean.
Norman women also wore pendants ('Saint-Esprit' representing a dove) and brooches.

Places to see...

AREA OF MANCHE

Ardevon and Mont-Saint-Michel : Atelier d'Art J. et M. Laurette Jewellery and ceramics.

L'Atelier de la Rive. Route de la Baie - **Ardevon** Tel (33) 2 33 60 08 01.

L'Atelier Galerie. Les Remparts. **Le Mont-Saint-Michel.** Tel (33) 2 33 60 14 22.

For a list of the numerous antiques markets, 'bric à brac' fairs, sales rooms, antiquarians and 'bric à brac' sales people... Contact the Tourist Offices.

V - TRADITIONAL NORMANDY

1 - The Norman identity

The authentic and traditional Normandy that we invite you to discover in the reading of this guide, does not surrender itself easily, one has to search for it, to seek it out from behind the stereotyped picture, the caricatures that are offered in the tourist guides and on post cards.

Normandy was a great nation *'the most advanced country in material, social and intellectual civilisation of western Christendom'* and even if it was annexed to France in 1204, it has never been totally assimilated.

Normandy is today part of France and intends to remain so, but that does not prevent the Normans from exalting in Viking gestures and their glorious past and claiming loud and clear, in a large majority, the reunification of the 'two' administrative regions, created arbitrarily in the 1960's, into one single Normandy demanding an acceptance of the Norman identity.

Even if from the Epte to Couesnon, they are convinced of being part of the same community, even if the blood of the Vikings still runs in the veins of the Normans, and even if the distant lands of the north of Europe, where they find certain major traits of their character, still retain around them today a great attraction, the Normans of the 21st century do not have the impertinence to affirm that they are all descendents of the 'North Men' and make up a separate ethnic group in France.

The Normans of the Third millennia have blended together their Celtic, Saxon and then Scandinavian origins, those of the fabulous ducal epoch, the extraordinary adventure of the Anglo-Norman kingdom but also those acquired over seven centuries as part of the French people during which time the province saw large migrations leading to a great mingling of populations. One has seen and still sees in Normandy that its inhabitants are not xenophobes. Remember on this subject the old adage : *'It is Normandy which makes the Norman and not the contrary !'*.

2 - The fundamental rights of the Normans

'A furore normanorum, libera nos, domine !' '(Lord, deliver us from the fury of the Normans)' : this prayer came from all the abbeys during the first raids which the Vikings made to our lands, but quickly the pillagers, who in reality had a very advanced civilisation, weary of their continual restless wandering and won over by this land of Cockaigne, integrated themselves into the native population and shared with them their values.

The *'North Men'* were above all peaceful peasants or traders, living in a system respectful of authority and justice, condition 'sine qua non' of the respect of individual liberties. The famous **'coutume normande'** was largely inspired by this system. It gave birth to the **droit normand** of which the first aspect is the protection of the rights of the 'citizens'.

Its principal objective was to ensure the continuity of properties in the same family. Men taking precedence to the detriment of women. The absolute law of primogeniture being the principal governing inheritances.

The 'Norman right' was exported to England and the British themselves exported it to the United States and to their dominions.

It is thus, also paradoxical that it is apparent, that from the Vikings the Normans learnt the great democratic principles but also that authority is the best shield against anarchy and tyranny.

Among the specific survivors of the Scandinavian inheritance in the rights of the Normans we can note the **'Danish style marriage',** a form evolved from cohabitation which recognised the rights of succession of children coming from these relationships (The three first Dukes of Normandy lived 'as man and wife") and slavery which disappeared in the time of William.

3 - The Institutions

When the 'men from the north' disembarked in Normandy, the inhabitants of that which was then still called Neustria, lived in pitiful conditions, in a country devastated by wars and invasions. A chronicler noted *'it was possible to effect there numerous leagues without hearing the barking of a dog...'* The only havens of peace and civilisation were the monasteries which had spread in the country since the 5th century. Some country squires caused terror here and there and in the depths of the forest which occupied the major part of the territory of the current Normandy, the druid cult and pagan gods were still a reality.

The Carolingian power had continued to slacken since the death of Charlemagne and the state was in a process of complete disintegration.

The church was the only protection against anarchy reigning throughout the country. To assert their authority, it was thus to the clerics that the Vikings went in the first place.

When the Vikings settled in Neustria, they found a feudal system established but as they did not accept serfdom, they fought it fiercely until its abolition.

From 911, the 'sons of the sea' broke the masts of their 'esnèques' to make the main wooden parts of their houses. They brought from their distant countries materials and animals. They set up on the coast and along the rivers and began to clear the forest to cultivate the land. They united with the indigenous population thus adopting the lifestyle, the language and the Christian faith following in that the example of their chief Rollon who was baptised! The Nordic, Christian and local traditions gave birth to the Norman state !

The Norman chiefs obliged the 'free' peasants to cultivate the land under threat of a fine, while they devoted themselves to hunting, their main pastime, in the numerous forests of their new homeland.

The Duke of Normandy held the highest rank among the lords of France and benefited from exceptional privileges.

He was present, topped with his gold crown, at the coronation of the kings of France, he appointed bishops, was the protector of the churches, dictated the laws applying in the Duchy which he governed as he wished, making his own justice, having over his subjects the right of life or death, having money produced *(the deniers were made in Rouen, Lisieux, Bayeux and Evreux, episcopal cities)*, decided on the measures, raised troops and levied taxes… to summarise he had all the powers of a sovereign.

To rule over this land that he had conquered, Rollon knew that he must make authority and justice reign there. Wanting to combat the crimes and offences by 'slanderous remarks' and the 'fear of torture' *(the smallest theft was punishable by death)* one of his first laws was to oblige the peasants to permanently leave their agricultural material in the fields where they worked to put his subjects to the test. *(This practice was still apparent some years ago in our countryside where one could see old ploughs and ancient reapers rusting in the middle of the fields)* It is said also that near Rouen, in the **forest of Roumare**, there was a gold chain placed on the branch of a tree which stayed there for three years ! After a certain time the Duke was able to affirm that *'theft no longer existed in his Duchy".*

In the range of punishments, often cruel, inflicted on the offenders, we can mention, among the 'honourable amend' according to anecdote, the particularly humiliating measure consisting of appearing before the judges without headgear.

It is said that it is for this reason that the Norman peasants today still always retain their hats, called 'la bâche', on the head.

In addition, the wars between local lords would be considerably reduced because of the ban made by the Duke on taking up arms during Advent, Lent, during the 'Octave' of feast days and every day of the year between Thursday and Monday.

Equally it was forbidden to attack or rob travellers and ecclesiastical persons.

To ensure the internal peace of his Duchy, William established the 'Fief de Chevalier'. The territory under his power was divided into several fiefs which each were obliged to put an armed knight at the service of the public security for at least a month.

The fiefs de Chevalier were grouped together under about ten 'fiefs d'honneur'.

In respect of the answerable rights, Henry 1st Beauclerc went further than his father, who alone exercised judiciary power, by creating a body of magistrates who were originally from the **'Exchequer'**, a symbol even of Norman institutions. It was at the same time a central court of justice and of accounts. This institution gave birth to the **'English Exchequer'**.

Soon, this institution acquired a fundamental role in the financial domain, all the administrators of the Duchy and of the Kingdom coming before it, to present their accounts.

Originally installed in the castle of Rouen, the Exchequer of Normandy was subsequently transferred to all the ducal residences. It met twice a year and each audience lasted three months.

Another judiciary institution existed beside the Anglo-Norman sovereigns, it was **'Parlement'**. The 'coroners' (that is to say those linked to the crown) were mandated there in the Counties to receive complaints from the inhabitants. The summons was made by the famous cry of **'Haro'** Haro ! mon duc, on me fait tort ! The Exchequer was a sort of court of appeal.

We can also note that the word 'Eyre", current today in England, described, in the ancient Norman custom the mobile tribunals made up of representatives of the Duke and presided over by a 'chef justicier".

To the justice of the Duke was added the 'trêve de Dieu' proclaimed by the Church. On the administrative side, decentralisation existed equally with the Bailiffs who represented the sovereign in his possessions.

To summarise, the respect for the law, the institutions and the authority of the Duke were the essential rules of organisation of Norman society. As a counterbalance the Normans benefited from numerous charters. This advance of Anglo-Norman institutions over those of neighbouring kingdoms would last until 1204.

After the unification with France, the King was obliged to accept for his subjects, by the 'Charte aux Normands', the recognition of their liberties and the right to be different notably on subjects such as : the respect of individual property, a principal dear to the inhabitants of the Province as we have seen previously.

This Charter, confirmed by successive Kings of France, would be invoked by the Normans up to the Revolution which put into place permanently, a centralised regime.

4 - The Norman customs

Over the years the principal traits of the Norman character were forged (for better or worse ?) as the people of Maupassant illustrate so well. Thus came the image of the man respectful of other people's property, attached fiercely to his land, to his property, to money, litigious, suspicious of the 'horsains', and generally of those who did not share the same values as he. The celebrated **'Ch'est mein drei'** (It's my right !), last parry of the Norman peasant is found again in the English expression : **'Dieu et mon droit'**, such that the British translated the expression **'P'têt' bein qu'oui, p't'êt bein qu'non !'** which marks prudence rather than indecision by the non less famous **'Wait and see !'**.

****

The Scandinavian origins of place names.
Numerous names of Norman communities have a Nordic origin. Those which date from the first invasions have as endings : tuit, gate, fleur (rain), tot (from the god Thor), beuf, Bec (the stream), ham (the port), Hogue (the heights), as in Blacquetuit, Houlgate, Honfleur, Barfleur, Lanquetot, Yvetot, Elbeuf, Orbec, le Bec, Ouistreham, La Hague, whereas Roumare and Rouville recall the memory of the first Duke of Normandy and Langrune has the same roots as Greenland : green earth.

****

If, in the ducal era, the Norman lords practised in their wooden and then stone castles, a certain 'art de vivre' or the 'bonne chère' held an important place, in the towns, very 'civilised', called 'communes' when they had 'jurisdiction', the existence was generally miserable, the population living in dark unhealthy houses. One found there traders whose activities were particularly controlled. In the centre of a settlement would be found the church and the cemetery and around those the 'corn market', the forges, the stalls of craftsmen working in wood, stone, copper or pewter... If the noble ladies dressed in clothes of satin or velvet, the common people wore shirts or dresses of hemp or linen made by humble tailors.

From the rudimentary clothes of the warrior Vikings, the Norman chiefs preferred little by little the rare fabrics and precious jewels, proving a refinement which dazzled the neighbours.

5 - The habitat

Humble dwellings : Under the protection of the lord, the peasants lived in humble thatched cottages made up of one main room. The walls were made of wood or cob. These primitive dwellings had only one door and no other openings or fireplace.

Fortified dwellings : The first fortifications built by the Viking chiefs from the 10th century were castral or feudal mounds. They were raised heaps of earth around which was cut a ditch. The mound was defended by a wooden palisade. It was surrounded by two courtyards to the north and south. On the first, a humble dwelling in wood was built, a chapel, a kitchen and sometimes a guard tower and the other was used to enclose the animals and the stables. Entry was by a bridge which crossed the ditch.

Military fortresses : Towards the middle of the 11th century real fortresses were built which would give way to imposing stone castles.

The stone Keeps in quadrangular form were very much in fashion in Normandy and in England (but also in the south of Italy) in the 12th century (Norman keeps of **Caen, Falaise, Domfront, Vire**... or English castles of Arundel or Colchester but also the Tower of London built of Caen stone).

These towers were not only defensive buildings but also dwellings of lords which could prove to be very comfortable.

6 - Education and letters

In the favoured circles, the Normans expressed themselves in 'French' but wrote in Latin. The children were taught from the age of nine by the clerics.

Certain abbeys had an international renown in the field of education like that at **Bec** from where came the teacher Lanfranc (future archbishop of Canterbury) in the 11th century but also those of **Saint-Evroult, Jumièges, Saint-Wandrille** or of **Fontenelle, *Fécamp*** or **Saint-Ouen** of **Rouen.** In the 'scriptoria' of the great Abbeys like that of **Mont-Saint-Michel**, the monks wrote above all, works destined for study. In the Norman abbeys they taught arithmetic, geometry, grammar, rhetoric and dialectic, astronomy and music.

On this subject we should note that The Music School of the Abbey of **Saint-Evroult** had a reputation which extended even to Italy.

Each abbey possessed, in addition, its school of Gregorian chant.

The descendents of the Vikings would forget little by little the 'Norois'', their original language to speak the *'French of Normandy'* and the children of the nobility began to be sent to the schools of Bayeux, *'only town of the Norman traditionalist' where it was still spoken* - to learn the language of their ancestors.

7 - The rites and customs of our ancestors

Were the Vikings abominable machos ? Everything leads us to believe so but what man wasn't in this era ? Examples are numerous of battered and humiliated wives but also of great passions. We know that our ancestors preferred to embark their cattle on their drakes (ships) than their women and that they 'married' in *'Danish style'* with the native women to ensure their posterity. Thus the red haired blue eyed colossi joined their destinies and their genes with those of the descendents of the Celts, the Gallo-Romans, the Saxons or the Francs who peopled Neustria. We should note that in the extreme south of the territory lived the offspring of the Arab tribes, 'the Moors' that the occupying Romans had brought from Africa as mercenaries to defend the steps of the 2nd Lyonnaise against Saxon invasions. The towns of **Mortagne,** in Orne, **Mortain** in La Manche recall this presence in certain family names : **Maurey, Morin, Morel**, very frequent in Normandy. Our Dukes, like their men, were at times total chauvinists as Robert with 'Arlette', Richard III with Gonnor and even William who, according to legend, doubting the fidelity of Mathilde during his long stays in England, dragged her one winter's day, naked behind his horse, in the steets of Caen to make her admit her misdemeanours. (It is said that she sneezed in one of the dark narrow lanes of the Ducal capital and that, for this reason, this place was called : Cold Road). All, mercifully, were not as cruel as the lord of the region of Argentan who killed his unfaithful wife, collected her blood, tore out her heart and had it cooked and had a chair recovered with her skin. He then invited the lover to dinner, sat him in the chair and served him the heart of his beloved. Afterwards he killed him, collected the blood, mixed it with that of his wife and used the mixture to repaint the columns of his manor... It was necessary to wait until the 12th century for Alienor of Aquitaine, who was Queen of France then

Duchess of Normandy and Queen of England to force the evolution of the place of women in her possessions. She was the originator of the 'fine amor' which forced the Anglo-Normans to more courtesy and gallantry in their relations with their wives. The woman, over the years, would play a more and more considerable role in Norman society.

8 - The sweet life in Normandy in the 19th century

The 'Norman wedding party'.

A marriage, in the country, was in the 19th century, the occasion for great celebrations and lavish festivities - the tradition of the banquet was inherited from the Viking era. After the religious ceremony, the 'fiddler' took the head of the cortege and led the guests across the countryside to a decorated table in the courtyard of the farm then after the meal, the bodies and spirits having been warmed by the 'maît cidre', the wines of Bordeaux and the Calvados, they danced. The country men wearing for the occasion their best 'blaude' (blue cotton shirts) starched, pleated and embroidered at the collar, without forgetting their high silk hat, around the neck a red and white chequered handkerchief and clogs on their feet. The 'petits' bourgeois wore a waistcoat in embroidered silk under a short belted jacket with a tall felt hat. In their hands they would carry the inevitable umbrella or cane. The women, for themselves, wore skirts in linen pleated to the waist, a cotton scarf, the shoulders being covered with the famous Norman shawl in cashmere. On their heads they delicately placed the lace headdress or a simple cotton bonnet. The choice of a wife, in most cases, was not as the result of a sudden love match, it was considered and negotiated at length. Before the marriage, the mothers kept their daughters around them to avoid excesses of affection from certain suitors. They helped their mothers in the home and made their trousseau.

= **The game of dominos, 'a national sport'.** In the last century and up to the 1950's, in the cafes or after the family meal, one played dominos, 'national sport' in Normandy. It was found in practically all houses. There one played 'for money', with great seriousness, long silences and various exclamations to follow. In certain Norman regions they gave names to the dominos. As in the Pays d'Auge the double four was called 'Curé du Sap'. In Upper Normandy in the clubs for the retired, they still gather several times a week to play dominos.

= **The placing on the marshes at Sainte-Mère-Eglise.** This practice still exists in certain locations of the Canton. In springtime, the breeders take their animals on to the communal marshes where they pass the fine season and are collected again before the rise of the water in winter. A guard is appointed daily to look after them and to flag up any problems to the owner.

VI - AGRICULTURE, CRAFTSMANSHIP AND INDUSTRY

As we have seen previously, Normandy was already an industrial country in the paleolithic era and a flowering agricultural country under the Roman occupation. Among the traditional activities we can mention :

1 - Activities related to wood

Places to see...

AREA OF MANCHE

Montjoie-Saint-Martin :

= **'Musée de l'Outil des Métiers du Bois'.** Between Saint-James and Saint-Hilaire-du-Harcouët (D 30) 'La Croix Siroux' - (D 570). Contact (33) 2 33 48 33 79 - Open from Easter to All Saints by appointment. Exhibition of more than 600 hand tools from 10 professions in woodwork, dates from the closure of the factory.

AREA OF ORNE

La Perrière : The town, leaning against the immense forest of Bellême, had for a long time drawn inspiration from the use of wood. The local economy rested essentially on this activity up to 1989, date of the closure of the factory.

AREA OF EURE

Bézu-Saint-Eloi :

= **The wooden toys of 'Père Jorelle'.** Founded in 1864, the workshop perpetuates the craftsmanship of toys of old the craftsman fashioned from wood coming from the nearby forest of **Lyons**, specially selected for this use. Certain pieces are reproductions of more ancient toys in wood from around the world and already figured in a catalogue in 1909 : games of croquet, cup and ball, 'établi d'enfant', solitaire, games of skittles, wooden horses, tops, spinning tops and games of frogs of which the workshop is the sole manufacturer in France today. Open all year except in August from 8 am-12 noon and from 1.30-5.30 pm every day except Sunday. Accessible for the disabled. 6, rue de la Vierge - Tel (33) 2 32 55 07 67.

La Haye-de-Routot :

= **'Musée du Sabotier'.** Church - Tel (33) 2 32 57 59 67. Open from March to 11th November : Sundays and national holidays from 2-6 pm. May, June, September : Saturdays, Sundays and national holidays from 2-6.30 pm ; July and August : every day from 2-6.30 pm. Presentation of the tools and techniques used in earlier times. The evolution of this ancient craft is also recounted and a film presents and brings to life the work of the clog maker. See also a beautiful collection of contemporary clogs coming from diverse regions of France.

2 - Craftsmanship related to straw

Places to see...

AREA OF ORNE

Alençon : In the region of Alençon, straw hats were made and there existed thatched mills.

Coulimer : Monsieur and Madame Dumas still practice the traditional straw work - La Grand Hersée - Tel (33) 2 33 25 49 35

AREA OF SEINE-MARITIME

Hautot-sur-Mer :

= **'Tresseurs de Paille'.** (weavers of straw) Sylvie and Etienne Varin in Pourville - Tel (33) 2 35 40 00 02.

3 - Metalwork

Numerous remains - notably in place names - testify still today in western Normandy to the existence of ancient forges.

It is a thousand year old industry which was particularly flourishing up to the end of the 19th century.

The first metalwork, that of the making of iron, without casting, - a new metal discovered only at the end of the Middle Ages - was very dispersed, in relation to the areas where the mineral was extracted. It was made in the low hearths or small furnaces ventilated by hand, the mineral of the area and, as fuel, charcoal. The Roman roads of the west, sometimes called in the mediaeval era, 'iron roads', were often ballasted with slag.

Places to see...

AREA OF MANCHE

Between Le Vast and Valcauville :

= **The making of zinc nails.** Information : Tel (33) 2 33 34 14 93 or (33) 2 33 24 60 09 - Fax (33) 2 33 24 60 09.

Villedieu-les-Poêles, capital of craft tourism

The reputation of Villedieu-les-Poêles, in the area of La Manche, as Capital of craft tourism, rests on the value of the knowledge linked to the working of copper in all its forms : pans, brass-work, boiler making, and casting.

'La Fonderie de Cloches' (The bell foundry) - In a workshop constructed in 1865 and which retains all its cachet, its floor of solid earth, its tools in copper characteristic of Villedieu, its wooden rolling bridge in perfect working order, one sees foundry craftsmen, casting 'au trousseau' the huge bells in moulds of clay, horse dung and animal skin, following the old methods of many centuries. Everywhere in the course of production, the bells destined for some Norman bell tower are alongside their sisters for all over the world : Africa, the United States, Haiti, Japan, Armenia…

Workshop open to the public from the school holidays in February to those of All Saints.Closed Sundays and Mondays except in summer. Visits in English. For information : La Fonderie de Cloches Cornille-Havard, rue du Pont Chignon. Tel (33) 2 33 61 00 56.

'L'Atelier du Cuivre'. (The Copper Workshop) - In watching the workmen, you admire and appreciate the ancient movements, the techniques, the tools of the 'repouseurs', the tinsmiths, the polishers, and the beaters. To make your visit even more enjoyable, the Copper Workshop has combined tradition and progress : a 15 minute film is shown on a large screen to appreciate all the techniques old and new of this ancient craft. Open all year from Monday to Saturday from 9 am-12 noon and from 1-5.30 pm. Open Sundays in the main season from 10 am-12 noon and from 2.30-5.30 pm. For information : 54, rue du Général Huard - Tel (33) 2 31 51 31 85.

'Musée de la Poeslerie'. 'La Cour du Foyer' : the centre of the ancient activity in copper. In authentic settings from the 12th, 15th and 17th centuries you can visit the Musée de la Poeslerie with ancient copper workshop. (Possibility of a joint ticket with the Musée de la Dentellière - lace museum).

Open every day except Monday mornings from Easter to All Saints from 10 am-12 noon and from 2-6.30 pm. In July and August open every day from 10 am-6.30 pm continuously. For information : Cours du Foyer - Tel (33) 2 33 90 20 92 - Fax (33) 2 33 61 11 78.

'La Maison de l'Etain'. The House of Pewter. (See previous chapter under the heading 'Pewter').

'Musée du Meuble Normand'. Museum of Norman furniture (See previous chapter under the heading 'Furniture').

'Musée de la Dentellière'. Lace Museum (See previous chapter under the heading 'Lace').

AREA OF CALVADOS

Potigny - Saint-Germain-le-Vasson - Soumont-Saint-Quentin : 1990 saw the end of the use of the most important deposit of iron ore in the west of France bringing to an end a hundred years of the industry in Calvados. There remain today, vestiges of this heritage and an ambitious museum project has been started. It is for the association 'Mines de Soumont, un patrimoine, un projet' to create a working structure with the help of the three communities concerned. An 80 metre gallery will be reconstructed and a pit-head frame will give realism to this reconstruction.

'Le Carreau du Livet' at *Saint-Germain-le-Vasson.* It is one of the sites of the Soumont mine, last iron mine in the west, where the great engines on wheels and on rails brought up from the depths and the materials of the miner are presented. One can also discover the last 'sale des pendus' in the region, the baths-showers and the lamp room in their original format as well as the descent system which took the miners to 250 metres below ground. Surrounded by communal forest paths , the 'carreau du Livet' is an ideal place for walking but also for relaxing or picnicking with the river close by and the shady places that it offers. Free visit, commentary on request. For information : Mairie - Tel (33) 2 31 90 53 44 - Fax (33) 2 31 40 88 33.

Saint-Rémy-sur-Orne :

= **'Mine de Fer'.** Iron mine. The tools, the work, the men - Video : 'Les Gueules Rouges' - Geological garden, arboretum, shop, picnic area. For information : Tel (33) 2 31 69 67 77. Open to the public from 1st June to 30th September every day from 10 am to 6.30 pm, from 1st October to 1st December every day except Tuesday from 2-5.30 pm, from 1st April to 1st June from 10-12 am and from 2-6 pm except Tuesday. Closed 25th December and 1st January.

AREA OF ORNE

Aube :

= **'La Grosse Forge d'Aube'.** The Great Forge of Aube. Rue de la Forge - Tel (33) 2 33 34 14 93. Set in the valley of the Risle, some six kilometres from L'Aigle, at the entrance to the town of Aube since the beginning of the 16th century, the great forge is among the best preserved in Europe. It gathers together on the same site, workshops for the production of iron and copper. Visits to the forge and an audiovisual presentation. Visit from 10th June to 1st October : Fridays, Saturdays, Sundays and Mondays from 2-6 pm and Wednesdays and Thursdays from 3-4 pm. From 1st January to 9th June and from 1st October to 21st December : Open from 1.30-3.30 pm from Monday to Thursday.

Le Champ-de-la-Pierre : **Site of Forges. 'The most important in the west of France".** For information : Madame Rivard, Tel (33) 2 33 39 72 94. Founded in 1572 by Claude de Broon on his land-holding at 'Champ de la Pierre' and at 'Joué du Bois'. The mineral was extracted in open cast mines from the woods of *Rânes* then the coal from the 'Forêt d'Ecouves' was taken from *La Bruyère-Saint-Brice*. It provided the nail makers, the lock-makers and the ironmongers of *Tinchebray-Chanu.* Important vestiges of the metallurgy industry in Orne in the 16th century. Large furnace of the great forge (17th century). Guided visits in July and August, Saturdays at 5 pm.

Champsecret :

= **'Les Forges de Varenne'.** Complete collection of wood fired ancient metallurgy from the 16th century. - (Great furnace - Walloon forges - Foundry). For information : Tel (33) 2 33 37 76 88. Open from 1st January to 31st December every day from 9 am-12 noon and from 2-5 pm. Guided visits.

Longny-au-Perche :

= **'Anciennes Forges de Beaumont'.**

Putanges :

= **Ancient canon foundry.** In 1756, a canon foundry was created in Putanges. The last master of the forge claimed in vain from the king, his ennoblement in recompense for his work in the defense of France.

Saint-Sulpice-sur-Risle :

= **Manufacture of needles.** An important manufacture of needles was created in this village in the 18th century. The activity is continued today in Aigle by the Company 'Bohin' which is one of the principal makers in France.

Le Sap :

= **'Forge' and ironworks.** Visit to the workshop of the traditional forge from the 18th and 19th centuries. From May to September. 1, rue Hubert-Laniel. Tel (33) 2 33 67 04 73. Ancient miners village at the place called : 'Le Sap-Mêle'. The mine of Sap-Mêle fed the great forges and the forges of all the region and principally the '800 forges' of Sap. See the 'boves' (caves).

Saint-Cornier-des-Landes :

= **Ancient 'City of nails'.** The little community of Saint-Cornier glories in having been until the 1920's the 'capital of forged nails'. At the beginning of the century, indeed, the craftsman nail makers were numerous in the community. They worked on piecework at home in little improvised forges situated at the end of the garden making nails on the 'billots' (blocks) of granite (many still exist in Saint-Cornier and used to decorate the entrances to properties) which were specially cut for this use. The bellows were operated by the dogs who, from the interior turned a wheel - like squirrels. At the beginning of each week a manufacturer delivered the shanks to the nail makers and would collect the finished product on Saturday. With the money received in payment for their work, they hastened to meet at the café where a 'warm ambiance' reigned until the morning. It is said that the wives placed themselves at the entrance to the bistro to recover, in passing the essential money. In Saint-Cornier they made the nails 'of the gardener'', the nails for shoeing horses (normal and specials for ice), the nails for boots and nails for marine carpenters.

Tinchebray :

= **'La Filière Quincaillerie'.** From the Middle Ages, the region of Tinchebray was a very diverse industrial sector (textiles, leather, wood, paper, horn, mother of pearl) they made knife handles in mother of pearl at *Saint-Jean-des-Bois*. In the 16th and 17th centuries, archive documents testify to the presence of wheelwright's forges throughout the region and individual nail forges at **Saint-Cornier-des-Landes.** It was these forges which helped the development of the iron industry in the region. Metallurgy could develop as all the necessary conditions for this type of industry were found there : great forests for heating (charcoal), proximity to the mineral sources (for the primary material), well fed rivers and streams (for the driving force). The metal craftsmen included : blacksmiths, trap-makers, workers in spiral metals, the makers of drills, steelworkers and those making iron artwork... At the beginning of the 20th century, more than 2000 workers worked with iron at Tinchebray and in the surrounding area. Tinchebray is today still the **French capital of ironmongery.** One still finds there, eleven enterprises in this area of activity which represent amongst them, 80% of the national production of garden utensils and 25% of ironmongery for building (decorative ironwork - decorative ironmongery - mechanical welding). We should say that they still make animal traps and spiral metalwork (European leaders). These companies are grouped together in the heart of the 'Système productif localisé'. For information : Tel (33) 2 33 62 20 59 - Internet site : www.quincaillerie.org.

= **'La Route du Fer'.** This signposted tour of the great furnaces, forges and foundries, testifies to the importance of the metal industry in the region of Orne from the 16th to the 20th century. Length of the tour : 143 kilometres. From Aube to **Ferrière-aux-Etangs**, passing through **Le Champ-de-la-Pierre, Rânes, Saint-Clair-de-Halouze, Dompierre** and **Champsecret.** Stopping points : **Bagnoles-de-l'Orne, La Ferté-Macé, Carrouges. Leaflet** available in the Tourist Offices.

AREA OF EURE

Le Neubourg :
= **Museum dedicated to the craft of the wheelwright forger**. For information : Tel (33) 2 32 35 93 95.

AREA OF SEINE-MARITIME

Auzouville-sur-Ry :
In earlier times they made, in this community, taps for barrels of cider or calvados called 'champleurs''. The tradition remains with a factory making taps.

Duclair :
There formerly existed in Duclair a 'production of horse nails' (Mustad) which closed its doors in 1990.

Forges-les-Eaux :
= **Ancient city of metallurgy.** The activity around iron prospered there up to the 16th century.

Lillebonne :
= **Ancient forges.**

Sainte-Croix-sur-Buchy :
= **Creation of ironwork and weathervanes. 'Néel Créations'.** 'Le Grand Pré' - Tel (33) 2 35 34 36 18.

4 - The Textile industry

With the metal industry, it was the principal activity to which the Normans devoted themselves throughout the Province.

In the area of Calvados alone, almost 100,000 people wove cotton or made lace and around thirty factories, employing 3,000 people, produced 3,000 tons of spun cotton. *(Falaise, Condé-sur-Noireau).*

Numerous reminders remain today of this industry which is now practically extinct, if one excludes the flax activity.

Places to see...

AREA OF MANCHE

Le Vast-Gonneville :
  = **Ancient cotton mill.**

AREA OF CALVADOS

Lisieux :
  = **Ancient textile city.** In the 18th century, the textile activity of Lisieux represented 30% of the French production. In the little cemetery of **Saint-Germain-de-Livet,** a marble grave carries the names of Rosenvald and Pilter, Anglican Pasteur. They came to set up in this region of Lisieux to create a textile factory and called on many English and Irish workers. These were at one time so important that the Journal de Lisieux published pages in English and the lexovian priests put together a catechism in the same language.

Beauvillers (near to Lisieux) :
  = **Textile village, ancient Laniel producer.**

Lisores :
  = **Ancient Laniel factory** where they bleached the materials in the fields.

Vire : Here in the 14th century they made linen cloth and wove wool.

AREA OF ORNE

Dompierre :
  = **'Maison de Fer et du Fil'.** Tel/Fax (33) 2 33 38 03 25. Traditions of mining and textiles in the Bocage from the 18th to the 20th century are recalled in this museum (Lace and Hemp from the seed to the cloth). Open from 1st May to 30th June and from 1st to 30th September Sundays from 3-6 pm. From 1st July to 31st August : every day from 3-6 pm. Guided visits.

Mortagne-au-Perche, in Orne and its surrounding areas, craftsmen made, up to the 19th century, the fabrics for boat sails. These fabrics were sent to Rouen. They also made there the fabrics called 'Mortagnes' which were known throughout France.

Alençon, Ecouché and Vimoutiers were important textile centres.

****

The cloth of Vimoutiers 'lasts a lifetime'

In the 16th century, around Vimoutiers, in Orne, an important cloth industry was born. The peasants, without work for a part of the year, installed at home the methods for weaving, at first hemp cloth, and then linen. Transported to Vimoutiers in bulk, the strands were woven on the farms in an area of forty kilometres around the town. In the 18th century this activity occupied more than 17,000 people. The cloth was marked and sold in the imposing 'Halles de Vimoutiers' to buyers who sent it to neighbouring areas and even abroad.

In the 17th century, a man living in a monastery invented a new cloth. He was called **Paul Creton** *and gave his name to the new 'toiles cretonnes which, at this time, were pure linen. At the beginning of the 18th century, another similar man, Pierre Aubert, invented a new means of weaving linen. These two inventions gave a considerable 'push' to this industry in the East of the area of Orne and the cloths of Vimoutiers had a reputation without equal. Fourcroy wrote at the time of the Revolution : 'The cloth of Vimoutiers is the most beautiful and of the finest texture'.*

In the 19th century, the bleachers of Vimoutiers, the Laniels, had the idea of creating a cloth mechanically, the first in the region. After a study trip to England, they prepared their plans for new installations and established their factory at Beuvillers, near to Lisieux. They continued to bleach their cloth 'in the field' at Lisores near Vimoutiers. Combining the old experience and the new procedures, they soon remained the only makers of the 'Toile de Vimoutiers' and made themselves a substantial fortune. Victim of the competition, the Cloth industry ended in Vimoutiers in the 1950's.

****

AREA OF EURE

Bernay :
> = **Ancient cloth making 'city'.** Bernay had a reputation in the 12th century for its wool cloth. They also made hats.

Brionne :
> = **Textile town from the 16th century.** Ancient factories on the banks of the Risle.

Evreux and Les Andelys :
> = **Textile 'cities'.** In Andelys they wove silk, thread.

Louviers :
> = **'Musée Municipal'.** Presentation of the history of the cloth industry in the region. Free visits every day except Tuesday from 10 am-12 noon and from 2-6 pm. Accessible to the disabled - Tel (33) 2 32 09 58 55.

Radepont :
> = **The textile mill of 'Cathedral' Levavasseur.** Close to the Abbey of Fontaine-Guérard, one can see the original ruins of the ancient Levavasseur mill which was built between 1855 and 1860 on the banks of the Andelle by Baron Charles

Levavasseur in an 'English neogothic' style marrying the brown brick with the white stone. The factory was almost entirely destroyed by a fire. There only remains today, a sort of industrial cathedral with four high towers.

AREA OF SEINE-MARITIME

Cany-Barville :
= **Ancient cotton mills. Eco-museum of 'Moulin-Saint-Martin'.** The linen activity was previously very important in the valley of the Durdent. In the 19th century, 18 workshops existed. The working of linen groups together with scenes of work by hand, using objects and machines authentic to the 1800's : seed drill, 'violon', 'braye', 'ecangeur', Flemish mill. At the same time you can watch the making of ropes, called 'longes de ferme' used to lead cows, calves and sheep. 3, rue de l'Abreuvoir - Tel (33) 2 35 97 59 71 - Open from April to October all the days except Saturday - Guided visits.

Barentin, Lillebonne :
= **Ancient textile factories.**

Doudeville :
= **Capital of Norman linen.** Information from the Tourist Office.

Elbeuf :
= **Ancient capital of the textile industry in Normandy.** Elbeuf was one of the great cloth making cities of France with an international renown.

Gruchet-le-Valasse :
= **Leading place of the 'Indiennes'.** They made handkerchiefs here.

****

Norman flax

For centuries, on the great plains of western Normandy but also and above all in eastern Normandy, they cultivated flax. Today this crop is still important as they harvest in the Pays de Caux half of the flax produced in France. The Flax of Caux benefits from a worldwide renown because of its quality (length, fineness, strength, colour and ease of working).

A demanding plant, flax is only grown every seven years on the same land. From germination to flowering you have to wait two months. In June you can admire the fields covered in blue flowers - the most productive - or white according to the variety. The flowers open in the morning and last half a day. 30 days later, the flax is ripe.

In mid July, at maturity, it is cut (to conserve all the length of the stem) and placed on the earth to soften : the actions of the micro-organisms separate the fibres of wood from the skin. Afterwards it is collected and taken to the 'usure' for 'teillage' which frees the fibres. Finally the long ribbons are combed, spun and bleached to obtain a thread ready to be woven by makers of clothing, of household linen or cloth for furnishings of the highest quality.

*In the Valley of the Dun, between **Fontaine-le-Dun** and **Bourg-Dun**, we advise you to stop, during the best season to discover freely the little blue flowers and their multiple uses.*

The Seine-Maritime is the principal flax producing area in France (14,900 hectares with 1442 cultivators). In five communities in Upper Normandy, in June and July, under the aegis of the 'Confrèrie des Maîtres du Lin du Pays de Caux', various events are organised for the promotion of this cloth (Presentation of the processes, visits to workshops, introduction to embroidery, cloth markets, exhibitions, embroidery competitions).

Routot *(Eure) 3ʳᵈ weekend of June :* **Festival of flax and its derivatives in the 'Maison du Lin'.**

Doudeville *(Seine-Maritime), 'Capital of flax' where you can buy linen clothing, the 3ʳᵈ weekend of June* **'The Fête du Lin'** *takes place.*

'Maison du Lin de Normandie'. *2, place du Général Leclerc - 27350 Routot - Tel (33) 2 32 56 21 76. Everything to do with flax, its growth, its history, its uses, both industrial and in craftwork. Open : March and October : Saturdays and Sundays from 2-6.30 pm. April, May, June and September : every day except Tuesday from 2-6.30 pm.*

Claville, *in the area of Eure :* **'Lin Passion',** *'Domaine de l'Hermitage' : Tel (33) 2 32 34 69 06 - Fax (33) 2 32 34 87 49. E.Mail : info@linpassion.com - Household items in linen and in cotton and linen cloth : table linen, bed linen, toiletry items, linen for religious services, accessories... Open throughout the year by appointment.*

Saint-Pierre-le-Viger : *Permanent information kiosk on flax (its history, its growth, its production, its transformation...).*

****

5 - The leather industry

Numerous tanneries existed in Normandy : at **Torigny, Montebourg, Saint-James**, in the Manche, at **Saint-Pierre-sur-Dives** and at **Vire**, in Calvados, at **Les Andelys, Gisors** in Eure and at **Auffay** in Seine-Maritime.

Thury-Harcourt, in Calvados, the Saint-Bénin quarter was renowned for its leather commerce and its 15 tanneries.

Places to see...

AREA OF CALVADOS

Vaux-sur-Seulles :

= **Leatherwork.** Denis Pimor, craftsman. Hameau de Vaussieux. Tel (33) 2 31 92 89 07.

AREA OF ORNE

Tourouvre :

= **'Tannerie du Perche'.** 'La Gazerie' - Tel (33) 2 33 25 70 18. Open from 9 am-12 noon and from 1.30-6 pm except Sundays. Inheritor of an ancient tradition, this family enterprise works with wholesalers but also with individuals. It has acquired a great renown in the tanning of all sorts of skins, also making leather clothing, sheepskin and furs to measure. Taxidermists and naturalists, the proprietors treat and transform all sorts of whole mammals, birds and fish into African hunting trophies. Exhibition and sales on site.

AREA OF EURE

Gisors :
= **'Fossé aux Tanneurs'.** From the 13th century, numerous tanneries already existed in Gisors.

Pont-Audemer :
= **Remains of ancient tanneries**.

6 - The making of wind vanes and weathercocks

The use of this ancient craft has become rare today, a craftsman in *Francheville,* in Eure, specialises in the making of wind vanes and weathercocks in zinc - Tel (33) 2 32 32 62 76.

7 - Lime kilns

Lime has been destined, since antiquity, for the improvement of agricultural land.

Places to see…

AREA OF MANCHE

Beuzeville-la-Bastille et Liesville :
= These two villages were great producers of lime. The 'blue stone' from which it was extracted came from a quarry situated near the kilns. It was transported to the centre in small wagons. One lit a large fire and walled up the entrance of the conduit before spreading the stones in the 17 metres of chimney alternating them with wood. At the base of the fireplace, a grill held the stones and their 'cooking' was activated by the trapped air in the base of the installation. The decomposition finished, one recovered the lime piled up on the grills as well as the pieces of stone having passed through them, which were then broken up in the grinders to be reduced to powder. The lime, thus obtained, then served to enrich the soils, to guard against parasites on the trunks of apple trees and as a basic product for butchers to help in the preparation, serving to clean the bellies of cattle. The port of Beuzeville-la-Bastille thus saw many 'gabares' carrying their cargo, sea fertiliser from the Bay of Veys. They returned loaded with the lime from Liesville or their own lime-kilns. The kilns ceased their activity in 1961. They also made lime at *Hauteville-sur-Mer*.

Orval :
= **Ancient lime kilns.**

Régneville-sur-Mer :

=**The lime kilns of Rey. 14, route des Fours à Chaux.** Tel (33) 2 33 46 82 18 - Fax (33) 2 33 46 03 74. External visit to the site of the lime kilns : this extraordinary testimony to the industrial architecture of the 19th century was conceived at the beginning of the second Empire. In the neighbouring museum, numerous models and reconstructions present the history of the techniques of the production and use of lime since antiquity. Throughout the season, the visits to the Museum and the kilns are further animated. On the site a reduced size model of a lime kiln allows one to better understand the work of the 'chaufourniers' and the process of transforming limestone into lime : cooking, extinction and expansion of the live lime, the making of lime mortar. Open : March : Sundays from 1-6 pm. April to the end of May and October : every day from 1-6 pm. June to the end of September : every day from 11 am-7 pm.

8 - The extraction of coal

Until quite recently they dug coal in Normandy, on the soil of Calvados. A souvenir of this is conserved at *Molay-Litry* : **Museum of the mine.** Rue de la Fosse Frandemiche - Tel (33) 2 31 22 89 10. Open to the public every day from 10 am-12 noon and from 2-6 pm. Annual closing in January. This museum evokes the history of this mine from 1743 to the 20th century through a variety of objects : a fire pump from the 18th century, unique in France…, a rebuilt mine gallery, an animated model at 1 :10 scale of the mine pithead. The museum has been entirely renovated.

9 - The cutting of stone

= The **'stone of Caen'** was principally worked in the quarries situated in the region of *Caen*, in the Bessin, in the region of *Argentan* and in Perche.

= The **'white stone'** was also extracted and dug in Upper Normandy, notably in the valley of the Seine.

In the west of the province, they used **granite** whereas in the Pays d'Ouche it was **flint**.

In certain areas, such as the region of *Vimoutiers*, they extracted a very soft, crumbly russet coloured stone called **'Roussier'** with which they constructed the bases of the Manors. It was with this russet stone that they built Battle Abbey in Hastings.

Places to see…

AREA OF CALVADOS

Le Gast :

= At the place called 'La Tuilerie' : **'Atelier d'un ancien Picaut'** (Cutter of granite stones). He makes sculptures which are displayed in the open museum. All year - Contact : Bernard Amplilhat. Tel (33) 2 31 66 06 88.

Le Mollay-Littry :
= **Stone cutting.** Grégory Baloche, Z.A. Les Planquettes, route de Balleroy. Tel (33) 2 31 92 39 73.

AREA OF ORNE

Occagnes :
= **'Atelier Bondon'.** - route de Falaise - Tel (33) 2 33 35 84 30.

10 - Plastics Industry

AREA OF ORNE

Alençon :
= **Plastics industry centre.** As a result of the ISPA's development initiatives, Alençon has now become the leading centre in the plastics processing sector.
The Alençon Plastics Industry Centre plays the role of intermediary and partner to many companies and organizations :
= Regional and local authorities.
= Research and training bodies
= Professional plastics industry organizations.
= Companies with plastics processing related activities.
The Alençon Plastics Industry Centre concentrates the skills and techniques of regional, economic, professional and technical partners in a single location. It encourages the development of companies involved in plastics conversion and processing.
Founding partners :
- Chambre de Commerce et d'Industrie d'Alençon.
- Groupe IPSA.
- Groupement de l'Industrie Plastique Normandie-Maine.

11 - Brick-works

Numerous artisan brick-works existed in Normandy in the 18th and 19th centuries. Made with the earth extracted from the land, they were often of mediocre quality. Porous, they spread dampness in the walls.

Places to see...

AREA OF ORNE

Tourouvre :
= **'Briqueterie des Chauffetières'.** L'Hôme-Chamondot - Tel (33) 2 33 25 71 26. This traditional brick works has been run by the same family since 1890 on a site more than two centuries old. They make bricks to order in the old style, all baked over a wood fire. This brick works is to our knowledge the last operating in Normandy. The earth is extracted nearby and the old ovens fed by logs collected from the nearby forest. The company recently provided the bricks for the up-keep of the castle of Versailles.

MUSEUMS OF ART AND POPULAR TRADITIONS

Places to see...

AREA OF MANCHE

Avranches :

= **'Musée d'Arts et Traditions populaires'.** Place Jean-de Saint-Avit - Tel (33) 2 33 58 25 15. This museum allows the discovery of an aspect of the richness of the heritage of the people of Avranches from the Middle Ages up to the 20th century.

= **'Trésor Saint-Gervais'.** Church of Saint-Gervais - Tel (33) 2 33 58 00 22. Conserved in the heart of the church of Saint-Gervais, the treasures include magnificent religious pieces of the goldsmith's art and the statuary of the people of Avranches. It displays notably the famous relic of the head of Saint-Aubert, founder of Mont-Saint-Michel, the relic where one can distinguish, according to tradition, the mark left by the finger of the archangel Saint-Michael.

= **Manuscripts from Mont-Saint-Michel.** Ancient library - 'Hôtel de Ville d'Avranches' - Tel (33) 2 33 68 33 18. The manuscripts from Mont-Saint-Michel have been kept in Avranches since the French Revolution. It is one of the most beautiful collections from the Roman era in Europe. The library holds around thirty mediaeval manuscripts (8th to 15th century).

Bricquebec :

= **'A la Recherche du Temps perdu'.** Museum of A.T.P. in an ancient farm. 'Les Brecqueries' (route de Saint-Sauveur). Tel (33) 2 33 04 07 53. Presentation of objects and utensils from life at the beginning of the century. Large natural scenes of life in the countryside - the village grocers, the rural school, the interior of the peasant home, the war time. Open from Easter to the end of October.

Coutances :

= **'Musée Municipal'.** 2, rue Quesnel-Morinière - Tel (33) 2 33 45 11 92. Paintings from the 17th - 20th century - Sculptures from the mediaeval era, Ancient costumes, Ceramics, Furniture.

Granville :

= **'Musée du Vieux Granville'.** - 2, rue Lecarpentier - Tel (33) 2 33 50 44 10.

Les Loges-Marchis :

= **'Musée Revoir le Passé'.** Humble and private museum dedicated to rural life which will astonish you by the variety of its collection of everyday objects. Contact : Tel (33) 2 33 49 27 67.

Milly :

= **Exhibition of paintings on pebbles and old Norman crafts.**

Saint-Lô :

= **'Musée Ethnologique'.** Le Bois Jugan - Tel (33) 2 33 56 26 98 - Fax (33) 2 33 56 09 12.

Saint-Martin-d'Aubigny :
   = **'Musée de la Brique'.** La Briqueterie - Tel (33) 2 33 07 61 95.

Sainte-Mère-Eglise :
   = **'La Ferme-Musée du Cotentin'.** Unique testimony to the rural traditions of an earlier time set in buildings from the 17th and 18th centuries. Everything that made up the lifestyle and peasant activity is preserved : the press, the tower in granite which served to crush the apples, a collection of regional ploughs made in relation to the soils, the bakery where they cooked the bread pies for the week. The farm-museum also offers temporary exhibitions and numerous activities throughout the year : local markets, festivals of the horse, the harvest, bread, crafts. Open : School holidays : every day from 1-6 pm. In March : Sundays from 1-6 pm. From April to the end of May and in October : every day from 1-6 pm. From June to the end of September : every day from 11 am-7 pm. For information : Tel (33) 2 33 95 40 20 - Fax (33) 2 33 95 40 24.- E.Mail musee.sainte.mere@wanadoo.fr

Brouains :
   = **'Le Moulin de la Sée'.** 'Ecomusée de la vallée de Brouains'. Ancient paper mill. Tel (33) 2 33 59 20 50 - Internet : www.moulin-de-la-see.com.

AREA OF CALVADOS

Caen : At the 'Logis' of the Governors inside the ducal castle. '**Musée de Normandie'.** The daily life of the Normans, their traditions since pre-history : are evoked here : rites and customs, work on the land, craftsmanship and industry. Admirable archaeological and ethnological collections are displayed. Open every day except Tuesdays and public holidays from 9.30 am-12.30 pm and from 2-6 pm. Guided visits by appointment - For information : Tel (33) 2 31 30 47 60 (opening times) (33) 2 31 30 47 50 (Conservation) (33) 2 31 30 47 62 (communication) Fax (33) 2 31 30 47 69.

Clécy :
   Museum of miniature railways. 'Les Fours à Chaux'. Tel (33) 2 31 69 07 13 - Fax (33) 2 31 67 98 10.

Courseulles :
   = **'Musée des médailles et du Vieux Courseulles'.** 17, rue Amiral-Robert - Tel (33) 2 31 37 70 00.

Crévecœur :
   = **'Fondation Schlumberger' - 'Musée du Pan de Bois'.** Tel (33) 2 31 63 02 45 - Fax (33) 2 31 63 05 96. E.Mail : musee.schlumberger@wanadoo.fr - The castle of Crévecœur was built on a feudal mound around the 15th century. This historic site comprises five hectares on which are a mound and a courtyard surrounded by moats which make up a stronghold from the mediaeval period. Nearby is the orchard which has 26 varieties of traditional apple trees and welcomes animals freely. One can also admire there an admirable square dovecote and the manor of the lord. For

information : Tel (33) 2 33 25 91 07 - Fax (33) 2 33 25 33 36. Open from 1ˢᵗ January to 31ˢᵗ August every day from 2-6 pm except Monday, Tuesday and Wednesday. All the rest of the year Saturday and Sunday from 2-6 pm.

AREA OF ORNE

La Madeleine-Bouvert :
= **'La Ferme de l'Aritoire'.** Free entry - Tel (33) 2 33 73 93 34. Open from 1ˢᵗ March to 15ᵗʰ September every day by appointment and week-ends from 6-8 pm. Collection of headdresses and bonnets from an earlier time.

Le Merlerault :
= **'Musée Municipal Ruchon-Morin'.** Rebuilding of a bourgeois house from the 19ᵗʰ century. For information : Tel (33) 2 33 35 42 67. Open all year, Wednesdays from 2-4 pm, Thursdays and Saturdays from 10.30 am-11.30 am - Free entry.

Le Sap :
= **'Ecomusée du Grand Jardin'.** rue du Grand-Jardin - Tel (33) 2 33 35 25 89. Internet site : http://www.le-grand-jardin.asso.fr

Mortagne-au-Perche :
= **'Musée Percheron'.** At the Maison des Comtes du Perche. Collection of objects of local history - Temporary exhibitions in summer. 8, rue du Portail Saint-Denis. Open from 15ᵗʰ June to 15ᵗʰ September from 3-6 pm. For information : Tel (33) 2 33 25 25 87.

Saint-Cyr-la-Rosière :

= **'Musée Départemental des Arts et Traditions Populaires du Perche'.** 'Prieuré de Sainte-Gauburge' (13th and 16th centuries). Architecture - Temporary exhibitions. Shop - specialist library. Tel (33) 2 33 73 48 06 - Fax (33) 2 33 73 18 94.

Sées :

= **'Musée Départemental d'Art religieux'.** One of the richest in Normandy. Learned and popular religious art. Place du Général de Gaulle - Tel (33) 2 33 28 59 73.

Tinchebray :

= **'Musée de l'ancienne Prison Royale'.** Art and popular traditions from Lower Normandy. Royal prison from the 17th century, tribunal. Rebuilding of an ancient Norman interior. 34, Grande-Rue - Tel (33) 2 33 66 78 00.

AREA OF EURE

Le Bec-Hellouin :

= **'Musée de la Musique Mécanique'.** Rue Lanfranc - Tel (33) 2 32 46 16 19.

Bosquentin :

= **'Musée de la Ferme et des Vieux Métiers'.** 1, chemin Sainte-Anne - Tel (33) 2 32 48 07 22 or (33) 2 32 49 35 25. In a typical farm of the Pays de Lyons, a collection of traditional objects and utensils to bring to life the old crafts and the Normandy of earlier times. The founder of this A.T.P. museum, Jean-Jacques Falher, is also an excellent 'raconteur' who evokes, through anecdotes, the history of the tools that he exhibits. Cider tasting and regional products in the courtyard. Visit from Easter to All Saints, weekends and public holidays from 2.15-6.30 pm.

Bourneville :

= **'Maison des Métiers'.** Le Bourg. Open in September and October Sundays and public holidays from 2-6 pm. May, June, July and August : every day except Wednesdays and the last weekend of the month from 2-6.30 pm. In July and August : every day from 10 am-12 noon and from 2-6.30 pm. (The entry ticket also gives access to the 'Musée des Terre-Neuvas'). Situated in an old town house, this museum offers an amazing collection of ancient paintings, landscape paintings from the 19th century, drawings, objets d'art : pottery, ivories, arms, Masonic objects, religious art but also an important collection of babies bottles from ancient times to the present day for you to discover. At the end of the visit, you are presented with a reconstruction of the interior of a typical house of the Pays de Caux. In the park there is an arboretum. Tel (33) 2 32 57 40 41

Conches :

= **'Musée Municipal'.** Route Sainte-Marguerite - Tel (33) 2 32 30 90 41.

La Couture-Boussey :

= **'Musée d'Instruments à Vent'.** 2, rue d'Ivry -Tel (33) 2 32 36 28 80.

Ezy-sur-Eure :

= **'Musée Municipal du Peigne Called des Peigneux'.** Known from the 15th century for making combs, the commune of Ezy-sur-Eure supplied the leading Parisian hairdressing salons. This unusual museum has a collection of the best models made in Ezy, out of boxwood, turtle shell, horn, ivory, cardboard and even hardened rubber. The old workshop site can be visited 71, rue Pasteur -Tel (33) 2 37 64 64 69. Open from February 1st to December 20th, on Wednesdays from 2-6 pm and on Saturdays, Sundays and public holidays from 10 am-12 noon and from 2-6 pm.

Hauville :

= **'Le Moulin'.** Dating back to the 12th century, it is one of the only stone windmills left in Upper Normandy. Nearby in the miller's house there is an exhibition about water and windmills in the region. Open : March, April and October : on Saturdays, Sundays, and public holidays from 2-6 pm May, June and September : Saturdays, Sundays and holidays. from 2-6.30 pm. July and August : every day from 2-6.30 pm.

Pont-Audemer :

= **'Musée Municipal A.-Canel'.** 64, rue de la République - Tel (33) 2 32 56 84 81

AREA OF SEINE-MARITIME

Cany-Barrille :

= **'Ecomusée J.-F. Martin'.** In an old 15th century flour mill : retrospective exhibition of country life (old trades, evolution of agricultural machinery...). The Eco-musée in Cany was founded by Charles Neufville in 1990 and a collection of 400 machines and 4,000 tools have been assembled over thirty years. On show : Tractors, (with wheel bands, tracks since 1915), harvesters, threshers, wooden ploughs, presses, stills, everything to do with the harvest (scythes, flails, a 1860 steam machine, a hand-driven flail), and many other tools to do with agriculture. The interior of an 1800 cottage in the Pays de Caux. A collection of horse drawn vehicles : a phaeton, an English cab, a hearse, a chariot.
A collection of old toys. A collection of wooden sculptures, paintings and engravings. Open from April 1st to October 30th from 2-7 pm. The first Sunday of each month with varied attractions. 3, rue de l'Abreuvoir - Tel (33) 2 35 97 59 71- Fax (33) 2 35 97 06.

Caudebec-en-Caux :

= **'Musée Biochet-Brechot'.** In the 'Maison des Templiers' dating back to the 13th century, a museum of local history and collection of fire back.

Fécamp :

= **'Musée des Arts et de l'Enfance'.** 21, rue Alexandre-Legros - Tel (33) 2 35 28 31 99. Open from September 1st to June 30th every day from 10 am-12 noon and from 2-5.30 pm except Tuesdays, January 1st, May 1st, and December 25th. In July and August : every day from 10 am-12 noon and from 2-6.30 pm. (The entry ticket also gives access to the 'Musée des Terre-Neuvas'). Situated in an old town house, this museum offers an amazing collection of ancient paintings, landscape paintings from the 19 century, drawings, objets d'art : pottery, ivories, arms. Masonic objects, religious art but also an important collection of babies bottles from antiquity to the present day for you toff discover. At the end of the visit, you are presented with a reconstruction of the interior of typical house of the Pays de Caux. In the park there is an arboretum.

Harfleur :
= **'Musée du Prieuré'.** 52, rue de la République - Tel (33) 2 35 45 40 62. Built in an old inn from the 15th century which used to welcome sailors, this museum contains collections relating to local history, from pre-history to the present day. Beautiful ceramics and glassware from the Roman period.

Lillebonne :
= **'Musée du Jardin Jean-Rostand'.** Open from 1st May to 30th October every day from 10 am-12 noon and from 2.30-6.30 pm and the rest of the year from 2.30-6.30 pm except Tuesdays. 7, rue Victor-Hugo - Tel (33) 2 35 38 53 73. Situated at the entrance to the public garden in a 19th century pavilion. This museum shelters archaeological and ethnographical collections. A Gallo-Roman tomb enriched with 45 objects, furniture, jewels from the Pays de Caux, various utensils including a complete set of materials for a wig/hair-piece maker, souvenirs from the textile factories, beautiful collections of utilitarian objects, a remarkable series of decorative bricks reborn from the pottery centre of Melamare.

Maniquerville :
= **'L'Agriculture au Fil du Temps'.** Tel (33) 2 35 29 31 28. Open to the public from Easter to All Saints. In an authentic farm, beautiful and interesting collection of tools and machines : more than 1,000 items are displayed often relating to the cider production, but also to livestock farming, the growth of beetroot, oilseed rape, wheat and the work of the foresters...

Martainville :
= **'Château-Musée Départemental des Traditions et Arts Normands'.** Bourg de Martainville - Tel (33) 2 35 23 44 70 - Fax (33) 2 35 23 16 84. In a sumptuous dwelling from the 15th and 16th centuries rich collections are exhibited retracing the daily life in eastern Normandy from the 16th to the 19th century : furniture, dishes, utilitarian items are grouped together according to their origin. A floor is given over to Norman costume. Open every day except Tuesdays and Sunday mornings. From 1st April to 30th September from 10 am-12.30 pm and from 2-6 pm (winter) and 2-6.30 pm (summer). Sunday afternoons from 2-5.30 pm (winter) and 2-6.30 pm (summer).

Neufchâtel-en-Bray :
= **'Musée Mathon-Durand'.** Grand-Rue Saint-Pierre - Tel (33) 2 35 93 06 55. Open from 15th June to 15th September all the days, except Monday, from 3-6 pm. From 1st October to 1st November only the Sunday from 3-6 pm. Five rooms of

an ancient bourgeois house from the 16th century are given over to popular arts and traditions of the Pays de Bray : glassware, furniture, pottery, work in the fields and the making of cheese from NeufchâTel.

Notre-Dame-de-Bondeville :

= **'Musée Industriel de la Corderie Vallois'.** 185, route de Dieppe. Tel (33) 2 35 74 35 35. Museum of Man and Industry in Seine-Maritime. A moving museum, this ancient factory has become a place to remember the regional textile industry. There is a wood panelled building, built in 1822 on the 'Cailly' which houses both English and French hydraulic spinning machines. These were used to make ropes and braided cotton between 1880-1978. Today one can see the hydraulic wheel, the mechanical transmissions and the machines of the era in operation. Open every day from 1.30-6 pm (except 1st January, 1st May, 1st November, 11th November and 25th December).

Rouen

= **'Musée Départemental des Antiquités'.** Square André-Maurois, 198, rue Beauvoisine - Tel (33) 2 35 98 55 10. In this cloister of a convent from the 17th century, this museum has been developed to house rich collections evoking the history of Rouen and its region from pre-history to the 19th century. See especially the important archaeological collections, 'protohistoriques', Gallo-Roman (mosaic from Lillebonne) and Merovingian. 'Objets d'Art' from the Middle Ages and the Renaissance, furniture (tapestry of the winged stags from the 15th century) and wood panels. Open all the days (except Tuesday, Sunday morning and public holidays) from 10 am-12.15 pm and from 1.30-5.30 pm, Sundays from 2-6 pm.

= **'Musée National de l'Education'.** 185, rue Eau-de-Robec - Tel (33) 2 32 82 95 95. This museum is devoted to children and their education since the 16th century through exceptional collections of paintings, engravings, furniture and scholastic material without forgetting games and toys. Reconstruction of a classroom from around 1900 in a beautiful wood panelled dwelling. Open all the days except Tuesday from 10 am to 0.30 pm and from 1.30-6 pm. Saturdays and Sundays from 1-6 pm.

= **'Centre d'Histoire Sociale Expotec 103'.** Museum spread over several sites. At the Moulin Saint-Gilles : a history of the techniques testifies to the industrial saga. Tools, steam machines, motors, a forge, weaving crafts... 13, rue Saint-Gilles - Tel (33) 2 35 08 08 41. Open from 2-5 pm, weekends and public holidays.

Rouvray-Câtillon :

= **'Le Randillon'.** In a Manor from the 16th century: Centre to the memory and the identity of the Pays de Bray.

Saint-Valery-en-Caux :

= **'Musée Maison Henri IV'.** In a beautiful wood panelled building in Renaissance style is presented a permanent exhibition of the local history as well as temporary exhibitions - Varied themes : local history, furniture, painting,... Open every day in July and August - In June and September : every day except

Mondays and Tuesdays -the rest of the year : open weekends and public holidays from 11 am-1 pm and from 3-7 pm. Closed in January. Tel (33) 2 35 57 14 13.

Sommery :

= **'Ferme de Bray'.** Traditional farm from the 17th century with cider press, 'auget' mill, bread oven, dovecote... Open from 15th April to 1st November, weekends and public holidays, July and August from 2-6 pm. Tel (33) 2 35 90 57 27.

Yvetot :

= **'Musée du Pays de Caux'.** 18, rue Grand-Fay - Tel (33) 2 35 95 03 69. Actually closed. Presentation of more than 20,000 objects, writings and documents ! Reconstruction of family settings : work in the fields, the harvest, the milk industry, the extraction of the marl, the café-grocery of olden times.

TOURIST CIRCUITS

AREA OF CALVADOS

= **'The route of the mills'.** Tour situated to the south of **Courseulles** around **Creully** and **Thaon** drawn between the valleys of the Seulles, the Thue and the Mue. This is the country 'of stone and water'. These watercourses previously fed numerous hydraulic mills. Leaflet available from Tourist Offices in Calvados.

= **'The Route of Traditions'.** Region of passage, situated in contact with the plain of Caen and the Norman Bocage, the pre-Bocage is one of multiple traditions : agricultural, crafts, industrial, popular, cultural and religious...
This tour based around **Villers-Bocage** and **Aunay-sur-Audon**, is an invitation to discover this land and its past. Leaflet available from Tourist Offices in Calvados.

VII - MARITIME TRADITION

1 - Places of history

Heirs of the courageous Vikings, the Normans have accorded, throughout their history, a major importance to the sea and everything concerned with it.

Normandy possesses a very rich maritime heritage and participated greatly in the constitution of the maritime heritages of France and England.

The Dukes of Normandy held a great interest particularly with maritime affairs and aided the development of four great ports which carried out almost entirely the exchanges, notably with England : *Barfleur,* 'the Royal Port', *Caen, Ouistreham* and *Dieppe.* Since then the maritime vocation of the province has never diminished.

Places to see…

AREA OF MANCHE

Barfleur : Historic port known in earlier times for its naval shipyards.

= **The sea rescue centre** gathers together numerous souvenirs.

****

Barfleur : First great anglo norman port

Founded well before the first Viking raids, the port of Barfleur became the first great port of the Norman coast before attaining great notoriety in the Middle Ages and then becoming the official port of the Anglo-Norman kings.

We know that the ship on which William made the crossing between Normandy and England in 1066, which was called 'Mora', had been ordered by Mathilde, from the shipyards of Barfleur. Some people think that William's fleet, before arriving at Dives was assembled in Barfleur. These ships, we should remember, were of typical Viking construction.

It was a sailor from Barfleur, Etienne, son of Airard, who had the honour of captaining the ducal ship to England.

Having become King of England, William used Barfleur as a transit port and it was thus that the port became the official embarkation point for the Anglo-Norman sovereigns.

The 'Esnecca Regis' was specially constructed and fitted out to transport the king, his court and the royal treasure. The crossing between Barfleur and Southampton lasted roughly one night.

The sons of the Conqueror retained the habits of their father.

It was off Barfleur that the dramatic wreck of the 'Blanche Nef' took place in 1120 on the rocks of Quillebeuf.

The port of Barfleur was subjected over seven centuries to the vicissitudes of the relations between England and France and that which the war did not destroy or kill was decimated by the sea and the plague. In fact, the important port from the 11th century which could accept a thousand ships has disappeared little by little under the floods, victim of the rising waters which eroded the banks and submerged the mediaeval town which accounted for 10,000 inhabitants at the time of William.

After the Hundred Years War, the great maritime city which had been Barfleur practically ceased to exist.

An enthralling 3 hours visit for the whole family !

La Cité de la Mer is the only one of its kind in Europe. Its a new scientific, cultural and touristic centre which seeks to answer many of the questions asked when man encounters the deep ocean.

*It has set up home in the **Transatlantic Ship Temminal**, a masterpiece of Art Deco design and an exceptional testimony to the transatlantic era.*

La Cité de la Mer gives new life to this monumental architecture and enhances it with two exhibitions showing different aspects of the conquest of the underwater world:

*'**Journey to the centre of the sea**' and '**The submarines' incredible adventure**'. By visiting both of them, visitors can listen, watch, immerse themselves and play an active role...to understand.*

*Dive gradually into the '**Journey to the centre of the sea**', that's the promise of an initiatory trail to the depths. With murals and magical aquariums, submarine charts and sparkling waves, interactive displays and thrilling exhibitions, the marvels of this other world invite you to penetrate their secrets. **The Abyssal Aquarium**, the deepest in Europe, and the sixteen pools show the surprising wildlife that demonstrate the limitless capacity for adaptation to the sea.*

*'**The submarines' incredible adventure**': Invention and creativity are transmitted in the submarine's lair. Alongside technological advances, the tale is told of the life under water. Visit '**Le Redoutable**', the world's largest submarine open to the public in its dry dock, and discover the numerous submarines that have been invented down the ages - from the Nautilus imagined by Jules Verne to modern submarines. The many interactive displays, games and simulations give you an opportunity to experience the vast and strange underwater forces.*

La Cité de la Mer, subaquatic sensation.

Tel (33) 825 33 50 50 - Internet : www.citedelamer.com

'La Rade de Cherbourg' (the Cherbourg sea wall)

The creation of the Rade de Cherboug is in the domain of great works, one of the most grandiose undertakings of the 18th century.

It was created on 1,500 hectares, the largest artificial sea wall ever constructed.

The first to see in Cherbourg, city nestled at the end of a bay, 'the Inn of the Channel', was the military engineer Vauban who persuaded Louis XIV to restore the fortress before deepening the outer port and a harbour. Three years later, in 1689, the king changed advisers and had the rebuilt ramparts destroyed for fear of an English landing. The defeat at La Hougue in 1692 was the event which convinced the military experts of the need to construct a great war port on the Channel. In 1776, Louis XVI leant in favour of Cherbourg.

It was necessary to completely build a wall in the sea some 3 kilometres from the estuary.

The building was entrusted in 1783 to an engineer of bridges and roads, Alexandre de Cessart, who imagined a wall formed by the juxtaposition of 90 wooden containers, in a conical form 20 metres high and 50 metres in diameter. But the storms destroyed the containers before they could be filled. In 1789, the foundation, situated at a depth of 12 metres, a width of 100 metres and a length of 3,700 metres was achieved. Interrupted during the Revolution, the work was recommenced with Napoléon Bonaparte in 1802.

The outer port (290 metres by 240) was opened in 1813. The Charles X harbour (290 metres by 220) was achieved in 1829 and the Napoléon III port was built between 1836 and 1864. The central wall was finished in 1853.

In 1860, the wall was reinforced by three forts at the two extremities and in the centre. To the central wall would be added a wall to the west coming from Querqueville and a wall to the east linking the island of Pelée. The Homet wall some 1,000 metres long was finished in 1914 and that of the 'flemish' in 1922. More than two centuries of work were thus necessary to construct the 'rade' accessible at all times. It has welcomed and still welcomes the greatest liners in the world.

****

Courtils :

= 'Maison de la Baie du Mont-Saint-Michel, Relais de Courtils'.

Route de la Roche Torin - Tel 02 33 89 66 00 - Fax 02 33 89 66 09. E.Mail : smet.courtils@wanadoo.fr - Information point, shop, meeting room Discovery activities, (crossing of the shores, outings…). Half day and full day excursions.

Fermanville :

= 'Phare du Cap Levy'. 28 metres high. It was built in 1947 to replace the lighthouse constructed in 1858 and destroyed during the Second World War.

Gatteville :

= 'Phare de Gatteville'. Tel/Fax (33) 2 33 23 17 97. On the point of Barfleur, built in granite in 1834. It is 71 metres high and the light carries some 90 kilometres. To reach the top and admire the coastline you must climb 365 steps !

Exhibition room on the history of lighthouses and beacons. Exceptional panorama over the 'Val de Saire' from the top of the lighthouse. Open from 1st April to 30th September from 10 am-12 noon and from 2-7 pm and open from 1st October to 31st March from 10 am-12 noon and from 2-4 pm. Closed from 15 November to 15 December and in January - visit : 30 minutes. Closed the 1st May and 25th December.

Goury :

= **'Phare de Goury'.** It stands 48 metres tall on the 'Cap de la Hague'. It protects ships in the dangerous passage of the Raz Blanchard. Its lifeboat station is famous.

Granville :

= **'Musée du Vieux Granville'.** Rue du Roc, in the ancient 'Logis du Roy'. Tel (33) 2 33 91 88 39. At the entrance to the upper town, this museum of art and popular traditions recounts the history of Granville, corsair city, cod fishing port and then tourist centre.

= **'Musée Maritime'.** Collections of ship models - Environmental and scientific space presenting the mechanism of the tides, the silting of the bay, the dangers and the protection of the bay.

Régneville-sur-Mer :

= **'Musée maritime des fours à chaux'** - 14, route des fours à chaux. Tel (33) 2 33 16 82 18. E.Mail : musee.regneville@wanadoo.fr - Open : School holidays : every day from 1-6 pm. March : Sundays from 1-6 pm - April to the end of May, October : every day from 1-6 pm. June to the end of September : every day from 11 am-7 pm. Régneville was one of the most important ports in the Cotentin. The brigs and schooners transported limestone all along the north coast of Brittany and brought from Wales, the coal destined for the lime kilns. Models, rope-making techniques, rigging, marine mementos, recall the activity which reigned in the port of Régneville at the beginning of the century.

Sainte-Mère-Eglise :

= **Les 'Gabares'.** Flat bottomed boats of between ten and twenty metres in length whose drive was provided by a sail installed on the mast (folding), set forward on the ship, or by towing with a rope (grelin) which was pulled by the ship's apprentice or a horse. When this was not possible, the chief handled the 'fourquet', with a long pole on which the sailor pushed against the bottom of the river. The average speed was thus not more than 4 kilometres an hour. They criss-crossed in earlier times the 25,000 hectares of marshland and represented the only means of transport to transport the 'tangue' of the Bay of Veys, the lime of Liesville or even the cattle and horses of the canton. At the end of the 19th century they numbered 200. Their use dates back to the 14th century since one can trace from this period, a delivery of barrels of wine to the Lord of Néhou coming from Carentan by this mode of transport. One must clearly understand the utility of these gabares, to have then only something horse-drawn, capable of transporting one or two tons at the maximum, then this boat which could be loaded with twenty. The use of the gabare (barge) in the marshes disappeared around 1930.

Recently, a gabare has been reconstructed in the marshes of Pont-l'Abbé and the local choir carries this somewhat abandoned name.

Tonneville :

= **'Ludiver'**. 1700, rue de la Libération. Tel (33) 2 33 78 13 80. Observatory-Planetarium of the Cap de la Hague. Open from 10 am-7 pm.

Tourlaville :

= **'Musée Maritime Chantereyne'**. Port des Flamands - quai Pierre-le-Comte Tel (33) 2 33 20 04 71.

Ile de Tatihou :

= **'Musée Maritime'**. Accueil Tatihou, quai Vauban. Tel (33) 2 33 23 19 92 - Fax (33) 2 33 54 33 47.
E.Mail : ile.tatihou@wanadoo.fr Internet : http://www.tatihou.com Access to the island : from the port of Saint-Vaast-la-Hougue, by amphibious boat : From May to September : every day, from October to April : weekends. Strong in the richness and diversity of its history, the island of Tatihou is today one of the reference points of Norman maritime culture.

= **'Musée Maritime'**, court of merchandise from the Lazaret era (18th century) ensures the conservation and value of the archaeological collections (property coming from the wrecks of the Battle of La Hougue in 1692) and deethnology (fishing boats and techniques on the Norman coasts).

= **The port (end of the 19th century)**. Discover a traditional boat : 'L'ami Pierre', 'bisquine' de Barfleur - Day trips in the bay of la Hougue in July and August.

= **'L'Atelier de charpente navale'**. They restore the collections there and enrich them by the reconstruction of traditional boats.

= **'La Halle aux bateaux'**.

= **'La Maison des douaniers'** (the Customs house) built around 1810.

= **'Le Jardin botanique'**. Three hectares on the island 'intra muros' laid out as a garden dedicated to the plants of the coastal region of La Manche and the Atlantic. 200 species of plant.

= **'Le Jardin maritime'**.

= **'Le Tour Vauban' built in 1694**.

= **'The Centre of scientific culture'**. Hospital of Lazaret built around 1825.

= **'La Caserne' 7,** restaurant.

= **'La Chapelle'** from the beginning of the 18th century.

= **'Les Poudrières'** from the end of the 19th century.

= **'The ornithological observatory'**.

= **'Le Fort de l'Ilet'** (beginning of the 19th century)

Vains :

= **'Maison de la Baie du Mont-Saint-Michel - Relais de Vains'** - St Léonard - This new 'Maison de la Baie' opened its doors in 2001. The museum has as a theme 'Life in the Bay', presentation of the great ecosystems and the human activities (fishing and the history of salt). Dates and opening hours : during the school holidays, every day from 1-6 pm. In March : Sundays from 1-6 pm. From April to the end of May and October : every day from 1-6 pm. From June to the end of September : every day from 11 am-7 pm. Free visits lasting an hour. Contact : Tel (33) 2 33 89 06 06 - Fax (33) 2 33 89 06 07. E.Mail : musee.courtils@wanadoo.fr

****

La Hague, country of contreband

Like most of the coastal regions, the history of La Hague has been marked by the exploits of the smugglers... and the customs officers. Smuggling was a very ancient activity in this area since the Middle Ages. The fraud was in salt, cloth and tobacco. The traffic was most often with the Channel Islands which had a less beneficial tax status.

The 'gravage' also existed on the coast. In the beginning it was a practice accepted by the authorities : that of collecting wood - which was rare and expensive in the Cotentin - on the beaches and on the shoreline. But when the wood became scarce, certain people were tempted to obtain it by demonic means : they lit fires on the shore where rocks were numerous and sharp and waited for ships , which believed they had found a harbour, until they broke up and the wood and the riches that they contained could be collected.

One still finds remains of this era, in the old dwellings on the coast, with hiding places behind the fireplaces to conceal the smuggled products.

****

AREA OF CALVADOS

Courseulles :

= **'Maison de la Mer'.** Place du Général de Gaulle - Tel (33) 2 31 37 92 58 - Fax (33) 2 31 37 34 84. Shellfish, cold water fish. Aquarium - sea tunnel - diorama on the oyster. Open from1st March to 30th April from 10 am-12 noon and from 2-6 pm. From 1st May to 30th June : from 9.30 am to 0.30 pm and from 2-7 pm (every day). In July and August : from 9.30 am-7 pm every day.

= **'Musée des Médailles et du Vieux Courseulles'.** 17, avenue Amiral-Robert - Tel (33) 2 31 37 70 00.

= **Ancient shipyards.** In this little Norman port, they built in earlier times, (1876-1922) wooden fishing boats and the 'doreys' called 'picoteaux'. In October they fish for sand eels. Returning from fishing, the chiefs of the trawlers sell on the quayside crustaceans and fish.

Lion-sur-Mer :

= **'La Maison du Fossile'.** 2, place des Victimes du 2 juillet 44. Tel (33) 2 31 96 88 00. Open from 1st May to 30th October every day (except Tuesday) from 10 am to 12 noon and from 2-6 pm. From 1st November to 30th April open during the week-end and school holidays. Important collection coming from the geological site in the cliff of the confessionals in Lion.

Dives-sur-Mer :

= **Traditional ships.** The 'Saint-Rémi' is the property of the town of Dives-sur-Mer. It was restored by the benefactors of the Sailing School. 'Anne Mathilde' has been acquired thanks to the participation of the regional 'conseil' and the three communities of Cabourg, Houlgate, Dives and the clubs of the estuary. These two magnificent boats represent the towns and the clubs of the estuary at festivals and major gatherings. If you want to discover movements of the past or share the pleasures of traditional sailing, you can travel on board. They wait for you in the yacht harbour of Port Guillaume. For information : Tel (33) 2 31 91 43 14.

Luc-sur-Mer :

= **'Maison de la Baleine'.** 45, rue de la Mer - Tel (33) 2 31 97 55 93. Museum of the world of marine mammals and whales. Open from 1st October to 31st May : weekends in the afternoon. From 1st June to 9th September : every day from 10 am-12 noon and from 2-7 pm. From 10th September to 1st October : every day from 2-6 pm and by appointment.

Honfleur :

= **Musée de la Marine'.** In the ancient Church of Saint-Etienne (14th-15th century). Quai Saint-Etienne - on the edge of the Vieux Bassin - Tel (33) 2 31 89 14 12. Disused, the oldest church of Honfleur has welcomed a 'Museum of the Sea' opened in 1976. It holds models, a rich iconographic documentation on the topography of the town in different eras and varied souvenirs of wooden ships. It evokes memories of the great sailors, discoverers, slave traders and smugglers : collection of model boats, objects and souvenirs of the sea …

Ouistreham :

= **'Le Phare'.** Built in 1903, it is 38 metres tall and has a view up to 18 miles. It has 171 steps. Visits by appointment from April to June and open to the public in July and August from 3 pm. The guide will retell numerous anecdotes at will.

Villerville :

= **'Mer et Désert'.** 10, avenue du Général Leclerc - Tel (33) 2 31 81 13 81.

AREA OF EURE

Poses :

= **'Musée de la Batellerie'.** 64, chemin du Halage. Evocation of the history of the shipping on the inland waterways in the era of towing on the Seine, this thanks to two floating museums, 'the Fauvette', river tug from 1928, classed as an historic monument, and the barge 'Midway II' which holds a museum dedicated to the local history of the Seine. Guided visits from 1st May to 1st October, Sundays and public holidays from 2.30-6 pm.

AREA OF SEINE-MARITIME

Caudebec-en-Caux :

= **'Musée de la Marine de Seine'.** Avenue Winston-Churchill - Tel (33) 2 35 95 90 13.

Dieppe :

= **'Château-Musée'.** Rue Chastes. Tel (33) 2 35 84 19 76. Rooms of the sea with model ships, maps, navigation instruments. See Château-Musée de Dieppe - Chapter 3).

= **E.S.T.R.A.N. 'Hissons la grande voile' - Cité de la Mer.** 37, rue de l'Asile Thomas - Tel (33) 2 35 06 93 20. Internet : citedelamer@online.fr. Its objective is to allow visitors to discover the identity of the Channel through four areas : The evolution of naval construction. The fish chain, 'from sea to plate'. Cliffs and pebbles. Marine aquariums unique in the region. Open every day from 10 am-12 noon and from 2-6 pm, except 24th and 31st December in the afternoon and 25th December and 1st January all day.

Etretat :

= **'Marine aquarium'.** Laid out in a tunnel with varied coloured species originating from the Channel but also from tropical seas. Open to the public weekends in the Spring from 2-6 pm ; from 15th June to the end of September every day from 1-7 pm. For information : Tel (33) 2 35 27 01 23.

Fécamp :

= **'Musée des Terre-Neuvas'.** 27, boulevard Albert Ier (facing the sea). Tel (33) 2 35 29 76 22. Open to the public every day from 1st September to 30th June from 10 am-12 noon and from 2-5.30 pm except Tuesdays and the 1st January, 1st May and 25th December. In July and August open every day from 10 am-7 pm. Through ancient models of authentic boats and old equipment, the museum presents a painful but fascinating adventure of the Fécamp Terre-Neuvas who, following the example of the Bretons would leave for several months to fish for cod in the glacial waters of the Atlantic. The museum also recalls the fishing for herring and the smoking of the fish in the 'boucanes'. A part of the museum is given over to the history of naval construction in Normandy since the Vikings. Beautiful collection of marine paintings.

Le Havre :

= **'Espace maritime et portuaire des docks Vauban'.** Quai Frissard - Tel (33) 2 35 24 51 00 - Fax (33) 2 35 26 76 69. Open to the public Tuesdays, Wednesdays, Saturdays and Sundays from 2.30-6 pm. Docks constructed in brick in 1846, with vast glass roofs. They retell the history of whale fishing but also the époque of the great liners and then the container ships.

= **'Maison de l'Armateur'.** 3, quai Ile - Tel (33) 2 35 19 09 85. <u>Closed for works</u>. One of the last witnesses of Le Havre from the 18th century. This dwelling, symbol of Le Havre's commercial prosperity but also witness of the architecture of the 18th century was built following the original plans with exceptional décor.

= **'Musée de l'ancien Havre'.** 1, rue Jérôme-Bellarmoto - Tel (33) 2 35 42 27 90. Open from Wednesday to Sunday from 10 am-12 noon and from 2-6 pm except public holidays. The Museum of Old Le Havre is set in a house from the 18th century which belonged to the ship owner Michel Dubocage from Bléville. Old officer of the national marine, he made a tour of the world and opened the route to China.

Presented here are :
- The history of Le Havre since 1517.
- Maritime life under the old regime.
- Maritime life from 1815 to 1914.
- Naval construction.
- Leisure and sea bathing.
- The town area from 1517 to 1838.
- The industrial revolution.
- The town space from 1850.
- The marine painters.
- Brass bands and orchestras.

****

The 'French line'

The Americans had reigned on the Atlantic up to 1840, the era of the birth of 'Cunard' (1869 : 'White Star Line'). Then the British took over the role.

France entered the competition from 1861 with the French Line (C.G.T. or the 'Compagnie Générale Transatlantique') on a level much more restrained than Southampton. Le Havre welcomed only a single French transatlantic company and only some foreign companies whereas the English port welcomed numerous national and foreign companies.

England was going to display its superiority (speed, length, capacity…) from 1840 with brief appearances from Germany and Italy up to 1935 when France launched the 'Normandie'.

The names of the greatest English liners remain celebrated even in Normandy : Mauretania, Lusitania, Aquitania, and still Olympic, Majestic and most sadly the famous Titanic.

A great difference separated the international fleets from the French fleet : the sister-ships. The French Line, contrary to the other companies would always launch ships that were radically different.

The company had a small immigrant clientele compared to other nations and a large clientele in First Class, above all American. France, except where the Normandy was concerned, would never be the strongest on the Atlantic and would play with success the cards of gastronomy, of chic and of the service 'à la française".

It was thus that the French Line could, up to 1974, rival the other countries represented on the ocean.

The great liners of the French Line were : 'La Touraine', 'La Savoie', 'La Lorraine', 'La Provence'… (the first launched the 'floating palaces' from 1890 to 1905).

The 'France I' in 1912 whose First Class cabins were sold to the highest bidders as well as that of the Captain. She made her maiden voyage on 20th April 1912. It was the first liner to provide more places in the lifeboats than the passengers on board. Remember that the Titanic had sunk five days earlier. This was the only

French liner with four funnels - a question of imitating the ships such as the Aquitania - being a reference to luxury.

The 'Paris' in 1921.

The 'Ile de France' in 1927, nick named the 'Saint-Bernard of the Atlantic' which had the best and the longest career of the French 'transat' and saved two wrecked ships. It is the only liner in the world to have received three triumphal welcomes to New York : that of its inaugural voyage, that of its return from the war and finally that after the rescue of the 'Andrea Doria'.

The 'Normandie', in 1935, was the biggest, longest and most prestigious liner in the world. The First Class restaurant was open through the height of three decks and through 86 metres of length (13 metres more than the Gallery of Mirrors in Versailles). It was a window for French Decorative Arts and it became famous by taking the 'Blue ribbon' for speed - held up to that point by England - on her inaugural voyage. This was a triumph, a long awaited revenge, to the delight of those on board. Sadly she sailed for only four and a half years, the liner alongside in New York at the entry of France into the war against Germany was burnt in 1942 by the American workers who wanted to change it into a troop carrier. Thus she finished her career miserably, submerged in the port and was lost totally. The 'Queen Elizabeth' and the 'Queen Mary' came back intact from the war and became again Masters of the Atlantic.

With the 'France' in 1964, France renewed her prestige. The liner was huge : 315 metres long ! Luxury in the new materials and French gastronomy were on the daily menu for the privileged passengers. But for the aeroplane and the petrol crisis forced in 1974, the proud ambassador of the French merchant navy was laid up and relegated to the 'quay of the forgotten' in the port of Le Havre. Under the name of the 'Norway' she took up a new career at the end of the 1970's. Today, only the Queen Elizabeth II continues the tradition of the great transatlantic liners. On the abandoned quays of the French Line there still resound the cheers of the people of Le Havre on the departure of the liners taking Trans-Atlantic journeys, with the greatest personalities of the political world, of business, of entertainment, giving the town a continual air of festivity.

****

Rouen :

= **'Musée maritime fluvial et portuaire'.** Boulevard Emile-Duchemin - Hangar portuaire 13 - Tel (33) 2 32 10 15 51. Museum set out near to the square clock tower in an ancient port building for holding merchandise, built in 1925 and having been owned by the company Schiaffino.

It presents beautiful collections linked to the Rouen maritime heritage, to the marine and river trade, to the pleasure traffic on the Seine. Thirty boats are exhibited including a barge 'Pompon Rouge'. Workshop for the restoring of ships.

Open from Monday to Friday from 10 am-12.30 pm and from 2-6 pm except Tuesdays. Saturdays and Sundays from 2-6 pm.

The close relations between the port of Le Havre and England

Le Havre and Great-Britain have a past which is strongly linked.

Officially created by François Iᵉʳ in 1517, Le Havre experienced the agonies of the Hundred Years War and the landing of Henry V in 1415, before really existing.

The most remarkable deeds : During the Wars of Religion, the Huguenots called successfully on the English to help push the Catholics out of Le Havre.

The development and enlargement of the port of Le Havre from 1838 was modelled on the English style which was more advanced than the French thanks to the industrial revolution.

Le Tréport :

= **'Musée d'Histoire locale et maritime'** : *'Les enfants du Vieux Tréport'*. 1, rue de l'Anguainerie, 'ancienne prison' - Tel (33) 2 35 86 25 45 or (33) 2 35 86 13 36. Open from Easter to the end of September every weekend and public holidays from 10 am-12 noon and from 3-6 pm. Situated near to the vaulted door of the ancient prison from 1563 (2 cells and a guard room) and in the old Mairie, this museum presents on three levels the history of 'the Maritime Door of Normandy'

= **The sea baths** (19th and 20th century) : reconstructed beach scene and model of the casino.

= **The life of the people of the sea :** models of boats, painted sailor's bags, traditional costumes, fishing materials…

= **The wrecks and safety at sea :** Objects from a ship which was wrecked in 1904, canon and rope firing guns.

= **Traditional activities that have, or have almost, disappeared :** the collection of pebbles, the kippering of fish, the marine carpenters…

Visit of the port and the recovery of trout and salmon. Ask at the Tourist Office - Tel (33) 2 35 86 05 69.

Varengeville-sur-Mer :

= **'Marine cemetery'.** One of the great places of Norman heritage.

2 - Fishing on foot

At low tide along the Norman coasts you can fish in the sand or on the rocks : shrimps, prawns, clams, cockles, razor clams, mussels, oysters, velvet crabs, whelks, red crabs, crabs…

IMPORTANT : often in summer, a ban from the préfet forbids the fishing on foot. Check always on the decisions taken by the authorities.

3 - Nautical activities

To have a list and the conditions of practice,
contact the Departmental Committees for tourism.

4 - Sea trips and the hire of boats

AREA OF MANCHE

Agon-Coutainville.
= **Trips on board the 'Charles Marie'** (traditional sailing boat built for cruising - 24 metres overall). Day trips : Bay of Mont-Saint-Michel, Chausey, Les Minquiers, Les Ecréhou... Trips of several days : The Channel Islands, northern Brittany, southern England... For information and bookings : Association 'Le Ponton' - 33, avenue des Pins. Tel (33) 2 33 46 69 54 - Fax (33) 2 33 45 84 75.

Barneville-Carteret :
= **Hire of sailing boats.**
= **Trips on board traditional boats (Neire Maôve and Goëlette du Cotentin).**
Coastal trips, journeys to the islands, cruises to the Channel Islands and the south of England. For information and bookings : Association des Vieux Gréements en côte des Isles - Le Cap - B.P. 24 - Tel (33) 2 33 04 69 77.-   E.Mail : goelette@chez.com - Internet site : http://www.com/goelette
= **Sea trips on board the 'Amarine'** - leaving from *Carteret* or *Port Bail* from 1st April to 30th September. Discovery and observation of the coastline (duration 1 to 3 hours) and sea fishing trips (duration 4-7 hrs) - Demonstration and introduction to fishing (capacity : 25 passengers) - Embarkation at the Port des Iles - Pontoon F. For information : Tel (33) 2 33 53 65 90 - Fax (33) 2 33 53 43 90.

Carentan :
= **Discovery of the Bay of Veys (mini cruises)**

Cherbourg-Hague :
= **Hire of sailing boats.**
= **Discovery of the Cherbourg sea wall by boat.** Aboard the launch 'Vega' (capacity 80 passengers), discover every day from 1st April to 30th September the largest artificial sea wall in the world. Tour with commentary around the harbour walls, the ports and the Island of Pelée. Embarkation in the Port Chantereyne - Pontoon J. Information and reservations : Cherbourg Tourist Office : Tel (33) 2 33 93 52 02 - Fax (33) 2 33 53 66 97 or (33) 2 33 93 75 27 or even 06 07 05 51 93 (boat).

Donville-les-Bains :
= **Trips on board the 'Courrier des Isles', traditional boat.** Destinations the Chausey islands, Plateau des Minquiers, the Bay of Mont-Saint-Michel, the Channel Islands... Contact : Gilbert Hurel - 7, Sentier des Blancs Arbres, 50350 Donville, Tel (33) 2 33 50 49 80 / (33) 2 33 50 45 06.

Granville : sailing station
= **Outings on board the 'Bisquine' 'La Granvillaise' (18 metres).** Destinations : The Bay of Granville, the bay of Mont-Saint-Michel, the Channel Islands, For information and reservations : Association des Vieux Gréements Granvillais -

Maison de la Bisquine - 43, boulevard des Amiraux ; Tel (33) 2 33 90 07 51, Fax (33) 2 33 90 03 77.

= **Outings on board the ship 'Le Lys Noir'.** Destinations : The Islands of Chausey, the Channel Islands, the Bay of Mont-Saint-Michel, Northern Brittany, For information and reservations : Association Le Lys Noir - 11, rue des Juifs. Tel (33) 2 33 90 48 63

= **Trips on board the 'Strang Hugg'.** Cruises, sea fishing… For information and reservations : Association Strang Hugg. M. Pierre Hédouin - 5, rue P.-Litan - Tel/Fax (33) 2 33 90 69 06.

Boat hire. Tourist Office.

Port Bail :

= **Sea trips** (see under *Barneville-Carteret*).

AREA OF CALVADOS

Colleville-sur-Mer :

= **Hire of sand yachts and speed sailing on the beach** - 'Le Cavey'. Tel (33) 2 31 22 26 21.

Courseulles :

= **French school of sailing.** 'Société des Régates de Courseulles' - Open every day in summer - 5, quai Est. Tel (33) 2 31 37 47 42. Nautical activities, regattas and trips on sailing ships - training and competition on FC8, dinghies and sports catamarans.

= **Trips along the Mother of Pearl coast and the landing beaches.** On the *'Ville de Courseulles II'* hours according to the tides - sea fishing. For information : Tel (33) 2 31 37 47 42 - 'Société des Régates de Courseulles', (33) 2 31 37 92 59.

= **Boat hire.** Locabat (boats with or without motors, with or without license) from April to September. 41, rue des Petits-Champs - Tel (33) 2 31 37 97 85.

Deauville :

= **Boat hire.** Centre nautique (on the board walks) - Only catamarans - Tel (33) 2 31 14 02 19.

= **Krischarter** - Port Deauville. Hire of sailing boats only - Tel (33) 2 31 88 67 32. **Boat and B.** Accommodation on boats at the quayside - Tel (33) 2 40 40 30 20.

Grandcamp-Maisy :

= **Outings on the 'Grandcopaise'.** The 'Grandcopaise' is a trawler of 14.65 metres built in 1949 and renovated. Visits and excursions possible from April to September (limited to 12 persons and by appointment). Tel (33) 2 31 22 18 47.

= **Trips along the Mother of Pearl coast and the landing beaches** on the **'Colonel Rudder'.** Mini cruises and excursions with commentaries from March to November dependent on the tides for the landing beaches or the Natural Park of the Bay of Veys, the regional natural park of the Marshes and of the Cotentin.

Covered launch with 65 seated places (W.C., Bar,...) - sea fishing. Departures from the north quay according to the hours of the tides from April to October. For information and bookings : Mme. Vicquelin - Tel (33) 2 31 21 42 93 and (33) 2 31 22 64 15.

= **Excursions (duration : around one hour).** Discovery of the Pointe du Hoc from the sea. Visit enlivened with real life anecdotes and those brought back by American Rangers and German veterans on the fierce combat that took place here.

= **Mini-cruises to the landing beaches with commentary** (Omaha Beach to the east or Utah Beach to the north-west), Tourist cruise around the Islands of Saint-Marcouf, discovery of the natural nesting place of the great black cormorant, or the Hermitage and the ancient fortifications.

Honfleur :

= **Visit with commentary of the different harbours of the port of Honfleur** on the **'Calypso'** (Capacity : 62 passengers). Departures from : Quai de la Planchette (Opposite the Lieutenance). Tel/Fax (33) 2 31 89 20 93 - (33) 2 31 89 07 77.

= **Sea trips.** On board the 'Evasion' (Capacity : 40 persons) : Passage of the locks, guided commentary on the estuary and the Pont de Normandie. Embarkation : Quai des passagers. Information : Tel (33) 2 31 89 41 80 - Fax (33) 2 31 89 41 80. On board the 'Stephanie' (capacity : 38 persons) : trips in the estuary, Pont de Normandie. Embarkation : Quai des Passagers. For information : Tel 02 31 89 21 10 - 06 14 96 37 95 - Fax 02 31 89 21 10.

Isigny-sur-Mer :

= **Sea trips with visits to the estuary of the Aure and the Vire.**

Ouistreham/Caen :

= **Boat Hire :** catamarans, sail boards, dinghies. During the season at the foot of the lighthouse. Tel (33) 2 31 97 00 25 or (33) 2 31 96 75 74 or (33) 2 31 96 52 31, **Mini cruise.** On board the **'Hastings'**, panoramic boat, on the canal of Caen to the sea. Return trip of two and a half hours along the waterway - Every day from March to November. Departures from the Bassin Saint-Pierre in Caen. Departures from the quai Charcot in Ouistreham by reservation. For information : Tel (33) 2 31 34 00 00.

Port-en-Bessin :

= **Sea trips :** with the Union Nautique du Bessin on board the 'Union', old schooner and on the 'Orion', 9 metre cruise ship, according to the hours of the tides. For information : Tel (33) 2 31 22 43 88. All year.

= **Visit to the port and its infrastructures.**

Visit accompanied by a 'guide médiateur' :

= 'To the heart of Port-en-Bessin from Tuesday to Sunday (timings vary in relation to the tides)

= 'To watch over and rescue' : at the semaphore and on the SNSM launch, Friday afternoons and Saturday mornings.

= 'From town crier to computer' : every other Wednesday from 6 am in the morning.

= 'The landing' : every other Tuesday from 9.30-11 pm. Bookings essential : Tel (33) 2 31 21 92 33 or (33) 2 31 51 96 58.

Trouville/Hennequeville :

= **Sea excursions** on board the **'Gulf Stream'** every day on the tide from Easter to mid-November. Departures from Quai Albert 1er, near to the Casino. Every day on the tide, two types of excursion are offered on board the launch 'Gulf Stream' : a 30 minute trip allowing you to discover the coastline of Trouville and Deauville and another of two hours which will take you as far as the Pont de Normandie. The departures take place every day on the tide (three hours before and after the times of the high tide) except in bad weather. For information : Tel (33) 2 31 65 23 30 or 06 07 47 14 12 - Fax (33) 2 31 65 11 33.

AREA OF SEINE-MARITIME

Dieppe :

= **Port visit.** Guided visit of the commercial ports, the fishing, cross-channel and pleasure harbours. Information from the Tourist Office. Tel (33) 2 35 84 11 71 - Fax (33) 2 35 06 27 66.

= **Sea and sea fishing trips.** In July and August, leaving from the Pont Ango approximately every hour. For information : Tourist Office of Dieppe. Tel (33) 2 35 84 11 77 - Two boats each with a capacity for 50 people. **Sea fishing.** M. Legros, 54, rue du Dauphin Louis XI. Tel (33) 2 35 84 82 85.

Fécamp :

= **Excursions and sea fishing.** On board the ship **'Ville de Fécamp'** - Capacity 63 persons. Contact M. Prenveille, 15, rue de la Vicomté. Tel (33) 2 35 28 99 53.

= **Sea trips.** On board the ship **'La Tante Fine',** old schooner, ancient lobster fishing boat. Excursions of between 2 and 4 hrs. For information : Tel (33) 2 35 29 78 01 or 06 09 28 70 71.

= **Albâtre plaisance.** Coastal trip, sea fishing, diving, sea scooters, cruise... For information : M. Lacheray - 2, rue du Commandant Rondel - Tel (33) 2 35 28 94 58. **Hire of boats and sailing boats.** For information : M. Preveille (see above - M. Lacheray (see above).

Le Havre :

= **Hire of boats and sailing boats.**

= **Ad hoc.** - 136, quai Frissard - Tel (33) 2 35 25 30 51.

Normandie Yachting, 10, rue du Maréchal-de Lattre de Tassigny. Tel (33) 2 35 74 90 00.

Trans Manche Loisirs. 59, rue Dicquemare - Tel (33) 2 35 41 14 49.

Saint-Valery-en-Caux :

= **Sea trips.** Excursions of between 1.5 hrs-3 hrs for 28 passengers - Cruises for ten people - The ship the 'Albarquel' old 25 metre Portuguese schooner, by appointment. Information and reservations from the Tourist Office of Saint-

Valery-en-Caux - Tel (33) 2 35 97 00 63 or (33) 2 35 57 21 58 or 06 11 97 56 50 - http://perso.wanadoo.fr/albarquel/ E.Mail : albarquel@wanadoo.fr

= **Sea sport fishing.** Ecole homologuée - Squale Club Valeriquais, 7, quai d'Aval. Tel (33) 2 35 97 77 54.

= **Cruises Tea fishing.** AVAP Mer - B.P. 6 - Tel (33) 2 35 97 34 99.

Le Tréport :

= **Excursions and sea fishing.** On board the 'Eden I' according to the timing of the tides. For information and reservations : M. Masson - 2, rue Saint-Laurent - Tel (33) 2 35 50 38 87 or (33) 2 35 86 82 62 or the Tourist Office : Tel (33) 2 35 86 05 69.

= **Hire of boats and sailing boats.** Loisirs yachting - 4, avenue des Canadiens. Tel (33) 2 35 50 16 70.

5 - The virtues of the sea... the thalassotherapy

AREA OF CALVADOS

Deauville : **'Institut de Thalassothérapie'.** 3, rue Sem - Tel (33) 2 31 87 72 00. Health cures, relaxation, fitness, care of the body and the face, aesthetics, aquaform space. Open all year 7 days a week.

Luc-sur-Mer : **'Institut de Cure Marine'.** Opposite the sea. Tel (33) 2 31 97 32 22. Fitness, health cures for a weekend or up to three weeks with or without accommodation and meals (dietetic) - Warm sea water pool, training room.

Ouistreham-Riva-Bella : **'Thermes marins'.** Avenue du Commandant Kieffer - Tel (33) 2 31 96 40 40. Five formulae to choose from : fitness, objective figure, bio relaxation, marine vascular medicine and post partum. Pool with activities, aquavital route and training centre.

6 - Maritime events and nautical festivals

AREA OF MANCHE

Barfleur : 2*nd Sunday of August :* **The Regattas,** traditional event over a hundred years old.

Barneville-Carteret : beginning of August : **'Fête de la Mer'.** Ceremony at the Calvary of sailors lost at sea - Blessing of the sea - placing of a crown of flowers - Open air meal - Regattas.

Granville : end of July, beginning of August **'Grand Pardon'.** Each year, in the church of Notre-Dame-du-Cap-en-Lihou, the sailors and their families come to pray to the protecting Virgin. Procession - Boats decked out in the decorated port - Blessing of the sea - Spreading of flowers on the water in homage to sailors disappeared at sea - Games - Activities - Tasting of sea food.

Lingreville : beginning of August : **'Fête des Coques d'Or'.** There was once a habit of painting in gold, the shells of the cockles, that were found in abundance on the beach. This tradition was the origin of the fête which it now perpetuates. After the religious service opposite the sea there takes place a rural fête with the tasting of shellfish and various entertainments.

Portbail : in the middle of August **'Fête du Port'. Fishing contest** (sea or 'au coup').

On the Ile de Tatihou : In July : **'Fête de la Mer'** (organised every 10 years. The next will take place in July 2011). **'Fête des Régates'.**

Saint-Georges-de-la-Rivière : beginning of August : **'Fête de la Plage... et de l'Ane !'** (Festival of the beach... and the donkey !)

AREA OF CALVADOS

Caen : 1ˢᵗ Saturday of September : **'Fête du Port'.** Throughout this traditional event, the town of William the Conqueror recalls that it is also a port and presents, in the 'bassin' Saint-Pierre, a collection of boats from the maritime conservatory, and in Place Courtonne, a 'market of the sea' and various other entertainments.

Courseulles : in August : **'Fête de la Mer'** in memory of sailors at sea.

Dives-sur-Mer : in the middle of August : At Port Guillaume : **'Grande Fête de la Mer'.** Religious service - placing of wreaths on the sea - Decorated boats - Nautical games - Recital of sailor's songs.

Honfleur : Sunday and Monday of Pentecost : **'Fête des Marins'** (106ᵗʰ occasion in 2003). Marked by a blessing of the sea, this ancient festival of more than 135 years, takes place the Sunday of Pentecost. The fishing boats, on this occasion, come in procession from the port then each embarkation is blessed by the clergy. Exhibition of model boats.

= **'Pilgimage to Notre-Dame-de-Grâce'.** On the heights above Honfleur, opposite to the mouth of the Seine one finds a small chapel dedicated to Notre-Dame-de-Grâce. For more than 1000 years, the sailors of Honfleur and their families have come to pray to the protecting Virgin. One finds there, numerous 'ex-voto', models of ships. The Monday of Pentecost, the sailors, their families, the clergy and the population go in procession to Notre-Dame-de-Grâce, the children participate in the procession carrying above their heads the models of boats. Beginning of June.

= **'Fête de la Crevette'.** 3ʳᵈ week of September : On foot or aboard the famous 'crevettiers' they have fished for the grey prawn in Honfleur for decades. Numerous entertainments take place on the occasion of this festival : recital of sailor's songs - jousting on water - demonstrations of practices linked in earlier times to fishing...

Ouistreham : in August : **'Fête de la Mer'.**

Trouville : end of July, beginning of August : **'Fête de la Mer et du Maquereau'.** Official ceremony - departure of decorated boats - Blessing of the sea and the ships - Nautical games. Saturday evening : tasting of grilled mackerel, sea songs - dancing.

Villerville : in July : **Blessing of the sea.** In homage to Norman sailors who have perished at sea. Religious service - procession of models - Blessing by the priest.

AREA OF EURE

Berville-sur-Mer : 14 and 15 August : **'Fête des Marins'.** Unique and narrow window of the area of Eure on the sea, the community of Berville organises each year its festival of the sea with a blessing of the sea, the placing of wreaths in homage to disappeared sailors and various festivities.

AREA OF SEINE-MARITIME

Fécamp : the Thursday of Ascension : **'Fête de la Mer'.** Mass in the ancient Abbey church of the Trinity, procession to Notre-Dame-de-Salut, blessing of the sea, official homage to sailors that have disappeared at sea - Fair in the town.

Le Havre : 1ˢᵗ weekend of September : **'Mer en fête' :** Various entertainments - Festival of sea songs - Decorated boats - Fireworks - Music hall show - Blessing of the sea - Parade of ships - Exhibition and sale of unique nautical material.

Regattas.

Le Tréport : 3ʳᵈ Sunday of July. **'Fête de la Mer'.** Musical parade of model ships, blessing of the sea, various entertainments, fireworks.

Yport : 14ᵗʰ August : **'Fête de la Mer'.** Mass, procession, blessing of the sea.

To know the exact dates of the events shown above and the details of the organisation, contact the Tourist Offices concerned.

7 - Fish markets

AREA OF CALVADOS

Caen-Mondeville : Exit from Caen in the direction of Pont-l'Evêque on the RN 175 : **'La Criée'** has sales of fish every morning from Tuesday to Saturday from 9-11 am. Tel (33) 2 31 70 35 35.

Port de Courseulles : Quai des alliés : every day (direct from the fishermen).

Port de Dives-sur-Mer : Every morning in July and August (direct from the fishermen - Kiosks in the port).

Port de Grandcamp-Maisy : Every morning (direct from the fishermen).

Port de Ouistreham : Every morning in the 'Halles' of the port (direct from the fishermen).

Port-en-Bessin : At the fish market, in the port Sunday mornings (direct from the fisherman).

Port de Trouville : Every day of the year, on the quayside (direct from the fishermen).

8 - Leisure ports

AREA OF MANCHE

Beach port of *Agon-Coutainville* : **'La Pointe d'Agon'** : 100 anchorages of which 20 are for visitors - Tel (33) 2 33 47 28 44.

Leisure port of *Barneville-Carteret* : **' The port the Islande'.** The privileged shelter. 2, promenade Barbey d'Aurévilly - Tel (33) 2 33 04 70 84 - Fax (33) 2 33 04 08 37. E.Mail : www.barneville-carteret.fr The Port of the Islands has been a novelty since it opened its doors in 1995. It is sited opposite to Jersey and Guernsey and offers 311 places in the harbour and 60 places for visitors. 95 places at anchor. Tel (33) 2 33 04 70 84.

The leisure port of *Carentan* : In the town : 270 places of which 50 are for visitors - minimum depth 3 metres - Open all year. Accessible by a marked channel crossing the Bay of Veys, practical for five hours during each tide. Before arriving in the Port of Carentan one passes over the canal bridge which spans the RN 13 which leads to Cherbourg. Offices : Tel (33) 2 33 42 24 44 - (Denis Leprevost).
E.Mail : port-carentan@wanadoo.fr
Internet site : http://www.sctefrance.com/portcarentan
The access is made by a channel crossing the Natural Park of the Marshes of the Cotentin and of the Bessin and opening into the bay of Veys.

'Port de mouillage' de *Barfleur* : 140 anchorages and 45 places for visitors. Tel Capitainerie (33) 2 33 54 08 29 or the Mairie : Tel (33) 2 33 23 43 00.

'Port de mouillage' de *Port-Bail* : 200 anchorages - 30 visitor places sheltered from the prevailing winds, beach port ideal for cruisers and launches of low draught. It is accessible by a signed channel immediately close to the Channel Islands of Jersey, Sark and Guernsey. Contact : Tel (33) 2 33 04 88 30 (Mairie) - Fax (33) 2 33 04 39 90. Capitainerie : Tel (33) 2 33 04 83 48. E.Mail : portbail@wanadoo.fr
Internet site : http://www.ville-portbail.fr

Chantereyne leisure port of *Cherbourg-Octeville* : Capitainerie : Tel (33) 2 33 87 65 70 - Fax (33) 2 33 53 21 12. The leisure port of Cherbourg welcomes on average 10,000 boats a year which makes it the **premier leisure port of France** in terms of visitors. A marina in the commercial harbour allows henceforth the acceptance of vessels from 10 to 20 metres.

Port of international level : Port with deep water enclosed by a majestic sea wall - 1200 places on pontoons - 1 waiting landing stage : 30 places - 300 places for visitors, accepts 'panne MNPQ. Access 24 hours a day.

'Port-Dièlette in *Tréauville'* : To the south of La Hague, sheltered by the Cap de Flamanville. 510 places - 420 in the floating basin accessible by a drop down door of which 80 are reserved for visitors - 40 places on pontoons in the outer port of which 20 are reserved for waiting. In direct line with the Channel Islands. Contact Patrik Guillard, Mâitre de Port - Tel (33) 2 33 53 68 78 - Fax (33) 2 33 53 68 79.

Beach port of *Goury* : 40 anchorages - Tel (33) 2 33 52 85 92.

Leisure port of *Granville* : **'Port de Hérel'** : 1000 places of which 150 for visitors (second port of La Manche after Cherbourg). An essential stopping point for a large number of seamen and amateur sailors coming from the islands. Access to the basin : floating port, two and a half hours before high tide and three and half hours after high tide. Capitainerie (M. Denis) Tel (33) 2 33 50 20 06 - Fax (33) 2 33 50 17 01.
E.Mail : cci@granville.cci.fr Internet site : http://www.granville.cci.fr

Port of *Omonville-la-Rogue* : Open sea port - minimum : 3.5 metres - 54 moorings on buoys - 4 safes for transit - Access 24 hours a day. Tel (33) 2 33 52 74 94 - Fax (33) 2 33 52 09 64.

Port Lévi : 80 moorings and two visitor places. Tel (33) 2 33 54 31 79.

Beach port of *Quinéville* - **Havre de la Sinope** : 130 moorings with one visitor place. Capitainerie : Tel (33) 2 33 21 16 68.

Beach port of *Régneville-sur-Mer* : **'Le Havre de Régneville'** : 60 moorings - 4 visitor places. Embarkation/disembarkation on a floating pontoon. Tel (33) 2 33 46 36 76.

Leisure port of *Saint-Vaast-la-Hougue* : Capacity : 665 places of which 160 are for visitors in the heart of an ultra modern marina. Choice stopping place. Tel (33) 2 33 23 61 00 - Fax (33) 2 33 23 61 04.
E.Mail : port.saint.vast@saint.vaast.reville.com
Internet site : http://www.saint.vaast.reville.com

Ports of *Tourlaville :* **Le Becquet** : Beach port. 85 moorings - Tel (33) 2 33 22 27 49. **'Port des Flamands'** : Deep water port - 109 moorings, more than forty beach moorings - Accesible 24 hours a day. Tel (33) 2 33 22 29 85.

AREA OF CALVADOS

Leisure port of *Cabourg* : 200 beach places, on 'corps morts'. Port Capitainerie : Tel (33) 2 31 91 23 55 - Fax (33) 2 31 24 71 60. E.Mail : cycabourg@aol.com

Leisure port of *Caen* : Bassin Saint-Pierre - 120 floating places. Capitainerie. Tel (33) 2 31 36 22 00 - Fax (33) 2 31 96 39 52. Port : Tel/Fax (33) 2 31 95 24 47.

Leisure port of *Courseulles* : Tel (33) 2 31 37 51 69 - two basins (800 places) - Numerous installations including service station and crane.

Leisure port of *Deauville* : 'Port Deauville' - 3, quai des Marchands - 900 floating places. Capitainerie : Tel (33) 2 31 98 30 01 - Fax (33)2 31 81 98 92.

Municipal port : 400 floating places - Tel (33) 2 31 98 50 40 - Fax (33) 2 31 87 30 62.

Leisure port of *Dives-sur-Mer* 'Port Guillaume" : Capitainerie : Tel (33) 2 31 24 48 00. 600 floating places - reception 24 hours a day. **SRDH - Club nautique :** 30 moorings + 120 beach places on 'corps morts' Capitainerie : Tel (33) 2 31 24 48 00. Port : Tel (33) 2 31 24 23 12.

Leisure port of *Grandcamp-Maisy* : 248 floating places. Port/Capitainerie : Tel (33) 2 31 22 63 16 - Fax : (33) 2 31 22 99 95 (mairie).

Leisure port of *Honfleur* : Capitainerie : Tel/Fax : (33) 2 31 14 61 09. Port : Tel/Fax : (33) 2 31 98 87 13. 75 floating places.

Leisure port of *Isigny-sur-Mer* : 70 floating places + 5 visitor places - Régisseur : Tel (33) 2 31 54 21 01 - Fax : (33) 2 31 51 24 09.

Leisure port of *Merville-Franceville* : 60 moorings + 120 beach places on 'corps morts'. Port : Tel (33) 2 31 21 21 97.

Leisure port of *Caen-Ouistreham* : Quai Georges-Thierry. Capitainerie : Tel (33) 2 31 36 22 02 - Fax (33) 2 31 96 39 52. Port : Tel (33) 2 31 96 91 37 - Fax (33) 2 31 96 91 47. Rectangular deepened basin to the east of the canal - 650 places on rings or floating.

<u>AREA OF SEINE-MARITIME</u>

Leisure port of *Dieppe* : Pont Jehan-Ango - Tel/Fax (33) 2 35 40 19. 450 places on rings, 50 of which are for visitors.

Leisure port of *Fécamp* : Chaussée Edouard-Levasseur et Fils. Tel (33) 2 35 28 13 58 - Fax (33) 2 35 28 60 46. 590 places on rings, of which 40 are for visitors.

Leisure port of *Le Havre* : Boulevard Clemenceau - Tel (33) 2 35 21 23 95. 1040 floating places on pontoons - 50 places for visitors - dry dock - lock - draught : 3 metres - guarded port - Entries at all times 24 hours a day. Ideal base from which to discover Normandy - Distances : Guernsey : 126 miles - Brighton : 81 miles - Portsmouth : 86 miles - Plymouth : 170 miles.

Leisure port of *Rouen* (River) : 40 places for visitors. Tel (33) 2 35 07 33 94.

Leisure port of *Saint-Aubin-les-Elbeuf* (River) : 150 places on rings, of which 50 are for visitors. Tel (33) 2 35 78 42 78.

Leisure port of *Saint-Valery-en-Caux* : Place du Marché - Capitainerie Tel (33) 2 35 97 01 30 or 06 07 31 56 95. Fax (33) 2 35 97 90 73. 600 rings on floating pontoons of which around thirty are for visitors, basin sheltered from the winds - 1.80 metres draught.

Leisure port of *Le Tréport* : Chamber of Commerce. Tel (33) 2 35 86 27 67. 205 places on rings, of which 10 are for visitors.

9 - Marine carpenters - shipyards

AREA OF CALVADOS

Mézidon : Marine carpenter. Olivier Oudry, craftsman 50, rue Pierre-Semard. Tel (33) 2 31 20 95 22.

****

Norman expressions in navigational terminology
The Normans, heirs of the ancient Vikings,
have strongly marked the vocabulary,
the techniques of navigation and other marine terms

Judge for yourselves :

= **Bèter :** which is said as 'appater' among the Normans and which came from the Nordic 'beita' and has become 'to bait' in English.

= **Bâbord** which is to say 'left' (or port side) came from the Norse.

= **'Bak-bordi'** (old Nordic) as starboard came from 'Stior-bord".

= **Crabe :** came from 'krabbi' and Homard (lobster) from 'humarr'.

= **Crique** (cove or creek) : came from 'kriki'.

= **Flotte :** signifying a gathering of ships came from the Norse 'floti'.

= **Gréer** (to rig) : came from the Norse 'greida'.

= **Haler** (to tow or haul) : came from 'hala'.

= **Hauban** (shroud) : came from 'böfud-benda'.

= **Tanguer :** came from 'tangi'.

= **Vareck :** which stands for the algae thrown up on the beach came from 'vagrek' which signifies 'object rejected by the sea'. The English 'to wreck' ?

****

With respect to...

It was a man from Le Havre called Augustin Normand (1839-1906), a knowledgeable naval technician, who was the first in France to adopt the propeller for the propulsion of ships.

2000 years before our time the Seine was the principal route for the trade in tin between Rome and Great Britain.

⌐HALLE¬
aux VINS

Wine in bulk or bottles- Spirits - Apéritifs - Champagne

10, quai de La Touques	6, rue du Bouloir
14800 DEAUVILLE	**14600 HONFLEUR**
Tel/Fax : (33) 2 31 98 33 85	Tel/Fax : (33) 2 31 89 11 60

En partenariat avec :

PAYS DE LOIRE - VAL DE LOIRE :

Muscadet :	*Château de l'Aiguillette*	44 Mouzillon
Sauvignon :	*Domaine Saint-Roch*	41 Meusnes
Saumur-Champigny :	*Domaine "Les Méribelles"*	49 Souzay-Champigny
Anjou :	*Domaine de la Belle Angevine*	49 Beaulieu/Layon
Sancerre :	*André Robineau - Cave du Fort*	18 Sancerre

BORDEAUX :

Côtes de Blaye :	*'Les Chevaliers d'Aliénor'*	33 Generac
Haut-Médoc :	*Château "Lenoine-Lafon-Rochet"*	
	Sabourin Frères	33 Cars
Saint-Emilion :	*Clos des Menuts* Maison Rivière	33 Saint-Emilion

SUD-OUEST :

Bergerac :	*'Les Grands Chais de Saint-Laurent'*	
		24 Saint-Laurent-des-Vignes

Vallée du Rhône :

Côtes du Rhône	*'Les Vignerons Visanais'*	84 Visan
Côtes du Ventoux	*'Les Vins de Sylla'*	84 Apt
Côtes du Lubéron	*Caves de Loumarin-Cadenet*	84 Cadenet

BOURGOGNE-MACONNAIS-CÔTE CHALONNAISE :

Bourgogne de Vigne en Verre - Group. de viticulteurs	71 Tournus

BEAUJOLAIS :

Beaujolais-Brouilly :	*Domaine Saint-Charles*	69 Saint-Etienne-la-Varenne

LANGUEDOC :

Vin des Sables :	*Domaine du Petit Chaumont*	30 Aigues-Mortes
Côteaux du Languedoc :	*Vignerons de Benovie*	34 Saussines
CHAMPAGNE : *Champagnes Christian Doulet*		51 Epernay
CALVADOS : *Calvados Roger Groult*		14 St-Cyr-du-Ronceray

Cider, Pommeau and Calvados from Normandy

VIII - NORMAN GASTRONOMY

Norman food products have a well-established reputation. Whatever the era, the farmers and craftsmen have always known how to get the best out of the natural assets of the region, and the knowledge inherited from ancestors, which allowed them to develop products of character and quality whilst still respecting tradition as well as perfecting manufacturing with new techniques.

Norman gastronomy is rich and varied. What is more normal in a country where eating well, is part of the art of living?

1 - Local Norman products

PRODUCE FROM THE SEA, RIVERS AND LAKES

People don't generally realise that Normandy is the French region with the most oyster farms in France with an annual production of around 35,000 tons, the equivalent of three million hampers. In fact one out of every four oysters eaten in France is Norman. In the Gaelic era, oysters were collected on the Norman coasts. Norman oysters are farmed at *Saint-Vaast-la-Hougue*, de *Blainville*, *Agon-Coutainville*, *Gouville* and to the west of Veys Bay. They are also found in Calvados in the area of *Isigny* but also at *Asnelles* and *Courseulles*.

Don't think twice about going to the different farms open to visitors where you can try the oysters. (Information from the Tourist Offices of Manche et Calvados).

With several hundred boats, fishing is still one of the main activities in Normandy and for centuries numerous riches from the sea were collected on foot or by boat, specially along its 600 kms of coastline.

Cockles from the 'Côte fleurie', mussels from *Barfleur*, (called 'Skies' in Manche) from *Lion, from Langrune*, ormeaux, clams (called 'Venus' in the West), 'palourdes' from *Granville*, *Carolles* and *Jullouville*, cockles from *Cabourg*... but also 'amandes', winkles, buccins, 'clams', clovisses clams, scallops from the *côte d'Opale*, grey shrimps from *Trouville and Honfleur*, pink shrimps, crabs (or 'sleepers"), velvet crabs and spider crabs from the *Côte de Nâcre*, sole from *Trouville*, lobsters from *Chausey*, from the Cape of Antifer, from *Cherbourg* (called the 'single ladies of Cherbourg"). Shellfish account for half the catch made by Norman fishermen.

255

Mussel farming

*Mussel farming known as 'Mytiliculture' was introduced to Normandy at the end of the XIX*th *century and has since made a large impact on the region today producing the most mussels in France with 25,000 tons being sold every year. On most of the western coast of Normandy at low tide you can make out the rows of wooden posts : these are 'bouchots' a very regimented sort of fishing. This variety is much appreciated by gourmets for its creamy iodised tasting flesh.*

Scallops from the Alabaster coast

Scallops provide the no. 1 resource for Norman fishermen.

Respecting a very severe 'dragnet' code, the scallop fishermen from Dieppe have been fishing this variety for centuries. They fish around 3,000 tons per year.

In the restaurants of the Alabaster coast scallops are served with fresh cream or flamed with calvados.

Fishermen from **Port-en-Bessin** - which still has a fleet of about fifty boats - from the Pays d'Auge or from the North of the Cotentin go further a field to find their fish, which are found in plenty and wriggling in the fish halls and markets like **Trouville :** it is still one of the biggest attractions on the 'côte fleurie' (the stalls are full of sea bass, plaice, codfish, ray, and yellow pollack, John Dory, whiting, grey dorada, gurnards, red mullet, monkfish, sole, turbot, mackerel, sardines, spotted dogfish, bream, grey mullet, salmon, trout and shellfish).

'Sea' bass from Cotentin

In the area round Saint-Vaast-la-Hougue, in the area of Manche, fishermen who still fish bass with a 'long line' have got together in an association which has adopted a special label so that their product and their age old tradition can be noticed.

In Upper Normandy, and specially in **Dieppe,** one fishes herring, whereas in **Fécamp**, the Norman fishermen go to the distant Banks of Newfoundland fishing for cod like the 'terre-neuvas' of Saint-Malo. You also find squid and cuttlefish fishing in Normandy.

Herring the poor man's steak

When the month of November comes along, fishermen from the Alabaster coast go looking for the schools of herring coming down from the North Sea to spawn off the Norman coasts.

Fish are still plentiful in the many rivers, streams and lakes in Normandy.

You can fish a tasty trout with its silver belly, salmon and other carp, roach, perch, gudgeon and eels...

Fish farming is an ancient activity in the region. The first trout and salmon farms were started by the monks near the big Norman abbeys which were always by a waterway. It was said that in the 18th century the monks at the Abbey of Bec(*)-Hellouin (near Brionne) protested solemnly to the Father Abbott because they were fed up of eating salmon.

(*)- Bec comes from the Scandinavian and can be translated by 'stream'.

The 'fishponds of Vatierville' near *Neufchâtel-en-Bray* carry on this tradition in a place which was already used for fishing in the 15th century.

For more than 70 years the 'Kot brothers' have farmed trout and salmon with passionate enthusiasm, which they sell alive or smoked in the old traditional fashion, marrying the Norman expertise with techniques used in Eastern Europe.

In the marvellous greenery, signed 'Madame Kot' - Michel Kot gives a warm welcome to his visitors when he shows them his set up and products , but he eternally gives out the same old message : a healthily reared trout, eaten fresh or smoked, is a succulent dish to be (re)discovered.

DAIRY PRODUCTS

For the Normans 'White Gold' is milk, an immaculate liquid producing unctuous cream and the fatty tasty Norman cheeses which have won over the most delicate of palates, starting with the most important **Camembert** both appreciated and renowned all over the world. As a result of the quality of its pastures and that of its race of Norman cattle, Normandy is one of the most privileged regions in Europe for dairy products.

NORMAN CHEESES

The cheese industry is the oldest and most well known of Norman industries.

We can confirm that the peasant farmers of the old Province were already making cheese in the 10th century.

The oldest of Norman cheeses, produced in the Touques valley in the 'Pays d'Auge' was called '**Angelot**'. It was named after an English coin which it looked like.

Pont-l'Evêque Cheese : The square shaped Pont-l'Evêque, which is the name of a Calvados commune between **Lisieux** and the 'Côte Fleurie', is particularly appreciated for its creamy body and its significant taste. It is a soft cheese, separated from the curd and then drained. Its ochre crust can be brushed or washed. It was originally made from the luke warm last milking, which goes to explain why its technique was so adapted to the traditional craft, which has been handed down to us today. Modern industrial producers have learnt how to accommodate cheese making, mixing different milk from different farms.

For a good Pont-l'Evêque cheese to ripen you need three litres of milk and five to six weeks.

It is said, that this cheese was invented by the monks from the area of Pont-l'Evêque as from the 12th century, but it was only in the 17th century that it acquired its ultimate denomination.

Pont-l'Evêque cheese exists in four sizes :

= The 'big' Pont-l'Evêque : 20 cm sided square.

= The Pont-l'Evêque : 10 cm sided square

= The little Pont-l'Evêque (returned to favour in the 80's) : 9 cm sided square.

= And the half Pont-l'Evêque : rectangle of 11 cm by 5.5.

Each cheese contains at least 45% fat. More than 3,500 tons a year are produced.

Livarot Cheese : This is a limited production, as it is made only in the limits of the town which gave it its name. Livarot is undoubtedly the most original of the 'great Norman Trilogy'. It was mentioned for the first time in 1690, and had its fame and glory in the 19th century, being at that time, the most eaten cheese in Normandy. Chroniclers of that period called it the 'worker's meat' because of its nutritive value and also its modest cost. Round and orange coloured, it is a very high cheese, maintained by sedges - five strips of reed - giving it the nickname of 'colonel". Amateurs are always on the lookout for it, because of its exceptional taste of quality.

Livarot is a soft cheese separated from the curd and then drained. Its crust is washed.

Originally it was made on the farms and sold when it was very 'young' to cheese ripeners on the Livarot market and above all in **Vimoutiers** which was the main cheese market in the region.

For a good Livarot cheese to ripen you need five litres of milk and eight weeks.

Neufchâtel-en-Bray Cheese : The town of **Neufchâtel-en-Bray** is renowned for the quality of it cheese and butter since the 11th century. Having conquered the best tables in the region it became established in Great Britain from the time of the Hundred Years War. The development of the production of cheese in the area was much helped by the drying out of the marshland and the introduction of Norman

258

cows to the Pays of Bray. From the end of the 18th century, the Neufchâtel cheeses were to be found in Paris and Belgium.

It was presented in three shapes each weighing 100 grams : the little brick, the bung and the heart, the most well distributed of the three. Before, the cheese was also sold as a double bung weighing 200 grams and as a large heart weighing 600 grams.

Because the problems of keeping it, in times gone by, the Neufchâtel could not be made in summer. Salting it eradicated this problem and enabled a standardised product.

At the beginning of the 19th century, sales dropped because of measures taken by the State in order to reduce the amount of milk reserved for making cheese in the Pays de Bray. This was to encourage making butter which was necessary for feeding the population.

Cheese from the Neufchâtel farmers are made from a mixture of curd with flour before being moulded. They are ripened in a cool cellar for three weeks.

It has been said that the Neufchâtel cheese has this special heart shape, because of a cheeky idea the young local farm girls had, to make their feelings known to the English soldiers occupying the area during the Hundred Years War. They had thus found an original way of showing their feelings. About 800 tons of Neufchâtel cheese are made per year.

Camembert Cheese : Although it is more recent, Camembert is undoubtedly the most well known of Norman cheeses. It is named after a little village in the canton of **Vimoutiers,** in Orne and was perfected by **Marie Harel (1761-1844)** during the French Revolution. Camembert from Normandy is made with non pasteurised milk never heated over 37°.

The cheese is self-drained. The curd is moulded with a ladle, discontinuously, and generally five successive times. This produces an elastic and unctuous matter. It is salted only with dry salt and 2.2 litres of milk are needed to make a Camembert. One month is necessary to obtain a fully ripened cheese.

Camembert is a soft cheese, with a flowery crust (originally blue), round shaped, weighing a minimum of 250 grams, containing a minimum of 45% fat and always in a wooden box.

The manufacturing of Camembert from Normandy alone represents a production of 10.000 tons per year.

Many other cheeses have seen the day, some of which are still made in areas of Normandy. Some of the most famous are the **'Pavé d'Auge'**, the **'Lisieux'** and the **'Trouville'** in the region of Calvados. The **'Brillat Savarin'** in Seine-Maritime and the *'Coutances'* in Manche.

In the Perche at *Le Pin-la-Garenne,* Marc and Marie-Agnès Ronfard manufacture and sell cheeses on the markets, particularly in *Mortagne ;* these are tomme and a farm cheese made from non pasteurised cow's milk (50% fat) which they have christened '**Le Petit Percheron**'. The old name for this cheese was 'Le Puant' (the Smelly).

MEAT PRODUCE

Raising animals for their meat is a very old practice in Normandy. It was at its height at the end of the 19th century - when the Parisians still had the means of eating meat at least once a week - until the Second World War. It was only natural that the inhabitants from the Capital turned to their closest neighbors, the Normans, from whom they bought live cattle - which was then slaughtered in Paris - or carcasses of meat coming from Norman slaughter houses.

People used to say there were as many cows as people in Normandy. We don't know whether this saying was true but it was certain that Normandy was one of the most important regions for raising beef stock in France. These peaceful ruminants can be found in their thousands in the numerous 'pays', starting with the Pays d'Auge, where they are part and parcel of the picture of this land of plenty but also in the Bocage, the rich grassy plains of the Orne Valley, of Bessin, Perche, the pastures of the Pays of *Merlerault*, of Ouche, of Bray, without forgetting the plain of the Pays of Caux.

The production of a meat of quality is helped by the gentle climate, the rich grass, the expertise of the stock breeders, but also and above all by the excellent Norman cows which give a particularly delicious melting taste.

This unanimously known quality of beef can also be attributed to veal (very much appreciated by the Italians). The 'Norman Red Label Veal' is exclusively raised with whole milk.

Normandy is the third most important region producing pork. Their quality is today recognizable by a Red Label ('Farm Pork from Normandy') and has greatly contributed to the reputation of charcuterie and Norman cooking, one of the tastiest in France. Nowadays these local breeds have been reintroduced like the **'Porc de Bayeux'**.

'Les agneaux de pré salé' called the 'Grévins' raised in the bay of *Mont-Saint-Michel* gives us legs, shoulders and cutlets unequal in taste.

Norman poultry is equally well known for its firm and tasty meat.

Thanks to the determination of skilled breeders, certain varieties of hens, geese, and Norman rabbits, which were mostly supposedly extinct, are now popular again with consumers : this is the case with hens belonging to some Cotentin breeds from *Merlerault*, from *Crevecœur,* from *Caumont*, from *Pavilly* and from *Gournay ;* as for rabbits of the **'white rabbit'** breed from *Hautot*, the **'Norman rabbit'** and for web footed birds such as duck from *Duclair* or *Rouen,* and the **Norman goose.**

People in the region generally raise rabbits, hen, chickens, quail, guinea fowl, turkey, capons, pullets, ducks, geese…

For several years now there has been 'Red Label farm poultry from Normandy'.

Goose and duck 'foie gras' from Normandy has been appreciated now for about ten years and is actively sought after by experts capable of discerning their subtle taste provided by the quality of their food and the rich soil. Over the last few years Normandy has become the third largest region producing 'foie gras' in France. Markets selling 'foie gras' take place each year all over the region at the end of autumn in anticipation of Christmas.

****

Her highness 'the norman cow'

The Norman breed is known and appreciated not only for the quality of its dairy products but also for the flavour of its 'marbled' meat and the nutritive properties of its milk ; just recently it has made an important comeback with breeders (who choose quality rather than quantity because of the quotas imposed by Brussels). Because of the 'mad cow' disease crisis, consumers today prefer good meat with known origins, even though it may be a little dearer on the scales, to a cheap meat which might be of high risk.

It has been said that the Norman beef race was introduced into our countryside from the 10th century by the Vikings who preferred bringing their cows with them in their drakkars rather than their women ! The origin of the breed appears to be from Norway, in the county of Telemark, although others claim that it arrived in the 19th century from a cross between the 'Cotentin' and the British 'Durham' breeds.

The Cotentin Cow

Rearing beef stock in Manche has existed for centuries. Over the years, due to empiric selection, a particular type of breed of cow emerged whose standard was defined in 1884.

A really mixed race, like the Norman, it offers the particularity of combining the qualities of a dairy cow with that of being an excellent animal for its meat. With its high fat content, it is the most suitable for the making of butter and cream.

Varieties of butter in Manche have their 'vintages' and those from the **Isigny** have a good reputation.

The '**Domaine de Saint-Hippolyte**' at **Saint-Martin-de-la-Lieue** near **Lisieux**, in a splendid Pays d'Auge Manor from the 16th century offers three circuits where visitors can discover a farm of 70 hectares which also shows the different steps of making local foodstuffs from the Pays d'Auge (meat, milk, cheeses and cider).

The Norman beef stock is particularly honored. (Many information boards. Visits of stables and cheese making. Tasting and sale of farm products).

Open every day from May 1st to September 30th from 10 am-6 pm. Guided tours at 11 am, 2 pm, 3 pm and 4 pm.

For information : Tel (33) 2 31 30 68 ou (33) 2 31 62 08 55. Fax : (33) 2 31 31 83 72). E.Mail : genois@wanadoo.fr

****

CIDER PRODUCTS

More than ten million apple trees still flower on the Norman soil. Every year they yield hundreds of thousands of tons of apples which are made into that exceptional drink called cider.

CIDERS

Normandy's climate and the make up of its soil have been very favourable to growing apples trees and to their quality since the 16th century.

The fruit can be classed into four sorts : the sweet, bitter, bittersweet, and acid apples which give it the special taste of the thick colored cider and has made its reputation.

Even in 1788, when the King Louis XVI visited Normandy, he exhorted the merits of this brew, which was thirst quenching and light in alcohol.

The Norman soil is very varied and the make up of the different 'pays' offer the orchards different nutritive elements and varied orientation to the natural elements.

These orientations can then have either a good or bad effect on the production of the orchards, allowing some to be bathed in the kind rays of the rising sun and that of noon, sheltering them from the dry, icy winds from the East which are so damaging to the pollination of the flowers during the month of May.

All of these elements contribute to make up the various qualities of Norman cider and is the result of two factors : **Soil** and **Orientation.**

The third very important factor which can increase the quality lies in the choice of the varieties grafted by the Normans over four centuries.

This difference magnifies the best qualities and improves the inferior qualities.

Traditional cider making

M. G. Warcollier, the Director of the Pomological Department in **Caen,** wrote, in the catalogue for the Easter Fair in **Vimoutiers** in 1938, that cider : *'well prepared, kept in good conditions, constitutes an excellent drink, pleasant, refreshing, tonic, stimulating, good for the digestion, nutritive, rich in vitamins and most healthy'.*

*Hauchecorne would say, **of all fermented drinks it is the most thirst quenching and the most hygienic for consumption during the summer heat.***

*Doctor Denis Dumont stated that a well made cider was, up to a certain point, protection if not a cure for a whole series of illnesses : gall stones, gout. **The malic acid contained in cider is a powerful diuretic which sharpens the functions of the liver and reacts against the formation of uric acid and to the constitution of coagulation of phosphate.***

Good cider is appreciated by all consumers. It is pleasant thanks to its gleaming amber colour, and to its transparency which sometimes is of perfect limpidity. It is appreciated because it sparkles in its glass, flattering one's sense of smell with its delicate and penetrating fragrance. 'Good cider satisfies everyone's tastes and whims'.

Julien Le Pulmier, Norman apple expert from the 16th century wrote a well known thesis : **'De vino et Pomalo'** (which can be translated as 'About wine and cider') : the 'sidre' or 'pommé' is a sort of drink common and familiar to the Normans, which is drawn from apples crushed by the stone wheel of the press...'

As for its manufacture, he declared : *'The press has one or two wooden wheels, which are made to turn using oxen or horses in a trough with a circumference of 50 to 60 feet... One shovels the required quantity of apples for the wheels to crush at one given time. When crushed, the apples are put in a vat where they remain 'for the time decided on by the head of the family, more often than not from 12 to 14 hours. Afterwards the marc is taken from the vat, it is laid on the press in layers called 'quarré' separated by beds of 'fairre"(which we think was 'Glui') which is then pressed and then distilled with an 'egoust'. The apple juice is made into 'sidre' in a vat from which it is put into 'vessels"(today called casks)'.*

From the 16th to the start of the 20th century traditional cider making has barely changed.

The development and the spread of cider to a larger amount of consumers has only really existed since the 1920's.

Cider has had to wait several hundred years to obtain the merit it deserved because, most of the time, it did not have the requisite quality compared to wine or beer and suffered from a lack of reputation.

There were several reasons for this lack of quality, basically the lack of knowledge of the properties of the raw matter : the apple. Moreover, the manufacturing was quite rudimentary and had maintained its empiric character.

It needs to be said that cider at that time was made almost only for family consumption. It was drawn out of the barrel when it was needed.

To make a cider good enough to be sold which could compete against other drinks, one had to work methodically, starting by studying the different varieties of apples used for making it. Important research was subsequently carried out by the French Apple Association, producing valuable results.

Eugéne Lecœur, a chemist and apple expert from **Vimoutiers** studied local apples in his spare time for over forty years and suggested this method and in 1924 he started a competition for experimental ciders made with one, two or three varieties.

Many tests were carried out. Some people thought this strange, but for others it was the beginning of a selection of the varieties capable of obtaining cider of a superior quality. A first vintage was created and the first labels appeared on bottles of cider, which was the first step towards better communication. It was the 'Cru de Malvoue' from the farm belonging to Maurice Duhamel in **Vimoutiers.**

In the following years, the idea of 'cru' was further developed in the Pays d'Auge.

Although the studying of a variety of fruit for pressing, brought an improvement to the quality of cider, many of them were unable to obtain perfection because of a poor manufacture or just simply because of the lack of care necessary in brewing.

In the 1930's there was, what one could call, a crusade to improve the making of cider. In parallel to the farm producers, large factories producing cider had emerged mostly as part of the euphoria of the 1918 victory and had got themselves organized making great progress in the industrialization of the manufacturing process of a standardized product but of honorable quality.

Both the development of the production and consumption of cider were interrupted abruptly by the Second World War. The results of abolition of the 'right to distill', the fight against alcoholism and different taxes put on alcoholic beverages by the State from the 1950's practically stopped farmers making cider and they were even encouraged to destroy their orchards.

When those called the 'Parisians' started buying secondary residences, arriving in droves in the 1970's, together with the development of tourism and the evolution of French consumer taste for authentic products, it provoked the revival of cider-making and the need for the manufacturers to satisfy the consumers.

Jean-Claude **FOURMOND-LEMORTON**
Producer-Gatherer

*Cider and Perry - Pommeau from Normandy
Calvados from Domfront - AOC aged in oak casks*

"Le Douët Gasnier" 61350 MANTILLY - Tel/Fax (33) 2 33 38 71 63

Vintage ciders

More and more producers today are looking to the same objective, which is to have a range of ciders to choose from. In fact, as with wine, there is no standard cider, but rather ciders whose taste, whose alcohol content vary not only because of the geological and climatic influence but also because of the make up of the orchards; the different varieties alter from one sort of soil to another (several thousands of existing varieties of cider apples have been identified). Through a reasonable selection of the varieties and by using methodical and rational manufacturing, cider manufacturers have become real professionals, like the winegrowers, who leave nothing to chance, thus always presenting a cider with the same characteristics, the same taste, while being able to maintain the qualities belonging to a good cider. The times when cider was made with water from the pond have gone.

Today Norman cider enjoys a national reputation with the most appreciated sorts being those from the **Pays d'Auge,** the **Domfrontais** and the region of **Dieppe.**

Calvados

As a tradition inherited from the Vikings, who gulped down strong spirits in the middle of a meal to help digest any fatty food, the **'Trou normand'** *('Norman hole')* is generally served between two meat courses. A young strong Calvados (between 60% and 70% proof) is used and is drunk 'bottoms up'.

Old Calvados (over 5 years old) about 45% proof is sipped as a digestive at the end of a meal.

Nowadays the 'Trou normand' is more often replaced by iced apple sherbet laced with calvados and served between entrées, (no comment).

Calvados is also used as a basis for cocktails.

'Eau-de-vie de cidre' (cider spirits) was used for the first time in 1553 in the 'Diary of Gilles de Gouberville', a gentleman and Norman agronomist from the Cotentin area talked about distilling cider in his village of **Mesnil-au-Val** *(Area of Manche)*. The name of Calvados was borrowed from that of the Norman region. Calvados is used a great deal in Norman cooking, like cider and pommeau because their aroma and cream go so well together.

Calvados is made from cider which has been obtained from naturally fermented apples.

Cider is distilled in three provinces in Western France, **Brittany, Maine** and of course **Normandy.**

The title 'calvados' is reserved for certain Norman soils, the other being 'cider alcohol'.

Calvados is classed into categories of controlled origin, and soils and distillery methods explain the differences between :

Calvados obtained in one distilling with a continuous flow.

Calvados from the **Pays d'Auge** made exclusively from fruit picked in the most reputed soils and distilled in two stages in a 'two pass' still.

Calvados reaches its fullness only when it has aged for a certain length of time in oak casks. The age of the Calvados on the label is that of the youngest spirit in its assembly.

Hence : '3 star' means a minimum age of two years. 'Sous bois', 'vieux' or 'reserve' means a minimum of three years. 'Hors d'âge' : six years or more. Certain manufacturers assemble much older Calvados.

'Pommeau', the Norman apéritif . Although pommeau, known by the Normans for centuries under this name or otherwise, was made on the farm for family needs, and its manufacture on a larger scale and its distribution only dates back to thirty years ago ; at that time the Norman distillers suffering from poor sales of Calvados due to heavy state taxes had to find alternative outlets to maintain their activity. The 'Anée' company in *Vimoutiers* was the first to show the example. It was a relatively cheap aperitif, made partly from Calvados and apple pulp, which were an excellent combination. It is only for sale after ageing for at least 18 months in an oak cask. It is from 16 to 18% proof and is drunk very cool.

'Poiré', (Perry) 'Norman Champagne'. Perry is a speciality from the Norman Bocage area and is made like cider from different selected varieties of pears. This drink is consumed during a meal or as an aperitif such as 'Norman Kir', using either blackberry or peach syrup, and is an excellent way of quenching one's thirst and has come into fashion again over the last few years. The biggest orchards are in the *Domfrontais* (Domfront area) which was severely damaged during the great storms of December 1999.

In days gone by, Perry was dyed with blackberry juice. Since the 1980's the production of Perry has increased considerably. Perry from the region of Manche also has an excellent reputation.

****

Wine in Normandy...

For the last few years we have seen, albeit timid we must confess, the revival of growing vines and wine producing in Normandy.

You will perhaps be surprised to know that from, the Middle Ages to the 16th century, wine was produced in the Norman countryside. There were many wines on the more sunny slopes.

Listening to the chroniclers of that time, it was of really poor quality but all the same it was drunk by all, including the Duke.

*A lot of villages and hamlets still have a souvenir of these past riches : **Sévigny**, **Cesny-aux-Vignes**, **Juvigny**, Ménil-Vin, 'Mont de la Vigne'…*

*However the Norman vineyards were condemned to disappear by in the 16th century by King Charles IXth. Every year in **Sévigny**, Mr de Quennetain grows and picks his grapes and makes his own wine as do the inhabitants of **Vingt-Hanaps,** near Alençon, who replanted vineyards on the slopes of their village where they hold a Wine Festival in the autumn.*

…and Beer

*In **Tosny**, near Château Gaillard in Eure, a brewer christened his beer 'Richard the Lionheart' in memory of the Anglo Norman sovereign.*

Since recent times he has been brewing successfully. He explains that his success comes from its quality : 'a malt beer which is 100% natural'.

It is a blond amber and fragrant beer.

Guy Duplessis likes showing you round his state-of-the-art brewery and in the factory shop he also has beer jam.

Open 7 days a week at n° 13 de la rue aux Moines - 27700 Tosny -Tel/Fax (33) 2 32 51 55 75.

*At **Joué-du-Bois**, in Orne, in the hamlet 'La Poêlerie', Steve Skews, an English master brewer has installed the 'Brewery' in a farm he bought in 1994. He brews blond beer ('Norman Gold') and dark amber beer ('Conqueror') in an English tradition with ingredients brought from his home country. As from 2002 he is planting hops on his land to make an almost 100% Norman beer.*

****

VEGETABLES

Producing vegetables is an old and important activity in Normandy. The major market gardens are in the East of Normandy around urban areas (**Rouen**, **Elbeuf**, **Dieppe** and **Le Havre**) and in the area of Manche all along the coast where vegetables benefit from sea fertilisers. Carrots, leeks, lettuces, cauliflower, cabbage, potatoes, turnips… are the main vegetables grown in Normandy.

The plains of Caen, of Argentan-Trun, of the Pays de Caux are known for the quality of the potatoes grown there.

The annual production reaches 220,000 tons.

On the markets in Eure, Calvados and Orne, consumers have recently discovered Norman endives called **'La Vikingnoise'**. These endives typically Norman, come from a farm near **Marbœuf**.

MUSHROOMS

Mushrooms are used a lot in Norman cooking with cream because of the rich pastures, the huge forests and the latent damp which give the Normans many different varieties of these delicious vegetables. : morels in the spring and in autumn, cepes, boletus, chanterelles, horns of plenty and pink field mushrooms.

The 'boves' or old caves - old chalk stone quarries - where the temperature is always kind and the density of damp remains constant and provides an environment for the development of many mushroom growing farms; this plus the horse manure from the many stud farms give us the culture of the 'champignon de Paris'.

To be seen…

AREA OF CALVADOS

Fleury-sur-Orne : **'Les Champignonnières de Fleury'**, 39, chemin des Côteaux. Tel (33) 2 31 84 36 78 - Fax (33) 2 31 34 56 97. One of the old white stone quarries called 'Caen stone' at Fleury-sur-Orne is used by a firm growing 'champignons de Paris'. Part of the stone extracted from these quarries was taken to England for certain buildings. These caves were also used to shelter inhabitants from Caen during the D-Day landings in 1944.

AREA OF EURE

Brionne : **'Champignonnière'** (mushroom growing cave) : situated in a cave in the slope of a hill it was used as a shelter for the homeless during bombing in August 1944 and took in 3000 people. Today oyster mushrooms are grown using modern methods. It is 43 meters deep and has 2 kms of tunnels. Guided tour lasting 30 minutes on Sundays from 3-6 pm from July 1st to the end of August and by appointment. Tel (33) 2 32 57 87 99.

AREA OF SEINE-MARITIME

Dieppedalle-Croisset - Canteleu, près de *Rouen :* **'Champignonnière'.** Rue Hardel - Tel (33) 2 35 36 61 82. (Visits possible on Sunday afternoons) In the old quarries used for building Rouen, on the banks of the Seine, white mushrooms are grown and sold in the local markets.

NORMAN BREAD

Although bread was banned from diet menus for years by dieticians, today it has been redeemed by the same 'good food specialists' who have at last accepted that the enemy of healthy food was not the bread eaten but what was mopped up with it.

After years of tasteless white soggy bread, thanks to the expertise of professionals in the bread industry, today we have reverted to quality bread which the whole family can eat.

In Eastern Normandy, an area of excellent wheat growing, farmers, millers, and bakers have got together to offer 'Norman Bread' identified by its own logo. This bread is made from selected flour. It is made as it was in the olden days : tasty and crusty. **'Pain Brié'** is a speciality from coastal parts of Caux and the area round *Honfleur* ; it has a dense quality and was originally made for keeping a long time on boats at sea for a long time, and is still appreciated in the region.

At *Argentan*, in Orne, for the 50th anniversary of the Battle of Normandy a baker introduced a 'war bread' made in the same way as in the 1940's. He is also the inventor of a 'camembert bread' and 'camembert chocolates'.

AREA OF ORNE

Autheuil : **'Moulin de la Pelletrie'.** On the river 'La Commanche' you can find one of the last mills grinding flour in Normandy. Visits are possible by phoning for appointment with Jean-Claude Leroy -Tel (33) 2 33 25 73 40.

AREA OF EURE

Fourmetot : **'Maison du Pain d'autrefois' - route du Bourg - (The house of bread as it was).** Tel (33) 2 32 57 12 52 - Fax (33) 2 32 42 54 36. Working demonstration and commentary by a baker, from kneading the dough to taking the bread out of the oven. Exhibition. Breakfast or country snack on appointment.

Saint-Ouen-de-Pontcheuil : **'Ecomusée de la Meunerie traditionnelle'.** (Museum of traditional flour milling). Au Moulin Amont - Tel (33) 2 32 35 80 27.

TRADITIONAL NORMAN PUDDINGS

= **'La Teurgoule'.** The Teurgoule recipe is three hundred years old. It was understood that this excellent Norman dessert was invented by wives of sailors who brought back from afar the rice and cinnamon needed for making it. They had the idea of making it with whole creamy milk from the Pays d'Auge. They used the bread oven to cook the mixture for hours in big earthenware terrines.

To make teurgoule you need : 125 grams rice. 85 grams of sugar powder. 1 teaspoonful of cinnamon. 1 pinch of salt. 2 litres of whole full cream milk.
You mix all the ingredients and pour into an earthenware terrine and cook it on a low light for four to five hours. Teurgoule can be eaten hot or cold with or without brioche.

= **'Le Bourdin'.** This is a sort of tart made by the bakers using bread dough with a knob of butter. Non-peeled apples, preferably from Calleville, are cut in two, with the core taken out, are placed onto the dough. The edges are covered over with the surplus dough and it is put into the oven. Once baked the apples are sugared and the dish is served lukewarm.
In the Bocage they make a variety of bourdin called **'Bourdelot'.** Bourdin and bourdelot can only be made in autumn.

= **'Le Douillon'.** *Speciality from the Pays of Caux.* Peel the cored apples, put them in a buttered earthenware dish then sprinkle with sugar. Prepare a short pastry with as much flour as butter. Add a pinch of salt, a drop of water and some sugar until one obtains a supple mixture of dough.
Cover up the apples with the dough which has been rolled until it is 5mm thick. Cover and bake for 30 minutes. Serve lukewarm after covering the douillon with a spoonful of fresh cream.

= **Brioche made with butter.** The brioche was practically part of any special festive meal in Normandy. It was eaten as a snack or at the end of the meal, after the tart or cake, with an egg custard, or chocolate sauce or 'fruit salad'

= **Gache or fallue or neurolle (Brioche).** Sort of brioche or butter bread either long shaped or not. It was made by bakers mainly in Western Normandy.

= **'Brasillé' or 'Beurré Normand'.** 'Brasillé' in Bessin, 'Beurré Normand' in the Bocage, It is a puff pastry made with a lot of butter.

= **Norman 'Crêpes'.** Made with whole milk and fresh eggs, they are eaten as a dessert, sprinkled with sugar, with jam or flamed with Calvados.

JAMS

Mulberries, blackcurrants, raspberries, strawberries, gooseberries, apples, pears, quinces... were previously picked to make excellent jams or jellies which schoolchildren spread on large slices of bread in winter and went very well with brioche on Sundays.

Some farmers and bakers have started making jams using the traditional recipes which they sell on the farms, on the markets or in the better grocers shops.

At the Ferme de la Houssaye at *L'Oudon-Garnetot*, Eric Ribot developed making ice creams about twelve years ago, using the milk from his parents farm nearby to make ice creams and sherbets. Using the name 'Au frisson normand' (*see advert*), he also makes fruit jam (specialities of calvados, apple, cinnamon, and tatin apple) and also flavoured milk, a product which has existed for a long time in Normandy but which has never really been commercialized.

He has **milk jam** with vanilla, chocolate, hazelnut, or apple flavours on offer.

Using an ancient recipe he has also invented the **'Raffiné de Pommes'** which is eaten like jam but is also used in cooking to make a sauce which goes really well with game, breasts of duck, white meats, sea scallops...

Having started with this product, he has also gone on to making other flavours using fruit from the area.

A.O.C. from Normandy

Several Norman products have an A.O.C. (label of certified origin) proof of their identity, of their originality and of their quality. Like all products with A.O.C. they are strictly controlled at regular intervals.

*It concerns : **Cider from the Pays d'Auge.** The A.O.C. Cider from the Pays d'Auge is made exclusively from about fifty local varieties of cider apples belonging to the sweet, bitter-sweet, or acid categories and coming from apple trees planted on the best soils of the region.*

Calvados. *In fact there are three different A.O.C.'s under the name of 'calvados' The oldest (1942) : 'Le Calvados du Pays d'Auge', le 'Calvados' which only had a reglementary label in 1942 but became an A.O.C. in 1984 and the most recent, the 'Calvados du Domfrontais'. Each of these three A.O.C.'s is linked to an area* strictly defined by the I.N.A.O. It is within this particular area that everything to do with the production of the spirits must take place : the picking of the apples, the transformation and the distilling of the cider.

Butter and cream from Isigny. Because of its particular pastures, its special breed of animals and the Norman soil, it has been one of the rare French regions to produce and consume butter and cream all through history.

The area of the Bay of Veys which is inside this zone has always been very well known for its very typical and high quality products. The fact that there was a large port in the heart of this area enabled many French and foreign lands to appreciate butter from Isigny. Butter and cream from Isigny received their A.O.C. in 1986.

Camembert from Normandy. Invented during the French Revolution in the little village of Camembert in Orne, Camembert has been imitated all over France and even abroad, because of the lack of any particular copyright protection. In 1924 the Court of Orleans confirmed that 'Camembert' had become a term of public property. Since 1983 'Camembert from Normandy' made with whole milk using ladles for moulding carries an A.O.C. This is valid in five Norman regions.

Livarot. Livarot carries three A.O.C.'s since 1975. The area concerned is very restrictive : the south of the natural Pays d'Auge area which represents several cantons of Calvados and Orne. This traditional cheese-making area has very rich pastures and a kind damp climate giving early grown grass for the cows.

Pont-l'Evêque. Pont-l'Evêque received its A.O.C. in 1976. It is made from milk coming from Normandy and Mayenne.

Neufchâtel Cheese. Cheese from Neufchâtel received it's A.O.C. in 1977. It is made in the country of Bray has unusual pastures with soil composed of marl and silex clay up as far as the chalk slopes. The milk was produced by an original collection of predominantly Norman cows which were rich in fat and proteins. The production zone is constituted by 135 communes, within a radius of 25 to 30 km around Neufchâtel

Pommeau from Normandy. Pommeau from Normandy received its A.O.C. in 1991 and is made all through the **Calvados A.O.C. area.** The subsoil of the orchards is made up from granite from the Armorican Massif in the Domfront region, from shale in the Pré-Bocage and silex clay on a chalk subsoil in the Pays d'Auge. Pommeau from Normandy must be made from fruit picked in selected orchards identified by the National Institute of A.O.C.'s There are currently procedures under way by the I.N.A.O. (Institut National des Appellations d'Origine) for a future recognition of Perry from the Domfront and Passais regions and for the Norman breed of beef.

****

'Bio' Products

A certain number of farmers have decided to devote themselves to bio farming, as they have done in other French regions, by not using synthetic chemical products in the soil and by giving biological food to their animals.

Thanks to natural means, using a lot of labour, they today propose a large range of products using the 'AB' logo including certain more or less well known products which are transformed for today's tastes.

Amongst these 'bio' products we can mention : eggs, butter, cream, cheese, meat, bread, vegetables, cider, apple and fruit juice.

****

Norman agri-business some figures...

Agri-business is the biggest employer in Normandy (13% of jobs in industry) representing more than 6 billion turnover per year..

65% of this figure comes from milk and meat products.

Normandy is the biggest producer in France for : Fresh cheeses, Soft cheese Butter, Cream, Cider apples, Oysters and mussels, Scallops, Sea snails, Cuttlefish.

2nd biggest producer in France of : Carrots and leeks.

3rd biggest producer in France of : milk and beef.

6 Norman products have labels of conformity guaranteeing regular and specific quality : cider made from cider apples, 'Cider from Normandy' or 'Norman cider', 'Maître Veau' veal, Beef from the 'Pays Normands', Norman Breed quality (Race Normande), 'Père Guillaume Rabbit' (There are currently procedures for 'certified Lamb, Oysters from Normandy, Vegetables from Manche, Tripes à la Mode de Caen, Traditional de Norman Breed Beef).

Biological farming in 1998 was represented by 340 producers on 15,000 hectares. The first figure should increase to 1,200 in 2005.

Normandy has 8 Red Labels : Farm poultry from Normandy, Farm pork from Normandy, Dry sausages ; dried sausage and rosette, Veal reared on whole milk from Normandy, Old, and very old Mimolette, Ciders from the 'pays normands', Carrots from Créances, Leeks from Créances, Sand Carrots.

(There are currently procedures for free range eggs, Norman scallops and andouille of Vire).

9 Collective trademarks have been created : Bouchot mussels, Oysters from Normandy, Seafresh, Fresh from the coast of Upper Normandy, Fresh garden vegetables from Upper Normandy, Red fruit from Normandy, Croquine, Ciders from the Pays de Haute Normandie, Fermiers des Becs, Lamb du Pays normand.

Master-butcher of Normandy.

(Origin : Chambre Régionale d'Agriculture - 2001)

****

What did our ancestors eat ?

From the middle ages, members of Norman aristocracy had a certain 'art de vivre' in their castles and manors, where good food played an important part.

People ate a lot of meat - using their fingers (beef, pork, mutton, poultry) served in wooden bowls.

One of the Norman specialities at that time was the buckwheat pancake.

Even at this time dairy products were ever present on Norman tables : butter, cream and cheeses were popular.

It was said that the Vikings taught the Neustrians how to make butter.

The 'angelots' or 'augelots', ancestors of Neufchâtel, Livarot and Pont-l'Evêque were appreciated accompanied by barley beer and wine.

The populace lived and ate in a more modest fashion.

The poorest ate little meat, because of the strict control the Dukes had imposed on hunting, and when they did it was pork, reared on acorns and nettles in their humble homes.

They ate black rye bread, peas, beans, onions and above all gruel. They owe the name of 'Norman gruel eaters' because of this 'national dish'.

From this time on Norman peasant became excellent in cultivating land and rearing stock.

They were the first to use horses for ploughing the land.

= *The more modest townsmen lived off 'Gros bœuf' ou 'Gros Porc' whilst the 'magistrates' ate mutton, veal and poultry.*

Game was reserved for nobles.

= **Collation** *(Light meal).*

At the start of the last century, the farmers got up early to milk the cows and then tend the beef stock. They would often only drink a bowl of milk before they left. When they came back home around 10 o'clock they would eat a 'light meal', a good breakfast with vegetable soup, bread and butter, charcuterie, jam and other farm products allowing them to carry on until lunchtime.

Food was of great importance in a farmers life.

The victuals were high calorie : 'fat' soup, pancakes, buckwheat gruel, potatoes...

= **The cross on the bread.**

In our countryside, when the master of the house cut into the bread, he drew a cross on it with point of his knife - one vertical and one horizontal stroke- this rite was undoubtedly a way of thanking God for providing the humblest with their daily food.

****

2 - The Capitals of Norman Gastronomy

<u>AREA OF MANCHE</u>

Annoville : **capital of Norman biscuits.** In this commune les 'Annovillaises' are made ; these are biscuits made with butter in traditional Cotentin fashion. Information : Office de Tourisme de **Hauteville-sur-Mer**. Tel (33) 2 33 47 51 80.

Avranches : **capital of salted meadow lambs and the pear called 'Louise Bonne'.**
Pre-salted lamb : The speciality of pre-salted lamb stems from the fact that the lambs graze on the 'herbus' of the Bay of **Mont-Saint-Michel**, vast stretches regularly covered over by the tides. The grass it eats is impregnated with sea salt which gives the lambsmeat a particularly pleasant taste.

Barfleur : **capital of Mussels called 'Blonde de Barfleur'.** A mussel from the deep of great quality. The 'Blonde de Barfleur' is fished off the East coast of the Cotentin. It is probably the biggest known field of wild mussels in France.

La Chapelle-en-Juger : **speciality of smoked ham.**

Cherbourg-Octeville : **speciality 'les Demoiselles de Cherbourg' : big shrimps fished off the North of the Cotentin.**

Cosqueville : **capital of the 'Bouquet'.** Le bouquet de Cosqueville is a very tasty big pink shrimp.

Coutances : **Speciality of black pudding ('boudin coutançais'), tripe with cream** (the tripe is folded in small packets in rind, **Buckwheat pancakes, and 'gache' or 'fallue'** (brioche).
Other specialities : Cheese 'le Coutances' and Meiss chocolates.

Créances : **capital of the Norman Carrot.** In the middle ages carrots were already grown in the Créances country. The excellent quality of the sandy soil made their growing easy. Onions and leeks are also grown there. 'Poireaux de Créances' and 'Carottes de Créances' carry the Red Label.

Ducey : **capital of salmon.** For centuries salmon swimming up the river Selune towards the nearby sea have been fished here. Today there is a salmon farm at the Moulin de Cerisel, Route des Chéris. - Visits on Wednesdays and Saturdays or by appointment. Salmon and trout hatchery - video commentary. Information, Tel (33) 2 33 48 47 17.

Granville : **capital of the sea snail. Other speciality : clam stuffed with garlic butter.**

Lessay : **speciality of smoked ham.** Norman smoked ham is a dried ham, smoked in the chimney so it may be kept for several months. It is usually eaten cooked in cider then fried, or cut up raw into long thin slices with salted butter.

Montebourg : **Capital 'Pigs trotters à la Cassine'. Speciality of tripe 'façon Montebourg'.**

Le Mont-Saint-Michel : **speciality : 'Omelette de la Mère Poulard'.** Mother Poulard's omelette is prepared on a wood fire, like Annette Poulard, who opened the inn at the foot of the ramparts in 1888 and which today bears her name. The omelette is beaten to the music of the rhythm of the 'omelettiers' whisks in the copper 'culs de poule' made in *Villedieu-les-Poêles*. Its recipe, a jealously kept secret, is handed down by the owners from father to son. Annette Poulard is buried in the small Mont Saint Michel parish church cemetery. On her grave you can read the following epitaph : *'Welcome Our Lord like she welcomed her clients'*.

Saint-Denis-le-Gast : **speciality of smoked 'andouille'.**

Saint-Georges-de-Livoye : **speciality of honey.** Commune situated on the circuit of the 'Route de la Table'.

Saint-Hilaire-du-Harcouët : **capital of onion sausages. Speciality of buckwheat pancakes** Buckwheat pancakes (galettes de Sarrasin), very popular in neighbouring Brittany, first appeared on the Saint-Hilaire-du-Harcouët market just after the last war. In olden times it was eaten at lunch and replaced bread. Folded or rolled into four, it could be eaten with salted pork, butter, a sausage, jam or even soaked in a 'moque' of beer.

Saint-Vaast-la-Hougue : **speciality of oysters.** The bay of Saint-Vaast is one of the main oyster producers in Normandy. Oysters produced here have a marked taste of hazelnut. **Other specialities : Vegetables.**

Ile de Tatihou : **speciality of oysters.**

Valognes : **specialities : cider, calvados, fruit jelly made by the 'Bénédictines' and 'Pierre de Valognes' (confectionery).**

AREA OF CALVADOS

Asnelles : **speciality of shortbreads.** The 'sablés d'Asnelles' were invented by Charles Bansard in 1904. **Other specialities: products from oysters 'La Calvadosienne'.**

Bayeux : speciality '**Le Porc de Bayeux**'.

Bény-Bocage : **capital of the goose. Specialities 'foie gras' goose potted meat. Promotion of force fed Norman geese. In olden times there was a goose potted meat contest in this commune. (100% goose meat)**

Beuvron-en-Auge : **capital of jam and cheese. Specialities cheese 'le Pavé d'Auge', cooking with cream** Quince and sweet cider jam are a great local speciality.

Cabourg : **speciality dried sausage (saucisson) with camembert cream.** Camembert cream is part of the composition of the original dried sausage. Although not apparent its taste is pronounced. It is a skinless sausage, made in a mould which always remains mellow. It is made by an emblematic craftsman from Cabourg who is an old hand at world records, such as 'whipping up the mayonnaise' or the tallest known pile of traditional charcuterie or even the number of onions he has peeled… He is to be found. 31, rue de la Mer à l'Enseigne 'Le Pôvre Dany'.

Caen : **capital of cooked tripe.** Tripe cooked 'à la mode de Caen' was invented by a monk in the Abbaye aux Hommes in the 16th century, which puts paid to the oral tradition that says that the Duke William liked this dish a lot. They became 'à la mode' in the 19th century and conquered the world thanks to restaurateurs, but above all thanks to the Norman butchers who manufacture them and make them known amongst the population. 'Tripe à la mode de Caen', is made from stomach, cow's trotters and is cooked for ten to twelve hours. They are preferably served at about 10 am in the morning, with dry cider or dry white wine. They are served with steamed potatoes or chips.

Cambremer : **capital of cider and A.O.C. produce** Real natural ciders from Cambremer made in the old fashioned way have a slightly bitter taste which makes them particularly thirst quenching. They are fragrant and richly coloured.

Clécy and in general all the **Suisse Normande : specialities 'Teurgoule', wheatbuck pancakes and shortbread biscuits.**

Clinchamps-sur-Orne : **speciality of 'Brasillé'.** Pure butter Norman dessert.

Courseulles : **Norman capital of the Oyster.** Already well known in Roman times, the Courseulles oyster is still appreciated by the finest of palates. It can be savoured and purchased directly in the different resorts along the seaside.

Deauville : **speciality of shellfish.** *'Deauville, also has the sea! From mussels and cream to shrimps served luke warm, without forgetting the velvet crabs and also, noblesse oblige, lobster and crayfish…'.*

Falaise : **Capital of 'crépinette' (flat onion sausage). Other specialities garlic sausage, long sausage, short breads.**

Grancamp-Maisy : **speciality scallops.** To eat them 'à la Normande' : 'cook the scallops in a court-bouillon the let them simmer for 10 minutes. Cook some finely chopped white mushrooms in water with some lemon juice and butter. Make a white sauce with the court-bouillon from the scallops and the water rendered by the mushrooms (add some flour). Add fresh cream and a raw egg yolk (without cooking it). Cover it all with bread crumbs, add a knob of butter and brown it in the oven'.

Honfleur : **capital of grey shrimps** On the quays, near the Lieutenance, there are wheeled stalls where fisherman still sell the famous live grey Honfleur shrimp.

Houlgate : **capital of the 'Teurgoule'.** Traditional Norman dessert.

Isigny-sur-Mer : **capital of Norman dairy products (1st dairy quality in France). Specialities : milk, fresh cream cheese, caramels, oysters.**

The oyster : the 'Isigny special' produced in the Bay de Veys is 'fleshy, with a big shell, sweet and firm and there was a time that retailers and consumers would know that they could acquire this 'super oyster' directly from where it was produced; that is to say in the region of Isigny and Grandcamp.

Lisieux : **capital of cooking with cream and calvados. Specialities : chicken and veal scallop Vallée d'Auge, with cream and mushrooms.**

Livarot : **capital of cheese.**

Noyers-Bocage : **speciality : country paté.** This is a paté manufactured solely using pork.

Pont-l'Evêque : **capital of cheese.**

Saint-Aubin-sur-Mer **and generally speaking the côte de Nâcre : speciality of 'gui-gui',** soft marshmallow in different flavours served on a stick - sold on the beaches.

Touques : speciality of trout.

Trouville-sur-Mer : **capital of 'Sole à la Normande'. Other specialities : grey shrimps, scallops and, 'Tarte Antoine''.**

Vire : **Norman capital of the 'andouille' sausage.** 'Number one' product of Norman charcuterie, the andouille from Vire is made from the digestive organs of the pig and include : the stomach, the small intestine, and the large intestine. Having been thoroughly cleaned, the guts are cut into strips then salted and marinated for several days. Then they are assembled, attached at one end and covered with a 'robe' (part of the large intestine which has been put aside for this purpose before being cut up). The sausages are hung in the chimney, over a fire made of beech and smoked for 6 to 8 weeks. After being smoked, they are soaked for up to 48 hours, before being tied up and cooked in water.These days, the real '**andouille from Vire**' is 'completely hand made' just as it was two centuries ago and that is the reason that this speciality has maintained its excellent reputation in spite of the invasion of industrial products calling themselves : '**Andouilles de Vire**'. **Other specialities : 'Pain de carême' et 'galette des rois briochée'.**

AREA OF ORNE

L'Aigle : **capital of 'Cervelas' sausages.** The '**cervelas**' is a sort of sausage made from pork (lean and fatty) which is slightly smoked with some Calvados added, thyme and laurel, onion and spices. It can be eaten grilled on the BarB-Q served with split peas and small pieces of smoked or non smoked bacon ; rolled in pastry, grilled and covered in apple jam or in puff pastry; boiled served with sauerkraut or cold, cut into slices for eating with aperitif.

'Our cervelas from l'Aigle is tasty ! With a bowl of cider, you will be tasted, and a gourmet stomach will appreciate your smokiness. But, what's your name ? I am Cervela from L'Aigle'.

The Cervelas from l'Aigle is in the limelight during the '4 Days in L'Aigle', a trade fair taking place during Ascencion weekend. You can try it in the 'House of Cervelas'.

Alençon : **capital of Norman 'andouillette'. (chitterling sausage).** The 'andouillette' from Alençon is different from that of Troyes. Because it is made of minced not sliced pork guts. Ingredients : crow, stomach, and pork throat. Seasoning : salt, white pepper, nutmeg, parsley, shallots, vinegar and mustard.

HALLE AUX VINS

Wine in bulk or bottles- Spirits - Apéritifs - Champagne

10, quai de La Touques	6, rue du Bouloir
14800 DEAUVILLE	**14600 HONFLEUR**
Tel/Fax : (33) 2 31 98 33 85	Tel/Fax : (33) 2 31 89 11 60

En partenariat avec :

PAYS DE LOIRE - VAL DE LOIRE :
Muscadet :	*Château de l'Aiguillette*	44 Mouzillon
Sauvignon :	*Domaine Saint-Roch*	41 Meusnes
Saumur-Champigny :	*Domaine "Les Méribelles"*	49 Souzay-Champigny
Anjou :	*Domaine de la Belle Angevine*	49 Beaulieu/Layon
Sancerre :	*André Robineau - Cave du Fort*	18 Sancerre

BORDEAUX :
Côtes de Blaye :	*'Les Chevaliers d'Aliénor'*	33 Generac
Haut-Médoc :	*Château "Lenoine-Lafon-Rochet"*	
	Sabourin Frères	33 Cars
Saint-Emilion :	*Clos des Menuts* Maison Rivière	33 Saint-Emilion

SUD-OUEST :
Bergerac :	*'Les Grands Chais de Saint-Laurent'*	
		24 Saint-Laurent-des-Vignes

Vallée du Rhône :
Côtes du Rhône	*'Les Vignerons Visanais'*	84 Visan
Côtes du Ventoux	*'Les Vins de Sylla'*	84 Apt
Côtes du Lubéron	*Caves de Loumarin-Cadenet*	84 Cadenet

BOURGOGNE-MACONNAIS-CÔTE CHALONNAISE :
Bourgogne de Vigne en Verre - Group. de viticulteurs   71 Tournus

BEAUJOLAIS :
Beaujolais-Brouilly :	*Domaine Saint-Charles*	69 Saint-Etienne-la-Varenne

LANGUEDOC :
Vin des Sables :	*Domaine du Petit Chaumont*	30 Aigues-Mortes
Côteaux du Languedoc :	*Vignerons de Benovie*	34 Saussines

CHAMPAGNE : *Champagnes Christian Doulet*	51 Epernay
CALVADOS : *Calvados Roger Groult*	14 St-Cyr-du-Ronceray

Cider, Pommeau and Calvados from Normandy

Each year there is an International White Pudding and Andouillette contest in Alençon.

Other specialities : **White Pudding, the 'Sieurs d'Alençon', 'le Bouchon d'Alençon' et 'les Pierres de Notre-Dame'** (confectionery and hand made chocolates).

Argentan : **speciality 'terrine from Argentan'. Other specialities : 'Norman spurs' (chocolates), 'war bread', 'camembert bread', 'chocolates... made with camembert', with mushrooms...**

Athis-de-l'Orne : **capital of 'Bourdelot'.** 'Bourdelot' is a typical Norman dessert served previously at the end of the Harvest Festival dinner symbolic of the end of harvesting. It is made up from natural products : dough, sugar, butter, Calleville apples or similar. Short or puff pastry can be used. Contest : There is a Bourdelot and Charlotte contest on 3rd Friday in October in Athis. **Other specialities : 'Charlotte' made with apples and calvados, Galette des Rois.** A 'galettes des rois' takes place in January.

Bagnoles-de-l'Orne : **speciality of 'Chocolate Macaroons' ('Macarons Lenoir').**

Camembert : **the capital of cheese.** Innformation : House of Camembert - 61120 Camembert.

Céaucé : **speciality of quails.**

Coulonces : **speciality of 'bourdin'.**

Domfront : **City of Calvados Other Specialities : 'Galette', Perry, pommeau, smoked ham, 'Les Rochers de Domfront' (chocolate), the Domfront short breads.** Products derived from cider are a Domfront speciality, thanks to its healthy soil responsible for its originality, above all the Perry, a tasty drink and a true speciality from neighbouring Passais.

Essay : **capital of 'Boudin Blanc' (white pudding). Le 'Boudin Blanc' :** in olden times it was only made at Christmas and is made up from ham, eggs, flour, whole milk and aromatic plants. For the last 15 years this community has organised the best white pudding contest.

Flers : **speciality of Duck pie. Duck pie** is made with puff pastry and stuffed with small pieces of duck cut up into cubes, and minced mushrooms.

Other specialities : 'Gousset' from Flers is a piece of beef with a beef based stuffing. Eaten with apples, cream and flamed with calvados.

The 'Bec of Flers' : puff pastry dessert with rhubarb and with apples cooked in blackcurrant and sugar.

The 'chiffoine' : calvados and fruit based liqueur.

And confectionery such as **Camembert cream caramels.**

La Ferté-Macé : **capital of skewered tripe.** Like Caen, the town of La Ferté-Macé has a speciality of cooked tripe. Its speciality is skewered tripe. Skewered tripe,

La Ferté style, is also called 'tripes en paquet' and is composed of pieces of cow's stomach from 15 cms long and 5 to 7 cms wide, inside which you roll up different ingredients : different parts of intestines, trotters, cuvier. The rolled packet weighing about 200 grams has a piece of wood going through it (beech or hazel). The uncooked tripe must be of prime quality and is cooked slowly in an oven for over 12 hours, preferably in a earthenware recipient called a 'Pote". La Ferté tripe has neither vegetables, nor tomato with it but should be eaten with steamed potatoes. **Other speciality : 'L'andouille fumée', (smoked sausage).**

Longny-au-Perche : **Norman capital of Terrine forestière and cooked tripe - Speciality of 'gâteau Longnicien'.** Traditionally in the old days in Longny, horse breeders and traders would get together round a bowl of tripe after the market.

Lonlay-l'Abbaye : **speciality butter short breads and dry Norman 'biscuits'.**

Mantilly : **capital of Perry.**

Le Mêle-sur-Sarthe : **speciality of 'Foie gras'.**

Le Ménil-de-Briouze : **'La galette du Ménil'.** The pancakes from le Ménil-de-Briouze started in the 20th century. A baker's daughter in the community thought up this speciality half cake, half brioche.

Le Merlerault : **speciality 'Pullet of le Merlerault'.**

Moulins-la-Marche : **capital of the butter 'Brioche'.** The brioche, sometimes called 'norolle' is the pastry preferred by the Normans. It was always part of a special meal or wedding dinner in the 19th century.

Mortagne-au-Perche : **Norman capital of 'Boudin noir'.** (black pudding). This speciality, made in Mortagne for over a 1000 years has contributed enormously to the reputation of the Perche capital. Each year in the Black Pudding Fair, **4 to 5 kilometers** of this speciality are sold.

Passais-la-Conception : **speciality of Cider and Perry.**

Rânes : **capital of the 'pirotte' or fattened goose.** At Saint-Rigobert, usually on the first Saturday in December, the farmers gather in Rânes to eat the fattened goose or 'pirotte".

Saint-Sauveur-de-Carrouges : **speciality of Norman 'Gruyère' 'Gruyère of Carrouges'.** A 'gruyère' type cheese was already made in Orne by the monks several centuries ago. This tradition has been started again by a farmer and producer, Gérard Mercier, who has perfected a 'Norman gruyère' which he has been making for the last 14 years and which is much appreciated by gourmets. You can acquire it directly from the farm. Gérard et Monique Mercier - Les Noës - Saint-Sauveur-de-Carrouges - Tel (33) 2 33 27 25 59. Sale on site on Saturday afternoons.

Treillebois : **speciality of cheese 'Le Pont de Treillebois'.**

Vimoutiers : **Capital of Norman produce for the Table : Apples, cider, calvados, pommeau** (large exhibition of everything to do with apples, apple tart and cakes – contest during the Apple Fair in October - Cider, calvados and pommeau

competitions at Easter - head qauarters of the 'Confrérie des Chevalier du Trou normand' and the 'Confrérie des Gentes dames du Pommeau' (today dormant), **'cité de la Race Bovine normande'** (well known contest of Norman beef stock and producers in October, **statue of the Norman Cow** in the Town Hall Square, **town of Camembert cheese and Norman Butter**
(Camembert Museum, Statues of Marie Harel, Camembert Route, headquarters of the 'Confrérie des chevaliers du Camembert' - 'Halle au Beurre' where the most important butter market in Normandy took place).

****

'Les Etriers Normands' (Norman Spurs) :
a speciality from Orne

Ten chocolate makers from Orne have put their experience together in inventing this speciality in honour of the Horse.

For information about this list of professionals, contact the chairman : Gilles Vacher, Rue du Moulin à Vimoutiers (28).

****

AREA OF EURE

Bernay : **Capital of trout. Specialities 'Foie gras' and trout 'pâté' - Norman bread.** Every year there is a big gastronomical feast at the end of June in the abbey at Bernay to commemorate these two products, and also all the products in the area.

Gisors : **speciality of Pullet 'à la crème'. Other speciality : 'Brioche' from Gisors.**

Louviers : **speciality : 'choux de Louviers'.** Choux pastries stuffed with stewed apple and custard with a calvados flavour.

Lyons-la-Forêt : **speciality 'pâtés' from Lyons. This speciality is more than 75 years old.** Lyons paté has been certified since the war. It is made from poultry livers, throat of pork and flavoured with port.

Pont-Audemer : **speciality of 'Rillettes de Lapin'** (rabbit potted meat). **Other speciality : 'Mirliton'** - cake generously laced with light tasty sugared almond and chocolate.

AREA OF SEINE-MARITIME

Autretot : **speciality 'Le Galuchon'** sort of puff pastry Galette des Rois.

Bolbec : **speciality : 'Le Pavé Bolbécais' et 'Les Bisous de Bolbec' (chocolates).**

Dieppe : **local speciality 'Marmite Dieppoise'.**

Other specialities sole, scallops, 'pain Duval' which stays fresh for several weeks - this bread was very well known in the 50's, and is still made today at *Chambois* in Orne near *Argentan.*

'La Marmite dieppoise' : ingredients : 1 minced onion, 1 minced leek white, 2 tomatoes, 3 spoonsful of olive oil, 40 gr of butter, 2 spoonsful of fresh cream, 30 gr of flour, cayenne pepper, fennel-salt, parsley, red pepper, curry powder, 4 slices of monkfish, 4 langoustines, 4 scallops, 4 fillets of sole, 1 litre of cooked mussels 'à la Marinière' and some shelled shrimps. Recipe : Cook the onion and the minced leek whites in olive oil, add the two peeled tomatoes and simmer until cooked. Add a litre of water, salt and cayenne and cook the fish in the order given previously. Melt 40 grams of butter in a pan, add 30 grams of flour, and gradually mix in the sauce from the fish and mussels. Cook for five minutes and add the cream, the fennel, curry powder, cayenne pepper and salt. Place the fish on a salver, coat with the sauce, decorate with the mussels, shrimps and red pepper. Concerning the latter, one must remember that the port of Dieppe had had spices for centuries, which were used in Norman cooking and also in making liqueurs like **Bénédictine**, 'elixir of health' invented by a Bénédictine monk in 1510.

Doudeville : **Capital of Linen.** The charming town of Doudeville, mentioned by Maupassant, is known today as the **Norman Capital of Linen**, but it generally ignored that the seeds of this plant, generally used for making thread, then cloth, from most ancient times, is also used for making foodstuffs bringing them both a special flavour and high nutritive quality. Several craftsmen from Doudeville have revived linen through different specialities of baking, pastries or charcuterie.

Duclair : **Capital of Duck. Speciality : of 'Canard au sang'.** It is said that the famous speciality of *'canard au sang'* by the means of the breeding ducks is a very old activity in Duclair. The breeder took the 'palmipedes' to Rouen in rowing boats where they were sold to the inns or to private people. During these trips it was not unusual that a certain number of ducks, squashed into wooden or wicker boxes, died by suffocation which meant a financial loss for the fatteners. It was then that a cook had the idea of inventing a new recipe with these ducks that had died, which took off very quickly with the local gourmets.

Elbeuf : **speciality 'La Caille au monstrueux' (quail and leeks).** An enormous leek grown in the alluvial plains of the Elbeuf area. **Other specialities : les 'navettes d'Elbeuf'** (sugar almond sweet in the shape of a shuttle to remind one of Elbeuf's former textile industry). And the **Douillon** (Apple in a short pastry).

Etretat : **speciality 'La Caudrée d'Etretat'.** Sort of Norman bouillabaisse.

Fécamp : **specialities mackerels cooked in liqueur 'Bénédictine'.** This liqueur, invented in the 16th century and revived in 1863 by Alexandre Legrand, was composed of at least 27 herbs and spices such as génépi, cinnamon, aloes, vanilla, juniper berries, pine buds.

Other speciality 'Filet de sole fécampoise' (fillet of sole served with mussels).

Gournay-en-Bray : **cradle of 'Petit Suisse'** cottage cheese invented by Charles Gervais.

Gruchet-le-Valasse : **speciality of chocolate 'Le Galet de la Côte'.**

Jumièges : **capital of Norman cherries and plums.**

Le Havre : **speciality 'L'Oscar' confectionery made with chocolate, nougatine, apples and almonds.** Oscar was the Christian name of the Brazilian architect Niemeyer who built the House of Culture in le Havre.

Le Tréport : **capital of the type of mussels called 'Cul bleu'.**

Neufchâtel-en-Bray : **One of the four capitals of cheese in Normandy.** It was in this important agricultural centre in the Pays de Bray that Neufchâtel cheese started. The 3rd weekend in September, every year since 1995, the 'Confrérie des Compagnons du Fromage de Neufchâtel' organises a Cheese Fair with chapter and enthroning - tasting and sale of cheese and local food products.

Rouen : **speciality 'Le Caneton à la Rouennaise. Duckling à la rouennaise'.** This speciality was already much appreciated by Voltaire in the 18th century. At the beginning of the 19th century this dish was served in the Restaurant de la Côte d'Or, situated Quai de Paris in Rouen. This restaurant no longer exists today. We know that the Duke de Berry, second son to Charles Xth used to go to this restaurant. At the end of that century, Père Denise prepared 'Caneton à la Denise' which came from his farmyard in Duclair. The bird was spit roasted. Served bloody, it was prepared 'à sa façon'. (his style).

Other specialities :

Apple sugar. For more than four centuries Rouen has been producing sticks of apple sugar. Its hand-made production is summed up in its cooking of the sugar, at 130°, extract of apple is added to give it its flavour. Although it seems simple, this recipe requires real experience. The little sticks are hand rolled until they cool down. This speciality can be found in most confectionery shops in Rouen.

Les 'Larmes de Jeanne d'Arc'. (Joan of Arc's Tears) Confectionery made by one of the oldest of the well known confectioners in Rouen. As are the chocolate called **Paillardises.**

Saint-Romain-de-Colbosc : **speciality of Black pudding and cream.**

Saint-Valery-en-Caux : **speciality of lobster.** If you listen to local fishermen, lobster fished off the coasts of Normandy is of exceptional quality because of the iodine content in the Channel waters.

Saint-Wandrille : **speciality of fruit jelly.** The Benedictine monks in Saint-Wandrille carry on this tradition and sell excellent fruit jellies in the Abbey shop, together with other products from the Monastery which are sold under the 'Monastic' label.

Veules-les-Roses : **speciality of cress.** *Sales direct to the public on Wednesday mornings on the Veules market and Saturdays from 3-6 pm* at la 'Cressonnière'. Tel (33) 2 35 96 50 89.

Yport : **speciality of Apple Tart, la 'Tarte Ledun'.** Served hot with whipped cream 'to make it lighter' **Other specialities : Smoked herring or 'safate', Salted cod and 'Le ragoût de roussette d'Yport'.**

Yvetot : **speciality Leg of lamb from Yvetot.** This is a leg of lamb cooked in a casserole with various vegetables and sprinkled with calvados.

3 - FOOD FAIRS

NB : For exact information on the dates of events and of their content, contact the Tourist Offices concerned.

AREA OF MANCHE

Barenton : Early November in the 'Maison de la Pomme et de la Poire' :

Fête au sirop. Syrup from Normandy, also called 'raisiné' in the Domfront area or 'pomé' in Gallo country, is well cooked fruit jam - the cooking time can last up to 48 hours ! -, with an apple and pear base , and whose recipe had practically been forgotten for about fifty years. It was revived in 2000 in Barenton. This is a friendly opportunity for Normans and Bretons to meet up.

Courtils : early July **'Fête du Mouton de Pré-salé'.** Information. Tel (33) 2 33 70 96 56.

Créances : First Sunday in August : **'Carrot Fair'.** Sale of vegetables - Chapter of the 'confrérie des Mouôgeous d'carottes de Crianches' - various attractions - country meals - carrots in all shapes and forms. Information. Tel (33) 2 33 46 30 18.

Denneville : End of July : **Oyster fair with tasting and attractions.**

Dragey : mid July : **Cider fair.** Information : Mairie de Dragey - Tel (33) 2 33 48 87 42 ou (33) 2 33 48 83 38.

Fierville-les-Mines : In May or June **Pig fair.**

Gouvets : First Sunday in August **Cider Fair.**

Lingreville : Early August **'Fête des Coques d'or'.** In olden times people would paint sea shells which were plentiful on the sandy beaches at low tide. This tradition gave birth to a festival which still exists today. The fair takes place after Mass which is celebrated opposite the sea with the possibility of tasting the shell fish.

Nez-de-Jobourg : First Saturday in August : **Sheep Festival.** Sheep contest - tasting of roast lamb. Information : Tel (33) 2 33 52 74 94.

Pontorson/Roz-Couesnon : Early August **Sacred meadow lamb.** Normans and Bretons from the Bay of Mont-Saint-Michel get together to celebrate the festival. Information. Tel (33) 2 99 80 21 79.

Saint-Lô : **Salon Horial.** Every two years the Horial Exhibition (Horizons agro-alimentaires de Normandie) takes place giving local companies in this field to show their goods to potential clients. This show, open to both professionals and to the public, is a veritable shop window for Norman Agri-business : for four days visitors can see and taste all the delicious local products.

Sainte-Mère-Eglise : End of July, au 'Musée de la Ferme' (Farm museum) : **Traditional dance and evening market with local.** Contact. Tel (33) 2 33 95 40 20.

Saint-Quentin-sur-le-Homme : Early December **Fair with local products.**

Saint-Sauveur-le-Vicomte : end of October, in the old castle **Apple festival : 'saveurs de Pomme, saveurs d'automne'.**

Torigny : In November **Fair with regional products.**

AREA OF CALVADOS

Argences : in October **Onion fair.**

Beuvron-en-Auge : Last Sunday in September **Cider Festival.** Tasting and sales - Market with local products - crafts of yesteryear. End of December : **Christmas market.** Information : Association 'Art et Traditions'.

Cambremer : First weekend of May **A.O.C. Festival.** Big festival of Norman products of quality in this capital of Norman gastronomy, mainly known for the quality of it cider based products. Information : Tourist office. Tel (33) 2 31 63 08 87.

Cuverville : in December : **Christmas market.**

Falaise : Ascension day **Marché gourmand.** In October : **Onion Fair dating from 12th century.** Beginning of December : **Christmas market.**

Fervaques : in October **Nut fair.**

Honfleur : 3rd weekend in September : **Shrimp festival.** Grey shrimps have been fished in Honfleur for centuries. At this event one can eat them in the delightful old town centre.

Lisieux : August 1st in the town streets. **'Foire aux Picots'**[1]. This traditional fair takes place in the Square de la République and brings together a large number of poultry producers, foie gras, and other food specialities. Information : Tourist Office : Tel (33) 2 31 48 18 10. Every Saturday morning : **The 'Marché cœur du Pays d'Auge'.** In the place de la République, farmers sell stock from their farms in a very colourful market. In July and August : **'Les Mercredis de l'Eté'.** Every Wednesday from 4 pm in summer, there is a market with local wares, attractions and outside country food and free concert. In December : **Christmas market** Craftsmen and farmers suggest ideas of gifts and gourmet menus for the festive season.

Livarot : 1st weekend in August : **Cheese festival.** Different attractions - tasting, sale of local produce in the presence of local members of the Norman 'confréries gastronomiques' - Fun fair - on Sunday : **contest of the biggest Livarot eater !** Information : Tourist Office, Tel (33) 2 31 63 47 39.

Maisoncelles-la-Jourdan : 3rd week in September **Cider festival.**

Pont-l'Evêque : 2nd weekend of May : **Cheese festival.** Tasting, sale of cheese from Pont-l'Evêque and local products - **Best Pont-l'Evêque contest.** Information. Tel (33) 2 31 64 00 02.

───────

(1) Le picot is a fattened turkey which is reared for Xmas.

Ouistreham : last weekend in October : **Sand eel and mussel festival.** Sand eels are long little fish, unfortunately rarer and rarer, which are found in the Orne estuary. They are fished in the sand using forks or spades. During this festival the restaurateurs invite you eat them fried or mussels Marinière. Contact. Tel (33) 2 31 97 18 63.

Pont-d'Ouilly : last weekend in October **Apple fair.** Cake and apple tart contest.

Trouville : end of July, beginning of August **Festival of the Sea and Mackerels.** Last week end of October : **Snail festival.** For the last few years, the seaside resort of Trouville has been having an escargot day where they can be tasted and cooked in different fashions. At the same time there is a snail buttering contest for the children, a snail race and a treasure hunt for the Golden Snail... Information : Tel (33) 2 31 14 60 70.

Villers-sur-Mer : 3rd weekend in October : **Shell and shellfish festival.** Tasting and sale of scallops and shell fish - Market with local products - various attractions (contests, parades) - food tasting contest -Information. Tel (33) 2 31 87 01 18.

Vire : All Saints weekend **'Foire à l'Andouille et Produits du Terroir'. (Vire Sausage festival).** The 'andouille de Vire' already existed at the beginning of the 18th century using a recipe which has never been changed . It has enhanced the town of Vire's reputation which has organised a sausage and local produce festival every year since 1989. Tasting and sale of charcuterie, cider, farm produce and craftwork from the Bocage. (50 exhibitors - 7000 visitors !).

AREA OF ORNE

Alençon : In the exhibition hall at the end of September : **Craft work, local produce and nature exhibition.** More than 300 exhibitors and 30,000 visitors come to this exhibition which is a shop window for agriculture and traditions from Orne.

Argentan : On the fair ground during the Quasimodo Fair, a week after Easter. **'Festival ornais de l'Elevage et de l'Agriculture'.** This exhibition includes a beef stock contest (Norman breed and beef cattle), horse parades and other animals, with tasting and sale of local products, A.O.C. cheeses.

Bagnoles-de-l'Orne : 2nd fortnight in September **Local product week.** Early October : **Mushroom days in the forest of Andaine.** Mushroom picking with guides.

Bellême : last weekend in September **International Mushroom Meeting in Bellême.** Bellême forest, one of the most beautiful wooded areas in France, is where an important mushroom event takes place at the start of autumn, where many specialists are present : picking mushrooms with guides - conferences - Professional Day for Chemists - Golden Cep Competition - mushroom exhibition (between 400 and 700 varieties).

Briouze : 3 days every year during the 3rd weekend in November. **Sainte-Catherine Fair and Festival.** As a traditional Norman fair the Sainte-Catherine honours local products and in particular the Norman beef breed. On the Monday there is a contest and veal market and also a sale of Norman heifers. **Win a bullock !** For years and years, guessing the weight of a bullock has been one of the main attractions. All you have to do to take part is to guess the animals weight, or be the nearest to the real weight- two tries for a very modest price.

Camembert : in April and November **Exhibition and sale of local produce.**

Carrouges : In July and August **'Gourmandises'.** Sale of local food produce. Mid October : **Apple exhibition.**

Coulonces : mid September **'Fête du Bourdin'.** For the last century, when this country fair takes place in this little community near *Argentan*, about 600 bourdins are made and eaten.

Courtomer : July 14th **Food fair.** Sale of farm produce and craft work - traditional dancing - rides in horse traps. Information : Syndicat d'Initiative. Tel (33) 2 33 31 87 70.

La Ferté-Macé : mid October **'Journées mycologiques d'Andaines (et du Houlme)'. (mushroom days).** Mushroom picking with guides, exhibition, conferences.

Le Ménil-de-Briouze : on the Sunday before July 14th **Pancake festival.** Attraction - outdoor country meal.

Le Sap : 2nd weekend in November **Cider festival.** Old style manufacturing - houses decorated to apple and cider themes - local produce market - old crafts exhibition - traditional country dancing.

Longny-au-Perche : usually May 1st **Tripe fair and French Tripe Championship.**

Mantilly : every second year, weekend following July 14th (2004). **Perry festival.** Outdoor country fair - tasting - sale of Perry and local produce - outdoor lunch and dinner - payment on admission. Information. Tel (33) 2 33 38 72 93.

Mortagne-au-Perche : For 4 days during the 3rd weekend of March. **'Foire au Boudin'. (Black pudding fair).** Agricultural fair (cattle contests, Percheron horses) - Exhibition - fun fair - cycle race. During the event, you can try tasting black pudding 'on every street corner''. Best black pudding contest and **biggest eater of black puddings. Boudin, (exceptionally no fair in 2002).** Information. Tel (33) 2 33 85 11 18.

Rémalard : end of October **Apple and pear festival.** More than 100 exhibitors ! Thousands of visitors each year.

Saint-Fraimbault : in September **Festival of local produce.**

Sées : in December on the Sunday nearest to Saint-Lucie. **Turkey fair.** One of the oldest and biggest in the region. In the open air : sale of turkeys and foie gras on makeshift stalls in anticipation of Christmas and New Year feasts. At the same time : regional produce fair, pate from Sées, pastries.

Trun : end of September, beginning of October **Onion fair.** The idea of this fair was to attract the populations of the Pays d'Argentan and the south of the Pays d'Auge to Trun, big centre for trade, so that they could stock up with onions before the arrival of winter. The highlight of the weekend is a cattle judging contest. **On the Sunday there is a competition for the heaviest vegetable and for the most original vegetable.**

Vimoutiers : **at Easter** During the old traditional **Easter Fair** there is the **Cider, Calvados and Pommeau Competition, the oldest and most well known in Normandy, having been created 70 years ago.** 2nd weekend in October **Apple fair :** This fair created before the war enabled apple producers to sell their produce to cider makers and distillers at the best price, using samples, but today no longer serves any purpose. Nowadays it is mainly a popular fair and fun fair. Every year there is a life size design made out of apples, using a different theme, which attracts several thousand visitors to the Butter Market Hall. During this fair there is : an apple exhibition, an apple tart and cake contest, and also of cattle for reproduction and for meat, where the Norman breed is at the foremost. There is also the contest for the longest apple peel organised by the Tourist Office. Every year in October in Orne there is the '**semaine du goût**", (taste week).

AREA OF EURE

Damville : end of August **Cider fair.**

Beaumesnil : end of September **Open House at the producers in the Canton.**

Bernay : last Sunday of June **'Rendez-vous des Becs fins'.** Market for 'foie gras' and local produce, promotion of local specialities in 'Belle époque' atmosphere. Information : Tourist Office : Tel (33) 2 32 43 32 08.

Cormeilles : On Sunday mornings from the end of June to the start of September **Country market.**

Lieurey : November 11th **Herring fair.** Herring market - tasting of grilled herring - contest for the eater of most herring. Several tons of herring are sold on that day to be marinated, following local tradition.

Morainville-Jouveaux : 3rd Sunday in June **Cider festival** and cider contest organised by the 'Confrérie des Goustes Cidre de France' (Commanderie de Normandie-Picardie). Different attractions. Information. Tel (33) 2 32 56 28 02.

Le Neubourg : in October, November and December **'Foie gras Market'.**

Pont-Audemer : end of May **Cooking festival.** Restaurant keepers from the town propose attractions and promote the local gastronomy. Information : Tourist office. Tel (33) 2 32 41 08 21.

Saint-Ouen-du-Tilleul : 2nd Sunday in October **Apple festival.** Local produce market - old fashioned cider making - special 'apple' meals.

Sainte-Opportune-la-Mare : early October **Apple festival .** Apple market - old fashioned cider making - cider competition - Tasting and sales - local produce market.

Tillières-sur-Avre : early October **Apple festival.**

Vernon : Pentecost weekend **Cherry festival.** Various attractions. Information. Tel (33) 2 31 51 39 60.

AREA OF SEINE-MARITIME

Bretteville-du-Grand-Caux : in October **Apple festival.** Information : Mairie Tel (33) 2 35 27 70 27 - Fax (33) 2 35 27 96 93.

Caudebec-en-Caux : last Sunday in September (uneven years) **Cider festival.** Old fashioned cider making, Tasting, sales.

Dieppe : Weekend following November 11th **Herring Fair and Scallop Festival.** The port of Dieppe used to be specialised in herring fishing but has gradually lost its importance in this field. The herring fair reminds us of this old tradition. Tasting and sale of herring on the piers - attractions in the town centre - fishing contest.

Forges-les-Eaux : All Saints' Day **The Week of the Apples.**

Gournay-en-Bray : end of September **Herring, Cheese & Cider Fair.**

Jumièges : *Base de loisirs* on the 1st Sunday every month in summer **Fruit festival.** In June and July the association of farmers and producers of the 'Route des Fruits' organise : **the cherry festival,** in August **the plum festival** and in September **the apple festival.** Information. Tel (33) 2 35 37 35 08.

Le Havre : 1st Sunday in November **Apple festival.** Founded in 1987 to highlight the value of the culinary heritage and folklore in the region of Le Havre. About 1000 exhibitors take part in this festival. You will find various craftsmen and artists alongside farm or small scale producers of meat or cider.

Londinière : end of November **Cheese and pleasures around the table Fair.**

Longueville-sur-Scie : end of March **Cider competition.**

Neufchâtel-en-Bray : mid September **Neufchâtel Cheese festival.**

Parc de Brotonne : in October **Apple festival.**

Pierrecourt : 3rd weekend in June **Strawberry fair.** Local produce fair - varied attractions - Information : Tel (33) 2 35 93 55 08.

Rouen : A Saturday in mid October in the historic heart of the town. **New 'Fête du Ventre'.** In October 2000, after 60 years of non existence, Pascal Monville, a dynamic tradesman from Rouen revived the Fête du Ventre, in an aim to give back its reputation concerning gastronomy to the Norman capital. The Association of 'Rouen Conquérant' with the help of local traders, the Town Hall and different sponsors have the ambition to promote the concept of **flavour, soil** and **taste** of producers by proposing the sale of authentic wares of quality. All through that day the 'place du Vieux-Marché' and the rue Rollon take on a traditional festive manner with exhibitors dressed in 14th century Norman clothes and with various other attractions. An event for 'gourmets' and 'gourmands' not to be missed under any circumstances.

Sept-Meule : In October **Apple festival.**

Le Tréport : 2nd Sunday in June **Mussel fair.** At the bottom of the cliffs, in this place blessed by the gods, one can fish large mussels called 'Culs Bleus'. During the fair nearly two tons are served.

November 11th **Herring Fair.** Tasting of fresh, grilled and smoked herring. Sale of fish.

Saint-Valery-en-Caux : end of November : **Herring and cider festival.** Information : Tourist Office. Tel (33) 2 35 97 00 63.

Valmont : end of October **Apple Festival.** Information : Tourist Office. Tel (33) 2 35 10 08 12.

4 - GASTRONOMICAL CIRCUITS

Over the whole of Normandy

The Norman Cheese Route Created by the Tourist Office of Vimoutiers, the Norman Cheese Route is an unmarked circuit which goes from *Neufchâtel-en-Bray*, in Seine-Maritime, to *Coutances*, in Manche, whilst passing through all the towns linked to the history of cheese in Normandy : *Pont-l'Evêque, Saint-Pierre-sur-Dives, Livarot, Vimoutiers, Camembert, Falaise, Condé-sur-Noireau, Vire* and *Saint-Lô*.

AREA OF MANCHE

'La Route du Cidre du Coutançais'. Created by an association of 'Producteurs récoltants de Cidre et de Produits agricoles des crus du Coutançais', this tourist circuit takes the visitor on a discovery of the apple country around Coutances.
'This land of hedgerows with its high places flanked by frothing waves and flowers stays attractive, in many varied ways, all through the seasons. In spring you can find the pink and white of the flowering apple trees and in autumn loaded with heavy golden or red fruit. The perfume from the heaps of ripe apples awaiting the press near the field grates. All along these shadowy roads and bumpy lanes, one can make out the unbelievable number of churches, manors, country residences of character. Worthy introduction to the flagships of a heritage amongst which one can note : **Coutances, Lessay, Hambye, Pirou, Gratôt, Chanteloup, Régneville-sur-Mer, Orval** and **Périers'.**
On the circuit, producers, identified by the sign **'Cru du Coutançais'** will open their gates to you and let you taste their cider. Information and a free brochure obtainable from Manche Tourist Offices.

'La Route de la Table'. Gastronomical and tourist circuit in the south of the region. Access via *Carentan* as from *La Haye-du-Puits*. The circuit is constituted by nine stages of visits of workshops making craft or gastronomical specialities from Manche : biscuits, hams smoked over an open wood fire, camembert from Normandy made from whole milk and moulded by ladle, apple based produce, red fruit, fresh dairy products, andouille sausage, culinary crockery.

DEPARTMENT OF CALVADOS

The Livarot Cheese Route. This tourist circuit invites you to discover the history of this highly appreciated cheese and the beautiful sites of this well known countryside. A free brochure is distributed by the *Livarot* Tourist Office.

The Cider Route. Be guided down the Cider Route linking the little towns of *Cambremer, Beuvron-en-Auge, Beaufour-Druval* and *Bonnebosq* and discover the landscapes and Pays d'Auge houses with their typical half timbers. This route is right in the heart of the geographical area of the A.O.C. (Appellation d'Origine Contrôlée) ciders from the Pays d'Auge.

A signpost '**Cru de Cambremer**' points out the entrance to 20 farms where you can, in most cases, visit the cellars and the press. You can also taste the cider, pommeau and calvados. The '**Cider de Cambremer**' is made from trees from a specific soil and its best products are selected in an annual contest at the start of May. Information : Cambremer Tourist Office -14340 Cambremer - Tel (33) 2 31 63 08 97 - Free brochure on demand.

The Gastronomical Route. Created by the Lisieux Tourist Office, this circuit is roughly 110 km long and lets you discover all the natural and gastronomical riches of the Pays d'Auge and its capital. Information : O.T.S.I. Lisieux -11, rue d'Alençon - Tel (33) 2 31 48 18 10.

The Route of Traditions The *route of traditions* is one of the most popular tourist routes used in Western Normandy. This sign-posted itinerary (sign post with a white background and a navy blue rim) is an invitation to find out about traditional farm produce.

Towns to stop at : *Cahagnes* ('crème de calvados' et Norman cocktails) - *Amayé-sur-Seulles* (Calvados, pommeau, cider, apple juice) - *Saint-Germain-d'Ectot* (Goats cheeses) - *Hottot-les-Bagues* (Weaving) - *Maisoncelles* - *Pelvey* (pottery, crockery) - *Jurques* (Foie gras, magret, rillettes, confit) - *Dampierre* (cider, apple juice, cider vinegar, rillettes, pigeon paté) - *La Vacquerie* (angora wool) - *Sept-Vents* (Old fashion style bread). Free brochure from the local Tourist Offices.

AREA OF ORNE

The Camembert Cheese Route. Sign-posted tourist circuit of about 50 kilometres around *Vimoutiers* which will allow you to discover the Camembert country. Free brochure given out by the Vimoutiers Tourist Office (28).

The Perry Route. You are invited to discover the Countryside of Domfront and Passais and Mortain reputed for the quality of their produce which assembles the biggest concentration of pear trees in France. Come in April and admire the pear trees changed into enormous white bouquets, and which constitute a magnificent décor. In autumn the flowers give way to the fruit which produces a beverage unique in France : poiré (Perry). Free brochure available in the Domfront (34) Tourist Office.

AREA OF SEINE-MARITIME

The Apple and Cider Route. Created by the 'Comité Departmental du Tourisme', of Seine-Maritime, this 38 km long tourist circuit stretches from the Pays de Caux to the Pays de Bray. It is best to join the circuit at *Auffay* then to follow the signs for *Le Catelier, Muchedent, Le Bois-Robert, Anneville-sur-Scie* and *Longueville-sur-Scie.* All along the visitor will find : cider for sale and discover the 'thousand faces of the apple and cider in Upper Normandy". Information from the Mairie of Auffay - Free brochure on request. Tel (33) 2 35 32 81 53.

The Neufchâtel-en-Bray Cheese Route. Non signposted tourist circuit of about 50 kilometres around NeufchâTel 'In the heart of the Pays de Bray, between *Neufchâtel-en-Bray* and *Forges- les- Eaux*, there is a well known cheese which has been appreciated for along time : the Neufchâtel'. Free brochure from the Tourist Offices or from the Comité du tourisme de Seine-Maritime.

The Fruit Route. The micro climate of the Jumièges peninsular makes it favourable for growing trees. Along the Seine, between *Duclair* and *Jumièges* one finds the 'Route des Fruits". Following what season it is, one can buy fruit straight from the small producers on the road side under the shade of a parasol : raspberries, gooseberries, strawberries, cherries, plums called 'verte bonnes', miarabelle.

'Guide l'Assiette du Pays'. In Normandy, discover the good addresses where you can be served a simple, swift good meal which will allow you to taste the real Norman flavours. The 'assiette du Pays' is one course meal, main course or dessert with a glass of something typical to drink and made from local Norman produce. Guide available from the 'Fédération Régionale des Pays d'Accueil touristiques' - BP 523 - 14035 Caen cedex. Tel (33) 2 31 06 98 04 - Fax (33) 2 31 06 97 81.

5 - MUSEUMS OF FOOD DELICACY

AREA OF MANCHE

Barenton : **'Musée de la Pomme et de la Poire'.** You can discover the different aspects of traditions linked to producing cider apples. Presentation and sale of farm produce. Museum orchard. 'Logerais' - Tel (33) 2 33 59 56 22 -Fax (33) 2 33 59 16 20.

Montebourg (55) *:* **'Musée du Lait'.** rue des Perruquettes - 50310 Montebourg Open in July and August from 2-6 pm. Tel (33) 2 33 41 13 48.

Saint-Jean-des-Champs : **Ferme de l'Hermitière.** Tel (33) 2 33 61 31 51. *Eco-museum - Manufacture of cider and calvados.*

Valognes : **'Musée Régional du Cider et du Calvados'.** Rue du Petit-Versailles. Tel (33) 2 33 40 22 73. Sale and tasting of regional produce.

'Musée du cidre' : *At the house in the 'Grand Quartier'.* Built around 1480, housing dyers of sheets, leather and skins, this house later became a barracks from 1700 to 1900. You will discover five centuries of history about cider with the presence of grinders, presses, pottery, material for transport and scenes from Norman life with clothes and furniture from the 18th and 19th centuries. Video.

'Musée du Calvados et des Vieux Métiers'. Built between the 17th and 19th centuries, the 'Hôtel de Thieuville' was alternatively a private house, a charity, lingerie factory, lace makers, Gendarmerie for mounted police, then fire station. You can see tools, equipment, machines and furniture in connection with the craft of distilling, working with stone iron, and leather. 18 different professions are represented in 15 rooms. (Collections from the 11th to the 20th centuries).

AREA OF CALVADOS

Livarot : **'Musée du Fromage'.** Manoir de L'Isle 68, rue Marcel-Gambier (Direction Saint-Pierre-sur-Dives). Tel/Fax (33) 2 31 63 43 13. Open to the public from March 1st to October 31st from 10 am-12 noon and from 2-6 pm. Closed from November 1st until February 28th. Reconstitution of farm cheese dairy, and an old fashioned cheese dairy. Audio-visual commentary about cheese making. Exhibition of labels.

Pont-l'Evêque : **'Chais des Calvados du Père Magloire et Musée des Métiers anciens'.** Open every day from April 1st to November 1st. Visit lasts one hour. Tel (33) 2 31 64 30 31 - Fax (33) 2 31 65 44 75. E.mail : info@pere-magloire.com Site internet : www.pere-magloire.com

Saint-Martin-de-la-Lieue : **'Domaine de Saint Hippolyte'.** Open every day from May to September from 10 am-6 pm. Tel (33) 2 31 31 30 68. There is a superb half timbered manor house in the heart of a large property in the Touques Valley, where you can go through all the stages of transformation of grass into milk, watch the cows being milked… and tasting the cheese made on the farm. You learn a great deal about cattle rearing. See section 'Produits carnés' (meat products) (Chapter 1).

Vire : **'Maison de l'Andouille'.** Route de Caen - Manufacturing technique of andouille sausage from Vire - Open every day except Sunday.

AREA OF ORNE

Camembert : **'Ferme Camembert'** - **'Le Bourg'** - Exhibition of labels and objects from yesteryear - Video - sale of local products. Information : (33) 2 33 12 17 45. **'Manoir de Beaumoncel'.** Visit 'The House Marie Harel' - Only in groups and by appointment. Tel (33) 2 33 39 27 01. **Farm production of camemberts.** Sale on site. 'Ferme de la Herronnière' - Tel (33) 2 33 39 08 08 - Fax (33) 2 33 39 35 67 31.

Le Sap : **'Ecomusée du Grand Jardin'** **'De la Pomme au Calva'.** Open from March to December from 10 am-12.30 pm and from 2-6 pm. Open or guided visits. - Closed on Sunday mornings and all day Monday and Tuesday. Rue du Grand Jardin - Tel (33) 2 33 35 25 89. Information : http : // www.le-grand-jardin.asso.fr

In a small old farm on 3 hectares of land, the eco-museum shows the public collections of what it was like in times gone by, in the stables and cider making. All that was left were the cement containers built in 1926 where the cider was kept. Today it has been turned into a perfect area for showing objects and documents dealing with apples, cider and its distilling.

You must see the two highlights of the museum which are the 'gadage' (stone apple press) and the 'pressoir longue étreinte". Both date from between the end of the 18th and the beginning of the 19th centuries ; made entirely of wood they are set into motion for the cider festival.

A 'boiler', which is completely renovated, shows how to distil cider and how to keep calvados. Various attractions.

*Vimoutiers : '**Musée du Camembert'.** 10, avenue du Général de Gaulle. Tel (33) 2 33 39 30 29 - Fax (33) 2 33 67 66 11. Reconstitution of a cheese-making dairy farm - Exhibition of labels (1500 !) - video - tasting.

AREA OF EURE

*Cormeilles : '**Maison du Pays d'Auge et des Calvados'.** In the heart of the Pays d'Auge and Normandy, the Busnel distillery 'bathed in the copper reflection of the stills' will reveal to you 'an ancestral know-how, issue of patience, rigour and sensitivity'. Tel (33) 2 32 57 38 80 - Fax (33) 2 32 42 50 52.

La Haye-Routot : **The Bread Oven.** A bread oven in 18th century building revives rural traditions and regional specialities at the same time as an exhibition of bread and traditional bread making. On Sunday afternoons from March to mid November, the baker shows how the old bread ovens worked and draws old fashion style bread and biscuits from the oven in front of the public ; open: on Sundays and holidays in March, April, October until November 11th from 2-6 pm. On Saturdays, Sundays and holidays in May, June, and September from 2-6.30 pm. Every day in July and August from 2-6.30 pm.

AREA OF SEINE-MARITIME

Fécamp : **'Palais de la Bénédictine'.** 110, rue Alexandre-Le Grand - B.P 192 - 76401 Fécamp Cedex - Tel (33) 2 35 10 26 10 - Fax (33) 2 35 28 50 81. Site internet www.bénédictine.fr E.mail Palais.Benedictine@bacardi.com.sit Visit of Art Museum, distillery, cellars. Tasting- sales. Open to the public every day from February 3rd to December 31st (Closed from January 1st to February 2nd and December 25th). At the end of the visit those adults that so wish, are offered a taste of Benedictine. (Abuse of alcohol is dangerous for one's health ; to be drunk with moderation).

Opening hours : From February 3rd to March 30th : 10 am-12.15 pm and 2-6 pm. From March to June 29th : from 10 am-1 pm and from 2-6.30 pm. From June 30th

to September 2nd : from 9.30 am-7 pm. From September 3rd to September 30th : from 10 am-1 pm and from 2-6.30 pm. From October 1st to December 31st : from 10 am-12.15 pm and from 2-6 pm.

The Museum is dedicated to the world famous liqueur invented by Alexandre Legrand. (Manufacturing with presentation of different plants used in its making, the distillery, cellars, advertising, patents, export, building of the palace) but also presentation of collections of paintings, sculptures, ivories, wrought iron, enamels...

Neufchâtel-en-Bray : '**Musée Mathon-Durand'**. Part of this museum is dedicated to the manufacture of Neufchâtel cheese. A.T.P. Tel (33) 2 35 93 06 55. Open all year round at week ends from 3-6 pm and every day in July and August except Mondays.

Rosay : **Museum of the Apple and Cider.** Route de Pommeréval. Tel/Fax (33) 2 35 94 31 66. Exhibition showing the history of the apple, of cider products from the start of the century up to today by means of different documents, postcards, objects, tools and materials. Discovery of old crafts. Tasting/sales. Open from Easter to All Saints day on Sundays and holidays, from July 14th to August 15th open every day from 2.30-6.30 pm.

Saint-Maclou-de-Folleville : '**Le Moulin d'Arbalète'**. Tel (33) 2 35 32 67 11. This living museum dedicated to bread is built round a working flour mill ; bread making and baking using wheat milled by the grindstones, bread and cake making. Open from April 1st to November 1st, on Wednesdays, Saturdays, Sundays and holidays from 2-6 pm. Every day in July and August from 2-6 pm.

Sommery : (Ferme de Bray in the Hameau de Bray) : '**Pressoir à pommes à longue étreinte de 1802' - Auge circulaire et roues - vaste cave.** (1802 Circular stone Apple Press - large cellars) Open all year. Tel (33) 2 35 90 57 27.

Sainte-Opportune-la-Mare : **House of the apple.** Parc Naturel régional de Brotonne. Tel (33) 2 32 57 16 48. To be seen : *apple press dated 1837 -apple mill dated 1746 - barrel maker's workshop.* Founded by priests in 1710, this old Presbytery shows the reconstitution of cellars, and stills.

To finish the visit : sale and tasting of cider, Perry, pommeau, calvados... and apples. Nearby a museum orchard with about 50 local and regional varieties.

Open at weekends from 2-6.30 pm in April, May, June and September. Open every day in July and August from 10.30 am-12.30 pm and from 1.30-6.30 pm.

IX - THE UNUSUAL AND SECRET NORMANDY

1 - Beliefs and superstitions

The almost solitary life of the first settlements in Normandy in the heart of the immense dark forest which covered almost all the land, the survival of Celtic and Viking beliefs are the origin of the great number of superstitions and legends which still haunt the countryside. Demons, white ladies, fairies, sorcerers, werewolves, debauched monks, dragons and other fantastic creatures are, following the example of neighbouring Brittany, the people of this strange universe and at times are still present in the depths of 'bocage'.

Even a few years ago, in our countryside, the sorcerer, who used 'Petit Albert' or 'Grand Albert' - very widespread works of witchcraft - had a reputation at the time for coming in the night and it has still not totally disappeared...

At the dawn of the 21st century, after 2,000 years of Christianity, certain magic practices still indeed hold court and priest exorcists still receive in each diocese numerous 'victims' or 'pseudo-victims' of 'j'teux d'sorts'. They also visit the 'bonesetters' or the healers to relieve a large range of ills.

If a farm animal is ill they think first that it is from a 'wrong doing'.

In numerous places pagan cults had their sanctuaries - generally sited close to a spring - where they came to worship and invoke the healing saints, the leader of which was Saint-Sébastien.

Here and there were born places of pilgrimage which endure and today still receive thousands of the faithful. Among the most ancient we can quote ***Mont-Saint-Michel*** but also that of ***Douvres-la-Délivrande,*** between ***Caen*** and the sea, where they give thanks to the black Virgin.

In the Cotentin, the 'Pays Bas-Normand' the 'Pays d'Auge' or the 'Pays de Caux', where the superstitions are still living, it is considered that the ill follows you to the grave.

In the cemeteries of the region of ***Lisieux,*** one must avoid the main entrances where the demonic spirits watch. They could transform the dead into a werewolf or a phantom.

Large numbers of legends have their origins in the gullibility born around the megaliths which exist in their thousands in Normandy.

AREA OF MANCHE

La Haye-du-Puits : beginning of July **Festival of 'Sorcery and the fantastic in Cotentin'.** Between 1668 and 1672 there took place at *La Haye-du-Puits* a legal hearing which local memory still recalls. Around twenty sorcerers and witches but also a priest known to be guilty of acts of sorcery were condemned to be burned but they were not executed on the orders of Louis XIV in 1682. Numerous legends of sorcery still circulate in the Cotentin : the witching hour, black masses, the transformation of people into animals, dubious persons, goblins, 'milloraines', white ladies,... (see the work of Barbey d'Aurevilly). The places linked to these legends are the Mont Etenclin, the wood of Limors, the commune of Varenguebec, the Mont de Doville (the inspired mountain).

Saint-Pierre-Eglise : Numerous sorcerers existed in the region of Saint-Pierre, notably Theil. The most celebrated amongst them had as a surname ' The toad'.

AREA OF ORNE

Around **Bagnoles-de-l'Orne** : **Tour of 'The country of Lancelot of the Lake'.** In a country rich in legends, find again the mysterious atmosphere linked to the history of the Knights of the Round Table and that of Lancelot of the Lake. Tours - conferences. For information : Tel (33) 2 33 37 84 59.

AREA OF SEINE MARITIME

Gruchet-le-Valasse : They have classified as an act of sorcery a strange phenomenon observed here some years ago. The body of Marie Bataille was found intact in its coffin… 40 years after her death !

Forges-les-Eaux : They tell here the story that an old horse would again find it's health after having drunk the waters of Forges…

****

The funeral associations or the Brotherhoods of Charity

Since the Middle Ages, at the time of the great epidemics, there were formed in Normandy, the 'charities' who would give as their mission, the accompanying of the grieving and the burial of the dead. The members, numbering around a dozen, carried at the centre of the ceremony the surplice and a cassock. They had the chest covered with a large embroidered 'échappe' the 'chaperon' (the hood). The 'tintenellier' (bellringer) would shake the 'tintenelles' (little copper bells).

*One held the velvet banner, embroidered with gold. Certain of the Brotherhoods still exist today. One of their great gatherings takes place at **Préaux-Saint-Sébastien** near **Meulles** in Calvados on the occasion of the pilgrimage of Pentecost where they come to venerate Saint Sébastien.*

****

THE HEALER SAINTS

Certain saints are invoked to heal a particular ill by their intercession with God, the 'illness of the saint', which cannot be relieved by traditional medicine. Each saint possesses, in some form, a special ability. One notes sometimes a phonetic resemblance between the name of the saint and the ill that he cures.

AREA OF MANCHE

Brucheville : In this parish, they call on the Saint-Eutrope to heal the dropsy and Saint-Gilles to whom one takes the children who suffer from nightmares. The children must 'toucher la bête Saint-Gilles' and take part in a mass celebrated in honour of the saint to make their fears disappear.

Carquebut : The fountain of Saint-Ouen holds, it is said, the power to heal maladies of the eyes.

Le Petit-Celland : **'Fontaine Saint-Gerbold'.** The people suffering from 'croup' came in earlier times to pray before the statue of the saint then going to the fountain to collect the water which would heal the lesions.

Sainte-Mère-l'Eglise : **Saint-Méen** is called upon in this parish of which he is the second patron. Born towards the end of the 5th century, originating from Wales, this man saint was obliged to flee before the invasion of the Saxons and took refuge firstly in Brittany. Acording to legend, Saint-Méen came to visit Saint-Marcouf. Being thirsty on the road, he struck the earth with his stick and a spring emerged at this place. This water source never dried up. Saint-Méen is called upon to heal the 'scabies of the hand' but his competencies have over the passage of time extended to all skin infections. Custom was that the sick person took home with him a little of the miraculous water from the spring in order to be able to continue the cure.

AREA OF CALVADOS

Lisieux : **Saint-Expédit and Saint-Antoine-de-Padoue called upon at the cathedrale Saint-Pierre.** One prays to Saint-Expédit to resolve urgent problems and especially for the healing after a shaky period of health. Saint-Antoine of Padua was the object of a special group. They asked him to cure absent mindedness by helping the 'return' of lost objects. They say at times the ritual words : 'Saint-Antoine, old crook, old 'grigou' (= miser) will you give back to me that which you have taken away from me !'. They also call on Saint-Antoine of Padua for the healing of shingles. In Lisieux, the pilgrims address him by writing their varied requests asking for above all that health should continue in their lives.

AREA OF ORNE

Corbon : **'Les Pouvoirs des Seigneurs de la Vove'**. It is said that the Lords of the Vove had the power to heal the illness of the 'carreau' (mines).

Flers : **Saint-Léonard and the children 'noués'.** They came in bygone days to the Church of Saint-Germain to invoke Saint-Léonard for the healing of disabled or retarded children.

La Madeleine-Bouvet : **'Fontaine Saint-Laumer'.** Saint-Laumer was invoked against fevers.

La Perrière : **Saint-Julien healer of illnesses of the eyes.** The water from the spring of Mauperthuis would have the power to heal all illnesses of the new born. It also cared for maladies of the eyes and burns. Saint-Julien was equally considered as the Patron of the 'bonesetters' and the sorcerers.

Saint-Cyr-la-Rosière : **'Notre-Dame-de-la-Clémence'.** There existed in earlier times an oak, in the trunk of which, was fixed a statue of Notre-Dame-de-la-Clémence. This virgin, venerated by all the population, was afterwards placed in a chapel (15th century) on the site of the oak. She was the origin of miraculous cures. A stained glass window evokes the ancient pilgrimage and the founder of the oratory, Madame de la Cornillère.

Saint-Evroult-Notre-Dame-du-Bois : **Saint-Evroult, protector of agriculture.** Saint-Evroult was a very popular saint in Normandy. He is called upon as the protector of the agriculture and more especially to safeguard the crops and the animals. The blessing of cowsheds, on the 29th December, feast day, is still practised even outside Normandy. He is also invoked, as Saint-Mathurin, for the healing of mental illnesses and people came from afar to the abbey to solicit his intercession. One also sought there the healing of skin ailments, notably the 'fleurs de Saint-Yvrou or 'fleurs de cimetière' and certain childhood illnesses.

Saint-Michel-des-Andaines : **Saint-Ortaire and the healing of lengthy illnesses.** At the oratory of Saint-Ortaire, close to the town of *Bagnoles-de-l'Orne*, one calls on Saint-Ortaire, Norman monk born around 480 who welcomed in his humble monastery in the Andaine Forest, numerous sick people. It is confirmed that he cured a great quantity.

AREA OF SEINE MARITIME

Gruchet-le-Valasse : In the valley of the Grès it is claimed that the iron containing waters made miraculous cures on children who had difficulty in walking. They went around the Calvary and left as an offering an old pair of shoes that had been worn by the child.

Jumièges : In the depths of the forest of Jumièges is hidden the 'chapelle de la Mère de Dieu', which one also calls in this region : 'Notre-Dame du gGos Ventre'. The future mothers coming, and still come, it seems, to pray there, to have beautiful babies.

Mauquenchy : One comes to the church and then to the spring of Sainte-Anne where the water is said to heal 'illnesses of the eyes'.

Quièvrecourt : In the parish church one finds the Chapel of Saint-Apolline called on for the healing of toothache. She was venerated in many places in the 'Pays de Bray' by statues and oratories.

'Sainte-Honorine et les Malentendants'. 'Honorine was martyred in 303 at Mélamre near to *Le Havre.* Her body was thrown into the Seine and came ashore at the foot of the cliff of *Graville.* There, the little religious community of men had built a chapel to Saint-Etienne. Having collected the remains of Honorine, they decided to dedicate the site to the latter. In the 9th century, in view of the Viking invasions, the community, taking with them the remains of the saint, went to take refuge near to Paris at Conflans which has since had the name of Conflans-Sainte-Honorine. The monks returned a few years later with a part of the saint's remains. Her stone sarcophagus is displayed in the church of the Priory of Graville (Museum), but it is empty ! Carbon 14 dating has confirmed the presence from the 4th century as well as the cut of a round window 'oculus' (bull's eye) towards the year 1000. Sainte-Honorine is the patron saint of boatmen and sailors, she also cures illnesses of hearing. Tradition affirms that one must pass the head through the oculus to be cured of deafness and even if one can hear, one says that 'one can hear better afterwards… !'

Quillebœuf : **Saint-Onuphre and the illnesses of the stomach.** Numerous Normans came to pray in the church of Saint-Onuphre against the illnesses of the stomach. In the 19th century, they plastered over his intestines, visible to all eyes, to avoid shocking the children.

Saint-Clair-sur-Epte : In this high place of Norman history but also in various other places in the province (*La Haye-Routot* in Eure, *Bonneville-sur-Ajon* in Calvados or Les Pieux in la Manche) one prays to and venerates Saint-Clair. Of aristocratic origin, the latter was born in the middle of the 9th century and chose, when very young, to give his life to God. He was based at first on the coast in a place that would become *Cherbourg.* He preached the good word in the countryside and obtained, it is said, miraculous cures. After having carried out good works throughout Normandy, he finally settled on the banks of the Epte, in eastern Normandy. It was there that he was assassinated, the head sliced open, in 884 by brigands sent by a woman whose advances he had repulsed. The legend of Saint-Clair tells that he collected his head, like Saint-Denis, and carried it in his hands to his hermitage and after having carefully washed it in the nearby spring, he placed it on the floor.

2 - The great Norman pilgrimage sites

Since the Middle Ages, Normandy has received numerous pilgrims going especially to the greatest pilgrimage place in Normandy, that of *Mont-Saint-Michel,* but there also exist in Normandy numerous 'roads of Compostela' taken to arrive in Saint-Jacques by the French 'pelerins' but also the Germans and the English, 'the pilgrims". The latter, to go to Saint-James generally disembarked in *Barfleur.*

There remain in Normandy, numerous names of places that recall the history of the pilgrimages. One thus finds many 'chemins montois', 'chapelles aux Jacquets'.

The Norman Benedictine monks had put into place a complete organisation throughout their abbeys and priories to receive and if necessary to come to the aid of the walkers. The sculpted scallop shells or a cross indicated the right direction.

The Association of the Roads of Mont-Saint-Michel proposes to rediscover the ancient roads taken by the 'miquelots' following the example of that which has already been done for the roads of Saint-James.

AREA OF MANCHE

Mont-Saint-Michel : **Spring Festival of Saint-Michael.** In May in the presence of the 'Confrèries de Charité' (who march at the head of the procession ringing their little copper bells) the orders of knighthood, the representatives of the government of Canada and the 'Duchesses' of Brittany and Normandy. A great mass is celebrated on this occasion in the Abbey church. For information : Tel (33) 2 33 60 14 30.

Annual pilgrimage to Mont-Saint-Michel. This has taken place at the end of July since 1946. For information : Tel (33) 2 33 89 64 00 or (33) 2 33 48 80 37. Departing from Genêts around 8.30 am - Pilgrimage of the parish and the diocese. One goes to the sanctuary on foot across the shore.

Autumn pilgrimage of Saint Michael, beginning of October.

La Pernelle : end of August, **Pilgrimage.**

Rauville-la-Place : Beginning of July, **Saint-Clair pilgrimage.**

Ravenoville : The black Virgin set on the banks of Ravenoville was in earlier times the object of great fervour and of important pilgrimages.

Régneville-sur-Mer : 17th September : **Pilgrimage to Notre-Dame-de-Pitié.**

Saint-Marcouf-de-l'Isle : Beginning of September in the Eglise des Gougins : **Pilgrimage to Notre-Dame-de-Bonsecours.**

Le Theil : end of July, **Pilgrimage to Saint-Clair.**

Villedieu-les-Poêles : **'Le Grand Sacre'.** Religious procession of the 'Fête-Dieu' which is surrounded by a special splendour because of the presence of a delegation from the Order of the Knights of Malta and dignitaries from the church. The next one will take place in 2004.

AREA OF CALVADOS

Bernières-d'Ailly : **Pilgrimage to Sainte-Anne** Patron saint of weavers, Sainte-Anne was particularly venerated in Normandy. Each year, on the last Sunday of July an important pilgrimage takes place to the Chapelle Sainte-Anne d'Entremont at ***Bernières-d'Ailly*** near to ***Falaise***.

Douvres-la-Délivrande : **Pilgrimage to the black Virgin.** This pilgrimage is said to be the **oldest in Normandy.** Since the Middle Ages thousands of pilgrims came there to pray and to invoke Notre-Dame-de-la-Délivrande. The ancient sanctuary has been replaced by a Neo-gothic Basilica. Each year, the black Virgin is crowned and dressed in a new fine and richly embroidered mantle. The Fête of the crowning takes place on the 1st Thursday following the 15th August. After the open air 'Messe pontificale' co-celebrated by numerous priests, a great procession takes place in the roads of the little town. In the evening, a vigil takes place in the Basilica and then a torchlight procession. Douvres, a town more than 2,000 years old, was already an important place of cults in the Gallo-Roman era. One paid homage there to the 'Déesse Mère' (statue found again at Saint-Aubin in 1942 and exhibited in Caen in the Museum of Normandy). After this pagan cult there came at the beginning of the 'christianisation' of the region a cult 'marial'. The primitive chapel was destroyed in 830 during the first Viking raids. Around 1150, the Chapel was rebuilt on the same site where, according to legend, they had rediscovered, thanks to a sheep, the first statue of the virgin which decorated the primitive sanctuary. Over the centuries, La Délivrande has developed. Numerous pilgrims coming to pray to Notre-Dame, humble or famous like the pious King Louis XI who came there in 1470 and in 1473.

Honfleur : **Pilgrimage to the Chapel of 'Notre-Dame-de-Grâce'.** Built in the 17th century, the chapel of Notre-Dame-de-Grâce was an important place of pilgrimage for the sailors asking for protection from the Virgin. The paintings, numerous ship models and ex-voto, testify to this religious place. A great annual pilgrimage has always taken place on the Sunday and Monday of Pentecost.

Lisieux : Last weekend of September : **'Les Fêtes Thérésiennes'.** 'Sister-Thérèse de Lisieux', born Thérèse Martin in Alençon in 1873, lived at the Carmel of Lisieux where she succumbed to tuberculosis, in 1897 at the age of 24. Beatified in 1923, that which inspired the great reform of Vatican II is today part of it, on the decision of Jean-Paul II in 1997, of a very limited circle of 'Doctors of the Church'. Patron Saint of Missions, she is venerated by millions of Catholics throughout the entire world. The chapel of the Carmel of Lisieux, where her ashes rest, is the object of numerous pilgrimages throughout the year. In September, with the 'Fêtes Thérésiennes', which commemorate her death, her remains are carried in procession from the Carmel to the Basilica and then the next day, at the end of the Pontifical Mass, they are taken back to the Carmel. This 'fête' is the occasion for conferences and debates relating to the life and work of Thérèse. **Visit the Museum of Thérèse Martin in Lisieux.**

Pont-d'Ouilly : The Sunday following the 15th of August, at the Chapel of Saint Roch : **'Pardon de Saint-Roch'.** In the morning an important cortege of pilgrims in Norman costumes forms, little copper bells at the front, followed by the clergy it moves towards the Chapel of Saint-Roch. After the open air mass a great picnic is organised. The procession reforms again in the afternoon to visit the surrounding countryside. The harvest is blessed by the Bishop. They make offerings of produce from the land. Saint-Roch was invoked against the plague but also against epidemics and for the protection of the crops. Building open every day.

Saint-Sébastien-de-Préaux : At Pentecost : **Pilgrimage to Saint-Sébastien.** In the presence of the 'confreries de charité Normandes', each year, for centuries, on the Monday of Pentecost, there takes place a traditional pilgrimage to the church of Saint-Sébastien-de-Préaux.

AREA OF ORNE

Batilly : **The Worship of Saint Roch.** The first pilgrimages to the Chapel of Saint-Roch, which is set in the rock on this steep site, took place in the Middle Ages because of the great plagues.

Céaucé : **Pilgrimage to Saint-Ernier.** Saint-Ernier was built in the 5th century on the place that would become Céaucé, a humble sanctuary dedicated to Saint-Martin and also founded a coenobite community. Every year, the parishioners of Céaucé celebrate Saint-Ernier with a procession of his relics. This procession is famous throughout the region for its itinerary in a long continuous loop. In earlier times, there were two processions : the 'little tour' and the 'great tour'', the first on the Monday of Pentecost and the second the next day. They have henceforth settled for the little tour. Saint-Ernier, for whom the fête is celebrated on 9th August, is invoked against bad weather, also against floods as well as drought.

Joué-du-Bois : **Pilgrimage to 'Notre-Dame-de-la-Raitière'.** Since the Middle Ages the Virgin Mary has been venerated in a little oratory set at the place called 'La Raitière'. A chapel was built in 1585 to shelter the statue of the virgin miraculously saved from a desecration of the place by the Huguenots. Enlarged at the end of the 19th century, the sanctuary is still honoured. The processions take place within its surroundings to the sound of the five bells of the chapel. Each year, on Ascension Day and on 15th August, at 11.00 am, pilgrimages take place which gathered together in earlier times all the 'confréries de charité' for the whole region. Throughout the year numerous pilgrims come to beseech the Virgin whose statue still adorns the alter of the chapel.

Longny-au-Perche : **Pilgrimage to 'Notre-Dame-de-la-Pitié'.** The first Sunday of September in the little chapel.

Monnai : At Pentecost and on 15th August, in bygone days, there took place an important **pilgrimage to 'Notre-Dame-du-Vallet'** whose chapel is found on the left when going from Monnai 'Le Sap' in the valley. Follow the dirt road beside the river. Virgin from the 16th century.

Montligeon : At the Basilica Notre-Dame, **Pilgrimages** on 1st May, 25th May, 1st June, 15th August and 12th November.

Passais-la-Conception : **Pilgrimage to 'Notre-Dame-de-la-Conception'.** A very ancient 'marial' pilgrimage has taken place each year in Passais-la-Conception. It owes its fame to Louis XI and was restored in 1851. It takes place on 25th May and 15th August.

Rânes : **Pilgrimage to Notre-Dame-du-Chêne.** In the heart of the wood of Rânes is found a place of pilgrimage that was very popular up to the beginning of the 20th century.

Saint-Céneri-le-Gérei : In this little community of the Alpes Mancelles, not far from *Alençon,* one finds, in a meander of the Sarthe, a little isolated chapel dating from the 16th century which holds a statue of the saint hermit. The young girls of the countryside came there in pilgrimage to push in needles in order to quickly find a husband.

Saint-Christophe-le-Jajolet : The first Sunday of July and the first Sunday of October : **Blessing of the cars.** A few hundred metres from the magnificent château of the 'Duc d'Audiffret-Pasquier', there takes place each year a particular type of pilgrimage to Saint-Christophe. In a place specially set out for this ceremony, the priest of the parish, after having celebrated mass, blesses one by one the numerous vehicles assembled, not forgetting the drivers who he exhorts to ' drive as good Christians".

Ticheville : **Pilgrimages to the Saint-Sauveur and to Saint-Vulfranc.** Saint-Vulfranc had his oratory near to the spring that one can still see today and which still receives a great number of pilgrims.

Les Tourailles : **Pilgrimage to 'Notre-Dame-de-la-Recouvrance'.** An important and ancient 'marial' pilgrimage takes place each year on the 31st May. Its origins merge with the beginnings of Christianity in Gaul. It is said that Saint-Adelin, Bishop of Sées, had restored the primitive sanctuary around 911. Among the illustrious pilgrims who came to the Tourailles we can note The 'Good King' Henry IV in 1590.

AREA OF EURE

Acquigny : **The field of Martyrs.** Saint-Mauxe and Saint-Vénérand were executed by the Romans at Acquigny in a place they still call today the 'Champs des Martyrs'. This point became a place of pilgrimage on the Monday of the Trinity and in 1724 a miracle occurred there. A young paralysed woman dragged herself to the megalith which was to be found there and found that she could again use her limbs. This belief is perpetuated up to today and the sick take part with the clergy in the processions. They cross and re-cross under the reliquaries and each collects seven stone dishes which they take to their homes to bring them good fortune...

Bernay : The Monday of Pentecost : **Annual pilgrimage to 'Notre-Dame-de-la-Couture',** presided over by the Bishop of Evreux, in the presence of the 'confreries de charité' of the region.

Pilgrimage to 'Notre-Dame-du-Vœu', where the pilgrims came to ask for the realisation of their wishes and desires.

Saint-Clair-sur-Epte : **Pilgrimage to Saint-Clair.** In this high place of Norman history but also in various other places in the province, one prays to and venerates Saint-Clair. Of aristocratic origin, the latter was born in the middle of the 9th century and chose, when very young, to give his life to God. He was based at first on the coast in a place that would become *Cherbourg.* He preached the good word in the countryside and obtained, it is said, miraculous cures. After having carried out good works throughout Normandy, he finally settled on the banks of the Epte, in eastern Normandy. It was there that he was assassinated, his head cut off, in 884 by brigands sent by a woman whose advances he had repulsed. The legend of Saint-Clair tells that he collected his head, like Saint-Denis, and carried it in his hands to his hermitage and after having carefully washed it in the nearby spring, he placed it on the floor. At the dawn of the 21st century, his fête is always celebrated by a night mass at the end of which they carry his relics to the place of his torture. They then light a great bonfire. Saint-Clair is called upon for the illnesses of the eyes and blindness.

AREA OF SEINE MARITIME

Allouville-Bellefosse : In this charming community close to *Yvetot,* one finds, in the cemetery, a thousand year old oak. 18 metres high and measuring 15 metres in circumference, they have put in its trunk two chapels one on top of the other, to which one can gain access by a spiral staircase. The first chapel was built in 1696 by the priest of the parish and was for a long time the object of a 'marial' pilgrimage, on the 2nd of July. The second oratory is called the 'Room of the hermit'

Cany-Barville : In bygone days, on the 1st September, there was a pilgrimage to Saint-Gilles and to Saint-Leu to the Chapel of Caniel - Road to *Veulette* - on the hill to safeguard themselves from fear.

Freneuse : In the region of *Elbeuf* : **Pilgrimage to Saint-Expédit,** 'patron saint of urgent and desperate matters'.

Grainville-la-Teinturière : **'La Procession Blanche'** - The third Sunday of July - To escape from the plague, at the beginning of the 17th century, the inhabitants of the parish made a vow. They would not give in to the plague and would come out of their houses in procession waving white sheets. From this is born the name of the 'procession blanche'.

3 - Legends and extraordinary stories of Normandy

THE MYTH OF THE FOREST OF SCISSY

The inhabitants of the south Cotentin affirm in earlier times that the Mont-Saint-Michel was at first surrounded by dense forest and that this was, around 710, enveloped by a huge tidal wave.

This legend had as its origin a bad reading of a manuscript in which it is said that on their return to Mont-Gargan the envoys of the Bishop Aubert, who were collecting precious relics, were not able to recognise the place because of the deforestation that had taken place. Over the years one no longer speaks of clearance but of tidal waves.

THE SECRETS OF THE ROCK OF TOMBELAINE

From high on the ramparts of Mont-Saint-Michel, one can see the rock of Tombelaine, an island transformed today into an ornithological reserve. It's name came from the funeral of a young woman, named 'Hélène', niece of the King of Brittany, which was on the rock, the 'Tomb of Helen' or even that of 'Tumbellana' which made this little tomb important.

In 1048, two monks isolated themselves there, building humble cells and a chapel dedicated to the Virgin. A priory was built there and the place was populated to become a village.

During the Hundred Years War, the English took over the place and built a fortress there.

'Le Pic de la Folie", 47 metres tall, is the highest point of the island.

One recalls the reminder of the 'Marquis de Tombelaine", in his real name of 'Jean Le Déluge', a modest foot fisherman, a highly coloured personality who served at times as a guide to visitors of the Bay. He lived at Tombelaine at the beginning of the century and has become a person of legend.

HOW GERBOLD WAS SAVED !

Towards the beginning of the 7th century, a monk called Gerbold lived close to the King of England. He was so handsome and intelligent that a rich princess who lived at the court was smitten with him and harassed him until he repulsed her resolutely. Furious, the noble lady demanded an audience with the king declaring that he had wanted to seduce her. The latter had him thrown into the sea after having tied him to a block of granite. God came to the help of his faithful servant and by a miracle the block of granite became a block of cork and carried the poor monk to the coasts of Neustria. When he had set foot, in the depths of winter, on the soil of a land unknown to him, the sand was covered with flowers and he gave the place the name of 'Ver' [1] which means 'Spring". Gerbold was later named as Bishop of **Bayeux.**

---

(1) today : **Ver-sur-Mer.**

305

THE LOVERS OF THE TOWER

The communities of **Ver-sur-Mer** and of **Graye-sur-Mer**, in Calvados are only separated by a small stream which carries the unctuous name of 'La Provence'. Near to the sea and close to the watercourse, the Romans had constructed a tower to protect the coast from pirates. This tower was called : 'Tour de Fol'. A Roman centurion, whose task was to survey the coast from this building, had a very beautiful daughter who according to spoken tradition had the traits : ivory forehead with a halo of long backcombed hair, blue eyes as deep as the clear sky...'

She was called Livie and her mother had died. If it was for her physique that she was appreciated, it was equally for the quality of her morals. Inside the tower, the Romans had imprisoned Gallic prisoners among whom was a chief of great renown. He was called Verbrenn. He was madly in love with Livie and she was not insensitive to the charm of this dark, handsome Celtic warrior. Profiting from a day of Gallic uprising against the occupying Romans, Verbrenn fled, having become chief of the revolutionaries he returned to take the tower by assault.

After the relentless battle, the Gauls took the place and Verbrenn rushed into the tower seeking his 'beautiful one'. He found her kneeling before the the body of her father killed during the fighting. She wanted to avenge him and ran on to the beach where the Gauls massacred her. Then, in his turn, Verbrenn killed himself, taking his last breaths over the body of she that he loved.

THE BURNING OF THE TOWER

Two centuries later, the tower sheltered a young couple who had come to be married. The husband was a young lord who had fallen madly in love with a 'moult gente damoiselle' who fully reciprocated his love.

They lived very happily together when one day, on the beach, the drakes landed a horde of Vikings.

The chief of the 'northmen' was a handsome and powerful young man named Wilkind. He fell in love with the young woman and wanted to make her his 'in Danish fashion'.

After having burnt the tower, Wilkind, his axe in his hand ran towards the bedroom of the couple. In spite of fierce resistance which the young lord put up to protect his dearest love, the Scandinavian pirate killed him and then turned his attention to the young women. He was going to take her when her husband, having the necessary energy in his last moments, planted his dagger in the back of Wilkind falling on him to force the blade totally into his body.

The Norman chief collapsed although the young woman tried desperately to save the life of her beloved then realising that he was dead stretched out beside him offering themselves to the flames which crackled around them. The next morning, there remained only the ruins and the ashes.

It is said at times, when the fine weather approaches, in the middle of the night, a tower of fire seems to appear in the middle of the night mist. In turn, one can perceive the shadow of the young lovers whose love was strong even to death.

NO SAINTE-ADRESSE FIGURES ON THE LIST OF SAINTS

It is said that the name of this village, on the heights of *Le Havre*, came from a Captain whose ship, pushed by the storm, was going to be wrecked on the cliff of Saint-Denis-Chef-de-Caux. Thus the members of his crew, as a last resort, invoked Saint-Denis, the Captain told them that they would be better off calling on their 'saint-adresse'.

Historians have another version. The name of 'Saint-Adresse' came from the old French 'adrece' which can be translated as 'the right road, the good route' which was indicated to ships by a continuous fire on the cliff.

THE CONVERSION OF THE VIKING 'VIEUL AUX ESPAULLES'

Around the year 900, off the coasts of the Cotentin, the esnecca of a Viking chief called 'Vieul aux Espaulles, had been caught up in a storm. The story of Rou recounts how Vieul 'being in peril on the sea vowed to become a Christian if he escaped from the storm". When he landed on the shore, our Viking remained true to his promise : he had built a chapel in honour of Sainte-Magdeleine (Road to Utah beach at *Sainte-Marie-du-Mont*) and was baptised there without delay. Of the primitive chapel nothing remains except the baptismal font which is, the legend says, that in which Vieul aux Espaulles had received his baptism. The current sanctuary was rebuilt in the 16th century as 'ex-voto' by English sailors who escaped, also miraculously, from a shipwreck.

THE PEOPLE OF YPORT SURNAMED 'THE GREEKS'

The inhabitants of *Yport*, in Seine-Maritime, are at times called 'the Greeks'. This title came from a legend according to which a Greek ship was beached there in ancient times. The crew established themselves in this place and created the town.

THE TURNED STATUE

The door of the church of Notre-Dame, in the heart of the ancient lace-making city of *Alençon* is a major work which is admired by all the visitors but note there a statue of Saint-Joan… turned. It is said that she would be thus turned after the pillaging of the sanctuary by the protestants during the wars of religion.

THE 'DAME A LA LICORNE' HAUNTS THE CHATEAU D'O

A legend has it that one of the rooms in the Château d'O at *Mortrée* in Orne is haunted by a young elegant woman : 'La dame à la Licorne' who returned from time to time, in velvet tunic holding in one hand a wolf and in the other a fan, to find François d'O, first owner of the castle and called 'the debauched'.

HELPS THE YOUNG WOMEN TO FIND A HUSBAND

At Saint-Céneri-le-Gérei, near to Alençon, in a meander of the Sarthe one finds a little isolated chapel from the 16th century which holds a humble statue of the saint-hermit.

The young girls of the countryside came to stick in pins to find a husband within the year.

A GARGANTUAN CHAIR IN THE SURROUNDINGS OF ANDELYS

Close to *Les Andelys,* overlooking the Seine, one finds a huge rock called 'Tête à l'homme". It is said that it served as a chair for Gargantua.

THE BENEFITS OF THE WATER OF BAGNOLES-DE-L'ORNE

Messire Essirard, Lord of Bonvouloir, near to *Bagnoles-de-l'Orne* got older without descendents. In spite of the charms of his young wife, he had no sexual appetite. Thus he was advised to dive into the fountain of bubbling water which gushed out in the heart of the forest and suddenly vigour returned to him. He had numerous children and had built on his property of *Juvigny-sous-Andaine,* a tower in the form of a phallus which one can still see today : **'The Lighthouse of Bonvouloir'.**

ONE MUST AT TIMES NOT TRUST INNKEEPERS !

On 7th October 1621, Antoine de Montchrétien, the impetuous chief of the protestants in the area, was dining peacefully with some friends at an inn in *Les Tourailles* near to *Flers.* He was in the process of gathering together an army of Huguenots to fight the Catholics. Suddenly, armed men entered the dining room. They were commanded by Charles Turgot, Baron of Les Tourailles who ordered Montchrétien to surrender. The latter refused and engaged in combat with the faithful followers of the Baron who killed him after having sustained important losses. The Baron of Tourailles had been informed of the presence of the chief Huguenot by the innkeeper!

THE BIRTH OF THE FIRST PERCHERON HORSE

It was in the little community of *Corbon,* in Perche, that the first percheron horse was born, if one believes the legend which affirms that it was the off-spring of 'Balius' and 'Hélidor' (the latter being the grandson of Enée) from their encounter with a golden horse, without rider or harness. A saying claims that 'At Corbon in the corbonnaise region, at the place of the three walnut trees, there was a massive golden horse…'.

THE KNIGHT OF SERANS

It is affirmed in the countryside that a knight, Lord of **Serans,** was buried standing up, dressed in golden armour, near to the old chapel at the start of a little shaded road.

THE HANGED PERSON OF DOMFRONT

Spoken tradition says that a certain Jean Barbotte, miller by trade and living on the banks of the Varenne, near to the church of Notre-Dame-sur-l'Eau, left his mill to give himself over, in company with the Huguenots, to acts of banditry in the region. He was blamed for having participated in acts of pillage and in the burning of the Abbey of Lonlay. In 1508, under the protection of Gabriel de Montgommery, 'the regicide', he was living in total impunity up to the day when armed catholics arrived in the area to re-establish civil peace. He fled but not without taking the fruits of his larceny in his belt.

He went to the neighbouring city of **Domfront** hoping to disappear in the crowd and then to hide himself under the shelter of the ramparts but he was very thirsty and forgetting the risk that he ran he went to assuage his vice at the inn of the 'Lion d'Or". Learning that the town was in the hands of the Catholics, he fled into the nearby forest of Andaines.

The new governor of Domfront, informed of the activities of Barbotte, had him tried and condemned to death, sending his men off in his footsteps.

When he had lived like a hermit for more than six months in the heart of the forest, Barbotte felt that the Catholics had forgotten him and that he could go without fear to the December Fair in Domfront and go to eat and drink one or two 'bolées' of cider at the 'Lion d'Or'. Unfortunately for him, when he entered the inn he came face to face with the governor who had him arrested immediately.

Put into detention, his sentence was immediately made known to him and the same day he was led to the gallows so that he could be 'hung on high and run until death followed him'.

At the moment when the executioner passed the rope around his neck, he pronounced these famous words : **'Ah ! Domfront. Town of misfortune ! Arrived at midday and hung at one-o'clock... Not even time to eat !'.**

Local historians affirm that this story is only legend but the inhabitants of Domfront do believe in it and there, some years ago, they thought that Madame Barbotte, who lived in the city, was the relative of the famous hanged man.

THE DAMNED CASTLE OF BARDOUVILLE

A humble monk from the Abbey of Saint-Georges at **Saint-Martin-de-Boscherville**, who found himself on the opposite bank of the Seine, fell one day frantically in love with the Lady of the Manor of **Bardouville**. Almost every evening he crossed the river to visit his hearts chosen one, up to the day when the Lord of the manor, discovering his misfortune decided to kill his wife's lover. His deed accomplished, he dipped the 'chemise' of his wife in the blood of the unfortunate monk and forced his unfaithful wife to get dressed in her corset from where the name of 'chateau du corset rouge' came into being.

THE ASSASSINATION OF THE LORD OF LIGNOIR

A cowardly assassination occurred in Couterne under the reign of Henry IV. The Lord of Lignoir was the victim of his steward who had decided to kill him in order to take over his wealth. Before dying, he gave his soul to the protecting virgin of the manor that he owned near to **Briouze**. The virgin then appeared to him, promised her assistance and changed into a statue. To respect his vows his servants took the statue to **Briouze** but she returned by magic to the places of the demise of the unfortunate Lignoir. The phenomenon occurred several times so well that they built a chapel on the place and put the statue there. The chapel was defiled under the Revolution and the 'infant virgin was broken'.

THE DEVIL'S HOLE

Behind the Chapel of Saint-Nicolas, in **Argentan,** there existed in earlier times a hole, a hole so deep that nobody managed to block it and people who fell into it were never found. It was called the 'Devil's Hole'.

THE FOX'S OAK

An important treasure was said to be buried in a place called 'the Fox's oak' in the middle of the Forest of Gouffern, near to **Argentan,** not far from the ruins of the Abbey of **Silly**. A fox was charged with watching over the treasure. Many hunters tried to kill the fox to take over there but none of them managed to kill it. In 1830, they discovered at this place 800 Roman medals in silver dating from the Emperor Nero to Septimus the Severe.

THE STONE OF THE FAIRIES

On one of the faces of the imposing menhir which is found at **Silly-en-Gouffern** on the road of **Alménêches** on the edge of the forest one can see round cavities. The inhabitants of the region said that they were the marks left by the giants who had transported this stone to this place. It is also said that a treasure is buried under the stone but that the fairies forbid anyone who approaches there. One can only try to appropriate it during the night of the nativity around midnight while the priest recites the genealogy of Christ, the stone moving and then turning on itself.

THE TRAP OF THE FAIRY OF THE SAINT QUENTIN ROAD

A very long time ago, in a dark and narrow road in **Bayeux** lived a very beautiful fairy called 'Dame d'Aprigny'. When a traveller got lost one evening in the roads of the old town he met her, she invited him to dance with her and made him disappear in a thick bush of brambles and thorns.

THE GOLDEN CALF OF SAINT VIGOR

At **Saint-Vigor-le-Grand**, neighbouring community of **Bayeux**, was buried, following the destruction of a pagan temple, a golden calf. This spoken tradition confirms the presence of a cult to Bélénus in this place.

THE FOREST THAT WAS SWALLOWED UP

There existed on the site of the Cove of Saint-Martin, at **Beaumont-Hague,** an ancient forest engulfed by the floods. The fishermen claimed that they could hang up their nets in the branches of the trees.

IN THE ERA OF THE SMUGGLERS

The caves called 'from lion to sorcerer' and 'the Great church' are found in the cliffs of *Nez-de-Jobourg*. One of the two is, it seems, very deep and extends up to the church of Jobourg. Up to the end of the last century these caves served as hideouts for smugglers who traded with the Channel Islands.

SACRIFICIAL STONES AT BELLÊME AND AT LE SAP

In the thick forest of *Bellême* (which takes its name from that of the famous Gallic goddess) one can find traces of an important Druid culture and a sacrifice stone on the highest point of the region.

Human sacrifice was practised there, as at *Le Sap* (in a field to the left of the road to *Monnai*) whose name was taken from the **'Sapin'** (pine tree) a tree which was rare and venerated in the Norman forest.

THE TRADITION OF WELCOME IN THE VILLAGE OF CHANDAI

In the centre of the village of *Chandai,* in the direction of Paris when leaving *L'Aigle,* there existed an ancient stagecoach inn earlier named the 'Auberge du Bœuf Couronné'. It is said that this country hostelry received travellers of note such as Louis XVI during his journey in Normandy in 1786 but also Saint-Louis-Philippe Le Bel, Henri III, le bon Sully, Napoléon 1st. One is assured that even Julius Caesar would have stopped in the village !

THE GHOST OF CRULAI

Those of you who take the roads that lead to *Crulai,* near to *L'Aigle,* beware ! A ghost haunts the countryside terrifying the night for travellers. This spectre responds to the nice name of 'Nicole'. The beautiful 'Nicole', before going to burn in hell, was condemned to haunt the wood of 'the stone' for having committed many sins in her lifetime.

THE PURSUED WOMEN OF BENOUVILLE

Between *Etretat* and *Bénouville* there exists the vestiges of an ancient Celtic camp. It is said that at times, in the night, women, chased by horses, try to flee from the ramparts but fall into the sea and drown.

THE TREASURE OF BEZU

Near to *Bezancourt,* at *Bézu-la-Forêt,* in Eure, a two metre tall megalith, turning slowly on itself - one turn in a century it is said - guardian of a subterranean entry where a treasure is to be found. One day the stone fell on a peasant who went there to force an entry.

THE STONE OF BOSGOUET

In the village of *Malmains,* at *Bosgouet,* in the forest of Londe, on a tumulus, was a 'turning stone'. Every 24th December, during the Christmas night, a cock goes there to 'sing'. In the Middle Ages, it is told that it was moved with the help of 300 horses but the next night it had returned to its original place.

THE MEETING PLACE OF THE POOL OF 'BOUILLON'

The pool of **Bouillon** was the meeting place of supernatural beings. The fairies came there for the witching hour under the trees of Bas des Perrons as well as the elves, the white ladies and the sorcerers prowling on the banks. In 1781, the Curé of Bouillon came to the pool wearing his stole. The appearances ceased but the priest got lost in the area and died some months later.

THE MUTE FROGS OF BRETEUIL

It is said that in the region of **Breteuil-sur-Iton** the frogs are mute since Saint-Meslain, who founded the hermitage of Notre-Dame-du-Desert in the forest of Breteuil, disturbed, in his prayer, by the croaking of the frogs obtained their silence by threatening them with hell.

THE UNDERGROUND CITY OF THE HILL OF 'GREAT ROCKS'

Not far from **Bricquebec** towards **Brix** one finds a hill of the 'Grosses Rochers' where one can see an enormous monolith set in the soil between two covered paths. An underground city existed at this place which enclosed immense treasures defended by a flame breathing sow.

THE LEGEND OF THE HOLE OF BALIGAN

At **Diélette,** at the foot of the high cliffs of **Flamanville,** is found the 'Hole of Baligan' which was, it is said in the area, inhabited by a horrible dragon with seven heads who caused panic among the population at the beginning of our era.

To calm his anger, the inhabitants of the neighbouring places had to regularly offer him a child. One day, the peasants saw arrive by the sea, a clergyman who said he was called Germain and come to preach the good word to the pagan population. The latter made a deal with him : 'We will believe in your god if you will rid us of the dragon'. Germain thus went to the cavern and went in. The sea then rose, the wind blew up into a storm and the villagers heard the beating of the dragons wings and saw the fire coming out of its wide open mouth. Germain made the sign of the cross and the beast drew back and calmed. Once it was peaceful, he encircled its neck with his stole and pulled so strongly that the dragon fell into an abyss filled with sea water.

The inhabitants holding to their promise all converted without exception. They gave their village the name of **Saint-Germain-la-Mer.**

THE FOUNTAIN OF AVERNES

Close to the ruins of the Castle of the Marquesses of Avernes, at **Avernes-Saint-Gourgon,** is a spring at the place called 'La Fontaine de Pougouse'. A local myth believes that its flow is regulated by a fairy who lives in the nearby forest. When the spring flows abundantly that announces abundant harvests but when it is slow, that signifies that the corn will be scarce !

THE 'OLD WOMAN' OF CLÉCY

If you climb 'la Houle', in the Suisse Normande, you will notice near to the Sugar Loaf a curious looking cave. This was the home of Sybille de Clecy. But this was not the only one. There were several in the 'bocage'. It was the old women that a great number of people regarded as venerable and inspired. They claimed to be in business with the spirits of the dead. They had at their command, fairies, spectres, goblins, elves, werewolves, grass that made them invisible, divining rods, the black hen, the horned ram… They knew all the secrets, discovering buried treasures, finding lost or stolen objects, understanding all illnesses, the husband that the young girl should marry and the rich heiress who made the young man sigh. Almost all lived in caves or solitary huts, real hovels where one saw the heads of the dead, snakes, toads, salamanders, stuffed owls, a black cat, wolf fat, old parchments, chamber pots full of urine… The most famous was called Méréa (It is not long ago that in Méré they consulted the urines). She conveyed her oracles on the cliffs of *Clécy,* at *Berjou* and in the wood of Pommeraye, in the caverns and crevices of the rocks. But this old woman did not give up her advice on an empty stomach. One had to bring her presents, such as wine, liquors, milk, cakes, meat or flour and it was when she had drunk large numbers of glasses that a sort of rage would take over and it was from her mind that the inspiration came and she unveiled great secrets…

THE MEETINGS OF THE SORCERERS AT CÉAUCÉ

At Mount Margautin, in the territory of the community of *Céaucé,* the sorcerers made meetings with the devil. They sacrificed a black bull and proceeded at times with the enthronement of new sorcerers before Satan, personified by a black goat.

THE AUTOMATONS IN THE BASILICA

Built in the 14th and 15th centuries, the **Basilica of Sainte-Trinité** in *Cherbourg* possesses a 'macabre dance' sculpted on the balustrade of the nave. One saw there up to the 18th century an even more curious monument which commemorated the liberation of the town in 1450. It was a collection of persons moved by a mechanism which mimicked, the 15th August, the Assumption of Mary.

THE SORCERER OF CIDEVILLE

It was in 1851 an extraordinary affair of witchcraft took place at *Cideville*.

A shepherd had put a curse on the presbytery of the parish where strange phenomena were produced (levitation, thrown stones…). To struggle against this curse, one of the priests, with the help of a group of friends, used iron spikes with which, in the different rooms, they struck in all directions producing sparks while the moaning could be heard. The next morning, the sorcerer presented to the 'curé' the face and hands covered with wounds which he tried to hide. Begging pardon on his knees from the curé, who did not want to let it rest there, he was seized and the Justice of the Peace sentenced him severely.

AT COLOMBIERS-SUR-SEULLES ONE PAYS TO FIND A HUSBAND

The young girls of *Colombiers-sur-Seulles* who in earlier times could not find a husband came to the **'standing stone'**, climbed on top and then jumped down with their feet tied together after having left a coin which they had placed on the top.

HERRINGS TO THE CHILDREN OF CONCHES

Before the First World War, on Maundy Thursday, they gave a de-salted herring to each of the children personifying the apostles at the ceremony of washing the feet. That in which Judas had appeared in receiving two in compensation for the bullying of which he had been the object on this occasion.

DANCE WITH THE FAIRIES AT CONDÉ-SUR-NOIREAU

On the left bank of the Durance, near *Pontécoulant*, a cavern called 'The fairies hole' was inhabited by 'white ladies'.

THE BELLS OF CORNEVILLE SOUND IN THE WATER

To avoid the English, at the beginning of the 15th century after the Battle of Azincourt, not melting down the bells of their old abbey to make canons, the inhabitants of *Corneville*, in the luxuriant valley of the Risle, threw them in the river. Henceforth, when the bell of the parish church sounds, the old bells replied from the depths of the water.

This legend gave birth to a celebrated operetta of Planquette entitled 'The Bells of Corneville'. The local hostelry today possesses a carillon of twelve bells !

AT COURGEON THE FAIRY TRIPPED UP PASSERS-BY

At 'Gué de la Demoiselle' on the Chippe, at *Courgeon* in Orne, the fairy 'Lo' rushing towards them as if appearing to flee, amused herself by making the passers-by who were crossing the gué (ford), fall into the water.

CONTEST BETWEEN GARGANTUA AND SAINT-PETER AT CRAMESNIL

At *Cramesnil,* in Orne, there exists one of the most beautiful menhirs in Normandy called 'l'affiloir de Gargantua' (the sharpening stone of Gargantua). The latter, who was none other than the devil, threw out in his place, a challenge to Saint-Peter. He, being clever, overcame the test and out of pique, Gargantua threw his stone to sharpen in the grass.

GLOOMY FISHING IN DIEPPE

At the beginning of the 19th century, the day of the dead in *Dieppe* was marked by a ban on fishing. If the fishermen overstepped this instruction, they risked encountering their double who accompanied them in all their actions. In their nets, they would only catch broken skeletons and crushed bones.

THE FORBIDDEN CATS ON THE BOATS OF DIEPPE

A very ancient *Dieppe* custom obliges a sailor to avoid speaking of cats at an embarkation or in the presence of a fisherman. Equally one must not say the names of hare, rabbit, wolf or fox on board the boats. This superstition exists equally among fishermen in the west of England and in Brittany.

IN DIEPPE, THE GULLS BRING BAD LUCK TO THE FISHERMEN

If one hears the cries of the seagulls one can stop fishing as one is sure not to catch another fish, it is said in *Dieppe.*

THE DWARF EATER OF CHILDREN

The former people of *Dieppe* affirmed that 'a red dwarf' haunted the shores of the Channel. 'Spirit of the Waters', he swallowed imprudent children who swam without their parents authority.

'BIDOCHE' THE HORSE INVITED TO MARRIAGES IN DOMFRONT

In the years before the war, one could still see in *Domfront,* prancing at the front of marriage processions, a carnival horse called 'Bidoche'.

THE ENGULFED MONASTERY OF FLERS

Close to the 'château-mairie' of *Flers,* in Orne, one finds a deep lake under which, it is said, lies a monastery that was swallowed up.

This monastery was established here a long time ago by a man to atone for his sins.

The monks led there an exemplary life up to the day, being considerably enriched, they took some liberties with the monastic rules. They did not get up early in the morning to sing their offices and more and more often the thick walls of the monastery echoed to the laughter and moans of women...

The night of the Nativity, the community that lived there, rather than celebrating mass, preferred the pleasures of the table, becoming intoxicated in the arms of corrupt creatures.

One Christmas eve, as night fell on the monastery, a single bell began to sound and to continue ever more loudly.

One of the monks got up, his glass in his hand and shouted : 'Jesus is born, drink to his health !'.

Before he and his friends could raise their glasses to their mouths the earth shook and the monastery disappeared under a flood. There, where it had stood, the inhabitants of Flers discovered the next morning a deep lake with dark waters.

Since then, each year, on Christmas night, one hears the bell of the monastery which invites the monks to mass.

THE FAIRY OF ARGOUGES AT THE CASTLE OF RANES

The powerful lord of Argouges, whose fortress was built opposite to the church of *Rânes*, in Orne, fell in love with a fairy who he married. So that their love would last, she made him swear to never pronounce the word 'dead' in her presence. Their life was totally happy until the day when Mr. d'Argouges reproached his companion for spending to much time in front of the mirror declaring : 'Madame, with all the time that you use to make yourself beautiful, one could believe that you were preparing yourself to rejoin the dead !' As soon as the word was uttered, the fairy disappeared leaving the outline of her foot on a stone, high up on the keep. On certain nights, the fairy of Argouges returns, it is said, to haunt the great park of the castle .

THE TREASURE OF THE FAIRIES OF LUNERAY

Between the charming little village of *Luneray* and the community of *La Gaillarde,* near to *Dieppe,* are found many wells of great depth. It is told that the fairies hid their treasures there and that they dance there at night and watch over them. Misfortune to all who disturb them !

THE MYSTERY OF THE TREASURE OF THE TEMPLARS AT GISORS

The castle of *Gisors* is one of the most beautiful jewels of Norman military architecture from the 12th century.

Its construction was undertaken at the end of the 11th century by the nephew of Hugues de Paynes, **founder of the Order of the Temple** and was finished by the Anglo-Norman sovereigns following the plans established by the redoubtable Robert of Bellême.

Philippe-Auguste, after the annexing of Normandy to France in 1204, enlarged the castle.

At the heart of the building, reputedly impregnable, was a powerful Keep. From this exceptional place emanated a special, disturbing atmosphere, which came to reinforce the fantastic story of **Roger Lhomois**.

This brave Norman was, some forty years ago, one of the guardians of the castle. Fascinated by this monument over which hovered a mystery he undertook, confidentially personal searches being persuaded that the famous Treasure of the Templars was buried at Gisors. Over several years he dug underground tunnels in the soil of the false mound of the Keep, at night, after his work, until daybreak where he discovered at a depth of more than twenty metres a chapel with a surface area of around 200 metres enclosing chests, statues and sarcophagi.

Lhomois was convinced that he had discovered the famous treasure.

In spite of the precise description that he made of these places, the details that he gave, (and that he could not have invented), to the town councillors no credit was given to his account and he was passed off as crank and they hastened, on the order of the Minister of Culture of the time to fill in the galleries dug by Lhomois. This affair made a great noise and many hypotheses were built on it but today the enigma of Gisors remains intact. It is also affirmed, after the precise facts, that the overall system made the fortress of Gisors a 'cosmic clock' !...

THE TREASURE OF THE WOOD OF LIVAROT

Between *Livarot* and *Fervaques,* in the heart of the forest, one finds the 'turning stone", a raised stone of around two metres in height at the foot of which was hidden a treasure jealously guarded by a demon. One could have access to this treasure once a year during Christmas night when the priest pronounced the words of the Creed : 'Et homo factus est', the stone then turning on itself. At the end of the 18th century, the Bishop of Lisieux banned the superstitious practices which took place around the stone. It was affirmed that the young people who came to make a leap were certain to marry within the year...

THE TURNING STONE AT MONTMERREI

At *Montmerrei* (= the Mount of the dead) in Orne, one can discover an important Celtic necropolis, there is found there the biggest dolmen in the whole region called **'La Pierre Tournoir'.** A legend says that it turns on itself on the eve of the Feast of Saint-John.

THE GEESE OF PIROU

When at the end of the 9th century the Vikings landed at *Créances*, the 'almost island' of the Cotentin, they besieged the **castle** of *Pirou* sited at the edge of the sea, where the lord, Godefroy le Rouge, was giving a feast.

To escape death, it is said that the occupants of the castle metamorphosed into wild geese and kingfishers and flew off into the countryside.

Another version suggests that the fairies built the castle of Pirou and that they lived there peacefully until the Vikings landed on their shores. Taking fright, they were changed into wild geese and flew away at the sight of the first Viking.

It is told that each year, at the beginning of March, the geese would return to the castle to take refuge in the nests that they had built but the new proprietors of the castle had destroyed the nests and hunted the geese.

THE MISFORTUNES OF LORD GIROIE AT SAINT-CENERI

The lord of **Saint-Céneri-le-Gérel**, Giroie or Giroye, had been invited by his worst enemy, Guillaume II Talvas, Lord of Alençon, to his marriage. Put on guard by his entourage, he believed naively in the sincerity of his powerful neighbour and decided to go to the nuptial ceremony simply accompanied by twelve knights. Hardly arrived at the castle of Alençon, Talvas had him arrested and imprisoned in one of the towers, called afterwards : 'the tower of chevalier Giroie' (it was destroyed in 1782). After the marriage Talvas departed for the hunt. He left his men instructions concerning Giroie.

While the Lord of Alençon and his guests rode in the nearby forest, his butchers cut off the nose and ears of the unfortunate Lord of Saint-Céneri. They then punctured his eyes and emasculated him.

Thus 'diminished', he was handed back to his family and was cared for by his brother, a great doctor of the period (he must have been one of the best to avoid him passing away !) who dressed his wounds and made 'another man".

To thank God for 'having recovered his health' Giroie departed on a pilgrimage to the Holy Land and on his return, he became a monk at **Bec-Hellouin.**

THE KISSES OF THE WEREWOLVES AT THE PONT-AUDEMER

During the period of Advent it was forbidden for the young girls of **Pont-Audemer** and its surroundings to walk alone in the nearby forests. They were it is said, peopled by werewolves who kissed them on the mouth thus freezing the body.

THE TREASURE OF THE ENGLISH AT TOUTAINVILLE
AND AT TRACY-BOCAGE

Following the sayings of the ancients, at **Toutainville,** in Eure, at some thirty kilometres from **Bernay**, in the ancient quarries are treasures which were hidden there by the English when they were obliged to leave Normandy after the Hundred Years War.

Another treasure was abandoned by your ancestors in an underground tunnel which links the castles of **Tracy** and **Vaudry** in Calvados.

✳✳

Arthurian legend in Normandy

*In the 13th century, at the court of Aliénor of Aquitaine, Duchess of Normandy and Queen of England, who liked to stay in her castle and dwelling at Domfront and Argentan, it was considered that it was necessary to put down in writing the exploits of the Knights of the Round Table. The region of Andaines (**La Ferté-Macé, Bagnoles-de-l'Orne, Domfront**) thus inspired the chroniclers who placed there the settings of the exploits of Merlin, King Arthur and Sir Lancelot of the Lake. It was the Norman, Robert Wace who wrote in the 12th century the 'Roman de Brut' which is a translation in verse and in French of the Legend of King Arthur which was going to be reborn in Normandy eight centuries later, thanks to work of René Bansard, a humble scholar of **La Ferté-Macé**.*

A tour allows one to follow their steps in the mythical places of this Arthurian legend which was one of the major themes of western mediaeval literature.

Leaflet available from the Comité du Tourisme of Orne.

✳✳

X - NORMANDY AND THE HORSE

When the Vikings, 'sons of the sea', arrived on the territory of Neustria they discovered... the horse !

Although Rollon, called 'the walker', first Duke of Normandy led his troops on foot as his nickname indicates, his illustrious descendant William the Conqueror realised the essential role that such a noble animal could play during a war and so made the horse 'his most noble conquest', the most precious ally of his hegemony, as the Saxons found out at Hastings.

Breeding horses is an ancestral activity in Normandy. If the climate and the quality of its pastures contributed to making the area privileged for the quality of the products, the great era of the horse began in the 18th century with the breeding of robust chargers for the Sun Kings army, with the height of their fame being the 18th century when the 'Haras du Pin' was created.

Initially intended for use in the wars, the Norman horse gradually became the faithful work companion to the Norman peasant, helping him to clear the land, for farming the fast growing industry of the country at that time.

This was the hour of glory of the 'Percheron' and the Norman Cob, both supporting roles of the majority of Flaubert's novels and Maupassant's tales.

From 1850 onwards, horse breeding was turned towards horses for the sport and racing, which brought about the creation of many stud farms and with many great champions to be found on the racecourses which sprang up at that time, firstly with creation of the Bergerie at the ***Pin au Haras*** in Orne in 1823, ***first race course in France !***

The Emperor Napoléon III liked going there often. The sovereign favoured rearing and improvement of the breeds of trotters and thoroughbreds and the development of horse racing and equestrian sports.

At the dawn of the IIIrd Millennium, Normandy is still the Country of Excellence of the Horse.

The 'Horse world' involves more than 7,000 people in Normandy and is made up of personalities, traditions, legendary stud farms, fairs, sales, races...

1 - Different breeds of horse

Racehorses

The Thoroughbred - 'The soil is responsible for the quality of the breed'. The Thoroughbred, aristocrat of the equine race, was created by English breeders in the 18th century. It was introduced into France, and more particularly into Normandy during the 19th century. The mild climate, the lie of its land and the quality of its grass have contributed to making Normandy, and specially the regions of the West, the land of the thoroughbred par excellence. Orne and Calvados, the two French areas with most stud farms and horse breeders, now produce horses outclassing the English thoroughbred. This horse is born to race. Racecourses have been built for him and the selection of the stallions depends on its success on the race course.

The French Trotter - The Trotter is of Norman creation, really from Orne in the 19th century. The performance of this champion has been improved by time, by the selection of the 'Anglo Normans' and the 'Norman halfbloods', by the attention brought to breeding and by its training. Nowadays this champion valiantly defends the colours of its province on the most well known race courses such as ***Vincennes*** with the ***'Grand prix d'Amérique'***. For more than a century Orne has been the region of excellence for breeding trotters.

Horses for sport and pleasure

Western Normandy has always been the French privileged region for breeding horses for sport. This is for three reasons : The National studs of the ***Haras du Pin*** and of ***Saint-Lô*** have the best stallions, private beeders have known how to choose products of great quality and a great number of cavaliers who participate in competitions have chosen to settle in the area.

There are several hundred events in the region every year.

French saddle horse - 'Le Selle français' has legally existed since 1958. All the sporting horses with 'Norman halblood' or 'Anglo Norman' ancestors coming from the area of Manche and the ***Country of the Merlerault*** have been grouped together under this name.

Amongst the most famous names representing this breed are : **'Lutteur B'** born near ***Vimoutiers*** who, when mounted by Pierre Jonquières d'Oriola won the only Gold Medal for France in the Olympic games in Tokyo in 1964 and **'Pomone B'** world champion in Buenos Airies in 1968.

Drays and plough horses

The Norman Cob - For many years this fine specimen was the faithful companion to the rich Norman farmer. If harnessed to a cart he could also be used for work in the fields. The rearing of these animals has known a new growth with the revival of the Horse and carriage.

'Le Percheron' The Percheron horse is one of the glories of Normandy and particularly of the Perche where its was born. Its origins are distant. It is said the breed benefited from oriental blood in the 7th century. Since then there have been other crossbreeding with Spanish and also Arab horses (at the time of Charles Martel). One has said that the Percheron was an *'arab strengthened by the rustical nature of the climate use it was put to for centuries'*. Its real history began in 1883.

A certain number of breeders got together to create the 'stud-book' concerning the breed. The 'father' of today's percherons was **'Jean Le Blanc',** a horse born in *Mauves-sur-Huisne*. His qualities of an untiring worker were reputed throughout the world and as from the 19th century the USA, imported a great number (3,000 in 1911) and today that is where they are the most numerous. One feared its disappearance because of the mechanisation of agriculture and transport ; but that was without accounting for man's infatuation for this magnificent horse that the breed owes its rebirth today. It is used in the forests to pull logs but also carts and for sport. The Japanese, who are big amateurs, develop its breed and come to Orne every year to acquire stallions.

****

'Le Haras National du Pin', 'Versailles of the Horse'
One of the most famous stud farms in the world

In a wonderful green setting, in the heart of the 'horse country' you must make a stop. Fifty years after Colbert, Minister to Louis XIVth was founded, the state stud farms, the 'Haras du Pin' was created in 1715. The alleys and terraces designed by a student of the famous Lenôtre, hamonises the beauty of the architectural ensemble. You can breathe nobility everywhere : court of honour in the shape of a horseshoe, vast stables in stone and brick, wide alleys amongst which the avenue Louis XIV with its view of the castle.

Around a hundred stallions of different breeds are to be found in this world famous temple to the horse.

Guided tours (lasting 1 hour, rides in light carts, shows 'Les Jeudis du Pin' - from June to September - at 3 pm (Presentation of stallions and Horse and carriage accompanied by music) - lasting 40 minutes - Information : Tel (33) 2 33 36 68 68.

****

2 - Main Equine Events

<u>AREA OF MANCHE</u>

Agon-Coutainville : on the racecourse. In July and August, **Horse races.** and 1st Sunday in October, **'Fête du Cheval'.**

Avranches : in July and August, **Horse races.**

Beauchamps : mid July, **'Journée du Poney'.**

Carentan : in August, **Horse races.**

Granville : in July, **Horse races.**

Brécey : last Sunday in September, **'Fête du Cheval'**.

Bréhal : in July and August, **Horse races.**

Graignes : in July and August, **Horse races.**

Granville : in August, **Horse races.**

Guilberville : end of August, **'Fête de l'Ane'**.

Querqueville : end of August, on the de la Coquerie land, **Donkey fair.**

Le Mont-Saint-Michel : in July and August, **Horse races.**

Portbail : in August, **Horse races.**

La Rondehaye : mid August, **Plough horse fair.**

Saint-Hilaire-du-Harcouët : in March, **Concours Jumping Nationale 1.**

Saint-Lô : mid August, at the 'Haras National', **Normandie Horse Show.**

This event brings more than 2,000 horses and ponies together with jumping competitions and competition for Horse and carriage models.
The French Championship for ponies of less than 3 years old takes place.
Information : Tel (33) 2 33 57 77 77.

End September : **'Journée nationale du Cheval et du Poney'.**

Sainte-Marie-du-Mont : 1st Sunday of August, **Races for trotters** at the racecourse.

Sainte-Mère-Eglise : At Easter, **'Concours Hippique National'**.

Villedieu-les-Poêles : **Horse Show. Horse Races (8 by year).**

AREA OF CALVADOS

Cabourg : in July and August, **Horse races.**

'EQUI'DAYS'

Organised in Autumn by the 'Conseil Général' of Calvados, this well known event demonstrates the merit of one of the main riches of Orne : the Horse.

Cabourg : **Night races at the racecourse - Festival 'Epona'** (contest for professional or amateur coverage about the theme of the horse (television, news or video).

Caen : **Jumping International** with the world's best riders.

Deauville : **Races - Sale of horses- Horse and carriage contests- Horse Parades - Horse Show and Exhibition.**

Saint-Pierre-sur-Dives : **Horse and carriage - Endurance - Technique for Excursion - Horse ball - Horse fair - Craftsmen's exhibition and demonstrations by blacksmiths.**

In the Region : **Days of free visit of the Stud - Musical evening at the Haras de Sens - Exhibition of Paintings.**

322

Cambremer : on15 August, **Horse Fair** - Basic element of this equestrian assembly is the Percheron horse. In the programme : Contest of elegance, dressage, Percheron model contest, Horse and carriage contest, old style hay making, log pulling, marathon in the orchards, theme show.

Condé-sur-Noireau : 1ˢᵗ Saturday in September, '**Foire Saint-Gilles'.** One of the oldest horse fairs in Normandy. Created in the Middle Ages. Accompanied by funfair.

Deauville : **Deauville Races** at the Racecourse of la Touques and at Clairefontaine with icing on the cake in August the famous **'Grand Prix de Deauville'.** Presented every year at the end of August in the Deauville Casino la '**Cravache d'Or'** for the best jockey of the year.

****

International Auctions of Deauville

Every year in August the famous sale of yearlings attracts numerous investors from all over the world. They like meeting up in this resort which for this time of the summer becomes the world capital of the horse with its prestigious days of the horse on its two race courses. Over the years the sales, one of the best ambassadors for Deauville, are held in Elie de Brignac establishment 'the most beautiful auction houses of Europe'. Their influence increases as the years go by. The Deauville sales are part of the four main international markets of thoroughbreds together with those of Lexington (Kentucky) in the USA, Newmarket in England, Kill (near Dublin) in Ireland. They have become a rendez-vous not to be missed for a buyer looking for a high class horse. Four times a year the biggest investors, amateurs of racing the world over, meet in Deauville.

Mixed sales : mid February and mid December. Yearling sales : end of August and end of October Information : l'Agence Française - BP 51 - 32, avenue Hocquart de Turtot - 14800 Deauville Tel (33) 2 31 81 81 00 - Fax (33) 2 31 81 81 01.

Website : www.deauville-sales.com *E .Mail :* af@deauville-sales.com

****

Dozulé : in August, **Horse races.**

Moyaux : end of March, **Donkey Races.** During the famous agricultural fair, the organisers organise a presentation of donkeys.

Saint-Pierre-sur-Dives : in August, **Horse races.**

AREA OF ORNE

Alençon : in November, **Jump'orne.** Information - Tel (33) 2 43 84 40 39.

Argentan : in March, '**Salon des Etalons'.** Well known event on the racecourse of the Pays d'Argentan. Most of the main stud farms in Orne are represented. Information from the Société des Courses d'Argentan - Tel (33) 2 33 67 08 02. At the end of April **'Critérium de Vitesse'.** At the racecourse of the Pays d'Argentan.

Bagnoles-de-l'Orne : in July and August - **Horse races on the Racecourse.**

Domfront : end of July - **Horse races.**

Flers : end of August, at the beginning of September - **'Jumping international de Flers'.** Information : Tel (33) 2 33 64 39 66.

Le Mêle-sur-Sarthe : in November - **Foal Fair.** More than a hundred years old this event, organised on Saint André's Day, is in honour of the Percheron horse. Every year the national contest for colts and fillies brings together numerous animals from the West and the Centre of France. Besides the Percheron race, all kinds of horses, pony or donkey are revered. The event has been able to maintain the décor and atmosphere of yesteryear.

Le Pin-au-Haras : Thursdays during the summer season at the Haras du Pin - **'Les Jeudis du Pin'.** Show - recalling the past life of the famous Norman stud farm 1st June to the end of September every Thursday at 3 pm. Presentation and commentary of stallions, and Horse and carriages in the court yard of honour of the stud. Proposed arrival at 2.30 pm. Information : Tel (33) 2 33 36 68 68.

End of September : **World Congress of the Percheron Horse** Every year the biggest national meeting concerning this breed is held at the Haras du Pin, an exceptional venue. The event draws 200 of the best of the years horses. Friday is dedicated to a contest of models and the aspect of the males and the purchase of stallions by the the national Haras administration. Saturday is reserved for the contest of models and the aspect of the females, for the cart driving competitions and a dray exhibition -Free entry- Information : Tel (33) 2 33 12 16 00 - Fax (33) 2 33 36 14 12.

In September and October : **Horse races at 'La Bergerie' racecourse.**

Races and showing of stallions - Horse and carriage procession. Information : Tel (33) 2 33 39 44 44.

Mortagne-au-Perche : in July - **'Fête du Cheval Percheron'** end August - (by appointment). '**Mondial de l'Âne'.** Information : Tel (33) 2 33 67 17 03 (Association de l'Âne Normand).

Moulins-la Marche : end of June - **Journée 'Perce Neige'** The town of Moulins la Marche has a fascinating souvenir of Jean Moncorgé alias 'Jean Gabin' well known personality from the French cinema who owned a large property here, residing for many happy years as an authentic gentleman-farmer rearing cattle and horses. The Moulins race course, which still belongs to the family, has for the last 10 years, held a friendly meeting reuniting percherons and stars from showbiz every year. The proceeds from this event go to an association which builds and manages hostels for young handicapped persons. On that date there are eight races including the Jean Gabin Stakes.

Rânes : in July and August - **Horse races.**

Le Sap : in August - **Racing for trotters.** To know more about international competitions in Orne : http//www.worldnand.fr/fhr

AREA OF SEINE-MARITIME

Cany-Barville : in July, **National and international Contest** at the same time as the Castle 'Fête".

Forges-les-Eaux : during last weekend of July, in the forest - **Horse fair.** Procession in the town - Horse and carriage contest - horse show - riding lessons - local products - outdoor food - various attractions - fireworks display.

Veules-les-Roses : 1ˢᵗ Sunday in October - **'Foire du Val'.** Famous horse fair with drays and riding horses.

3 - Race Courses

AREA OF MANCHE

Agon-Coutainville : Racing for trotters.

Avranches : Races for trotters and fences.

Bourigny : Racing for trotters.

Bréhal : Flat racing, trotting, and fences.

Carentan : Racing for trotters. 32, chemin du Grand Bas Pays - Tel (33) 2 33 42 41 07

Cherbourg-Octeville : Racing for trotters.

La Glacerie (near Cherbourg/Octeville) : **Race course de la Glacerie** - Racing for trotters. 'La Banque à Genêts'. Tel (33) 2 33 22 09 80 - Fax (33) 2 33 43 32 54.

Graignes : trotting and fences. **Société des Courses de Graignes,** 25-27-31, rue du Vieux Château. Tel (33) 2 33 55 45 26 - Fax (33) 2 33 56 37 59

Granville : Flat racing, trotting and fences.

Jullouville : Racing for trotters.

Le Mont-Saint-Michel : Racing for trotters.

Portbail : Racing for trotters.

Sainte-Marie-du-Mont : Racing for trotters.

Valognes : Racing for trotters.

Villedieu-les-Poèles : Racing for trotters.

AREA OF CALVADOS

Cabourg : avenue Michel-d'Ornano. Tel (33) 2 31 28 28 80 - Fax (33) 2 31 28 07 36. Magnificent race course opened in 1991 with 5,000 seats in covered stands. A reference to the world of trotting with more than 20 evening events and day events of a high level.

Caen : Racing for trotters. 'Société du Cheval Français', La Prairie. Tel (33) 2 31 85 42 61 - Fax (33) 2 31 86 76 90.

Deauville : **Racecourse de la Touques** - flat racing. 45, avenue Hocquart de Turtot BP 43300. Tel (33) 2 31 88 09 07.

Racecourse de Clairefontaine - flat racing, trotting and fences. Tel (33) 2 31 14 69 00.

'Société des Courses du Pays d'Auge' Clairefontaine. Tel (33) 2 31 14 69 00 - Fax (33) 2 31 14 69 01.

****

Deauville, Capital of the Horse

When summer arrives, Deauville becomes the world capital of the Horse living for and from the races. At the Deauville-La Touques race course, as in Clairefontaine the international big brass of the world of racing mix with thousands of race goers. On the lawns of the weigh-in paddock, tourists in sandals rub shoulders with owners of the biggest stables of the planet, Texan millionaires or Arab Emirs, and personalities from show-biz, politics, or big business.

It's in Deauville where the most prestigious races take place, as does the Polo World Championships, Horse Shows, without forgetting the Yearling Auctions where prices sometimes reach more than a million euros.

****

Dozulé : Racing for trotters.

Lisieux : Flat racing and trotting. Route de Paris - Tel (33) 02 31 31 03 28.

Saint-Pierre-sur-Dives : Racing for trotters.

Saint-Martin-de-Tallevende : route de Pont-Farcy - Martilly **Racecourse de Vire**. From April to November : 13 days of reputed racing (trotting, fences and flat racing).
'Société des Courses de Vire' Same address -Tel (33) 2 31 68 14 50 - Fax (33) 2 31 68 89 60.

AREA OF ORNE

Alençon : Racing for trotters. 104, rue d'Argentan.
Société des Courses d'Alençon Same address - Tel (33) 2 33 28 02 90.

Argentan : in Urou-Crennes - **Racecourse of the Pays d'Argentan** : trotting, fences and flat racing. 4, route de Chambois - Point Courses. Tel (33) 2 33 39 77 05.
'Société des Courses du Pays d'Argentan'. Same address - Tel (33) 2 33 67 08 02 - Fax (33) 2 33 39 59 84.

Bagnoles-de-l'Orne : Races for trotters and fences.

Domfront : Racing for trotters.

Ginai : **'Racecourse du Pin'** - flat racing and fences. 'La Bergerie'. Tel (33) 2 33 39 94 32.

Moulins-la-Marche : Racing for trotters. *This private race course belongs to the family of the actor Jean Gabin, now deceased. His son continues horse breeding*

which he started in Orne in the 50's. Each year the 'Journée des Courses Perce neige' takes place with the presence of stars from cinema and Music Hall.
'Société des Courses du Perche'. Le Clos Mottay - Tel (33) 2 33 24 46 27.

Rânes : Racing for trotters. The Castle. **'Société des Courses de Rânes'** Same address - Tel (33) 2 33 36 26 20.

Le Sap - Racing for trotters.

AREA OF EURE

Mandres : **'Société des Courses de Francheville'.** Chemin de la Lande. Tel (33) 2 32 60 13 95.

AREA OF SEINE-MARITIME

Rouxmesnil-Bouteilles : **Dieppe Racecourse - 'Société des Courses de Dieppe'** - Avenue de Bréauté. Tel (33) 2 35 84 29 28 or (33) 2 35 84 11 49.

Saint-Aubin-lès-Elbeuf : **'Société des Courses de Saint-Aubin-lès-Elbeuf'.** Avenue Pasteur - Tel (33) 2 35 81 81 87

Saint-Etienne-du-Rouvray : **Racecourse des Bruyères.** Avenue des Canadiens - Tel (33) 2 35 64 15 54.

'Société des Courses Rouennaises'. Racecourse des Bruyères -Tel (33) 2 35 64 15 54 ou (33) 2 35 66 48 61 ou (33) 2 35 66 88 69.

'Fédération des Sociétés de Courses d'Ile-de-France and de Haute-Normandie'. Bureau Technique Régional de Haute-Normandie Tel (33) 2 35 66 58 28 - Fax (33) 2 35 65 09 66.

Places to see...

AREA OF MANCHE

Saint-Lô : **Haras National. (National Stud Farm).** Avenue du Maréchal Juin. Tel (33) 2 33 55 29 09 ou (33) 2 33 77 60 35. Magnificent group of buildings from the 19th century enclosing a court of honour. This stud farm is the cradle of the French riding horse. Around a hundred stallions for reproduction are housed here, thus making it the first stud farm in France. Tel (33) 2 33 77 88 77 - Fax (33) 2 33 55 26 14.

Guided tours, each Thursday during the season *: 'The Gardens of the Haras'.*
Presentation of Horse and carriages and mounted and handheld stallions in the courtyard of honour. From the last Thursday of July to the first Thursday of September at 3 pm. Information : Tel (33) 2 33 36 68 68.

AREA OF CALVADOS

Thury-Harcourt : Horse and carriage, promenades by trap.

AREA OF ORNE

Alménèches : '**Haras de Fligny**'. Private trotting stables - station de monte - Possibility of a guided tour by appointment - Tel (33) 2 33 35 62 58.

Brullemail : '**Haras de Brullemai'l** - In the heart of the Pays du Merlerault, excellent land for horses, there is the possibility to visit this breeding station for horses for sport (French saddle horses) - station de monte - By appointment only - Tel (33) 2 33 28 42 56.

Corbon : **Birth Cradle of the Percheron Horse.**

Dorceau : La '**Ferme Neuve**'. Rebuilt in 1851 by Mr Joseph Aveline, a century ago this farm was well known for its breed of percherons.

Heugon : '**Haras du Taillis**' - Rearing of thoroughbreds - Visits possible by appointment. Tel (33) 2 33 39 40 22.

Juvigny-sous-Andaine (Near *Bagnoles-de-l'Orne*) : '**La Ferme du Cheval de Trait**'. **(The Plough Horse Farm)** 'La Michaudière' - Tel (33) 2 33 38 27 78 - Fax (33) 2 33 30 43 33. Show with harnessed percheron horses (trick riding, chariot races) - Horse drawn agricultural material from 1830 to the present day. Exhibition of miniature agricultural machines(1/10th) - smithy - saddle making - open from April to October.

La Perrière : '**Promenades**' (Horse and carriage percheron).

AREA OF SEINE-MARITIME

Blosseville-sur-Mer : '**Exposition de voitures hippomobiles**' - At the heart of this picturesque village of Caux in an ancient stone cottage-cum-sheep pen. Weekends and holidays during summer.

Crasville-la-Rocquefort : '**Ballade à cheval et en char à bancs**'. Guided trips on carts equipped with benches for up to fifty persons. Visit of the village and its heritage, horse-drawn like yesteryear. All year round by appointment : Tel (33) 2 35 97 41 76.

Forges-les-Eaux : '**Musée des Maquettes Hippomobiles J. Guillot**' - Mondory Park - Town Hall - Open from April 1st to October 31st every day except Monday from 2-5.30 pm and Sunday from 2.30-6 pm. Information : Tourist Office - Tel (33) 2 35 90 52 10. More than 100 models are shown ! Presentation of farm transport and old fashioned merchandise. 45 exhibition rooms.

Saint-Saëns : **Horse shows** - Company 'Il était une fois' Ferme de Saint-Denis-Perduville. Tel/Fax (33) 2 35 34 78 95.

TO FIND OUT MORE...

To find out about the list of equestrian centres, farms or equestrian gites
in Normandy or private stud farms open for visitors :
contact the Tourist Offices or :

'Ligue de Normandie des Sports Equestres' : 180, rue d'Auge - 14000 Caen. Tel (33) 2 31 84 61 87 - Fax (33) 2 31 84 61 91.

'Comité Départemental de Tourisme Equestre de la Manche' : Le Presbytère - 50160 Brectouville. Tel/Fax (33) 2 33 56 76 03.

'Comité Départemental de Tourisme Equestre du Calvados' : Ferme de la Dîme - 14480 Colombiers-sur-Seulles. Tel (33) 2 31 80 10 28 - Fax (33) 2 31 80 31 73

'Comité Départemental de Tourisme Equestre de l'Orne' : Ferme de Sainte-Yvière 61570 Montmerrei. Tel (33) 2 33 35 31 75 - Fax (33) 2 33 35 60 80.

'Comité Départemental du Tourisme Equestre de l'Eure' : Centre équestre du Bec-Hellouin - 27800 - Le Bec-Hellouin. Tel (33) 2 32 44 86 31 - Fax (33) 2 32 46 45 59.

'Comité Départemental du Tourisme Equestre de Seine-Maritime' : La Valandte - Le Fond du Bois - 76280 Villainville.

XI - HAVE FUN IN NORMANDY

1 - Agricultural shows, shows, and fairs in Normandy, 'Assemblees'

The origin of fairs or Norman 'assemblies', dates from afar, although chroniclers agree that they were mainly developed from the 12th century. One of the oldest and most famous is the one from **Guibray** in *Falaise* which takes place for a fortnight in August but also the **Motmartin Fair** in early July, and the **Foire du Pré** in Caen which takes place in early October. Just in the Conqueror's birthplace there are at least five well known fairs per year. In times gone by, these events were places for meeting and exchange and sometimes lasted more than a week, like **Saint-Catherine's Fair** in *Honfleur* which sometimes lasted more than a fortnight.

Apart from those fairs keeping to the liturgical calendar the others are always on fixed dates.

They took place all year round except for an interruption during the winter months when the bad weather was likely to hamper travelling - mostly on foot for most - both men and cattle.

The agricultural fair with the sale of cattle, of horses and its competitions, in the 19th century almost always constituted the main event of Norman fairs, the majority of whose visitors were masculine.

Important 'Horse fairs' took place in different parts of Normandy. Breeder and dealers would rub shoulders. There were also calf, pig, and sheep fairs…

These events generally took place at the same time as local village fêtes and in a rural setting. From the morning onwards, the village would seeth with excitement, itinerant musicians would 'violin' on makeshift stages, the local town and country bourgeois mixing with the peasant farmers. These fairs were full of conviviality. The entries into tents were equipped with roasts where people ate and drank until they were drunk.

At the end of the 19th century, the musicians were gradually replaced by brass bands and the fairs lost their original reason for existence, being converted into popular fairs, accompanied at the beginning of the 20th century by processions. On these occasions the itinerants would get together and provide varied attractions :

travelling theatres, circuses, acrobats, jugglers, and merry go rounds, which at that time were not just for children. Heirs to the older assemblies, the Norman fairs would sometimes enable young men and women to offer their services in the *'louées'* to be taken on for hay making, for the harvest season or for the whole year. With this in mind they would wait in a corner of one of the fields of the fair waiting for proposals.

The most well known of Norman fairs, as it was one of the oldest and because it took place in the Norman capital, was undoubtedly the **Foire Saint-Romain** in *Rouen*. We speak of this event in the past tense since it has been temporarily suspended.

Established by Duke William in honour of the Patron Saint of Rouen, from the 20th century this event became an ordinary basic funfair running for a month from the second weekend of November on the banks of the Seine.

Also an ancestral fair is that of the **'Sainte-Croix'** in *Lessay* in Manche, which founded by the Benedictine monks in the 13th century has never ceased since, and always in a similar form. It takes place at the end of summer on the heath on the way out of the town. The merchants' tents can still be found on both sides of the Coutances road, each street assembling a particular trade.

This rural fair was one of the most important horse fairs in France for a long time.

Amongst the most picturesque of events,

To be seen...

AREA OF MANCHE

Auvers : Early August, **'Fête des Foins'** (Evolution of farming over the centuries).

Avranches : During the month of July, **Cavalcade 'Les Eclats de Rire'.** Early December, in the multi-purpose hall. **'Art Floral'.**

Bacilly : early August, **'Foire aux Béliers'.**

Champcey : mid August, **'Fête Champêtre'.**

Cherbourg-Octeville : Early December, **Foire from Cherbourg.**

Ducey : three days from the first weekend of August, **'Fête Locale'** Funfair - Big jumble sale - Various parades and activities. Dancing and fireworks on the Monday.

Ecocqueneauville : **'Foire Saint-Laurent'.** *Well known fair in the 16th century.*

Fermanville : early May, **Flea Market.**

Gavray : Third Thursday, Friday, and Saturday of October, **'Foire Saint-Luc'.** *For scores of years the town of Gavray has been known as one of the main markets for cattle and horses in the west of Normandy.* **'The Grande Saint-Luc'** *has existed for more than six centuries. During the last century it brought together 4000 cattle and 3000 horses. Today it is still one of the most biggest farming fairs in the west, drawing 800 cattle and 1500 horses. The dog fair is open Fridays and*

Lamb market on Saturdays. There are various activities during the farm fair : the onion and pumpkin fair - trade fair - horse show- country kitchen - Bar-B-Q.

Granville : in spring, **'Carnaval'.** *An old country custom had it that fishermen would spend all their money before leaving for the Banks of Newfoundland. They would also wear grotesque costumes. This event dating from the end of the 19th Century is the origin of this fair. Today it is more a procession of floats and groups of musicians and takes place on the Sunday before Shrove Tuesday.*

La Haye-du-Puits : end of August, **Dog fair.**

Le Fresne-Poret : 3rd week in June, **'Fête de la Saint-Jean'.** *Old fashioned haymaking.*

Lessay : for 3 days the second week of September, **Foire Sainte Croix.** *Founded by Benedictine monks a thousand years ago, it is one of the major fairs in Normandy attracting up to 500,000 visitors. In times gone by, a lot of business was done. Today visitors come more to have fun and to amble along the 10 kilometres of alleys each with its own speciality. Ever present roasters under tents offer roast lamb as in yesteryear and good 'bère' (2000 stands, 50 roasters and many funfair attractions) The Sainte-Croix was well known for it horse fair with many dealers, notably from England. This fair always takes place on Friday and Saturday morning. - Dog fair. Information : Tel (33) 2 33 46 46 18 ou (33) 2 33 46 14 69.*

Montebourg : 1st weekend in February, **Candelmas Fair. Norman Cattle Fair. Antique Show.** In August; **Foals, Cattle and Sheep Competition.**

Mont-Saint-Michel : end of September, beginning of October, **'Music under the Archangels Wings' Festival** - Information : Tel (33) 2 33 89 80 00.

Munneville-le-Bingard : mid-August on the heath **Harvest festival - old time harvesting.**

Nez-de-Jobourg : first Saturday in August, **Roussins Fair (black headed sheep).** *Agricultural fair - cattle competitions - local food products - country food.*

Ouville : mid-July, **District fair with Agricultural.**

Percy : mid November, **'Foire Exposition'.**

Picauville : 2nd Sunday in May, **'Fête sainte Jeanne d'Arc'.**

Pontorson : in September, **'Fête de la Moisson'.**

Port-Bail : mid July, **'Journée Normande, Son et Lumière'.** Early August, **'Fête de la Moisson'.**

Rauville-la-Place : early November : la Lande, **'Foire traditionnelle.**

Régneville-sur-Mer : August 15th, **'Fête Champêtre'.** About August 20th, **'Comice agricole cantonal'.**

Rocheville : early August, **'Fête des Roches'.**

Sacey : mid August, **'Fête de la Moisson'.** Information - Tel (33) 2 33 60 20 65.

Saint-Georges-from-Rouelley : mid August, at the Fosse Arthour **Craft Festival with Water Show.**

Saint-Hilaire-du-Harcouët : 1ˢᵗ Saturday in November, **'Foire Saint-Martin'.** *Agricultural fair with origins going back to the Middle Ages, but also an important commercial fair (800 exhibitors) and funfair. Over the five days it attracts more than 100,000 visitors.*
And three days later, **'Petite Foire Saint-Martin'.**

Saint-James : 4ᵗʰ weekend of September from Saturday to Monday - **'Foire Saint-Macé'.**

Saint-Laurent-from-Cuves : early August, **Medieval Fête.**

Saint-Lô : early October, **Saint-Lô Exhibition and fair.**

Sainte-Marie-du-Mont : August 15ᵗʰ, **'Fête Patronale'.** *Race- funfair- procession and firework display.*

Saint-Michel-from-Montjoie : end of July, **Granite festival.**

Saint-Pierre-Eglise : the first Sunday in July, **'Fête Saint-Pierre'.** *Originally organised in the 16ᵗʰ century for hiring out servants and farm workers before the harvests. Today it is just a fun fair with floats and bands.*

Saint-Sauveur-le-Vicomte : in July and August, **'Soirées normandes'.**
Early August : **Crafts and local products Fair.**

Sourdeval : last weekend in October, **'Foire Saint-Crépin'.** *Mainly well known for its important cattle fair (beef, horses, calves, pigs and sheep).*

Savigny : end of August, **Old fashioned festival.**

Surtainville : early July, **Country Fête.**

Torigni-sur-Vire : in September, **Agricultural Show.** Early November : **Exhibition of local and regional produce.**

Vains-Saint-Léonard : early July, **'Fête de la Baie du Mont-Saint-Michel'.** Exhibitions, jumble sale, popular dancing.

Varouville : early July, **'Fête champêtre'.**

Villedieu-les-Poèles : **'Corso fleuri'.** *Town fair with exceptional decorations.*

Ile de Tatihou : in August, **Festival 'Les Mousquetaires du Large'.**

AREA OF CALVADOS

Argences : in October, **'Foire de la Saint-Luc ou Foire aux Oignons'.**

Balleroy : 3ʳᵈ weekend in June at the Castle, **'Grande Fête - Rassemblement international de Ballons'.** *In the 70's the American millionaire Malcolm S Forbes, a rather eccentric businessman, fell in love with Normandy, and in particular with Balleroy Castle which he bought. Being a collector of hot air* balloons, every year he organised a meeting of aeronauts from all over the world. Since his death the meeting no longer takes place each year.

Bayeux *:* First weekend in July in the old town centre, **Medieval Festival.** *Large medieval market with attractions - fancy dress. Information : Tel (33) 2 31 92 03 30.*

Caen *:* last two weeks in September, Parc des Expositions, **Caen International Fair.** *This old local fair is known today as the shop window for business in western Normandy. Industry, agriculture, gastronomy, nautical activities are to be found. Each year a guest of honour is invited. The aisle of the 'sales talkers' is the one the visitors prefer.*

Equemeauville *:* first weekend in September, **Harvest Festival.** *Old fashioned harvesting - exhibition of old tools - fun fair -outdoor country food.*

Falaise *:* 1st weekend in October, **'Foire Saint Michel'.** *This basically trade fair was founded in the XIIth century. There is also a funfair.*

Honfleur *:* from 3rd Sunday in November, **'Foire Sainte-Catherine'.** Funfair.

Lisieux *:* end of December, beginning of January, Place de la République, **Fête Foraine.**

First weekend in March : **'Foire aux Arbres'** *Ancestral event (543rd edition in 2002) the stands are in the town squares and on most of the pavements in the town centre.*

Last weekend in May : **'Foire de Lisieux et du Pays d'Auge'.** *At the Halle des Expositions - Route de Paris Major trade exhibition - open to the public for one week. Shop window for the Pays d'Auge - agricultural and craft products (competitions).*

In June : 'Fête de la Saint-Ursin'.

Livarot *:* first weekend of July : **'Foire Saint-André'.** *Agricultural fair dating back tothe 16th century is still an important event with cattle show and traditional meals of tripe.*

Maltot *:* early March in the Castle, **'Foire aux Plantes'.** Saturday and Sunday from 9 am-7 pm without interruption : Sale of shrubs, roses, fruit trees, hedges, creepers, conifers…

Pont-l'Evêque *:* in May, **Cheese Festival.**

La Rivère-Saint-Sauveur *:* in July, **Fête de la Saint-Clair.**

Orbec *:* 1st November, **All Saints' Day Fair.** Funfair. In November : **Tree fair.** Sale of trees, plants, local natural products - Apple pie contest.

Trouville *:* in August, **Donkey races.** *Donkey races used to be frequent in Normandy. Trouville has reintroduced this tradition. Several races are organised on the beach for the pleasure of adults and children.*

Villerville *:* last weekend in August, **'Fête de la Saint-Roch'.** Old fashioned wedding in period clothes.

Saint-Aubin-sur-Mer *:* in July, **'Foire aux Greniers'** *(well known jumble sale).*

AREA OF ORNE

L'Aigle : on Ascension Day, **4 Days of L'Aigle.** Exhibition - fun fair - numerous attractions.

Alençon : in February or March, at the Hall des Expositions, **'Foire d'Alençon 'Orne Expo'.**
In July : **'Festival international de Folklore'.**
End of September, early October : **'Foire Artisanat-Terroir et Nature'.**

Argentan : one week after Easter, **'Foire de la Quasimodo'.** Funfair and exhibition - fun fair -agricultural fair. Founded in the Middle Ages.

Briouze : 3rd weekend in November, **'Foire Sainte-Catherine' :** the town of Briouze is known for its weekly calf fair, as far away as in Italy. Every year the Saint Catherie Fair takes place as it has for many years with the same programme : concert in the church - tree fair - market with local products - rambling - fun fair - exhibition - cattle contests

Carrouges : early August, **Hunting Fair.** With the participation of the Parc Naturel régional 'Normandie-Maine".

Exceptional event ! This highly colourful fair takes place in the admirable Castle grounds: beginning in the morning with Grand Mass of St-Hubert it is accompanied by a group of Bellringers. During the day : presentation of packs of hounds - equipages - competition including that of Hunting horns - Attractions - Night show. Information : Tel (33) 2 33 37 15 88.

Cerisy-Belle-Etoile : last Sunday in May, **'Fête des Rhodos' (Rhododendrons)**
On top of the Mount Cerisy (265 metres) a well off beautiful British couple had a beautiful house built in the thirties around which they planted a few young rhododendrons. The house was destroyed during the war and was never rebuilt. As for the rhodos, they proliferated in the 105 hectares of sandy ground, and today give this 300 metre high promontory, a strange look in the surrounding 'bocage' when they are in flower. An association was created to protect the site. Every year it organises a popular fair and music hall. During this event you are allowed to pick the flowers. Information. : Tel (33) 2 33 66 52 62- Fax (33) 2 33 65 54 09

Domfront : in March or April, **La Foire des Rameaux.** Trade fair, funfair every Palm Sunday weekend, this event was in times gone by, the rendez-vous for unmarried young people to find their match.
Early August : **'Les Médiévales de Domfront'.** Craftsmen's market, local products, street theatre, attractions, evening show. Contact : Tourist Office -Tel (33) 2 33 38 53 97

La Perrière : mid July, **Agricultural fair. 'Fête du Rosaire'.**

Montilly : in October, **Foire Saint-Denis.** Trade fair, country show. Left over from the old Norman assemblies, the Montilly Fair brings several thousand people together in a little 'Bocage' community. Large cattle and horse fair - Dog fair - Exhibition - market- country food - torchlight procession - firework display.

Rémalard : last weekend in October, **Autumn Fair.** Based on local natural products, craft work and jumble sale.

Saint-Fraimbault : mid August, **'Flories d'Antan'.** Over 200 volunteers relive the great rural traditions, beginning with harvesting.

Saint-Nicolas-des-Bois : Early July : **Lumberjack Fair.** Logging contest with candidates from all over France using both axe and chainsaws.

Tinchebray : in October, **'Fête Saint-Luc'.** Jumble sale and exhibition…
Agricultural Show every 8 years with fair and procession.

Vimoutiers : at Easter, (from Saturday to Tuesday inclusive), **Easter Fair.** This event dating back to the 17th century had King Louis XVth's personal authorisation and today this well known trade fair (the oldest in the region) takes place alongside a funfair in the town centre. On the Saturday morning there is a Cider, Pommeaux, and Calvados, competition, (the oldest and most reputed in Normandy). It ends on the Tuesday afternoon with the arrival of a professional 1st category international cyclist race **'Paris-Camembert'.**

AREA OF EURE

Les Andelys : early June, **'Fête Sainte-Clotilde'.** This saint is venerated and is supposed to have transformed the taste of water into that of wine, for those workers building the church which is dedicated to her. The water from the Sainte Clothilde Fountain is said to possess curative powers.
End of June : **'Journées Médiévales'.**
End of July, early August : **'Fête Saint-Sauveur'.**

Beaumont-le-Roger : July 14th, **'Fête de la Madeleine'.**

Bernay : Saturday before Palm Sunday, **Agricultural contest.** This important agricultural rendezvous in the Pays d'Ouche is also accompanied by a funfair and varied attractions.

La Haye-from-Routot : July 16th, **'Feu de Saint-Clair'.** Bonfire dedicated to the Norman martyr, Saint-Clair, organised by the brotherhood of the Charitons of la Haye-de-Routot.

In the village of *Le Marais-Vernier :* May Day, **Punching Fair.** This village of the Marais-Vernier relives the tradition of marking cattle on their horns before putting them out to pasture in the fields of Marais.

Lisors : August 15th à l'Abbaye from Mortemer, **'Fête Médiévale'.** Medieval market 'son et lumière'.

Lyons-la-Forêt : in May, **The Single's Fair.** Château de Fleury-la-Forêt et Abbaye de Mortemer- Information, Tel (33) 2 32 49 54 34 You would think this is very ancient, but in fact this original and unique event is very recent. However it is inspired by an old legend which said that the Fountain of Mortemer had the virtue *of encouraging people meeting each other and weddings .You can eat, drink and dance all through the day.*

Quillebeuf : 1ˢᵗ Sunday in July, **'Fête Saint-Pierre'**. *Funfair, dance, jumble.....*

Le Neubourg : in April, **Agricultural Fair.** In June, **'Fête Saint-Paul'.**

Vascœuil : 3ʳᵈ weekend in September (odd numbered years), **'Les Montgolfiades'.** *At the Castle : hot-air balloons take off, first flights.*
3ʳᵈ weekend of September (even numbered years) : **Hunt Fair.** *At the castle : équipages of big game hunting - horn blowing competition - archery - country food.*

AREA OF SEINE-MARITIME

Allouville-Bellefosse : first weekend in September every second year, the next in 2004). **'Fête de la Forêt, du Bois et de la Chasse'.** *St-Hubert Mass, log chopping competition, display of logging with horses, hunting horns, and demonstration of setters.*

Auffay : 3ʳᵈ weekend of November, **Fun fair.**

Cany-Barville : in March, **Cattle market at Monday Gras.**

Duclair : in September, **'Fête Médiévale'** dite **'Médiévales en Seine'.** *Medieval market, street attractions, food, night attractions... all the shopkeepers and inhabitants wear period clothes.*

Elbeuf : in September, **'Foire Saint-Gilles'.** *Dates back to the Middle Ages. Today it is only a funfair and sport.*

Forges-les-Eaux : first Sunday in October, **'Fête Brévière'.**

Le Havre : for 9 days in early November in the Parc des Expositions, **'Foire du Havre'.** *Showcase for the activities in the Le Havre area, the show has about 300 exhibitors.*

In August : **'Corso Fleuri'.** The most important in Normandy.

Jumièges : end of June, **'Fête Saint-Pierre'.** *Now a fun fair.*

Lillebonne : in spring, **Large agricultural fair.**

Neufchâtel-en-Bray : first weekend in June, **Agricultural Fair.**
Early November : **'Foire Saint-Martin'.**

Ourville-en-Caux : in March, **Cattle fair.** In July : **Donkey fair.**

Rouen : in May, Parc des Expositions - (Left bank near A 13), **International Fair of Rouen. Large region trade venue - 1500 m.** 3ʳᵈ week in May : - More than 170,000 visitors - Information : Tel (33) 2 35 18 28 28

'Fête Jeanne d'Arc'. *Over a week, Rouen honours the memory of the famous 'Maid of Orleans' (medieval fair, music, conferences) in April or May.*

Saint-Valery-en-Caux : on Easter Tuesday, **Cattle fair.**

Veules-les-Roses : in October, **'Foire du Val'.**

2 - Places of conviviality

Bowling Alleys

AREA OF MANCHE

Cherbourg-Octeville : 'Bowling Chantereyne' - port Chantereyne -Tel (33) 2 33 78 17 20. Open every day from 2 pm to 2 am.

Donville-les-Bains (near Granville) : 'Bowling de l'Ermitage' - L'Ermitage -Tel (33) 2 33 90 61 38.

Saint-Lô : ı 'Le Macao' - 2, rue du Maréchal Leclerc -Tel (33) 2 33 57 40 00.

AREA OF CALVADOS

Courseulles : 'Bowling de la Mer' - place du 6 juin - Tel (33) 2 31 37 48 58. 10 alleys - Billiard tables - Giant television screen - Pin ball machines - Open every day except Monday from 10 am-1 am and 4 pm-4 am at weekends.

Honfleur : 'Bowling' - La Fosserie - Tel (33) 2 31 14 66 66.

Lisieux : 'Bowling' - 69, route from Paris - Tel (33) 2 31 62 19 30. 8 alleys. Open every day.

Mondeville (near Caen) : 'Bowling du Calvados' - 6, rue Charles de Coulomb - (near exit RN 13) - Tel (33) 2 31 82 53 58. 18 computerised alleys - billiard tables - bar. Open during the week from 3 pm-3 am in the morning, and on Saturdays from 3 pm-4 am and Sundays from 3 pm-1 am.

AREA OF ORNE

L'Aigle : 'Cap'Orne' - Avenue Kennedy - Tel (33) 2 33 24 12 60.

Alençon : 'Bowling d'Arçonnay' - Le Petit Coudray - route du Mans - Tel (33) 2 33 28 94 76.

AREA OF EURE

Evreux : 'L.E.L'. - 1, rue Jean-Jaurès - Tel (33) 2 32 62 42 33. *8 alleys, ' automatic scoring" - Amusement arcade - French and American billiard tables.*
'Le Parvis' - 2, rue Franklin-Roosevelt - Tel (33) 2 32 62 42 33. *8 alleys, 'automatic scoring' Amusement arcade - French and American billiard tables.*

Louviers : 'Le Drugsport' - 23, avenue François-Mittérand - Tel (33) 2 32 25 33 80.

AREA OF SEINE-MARITIME

Amfreville-la-Mivoie : **'Bowling'** - 177, route de Paris - Tel (33) 2 35 07 18 76.

Dieppe : **'Dieppe Bowling'** - Belvédère - Tel (33) 2 32 14 00 20.

Le Grand-Quevilly (near *Rouen*) : **'Bowling du Bois-Cany'** - 22, boulevard Pierre-Brossolette - Tel (33) 2 32 11 58 58.

Le Havre : **'Bowling du Havre -** 47, rue Mazeline - Tel (33) 2 35 24 32 52.

Montivillers : **'Le Looping'** - 6, rue des Hérons - Tel (33) 2 35 13 90 00. 18 alleys - alleys for chidren - 12 billiards.

Rouen : **Bowling international from Rouen** - 130, rue Constantine- Tel (33) 2 35 71 24 47 - 16 alleys ! Electronic scoring - Open from 2.30 pm.

Billiard Halls

AREA OF MANCHE

Avranches : **'Big Ben Club'** - 20, place Littré - Tel (33) 2 33 60 55 90.

Cherbourg - Octeville : **'Le Dakota'** - 11, rue de la Paix - Tel (33) 2 33 94 74 55.

Coutances : **'Le Newton'** - 58, rue Saint-Nicolas -Tel (33) 2 33 45 95 95.

Gouville-sur-Mer : **'Club de Billiard Gouvillais'** - 35, rue du Littoral - Tel (33) 2 33 47 92 25.

Equeurdreville-Hainneville :
'Le Willy Hop' - 65, rue Hervé-Mangon - Tel (33) 2 33 08 09 09.

Saint-Lô : **'Le Shetland'** - 136, rue de Tessy - Tel (33) 2 33 72 04 35.

Urville - Nacqueville : **'Club Assun Billiard'** - 325, allée Avoinerie - Tel (33) 2 33 03 53 83.

AREA OF CALVADOS

Bayeux : **'Le Loch Ness'** - 67, rue Montfiquet - Tel (33) 2 31 51 71 71.
10 billiard tables (French, snooker, pool, American). Bar with video - open Monday to Saturday from 11 am-1 am, and 11 am-3 am at weekends.

Cabourg : **'Les Ormettes'** - Le Bas Cabourg - Tel: (33) 2 31 91 28 16. French billiard tables - 8 mini American billiard tables - 10 pin bowling- amusements. Open all year round.

Caen :
'L'Orient-Express' - 24, rue du 11 novembre - Tel (33) 2 31 72 81 64. 38 billiard tables (French, pool, American, snooker) - bar. Open all year from 2.30 pm-3.30 am.

'L'Academy Caen' - 43, quai de juillet - Tel (33) 2 31 84 76 13. Open on Mondays, Tuesdays, Wednesdays and Sundays from 12 noon-1 am and Thursdays from 12 noon-3 am.

'Le Dakota' - 54, rue de Bernières - Tel (33) 2 31 50 05 25. 8 French and 8 English billiard tables. Open all year round from Monday to Thursday from 4 pm-1 am. On Friday and Saturday from 2 pm-4 am and Sunday and Monday from 8 pm-1 am.

Deauville : **'French Billiard Tables'** - 52, Rue Gambetta -Tel (33) 2 31 87 03 65.

Lisieux : **'New Solaris'** - 32, boukevard. Jeanne d'Arc -Tel (33) 2 31 31 30 95.

Ouistreham-Riva-Bella : **See Casino 'Queen Normandy'.**

Touques : **'Billard's Club'** - 26, rue du Docteur Lainé.

Ver-sur-Mer : **'French Billiards'** - Voie du Débarquement - Tel (33) 2 31 22 21 86.

Villers-sur-Mer : **'L'Illusion'** - 6, rue des Grives - Tel (33) 2 31 87 62 26.

AREA OF ORNE

Alençon : 'The Twenty Club' - 4, rue Demées - Tel (33) 2 33 28 81 09. *I*n a somewhat torrid atmosphere amateurs can play French or American billiards.

Flers : **'Le Bizon'** - Rue de la Gare.

AREA OF EURE

Evreux :

'Le Parvis' - French and American billiard tables. Tel (33) 2 32 62 42 33
'Le 8ᵉ Art' - 67, rue Joséphine - Tel (33) 2 32 38 27 06.

Gaillon : **'Billard Club Gaillonnais'** - 101, rue du Général de Gaulle - Tel (33) 2 32 53 89 73.

Vernon : 'Le 8ᵉᵐᵉ Art' - 111, rue Carnot - Tel (33) 2 32 21 62 29.

AREA OF SEINE-MARITIME

Le Havre :

'Beer and Billiard' - 96, rue René-Coty - Tel (33) 2 35 42 44 88. Open every day from 2 pm-2 am except Sundays (closed at 10.30 pm). Large choice of billiards (snooker, American, pool or English) or if you like you can watch a direct screening of the Le Havre Football Club whilst enjoying a beer or two.

'Aux Olympiades' - 5, quai de Southampton - Tel (33) 2 35 42 59 73.

Le Petit Quevilly : **'Billard Sportif Quevillais'** - Académie de Billard - 27 F, avenue Jean-Jaurès - Tel (33) 2 35 63 86 51.

Oissel : **'Billiard Club Osselien'** - 8, rue du Manoir - Tel (33) 2 35 66 85 72.

Rouen : **'Rouen Billiard Club'** - Domaine de la Petite Bouverie - Allée Pierre-de Coubertin. Tel (33) 2 35 61 30 82.

To find out more : Ligue de Normandie de Billard : 8, rue du Manoir - 76350 Oissel. Tel (33) 2 35 66 85 72.

Pubs - Night Bars - Piano Bars

AREA OF MANCHE

Anneville : **'Aux deux Anes'** - 16, rue Bourgainville - Tel (33) 2 33 47 87 64.
Avranches :
    'The Big Ben Club' - 20, place Littré - Tel (33) 2 33 60 55 90.
    'The Liberty's' - 16, place d'Estouville - Tel (33) 2 33 58 10 01.

Bréal : **'Bar de la Vanlée'** - Tel (33) 2 33 91 86 00.
Cherbourg-Octeville :
    'Normandie Bar' - rue Ile-de-France - Tel (33) 2 33 53 43 27.
    'Space Boys' - 2, impasse Couppey - Tel (33) 2 33 53 37 37.

Ducey : **'Le Clapton'** - 18, rue du Génie - Tel (33) 2 33 48 16 64.
Granville :
    'La Citrouille' - 8, rue Saint Sauveur - Tel (33) 2 33 51 35 51.
    'Le Jupiter' - 3, rue des corsaires - Tel (33) 2 33 51 89 69.
    'Les Amiraux' - rue Fontaine Bedeau - Tel (33) 2 33 50 12 83.
    'The Welcome Pub' - 44, rue aux juifs - Tel (33) 2 33 50 13 70.
La Haye-du-Puits : **'Welcome'** - 1, avenue de Verdun - St Symphorien-le-Valois - Tel (33) 2 33 46 04 22.
Précey : **'Pub Montgomery'** - 39, route du Logis - Tel (33) 2 33 48 37 38.
Saint-Vaast-la-Hougue : **'L'Orastel'** - 13, quai Tourville - Tel (33) 2 33 20 12 23.
Tourlaville : **'Bar de la Place'** - 2, rue de Gaulle - Tel (33) 2 33 20 00 51.
Vains : **'La Boissonnerie de Saint-Léna'** - La Chaussée - Tel (33) 2 33 48 65 37.

AREA OF CALVADOS

Arromanches : **'The Mary Celeste'** - 5,rue René Michel - Tel (33) 2 31 21 51 19.
Bayeux : **'Loch'Ness Café'** - 67, rue Montfiquet - Tel (33) 2 31 51 71 71
Cabourg :
    'Le Pub' - 9, avenue de la Mer - Tel (33) 2 31 28 11 69.
    'Piano-Bar du Grand Hôtel' - en bord de mer. In this old and luxurious palace, otherwise frequented by Marcel Proust, you can discover the atmosphere of the Belle Epoque.
Caen :
    'The Glue Pot' - 18, quai Vendeuvre- opposite the Marina - Tel (33) 2 31 86 29 15. Air conditioning.
    'Why not ?' - 10, rue Buquet - Tel (33) 2 31 94 05 06.
    'Le Zinc' - 12, rue du Vaugueux - Tel (33) 2 31 93 20 30.
    'El Cubanito Café' - 12, avenue de la Libération - Tel (33) 2 31 94 34 16.

'O'Donnell's Irish Pub' - 20, quai Vendeuvre - Tel (33) 2 31 85 51 50. Traditional Irish gigs every Thursday.Happy hours : from 5 pm-7.30 pm Open every day.

'O'Zone Café' - 22, rue du 11 Novembre - Tel (33) 2 31 84 11 22.

'WPM' - 46, rue des Chanoines - Tel (33) 2 31 95 33 21.

'Apollon' - 16,rue Vangion - Tel (33) 2 31 93 00 82.

'Le Bodega' - 11, rue des Croisiers - Tel (33) 2 31 85 22 33.

'Le Dakota' - 54, rue de Bernières - Tel (33) 2 31 50 05 25.

'Le Notilus' - 56, rue d'Auge - Tel (33) 2 31 78 12 21.

'La Poterne' - 9,rue du Vaugueux - Tel (33) 2 31 93 57 46. Open from 6 pm-2.30 am.

'French Cafe' - 32, quai Vendeuvre - Tel (33) 2 31 50 10 02.

'At the Cafe' - 33, rue Basse - Tel (33) 2 31 94 71 65.

'Pub Concorde' - 7, rue Montoir Poissonnerie - Tel (33) 2 31 93 61 29.

'Le Tanaïs' - 40, boulevard des Allées - Tel (33) 2 31 85 79 87.

'Gibus Café' - 17 bis, rue des Tilleuls - Tel (33) 2 31 86 01 33.

Colleville-Montgomery : **'Le Club'** - Grande-Rue.

Courseulles-sur-Mer : **'Aux trois Matelots'** - Rue de la Marine - Tel (33) 2 31 97 53 13.

Deauville :

'Le Dundee's'. - Place Morny - Tel (33) 2 31 81 02 02.

'Brok Cafe' - 14, avenue du Général de Gaulle - Tel (33) 2 31 88 00 55.

'Chez Toit' - 94, avenue de la République - Tel (33) 2 31 14 88 85.

'Le 200' - 53, rue Désiré Le Hoc - Tel (33) 2 31 31 02 61.

Le **'Up and Down Cafe'** - 90, rue Eugène Colas - Tel (33) 2 31 87 47 47.

Douvres-la-Délivrande : **'The Cotton Pub'** - 4, rue Général de Gaulle - Tel (33) 2 31 37 38 39.

Honfleur :

'Le Lord' - 20, rue de la République - Tel (33) 2 31 89 12 22.

'Le Bounty's' - 25, boulevard Charles V - Tel (33) 2 31 89 03 20.

Lisieux :

'Le Retro' - 100, rue Henry-Chéron - Tel (33) 2 31 31 28 27.

'Le Français' - 3, place François Mittérand - Tel (33) 2 31 31 01 66.

'L'entract' Cafe' - 7bis, rue au Chat - Tel (33) 2 31 31 78 49.

'The Victoria' - 76, avenue Victor-Hugo - Tel (33) 2 31 62 11 13.

Mondeville :

'Manaïki Bar' - 2, rue Chapron - (near the Town Hall) - Tel (33) 2 31 52 06 03. *Open every evening.*

'Les Trois Brasseurs' - route de Paris - Tel (33) 2 31 35 49 49. Beer making. E.Mail : les3brasseurs@wanadoo.fr

Ouistreham- Riva-Bella : **'Le Sweety Loft'** - Route de Caen - Tel (33) 2 31 96 58 42.

Saint-Laurent-sur-Mer : **'D. Day House'** - 2, rue Désiré Lumière - Tel (33) 2 31 92 66 49.

Trouville-sur-Mer :
    'La Maison' - 66, rue des Bains - Tel (33) 2 31 81 43 10.
    'The Dickens' - 12, rue des Bains - Tel (33) 2 31 88 04 00.

Vire :
    'Le Shaman' - 7, rue Zimmermann - Tel (33) 2 31 67 12 42.

AREA OF ORNE

Alençon :
    'The Shetland' - 4, rue de la Halle aux Toiles - Tel (33) 2 33 26 05 39.
    'The Loch Ness' - 33, rue de Sarthe. - Tel (33) 2 33 29 01 83.

Argentan : ı**'Bentley's Pub'** - 22, boulevard Carnot - Tel (33) 2 33 67 20 01.

Flers :
    'Marmara Café' - 34, rue du Mont-Saint-Michel - Tel (33) 2 33 65 98 74.
    'Sédona Café' - 2, place Général de Gaulle - Tel (33) 2 33 65 49 90.

Mortagne-au-Perche : **'Le Caribou'** - 11, rue Ravenelles - Tel (33) 2 33 83 78 79. *A wink at our Canadian.*

Rai : **'The Clipper Pub'** - rue du Général Desticker - Tel (33) 2 33 24 30 31.

Sées: **'Le Baroque'** - 27, rue du Général Leclerc - Tel (33) 2 33 28 95 62.

Vimoutiers : **'Le Pub du Moulin'** - 8, route du Moulin - Tel (33) 2 33 67 03 08.

AREA OF EURE

Les Andelys : **'5e Avenue'** - quai de Seine - Tel (33) 2 32 21 92 63.

Bernay :
    'Piano-Bar' - 32, rue G.-Foloppe - *Cocktails, beers from round the world, billiards,... and concerts ! Open until 1 in the morning. Closed on Mondays.*
    'Jack's Pool' - 9, rue Lobrot - Tel (33) 2 32 45 55 92.
    'L'Autre Café' - 12, rue Gaston Foloppe - Tel (33) 2 32 44 95 73.

Brionne : **'Pub Saint-Denis'** - 6,rue Saint-Denis - Tel (33) 2 32 45 96 52.

Evreux : **'The London Pub Tavern'** - 8, rue Borville-Dupuis. *Open 7 days out of 7 until 1 am* - Tel (33) 2 32 38 07 00.

Ezy-sur-Eure : **'Black bird Pub'** - 15, rue Maurice-Elet - Tel (33) 2 37 64 64 64.

Louviers : **'The Butterfly'** - 16, rue des Quatre Moulins - Tel (33) 2 32 40 14 13.

Verneuil-sur-Avre : **'The Barn's Club'** - 182, rue de la Tour Grise - Tel (33) 2 32 32 39 87.

AREA OF SEINE-MARITIME

Bois-Guillaume : '**Bar-Cottage de la Bretèque**' - 2162, chemin de la Bretèque - Tel (33) 2 35 60 08 91.

Dieppe :
'**Le Régent**' - 160, Grande-Rue - Tel (33) 2 35 84 75 49.
'**l'Epsom**' - 11, boulevard de Verdun - Tel (33) 2 35 84 12 27.
'**The Scottish Pub**' - 14, rue Saint-Jacques - Tel (33) 2 35 84 13 16.

Etretat : '**The Highlander**' - 15, rue Adolphe-Boissaye - Tel (33) 2 35 27 04 46.

Fécamp : '**Pub Anglais**' - 93, rue de la Plage - Tel (33) 2 35 28 01 60.

Le Havre :
'**Beer and Billiard**' - 96, rue René-Coty - Tel (33) 2 35 42 44 88.
'**Les Capucines**' - 75, cours de la République - Tel (33) 2 35 26 61 71. Situated near the University, it is frequented by students.
'**Le King's**' - 58, rue de l'Abbé Herval - Tel (33) 2 35 41 38 63.
'**Le Plazza**' - 159, boulevard de Strasbourg - Tel (33) 2 35 43 04 28.
'**The Loft**' - Jardin de l'Hôtel de Ville - Tel (33) 2 35 22 40 84.
'**Funtime**' - 66, rue du Maréchal Galliéni - Tel (33) 2 35 42 31 71.
'**Actor Studio**' - 29, rue de l'Alma - Tel (33) 2 35 19 03 89.
'**Le Divin**' - 61, rue du Général Faidherbe - Tel (33) 2 35 42 52 58.
'**Del Rio Cafe**' - Espace Oscar Niemeyer - Tel (33) 2 35 43 35 55.
'**The night club**' - 71, rue du Général Faidherbe - Tel (33) 2 35 22 73 90.
'**Les Dunes**' - 48, rue Arthur-Honegger - Tel (33) 2 35 21 55 52.
'**The Black Horse**' - 71, rue Guillemard - Tel (33) 2 35 22 96 23.
'**The Pub**' - 68, rue Frédéric-Bellanger - Tel (33) 2 35 43 59 37.
'**Le Cap**' - Piano bar - quai Georges-V - Tel (33) 2 35 42 71 94.
'**The News**' - 101, rue de Paradis - Tel (33) 2 35 22 83 84.
Open every day from 8 am-9 pm, Friday and Saturday until 2 am. Bar with warm atmosphere where you can chat to friends and enjoy the setting.

Lillebonne : '**The Bridge Pub**' - 42, rue Victor-Hugo - Tel (33) 2 32 84 32 66.

Le Mesnil-Esnard : '**Le Neptune**' - 108, route de Paris - Tel (33) 2 35 80 19 44.

Pavilly : '**La Caravelle**' - 42, rue Delalandre - Tel (33) 2 35 92 77 46.

Rouen :
'**Au Glamour**' - 21, place Saint-Amand - Tel (33) 2 35 88 53 30.
'**Ibiza Club**' - 29, boulevard des Belges - Tel (33) 2 35 07 76 20.
'**Moon's Cafe**' - 4, rue Percière - Tel (33) 2 32 10 04 51.
'**La Luna**' - 26, rue Saint Etienne des Tonneliers - Tel (33) 2 35 88 77 18.
'**Le Double You**' - 16, quai Cavelier de la Salle - Tel (33) 2 35 73 04 99.
'**Le Jackson**' - 26, quai Gaston Boulet - Tel (33) 2 35 88 47 00.
'**Le Phil' Ing**' - 79, rue des Bons Enfants - Tel (33) 2 35 70 12 32.

'**Cocktails Bar**' - 23, place de la Basse Vieille Tour - Tel (33) 2 35 89 95 55.

'**Le Baccara** - 46 rue Buffon - Tel (33) 2 35 08 49 91.

'**L'Insolite**' - 58, rue d'Amiens - Tel (33) 2 35 88 62 53.

'**Bar Adelshoffen**' - 57, place du Vieux-Marché - Tel (33) 2 35 70 25 22.

'**Le Neptune**' - 1 bis, rue du Père Adam - Tel (33) 2 35 71 59 59.

'**The Big Ben Pub**' - 958, rue du Gros-Horloge - Tel (33) 2 35 88 44 50.

'**El Guevara Café**' - 31, rue des Bons-Enfants - Tel (33) 2 35 15 97 67.

'**Electro Spiral Pub**' - 50, rue Beauvoisine - Tel (33) 2 35 98 17 71.

'**Emporium Galorium**' - 151, rue Beauvoisine - Tel (33) 2 35 71 76 95.

'**Le Maceo**' - 28, rue Crevier - Tel (33) 2 35 07 47 35.

'**Le Swing**' - 17, boulevard de la Marne - Tel (33) 2 35 15 15 98.

'**Le Trio**' - 5, rue Ecuyère - Tel (33) 2 35 70 02 97.

'**Le Welcome**' - 32, rue des Augustins - Tel (33) 2 32 10 07 32.

'**Pub Alexander**' - 85, rue de Martainville - Tel (33) 2 35 71 33 57

'**Pub au Bureau**' - 2, place du Vieux-Marché - Tel (33) 2 35 98 68 69.

'**The underground Pub**' - 26, place des Champs-Maillets - Tel (33) 2 235 98 44 84.

'**The XXL Bar**' - 25, rue de la Savonnerie - Tel (33) 2 35 88 84 00.

Saint-Romain-de-Colbosc : '**Le Green**' - 2, rue de la République - Tel (33) 2 35 20 35 54.

Yvetot : '**The Macadam Cafe**' - av. du Maréchal Leclerc - Tel (33) 2 35 56 44 07.

American Bars

AREA OF SEINE-MARITIME

Rouen : '**L'Imprévu**' - 8, rue de l'ancienne Prison - Tel (33) 2 35 89 00 00. Open from 3 pm-2 am.

Country Cafes

AREA OF CALVADOS

Saint-Pierre-de-Mailloc : '**Le Saint-Pierre**' - Le Bourg - Tel (33) 2 31 63 11 93.

AREA OF EURE

Chauvincourt-Provemont : '**L'Escale**' - 6, rue de la Mairie - Tel (33) 2 32 55 82 60.

AREA OF SEINE-MARITIME

La Chapelle-sur-Dun : '**Le Champêtre**' - Tel (33) 2 35 57 08 34. Café, grocers and tobacco shop from yesteryear in a lovely building in the heart of a typically Caux village. Open every day from 7 am-9 pm except Wednesday afternoons.

Ermenouville : **'Café de la Paix'** - Tel (33) 2 35 97 96 24. Café, grocers and tobacco shop - A pleasant stop off with nice hospitality. Open every day from 7 am-9 pm.

Héricourt-en-Caux : **'Café de la Poste'** - Tel (33) 2 35 96 41 00. At the heart of a picturesque village, in a Norman setting, try a pancake with a cup of cider. Open every day, except Monday out of season.

Coffee and Tea Salons

AREA OF CALVADOS

Bayeux :
　'Au petit Duc' - 2, impasse Prud'homme - Tel (33) 2 31 92 95 09.
　'Café'inn' - 67, rue Saint-Martin - Tel (33) 2 31 21 11 37.

Beaufour :
　'Les Puces Gourmandes' - route de Dozulé - Tel (33) 2 31 65 12 91.

Caen :
　'Pâtisserie Stiffler' - 72, rue Saint-Jean - Tel (33) 2 31 86 08 94.
　'Pâtisserie Mésenge' - 153, rue Saint Pierre - Tel (33) 2 31 85 23 92.
　'Les Canotiers' - 143, rue Saint-Pierre - Tel (33) 2 31 50 24 51.
　'La Pastilla' - 3, rue Montoir Poissonnerie - Tel (33) 2 31 93 82 02.

Deauville :
　'Marybeth's' - 42, rue Hoche - Tel (33) 2 31 98 26 72
　'Haagen Dazs' - 43, rue Désiré - Le Hoc - Tel (33) 2 31 81 50 05.

Criquebœuf :
　'Manoir de la Poterie' - Chemin Paul-Ruel - Tel (33) 2 31 88 10 40.

Honfleur :
　'Espace Café' - 9, quai Lepaulenier - Tel (33) 2 31 89 18 19.
　'La Petite Chine' - 14, rue du Dauphin - Tel (33) 2 31 89 36 52.

Luc-sur-Mer :
　'La Digue' - 6, place du Petit-Enfer - Tel (33) 2 31 36 03 34.

Port-en-Bessin-Huppain :
　'Le Clipper' -12, quai Félix-Faure - Tel (33) 2 31 22 21 00.

Saint-Auin-sur-Mer :
　'La Coquille de Nacre' - 18, boulevard Léon-Favreau - Tel (33) 2 31 97 59 00.

Trouville-sur-Mer :
　'Le Vieux Normand' - 124, quai Moureaux - Tel (33) 2 31 88 38 79
　'Crêperie Bécassine' - 140, quai Moureaux.

AREA OF ORNE

Flers : **Pâtisserie Sautreuil** - 13, rue de Warminster - Tel (33) 2 33 65 01 27. Chocolates and ice cream - European Golden Laurels Award.

AREA OF EURE

Bernay : **'La Brûlerie'** - 12, rue Général de Gaulle - Tel (33) 2 32 46 47 74. Ground coffee from every origin. Tea and coffee salon. Closed Sunday and Monday.

Conches : **'Le Saint Jacques'** - 12, rue Saint Foy - Tel (33) 2 32 30 20 50.

Evreux : **'Camomille'** - 23, rue de Grenoble - Tel (33) 2 32 38 30 90.

Pont-Audemer : **'L'Echaudière'** - 12, place de l'Hôtel de Ville - Tel (33) 2 32 41 46 21.

Val-de-Reuil : **'Agri' -** Place des Quatre Saisons - Tel (33) 2 32 61 22 40.

AREA OF SEINE-MARITIME

Canteleu : **'Ozen Mahmut'** - 14, rue Alexandre-Dumas - Tel (33) 2 35 36 28 64.

Dieppe : **'La Coupole'** - 106, Grande-Rue - Tel (33) 2 35 84 65 85.

Eu :
    'Bardoux Mondie' - 40, rue Charles-Morin - Tel (33) 2 35 50 75 55.
    'Le Bragance' - Parc du Château- in the ancient royal cold rooms - Tel (33) 2 35 50 20 01.

Le Havre : **'Côté Jardin'** - 9, place de l'Hôtel-de-Ville - Tel (33) 2 35 43 43 04.

Mont-Saint-Aignan : **'Le viennois'** - 32, place Colbert - Tel (33) 2 32 10 34 28.

Rouen :
    'Vieux Carré' - 34 rue de la Gastine - Tel (33) 2 35 71 67 70
    'Marianne' - 6, rue du Massacre - Tel (33) 2 35 89 33 36.
    'On Shanti - 66, rue de Fontenelles - Tel (33) 2 35 07 51 33.
    'Dame Cakes' - 70, rue Saint Romain - Tel (33) 2 35 98 14 77.
    'Le Strudel' - 18, rue Petit-de-Julleville (in the centre, near the Cathedral) - Tel (33) 2 35 15 58 26.
    'Maud et Dinette' - 20, place du Vieux-Marché - Tel (33) 2 35 15 96 22.
    'Pain, Amour et Fantaisie' - 25, rue Cauchoise - Tel (33) 2 35 07 52 74.
    'Thé Majuscule' - 8, place Calende - Tel (33) 2 35 71 15 66.
    'Aux caprices' - 7, place des Emmurés - Tel (33) 2 35 73 49 36.
    'Chez la Mère Michel' - 33, rue des Carmes - Tel (33) 2 35 89 47 57.
    'The Five O'Clock' - 243, rue Eau-de-Robec - Tel (33) 2 35 88 41 18.

Saint-Valery-en-Caux :
    'Dorine' - 14, place de la Chapelle - Tel (33) 2 35 97 03 20.

Veules-les-Roses :
    'Un Jour d'Eté' - 25, rue Victor-Hugo - Tel (33) 2 35 97 23 17.
    'Le Tropical' - 3, place Mélingue - Tel (33) 2 35 57 17 36.

Casinos

English friends, you sometimes think twice about going into a casino because you think it is reserved for members only. In France it is not so, you can enter and play if you are 18 or over..

AREA OF MANCHE

Agon-Coutainville : **'Casino de Coutainville'** - 1, avenue du Président-Roosevelt. Tel (33) 2 33 47 06 88. One armed bandits - boule - piano bar.

Cherbourg-Octeville : **'Casino de Cherbourg'** - 6, rue Biard - (in centre near Town Court) - Tel (33) 2 33 43 00 56. Establishment recently renovated. Boule - one armed bandits - pub - discotheque.

Granville : **'Casino-club'** - 1, place du Maréchal Foch - Tel (33) 2 33 50 00 79. On the sea front… Boule - Black Jack - One armed bandits - roulette.

Saint-Pair-sur-Mer : **'Casino de Saint-Pair'** - 2, rue de la Plage - Tel (33) 2 33 91 34 00.

AREA OF CALVADOS

Cabourg : **'Casino'** - Promenade Marcel-Proust (on the sea front). Tel (33) 2 31 28 19 19. One armed bandits - Bar - Discotheque - Club - Gambling saloon : boule - English and French Roulette - Black-Jack - Baccarat - Stud Poker - Banco - Chemin de fer.

Deauville : **'Casino Barrière'** - 2, rue Edmond-Blanc - Tel (33) 2 31 14 31 14. In sumptuous decor, the most well known of French Casinos: boule - baccarat - banco - English and French Roulette - 30/40 - Black-Jack - Chemin de fer… 325 One armed bandits ! - Salons able to take up to 1000 people. Night club - Music Hall - Cinema.

Houlgate : **'Casino'** - 41, rue Henri-Dobert - Tel (33) 2 31 28 75 75. Boule - Vidéo-Bar every evening except Monday and Tuesday - Discothèque 'Le Wilys' - 30 one armed bandits open every day from 11 am-2 am. (Closed 3 am at the weekend and holidays).

Luc-sur-Mer : **'Casino'** - Rue Guynemer (bord de mer) - Tel 02 31 97 32 19. English -Roulette - Black-Jack - Boule - 104 one armed bandits - Discotheque - Piano bar - Terrace pointed towards seafront.

Ouistreham : **'Casino Barrière'** **'Le Queen Normandy'** - 51, place Alfred-Thomas (bord de mer) - Tel (33) 2 31 36 30 00. 130 one armed bandits - Boule - Billiards - 2 Bars - Discotheque.

Saint-Aubin-sur-Mer : **'Casino de Saint-Aubin'** - 128, rue Pasteur - Tel (33) 2 31 96 78 82. One armed bandits - Boule - Discotheque - Piano - Bar - Cinema - Club.

Trouville-sur-Mer : **'Casino Barrière'** - 1, place Foch - Tel (33) 2 31 87 75 00. 200 one armed bandits! English and French roulettee - craps - Punto Blanco -

Black-Jack - Boule - Stud Poker - Bars - Shows, Concerts, Discotheques, Cinemas… Open every day at 10 am.

Villers-sur-Mer : **'Casino de Villers'** - 4, place Lieutenant Fanneau - Tel (33) 2 31 14 44 88.- 50 one armed bandits - Boule - Piano-Bar - Cinema.

AREA OF ORNE

Bagnoles-de-l'Orne : **'Casino du Lac'** - 6, avenue Robert-Cousin - Tel (33) 2 33 37 84 00. - 80 one armed bandits - Boule - English and French Roulette Cinema - Terraces overlooking the lake.

AREA OF SEINE-MARITIME

Dieppe : **'Casino'** - 3, boulevard de Verdun - Tel (33) 2 32 14 48 00. Panorama overlooking the sea. One armed bandits - Boule - Roulette - Baccara - Banque - Chemin de fer - Black-Jack.

Etretat : **'Casino'** - Tel (33) 2 35 28 01 06 or (33) 2 35 28 55 21 - *23* one armed bandits - Boule.

Fécamp : **'Casino'** - Tel (33) 2 35 27 47 61. One armed bandits - Boule.

Forges-les-Eaux : **'Casino'** - Avenue des Sources - Tel (33) 2 32 89 50 50. 230 one armed bandits ! - Boule - Roulette - Baccara - Black-Jack.

Saint-Valery-en-Caux : **'Casino'** - Le Perrey (on the sea front) - Tel (33) 2 35 57 84 10. Open every day. One armed bandits - Boule - Bar - Discotheque - Cinéma - Orchestra - Karaoke - Piano-Bar.

Le Tréport : **'Casino'** - Esplanade Aragon - Tel (33) 2 35 86 35 45. One armed bandits - Boule - Billiard - Bowling - Cinema- Discotheque.

Veules-les-Roses : **'Casino'** - 1, place Mélingue - Tel (33) 2 35 97 64 33.

Veulettes-sur-Mer : **'Casino'** - Tel (33) 2 35 57 93 00. One armed bandits - Black-Jack - Roulette - Boule - Open all year round from 11 am-4 am.

Yport : **'Casino'** - Promenade Roger-Desnouet - Tel (33) 2 35 28 77 36. Boule.

Discotheques - Dancings

AREA OF MANCHE

Angoville-sur-Ay : **'La Campagnette'** - Tel (33) 2 33 46 01 92.

Barfleur : **'La Mora II'** - 14, rue Saint-Nicolas - Tel (33) 2 33 20 31 97.

Barneville-Carteret : **'Le Barnevill's'** - 33, boulevard des Ecrehous - Tel (33) 2 33 04 46 46.

Baudre : 'Le Milton' - La Renaumière - Tel (33) 2 33 05 08 88.

Bréville-sur-Mer : 'Le Kepler Club Retro' - 2, route de la Mer - Tel (33) 2 33 51 23 04.

Brix : 'Aston Club' - Le Mont à la Quesne - Tel (33) 2 33 41 99 69.

Cherbourg-Octeville : 'L'Amirauté' - 18, quai Alexandre III - Tel (33) 2 33 43 00 56.

Cherbourg-Octeville (Village of *La Glacerie*) *:* 'Le Vince's Club' - 18, rue Larsonneur - Tel (33) 2 33 20 50 62.

Giéville : 'L'Echo du Lac' - La Grandville - Tel (33) 2 33 55 89 46.

Gouberville : 'Key Largo' - 1, Le Bas de la Rue - Tel (33) 2 33 43 90 70.

Granville : 'George's Pub' - 3, rue des Corsaires - Tel (33) 2 33 51 89 69.

Gratot : 'La Soifferie' - 117, rue d'Argouge - Tel (33) 2 33 47 88 34.

Hambye : 'L'Apocalypse' - 10, route des 4 sapins - Tel (33) 2 33 51 20 13.

Lessay : 'Le Gipsy» - 59, route des Marais - Tel (33) 2 33 46 30 07.

Poilley : 'Le Moulin' - Moulin de Quincampoix - Tel (33) 2 33 48 53 91.

Quineville : 'Le Moulin Normand' - 34, route de Gougins - Tel: (33) 2 33 21 43 20.

Saint-Hilaire-du-Harcouët : 'La Taverne' - La Croix de l'Epine - Tel (33) 2 33 49 13 59.

Saint-Jean-de-la-Rivière : 'Le Kissing' - 'La Bamba' - 3, route de Barneville-Portbail - Tel (33) 2 33 04 63 27.

Saint-Lô : 'Le Sunset Club' - 2, rue des Fossés - Tel (33) 2 33 05 13 60.

Saint-Patrice-de-Claids : 'Le Sixties Dance' - 2, La Quesnerie - Tel (33) 2 33 47 77 69.

Saint-Vaast-la-Hougue : 'L'Orastel' - 13, quai Tourville - Tel (33) 2 33 20 12 23.

Tanis : 'La Bodéga' - 4, rue Rouvre - Tel (33) 2 33 48 17 94.

Teurtheville-Hague : 'Le Tin Open' - Le Pont Chauvin - Tel (33) 2 33 53 53 77.

Vaudrimesnil : 'Le Moonlight' - 11, rue des landes - Tel (33) 2 33 07 22 91.

Ver : 'L'Agrion' - 'Le Moulin' - Tel (33) 2 33 51 99 40.

AREA OF CALVADOS

Blonville-sur-Mer : 'Les Planches' - Les Longs-Champs - Tel(33) 2 31 87 58 09.

Bretteville-l'Orgueilleuse : 'Le Mirage 2000' - 86, route de Bayeux - Tel (33) 2 31 80 06 06.

Caen :

'Euro Caen' - 10, place du 36ème Régiment d'Infanterie - Tel (33) 2 31 83 68 11.
'Le Carré new Club' - 32 bis, quai Vendeuvre - Tel (33) 2 31 38 90 90. Open every day except Mondays from 10 pm-5 am - 'navy' atmosphere.

'**Le Chic**' - 19, rue des Prairies Saint-Gilles - Tel (33) 2 31 94 48 72.

'**Le Venois**' - 69, avenue Henry-Chéron - Tel (33) 2 31 73 32 80.

Cabourg : '**Casino**' - alongside the sea - Tel (33) 2 31 28 19 21.

Courseulles-sur-Mer : '**Le Galaxy**' - Avenue de la Combattante - Tel (33) 2 31 37 48 40. Open Friday and Saturday from 11 pm.

Deauville :

'**Chabada**' -13, rue Albert-Fracasse - Tel (33) 2 31 88 40 50

'**Y Club**' - 14 bis, rue Désiré Le Hoc - Tel (33) 2 31 88 30 91. Open every evening - Proper dress expected.

'**Régine's Club**' - rue Edmond-Blanc - Tel (33) 2 31 88 07 21. One of the most 'in' places in Normandy.

Dives-sur-Mer : '**Le Tango Dancing**' - 42, rue de Gaulle - Tel (33) 2 31 91 28 81.

Etreham : '**Club Ramsès**' - route de Port-en-Bessin - Tel (33) 2 31 92 67 40.

Heurtevent (Near Livarot) : '**Le Laser Night**' - Les Vannes - Tel (33) 2 31 32 83 38.

Jurques : '**Le Monaco**' - Migny - Tel (33) 2 31 77 35 46.

Lisieux : '**Club 98**' - 131, rue Henry-Chéron - Tel (33) 2 31 61 07 07.

Hérouville-Saint-Clair (near Caen) : '**La Mare au Diable**' - 214, rue Verte - Tel (33) 2 31 44 02 07.

Merville-Franceville-Plage : '**La Noche**' - Route de Cabourg - Tel (33) 2 31 24 22 95.

Perrières : '**Le Lagon Bleu**' - On the rocks - Tel (33) 2 31 40 10 97.

Ouistreham :

'**Le Cercle**' - Casino - Place A-Thomas - Tel (33) 2 31 36 30 00.

'**Le Ferry Night**' - 6-7-8 rue Pasteur - Tel (33) 2 31 97 19 22.

Every Saturday with retro band. Every Sunday afternoon during high season, tea dance. Every Tuesday and Friday during high season : aperitif and dancing from 6-10 pm.

Pont-l'Evêque : '**Le Festival**' - Route de Rouen - Tel (33) 2 31 64 35 94.

Saint Martain aux Chartrains : '**Le Paradis Bleu**' - Hameau Ponchains - Tel (33) 2 31 65 49 97.

Subles (prés de Bayeux) : '**L'Aurore**' - Route de Saint-Lô - Le Bas de Subles - Tel (33) 2 31 92 64 33.

Vauville : '**Le Moulin**' - Cour de Vauville - Tel (33) 2 31 81 38 38.

Vire :

'**Far West Discothèque**' - 79, avenue de la Gare - Tel (33) 2 31 68 91 51.

'**Le Tiffany**' - Vanvie - Tel (33) 2 31 68 62 27.

AREA OF ORNE

L'Aigle : 'Le Moulin d'Antan' - 35, rue des Jetées - Tel (33) 2 33 24 55 24.

Alençon : 'L'Arc-en-Ciel' - 11, rue de la Halle aux Toiles - Tel (33) 2 33 26 32 15. Open every evening from Wednesday. Something for everybody's taste and all sorts of music. Nice atmosphere and staff.

Alménèches : 'Tub Discothèque' - Saint-Hippolyte - Tel (33) 2 33 35 78 54.

Antoigny (near Bagnoles-de-l'Orne) : 'La Vallée de la Cour' - Tel (33) 2 33 37 27 72.

Bagnoles de l'Orne : 'Le Privé' - 6, avenue Robert Cousin - Tel (33) 2 33 37 84 30.

Batilly : 'L'Eclipse' - Route de Flers - Tel (33) 2 33 35 43 40.

La Ferté-Macé : 'Cap'Orne' - Route de Domfront - Tel (33) 2 33 37 62 32.

Flers : 'All Access' - 3, rue de la Chaussée - Tel (33) 2 33 64 83 07.

Livaie (près d'Alençon) : 'Le Lipstick' - Le Bourg - Tel (33) 2 33 27 98 43. Open Fridays, Saturdays and the day before holidays from 10.30 pm-4 am. Pleasant décor and relaxed atmosphere for an excellent evening with friends.

Montchevrel : 'Le Tempo' - La Croix - Tel (33) 2 33 28 93 93.

Saint-Germain-du-Corbeis (near Alençon) : 'Le Saint-Germain' - 5, rue du Général Leclerc - Tel (33) 2 33 26 25 19. Inhabitants call it the 'si..nge' (mon..key) 'In' Alençon discotheque.

Saint-Michel-Thubeuf : 'La Mare' - Le Lesme - Tel (33) 2 33 24 54 29.

Sérans : 'Le Saint-Georges' - Le Mesnil-Glaise - Tel (33) 2 33 67 25 94.

Urou et Crennes (near Argentan) : 'Le Monopol' - Route Nationale in the direction of Paris - Tel (33) 2 33 36 91 03.

AREA OF EURE

Avrilly : 'L'Escapade' - 6, rue Bordes - Tel (33) 2 32 67 41 90.

Les Baux-Sainte-Croix : 'Club Saint-Hubert' - 79, rue des Petits-Baux. - Tel (33) 2 32 67 84 96.

Beaumesnil : 'Baraba's Club' - 3, route de la Ferrière-sur-Risle - Tel (33) 2 32 44 45 02.

Bernay : 'Le France' - Le Bois d'Alençon - Tel (33) 2 32 43 12 21.

Bourneville : 'The Black Bottom' - Mairie - Tel (33) 2 32 57 49 13.

Chavigny-Bailleul : 'Le Sweet' - 2, route Fleurie - Tel (33) 2 32 30 28 75.

Colletot : 'Le Campbell Club' - La Mare Colletot - Tel (33) 2 32 42 71 97.

Coudray : 'Le Lagon Bleu II' - 39, rue de la Mairie - Tel (33) 2 32 55 80 02.

Etrepagny : 'Château de la Broche' - au hameau de la Broche - Tel (33) 2 32 55 77 10.

Ecardenville-la-Campagne : 'Le Trianon Club' - 28, rue Parissot - Tel (33) 2 32 35 11 92.

Evreux :
    'Le New World' - 15, boulevard De Normandie - Tel (33) 2 32 62 36 43.
    'Le Winston' - 33, avenue Winston-Churchill - Tel (33) 2 32 31 17 00.

Igoville : **'Le Pim's'** - 24, rue du 8 Mai 1945 - Tel (33) 2 35 123 02 56.

Le Chêne : **'Le Cristy'** - 25, route de Breteuil - Tel (33) 2 32 29 82 72.

Le Mesnil Jourdain : **'Les Templiers'** - RN 154 - Tel (33) 2 32 40 63 74.

Le Sacq : **'Le Pirate'** - 2, rue du Dolmen - Tel (33) 2 32 34 52 80.

Merey : **'Le Moulin de Merey'** - 11, rue de Neuilly - Tel (33) 2 32 26 08 50.

Saint-Ouen-de-Thouberville : **'Club 83'** - Hameau chouque - Tel (33) 2 35 18 03 08.

Saint-Germain-Village : **'Boccacio Life'** - 79, route de Lisieux - Tel (33) 2 32 42 31 44.

Sainte-Marthe : **'La Belle Epoque'** - 8, place de la Mairie - Tel (33) 2 32 30 02 38.

Thiberville : **'Loca Son Music and Light'** - 3, rue de Lisieux - Tel (33) 2 32 46 17 11.

Vernon : **'Le Moulin Vert'** - Quai Caméré - Tel 02 32 51 03 61.

Vitot : **'Le New Kheops'** - Chemin de la Porte-Verte - Tel (33) 2 32 35 70 88.

AREA OF SEINE-MARITIME

Auzebosc : **'Le Nautilus'** - Le Bourg - Tel (33) 2 35 56 81 11

Cauville sur Mer : **'Le Marina'** - RD 940 - Tel (33) 2 35 30 58 80.

Derchigny-Graincourt : **'Sloogi'** - 27, route de Dieppe - Tel (33) 2 35 83 62 97.

Foucart : **'Feeling'** - La Gare - Tel (33) 2 32 70 48 13.

Le Havre :
    'Le Cap' - Le Cap - 182, quai Georges-V - Tel (33) 2 35 21 15 36.
    'Lalexia club' - 26, rue Georges-Heuillard - Tel (33) 2 35 21 28 70. For people liking a 'young' evening. Free entry for girls until midnight.
    'Le Floston' - 34, rue Eugène Mopin - Tel (33) 2 35 51 41 17.
    'Le Siècle'- 17, rue des Magasins Généraux - Tel (33) 2 35 24 55 67. Special evening with themes - Decor and nice hospitality - Free entry for girls before midnight.

Le Hanouard : **'Le Calypso'** - Les Trois Colombiers - Tel (33) 2 35 96 93 25.

Grémonville : **'L'Excalibur'** - Bois Saint-Jacques - Tel (33) 2 35 56 01 34.

Gournay-en-Bray : **'Cesar's'** - Les Bruyères - Tel (33) 2 35 90 01 51.

Merey : **'Le Moulin de Merey'** - 11, rue Neuilly - Tel (33) 2 32 26 08 50. Karaoké.

Neufchâtel-en-Bray : **Dancing municipal** - rue Baron d'Haussez - Tel (33) 2 35 94 53 33.

Le Petit-Quevilly : **'Exo 7'** - 13, Place des Chartreux - Tel (33) 2 35 03 32 30.

Oudalle : **'Le Zénith'** - route de la vallée d'Oudalle - Tel (33) 2 35 20 00 28.

Rouen :
- **'Ibiza Club'** - 29, boulevard des Belges- Tel (33) 2 35 07 76 20. Karaoké - open until 5 am in the morning.
- **'Le Traxx'** - 4 bis, boulevard Ferdinand-de Lesseps - Tel (33) 2 32 10 07 80.
- **'KU'** - 2, rue Malherbe - Tel (33) 2 35 03 29 36.
- **'XXL'** - 25, rue de la Savonnerie - Tel (33) 2 35 88 84 00.
- **'Le New Boy'** - 16, avenue de Bretagne - Tel (33) 2 35 03 29 36.
- **'Le Coconut's'** - 9, rue de Malherbe - Tel (33) 2 35 73 45 88.
- **'L'Euro Club 76'** - 5, rue de la Tour - Tel (33) 2 35 89 64 01
- **'Le Kiosque'** - 43 C, boulevard de Verdun - Tel (33) 2 35 88 54 50.
- **'Le Smart'** - 66, route de Bonsecours - Tel (33) 2 35 71 12 18.
- **'La Luna'** 26 rue Etienne-des-Tonneliers - Tel (33) 2 35 88 77 18
- **'La Bohême'** - 12, place Saint-Amand - Tel (33) 2 35 71 53 99.

Roumare : **'La Brocherie'**- hameau Saint-Thomas - Tel (33) 2 35 33 14 14.

Roncheville-en-Bray : **'Le Jack'** - Mont Dugars - Tel (33) 2 35 90 66 87.

La Rue-Saint-Pierre : **'Keetch Coco'** - Le Village - Tel (33) 2 35 34 90 58.

Saint-Adrien : **'Le Moulin Rose'** - 68, route de Paris - Tel (33) 2 35 23 71 19.

Saint-Arnoult : **'L'Abreuvoir'** - La Croix Blanche - Tel (33) 2 35 56 09 19.'

Sept-Meules : **'Le Millénaire'** - 16, rue de Normandie - Tel (33) 2 35 50 87 09.

Saint-Pierre-lès-Elbeuf : **'L'Hacienda'** - 247, chemin de Halage - Tel (33) 2 35 81 05 34.

Sainte-Marie-des-Champs *(near Yvetot) :* **'Le Must'** - Rue Renard - Tel (33) 2 35 56 92 04.

Veules-les-Roses : **'Beach Club'** - 1, place Mélingue - Tel (33) 2 35 97 64 33.

Country Cafe with Music
Dancing and concerts

AREA OF MANCHE

Régneville-sur-Mer : **Music Bar 'Le Jules Gommes'** - 34, rue Vaurredoux - Tel (33) 2 33 45 32 04

AREA OF CALVADOS

Amayé-sur-Orne : **'Guinguette du Pont du Coudray'** - Le Pont du Coudray - Tel (33) 2 31 80 53 55. - Dancing, music on Sunday afternoons and evenings, with dinner dances on Saturdays and Sundays.

Cabourg : **'Thé Dansant'** - Orchestra on Sunday afternoon in the grand Casino.

Clécy : **'Au Fil de l'Eau'** - La Cambronnerie - Cafe with music and dancing - on Sunday afternoons from Easter until autumn - Tel (33) 2 31 69 71 13

Ouilly-le-Vicomte (près de Lisieux) : **'Le Chaudron Magik'** - 3, route de Deauville - Tel (33) 2 31 32 32. - Dinner dance with floor show.

Hérouville : **'Big Band Cafe'** - 1, avenue Haut Crépon - Rond point du Drakkar, behind the foundry - Tel (33) 2 31 47 96 13. Every Tuesday evening : rock concerts, blues, jazz.

Pont-d'Ouilly : **Musical Intertainement** - Every Sunday afternoon and holidays from the end of May to mid September on the banks of the Orne - Tel (33) 2 31 69 80 20. (Mairie)

Touques : **'Le Stephen'** - Route de Paris - Tel (33) 2 31 81 96 78 - Show with singer, transformists.

AREA OF ORNE

Alençon : **'La Luciole'** - 171, avenue de Bretagne - Two concerts every week : rock, jazz, modern music. Tel (33) 2 33 32 83 33

Bagnoles-de-l'Orne : **Casino du Lac** - Dancing with orchestra, tea dance on Sunday afternoons - Show, music hall.

AREA OF EURE

Amfreville-sous-les-Monts : **Guinguette 'Chez Dédé'** - Tel (33) 2 32 49 80 06. Go to the banks of the Seine, near the locks. For the time of an afternoon or of an evening to the accompaniment of an accordion you can relive the atmosphere of the Norman guinguettes which were so dear to Maupassant. Open all year round, except for January, every day except for Tuesdays. Matinee dance on Sunday and Thursday afternoons. Evening dance on Saturdays.

Jouy-sur-Eure : **'La Guinguette'** - 49, rue de l'Ancienne Abbaye - Tel (33) 2 32 36 18 99.

Louviers : **'Le Romantica'** - 8, rue François-le Camus - Tel (33) 2 32 50 45 83. E.Mail : www.tassili-romantica.com

AREA OF SEINE-MARITIME

Le Hanouard : **'Le Calypso'** - Les Trois Colombiers - Tel (33) 2 35 96 93 25. Dinner dances - Special evenings.

Le Havre :

'L'Agora' - Espace Oscar-Niemeyer. - Tel (33) 2 32 74 09 70. Café with music - contemporary music on stage.

'Le Music Bar' - 28, rue François-Arago - Tel (33) 2 35 53 14 59. This little bar out on the limb in the Eure quarter attracts amateur music lovers from the town centre with its reggae, ska, dub, music of the 70's, and groups from le Havre and elsewhere. They are given the same hospitality as are the clients. Open until 2 am in the morning.

'The BlackHorse' - 71, rue Guillemard - Tel (33) 2 35 22 96 93. In times gone by sailors called this the 'Street of Thirst'. Concerts and pleasant atmosphere Open every day from 6 pm-2 am.

'Le Brazil Café' - 78, rue Voltaire - Tel (33) 2 35 21 02 21. Concerts, French and foreign varieties.

'Le Camp Gourou' - 163, rue Victor-Hugo - Tel (33) 2 35 22 00 92. Music... house cocktails, all in a happy atmosphere Open in the evening, closed on Mondays.

'Couleur Café' - 1, rue des Gobelins - Tel (33) 2 35 21 38 84. Concerts. Open every day except Sundays from 6 pm-2 am.

'Le Havana Café' - 173, rue Victor-Hugo - Tel (33) 2 35 42 35 77. Open from Tuesday to Saturday from 6-10 pm. - Initiation to salsa.

'L'Hermès' - 348, rue Aristide-Briand - Tel (33) 2 35 24 35 84. This establishment is a part of Le Havre's 'institutions' Small rock concerts. Open every day except Tuesdays from 5 pm-2 am.

'Le Transept' - 77, rue Guillemard - Tel (33) 2 35 42 11 51. Pop music in an intimate decor.

'Le Crocus' - 67, rue Jules-Tellier - Tel (33) 2 35 53 25 96. Meal with show - Café-théâtre.

Gonneville-la-Mallet (near Le Havre) : **'Auberge le Canotier'** - Rue Faidherbe -Tel (33) 2 35 55 97 89.

Rouen :

'Les Caradas' - 64, rue de Fontenelle - Tel (33) 2 35 98 04 74.

XII - SPORT AND LEISURE IN NORMANDY

The coastal regions and the interior

Whether it is for a weekend or for the main holidays, Normandy offers to the enthusiast a rich palette of physical, sportive or leisure activities. At the seaside or inland, activities in the open air or inside, the choice is vast depending on your interests. Strong in its rich natural heritage, Normandy offers magnificent places and countryside to discover for everyone enjoying their favourite pastimes.

On foot, on horseback, by bike, on the sea or in the air, multiple activities are offered across the five areas. There are numerous seaside resorts, where one can enjoy all the sea sports along the 600 kilometres of coast that Normandy offers, from Le Tréport to Mont-Saint-Michel.

The companies, the sporting and cultural associations, the sports centres, the leisure centres, the open air bases… will allow you to organise and to practise to the best your favourite leisure and sports activities.

1 - Excursions, walks and hiking

For short or long expeditions, whether you are walkers, riders or cycle tourists, Normandy offers the possibility of discovering the Norman countryside in the rhythm and pattern of your wishes. Normandy has an important network of itineraries (roads and little byways) on the thousands of kilometres of pathways (around 5,000 kilometres) and tours are waiting for you.

Ideal for the family, the tours and excursions of an hour or a day or even trips or expeditions of several days which are organised by the professionals.

On foot, thousands of kilometres of sign-posted paths criss-cross the regions and allow the discovery of the magnificent Norman countryside at your chosen pace. Many paths, registered by the 'Fédération Française de Randonnée Pédestre' (F.F.R.P.), offer major itineraries or short circular tours, for excursions going from some hours to a full day or even trips lasting for a weekend or several days.

The long distance paths, called 'GR' ('Grandes Randonnées'), are national itineraries, often linear, and sign-posted. The long distance paths of the region, GRP ('Grandes Randonnées de Pays'), are for themselves regional itineraries and are also sign-posted. The smaller walks and excursions, equally signposted and in a circle, are family tours and make perfect walks of an hour or a day.

In Practice : all the itineraries are described in the topograpgical guides with routes marked on the 'IGN' (National Geographical Institute) maps and are sold in bookshops, newsagents, information offices : Tourist Offices.

Themed tours to see a special site or even nature trips to discover the fauna and flora are also organised by the different departments.

The Natural Regional Park of 'Normandy-Maine', the associations for the protection of nature and the National Forestry Office, offer nature excursions from April to October. For Information : 'Parc Naturel Régional Normandie-Maine, Maison du Parc' - B.P. 5 - 61320 Carrouges. Tel (33) 2 33 81 75 75.

Useful addresses : 'Comité Départemental du Tourisme de l'Orne', 88, rue Saint-Blaise - B.P. 50 - 61002 Alençon Cedex. Tel (33) 2 33 28 88 71 - Fax (33) 2 33 29 81 60. E.mail : orne.tourisme@wanadoo.fr

Equally **in Orne** discover the grandiose sites of the 'Suisse Normande' and the Valley of the Orne. The excursions will allow you to see from east to west the massive forest areas of Ecouves and Andaines and the spa centre of Bagnoles-de-l'Orne. A place to also visit is the world renowned National Stud of Pin ('Haras national du Pin'). Useful addresses : The Departmental Committee for Walking Tours ('Comité Départemental de Randonnée Pédestre'), 2, rue René-Fonk, 61000 Alençon. Tel (33) 2 33 29 33 74. Other information is available from Tourist Offices, Information Centres and Walking Associations.

In Manche, from the Bay of Mont-Saint-Michel to the Bay of Veys by the roads which criss-cross the regions of Mortain, Coutance, the Valley of the Vire and the Natural Regional Park of the Marshes of the Cotentin and Bessin, numerous itineraries will allow you to discover the multiple country-sides of the area.

Places to see...

'Le Chemin de Halage sur les Bords de la Vire' (The towpath on the banks of the Vire). Accessible to walkers, riders and cross-country bikers... Trips over more than 40 kilometres.

'Le Sentier littoral' (the coastal path). Created over around 230 kilometres, it follows the route of the customs officers. Places to see : the Bay of Mont-Saint-Michel, the Cape of Carteret, La Hague... on foot, by horse or on a bike.

The region of Mortain through the ancient railway tracks made into walking paths.

'Les Chemins aux Anglais' (The paths of the English). Mont-Saint-Michel was in earlier times one of the great centres of pilgrimage for Christianity. The 'Miquelots' the name given to the pilgrims travelling to the feet of the Archangel, came from the Kingdom of France, from England, from Germany, from Italy... The paths cross the region of La Manche from England to Mont-Saint-Michel. In total, almost 400 kilometres of paths and little country roads to discover the countryside and legends of (La Manche), its inherited riches which testify to the passage of the 'Miquelots'.

Useful addresses : For all information concerning walking tours, events, guided visits, commentaries… contact the 'Comité Départemental de la Randonnée de la Manche', Maison du Département, Route de Villedieu - 50008 Saint-Lô Cedex. Tel (33) 2 33 05 98 70 - Fax (33) 2 33 56 07 03. E.mail : manchetourisme@cg50.fr

In Calvados, 'Pays d'Auge', 'Suisse Normande', 'Pays de Falaise', 'Bocage Virois'…

Places to see…

Discovery walks from the (Centre Permanent d'Initiation à l'Environnement) (CPIE).

Itineraries presented on site by information panels. Leaflets and topographical guides available from CPIE, 'Vallée de l'Orne', Hôtel de Ville de Caen.

Tel (33) 2 31 30 43 27 - Fax (33) 2 31 30 43 45.

Useful address : 'Comité Départemental de Tourisme du Calvados', place du Canada - 14000 Caen. Tel (33) 2 31 27 90 30 - Fax (33) 2 31 27 90 35. E.mail : calvatour@mail-cpod.fr

In Upper Normandy, and more precisely **in Eure**, set off to discover the valleys and forests.

Useful address : 'Comité Départemental de Tourisme de l'Eure', boulevard Georges-Chauvin, B.P. 367 - 27003 Evreux Cedex. Tel (33) 2 32 62 04 27 - Fax (33) 2 32 31 05 98. E.mail : CDT-EURE@wanadoo.fr

In Seine-Maritime, 'Côte d'Albâtre', 'Pays de Caux', 'Vallée de la Seine', 'Pays de Bray', 'Parc Naturel Régional de Brotonne'.

Useful address : 'Comité Départemental de Tourisme de la Seine-Maritime', 6, rue Couronné - B.P. 60 - 76420 Bihorel. Tel (33) 2 35 12 10 10 - Fax (33) 2 35 59 86 04. E.mail : seine.maritime@wanadoo.fr

Health and orientation tracks. To stay fit during the holidays and discover the woods and forests, alone or in a group, the health routes with tracks including various obstacles or the orientation courses with itineraries marked on maps are also offered in all the Norman areas.

On a bike, whether you are cycle tourists or cross country bikers, the routes are effectively the same except for the possible length of the trips. Arrowed tourist routes have been specially conceived and selected for the interest of the places and countryside that they cross. These cycle routes (veloroutes), (circular tours each of about 20 kilometres) or cycle discoveries (cyclo-découvertes), (trips of 20 to 30 kilometres accompanied and at a moderate speed) propose itineraries away from major roads. These are permanent tracks, allowing on the way, the 'tour' of the regions.

For information : Contact the 'Comités Départementaux de Tourisme'.

Something to do in **South Manche, 'Vélo-route'** 'the tour of the lakes', the lakes of Vezins and of la Roche-qui-Boit.

Contact : 'Pays d'accueil du Sud-Manche', mairie, 50240 Saint-James.

Tel (33) 2 33 89 62 10 - Fax (33) 2 33 89 62 11.

'**Vélo-rails**'. These original trips made on pedal powered machines installed on a disused railway track allow you to explore the unusual sites. The 'vélo-rail' of Pont-Erambourg (Orne) in the Valley of the Noireau. On 6 kilometres of track between Pont-Erambourg and Berjou to discover the 'Suisse Normande'.

On horseback, from short trips to excursions of several days, for the experienced and the beginner and organised by professionals, will allow you to discover the Norman countryside. Depending on the length of the trip, numerous establishments offer somebody from equestrian tourism to accompany you to visit the different places with lodging in riding 'farms', gîtes or private homes... Above all and to better profit from your short excursions or longer trips the riding schools propose to teach you ride or to perfect your technique. Teaching is carried out by person with a state diploma. Other riding establishments such as the 'clubs hippiques', the pony clubs... also are charged with guiding you whether for the hire of horses, donkeys, the preparation of a brief excursion or a longer trip. Packages for a day, a weekend or longer stays are also offered. These establishments also provide opportunities for equestrian tourism and carriage driving. Formidable harnessed excursions, calash rides, cart trips... await you to discover the exceptional countryside of the five Norman areas. Still in the domain of equestrianism, guided visits to some of the most beautiful Studs in the world are offered throughout the year.

Practical information from the various Departmental Committees of Tourism, regional associations and Tourist Offices.

Topographical guides, maps and works concerning a precise itinerary, an organised excursion... have been specially produced. Certain centres have combined excursions, visits and discovery of the region and regional products.

Useful addresses : (See the chapter devoted to the horse).

Useful address : for programmes on foot, on horseback and by bike in all five areas, contact the 'Comité Régional de Tourisme de Normandie'. Tel (33) 2 32 33 79 00 - Fax (33) 2 32 31 19 04.

Excursions and outings.

Another way of discovering the Norman regions is on the little tourist trains, for example :

In Manche, several tourist railway associations offer short excursions over a few kilometres.

'***Le Train de la Côte des Isles***'. Carteret to Portbail, a 9 kilometre trip, opposite to the Channel Islands, in carriages from 1930. Excursions are offered by the 'Association Tourisme et Chemins de Fer de la Manche' (A.T.C.M.). Regular trains and themed, trains for markets, evening tourist trains. For information and reservations : 'Train Touristique du Cotentin' - Clos Saint-Jean - 50270 Saint-Jean-de-la-Rivière. Tel (33) 2 33 04 70 08.

'***Le Mini-Train des Marais***'. Offered by the 'Société des Chemins de Fer Touristiques du Cotentin'. Miniature village from the 1930's. A magnificent visit recreated by modellers to travel as in another time. It is situated at the 'Base Touristique Centre Manche' on the D900, on the axis Saint-Lô/Périers.

For information : 'Mini-Train des Marais'. Tel (33) 2 33 05 15 54.

In Eure :

= *'Le Train Touristique de la Vallée de l'Eure'*. At Pacy-sur-Eure. Trips in a little train of an earlier time along the valley of the Eure to discover a country station and collection of old carriages and wagons. Tel (33) 2 32 36 04 63 - Fax (33) 2 32 26 40 43.

= *'Pontaurail'* Travel on motorail from 1952 between Pont-Audemer and Honfleur with a stop at the Pont de Normandie. Departures from both towns. Tel/Fax (33) 2 32 41 00 64. E.mail : pontaurail@libertysurf.fr

In Seine-Maritime :

= *'Le Train Routier Touristique'*, to discover the three sister towns, Eu, Mers-les-Bains and Le Tréport. A journey of one hour. Information from the Tourist Office of the town of Eu, 41, rue Paul-Bignon - B.P. 82 - 76260 Eu. Tel (33) 2 35 86 04 68.

2 - Individual or collective pastimes, sporting activities in the open air or indoors

On the menu of your holidays or your weekends, the practice of sports such as polo, golf, tennis, rock climbing, mountaineering... will complete your visits to Normandy. The regions are particularly favourable for sporting activities and will allow you to ally physical activities with cultural pastimes and activities profiting overall from the magnificent countryside of the region.

Golf. The ideal topography of Normandy contributes to the good reputation of the thirty seven golf courses which it possesses. The beauty of the sites on which they are set, the originality of the layout and the variety of the courses class a good number of them among the most beautiful golf courses in France. With a reputation recognised more and more by golfers, **Normandy was named in 2000 among the ten best golfing destinations in the world**. Among the numerous courses, twenty three are 18 hole or even more, and will satisfy the 'aficionados'. The greens, green throughout the year, will bring good fortune to the enthusiasts, who for a first try or for the more confirmed can take advantage of individual or collective lessons given by the teachers. Introductory courses or for those who want to perfect their game are also available over longer periods with a choice of programmes or specially selected packages. According to the type of terrain, wooded, valleys, flat, urban, with the presence or not of obstacles such as lakes, rivers, forests... the courses offer varying levels of difficulty. Some golf courses of 18 and 27 holes :

In Seine-Maritime : The golf course of Etretat, situated in the heart of a seaside town with an international renown or the golf course of Saint-Saëns, situated in the depths of the Norman countryside, are part of the exceptional golf courses.

= *Golf d'Etretat*, route du Havre, B.P. 7, 76790 Etretat.
Tel (33) 2 35 27 04 89 - Fax (33) 2 35 29 49 02.
E.mail : golf.d.etretat@wanadoo.fr

= *Golf de Saint-Saëns*, Domaine du Vaudichon, B.P. 20 - 76680 Saint-Saëns.
Tel (33) 2 35 34 25 24 - Fax (33) 2 35 34 43 33.
Web site : http://www.golfstsaens.com
E.mail : golf-st-saens@infonie.fr

In Eure : The **golf course of Vaudreuil**, on a course designed by an English architect, situated in the middle of a vast park planted with thousands of ancient trees.
The **golf course of Champ de Bataille**, some 25 kilometres from Evreux, is set in the interior of a vast state-owned forest with a variety of tree types.

= *Golf de Vaudreuil*, 27100 Le Vaudreuil.
Tel (33) 2 32 59 02 60 - Fax (33) 2 32 59 43 88.
E.mail : gvaudreu@club-internet.fr

= *Golf du Champ de Bataille*, 27110 Le Neubourg.
Tel (33) 2 32 35 03 72 - Fax (33) 2 32 35 83 10.
Web site : http://www.golf-en-Normandie.com

In Orne : The **golf course of Bellême,** situated within the confines of the Perche Normand, it is a natural and undulating course. Tennis and swimming pool close by.

= *Golf de Bellême,* 'Les Sablons', 61130 Bellême.
Tel/Fax (33) 2 33 73 12 79. Résagolf : 02 33 85 13 20.
Web site : www.golfdebelleme.com E.mail : dir@golfdebelleme.com

= The *Golf course of Bagnoles-de-l'Orne*, the **oldest** in Normandy, on the other hand it is a 9 hole course.
Route de Domfront - 61140 Tessé-La-Madeleine. Tel (33) 2 33 37 81 42.

In Calvados, two golf courses of 27 holes (18 and 9) will seduce all golfers from beginners to the most confirmed. The **golf course of Deauville-Saint-Gatien**, 8 kilometres from Honfleur and Deauville, is set in a superb forested environment offering views over the estuary of the Seine. Its club house has been established in an ancient 'pressoir' from the 18th century. The **golf course of Saint-Julien**, in the heart of the Pays d'Auge is a half hour from Caen or from Le Havre and about ten kilometres from Deauville. It is set in a classified site. As for the **Golf of Deauville-l'Amirauté**, 5 minutes to the south of Deauville, it was built on an ancient stud farm. A true championship course, water obstacles are ever present. Finally, unique in Europe, it offers courses equipped for night-time play. To the south of the region, the **golf course of Clécy** is one of the most natural of French golf courses.

= *Golf de Deauville-Saint-Gatien* - La Ferme du Mont-Saint-Jean, 14130 Saint-Gatien-des-Bois.

Tel (33) 2 31 65 19 99 - Fax (33) 2 31 65 11 24
Web site : www.best-channel-golfs.com
E.mail : deauville-st-gatien@best-channel-golfs.com

= *Golf de Saint-Julien* - Open Golf Club - Saint-Julien-sur-Calonne - 14130 Pont-l'Evêque - B.P. 76. Tel (33) 2 31 64 30 30 - Fax (33) 2 31 64 12 43.
E.mail : saintjulien@opengolfclub.com
Web site : wwwopengolfclub.com/gsj/

= *Golf of Deauville-l'Amirauté*, Tourgeville, 14800 Deauville.
Tel (33) 2 31 14 42 00 - Fax (33) 2 31 88 32 00.

Golf of Clécy-Cantelou, Manoir de Cantelou, 14570 Clécy.
Tel (33) 2 31 69 72 72 - Fax (33) 2 31 69 70 22.
Web site : http://www.golf-de-clecy.com
E.mail : golf-de-clecy@golf-de-clecy.com

= **Omaha Beach Golf Club** - La Ferme Saint-Sauveur - 14520 Port-en-Bessin.
Tel (33) 2 31 22 12 12 - Fax (33) 2 31 22 12 13.
Web site : http://www.best-channel-golfs.com

In La Manche : the **golf course of Granville,** situated in the Bay of Mont-Saint-Michel is a club with 27 holes on a course in 'Scottish' style.

= *Golf course of Granville* - Bay of of Mont-Saint-Michel - Chalet du Golf - 50290 Breville-sur-Mer. Tel (33) 2 33 50 23 06 - Fax (33) 2 33 61 91 87.
Web site : http://www.best-channel-golfs.com/granville/acces/htm
E.mail : granville@best-channel-golfs.com

Polo. This sport dates from the tenth century B.C. It had been imported into the Indian Empire and was discovered by you, the British, in the north west of India. It was in 1880 that the first match was played against France, in Dieppe. 1892 saw the creation of the polo ground of Bagatelle. This sport was introduced into Argentina and to the USA around 1900. In 1921 the 'Fédération Française des polos de France' was created.

For the teams of 'bambins' or the very young riders, the polo pony can equally be practised in certain clubs. For all information, enquire at the Union des polos de France, route des Moulins, Bois de Boulogne, 75016 Paris.

To see. = The **World Championship of** *Polo of Deauville* (created in 1895 by the Duke of Gramont). It takes place in two parts, the Silver Cup and the Gold Cup, on the racecourse of Deauville-La Touques. This year, the championship will take place from 30th July, the final, taking place on 25th August. Information from the Tourist Office of Deauville, 11 bis, avenue de la République. Tel (33) 2 31 14 40 00 - Fax (33) 2 31 88 78 88.
Internet address : http://www.deauville.org
E.mail : info-deauv@deauville.org

Tennis and Squash. As far as tennis is concerned numerous towns and communities of the areas offer the possibility of practising this sport on exterior or covered courts or in halls by the efforts of clubs affiliated to the 'Fédération Française de Tennis'.

For all information in relation to the playing of tennis or squash, contact the Tourist Offices or Information points where you are staying.

Useful addresses :

*'Comité Départemental de Tennis de la Manche', 35, rue Tour Carrée - B.P. 337 - 50103 Cherbourg Cedex. Tel (33) 2 33 03 97 67 - Fax (33) 2 33 03 28 48.
E.mail : comité.manche@fft.f

*'Comité Départemental de l'Orne de Tennis', 5, rue Auguste-Mottin - 61500 Sées. Tel (33) 2 33 81 95 89 - Fax - 02 33 81 95 92.

*'Comité Départemental du Calvados de la Fédération Française de Lawn Tennis', 82, avenue Thiès - 14000 Caen. Tel (33) 2 31 93 20 05 - Fax (33) 2 31 93 20 87.

*'Comité Départemental de Tennis de Seine-Maritime', 37, rue Croix Vaubois - 76130 Mont-Saint-Aignan. Tel (33) 2 35 76 32 60 - Fax (33) 2 35 74 88 77.

Hunting. For lovers of hunting, on the track of small or large game or migratory birds, numerous associations have been created. They will advise you and guide you in the leisure activity.

Useful addresses :

* 'Fédération des Chasseurs' : Web site : http://www.chasseurdefrance.com
Fédération des Chasseurs de l'Orne, 46, rue de Bretagne - B.P. 177 - 61000 Alençon. Tel (33) 2 33 80 05 05 - Fax (33) 2 33 32 21 02.
E.mail : fdc61@chasseurdefrance.com

* 'Fédération Départementale des Chasseurs de Calvados', rue des Compagnons - 14000 Caen. Tel (33) 2 31 44 24 87 - Fax (33) 2 31 43 70 63.
E.mail : fdc14@chasseurdefrance.com

* 'Fédération Départementale des Chasseurs de la Manche', ZAC de la Chevalerie - 745, rue Jules-Vallès - 50009 Saoin-Lô Cedex. Tel (33) 2 33 72 63 63 - Fax (33) 2 33 72 04 84.
E.mail : fdc50@chasseurdefrance.com

* 'Fédération Départementale des Chasseurs de l'Eure', rue de Meleville - 27930 Angerville-la-Campagne. Tel(33) 2 32 23 03 15 - Fax (33) 2 32 23 22 75.
E.mail : chass.eure@wanadoo.fr

* 'Fédération Départementale des Chasseurs de la Seine-Maritime', 216, route de Neufchâtel - B.P. 57 - 76420 Bihorel. Tel (33) 2 35 60 35 97 - Fax (33) 2 35 61 82 14. E.mail : president@fdc76.com

3 - Fishing (rivers and streams). Fishing in ponds and lakes. Sea fishing (land, boat, underwater fishing)

The rich amount of fishing also enhances Normandy's reputation. One of the reasons for this is its large network of rivers, marshes, canals, lakes and others. The second, not the least, is to do with its fish population. The famous 'fario' brown trout, which has one of the greatest increases in its numbers in France, the salmon, and its carnivorous fish are also one of its trump cards.

Many fishing associations protecting the aquatic environment (AAPPMA) exist in all the regions. To find out about the best fishing spots, lodgings, different kinds of fishing, how to get to the fishing grounds... the

* 'Comité Régional de Tourisme de Normandie' has organised the 'Club Pêche de Normandie'.

Contact : 'Comité Régional de Tourisme de Normandie'. Le Doyenné, 14, rue Charles-Corbeau. F-27000 Evreux. Tel (33) 2 32 33 79 00. Fax (33) 2 32 31 19 04
E-mail : normandy@imaginet.fr

Trout fishing, for the whole day or for just part of it, fishing by the kilo, fly fishing... there's nothing missing for amateurs of 1st and 2nd category fishing. Normandy is full of sites for river, pool, natural or manmade lake fishing. The following should be noted :

1st category : predominantly from the salmon family (trout, sea trout, salmon).
2nd category : predominantly fresh water (roach and carp).
River fishing.

Seine-Maritime has about 1500 km of rivers classed as being in the 1st category. As far as the 2nd category is concerned there a possibility of excellent fishing along 150 kms of the large river Seine and 1000 hectares of pools and lakes.

One of the best trout rivers in Upper Normandy, the Bresle, is also well stocked with salmon. At Guimerville, the 'Val Doré' is a site covering 20 hectares. It is made up of five lakes where you can find big specimens : pike of 15 kilos, white and silver 'amours' of 25 kilos, and silurids weighing up to 50 kilos ! One lake is reserved for fly fishing. For the comfort of fishermen and followers there are rowing boats for hire, sale of bait, toilets and showers for those fishing.

La Béthune, all around Neufchâtel, there are courses and specific areas for all sorts of fishing.

Further north near Dieppe, there is the Arques basin, a river made up of three others that join together : the Varenne, l'Eaulne and the Béthune, which will really delight fishermen.

Useful addresses : Information from the 'Fédération des APP de Seine-Maritime'. 10, rue d'Harcourt, 76000 Rouen. Tel (33) 2 35 07 57 28.

In Eure. The 'Andelle' and the 'Lieure' are two rivers classed into the first category. Amateur fly fishermen will be really pleased with the different courses near the village of Charleval and managed by the fly fishing club La Mouche Charlevalaise, which has more particularly created a very well known fishing school.

Other rivers such as the 'Risle', the 'Iton', the 'Rouloir' and the 'Avre', are a paradise for amateur fly fishermen. Especially on the Risle there is a superb fly fishing course managed by the 'AAPPMA' of Brionne with 10 km of banks totally reserved for fly fishing. Information and booking : 'La Truite Risloise'. Tel (33) 2 32 45 00 28. Fax (33) 2 32 46 59 16.

* 'Fédération de Pêche de l'Eure', BP 411, 27504 Pont-Audemer, cedex. Tel (33) 2 32 57 10 73. Fax (33) 2 32 41 04 47.

In Orne. Fishing in lakes and pools. 'Fly fishing Course on the Varenne', 3 kms from Domfront. Tel (33) 2 33 38 53 97.

'Fly fishing Course' on the Touques at Canapville. Tel (33) 2 33 35 59 47.

Rabodanges lake covers 100 hectares and is classed into the second category for fishing. There are all sorts of fish, but it has a reputation for its carnivorous fish and its carp fishing course which is open at night.

Full of rainbow and brown trout, the 'Reservoir du Rocher' is especially for fly fishing and is a lake of 5 hectares situated near the village of Radon close to Alençon. It has been equipped with pontoons for the satisfaction of all levels of fishing. Boats can be rented. Site open all year round. Bookings and information : 'Normandie Pêche Sportive'. 61250 Radon. Tel (33) 2 33 28 11 86. Fax (33) 2 33 31 81 56.

For any other information contact : * the 'Fédération de l'Orne pour la Pêche et la Protection du Milieu Aquatique'. 59, rue Julien. BP 91. 61003 Alençon cedex. Tel/Fax (33) 2 33 26 10 66.

* The 'Maison de l'Eau et de la Rivière' takes in groups, individuals or holiday classes. Amongst others, it offers youngsters and adults a day of initiation to fishing techniques. Guided fly fishing course. Carnivorous fishing... Booking and information :' Maison de l'Eau et de la Rivière'. Le Moulin. 61100 Ségrie-Fontaine. Tel (33) 2 33 64 94 89. Fax (33) 2 33 65 93 95.

In Manche. The many authorised associations for the protection of fish of the environment will help you discover the existing 4800 kms of rivers classed into the 1st category. Other than the Sée which is well known as a salmon river and also classed as the second best river in France for this sort of fishing, there is another excellent river called the Selune, a few kilometres from there and is also thought of one of the best rivers in France.

Possibility of fishing using boats (rental on site) on the lakes of 'La Roche-qui-Boit' and 'Vézins', two reservoirs belonging to 'Electricité de France'.

As far as the Vire is concerned, it is well known for its coarse fishing. It is in the second category. The 'Vire' is also well endowed in carnivorous and migrant species of fish. For amateurs of late night carp fishing there are certain special reserves such as the Saint-Lô reach and that of Pont-Hébert.

Useful address : 'Fédération de la Manche pour la Pêche et la Protection du Milieu Aquatique'. 16, rue du Pont-l'Abbé. BP 89. 50190 Périers. Tel (33) 2 33 46 96 50. Fax (33) 2 33 46 96 62.

In Calvados. The 'Touques' **is classed as the best sea trout river in France.** There are all kinds of fishing. From Touques to Breuil-en-Auge the river is free to the public and belongs to the first category.

The private part of the 'Touques' is 50 km in length and is equipped and offers some exceptional fishing.

The 52 hectare federal lake in Pont-l'Evêque is worth seeing as well. It is abundant with carp, perch and rainbow trout.

For any information about fishing in the area contact the 'Fédération Départementale des Associations de Pêche et de Pisciculture du Calvados', 18, rue de la Girafe, 14000 Caen. Tel 02 31 44 63 00.

Scaling. Rock climbing. There are many natural sites which have been equipped for all levels of climbing. It is also possible to carry out this leisure sport indoors on man made climbing walls. Information from the clubs. Useful address : 'Fédération Française de la Montagne et de l'Escalade' (FFME), 8-10, quai de la Marne - 75019 Paris. Tel (33) 1 40 18 75 50. Fax (33) 1 40 18 75 59.

In Calvados. In the 'Gorges de la Vire', at Carville, there is a natural site equipped for scaling with or without supervision. There are about sixty passages, from levels 3 to 7.

A few places for scaling : 'Les Rochers des Parcs', at Clécy ; 'Mont Myrrha', at Falaise ; 'La Brèche au Diable', near Falaise ; the 'Centre Houlgatais d'Animation et de Loisirs' (CHAL) proposes interior scaling on man made walls for children and adults.

Useful address : 'Fédération Française de la Montagne et de l'Escalade' (FFME), 'Comité départemental du Calvados', 10-18, quartier du Grand Parc - 14200 Hérouville-Saint-Clair. E-mail : cd-ffme-14@voilà.fr

Information from the 'Union Départementale des O.T.S.I du Calvados', rue du Docteurr Charcot - B.P. 20 - 14 530 Luc-sur-Mer. Tel (33) 2 31 97 33 25. Fax (33) 2 31 96 65 09.

In Manche. A few sites : 'La Glacerie', near Cherbourg, 80 passages have been fitted out. 'La Roche-qui-Pend', at Cherbourg, 15 passages. The 'Sémaphore' cliff, at Flamanville, levels from 4 to 7, for experienced climbers. 'Les Roches-du-Ham', à Condé-sur-Vire, the Montmartin-sur-Mer quarries…

Useful address : 'Comité départemental' - Manche - FFME, 5, rue du Champ Dolent - 50590 Montmartin-sur-Mer. Tel (33) 2 33 45 52 20.

In Eure. The cliffs : 'ondoles' (Amfreville, Vatteville), 300 passages from 20 to 35 m, from levels 3 to 7 ; 'Roque' (Le Thuit), 300 passages from 20 to 30 m, level 3 to 8 ; 'Val-Saint-Martin' (Les Andelys), 130 passages, level 4 to 7.

Useful address : 'Comité Départemental Eure' (FFME), 14, route de Gaillon - 27120 Pacy-sur-Eure.

In Orne. Sites for climbing by the 'Parc naturel régional Normandie-Maine' : the rocks in the forest of Andaines, 120 climbing passages, from level 3 to 8, 'La Fosse Arthour', 171 passages, level 3 to 7, 'La Cluse de Domfront', the 'site l'Aiguille de Mortain' (80 passages from level 3 to 7)… Topo-guides available at the 'Maison du Parc', Tel (33) 2 33 81 75 75.

At Saint-Clair-de-Halouze, 40 passages from 5 to 15 m ; from level 2 to 6.

Useful address : 'Comité départemental - Orne' - FFME, 25, rue André-Letard, Le Caim - 61100 Saint-Georges-des-Groseillers.

In Seine-Maritime. Useful address : 'Comité départemental - Seine-Maritime' - FFME, 27, allée Daniel Lavallée - 76000 Rouen.

Car racing, Go-karting. For any information on automobile sports, contact the
* 'Fédération Française du Sport Automobile', 17-21, avenue du Général Mangin - 75781 Paris cedex 16. Tel (33) 1 44 30 24 00. Fax (33) 1 42 24 16 80.

Useful address : in order to obtain the precise information about automobile sports in each area, contact the
* 'Comité de Normandie du Sport Automobile', 292, route de Dieppe - 76960 Notre-Dame-de-Bondeville. Tel (33) 2 35 74 39 35. Fax (33) 2 35 76 95 49.

* In order to obtain the precise information about sporting associations of Go-Karting, contact the' Comité de Normandie de Karting', 10, avenue du Roi de Serbie - 14390 Cabourg. Tel (33) 2 31 85 32 74. Fax (33) 2 31 38 95 26.

In Seine-Maritime.
* Outdoor 'Circuits : Circuit de l'Europe', Les Bocquets - 76410 Sotteville-sous-le-Val. Tel (33) 2 35 78 72 17.
* 'Circuit d'Anneville-Ambourville'. Tel (33) 2 35 74 54 10. Dieppe Karting, (circuits Outdoor and Indoor), Zone Louis-Delaporte - 76370 Rouxmesnil-Bouteilles. Tel (33)2 35 06 13 33.

Indoor Circuits : * 'Normandie Karting', Quenneport - 76380 Val-de-la-Haye. Tel (33) 2 35 34 98 16. 'Circuit Le Réservoir', 581, boulevard Jules-Durand - 76600 Le Havre. Tel (33) 2 35 26 04 48.

In Orne.
* 'Circuit of the Pays d'Essay', La Branle - 61500 Aunay-les-Bois. Tel (33) 2 33 27 65 87. Circuit for car racing, Go-karts, quads and also moto trials.

Useful address : 'Association Sportive de Karting', K61, 'La Fuie' - 61200 Aunou-le-Faucon. Tel/Fax (33) 2 33 36 88 10. Mobile : 06 82 02 19 11.
E-mail : K61@club-internet.fr

In Eure.
* 'Euro Kart Espace Automobile', 20, rue de Gaillon - 27930 Gravigny. Tel (33) 2 32 62 69 13 ; (33) 2 32 33 18 25 ; (33) 2 32 62 90 64. Fax (33) 2 32 62 33 17.

In Manche.
Useful address :
* 'Association Sportive de l'Automobile Club de l'Ouest de Basse-Normandie', 5, rue des Ecoles - 50370 Brécey. Tel (33) 2 33 48 99 71. Fax (33) 2 33 48 11 22. E-mail : ASACOBN@Compuserve.com
The Association will pass on details to you about affiliated stables.

Other address : * 'Association Sportive de l'Automobile du Bocage', 9, rue Léon-Fauvel - 50430 Lessay. Tel (33) 2 33 46 54 76. Fax (33) 2 33 46 66 16. They will let you know about affiliated Go-Kart clubs ; two clubs represent the 'Ligue de Normandie de Karting in Manche' :
* 'Association Sportive de Karting Saint-Lô/Coutances', 2, rue du Stade Albert-Bossard - 50750 Saint-Romphaire. Tel (33) 2 33 55 76 82.
* 'Association Sportive Karting du Circuit de La Hague', Saint-Nazaire - 50440 Gréville-Hague. Tel (33) 2 33 08 45 40.

In Calvados. * 'Espace International Automobile' (EIA), Domaine de Betteville - 14130 Pont-l'Evêque. Tel (33) 2 31 64 39 01. Fax (33) 2 31 64 39 02. Six circuits opposite the Pont-l'Evêque lake. Open every dayl.

Site Internet : www.eia.fr Messagerie Internet : circuit-eia@wanadoo.fr

Duprat Concept, Chemin de la Performance - 14800 Saint-Arnoult (près de Deauville). Tel (33) 2 31 81 31 31. 'Circuit Honda', same address, Tel (33) 2 31 81 60 51. Fax (33) 2 31 81 26 00. Open every day.

4 - Airborne and Wind sports

Airborne trips, discovery of the regions, first flight, or tourist circuits, trips…, professionals from flying clubs and piloting schools will take you up for the first time in a plane, in a ULM , or helicopter. Lessons in piloting lessons are also possible. Numerous associations also organise parachute jumping, delta plane, gliding, or hot air ballooning. For information contact the Tourist Offices, 'Comités Départementaux de Tourisme et autres organismes agréés' (cf. other chapters).

In Eure. Some 'Aero-clubs' : at Etrepagny, Bernay, Evreux-Les Authieux, Saint-André-de-l'Eure.

Hot air balloons : without monitor, individual, in groups at Aclou - 27800. For information : 'France Montgolfières', 24, route de Paris - 77420 Champs-sur-Marne. Tel 01 60 95 15 86. Fax : 01 60 06 28 07.

E-mail : reservations@franceballoons.com

To be seen : the 'Montgolfiades' at the castle de Vascœuil in the area of Eure. For information contact the 'Comité Départemental du Tourisme de l'Eure', B.P. 367, Boulevard Georges-Chauvin --27003 Evreux cedex. Tel (33)2 32 62 04 27. Fax (33) 2 32 31 05 98. E-mail : cdt-eure@wanadoo.fr Site Internet : www.cdt-eure.fr

In Manche. Hot air baloons : at Carentan, Flight over the 'Parc Naturel des Marais du Cotentin et du Bessin' by the association 'Les Vents d'Ouest', certified by the 'Fédération Française d'Aérostation'. Duration : 3 h of one of which is in free flight. All year round depending on the weather. Departures from the 'Manoir de Cantepie', between Isigny-sur-Mer (14) and Carentan (50). For information : 'Association 'Les Vents d'Ouest', Le Presbytère, 34, rue de Beuzeville - 50500 Les Veys. Tel (33) 2 33 42 49 08. Fax (33) 2 33 42 49 06, Te mobile : 06 08 33 42 07. E-mail : lesvents-douest@aol.com - Website : www.multimania.com /lesventsdouest/

Paragliding and delta-plane : Information at the 'Mairie de Vauville', Le Bourg --50440 Vauville.

Planes, ULMs, flying lessons: flying clubs at Avranches, Cherbourg, Dragey, Granville, Lessay and Portbail.

Useful address : 'Comité Départemental du Tourisme. Maison du Département'. Route de Villedieu. 50008 Saint-Lô cedex. Tel (33)2 33 05 98 70. Fax (33) 2 33 56 07 03. E-mail : manchetourisme@cg50.fr , Website : www.manchetourisme.com

Dans l'Orne. Flying club and piloting schools : at Alençon, Le Mêle-sur-Sarthe, Flers, Mortagne-au-Perche… Useful address : 'Comité Départemental Aéronautique de l'Orne'. 66, Grande-Rue - 61170 Le Mêle-sur-Sarthe. Tel (33) 2 33 27 61 83. Fax (33) 2 33 31 09 62.

Hot air balloons : 'Montgolfières Club de l'Orne', 61200 Argentan. Tel (33) 2 33 26 08 04 mobile 06 08 72 88 41.

'Orne Montgolfières'. La Clais. La Sauvagère, 61600 La Ferté-Macé. Tel (33) 2 33 37 33 08 or 06 03 69 99 59. For these christening flights, numerous departures are organised from Bagnoles-de-l'Orne, la Ferté-Macé, Flers, Domfront or another site : contact on (33) 2 33 37 33 08.

In Seine-Maritime. Flying clubs, flying schools : at Rouen-Boos, Eu, Gommerville, Saint-Aubin-sur-Scie, Le Havre... For information contact the 'Comité Départemental de Tourisme'.

In Calvados. Parachute jumping, a few addresses : 'Abeille Parachutisme', 37, boulevard Charles-V - 14600 Honfleur. Tel (33) 2 31 89 77 66. Fax (33) 2 31 89 77 66. 'Centre Ecole Régionale de Parachutisme de Normandie', Flying club, B.P. 4 - 14650 Carpiquet. Tel (33) 2 31 80 65 59.

Helicopter trips : 'Héli Time' ; Les Ruelles - 27500 Corneville-sur-Risle. Tel (33) 2 32 57 00 38 or (33) 2 31 81 82 83. Tourist flights from Deauville. On the programme : Mont-Saint-Michel ; D-Day landing beaches, 'La Côte Fleurie'...

A few flying clubs : 'Flying club Régional de Caen' - 14650 Carpiquet. Tel (33) 2 31 26 52 00. 'Flying club de Deauville Saint-Gatien' - 14130 Saint-Gatien-des-Bois. Tel (33) 2 31 64 00 93.

5 - Nautical sports of all sorts Canoeing-Kayaking

With the many rivers, lakes, leisure and sports centres in all the areas, you can go on enlivening trips by canoe or kayak. Many clubs with the label F.F.C.K. 'Fédération Française de Canoë-Kayak' and associations will propose an hour or two, or half day trips when you can discover magnificent countryside. You can go down the river on your own or under supervision.

Useful address : Lists of Clubs and information at the 'Comité Régional de Canoë-Kayak de Normandie', 40, rue des Mouettes - 76960 Notre-Dame-Bondeville. Tel (33) 2 35 75 16 10

E-mail : normandie@ffcanoe.asso.fr , Website : www.crck.normandie.online.fr or contact the Comités départementaux de Canoë-Kayak.

In Calvados. Discovery of the 'Vallée de l'Orne' and the 'Suisse Normande'. Trips into the 'Gorges de la Vire'.

For information, contact the 'Comité Départemental de Canoë-Kayak du Calvados', B.P. 347 - 14000 Caen. Tel/Fax (33) 2 31 52 87 92.

In Manche. Trips down the 'Vallée de la Vire' : 'La Base de Loisirs L'Ecluse' - B.P. 17 - 50890 Condé-sur-Vire. Tel/Fax 02 33 57 33 66, offers trips of 4 to 26 km unaccompanied or under supervision.

For information : 'Comité Départemental de Canoë-Kayak de la Manche', 5, rue de La Grande Hurberderie - 50360 Quettehou. Tel/Fax (33) 2 3354 76 67.

In Orne. Discovery of the 'Pays d'Ouche', of the Risle, of Orne, of the Suisse Normande…

For information : 'Comité Départemental de Canoë-Kayak de l'Orne', Mr Marcel Broudin, 61200 Argentan. Tel (33) 2 33 35 39 19.

In Eure. Trip down de la Risle, with discovery of the 'Vallée de l'Eure' : the clubs offer many different trips. Possibility of some lasting several days. For information : 'Comité Départemental de Canoë-Kayak de l'Eure', 44, rue de l'Eglantier - 27200 Vernon. Tel (33) 2 32 51 14 93 - Fax (33) 2 32 21 94 97.

In Seine-Maritime. Trips on the Varenne, the Béthune, down the river to the 'Vallée de l'Austreberthe'… For information : 'Comité Départemental de Canoë-Kayak de la Seine-Maritime', Mr Reygner Jean-Pierre, 76000 Rouen. Tel (33) 2 35 07 07 06.

Seaside resorts and lakes… For sailing, jet skiing, sea scooter… Norman seaside resorts and the many lakes in the areas can fulfil all your nautical plans.

To find about the list of Clubs and Sailing schools, where you are staying contact the 'Fédération Française de Voile' (FFV), 55, avenue Kléber, 75116 Paris. Tel (33) 1 44 05 81 00. Fax (33) 1 47 04 90 12.

'Ligue Basse-Normandie' : 'Fédération Française de Voile, Pavillon de Normandie', 14, quai Caffarelli, 14000 Caen. Tel (33) 2 31 84 41 81.

In Seine-Maritime. The seaside resorts of the 'Côte d'Albâtre' at Saint-Valery-en-Caux, Veules-les-Roses, Veulettes-sur-Mer, Saint-Aubin-sur-Mer.

'Lac de Caniel' - 76450 Cany-Barville (between Dieppe and Fécamp). Tel (33) 2 35 97 40 55. Fax (33) 2 35 97 40 73. E-Mail : lac.de.caniel@freesbee.fr

For information contact the 'Comité Départemental de Tourisme', and tourism offices.

In Calvados. For Jet-skiing, and water skiing… 'Lac de Pont-l'Evêque', (cf. V-'Centres de Loisirs et Bases de plein air').

For moto-skiing and water skiing : information from the 'Motonautique Club de Basse-Normandie', Lac de Rabodanges - 61210 Les Rotours. Tel (33) 2 33 39 16 53 or (33) 2 33 35 00 33.

In Eure. Nautical teleski, windsurfing… 'Lac des Deux Amants' (cf. V - 'Centres et Bases de Loisirs').

In Manche. For any information to do with sailing contact the 'Comité Départemental de Voile de la Manche', La Halotière - 50380 Saint-Aubin-des-Préaux. Tel (33) 2 33 51 65 51.

'Centre Régional de Nautisme', boulevard des Amiraux - 50400 Granville. Tel (33) 2 33 91 22 60 - Fax (33) 2 33 50 51 99. E-mail : crng@dial.oléane.com

<u>**Some Aquatic Centres.**</u>

In Calvados. 'Nautical Centres' : at Condé-sur-Noireau, route de Vire. Tel (33) 2 31 69 02 93. Three pools, opening roof, giant slide... 'Le Nautile', Aquatic Centre, slide, swimming pool in breakwater, bubbling jacuzzis, saunas, solarium... 14107 Lisieux. Tel (33) 2 31 48 66 66.

'Aquatic Centre de la Suisse Normande', 'Parc de Loisirs du Trapsy', route de Caen - 14220 Thury-Harcourt. Tel (33) 2 31 79 03 18 - Fax (33) 2 31 79 93 05.

In Eure. Aquatic Centre 'Aquaval', Les Artaignes, route Garenne - 27600 Gaillon. Tel (33) 2 32 77 47 00 - Fax (33) 2 32 77 40 73. Slide, river, fun pool , varied other activities.

In Seine-Maritime. Aquatic Centre 'L'Archipel', 14, rue de la Pierre Naudin - 76650 Petit-Couronne. Tel (33) 2 35 18 42 42. Tropical temperature, 29° all year round, slide, geysers, massage with water jets...

In Manche. Aquatic Centre 'Aqua-Baie', rue Guy-de Maupassant - 50300 Avranches. Tel (33) 2 33 58 07 20. Giant slide, sauna, Roman bath, rapid river, geysers...
'Aquatic Centre', rue du 8 Mai 1945 - 50800 Villedieu-les-Poêles. Tel (33) 2 33 50 17 00, giant slide of 30 m, sauna, aquatic garden...

In Orne. Aquatic Centre of the District du Pays d'Argentan, rue du Paty - 61200 Argentan. Tel (33) 2 33 12 15 45. Fun pool, slide, jacuzzi...
Aquatic Centre 'Aquarel', 3, rue des Filles Saint-Claire - 61000 Alençon. Tel (33) 2 33 32 15 45 - Fax (33) 2 33 32 09 35. Aquatic activities, sauna, solarium...

6 - Leisure centres and centres with open air activities ; connected to sport and tourism

Ideal for spending a day or a weekend with plenty of sporting activities going on, you have a programme of varied activities, with sports and tourist equipment at your disposal : swimming, pedalos, rowing boats, games for children, fishing, boules, tennis, mini golf, golfing, horse riding.

In Orne. The open air activities centre of la Ferté-Macé, with the arrival of the fine weather covers a surface of 65 hectares, and a lake covering 28 hectares. It is six kilometres from Bagnoles-de-l'Orne : it has supervised bathing, (from June to September), windsurfing, horse riding, mini golf, picnic areas, 18 hole golf course with club house, restaurant... Information at the Tourist Office, Tel (33) 2 33 37 10 97. Tourist Complex reception desk, 61600 la Ferté-Macé. Tel (33) 2 33 38 99 00.
'L'Escale du Vitou', one of the most beautiful sites in the pays d'Auge. Situated at the entrance to Vimoutiers, there is a lake 6 hectares in size. On the programme : supervised bathing, 2 tennis courts, riding centre, rowing boats, pedalos, games for children, fishing, Deval-Kart, port with miniature ships, mini-golf... For information : Escale du Vitou, route d'Argentan, 61120 Vimoutiers. Tel (33) 2 33 39 12 04.

At the Mêle-sur-Sarthe, lake covering 23 hectares : sailing, wind surfing, supervised bathing, tennis courts, miniature golf... For information : (33) 2 33 27 61 02 or (33) 2 33 27 63 97. Fête du Lac, on August 15th.

In Calvados. The Leisure Centre of the 'Plan de d'eau de Pont-l'Evêque', covering 97 hectares, is composed of a nautical centre with sailing schools, wind surf rentals, pedalos. Possibility of canoeing, kayaking, jet-skiing, water skiing, skibus, and parascending. For information : 'Normandie Challenge'. Tel (33) 2 31 65 29 21 - Fax (33) 2 31 65 03 46.

Leisure centre, Camping - 14380 Pont-Farcy. Tel (33) 2 31 68 32 06. Canoes, kayaks, tennis courts, mountain bike rental, pedalos, mini-golf. The Vallée de Craham leisure park has two lakes, one for fishing and the other reserved for boats and pedalos. There is also a health course, a miniature train and games for the children. For information : 'Parc de Loisirs de la Vallée de Craham', 14240 Cahagnes. Tel (33) 2 31 77 88 18.

In Manche. Sports and leisure park et Loisirs, at Saint-James, on an area of 5 hectares : football, table tennis, volley ball, badminton, frisbee, mini-golf, boules, play ground for children... For information and booking ring (33) 2 33 60 82 74.

At Saint-Martin-de-Landelles, the 'L'Ange Michel', leisure park is situated between Saint-Hilaire-du-Harcouët and Avranches with more than thirty different sporting activities and attractions in an exceptional environment. Quads, pedal go-karts, dodgem boats, electric cars and motor bikes, round-a-bout, summer sledges, tourist train...Visit lasts 4 hours. The 'L'Ange Michel' leisure park, 50730 Saint-Martin-de-Landelles. For information on (33) 2 33 49 04 74, Fax (33) 2 33 49 29 56.

The 'Lac de Vezins'. 'La Mazure' leisure park - Les Biards. 50540 Isigny-le-Buat. Tel (33) 2 33 89 19 50. Canoes, kayaks, rowing, sailing, boats used without needing a licence, pedalos, tennis courts, moutain bikes, archery...

In Eure. As in all the Norman regions where there is a leisure park with lakes, tourists can enjoy a variety of activities during the summer 'rendez-vous'.

At the 'Lac des Deux Amants' : 1,500 ha next to the Seine. On the programme : beach with supervised bathing, play ground for children, nautical teleski, pedalo rental, kayaks, windsurfing, catamarans, rowing (all year round), boule, mini-golf, 18 hole golf course, tennis courts, fishing...

'Lac du Mesnil'. Courses all year round, archery, mountain bikes, scaling, pot-holing, kayak, windsurfing, rowing.

For information : 'Lac des Deux Amants'. 'Lac du Mesnil'. 27740 Poses. Tel (33) 2 32 59 13 13 - Fax (33) 2 32 61 00 97.

'Brionne Leisure Centre' : supervised bathing, beach games, pedalo rental, canoes, windsurfing, horse riding, picnic areas, health course, fishing... For information ring (33) 2 32 43 66 11. 27800 Brionne. Base open from May to September.

In Seine-Maritime. La Varenne Open Air Activities Base - 76510 Saint-Aubin-le-Cauf. Tel (33) 2 35 85 69 05. Stretching over 19 ha, open all year round. Sailing, windsurfing, archery, rowing...

'Lac de Caniel' - 76450 Cany-Barville (between Dieppe and Fécamp). Tel (33) 2 35 97 40 55. Fax (33) 2 35 97 40 73. E-Mail : lac.de.caniel@freesbee.fr

7 - Extreme Sports

Some of these extreme sports will delight even the bravest of amateurs who enjoy strong sensations. In the Vire valley, there is world reference in **elastic bungy jumping** (61 metres high) ; from a gangway on the **Viaduc over the Souleuvre**. '**La tyrolienne géante' 'Le Scable' :** another very exciting sport invites you to cross over the Souleuvre valley attached to the end of a 400 metre long cable. '**Saut à l'élastique, tyrolienne géante'**. Viaduc de la Souleuvre - 14350 La Ferrière-Harang. Tel (33) 2 31 66 31 66. Fax (33) 2 31 66 31 67. E-mail : info@ajhackett.fr Website : www.ajhackett.fr

Parachute jumping : Christening jump by '**parachute tandem'**, from a height of 3,000 m, free fall at 200 km/h. For information : Abeille-Parachutisme, 27170 Le Tilleul-Dame-Agnès, Tel 06 11 62 40 06 or (33) 2 32 30 27 46.

From Garden to Garden

Many old ties exist between Normandy and Great Britain. The *love of gardens* is a mutual tradition and more and more gardeners from both sides of the Channel are eager to show off their originalities... *'Connaissance des Jardins'* specializes in books which enable their readers to discover 'good addresses', many of which have never been published :

● Well-known *parks and gardens*, traditionally open to the public,

● *Private gardens* which are sometimes open to the public for the first time,

● *Professionals* such as nursery gardeners, landscape gardeners, decorators which we consider particularly competent in their own specialities,

● *Bed and breakfast* and *hotels* which are situated in an attractive setting or surrounded by gardens,

● *Remarkable trees, associations* and other **various information,** as well as the authors' own preferences...

The following books are available :

● **Jardins en Basse Normandie** (Gardens in Lower Normandy) : 350 addresses - 24,24 €

● **Jardins de l'Eure** (Gardens in the Eure department) : 112 addresses - 15,09 €

● **Jardins en Seine-Maritime** (Gardens in the Seine-Maritime) : 112 addresses - 13,57 €

Some of the above are bilingual (English and French).

For more information about these guides which provide a new insight into the world of gardens, please contact :

Connaissance des Jardins - 26 avenue de Thiès - 14000 Caen (France)

Tel/fax : (33) 2 31 08 27 21 - Email : connaissance-des-jardins@wanadoo.fr

XIII - SHOPPING IN NORMANDY

1 - Specific shops

AREA OF MANCHE

Tourlaville : The authentic umbrella from Cherbourg, Mapache (manufacture of Cherbourg umbrellas), Manufacturing of umbrellas, and walking sticks. Mapache 8, rue Camot, 50110 Tourlaville - Tél (33) 2 33 44 84 00.

Saint-Vaast-la-Hougue : **Epicerie Gosselin**, traditional grocery belonging to the same family for more than a century. Many regional specialities and an exceptional wine cellar. Caves Saint-Vincent, rue de la Verrue. Tel (33) 2 33 54 40 06.

Argentan : Restoration of old clocks **Bijouterie Flament**, 15, place Henri-IV - Tél. (33) 2 33 67 0139

Le Diable au Cadran. Restauration of old clocks - Jean-François Lefèvre, 15, rue de la Vicomté - Tél (33) 2 33 36 07 93 - Internet : jflefevre@pendulier.com

Flers : **Ekcstasya** - Craftsman in Art smelting. Creation of art objects (lights, chess sets , statuettes, figurines, various reproductions) ; restoration (pewter, clocks…) 31, place Saint-Germain - Tél (33) 2 33 96 36 22.

Flers : **La Brûlerie,** Coffee roasting, tea in bulk. 10, rue du 6 Juin - Tel (33) 2 33 65 20 72 - Fax : (33) 2 33 65 28 14.

*Sées : **La Charrette,*** Hand made decorations, small painted furniture, decorated milk churns. Ghislaine Ratier, 1, rue Lévêque - Tél./Fax (33) 2 33 27 95 87.

AREA OF CALVADOS

Bavent : **Cabinet Maker, restoration of furniture.** Jacques Fontaine, craftsman - Tél (33) 2 31 34 00 22

Bayeux : **Yvette Bellée,** upholsterer, decoration. 4, rue Tardif - Tél (33) 2 31 92 09 62.

Bernesq : **'La Grange au Mohair'.** Mohair clothes. La Harmonière - Tél (33) 2 31 22 70 39.

Bernières-le-Patry : **Gérard Leroy** - Cabinet maker. Artisan à 'Les Carrières' - Tél (33) 2 31 67 80 79.

Cabourg :

'A la Recherche du Temps Perdu'. Gift Shop, 3, avenue du Commandant Touchard. Tel (33) 2 31 91 59 96.

'La Licorne'. Navy decoration, 49, avenue de la Mer. Tel (33) 2 31 24 73 62.

Caen :

English Shop & Dolly's. Tea rooms, grocers shop. If you are homesick, you can take comfort in a typical breakfast 'like over there', or a brunch, or even 'fish and chips'. 16-18, avenue de la Libération - Tél (33) 2 31 94 03 19.

Cohier Upholsterer-Interior Decoration. Sabine Cohier, 90, rue Eugène-Boudin - Tél (33) 2 31 86 49 51.

Jean-Yves Tanguy, Lute maker. 15, rue Demolombe - Tel (33) 2 31 85 73 40.

Colombelles : **Clocks and watches repairs.** Jacques Le Dorner, 17, avenue de la Liberté - Tel (33) 2 31 72 62 17.

Creully : **Umbrellas H20.** Hand made umbrellas. Hameau de Creullet - Tel (33) 2 31 80 31 35.

Deauville :

Arfan. Jeweller. 92-96, rue Eugène-Colas. Tel (33) 2 31 81 12 13.

Antiques Lebreton. 15-16, Quai de la Touques. Tel (33) 2 31 81 03 03.

Hermès Deauville. And its famous silk scarves. 16, Place du Casino. Tel (33) 2 31 88 04 42.

Douvres-la-Délivrande : **Angorastyle.** Manufacture of angora sweaters. Route de Bény-sur-Mer - Tel (33) 2 31 37 63 00.

La Cambe : **Manufacture of Norman furniture.** Cabinet maker. Jean-Pierre Pesquerel, ancienne route nationale 13 - Tel (33) 2 31 22 79 22

Ifs : **Déco Meuble.** Gérard Levêque. Cabinet maker, sculptor. Z. A. de la Dronnière, 2, rue des Carriers - Tel (33) 2 31 34 22 66.

Langrune-sur-Mer : **Restoration of antique furniture.** Pierre Neutre. 1, route de Courseulles - Tel (33) 2 31 96 79 01.

Putot-en-Auge : **Hand made manufacture of lamps and shades.** Chemin des Bonnements - Tel (33) 2 31 39 61 46.

Le Mesnil-Mauger : **Cabinet making.** Jacques Alleaume, Craftsman.'Le Cléry' - Tel 02 31 63 85 21.

Sainte-Honorine-des-Pertes : **'Atelier de la Flambardière'.** Manufacture of music boxes. Le Grand Hameau - Tel (33) 2 31 22 87 81.

Thury-Harcourt : **'Emaillerie Normande'.** Jean Opderbeck. Enamelling on metal, kitchen utensils, name plates.10, impasse des Lavandières - Tel (33) 2 31 79 70 15.

Trouville-sur-Mer :

'Baby ßulle'. Toy shop.1, rue Victor-Hugo - Tel (33) 2 31 98 32 00.

'Au Cygne'. Navy style clothes. 94, boulevard Fernand Moureaux - Tel (33) 2 31 88 13 90 ; Fax (33) 2 31 81 30 49.

Henri Pennec-Cheesemaker. This poet-cum-cheese maker has invented around forty different cheeses. At the Trouville market (on Wednesdays and Sundays) the Deauville market (Saturday) and that of Honfleur (Saturday) Sold on the farm at *Saint-Benoît d'Hébertot :* Tel (33) 2 31 64 25 38 or (33) 2 31 64 39 49.

La Vacquerie : **'Angorella'.** Hand made knitting in angora wool. Route de Saint-Lô - Tel (33) 2 31 77 46 85.

AREA OF EURE

Les Barils : **'L'Epicier Normand'.** Local and home made produce (jams, jars of fruit and vegetables, terrines…).2, rue de Verneuil - Tel (33) 2 32 60 05 88. Fax: (33) 2 32 60 27 60.

Bernay : **'La Cour des Miracles',** home made produce. Fine wine cellar (50 sorts of Calvados and 100 sorts of whisky). Cobble courtyard dating back to the 15th century - Tel (33) 2 32 43 25 34.

Evreux : **'Au Jardin de Pomone'.** All produce is from the Norman region.15, rue Edouard-Feray - Tel (33) 2 32 33 06 81. Fax (33) 2 32 62 61 64.

Conches-en-Ouche : **'Maison Thoumyre - Since 1928 ...'.** Big choice of period and country furniture, knick-knacks and English furniture, ancient and modern paintings. 3, rue Grand Mare - Tel (33) 2 32 30 04 38.

Ménilles : **'Boutique René Verdière',** this is a professional, who has assembled period furniture, knick-knacks, paintings and antique jewellery and silverware. Open every day except on Sundays mornings. Wednesdays and Thursdays by appointment.17, rue aux Honfroy - Tel (33) 2 32 36 17 93.

AREA OF SEINE-MARITIME

Le Havre :

'Comptoir des Arômes'. 65, rue Président Wilson - Le Havre - Saint-Vincent. Fine grocery with possibility of tasting goods: bulk tea, marzipan, marshmallow, old style mustards, cloves of vanilla, aromatic and medicinal herbs in bulk, home made gingerbread, pink pepper chocolate, crystallised lemon… All this produce can be sold in small quantities.

'Bois d'Enfer' 39, rue Racine. Pedestrian quarter. Situated on two levels, you find the narrow workshop of an artist who sells his own works : lamps, little, tables, chairs, frames, strange or functional objects made with materials salvaged from the beach around Le Havre (rusty metal, flotsam, cord, coloured glass, shingles..) Open from Monday to Saturday.

'La Maison de Jade'. 65, rue Paul Doumer, Central quarter. Up market interior decoration (furniture, carpets, tablecloths, varied objects) which display objects made by local creators all year round. All this is shown in a vast luminous area with paving stones from an abbey. Open from Monday to Saturday.

'Cyrille Plate'. 30bis, rue Jean-Baptiste Eyriés, Notre-Dame quarter. Utilisation of material found mostly on the le Havre beach. Cyrille Plate is a specialist of totems, lighting, from bedside lamps to strange shaped lamps.

'Le Salon des Navigateurs'. 1, rue du Petit Croissant, Quartier Saint-François. An original men's hairdressers. A few hundred metres from the fishing port, there are deckchairs in front of the salon. Inside you can find the universe of someone madly enthusiastic about the sea and hairdressing. The outside shop windows display a veritable museum of hairdressing implements from 1900 to the present day. Next to the salon there is a room entierely devoted to the mythical treasures of le Havre's transatlantic memories. 'Tel (33) 2 35 42 12 71.

Rouen : **English Shop.** 103, rue de la Ganterie - Tel (33) 2 35 71 72 80.

2 - Commercial centres and pedestrian precincts

AREA OF MANCHE

Avranches : Saint-Gervais quarter (old town, pedestrian streets).

Cherbourg-Octeville : Central quarter, Old restored Cherbourg with its streets for pedestrians near the port.

Coutances : Old Saint-Pierre quarter. Shopping area around the cathedral. Picturesque quarters : Rues Quesnel-Morinière, St Pierre, Geoffroy-de-Montbray, des Piliers (old quarter).

AREA OF ORNE

Alençon : In the town centre around the Notre Dame church, pedestrian streets (Grande rue, rue du bercail, rue aux Sieurs...).

AREA OF CALVADOS

Caen : Saint-Pierre, Vaugueux, Saint-Jean quarters. Shopping area near the Saint-Pierre church, opposite the castle ramparts as far as the Town Hall. To the south, going towards the railway station the Saint-Jean quarter. Pedestrian streets: rue Saint-Pierre, rue Froide...

Dives-sur-Mer : The Guillaume-le-Conquérant. Village of art. This original quarter of Dives, with its flowers during summer is open to the public free of charge. There are antique shops, jewellers, art galleries, creators of scarves, book shops, leather goods, engravers, upholsterers, wood turners.....

Lisieux : a short walk away from the place François Mitterand (previously Place Royale !) and from the magnificent cathedral where Henry, Duke of Normandy, King of England married Aliénor of Aquitaine; wander down the rue Pont-Mortain which is the main shopping street in town.

AREA OF EURE

Evreux : The main shopping in the town centre : rue de la Harpe, rue Chartraine, rue du Docteur Oursel.

AREA OF SEINE-MARITIME

Rouen : Historic *heart* of Rouen (Old Rouen), quarter surrounding the Notre-Dame cathedral. To the north of the cathedral go down the rue Saint-Romain which is alongside the building and the archbishop's palace.

The narrow street has magnificent half timber houses with double or even triple corbelling and indicates that you are in the quarter of antique dealers, bric à brac, book shops and crockery dealers who are mostly grouped together around the Barthélémy Square, in front of the Saint-Maclou church courtyard. The rue Gros-Horloge (Big Clock) is a pedestrian street leading you to the square, le Vieux-Marché. In the rue Saint-Romain there is a workshop where the expertise of the old Rouen ceramists is perpetuated.

Le Havre : there are many shops in the town centre around the Hôtel-de-Ville. Pedestrian streets : rue Victor-Hugo and rue Louis-Brindeau.

Dieppe : The oldest Norman seaside resort still carries traces of medieval times although the inner city was rebuilt at the end of the 17th century after a great fire had destroyed Dieppe. The main shopping street, much appreciated by tourists runs parallel to the sea front. Right in the heart of Dieppe, it crosses over the 'Place du Puits Sale", reminding us that in olden times, sometimes at high tide, salt water would get mixed up with the fresh water in the town drinking well. In a typically Norman, 18th century building, you will come across the Café des Tribunaux; it's worth spending a few minutes on its terrace to cast a glance at the town and the sight of it's heaving population.

3 - Picturesque Markets

Other than the traditional markets, there are many picturesque markets as well as temporary markets, old fashioned style, special markets, night markets… take place in most towns in the different regions. Information in the Tourist Offices.

NB : some old style markets and special markets can take place during the week and even on Sundays in July and August.

Things to do : **in the area of Calvados.**

Old style markets in July and August : at *Amaye-surseulles,* 'Le Clos d'Orval", on Wednesday afternoons. At ***Cambremer,*** *every* Sunday morning. At ***Lisieux,*** 'Summer Wednesdays' every Wednesdays from 4 pm in the Cour Matignon, near the cathedral. At *Le Molay-Littry,* on Sundays mornings at the Moulin de Marcy. At *Orbec,* country market on Sundays mornings, place de la Poissonnerie. At ***Pont-l'Evêque,*** place des Dominicaines, on Sundays mornings. At ***Saint-***

Pierre-sur-Dives : 'Les animations du cloître de Saint-Pierre-sur-Dives', every Friday from 5-8 pm.

Also in Calvados, the **Fish Market**, at ***Caen Mondeville***, 'La Criée", every morning from Tuesday to Saturday from 9-11 am. At ***Courseulles***, Quai des Alliés, every day. At ***Dives-sur-Mer,*** at the port, every morning in July and August. At ***Ouistreham*** and ***Grandcamp-Maisy***, every morning, in the port. At ***Port-en Bessin***, in the port, on Sunday morning. At ***Trouville***, on the piers, every day of the year. **Antique Markets** : on the 2nd Sunday of each month: ***Honfleur,*** bric à brac , parvis Léonard and rue Cachin (all day) and at ***Ouistreham*** at the Grange-aux-Dîmes. At ***Saint-Pierre-sur-Dives***, antique market every Sunday of each month in the Halles de Saint-Pierre. Art Market, at ***Caen***, the last Saturday of each month, Quartier des Quatrans.

Weekly Markets

AREA OF MANCHE

Agneaux : on Mondays

Agon-Coutainville : on Tuesdays, Thursdays, Fridays and Saturdays

Avranches: on Tuesdays (during the season), on Saturdays

Barneville-Carteret : on Saturdays

Brécey : on Thursdays and Fridays

Bréhal : on Tuesdays

Bricquebec : on Mondays

Canisy : on Fridays

Carentan : on Mondays and Fridays

Carolles : on Thursdays

Cérences : on Thursdays

Cerisy-la-Forêt : on Wednesdays

Chef-du-Pont : on Wednesdays (during the season)

Cherbourg-Octeville : on Tuesdays and Thursdays

Condé-sur-Vire : on Wednesdays

Coutances : on Thursdays

Créances : on Saturdays

Dragey : on Mondays

Ducey : on Tuesdays and Sundays (during the season)

Flamanville : on Wednesdays

Genêts : on Sundays (during the season)

Ger : on Thursdays

Gouville-sur-Mer : on Fridays

Granville : on Wednesdays and Saturdays

Hambye : on Tuesdays

Jullouville : on Tuesdays (during the season) and Fridays

Juvigny-le-Tertre : on Mondays

Kairon : on Sundays (during the season)

La Haye-Pesnel : on Wednesdays

La Haye-du-Puits : on Wednesdays

Lessay : on Tuesdays

Marigny : on Wednesdays

Montbray : on Thursdays

Montebourg : on Saturday mornings

Montmartin-sur-Mer : on Wednesdays

Mortain : on Saturdays

Octeville-Cherbourg : on Wednesdays and Saturdays

Picauville : on Fridays

Les Pieux : on Fridays

Pontorson : on Wednesdays

Port-Bail : on Tuesdays

Quettehou : on Tuesdays

Roncay : on Fridays

Ronthon : on Mondays (during the season)

Saint-Denis-le-Gast : on Fridays

Saint-Hilaire-du-Harcouët : on Wednesday mornings, market and cattle market (calves, sheep, and piglets)

Saint-James : on Mondays

Saint-Jean-de Daye : on Fridays

Saint-Jean-le-Thomas : on Sundays (during the season)

Saint-Lô : on Saturdays

Saint-Marie-du-Mont : on Wednesdays (during the season)

Sainte-Mère-Eglise : on Thursdays since the 16th century

Saint-Pair-sur-Mer : on Thursdays

Saint-Pierre-Eglise : on Wednesdays
Saint-Pois : on Thursdays
Saint-Sauveur-Landelin : on Thursdays
Sartilly : on Fridays
Sourdeval : on Tuesdays
Le Teilleul : on Thursdays
Tessy-sur-Vire : on Wednesdays
Torigny : cattle market, every Monday morning
Tourlaville : on Wednesdays
Valognes : on Fridays
Villedieu-les-Poêles : important market every Tuesday, Friday and Saturday

AREA OF CALVADOS

Argences : on Thursdays
Arromanches : on Wednesdays (during the season) and on Saturdays
Aunay-sur-Odon : on Saturdays
Balleroy : on Tuesdays
Bayeux : on Wednesdays, on Saturdays
Beaumont-en Auge : on Saturdays
Le Bény-Bocage : on Thursday mornings
Bernières-sur-Mer : on Wednesday mornings
Beuvron : on Saturday afternoons
Blainville-sur-Orne : on Fridays
Blangy-le-Château : on Thursdays
Blonville-sur-Mer : during the season, on Tuesdays and Fridays
Bonnebosq : on Wednesdays
Bretteville--sur-Laize : on Mondays and Thursdays
Cabourg : every Wednesday, during the season : on Mondays, Tuesdays, Thursdays and Fridays.
Caen (Calvaire-Saint-Pierre) : on Wednesdays, Sundays.
Caen (Chemin vert) : on Thursdays.
Caen (Grâce de Dieu) : on Tuesdays.
Caen (rue de Bayeux) : on Tuesdays.
Caen Guérinière) : on Thursdays.
Caen (Boulevard Leroy) : on Wednesdays and on Saturdays.
Caen (Pierre-Heuzé) : on Thursdays and on Saturdays.
Caen (Saint-Sauveur) : on Fridays.
Caen (Vénoix) : on Wednesdays.
Cahagnes : on Fridays
Cairon : on Thursdays and Sundays

La Cambe : on Thursdays (during the season), and Fridays
Cambremer : on Fridays, old style market every Sunday morning (during the season) as well as Easter and Pentecost. Local produce, from the Pays d'Auge (fruit, vegetables, cheeses, cider, pommeau, jam)
Carpiquet : on Sundays
Caumont-l'Eventé : on Thursdays
Clécy : market with local produce, every Sunday mornings (during the season)
Condé-sur-Noireau : on Thursdays
Courseulles-sur-Mer : on Tuesdays and Fridays
Creully : on Wednesdays
Deauville : on Tuesdays, Fridays and Saturdays. During the season: on Mondays, Wednesdays and Thursdays.
Démouville : on Tuesdays
Dives-sur-Mer : on Saturdays. On Tuesdays (during the season)
Douvres-la Délivrande : on Thursdays and Saturdays
Dozulé : on Tuesdays
Evrecy : on Wednesdays
Falaise : on Saturdays
Fleury-sur-Orne : on Saturdays
Fontenay-le-Marmion : on Thursdays
Giberville : on Wednesdays
Grandchamp-Maisy : on Tuesdays and Saturdays
Graye-sur-Mer : on Fridays
Hermanville-sur-Mer : on Tuesdays
Hérouville-Saint-Clair : on Tuesdays, Wednesdays and Saturdays
Honfleur : on Wednesdays, Saturdays mornings around the Sainte-Catherine Church.
Houlgate : on Mondays and Thursdays. During the season: on Tuesdays, Wednesdays, Fridays and Saturdays.
Ifs : on Wednesdays
Isigny-sur-Mer : on Wednesdays and Saturdays
Landelles-et-Coupigny : on Wednesdays
Langrune-sur Mer : on Mondays (during the season), on Friday mornings
Lion-sur-Mer : on Thursdays (during the season)
Lisieux : on Saturdays (Place de la République), on Wednesdays (Hauteville).
Livarot : on Thursdays

Louvigny : on Saturdays

Luc-sur-Mer : on Wednesdays (during the season), on Saturdays

May-sur-Orne : on Fridays

Merville-Franceville : on Thursdays (during the season)

Le Mollay-Litry : on Thursdays

Mouen : on Saturdays

Mondeville : on Tuesdays and Thursdays

Orbec : on Wednesday mornings. Flower Market in May.

Ouistreham-Riva-Bella : every day (during the season) except on Mondays

Pont-l'Evêque : on Mondays

Port-en-Bessin : on Sunday mornings

Potigny : on Wednesdays

La Rivière-Saint-Sauveur : on Sunday mornings (during the season)

Saint-Aubin-sur-Mer : on Thursdays (during the season), on Sundays

Saint-Martin-des-Besaces : on Saturdays

Saint-Pierre-sur-Dives : on Mondays

Saint Martin-de-Tallevende : on Saturdays

Saint-Sever : on Saturdays

Soliers : on Fridays

Thaon : on Wednesdays

Thury-Harcourt : on Tuesdays

Tilly-sur-Seulles : on Sundays

Touques : on Saturdays

Trévières : on Fridays

Troarn : on Saturdays

Trouville-sur-Mer : on Wednesdays and Sundays. During the season : on Mondays, Tuesdays, Thursdays, Fridays and Saturdays.

Verson : on Saturdays

Vers-sur-Mer : on Wednesdays (during the season)

Vierville-sur-Mer : on Mondays

Villers-sur-Mer : Every Tuesday. During the season : on Mondays, Wednesdays, Thursdays, Fridays and Saturdays.

Villerville : on Tuesdays and Fridays

Vire : on Tuesdays and Fridays

AREA OF ORNE

Alençon : on Tuesdays, Thursdays, Saturdays and Sundays

Argentan : on Tuesday and Friday mornings (Place de l'Eglise Saint-Germain), on Sunday mornings (Quartier Saint-Martin)

L 'Aigle : on Tuesday mornings and Saturdays. L'Aigle Market : classed as the 3rd biggest and most important market in France. Every Tuesday morning, it consists of a cattle market (+ than 1000 animals) in a covered market situated on the route d'Argentan and a big traditional market in the town centre.

Athis-de-l'Orne : on Tuesdays

Bagnoles-de-1'Orne : on Tuesdays and Saturdays

Bellême : on Thursdays

Bretoncelles : on Thursdays and Saturdays

Briouze : on Monday mornings (calf market)

Carrouges : on Wednesdays

Céaucé : on Thursdays

Céton : on Sundays

La Chapelle-d'Andaine : on Fridays

Condé-sur-Huisne : on Fridays

Courtomer : on Fridays

Damigny : on Wednesdays

Domfront : on Fridays. Medieval Market in August.

Ecouché : on Fridays

Le Ferté-Fresnel : on Thursdays

La Ferté-Macé : on Thursdays

Flers : on Wednesdays. Last Wednesday in August there is the traditional Saint-Gilles Market, rue de Paris.

Gacé : on Saturday afternoons

Longny-au-Perche : on Wednesday mornings Sunday mornings for farm produce.

Le Mêle-sur-Sarthe : on Wednesdays

Le Merlerault : on Thursdays

Messei : on Thursdays

Mortagne-au-Perche : on Saturdays

Moulins-la-Marche : on Thursdays

Nocé : on Tuesdays

Passais-la-Conception : on Tuesdays

Pervenchères : on Tuesdays

Putanges-Pont-Ecrepin : on Thursdays

Reines : on Saturdays

Rémalard : on Mondays

Sainte-Gauburge/Sainte-Colombe : on Wednesdays and Saturdays

Le Sap : on Saturdays

Sées : on Saturdays

Soligny-la-Trappe : Tuesday all day, market 'au cadran' (cattle).

Le Theil-sur-Huisne : on Wednesdays

Tessé-la Madeleine/Bagnoles : on Wednesdays and Fridays

Tinchebray : on Mondays

Tourouvre : on Fridays

Trun : on Thursdays

Vimoutiers : on Monday afternoons and Friday mornings. It is one of the oldest markets in Normandy, as it was created in the 10th century. The butter market which took place there until the 60's was the biggest in the region.

AREA OF EURE

Les Andelys : on Saturdays

La Barre-en-Ouche : on Wednesdays

Beaumont-le Roger : on Tuesdays and Fridays

Bernay : on Saturday mornings

Beuzeville : on Tuesday mornings

Breteuil-sur-Iton : on Wednesdays

Brionne : on Thursdays and Sundays

Cormeilles : on Friday mornings. Country market every Sunday morning (during the season).

Damville : on Tuesdays and Sundays

Drucourt : on Saturdays

Evreux : on Wednesday, Saturday and Sunday mornings

Gisors : on Mondays

Giverville : on Sundays

Louviers : on Saturdays

Lyons-la-Forêt : on Thursdays

Le Neubourg : on Wednesdays

Nonancourt : on Wednesdays

Pont-Audemer : on Monday and Friday mornings

Saint-Rémy-sur-Avre-: on Saturdays

Thiberville : on Mondays

Verneuil-sur-Avre : on Saturdays

AREA OF SEINE-MARITIME

Auffay : on Friday mornings - big country market

Aumale : on Saturday mornings - country market

Bacqueville-en-Caux : on Wednesday mornings - country market

Barentin : on Saturday mornings

Bellencombre : on Tuesday mornings

Blangy-sur-Bresle : on Sunday mornings - country market

Bolbec : on Monday mornings

Bonsecours : on Friday mornings

Bosc-le Hard : on Wednesday mornings

Bouille (La) : on Wednesday mornings

Buchy : on Monday mornings in the 17th century Halles

Cany-Barville : on Monday mornings - country market

Caudebec-en-Caux : on Saturday mornings

Caudebec-lès-Elbeuf : on Sunday mornings

Criel-sur-Mer : on Wednesday and Thursday mornings (on Sunday mornings from July to September) - country market

Clères : on Fridays afternoons

Criquetot-l'Esneval : on Friday mornings - country market

Darnétal : on Saturday mornings afternoons and Sunday mornings

Dieppe : on Saturday mornings - big country market

Duclair : on Tuesday mornings - big country market

Elbeuf : on Saturday mornings

Envermeu : on Saturday mornings - country market

Etretat : on Thursdays - country market

Eu : on Friday mornings - country market

Fauville-en-Caux : on Friday mornings - country market

Fécamp : on Saturdays, all day long - country market

Fontaine-le-Dun : on Thursday mornings - country market

Foucarmont : on Tuesday afternoons - country market

Goderville : on Tuesday mornings - country market

Gonneville-la-Mallet : on Wednesday mornings - country market

Harfleur : on Sunday mornings

Le Havre : many markets

Lillebonne : on Wednesday mornings

Longueville-sur-Scie : on Sunday mornings - country market

Luneray : on Sunday mornings - country market

Montivilliers : on Thursday mornings - country market

Montville : on Saturday mornings

Neufchâtel-en-Bray : on Saturday mornings - big country market

Offranville : on Friday mornings - country market

Pavilly : on Thursday mornings - big country market

Rouen : Place du Vieux-Marché : every day (except Mondays), (large choice of Norman cheese). - Place Saint-Marc : on Tuesday, Friday, Saturday and Sunday mornings. - Place des Emmurés : on Tuesday, Thursday ('bric-à-brac') and Saturday mornings

Ry : on Saturday mornings

Saint-Jacques-sur-Darnétal : on Saturday mornings

Saint-Léger-du-Bourg-Denis : on Sunday mornings

Saint-Nicolas-d'Arliermont : on Sunday mornings - country market

Saint-Romain-de-Colbosc : on Saturdays mornings

Saint-Saëns : on Thursday mornings

Saint-Valery-en-Caux : on Friday mornings (on Sunday mornings from June to September)

Tôtes : on Wednesday mornings - country market

Trait (Le) : on Saturday afternoons

Tréport (Le) : on Tuesday and Saturday mornings - country market

Valmont : on Wednesday mornings - country market

Veules-les-Roses : on Wednesday mornings - country market

Yerville : on Tuesday mornings - country market

Yport : on Wednesday mornings - country market

Yvetot : on Wednesday and Saturday mornings - big country market

LONDRES

CALAIS

BRUXELLES

ALLEMAGNE

CHERBOURG

LE HAVRE

CAEN

ROUEN

PARIS

LE MONT SAINT MICHEL

BRETAGNE

RN 12

Alençon

LE MANS

CHATEAUX DE LA LOIRE

BORDEAUX - ESPAGNE

385

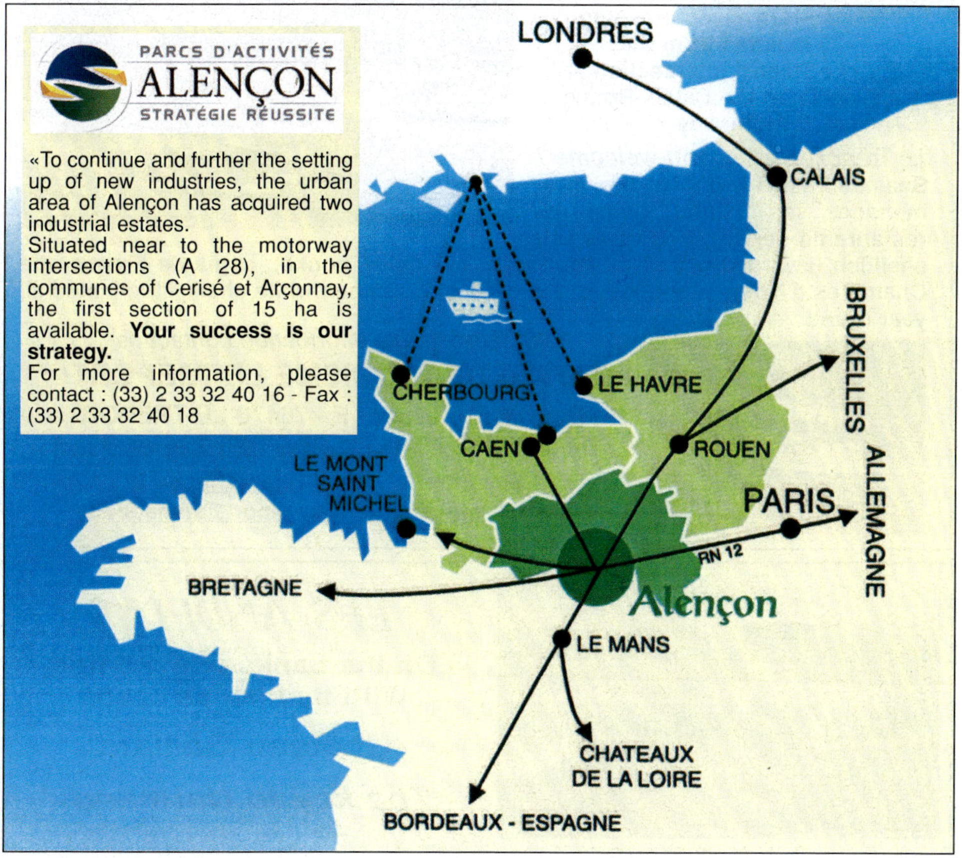

ÉVREUX
town of tradition and history

Contact :
(33) 2 32 31 82 60

LE TRÉPORT
Enjoy life on the open sea !

**20 minutes away to the north
of landing of the
Dieppe-Newhaven crossing
30 minutes from the
Eu - Le Tréport intersection at
Abbeville on the Calais-Rouen
motorway**

Le Tréport wishes you welcome !
Seaside resort with Casino, promenades sea fishing, numerous restaurants serving fresh fish and shellfish (awarded prizes or figuring in the guide books), Logis de France and Chambres d'Hôtes at the foot of the cliffs of European white chalk, illuminated all year round

ERIC-PHOTO

B. FARCY-PIXELL LE HAVRE

For more ample information contact us :
OFFICE DE TOURISME LE TRÉPORT***
**Quai Sadi-Carnot - F - 76470 LE TRÉPORT
Tel (33) 2 35 86 05 69 - Fax (33) 2 35 86 73 96**
Site Internet : www.ville-le-treport.fr
E-mail : officetourismeletreport@wanadoo.fr

LES ANDELYS

On the banks of the Seine
With its famous castle

'Château Gaillard'

'The key to Normandy'

Tourist Office : (33) 2 32 54 41 93 - Mairie : (33) 2 32 54 04 16
www.ville-andelys.fr

VILLEDIEU-LES-POÊLES

MUSEUM OF NORMAN FURNITURE
(150 models of typical period furniture)

MUSEUM OF LACE AND MUSEUM OF PANS

9, rue du Reculé
Tel (33) 2 33 61 11 78

Cour du Foyer
Tel (33) 2 33 90 20 92

CULTURE, ART and TRADITION form our HERITAGE

MEM RIAL PEGASUS

Relive the dawn of June 6th 1944 !

This new historical site is dedicated to the men of the British 6th Airborne, first of the liberators landing in Normandy during the night of June 5th to the 6th 1944. Situated in a park of 12.000m² the Memorial associates a modern museum exhibiting an exceptional collection and the original Pegasus Bridge.

Open every day except December and January. Open all through the day in summer.

Guided visit and screening of filmed archives.

Entrance fee : Individuals 5 € per person. Groups 3,5 € per person.

Tel (33) 2 31 78 19 44 - Fax (33) 2 31 78 19 42
Avenue du Major Howard - 14860 RANVILLE
E-mail : memorial.pegasus@wanadoo.fr

Museum of the D-Day Landing in Arromanches

The permanent landing exhibition is situated opposite the remains of the extraordinary artificial port, real life souvenirs, relief plans, animated models, diorama, and filmed archives from the British Admiralty.

Open every day. The visit of 1h15 is commented by a guide.

The price is modest : 5 € per person (group tariff), 6 € per person (individual tariff).

Tel (33) 2 31 22 34 31 - Fax (33) 2 31 92 68 83 - 14117 ARROMANCHES
Internet : http://www.normandy1944.com

Experience our short breaks packages :

La Manche,
it's just across the water !

From Cherbourg
to Mont Saint-Michel,
for those who take the time to explore,
this little corner of Normandy
has many hidden delights...

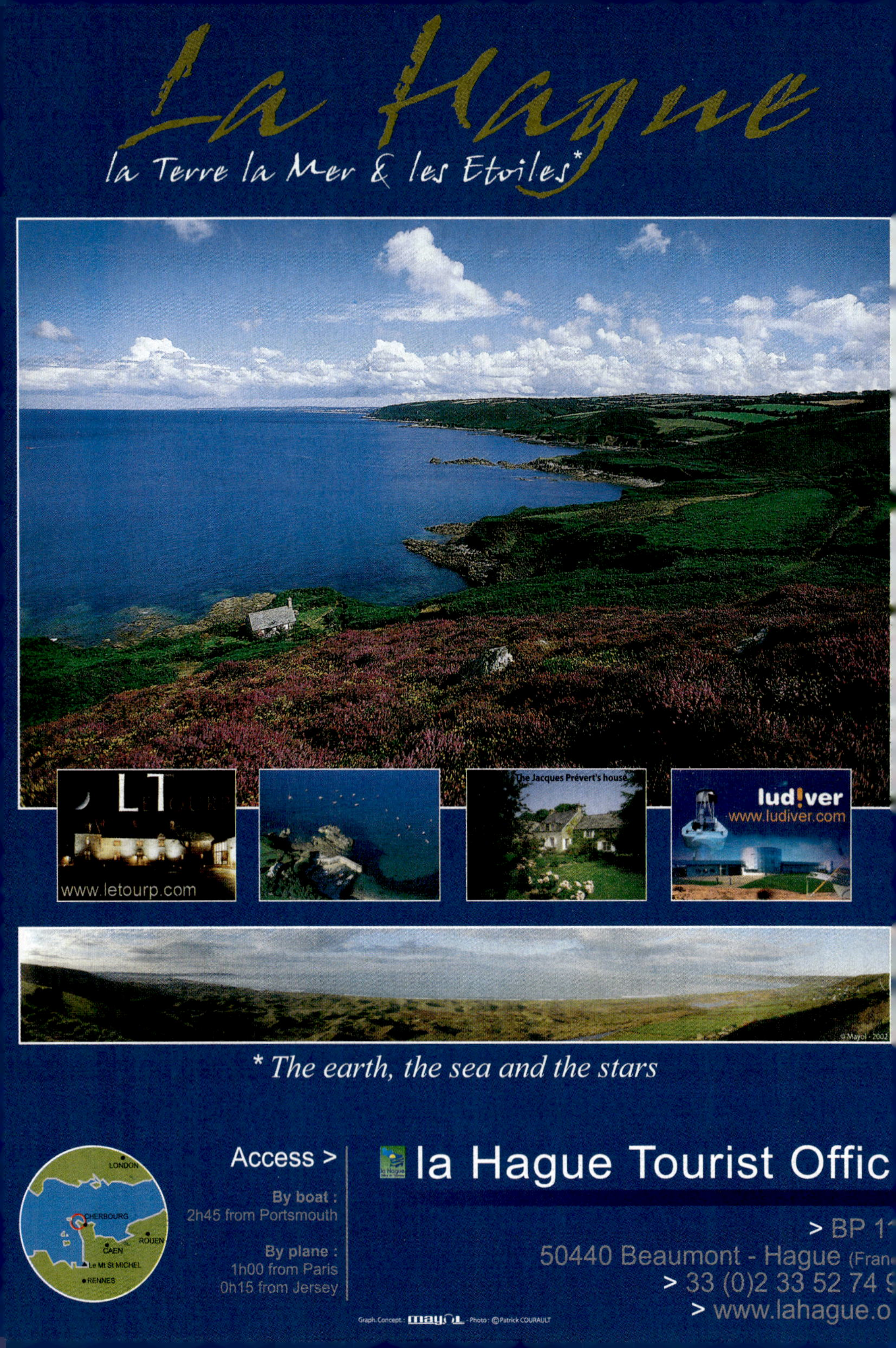

La Hague

la Terre la Mer & les Etoiles*

www.letourp.com

The Jacques Prévert's house

lud!ver
www.ludiver.com

* The earth, the sea and the stars

Access >

By boat :
2h45 from Portsmouth

By plane :
1h00 from Paris
0h15 from Jersey

la Hague Tourist Offic

> BP 1
50440 Beaumont - Hague (Fran
> 33 (0)2 33 52 74 9
> www.lahague.o

Graph. Concept.: mayol - Photo : © Patrick COURAULT

LA CITÉ DE LA MER
CHERBOURG

Dive into a world of sensations and emotions…

On the historic site of the **Transatlantic Ship Terminal**, La Cité de la Mer is more than three hours of adventure for all the family. **Explore Le Redoutable**, the world's largest submarine open to the public, and pilot a virtual submarine in a dynamic dive situation in a reconstituted operations room. **Discover the Abyssal Aquarium**, a giant trench of 350,000 litres of seawater, and the 16 theme tanks and meet the Denizens of the sea.
The whole extent of underwater conquest awaits you.

www.citedelamer.com

Tel : + 33 825 33 50 50

La Cité de la Mer, subaquatic sensation.

ÉCOMUSÉE DU PERCHE

The living museum of the Perche is situated in a Benedictine Priory founded in the XIth century. It maintains simultaneously both remarkable architecture and the testimony of peasant culture.

It is possible to visit the Priory during weekends and school holidays. Nearby, paths for ramblers.

Open every day from 14h to 18h except Tuesdays. Shop, bookshop, light drinks, sweets. Bicycle park, enclosure for horses, picnic area.

ÉCOMUSÉE DU PERCHE
Prieuré de Sainte-Gauburge
61130 SAINT-CYR-LA-ROSIÈRE
Tel (33) 2 33 73 48 06

vranches
keeper of the manuscripts
of Mont Saint-Michel

Let's share our treasures...

Within a stone's throw to Mont Saint-Michel, discover the treasure of the Saint-Gervais Basilica, the thousand-year old manuscripts from Mont Saint-Michel, the Municipal Museum and its collections, the Public Gardens with its unique view over the Bay of Mont Saint-Michel.

AVRANCHES
is located on the A84 (Estuary Motorway),
1 hour drive from Rennes - 1 hour drive from Caen
and 20mm drive from Mont Saint-Michel.
Tel : +33(0)233 58 00 22.
www.ville-avranches.fr

Création : GENOT communication - 33 (0) 1 16 00 Crédit photos : Ville d'Avranches et Paul Hay.

Make Caen your port of call

CAEN
NORMANDY

CAEN
NORMANDIE
CITY COUNCIL
14027 CAEN CEDEX
02 31 30 45 70
www.ville-caen.fr

TOURIST OFFICE
14000 CAEN
02 31 27 14 14

Caen   *City of William the Conqueror*

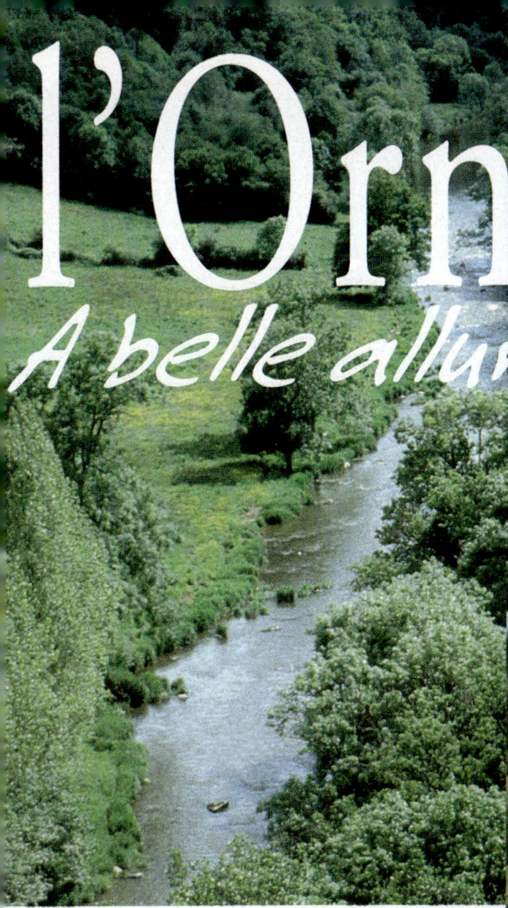

Take a breath of fresh air and vitality !

The Orne region, as a giant garden "à la française" is the ideal place to spend just one week-end or more, and to re-discover the real meaning of serenity and tranquillity. The region offers all of the charm unique to the area, with a large selection of dynamic, sportive activities and gastronomy.

- Bagnoles-de-l'Orne, medical watering and holidays place.

The foremost French spa with its natural therapeutic qualities for the treatment of blood disorders and circulatory troubles, and are suitable for all ages. It is a great place for relaxing and rest, on the edge of a beautiful 2 834 acre forest.

- Gastronomy

Enjoy the pleasures of eating with friends and discover our regional specialities such as the famous Camembert, cider, poiret and calvados.

- Take a good gallop in wide and wooded landscapes or simply walking or biking... The Normandy Maine Regional Nature Park offers many open-air activities :

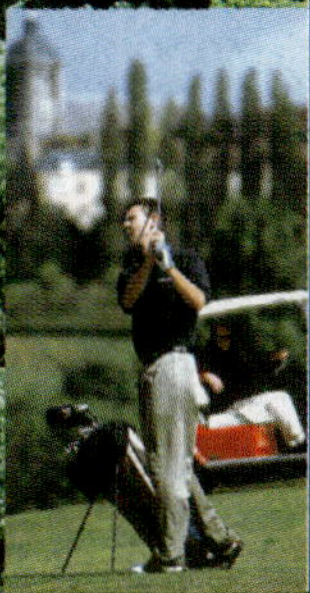

- 18 000 miles of signposts routes for walkers and horsemen
- Organised over-night lodging and stabling
- Horse-drawn caravans for hire
- Cyclists' touring itineraries
- More than 2 500 miles of waterways for fishermen
- Beautiful 18 holes Par 72 5935 m international golf course of Bellême

Don't miss the 2nd edition of great horse festival "La Licorne" taking place in the most beautiful French stud farm, "Haras du Pin", on july 19th and 20th !

Interactive videos to prepare your next holidays !

- Discover our department with interactive streaming videos on our web site :

http://www.cg61.fr

- Contacts

- Comité départemental du tourisme de l'Orne tél : 02 33 28 88 71
- Comité départemental de la randonnée pédestre - tél : 02 33 80 49 00
- Comité départemental de la randonnée équestre - tél : 02 33 35 31 75
- Station thermale de Bagnoles de l'Orne tél : 02 33 37 85 66
- Golf de Bellême - tél : 02 33 73 12 79
- Conseil général : 27, boulevard de Strasbourg 61017 Alençon cedex - tél : 02 33 81 60 00 (Poste 1224).

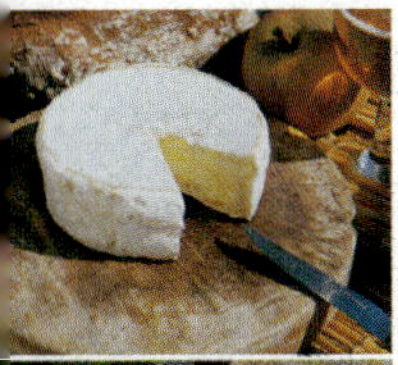

festival équestre la Licorne

L'ORNE
Conseil Général

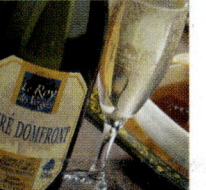

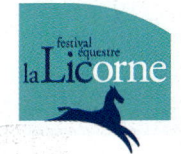

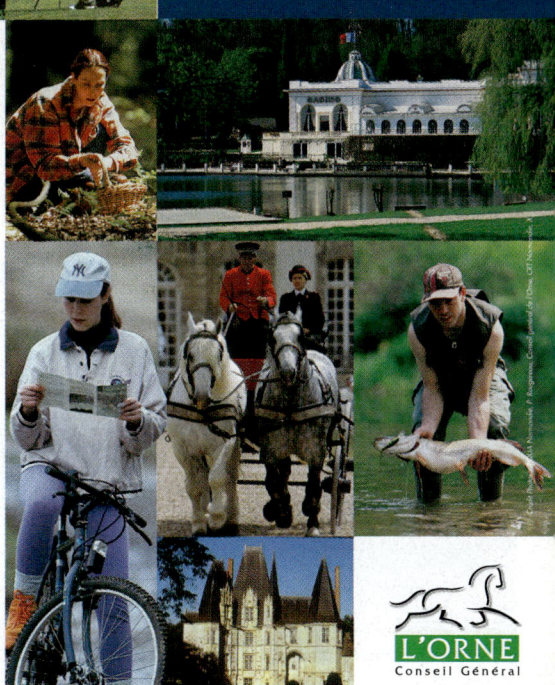

The most
relaxing...

Aaaaãhhh

...or the fastest way
to Normandy

Woooosh

POOLE PORTSMOUTH
CHERBOURG
CAEN

Ease across to Cherbourg or Caen and take full advantage of our award winning service. Or tear across to Cherbourg in just over 2 hours, and start your holiday sooner.
And all for less than you'd expect.

Reservations & Information **0870 908 9699**

Brittany Ferries

Logis de France in Normandy

These are small or medium family-run hotels, almost all of which are situated outside urban aeras, in Normandy's lovely villages.
The Logis de France, mainly classified as 1, 2 or 3 'chimney',
are hotels-restaurants united by a Quality Charter with garantees :
A warm personal welcome as a 'paying guest',
cooking that makes a feature of regional dishes and the chef's own specialities, Prices listed inclusive of service.

For booking in logis de France Hotels :
(33) 1 45 84 83 84
or www.logis-de-france.fr

XIV - GITES AND ACCOMMODATION

AREA OF MANCHE

Le Château d'Agneaux *** - *Agneaux (near Saint-Lô)* - 50180 -
(2 'chimney') - 12 rooms -
Tel (33) 2 33 57 65 88 -Fax (33) 2 33 56 59 21
E.mail : chateaux.agneaux@wanadoo.fr

La Croix d'Or ** - *Avranches* - 50300 -
(3 'chimney') - 27 rooms -
Tel (33) 2 33 58 04 88 - Fax (33) 2 33 58 06 95

Le Jardin des Plantes ** - *Avranches* - 50300 -
(2 'chimney') - 26 rooms -
Tel (33) 2 33 58 03 68 - Fax (33) 2 33 60 01 72
E.mail : jardin.des.plantes@wanadoo.fr

Le Motel des 13 assiettes** - *Pontaubault* (Avranches) - 50300 -
(2 'chimney') - 34 rooms -
Tel (33) 2 33 89 03 03 - Fax (33) 2 33 89 03 06
www.hotel-mont-saint-michel.com - E.mail : regine-baudu@wanadoo.fr

Le Paris ** - *Barneville-Carteret* - 50270 -
(1 'chimney') - 22 rooms -
Tel (33) 2 33 04 90 02 - Fax (33) 2 33 04 01 13

Les Isles ** - *Barneville-Carteret* - 50270 -
(2 'chimney') - 30 rooms -
Tel (33) 2 33 04 90 76 - Fax (33) 2 33 94 53 83

Le Beauvoir ** - *Beauvoir* - 50170 -
(2 'chimney') - 18 rooms -
Tel (33) 2 33 60 09 39 - Fax (33) 2 33 48 59 65

La Gare ** - *Bréhal* - 50290 -
(2 'chimney') - 9 rooms -
Tel (33) 2 33 61 61 11 - Fax (33) 2 33 61 18 02
www.logisdefrancebrehal.com

L'Hostellerie du Château *** - *Bricquebec* - 50260 -
(2 'chimney') - 16 rooms -
Tel (33) 2 33 52 24 49 - Fax (33) 2 33 52 62 71
www.hotelrestvieuxchateau.com

L'Aire de la Baie ** - *Les Veys* - 50500 - Carentan
(2 'chimney') - 40 rooms -
Tel (33) 2 33 42 00 99 - Fax (33) 2 33 71 06 94
www.aire-de-la-baie.com - E.Mail : info@aire-de-la-baie.com

Au P'tit Quinquin ** - *Ceaux* - 50220 -
(1 'chimney') - 18 rooms -
Tel (33) 2 33 70 97 20 - Fax (33) 2 33 70 97 42

Le Pommeray ** - *Ceaux* - 50220 -
(1 'chimney') - 20 rooms -
Tel (33) 2 33 70 92 45 - Fax (33) 2 33 70 95 33
www.le-pommeray.com - E.mail : le pommeray@wanadoo.fr

Le Relais du Mont ** - *Céaux* - 50220 -
(3 'chimney') - 25 rooms -
Tel (33) 2 33 70 92 55 - Fax (33) 2 33 70 94 57
E.mail : contact@mont-saint-michel.com

La Régence ** - *Cherbourg/Octeville* -50100 -
(2 'chimney') - 21 rooms -
Tel (33) 2 33 43 05 16 - Fax (33) 2 33 43 98 37

Le Manoir de la Roche Thorin *** - *Courtils* - 50220 -
(2 'chimney') - 15 rooms -
Tel (33) 2 33 70 96 55 - Fax (33) 2 33 48 35 20
www.manoir-rochetorin.com - E.mail : manoir-rochetorin@wanadoo.fr

Cositel ** - *Coutances* - 50200 -
(3 'chimney') - 55 rooms -
Tel (33) 2 33 19 15 00 - Fax (33) 2 33 19 15 02
www.hotelcositel.com - E.mail : hotelcositel@wanadoo.fr

Les Pins ** - *Denneville* - 50580 -
(1 'chimney') - 21 rooms -
Tel (33) 2 33 76 54 54 - Fax (33) 2 33 07 19 39

La Sélune ** - *Ducey* - 50220 -
(2 'chimney') - 20 rooms -
Tel (33) 2 33 48 53 62 - Fax (33) 2 33 48 90 30
www.selune.com - E.mail : info@sélune.com

Motel du Bocage ** - *Gieville* - 50160 -
(2 'chimney') - 20 rooms -
Tel (33) 2 33 56 06 01 - Fax (33) 2 33 56 05 01

Les Bains *** - *Granville* - 50400 -
(2 'chimney') - 47 rooms -
Tel (33) 2 33 50 17 31 - Fax (33) 2 33 50 89 22

Auberge de l'Abbaye ** - *Hambye* - 50450 -
(2 'chimney') - 7 rooms -
Tel (33) 2 33 61 42 19 - Fax (33) 2 33 61 00 85

La Digue *** - *Le Mont-Saint-Michel* - 50170 -
(2 'chimney') - 36 rooms -
Tel (33) 2 33 60 14 02 - Fax (33) 2 33 60 37 59
www.la-digue.fr - E.mail : hotel-de-la-digue@wanadoo.fr

Le Duguesclin ** - *Le Mont-Saint-Michel* - 50170 -
(2 'chimney') - 10 rooms -
Tel (33) 2 33 60 14 10 - Fax (33) 2 33 60 45 81

Le Motel Vert ** - *Le Mont-Saint-Michel* - 50170 -
(2 'chimney') - 53 rooms -
Tel (33) 2 33 60 09 33 - Fax (33) 2 33 60 20 02
www.le-mont-saint-michel.com
E.mail : stmichel@le-mont-saint-michel.com

Le Relais du Roy *** - *Le Mont-Saint-Michel* - 50170 -
(2 'chimney') - 27 rooms -
Tel (33) 2 33 60 14 25 - Fax (33) 2 33 60 37 69
www.le-relais-du-roy.fr - E.mail : le.relais.du.roy@wanadoo.fr

Le Saint-Pierre *** - *Le Mont-Saint-Michel* - 50170 -
(2 'chimney') - 21 rooms -
Tel (33) 2 33 60 14 03 - Fax (33) 2 33 48 59 82
www.auberge-saint-pierre.fr

La Poste ** - *Periers* - 50190 -
(1 'chimney') - 10 rooms -
Tel (33) 2 33 46 64 01 - Fax (33) 2 33 46 77 11
E.mail : hoteldelaposte2@wanadoo.fr

Le France et Vauban ** - *Pontorson* - 50170 -
(1 'chimney') - 27 rooms -
Tel (33) 2 33 60 03 84 - Fax (33) 2 33 60 35 48
www.hotel-france-vauban.fr

La Tour Brette * - *Pontorson* - 50170 -
(1 'chimney') - 10 rooms -
Tel (33) 2 33 60 10 69 - Fax (33) 2 33 48 59 66
La Bretagne ** - *Pontorson* - 50170 -
(2 'chimney') - 14 rooms -
Tel (33) 2 33 60 10 55 - Fax (33) 2 33 58 20 54
E.mail : debretagne@destination-bretagne.com
Le Montgomery * - *Pontorson* - 50170 -**
(2 'chimney') - 32 rooms -
Tel (33) 2 33 60 00 09 - Fax (33) 2 33 60 37 66
E.mail : hotel.montgomery@wanadoo.fr
info@hotel-montgomery.com
Le Sillon de Bretagne ** - *Pontorson* (Tanis) - 50170 -
(2 'chimney') - 7 rooms -
Tel (33) 2 33 60 13 04 - Fax (33) 2 33 70 91 75
E.mail : hotel@sillon-de-bretagne
Au Moyne de Saire ** - *Reville* - 50760 -
(1 'chimney') - 11 rooms -
Tel (33) 2 33 54 46 06 - Fax (33) 2 33 54 14 99
www.au-moyne-de-saire.com
E.mail : au.moyne.de.saire@wanadoo.fr
Le Cygne * - *Saint-Hilaire-du-Harcouët* - 50600 -**
(2 'chimney') - 29 rooms -
Tel (33) 2 33 49 11 84 - Fax (33) 2 33 49 53 70
www.hotellecygne.com - E.mail : hotel.le.cygne@wanadoo.fr
Le Normandy Hôtel * - *Saint-James* - 50240 -
(2 'chimney') - 10 rooms -
Tel (33) 2 33 48 31 45 - Fax (33) 2 33 48 31 37
Les Bains ** - *Saint-Jean-le-Thomas* - 50530 -
(2 'chimney') - 30 rooms -
Tel (33) 2 33 48 84 20 - Fax (33) 2 33 48 66 42
E.mail : hdesbains@aol.com
Les Voyageurs * - *Saint-Lô* - 50000 -**
(3 'chimney') - 31 rooms -
Tel (33) 2 33 05 08 63 - Fax (33) 2 33 05 14 34
Le Gué du Holme * - *Saint-Quentin-sur-le-Homme* - 50220 -**
(3 'chimney') - 10 rooms -
Tel (33) 2 33 60 63 76 - Fax (33) 2 33 60 06 77
www.le-gue-du-holme.com
Le France et Fuschias ** - *Saint-Vaast-la-Hougue* - 50550 -
(2 'chimney') - 32 rooms -
Tel (33) 2 33 54 42 26 - Fax (33) 2 33 43 46 79
www.france-fuschias.com - E.mail : france.fuschias@wanadoo.fr
Le Sainte-Mère ** - *Sainte-Mère-Eglise* - 50480 -
(2 'chimney') - 41 rooms -
Tel (33) 2 33 21 00 30 - Fax (33) 2 33 41 38 40
E.mail : hotel-le-ste-mère@wanadoo.fr

**Le Temps de Vivre ** - *Sourdeval* - 50150 -
(1 'chimney') - 10 rooms -
Tel (33) 2 33 59 60 41 - Fax (33) 2 33 59 88 34
E.mail : le-temps-de-vivre@wanadoo.fr
**La Clé des Champs ** - *Le Teilleul* - 50640 -
(2 'chimney') - 16 rooms -
Tel (33) 2 33 59 42 27 - Fax (33) 2 33 59 33 71
**L'Orangerie - *Torigni-sur-Vire* - 50160 -
(1 'chimney') - 5 rooms -
Tel (33) 2 33 56 70 64 - Fax (33) 2 33 56 70 64
**Le Grand Hôtel du Louvre ** - *Valognes* - 50700 -
(2 chimney") - 12 rooms -
Tel (33) 2 33 40 00 07 - Fax (33) 2 33 40 13 73
**Le Fruitier ** - *Villedieu-les-Poêles* - 50800 -
(3 'chimney') - 48 rooms -
Tel (33) 2 33 90 51 00 - Fax (33) 2 33 90 51 01
E.mail : hotel.le.fruitier@wanadoo.fr
**Le Saint-Pierre ** - *Villedieu-les-Poêles* - 50800 -
(2 chimney") - 21 rooms -
Tel (33) 2 33 61 00 11 - Fax (33) 2 33 61 06 52
www.st-pierre-hotel.com - E.mail : info@st.pierre.hotel.com
**Le Manoir de l'Acherie ** - *Villedieu-les-Poêles/Sainte-Cécile* - 50800 -
(3 'chimney') - 15 rooms -
Tel (33) 2 33 51 13 87 - Fax (33) 2 33 51 33 69
E.mail : manoir@manoir-acherie.fr

AREA OF CALVADOS

**Le Cardinal ** - *Annebault* (Dozulé) - 14430 -
(2 'chimney') - 6 rooms -
Tel (33) 2 31 64 81 96 - Fax (33) 2 31 64 64 65
www.lecardinalonline.fr - E.mail : cardinal@club-internet.fr
**La Marine ** - *Arromanches* - 14117 -
(2 'chimney') - 28 rooms -
Tel (33) 2 31 22 34 19 - Fax (33) 2 31 22 98 80
www.hotel-de-la-marine.fr - E.mail : hotel.de.la.marine@wanadoo.fr
**Hôtel d'Arromanches ** - *Arromanches* - 14117 -
(2 'chimney') - 9 rooms -
Tel (33) 2 31 22 36 26 - Fax (33) 2 31 22 23 29
www.hoteldarromanches.fr - E.mail : hoteldarromanche@ifrance.com
**Hôtel de Normandie * - *Arromanches* - 14117 -
(1 'chimney') - 20 rooms -
Tel (33) 2 31 22 34 32 - Fax (33) 2 31 21 57 56
www.hoteldenormandie.fr - E.mail : hoteldenormandie@wanadoo.fr
**Le Saint-Michel ** - *Aunay-sur-Odon* - 14260 -
(2 'chimney') - 6 rooms -
Tel (33) 2 31 77 63 16 - Fax (33) 2 31 77 05 83

La Place ** - *Aunay-sur-Odon* - 14260 -
(1 'chimney') - 19 rooms -
Tel (33) 2 31 77 60 73 et (33) 2 31 77 47 46 - Fax (33) 2 31 77 90 07

Le Lion d'Or *** - *Bayeux* - 14400 -
(3 'chimney') - 25 rooms -
Tel (33) 2 31 90 06 90 - Fax (33) 2 31 22 15 64
www.liondor-bayeux.fr - E.mail : lion.d-or.bayeux@wanadoo.fr

La Glycine ** - *Bénouville* - 14970 -
(2 'chimney') - 25 rooms -
Tel (33) 2 31 44 61 94 - Fax (33) 2 31 43 67 30

L'Epi d'Or ** - *Blonville-sur-Mer* - 14910 -
(2 'chimney') - 40 rooms -
Tel (33) 2 31 87 90 48 - Fax (33) 2 31 87 08 98
www.hotel-normand.com - E.mail : epidor@hotel-normand.com

Hôtel du Parc ** - *Cabourg* - 14390 -
(2 'chimney') - 17 rooms -
Tel (33) 2 31 91 00 82 - Fax (33) 2 31 91 00 18
www.hotelduparc-cabourg.com - E.mail : hotel-du-parc1@wanadoo.fr

Hôtel du Golf ** - *Cabourg* - 14390 -
(2 'chimney') - 40 rooms -
Tel (33) 2 31 24 12 34 - Fax (33) 2 31 24 18 51

Otelinn/rest. Le Montgomery ** - *Caen* - 14000 -
(3 'chimney') - 50 rooms -
Tel (33) 2 31 44 34 20 - Fax (33) 2 31 44 63 80
E.mail : otelinn-caen@wanadoo.fr

Din'Hôtel ** - *Caen* - 14000 -
(1 chimney") - 52 rooms -
Tel (33) 2 31 74 20 20 - Fax (33) 2 31 73 13 00

Le Site Normand ** *Clécy* - 14570 -
(2 'chimney') - 18 rooms -
Tel (33) 2 31 69 71 05 - Fax (33) 2 31 69 48 51

Le Cerf ** - *Condé-sur-Noireau* - 14110 -
(2 'chimney') - 9 rooms -
Tel (33) 2 31 69 40 55 - Fax (33) 2 31 69 78 29
www.le-cerf.com - E.mail : restcerf@wanadoo.fr

La Belle Aurore ** - *Courseulles-sur-Mer* - 14470 -
(2 'chimney') - 7 rooms -
Tel (33) 2 31 37 46 23 - Fax (33) 2 31 37 10 70

Hôtel de Paris ** - *Courseulles* - 14470 -
(2 'chimney') - 27 rooms -
Tel (33) 2 31 37 45 07 - Fax (33) 2 31 37 51 63
E.mail : hoteldeparis-normandie@wanadoo.fr

La Crémaillère - Le Gytan ** - *Courseulles* - 14470 -
(2 'chimney') - 40 rooms -
Tel (33) 2 31 37 46 73 - Fax (33) 2 31 37 19 31
www.la-cremaillere.com - E.mail : cremaillere@wanadoo.fr

La Pêcherie ** - *Courseulles* - 14470 -
(3 'chimney') - 6 rooms -
Tel (33) 2 31 37 45 84 - Fax (33) 2 31 37 90 40
www.la-pecherie.com - E.mail : pecherie@wanadoo.fr

La Ferme de la Rançonnière ** - *Crépon* - 14480 -
(2 'chimney') - 34 rooms -
Tel (33) 2 31 22 21 73 - Fax (33) 2 31 22 98 39
www.ranconniere.com - E.mail : ranconniere@wanadoo.fr

Hôtel Saint-Martin ** - *Creully* - 14480 -
(2 'chimney') - 12 rooms -
Tel (33) 2 31 80 10 11 - Fax (33) 2 31 08 17 64
www.hostelleriesaintmartin.com
E.mail : hostellerie.st.martin@wanadoo.fr

Auberge du Cheval Blanc - *Crevecœur-en-Auge* - 14340 -
(2 'chimney') - 4 rooms -
Tel (33) 2 31 63 03 28 - Fax (33) 2 31 63 41 58
E.mail : aubchevalblanc@aol.com

L'Espérance ** - *Deauville* - 14800 -
(2 'chimney') - 10 rooms -
Tel (33) 2 31 88 26 88 - Fax (33) 2 31 88 33 29

Le Trophée ** - *Deauville* - 14800 -
(3 'chimney') 35 rooms -
Tel (33) 2 31 88 45 86 - 88 28 46 - Fax : (33) 2 31 88 07 94
www.letrophee.com - E.mail : information@letrophee.com

L'Aubergade ** - *Deauville/Canapville* - 14800 -
(2 'chimney') - 12 rooms -
Tel (33) 2 31 65 22 59 - Fax (33) 2 31 65 08 14

Le Village ** - *Deauville/Touques* - 14800 -
(2 'chimney') - 8 rooms -
Tel (33) 2 31 88 01 77 - Fax (33) 2 31 88 99 24

Hôtellerie Normande * - *Dozulé* - 14430 -
(1 'chimney') - 12 rooms -
Tel (33) 2 31 79 20 18 - Fax (33) 2 31 39 65 02

Hôtel de la Poste ** - *Falaise* - 14700 -
(2 'chimney') - 15 rooms -
Tel (33) 2 31 90 13 14 - Fax (33) 2 31 90 01 81
E.mail : hotel.delaposte@wanadoo.fr

Auberge du Pont de Brie ** - *Goupillères/Halte de Grimbosq* - 14210 -
(2 'chimney') - 7 rooms -
Tel (33) 2 31 79 37 84 - Fax (33) 2 31 79 87 22
www.pontdebrie.com - E.mail : contact@pontdebrie.com

Le Belvédère ** - *Honfleur* - 14600 -
(2 'chimney') - 9 rooms -
Tel (33) 2 31 89 08 13 - Fax (33) 2 31 89 51 40

La Claire ** - *Honfleur* - 14600 -
(1 'chimney') - 20 rooms -
Tel (33) 2 31 89 05 95 - Fax (33) 2 31 89 11 37
E.mail : auberge.de.la.claire@wanadoo.fr

Auberge de la Source ** - *Honfleur/Barneville-la-Bertan* - 14600 -
(2 'chimney') - 13 rooms -
Tel (33) 2 31 89 25 02 - Fax (33) 2 31 89 44 40

Ferme de la Grande Cour ** - *Honfleur/Equemauville* - 14600 -
(2 'chimney') - 15 rooms -
Tel (33) 2 31 89 04 69 - Fax (33) 2 31 89 27 29
www.fermedelagrandecour.com

Le Romantica ** - *Honfleur/Pennedepie* - 14600 -
(3 'chimney') - 34 rooms -
Tel (33) 2 31 81 14 00 - Fax (33) 2 31 81 54 78

Le Clos Saint-Gatien *** - *Honfleur/Saint-Gatien-des-Bois* - 14130 -
(3 'chimney') - 55 rooms -
Tel (33) 2 31 65 16 08 - Fax (33) 2 31 65 10 27
www.clos-st-gatien.fr - E.mail : hotel@clos-st-gatien.fr

Le Bellevue ** - *Honfleur/Villerville* - 14113 -
(2 'chimney') - 21 rooms -
Tel (33) 2 31 87 20 22 - Fax (33) 2 31 87 20 56
www.bellevue-hotel.fr - E.mail : resa@bellevue-hotel.fr

Ferme des Aulnettes - *Houlgate* - 14510 -
(1 'chimney') - 15 rooms -
Tel (33) 2 31 28 00 28 - Fax (33) 2 31 28 07 21

Au 1900 ** - *Houlgate* - 14510 -
(2 'chimney') - 12 rooms -
Tel (33) 2 31 28 77 77 - Fax (33) 2 31 28 08 07
www.hotel-1900.fr

Hôtel de France ** - *Isigny-sur-Mer* - 14230 -
(2 'chimney') - 18 rooms -
Tel (33) 2 31 22 00 33 - Fax (33) 2 31 22 79 19
www.hotel-france-isigny.com
E.mail : contact@hotel-france-isigny.com

Hôtel de la Mer * - *Langrune-sur-Mer* - 14830 -
(1 'chimney') - 12 rooms -
Tel (33) 2 31 96 03 37 - Fax (33) 2 31 97 57 94
www.hoteldelamer.fr - E.mail : hoteldelamer@wanadoo.fr

La Coupe d'Or ** - *Lisieux* - 14100 -
(2 'chimney') - 14 rooms -
Tel (33) 2 31 31 16 84 - Fax (33) 2 31 31 35 60
www.la-coupe-d-or.com - E.mail : odile@la-coupe-d-or.com

Terrasse Hôtel ** - *Lisieux* - 14100 -
(2 'chimney') - 17 rooms -
Tel (33) 2 31 62 17 65 - Fax (33) 2 31 62 20 25

**Le Vivier ** - Rest. Le Cottage - *Livarot* - 14140 -
("1' chimney") - 9 rooms -
Tel (33) 2 31 32 04 10 - Fax (33) 2 31 32 27 85
www.hotel-du-vivier.com - E.mail : vivier14@club-internet.fr
Hôtel des Thermes et du Casino * - *Luc-sur-Mer* - 14530 -
(3 'chimney') - 48 rooms -
Tel (33) 2 31 97 32 37 - Fax (33) 2 31 96 72 57
www.hotelresto-lesthermes.com
E.mail : hotelresto@hotelresto-lesthermes.com
**Le Beaurivage ** - *Luc-sur-Mer* - 14530 -
(1 'chimney' - 21 rooms -
Tel (33) 2 31 96 49 51 - Fax : (33) 2 31 96 86 15
Chez Marion * - *Merville-Franceville* - 14810 -
(3 'chimney') - 14 rooms -
Tel (33) 2 31 24 23 39 - Fax (33) 2 31 24 88 75
www.chez-marion.com - E.mail : chezmarion@free.fr
**Le Vauban ** - *Merville-Franceville* - 14810 -
(2 'chimney') - 15 rooms -
Tel (33) 2 31 24 23 37 - Fax (33) 2 31 24 54 40
**Le Relais de la Forêt * - *Montfiquet* - 14490 -
(1 'chimney') - 23 rooms -
Tel (33) 2 31 21 39 78 - Fax (33) 2 31 21 44 19
www.relais-de-la-foret.com - E.mail : info@relais-de-la-foret.com
**Le Relais Normand ** - *Noyers-Bocage* - 14210 -
(2 'chimney') - 7 rooms -
Tel (33) 2 31 77 97 37 - Fax (33) 2 31 77 94 41
**Le Normandie - Chalut ** - *Ouistreham* - 14150 -
(2 'chimney') - 22 rooms -
Tel (33) 2 31 97 19 57 - Fax (33) 2 31 97 20 07
www.lenormandie.com - E.mail : hotel@lenormandie.com
**Le Saint-Georges ** - *Ouistreham* - 14150 -
(2 'chimney') - 18 rooms -
Tel (33) 2 31 97 18 79 - Fax (33) 2 31 96 08 94
**Hôtel du Commerce ** - *Pont-d'Ouilly* - 14690 -
(1 'chimney') - 11 rooms -
Tel (33) 2 31 69 80 16 - Fax (33) 2 31 69 78 08
**Auberge Saint-Christophe ** - *Pont-d'Ouilly* - 14690 -
(2 'chimney') - 7 rooms -
Tel (33) 2 31 69 81 23 - Fax (33) 2 31 69 26 58
**Eden Park ** - *Pont-l'Evêque* - 14130 -
(2 'chimney') - 50 rooms -
Tel (33) 2 31 64 64 00 - Fax (33) 2 31 64 12 28
www.edenparkhotel.com - E.mail : edenpark@wanadoo.fr
**La Taverne ** - *Potigny* - 14420 -
(1 'chimney') - 6 rooms -
Tel (33) 2 31 40 75 47 - Fax (33) 2 31 40 99 89

**Auberge de la Jalousie ** - *Saint-Aignan-de-Crasmesnil* - 14540 -
(2 'chimney') - 8 rooms -
Tel (33) 2 31 23 51 69 - Fax (33) 2 31 23 95 55
Hôtel de Normandie - *Saint-Aubin-sur-Mer* - 14750 -
(1 'chimney') - 22 rooms -
Tel (33) 2 31 97 30 17 - Fax (33) 2 31 97 57 37
**Le Clos Normand ** - *Saint-Aubin-sur-Mer* - 14750 -
(3 'chimney') - 31 rooms -
Tel (33) 2 31 97 30 47 - Fax (33) 2 31 96 46 23
E.mail : closnormand@compuserve.com
**Hôtel Saint-Aubin ** - *Saint-Aubin-sur-Mer* - 14750 -
(2 'chimney') - 22 rooms -
Tel (33) 2 31 97 30 39 - Fax (33) 2 31 97 41 56
Le Lighthouse - *Saint-Aubin-sur-Mer* - 14750 -
(2 'chimney') - 5 rooms -
Tel (33) 2 31 97 72 40 - Fax (33) 2 31 97 72 41
E.mail : info@lelighthouse.com
**Auberge Saint-Germain ** - *Saint-Germain-du-Crioult* - 14110 -
(2 'chimney') - 9 rooms -
Tel (33) 2 31 69 08 10 - Fax (33) 2 31 69 14 67
**Les Agriculteurs ** - *Saint-Pierre-sur-Dives* - 14170 -
(1 'chimney') - 10 rooms -
Tel (33) 2 31 20 72 78 - Fax (33) 2 31 20 62 74
E.mail : les.agriculteurs@wanadoo.fr
**La Grande Bruyère ** - *Touffreville-Troarn* - 14940 -
(2 'chimney') - 12 rooms -
Tel (33) 2 31 23 32 74 - Fax (33) 2 31 23 69 79
E.mail : la.grande.bruyere@wanadoo.fr
Le Clos Normand * - *Troarn* - 14670 -
(2 'chimney') - 20 rooms -
Tel (33) 2 31 23 31 28 - Fax (33) 2 31 23 15 72
**Hôtel Carmen ** - *Trouville-sur-Mer* - 14360 -
(2 'chimney') - 16 rooms -
Tel (33) 2 31 88 35 43 - Fax (33) 2 31 88 08 03
E.mail : l.b.carmen@wanadoo.fr
**Hôtel du Casino ** - *Vierville-sur-Mer* - 14710 -
(2 'chimney') - 12 rooms -
Tel (33) 2 31 22 41 02 - Fax (33) 2 31 22 41 12
**Les 3 Rois ** - *Villers-Bocage* - 14310 -
(2 'chimney') - 9 rooms -
Tel (33) 2 31 77 00 32 - Fax (33) 2 31 77 93 25
**Hôtel de France ** - *Vire* - 14500 -
(3 'chimney') - 20 rooms -
Tel (33) 2 31 68 00 35 - Fax (33) 2 31 68 22 65

L'Industrie ** - *Alençon* - 61000 -
   (1 'chimney') - 7 rooms -
   Tel: (33) 2 33 27 19 30 - Fax (33) 2 33 28 49 56
Le Grand Saint-Michel ** - *Alençon* - 61000 -
   (2 'chimney') - 12 rooms -
   Tel (33) 2 33 26 04 77 - Fax (33) 2 33 26 71 82
Le Grand Cerf ** - *Alençon* - 61000 -
   (3 'chimney') - 22 rooms -
   Tel: (33) 2 33 26 00 51 - Fax (33) 2 33 26 63 07
   E.mail : legrandcerfalençon@wanadoo.fr
Hôtel de France ** - *Argentan* - 61200 -
   (2 'chimney') - 10 rooms -
   Tel (33) 2 33 67 03 65 - Fax (33) 2 33 36 62 24
Hôtel des Voyageurs ** - *Argentan* - 61200 -
   (2 'chimney') - 41 rooms -
   Tel (33) 2 33 36 15 60 - Fax (33) 2 33 39 93 29
Hôtel Beaumont ** - *Bagnoles-de-l'Orne* - 61140 -
   (3 'chimney') - 34 rooms -
   Tel (33) 2 33 37 91 77 - Fax (33) 2 33 38 90 61
   E.mail : lebeaumont@compuserv.com
Hôtel de Normandie ** - *Bagnoles-de-l'Orne* - 61140 -
   (2 'chimney') - 22 rooms -
   Tel (33) 2 33 30 71 30 - Fax (33) 2 33 30 71 31
   E.mail : hotel-le-normandie@wanadoo.fr
Le Nouvel Hôtel ** - *Bagnoles-de-l'Orne* - 61140 -
   (3 'chimney') - 30 rooms -
   Tel (33) 2 33 30 75 00 - Fax (33) 2 33 30 75 13
   E.mail : nouvel.hotel@wanadoo.fr
Alirol Celtic ** - *Bagnoles-de-l'Orne* - 61140 -
   (2 'chimney') - 11 rooms -
   Tel (33) 2 33 37 92 11 - Fax (33) 2 33 38 90 27
   E.mail : leceltic@club-internet.fr
Albert Ier ** - *Bagnoles-de-l'Orne* - 61140 -
   (1'chimney') - 22 rooms -
   Tel (33) 2 33 37 80 97 - Fax (33) 2 33 30 03 64
La Potinière du Lac ** - *Bagnoles-de-l'Orne* - 61140 -
   (1 'chimney') - 17 rooms -
   Tel (33) 2 33 30 65 00 - Fax (33) 2 33 38 49 04
   E.mail : Lapotinieredu.lac2@wanadoo.fr
Le Roc au Chien ** - *Bagnoles-de-l'Orne* - 61140 -
   (2 'chimney') - 40 rooms -
   Tel (33) 2 33 37 97 33 - Fax (33) 2 33 37 59 29
Hôtel de Tessé ** - *Bagnoles-de-l'Orne* - 61140 -
   (2 'chimney') - 42 rooms -
   Tel (33) 2 33 30 80 07 - Fax (33) 2 33 38 51 92
   E.mail : hotedetesse@aol.com

**Hôtel du Nord ** - *Carrouges* - 61320 -
(2 'chimney') - 15 rooms -
Tel (33) 2 33 27 20 14 - Fax (33) 2 33 28 83 13
**Le Cheval Blanc ** - *La Chapelle-d'Andaine* - 61140 -
(1 'chimney') - 8 rooms -
Tel (33) 2 33 38 11 88 - Fax (33) 2 33 38 78 60
E.mail : michel.jacquet29@wanadoo.fr
**Hôtel de France ** - *Domfront* - 61700 -
(1 'chimney') - 19 rooms -
Tel (33) 2 33 38 51 44 - Fax (33) 2 33 30 49 54
**Le Relais Saint-Michel ** - *Domfront* - 61700 -
(1 'chimney') - 13 rooms -
Tel (33) 2 33 38 64 99 - Fax (33) 2 33 37 37 96
E.mail : relais.saint.michel.prodhomme@wanadoo.fr
**Le Paradis ** - *La Ferté-Fresnel* - 61550 -
(2 'chimney') - 12 rooms -
Tel (33) 2 33 34 81 33 - Fax (33) 2 33 84 97 52
E.mail : choplin.le.paradis@wanadoo.fr
**Auberge d'Andaine ** - *La Ferté-Macé* - 61600 -
(2 'chimney') - 15 rooms -
Tel (33) 2 33 37 20 28 - Fax (33) 2 33 37 25 05
E.mail : auberge-andaines@hotmail.fr
**Auberge de Clouet ** - *La Ferté-Macé* - 61600 -
(1 'chimney') - 6 rooms -
Tel (33) 2 33 37 18 22 - Fax (33) 2 33 38 28 52
**L'Hostellerie des Champs ** - *Gacé* - 61230 -
(2 'chimney') - 7 rooms -
Tel (33) 2 33 39 09 05 - Fax (33) 2 33 36 81 26
**Au Bon Accueil ** - *Juvigny-sous-Andaines* - 61140 -
(3 'chimney') - 8 rooms -
Tel (33) 2 33 38 10 04 - Fax (33) 2 33 37 44 92
**La Lentillère ** - *La Lacelle* - 61320 -
(2 'chimney') - 6 rooms -
Tel (33) 2 33 27 38 48 - Fax (33) 2 33 27 38 30
**Hôtel de la Poste * - *Le Mêle-sur-Sarthe* - 61270 -
(2 'chimney') - 18 rooms -
Tel (33) 2 33 81 18 00 - Fax (33) 2 33 27 67 20
**Hôtel de la Cloche ** - *Le Theil-sur-Huisne* - 61260 -
(2 'chimney') - 8 rooms -
Tel (33) 2 33 37 49 64 86 - Fax (33) 2 33 37 49 60 25
**Hôtel du Tribunal ** - *Mortagne-au-Perche* - 61400 -
(3 'chimney') - 21 rooms -
Tel (33) 2 33 25 04 77 - Fax (33) 2 33 83 60 83
E.mail : hotel.du.tribunal@wanadoo.fr
**Le Genty Home ** - *Mortagne-au-Perche* - 61400 -
(2 'chimney') - 8 rooms -

Tel (33) 2 33 25 11 53 - Fax (33) 2 33 25 41 38
E.mail : g.palmade@wanadoo.fr

Le Lion Verd ** - *Putanges-Pont-Ecrepin* - 61210 -
(1 'chimney') - 18 rooms -
Tel (33) 2 33 35 01 86 - Fax (33) 2 33 39 53 32
E.mail : hote.lionverd@wanadoo.fr

Le Relais d'Ecouves - *Radon* - 61150 -
(1 'chimney') - 3 rooms -
Tel (33) 2 33 28 41 41 - Fax (33) 2 33 28 41 41
E.mail : relais.decouves@wanadoo.fr

Hôtel Saint-Pierre ** - *Rânes* - 61150 -
(3 'chimney') - 12 rooms -
Tel (33) 2 33 39 75 14 - Fax (33) 2 33 35 49 23

La Normandière - *Saint-Denis-sur-Sarthon* - 61420 -
(1 'chimney') - 3 rooms -
Tel (33) 2 33 27 30 24 - Fax (33) 2 33 27 32 70

Auberge le Valburgeois ** - *Sainte-Gauburge-Sainte-Colombe* - 61370 -
(1 'chimney') - 7 rooms -
Tel (33) 2 33 34 01 44 - Fax (33) 2 33 34 19 24

Le Dauphin ** - *Sées* - 61500 -
(3 'chimney') - 6 rooms -
Tel (33) 2 33 80 80 70 - Fax (33) 2 33 80 80 79

L'Île de Sées ** - *Macé* (Sées) - 61500 -
(3 'chimney') - 16 rooms -
Tel (33) 2 33 27 98 65 - Fax (33) 2 33 28 41 22
E.mail : ile.sees@ile-sees.fr

L'Escale du Vitou ** - *Vimoutiers* - 61120 -
(2 'chimney') - 17 rooms -
Tel (33) 2 33 39 12 04 - Fax (33) 2 33 36 13 34

AREA OF EURE

Hôtel de Paris ** - *Les Andelys* - 27700 -
(2 'chimney') - 8 rooms -
Tel (33) 2 32 54 00 33 - Fax (33) 2 32 54 65 92
E.mail : thierry.augustin@libertysurf.fr

Château de la Râpée * - *Bazincourt-sur-Epte* - 27140 -**
(3 'chimney') - 13 rooms -
Tel (33) 2 32 55 11 61 - Fax (33) 2 32 55 95 65
E.mail : info@hotel-la-rapee.com

Hôtel le Lion d'Or ** - *Bernay* - 27300 -
(1 'chimney') - 23 rooms -
Tel (33) 2 32 43 12 06 - Fax (33) 2 32 46 60 58
E.mail : hotelliondor@wanadoo.fr

Cochon d'Or et Petit Castel ** - *Beuzeville* - 27210 -
(2 'chimney') - 20 rooms -
Tel (33) 2 32 57 70 46 - Fax (33) 2 32 42 25 70
E.mail : auberge-du-cochon-dor@wanadoo.fr

Hôtel de la Poste ** - *Beuzeville* - 27210 -
(2 'chimney') - 14 rooms -
Tel (33) 2 32 20 32 32 - Fax (33) 2 32 42 11 01
La Corne d'Abondance ** - *Bourgtheroulde* - 27520 -
(2 'chimney') - 11 rooms -
Tel (33) 2 35 78 68 01 - Fax (33) 2 35 78 50 41
E.mail : corne.d.abondance@libertysurf.fr
Hôtel Le Logis ** - *Brionne* - 27800 -
(3 'chimney') - 12 rooms -
Tel (33) 2 32 44 81 73 - Fax (33) 2 32 45 10 92
E.mail : lelogisdebrionne@free.fr
Hôtel des 2 Sapins ** - *Cailly-sur-Eure* - 27490 -
(2 'chimney') - 15 rooms -
Tel (33) 2 32 67 75 13 - Fax (33) 2 32 67 73 62
E.mail : juhel.eric@wanadoo.fr
Hôtel du Cygne ** - *Conches-en-Ouche* - 27190 -
(2 'chimney') - 15 rooms -
Tel (33) 2 32 30 20 60 - Fax (33) 2 32 30 45 73
Auberge du Président ** - *Cormeilles* - 27260 -
(2 'chimney') - 13 rooms -
Tel (33) 2 32 57 80 37 - Fax (33) 2 32 57 88 31
E.mail : aubergedupresident.27@wanadoo.fr
Hôtel de France ** - *Evreux* - 27000 -
(2 'chimney') - 16 rooms -
Tel (33) 2 32 39 09 25 - Fax (33) 2 32 38 38 56
E.mail : info@hoteldefrance-evreux.com
Hôtel Normandy ** - *Evreux* - 27000 -
(2 'chimney') - 20 rooms -
Tel (33) 2 32 33 14 40 - Fax (33) 2 32 31 24 74
E.mail : norman.hotel@wanadoo.fr
Hôtel le Trois Saint-Pierre ** - *Le Goulet* - 27600 -
(2 'chimney') - 20 rooms -
Tel (33) 2 32 52 50 61 - Fax (33) 2 32 52 50 74
E.mail : cannisses@wanadoo.fr
Au Grand Saint-Martin - *Ivry-la-Bataille* - 27540 -
(2 'chimney') - 9 rooms -
Tel (33) 2 32 22 35 95 - Fax (33) 2 32 22 35 90
Hôtel La Haye Le Comte *** - *Louviers* - 27400 -
(2 'chimney') - 16 rooms -
Tel (33) 2 32 40 00 40 - Fax (33) 2 32 25 03 85
E.mail : hotel-la-haye-le-comte@wanadoo.fr
Domaine Saint-Paul ** - *Lyons-la-Forêt* - 27480 -
(2 'chimney') - 17 rooms -
Tel (33) 2 32 49 60 57 - Fax (33) 2 32 49 56 05
E.mail : domaine-saint-paul@libertysurf.fr

Au Grand Saint-Martin ** - *Le Neubourg* - 27110 -
(2 'chimney') - 9 rooms -
Tel (33) 2 32 35 04 80 - Fax (33) 2 35 35 02 30
Hôtel Altina ** - *Pacy-sur-Eure* - 27120 -
(2 'chimney') - 29 rooms -
Tel (33) 2 32 36 13 18 - Fax (33) 2 32 26 05 11
E.mail : altinasa@aol.com
La Bonne Marmite *** - *Pont-Saint-Pierre* - 27360 -
(3 'chimney') - 9 rooms -
Tel (33) 2 32 49 70 24 - Fax (33) 2 32 48 12 41
E.mail : la.bonne.marmite@wanadoo.fr
Hôtel Le Soleil d'Or - *La Rivière-Thibouville* - 27550 -
(2 'chimney') - 12 rooms -
Tel (33) 2 32 45 00 08 - Fax (33) 2 32 46 89 68
E.mail : le.soleil.dor@wanadoo.fr
Hôtel de France - *Saint-Georges-du-Vièvre* - 27450 -
(1 'chimney') - 4 rooms -
Tel (33) 2 32 42 81 13 - Fax (33) 2 32 42 81 13
Hôtel Le Saumon ** - *Verneuil-sur-Avre* - 27130 -
(2'chimney') - 29 rooms -
Tel (33) 2 32 32 02 36 - Fax (33) 2 32 37 55 80
E.mail : hotel.saumon@wanadoo.fr
Hôtel d'Evreux ** - *Vernon* - 27200 -
(2 'chimney') - 12 rooms -
Tel (33) 2 32 21 16 12 - Fax (33) 2 32 21 32 73
E.mail : hotel.devreux@libertysurf.fr

AREA OF SEINE-MARITIME

La Villa des Houx ** - *Aumale* - 76390 -
(3 'chimney') - 22 rooms -
Tel (33) 2 35 93 93 30 - Fax (33) 2 35 93 03 94
E.mail : villa-des-houx@wanadoo.fr
Le Cheval Blanc * - *Caudebec-en-Caux* - 76490 -
(2 'chimney') - 15 rooms -
Tel (33) 2 35 96 21 66 - Fax (33) 2 35 95 35 40
Le Normandie ** - *Caudebec-en-Caux* - 76490 -
(2 'chimney') - 15 rooms -
Tel (33) 2 35 96 25 11 - Fax (33) 2 35 96 68 15
Normotel - La Marine ** - *Caudebec-en-Caux* - 76490 -
(2 'chimney') - 31 rooms -
Tel (33) 2 35 96 20 11 - Fax (33) 2 35 56 54 40
E.mail : lamarine@libertysurf.fr
Les Arcades ** - *Dieppe* - 76200 -
(2 'chimney') - 21 rooms -
Tel (33) 2 35 84 14 12 - Fax (33) 2 35 40 22 29
E.mail : contact@lesarcades.fr

Le Grand Duquesne * - *Dieppe* - 76200 -
(1 'chimney') - 12 rooms -
Tel (33) 2 32 14 61 10 - Fax (33) 2 35 84 29 83
Hôtel Windsor ** - *Dieppe* - 76200 -
(2 'chimney') - 48 rooms -
Tel (33) 2 35 84 15 23 - Fax (33) 2 35 84 74 52
E.mail : windsor@hotelwindsor.fr
Le Relais du Puits Saint-Jean - *Doudeville* - 76560 -
(1 'chimney') - 4 rooms -
Tel (33) 2 35 96 50 99 - Fax (33) 2 35 95 61 82
Le Dormy House *** - *Etretat* - 76790 -
(3 'chimney') - 61 rooms -
Tel (33) 2 35 27 07 88 - Fax : (33) 2 35 29 86 19
E.mail : dormy.house@wanadoo.fr
Hôtel-Restaurant Maine ** - *Eu* - 76260 -
(2 'chimney') - 18 rooms -
Tel (33) 2 35 86 16 64 - Fax (33) 2 35 50 86 25
E.mail : info@hotel-maine.com
Le Commerce ** - *Fécamp* - 76400 -
(1 'chimney') - 23 rooms -
Tel (33) 2 35 28 19 28 - Fax (33) 2 35 28 70 50
E.mail : lecommerce@hotel-lecommerce.com
Hôtel Normandy ** - *Fécamp* - 76400 -
(1 'chimney') - 30 rooms -
Tel (33) 2 35 29 55 11 - Fax (33) 2 35 27 48 74
Info@normandy-fecamp.com
La Paix ** - *Forges-les-Eaux* - 76440 -
(2 'chimney') - 18 rooms -
Tel (33) 2 35 90 51 22 - Fax (33) 2 35 09 83 62
E.mail : contact@hotellapaix.com
Le Vert Bocage ** - *Franqueville-Saint-Pierre* - 76520 -
(2 'chimney') - 19 rooms -
Tel (33) 2 35 80 14 74 - Fax (33) 2 35 80 55 73
Au Souper Fin - *Frichemesnil* - 76690 -
(2 'chimney') - 2 rooms -
Tel (33) 2 35 33 33 88 - Fax (33) 2 35 33 50 42
E.mail : eric.buisset@free.fr
Hostellerie de la Vieille Ferme ** - *Mesnil-Val* - 76910 -
(2 'chimney') - 31 rooms -
Tel (33) 2 35 86 72 18 - Fax (33) 2 35 86 12 67
Le Relais *** - *Montigny* - 76380 -
(3 'chimney') - 22 rooms -
Tel (33) 2 35 36 05 97 - Fax (33) 2 35 36 19 60
E.mail : info@relais-de-montigny.com
Les Airelles ** - *Neufchatel-en-Bray* - 76270 -
(2 'chimney') - 14 rooms -

Tel (33) 2 35 93 14 60 - Fax (33) 2 35 93 89 03
E.mail : les-airelles-sarl@wanadoo.fr
Le Grand Cerf ** - *Neufchatel-en-Bray* - 76270 -
(1 'chimney') - 12 rooms -
Tel (33) 2 35 93 00 02 - Fax (33) 2 35 94 14 92
E.mail : grand-cerf.hotel@wanadoo.fr
Hôtel des Elfes * - *Notre-Dame-de-Bondeville* - 76960 -
(1 'chimney') - 6 rooms -
Tel (33) 2 35 74 36 21 - Fax (33) 2 35 75 27 09
L'Eolienne ** - *Rouxmesnil-Bouteilles* - 76370 -
(2 'chimney') - 15 rooms -
Tel (33) 2 32 14 40 00 - Fax (33) 2 32 14 40 18
E.mail : grosset.philippe@wanadoo.fr
Auberge de la Rouge ** - *Saint-Léonard* - 76400 -
(2 'chimney') - 8 rooms -
Tel (33) 2 35 28 07 59 - Fax (33) 2 35 28 70 55
E.mail : auberge-rouge@wanadoo.fr
Au nom de Jésus ** - *Saint-Romain-de-Colbosc* - 76430 -
(1 'chimney') - 14 rooms -
Tel (33) 2 35 20 04 79 - Fax (33) 2 35 20 87 98
E.mail : au-nom-de-jesus@wanadoo.fr
La Marine - *Saint-Valery-en-Caux* - 76460 -
(1 'chimney') - 7 rooms -
Tel (33) 2 35 97 05 09 - Fax (33) 2 35 97 05 09
http : //lemurmure.free.fr/la marine.htm
Le Relais des Dalles - *Sassetot-le-Mauconduit* - 76540 -
(3 'chimney') - 4 rooms -
Tel (33) 2 35 27 41 83 - Fax (33) 2 35 27 13 91
E.mail : le-relais-des-dalles@wanadoo.fr
La Marine ** - *Tancarville* - 76430 -
(2 'chimney') - 9 rooms -
Tel (33) 2 35 39 77 15 - Fax (33) 2 35 38 03 30
E.mail : la.marine@wanadoo.fr
Le Saint-Yves ** - *Le Tréport* - 76470 -
(1 'chimney') - 16 rooms -
Tel (33) 2 35 86 34 66 - Fax (33) 2 35 86 53 73
Hôtel Normand ** - *Yport* - 76111 -
(1 'chimney') - 13 rooms -
Tel (33) 2 35 27 30 76 - Fax (33) 2 35 28 70 37
Auberge du Val au Cesne - *Yvetot-Croixmare* - 76190 -
(3 'chimney') - 5 rooms -
Tel (33) 2 35 56 63 06 - Fax (33) 2 35 56 92 78
E.mail : val-au-cesne@hotmail.com
Hôtel du Havre ** - *Yvetot* - 76190 -
(2 'chimney') - 28 rooms -
Tel (33) 2 35 95 16 77 - Fax (33) 2 35 95 21 18

Local Speciality Menu

In all Logis de France restaurants,
Local specialities are based on a **search of authenticity** and the **optimisation of the region's own recipes.** The dishes are prepared using **fresh produce** for a combination of **quality** and **flavour.**

Fédération Régionale des Logis de France
Maison du département de la Manche
50008 Saint-Lô Cedex
Tel (33) 2 33 05 94 54 - Fax (33) 2 33 05 98 16

Fédération Nationale des Logis de France
83, avenue d'Italie - 75013 Paris
Tel (33) 1 45 84 70 00 - Fax (33) 1 45 83 59 66
www.logis-de-france.fr

USEFUL ADDRESSES

British Embassy in France
35, rue du Faubourg Saint-Honoré 75383 - Paris cedex 08
Switchboard : Tel (33) 1 44 51 51 31 00 - Fax (33) 1 44 51 31 27
- Visa service : 16, rue d'Anjou - Tel (33) 1 44 51 31 01
- Consular services :18 bis, rue d'Anjou - Tel (33) 1 44 51 31 02
- Trade office : Tel (33) 1 44 51 34 56
- Press office amd information : Tel (33) 1 44 51 32 81
Web Site : www.amb-grandebretagne.fr
Minitel: 3615 GBRETAGNE (0,20 ~ per minute)

Tourism
- Comité Régional du Tourisme de Normandie
Le Doyenné - 14, rue Charles-Corbeau - 27000 Evreux
Tel (33) 2 32 33 79 00 - Fax (33) 2 32 31 19 04 - www.normandy-tourism ora

- Comité Départemental du Tourisme de la Manche
Maison du département - Rond-Point de la Liberté - 50008 Saint-Lô cedex
Tel.: (33) 0 33 05 98 70 - Fax (33) 2 33 56 07 03 - www.manchetourisme.com

- Comité Départemental du Tourisme du Calvados
Place du Canada - 14000 Caen cedex
Tel (33) 2 3 1 27 90 30 - Fax (33) 21 27 90 35

- Comité Départemental du Tourisme de l'Orne
88, rue Saint-Blaise - BP 50 - 61002 Alençon cedex
Tel (33) 2 33 28 88 71 - Fax (33) 2 33 29 81 60
Internet : ornetourisme.com

- Comité Départemental du Tourisme de l'Eure
Hôtel du Département - Boulevard Georges-Chauvin - BP 367 27000 Evreux cedex
Tel (33) 2 32 62 04 27 - Fax (33) 2 32 31 05 98 - www.cdt-eure.fr

- Comité Départemental du Tourisme de Seine-Maritime
6, rue Couronné - BP 60 - 76420 Bihorel
Tel (33) 2 35 12 10 10 - Fax (33) 2 35 59 86 04.

- Fédération Régionale des Pays d'Accueil Touristique de Normandie.
Conseil Régional de Basse-Normandie - Abbaye aux Dames
Place Reine-Mathilde - 14035 Caen cedex
Tel (33) 2 31 06 98 04 - Fax (33) 2 31 06 97 81

Transports

- Axe Calais-Bayonne
Chambre de Commerce et d'Industrie d'Alençon - BP 42 - 61002 Alençon cedex
Tel (33) 2 33 82 82 82 - Fax (33) 2 33 32 10 16 - www.axe-calais-bayonne.com

- Caen Airport
Route de Caumont - 14650 Carpiquet
Tel (33) 2 31 71 20 10 - Fax (33) 2 31 26 01 92 - www.caen.cci.fr

Cherbourg - Octeville - Maupertus Airport
50330 Gonneville - Te (33) 2 33 88 57 60 - Fax (33) 2 33 22 90 64

- Deauville - Saint-Gatien Airport
14130 - Saint-Gatien-des-Bois - Tel (33) 2 31 65 65 65 - Fax (33) 2 31 65 46
46www.aeroport.fr - Regular flights to London during the season.

- Le Havre Airport
Rue Louis-Blériot - 76620 Le Havre
Tel (33) 2 35 54 65 00 - Fax (33) 2 35 54 65 29 www:havre.aeroport.fr
Regular flights to England.

- Rouen - Vallée de Seine Airport
Rue Maryse-Bastié - 76520 Boos
Tel (33) 2 35 79 41 00 - Fax (33) 2 35 79 41 22 - www.rouen.aeroport.fr

- SNCF (Société Nationale des Chemins de Fer Français)
Direction régionale : 19, rue de l'Avalasse - BP 696 - 76089 Rouen cedex
Tel (33) 2 35 52 10 00 - Fax (33) 2 35 52 18 49 - www.sucf.com

- Brittany Ferries Normandie

At Ouistreham/Caen
Avenue du Grand Large - 14150 Ouistreham
Tel (33) 2 31 36 36 36 - Fax (33) 2 31 36 36 12 - www.britanny-ferries.fr

At Cherbourg-Octeville
Quai de Normandie - 50100 Cherbourg-Octeville
Tel (33) 2 383 88 44 44 - Fax (33) 2 33 88 44 05

Agri-business

IRQUA Normandie (Institut de la Qualité Agroalimentaire de Norrnandie),
Agropole Normandie Chambre Régionale d'Agriculture - 6, rue des Roquemonts -
14053 Caen cedex 4 - Tel (33) 2 31 47 22 47 - Fax (33) 2 31 47 22 60.

LIST OF TOWNS MENTIONED IN THE GUIDE

For more information consult our map or 'Michelin' map of Normandy

MANCHE

Agneaux B9
Agon-Coutainville B3
Angoville-sur-Ay B3
Anneville-sur-Saire B1
Annoville B3
Ardevon A4
Auderville A1
Avranches B3
Azeville B2
Auvers B2
Bacilly B3
Barenton B3
Barfleur B1
Barneville-Carteret A2
Baudre B3
Beauchamps B3
Beaumont-Hague A1
Beauvoir A4
Beuzeville-la-Bastille B2
Blainville-sur-Mer A3
Brécey B3
Bréhal A3
Bréville-sur-Mer A3
Bricquebec A2
Brix A2
Brouains B3
Brucheville B2
Canisy B2
Carentan B2
Carquebut B2
Carolles A3
Cérences A3
Ceaux B4

Cerisy-la-Forêt B2
Champcey B3
Chanteloup A3
La Chapelle-en-Juger B3
Chaulieu B3
Île Chausey A3
Chef-du-Pont B2
Cherbourg - Octeville A1
La Colombe B3
Condé-sur-Vire B3
Contrières B3
Cosqueville B1
Courtils B4
Coutances B3
Créances A2
Denneville A2
Donville-les-Bains A3
Dragey A3
Ducey B4
Ecoqueneauville B2
Equeurdreville-
   Hainneville A1
Fermanville B1
Fierville-les-Mines A2
Flamanville A2
Foucarville B2
Le Fresne-Poret B3
Gatteville B1
Gavray B3
Genêts A3
Ger B3
Giéville B2
La Glacerie A1
Gouvets B3
Gouville-sur-Mer A2

Goury A1
Graignes B2
Le Grand-Celland B3
Granville A3
Gratôt A2
Gréville-Hague A1
Hambye B3
Hauteville-la-Guichard B3
La Haye-Pesnel B3
La Haye-du-Puits A3
Herenguerville A3
Hiesville B2
Huisne-sur-Mer B4
Isigny-le-Buat B4
Jullouville A3
Juvigny-le-Tertre B3
Lessay A2
Liesville-sur-Douve B2
Lingreville A3
Les Loges-Marchis B4
La Lucerne-d'Outremer A3
Marigny B2
Marchesieux B2
Martinvast A2
Le Mesnil-au-Val B1
Milly B4
Montbray B3
Montchaton A3
Montebourg B2
Montjoie-Saint-Martin B4
Montmartin-sur-Mer A3
Montpinchon B3
Le Mont-Saint-Michel A4
Mortain B4
Muneville-le-Bingard A3

Le Nez-de-Jobourg A1
Omonville-la-Petite A1
Omonville-la-Rogue A1
Orval A3
Ouville B3
Percy B3
Périers B2
La Pernelle B1
Le Petit-Celland B3
Picauville B2
Les Pieux A2
Pirou A2
Poilley B4
Pontaubault B4
Pont-Hébert B3
Pontorson A4
Port-Bail A2
Précey B4
Querqueville A1
Quettehou B2
Quettreville-sur-Sienne A2
Guilberville B3
Quineville B2
Rauville-la-Place B2
Ravenoville B2
Régneville-sur-Mer A3
Réville B2
Rocheville A2
Roncey B3
Ronthon A3
La Rondhaye A2
Sacey B4
Saint-Aubin-des-Préaux A3
Saint-Côme-du-Mont B2
Saint-Denis-le-Gast B3
Saint-Georges-de-la-
    Rivière A2
Saint-Georges-de-Livoye B3

Saint-Germain-des-Vaux A1
Saint-Germain-sur-Ay A2
Saint-Hilaire-du-Harcouët B4
Saint-Hilaire-Petitville B2
Saint-James B4
Saint-Jean-des-Champs A3
Saint-Jean-de-Daye B2
Saint-Jean-la-Rivière A2
Saint-Jean-le-Thomas A3
Saint-Laurent-de-Cuves B3
Saint-Lô B3
Saint-Marcouf-de-l'Isle B2
Sainte-Marie-du-Mont B2
Saint-Martin-d'Aubigny A2
Saint-Martin-de-Landelles B4
Sainte-Mère-Eglise B2
Saint-Michel-de-Montjoie B4
Saint-Pair-sur-Mer A3
Saint-Patrice-de-Claids B2
Saint-Pierre-Eglise B1
Saint-Pois B4
Saint-Quentin-sur-le-Homme B4
Saint-Romphaire B2
Saint-Sauveur-Landelin A2
Saint-Sauveur-le-Vicomte B2
Saint-Vaast-la-Hougue B2
Sartilly A3
Saussey B3
Savigny B3
Sebeville B2
Sourdeval B3
Surtainville A2
Île de Tatihou B2
Tanis B4
Le Teilleul B4
Tessy-sur-Vire B2
Teurtheville-Hague A2
Le Theil B1

Tocqueville B1
Tonneville A1
Torigni-sur-Vire ou
    Torigny B3
Tourlaville B1
Tréauville A2
Urville-Nacqueville A1
Vains B4
Valcanville B1
Valognes B2
Le Val-Saint-Père B4
Varouville B1
Le Vast B1
Vaudrimesnil A2
Vauville A1
Ver B3
Les Veys B2
Vierville B2
Villedieu-les-Poêles B3
Vindefontaine B2

CALVADOS

Amayé-sur-Seulles C3
Annebault D2
Argences C3
Arromanches C2
Asnelles C2
Aubigny C3
Auberville D2
Aunay-sur-Odon C3
Balleroy B2
Bavent C2
Bayeux C2
Beaufour-Druval D2
Beaumont-en-Auge D2
Bellengreville C2
Bellou D3

Bénouville (Val-es-Dunes) C2
Bény-Bocage B3
Bernesq B2
Bernières-d'Ailly C3
Bernières-sur-Mer C2
Bernière-le-Patry C3
Beuvillers D3
Beuvron -en-Auge C2
Blainville-sur-Orne C2
Blangy-le-Château D2
Blonville-sur-Mer D2
Bonnebosq D2
Bonneville-sur-Touques D2
Bretteville-sur-Laize C3
Bretteville-l'Orgueilleuse C2
Le Breuil-en-Auge D2
Cabourg C2
Caen C2
Cahagnes B3
Cairon C2
La Cambe B2
Cambremer D3
Campeaux B3
Canapville D2
Canon C3
Carpiquet D2
Carville B3
Caumont-l'Eventé B3
Cesny-aux-Vignes C3
Chicheboville C3
Chiffretot D3
Chouains C2
Clécy C3
Clinchamps-sur-Orne C3
Colleville-sur-Mer B2
Colleville-Montgomery C2
Colombelles C2
Colombiers-sur-Seulles C2

Condé-sur-Noireau C3
Coquainvilliers D3
Coupesarte D3
Courseulles-sur-Mer C2
Courtonne-la-Meurdrac D3
Crépon C2
Creully C2
Crévecœur-en-Auge D2
Criquebœuf D2
Cuverville C2
Dampierre B3
Deauville D2
Démouville C3
Dives-sur-Mer C2
Douvres-la-Délivrande C2
Dozulé C2
Equemeauville D2
Etreham B2
Evrecy C3
Falaise C3
La Ferrière-Harang B3
Fervaques D3
Fleury-sur-Orne C3
Fontaine-Henry C2
Fontenay-le-Marmion C3
Formentin D2
Formigny B2
Le Gast B3
Giberville C3
Goupillères C3
Grainville C3
Grandcamp-Maisy B2
Graye-sur-Mer C2
Grimbosq (forêt de) C3
Heurtevent D3
Hermanville-sur-Mer C2
Hérouville-Saint-Clair C2
Honfleur D2

Hottot-les-Bagues B3
Houlgate D2
Ifs C3
Isigny B2
Jurques B3
Landelles et Coupigny B3
Langrune-sur-Mer C2
Lantheuil C2
Lion-sur-Mer C2
Lisieux D3
Lisores D3
Livarot D3
Longues-sur-Mer C2
Louvigny C3
Luc-sur-Mer C2
Malloué B3
Maltot C3
Maisoncelles-la-Jourdan B3
Maisoncelles-Pelvey B3
May-sur-Orne C3
Merville-Franceville C2
Le Mesnil-Guillaume D3
Le Mesnil-Mauger D3
Mézidon C3
Le Molay-Littry B2
Montfiquet B2
Mouen C3
Mondeville C2
Mont-Bertrand B3
Montpinçon D3
Moyaux D3
Norrey-en-Auge D3
Norrey-en-Bessin C2
Noron-la-Poterie B2
Noyers-Bocage C2
L'Oudon-Garnetot D3
Orbec-en-Auge D3
Ouilly-le-Vicomte D3

Saint-Denis-sur-Sarthon C4

Sainte-Eugénie D3

Saint-Evroult-Notre-
Dame-du-Bois D3

Saint-Fraimbault B4

Sainte-Gauburge/Sainte-
Colombe D4

Saint-Georges-des-
Groseillers C3

Saint-Jean-des-Bois B3

Saint-Lambert-sur-Dives D3

Sainte-Marie-du-Vieux-
Bellême D4

Saint-Ouen-sur-Iton E3

Saint-Sauveur-de-Carrouges
C4

Saint-Sulpice-sur-Risle D3

Saint-Victor-de-Réno E4

Le Sap D3

La Sauvagère C4

Ségrie-Fontaine C3

Sées D4

Sérans D3

Sévigny D3

Silly-en-Gouffern D3

Soligny-la-Trappe E4

Le Theil-sur-Huisne D4

Ticheville D3

Tinchebray C3

Les Tourailles C3

Tournai-sur-Dives D3

Tourouvre E4

Trun D3

Urou-et-Crennes D3

Villers-en-Ouche D3

Vimoutiers D3

Vingt-Hanaps D4

Vitrai-sur-l'Aigle E3

EURE

Acquigny E3

Amfreville-sur-les-Monts E3

Les Andelys E2

Avrilly E3

La Barre-en-Ouche D3

Les Barils E3

Les Baux-Sainte-Croix D3

Bazincourt-sur-Epte F2

Beaumesnil D3

Beaumont-le-Roger D3

Le Bec-Hellouin D2

Bernay D3

Berville-sur-Mer D2

Berthouville D2

Beuzeville D2

Bézu-la-Forêt E2

Bézu-Saint-Eloi F2

Bonneville E3

Bourg-Achard E2

Bourgtheroulde E2

Breteuil-sur-Iton E3

Brionne D2

Broglie D3

Cailly-sur-Eure E3

Le Chamblac D3

Château-sur-Epte F2

Chauvincourt-Provemont F3

Chavigny-Bailleul E3

Colletot D2

Conches-en-Ouche E3

Conteville D2

Cormeilles D2

Corneville-sur-Risle D2

Courcelle F3

Coudray F2

Damville E3

Drucourt D3

Ecardenville-la-Campagne
D3

Ecouis F3

Etrepagny F3

Evreux E3

Ezy-sur-Eure E3

Francheville E3

Fatouville D2

Fourmetot D2

Gaillon E3

Gisors F2

Giverny E3

Giverville D2

Goupillères D3

Gravigny E3

Harcourt D2

Hardencourt-Cocherel E3

La Haye-de-Routot D2

Igoville E2

Ivry-la-Bataille F3

Lieurey D2

Lisors E2

Louviers E2

Lyons-la-Forêt E2

Mandres E3

Marbœuf E3

Menesqueville E2

Ménilles E3

Merey E3

Montfort-sur-Risle D2

Morainville-Jouveaux D2

Mortemer E2

Moulineaux E2

Neauphles E3

Le Neubourg E3

Nonancourt E3

Pacy-sur-Eure E3
Parville E3
Perriers-sous-Andelle E2
Plasnes D3
Pont-Audemer D2
Pont-de-l'Arche E2
Pont-Authou D2
Pont-Saint-Pierre E2
Poses E3
Quillebœuf D2
Radepont E2
Routot D2
La Rivière-Thibouville E3
Saint-André-de-l'Eure E3
Saint-Armand-des-Hautes-Terres E2
Saint-Clair-sur-Epte F2
Saint-Georges-Motel E3
Saint-Georges-du-Vièvre D2
Saint-Germain-de-Pasquier E2
Saint-Germain-Village D2
Sainte-Opportune-la-Mare D2
Saint-Ouen-de-Pontcheuil E2
Saint-Ouen-du-Teilleul E2
Saint-Ouen-de-Thouberville E2
Saint-Rémy-sur-Avre E3
Thiberville D2
Tillères-sur-Avre E3
Le Tilleul-Dame-Agnès E3
Tosny F3
Toutainville D2
Val-de-Reuil E2
Vascœuil E2
Vatteville E2
Le Vaudreuil E2
Verneuil-sur-Avre E3
Vernon E3

Vieux-Port D2
Vitot E3

SEINE-MARITIME

Allouville-Bellefosse D2
Amfreville-la-Mie-Voie E2
Angerville-Bailleul D2
Anneville-sur-Scie E1
Ardouval E1
Arques-la-Bataille E1
Auffay E1
Aumale F1
Autretot D2
Auzouville-sur-Ry E2
Bacqueville-en-Caux E1
Bardouville E2
Barentin E2
Beaumont-le-Hareng E1
Beauval-en-Caux E1
Bellencombre E1
Bénouville D1
Bézancourt E2
Blangy-sur-Bresle F1
Blosseville-sur-Mer E1
Bois-Guilbert E2
Bolbec D2
Bois-Guillaume E2
Le Bois-Robert E1
Boissay E2
Bonsecours E2
Bosc-Guérard Saint-Adrien E2
Bosc-le-Hard E2
Bosc-Roger-sur-Buchy E2
La Bouille E2

Le Bourg-Dun E1
Bourville E1
Brémontier-Merval F2
Bretteville-du-Grand-Caux D2
Buchy E2
Canteleu E2
Cany-Barville D1
Canville-les-Deux-Eglises E1
Le Catelier E1
Caudebec-en-Caux E2
Caudebec-lès-Elbeuf E2
La Chapelle-sur-Dun E1
Cideville E2
Claville-Motteville E2
Clères E2
Crasville-la-Rocquefort E1
Criel-sur-Mer E1
Criquetot-l'Esneval D2
Darnétal E2
Derchigny-Graincourt E1
Dieppe E1
Dieppedalle-Croisset E2
Doudeville E1
Duclair E2
Elbeuf E2
Envermeu E1
Ermenouville E1
Etaimpuis E2
Etretat D1
Eu E1
Fauville-en-Caux D2
Fécamp D1
Fontaine-le-Dun E1
Forges-les-Eaux F2
Foucarmont F1
Franqueville-Saint-Pierre E2
Fréneuse E2

Frichemesnil E2
Goderville D2
Gonfreville-l'Orcher D2
Gonneville E1
Gonneville-la-Mallet D2
Gournay-en-Bray F2
Grainville-la-Teinturière D2
Grainville-Ymauville D2
Le Grand-Quevilly E2
Les Grandes-Ventes E1
Luneray E1
Graville D2
Grémonville E1
Grigneuseville E2
Gruchet-le-Valasse D2
Gueuteville-les-Grés E1
Harfleur D2
Hautot E1
Jumièges E2
Le Hanouard D1
Le Havre D2
Hautot-sur-Mer E1
Héricourt-en-Caux D1
Lillebonne D2
Londinières E1
Longueville-sur-Scie E1
Luneray E1
Maniquerville D1
Martainville D2
Mauquenchy E2
Mesnières-en-Bray E2
Le Mesnil-Durdent E1
Le Mesnil-Esnard E2
Le Mesnil-Follemprise E1
Le Mesnil-Jourdain E2
Le Mesnil-sous-Jumièges E2
Mesnil-Val E1
Montigny E2
Montivilliers D2
Montville E2
Montmain E2

Monterolier E2
Mont-Saint-Aignan E2
Montvilliers D2
Moulineaux E2
Muchedent E1
Neufchatel-en-Bray E1
Notre-Dame-de-Bondeville E2
Oherville D1
Offranville E1
Oissel E2
Orival E2
Ourville-en-Caux D1
Pavilly D2
Petit-Couronne E2
Le Petit-Quevilly E2
Port-Jérôme D2
Pierrecourt F1
Pourville E1
Quevillon E2
Quiévrecourt E2
Quillebœuf D2
Rosay E1
Rouen E2
Rouen-Boos E2
Roumare E2
Roncheville-en-Bray E2
Rouxmesnil-Bouteilles E1
Rouvray-Catillon E2
La Rue-Saint-Pierre E2
Ry E2
Saint-Aubin-lès-Elbeuf E2
Saint-Aubin-sur-Mer E1
Saint-Aubin-sur-Scie E1
Saint-Aubin-le-Cauf E1
Saint-Denis-Chef-de-Caux E2
Saint-Denis-le-Thiboult E2
Saint-Etienne-du-Rouvray E2
Saint-Jacques-sur-Darnétal E2
Saint-Jean-du-Cardonnay E2

Saint-Léger-aux-Bois F1
Saint-Léger-du-Bourg-Denis E2
Saint-Léonard D1
Saint-Maclou-de-Folleville E1
Saint-Martin-de-Boscherville E2
Saint-Martin-des-Champs D2
Saint-Nicolas-d'Aliermont E1
Saint-Pierre-lès-Elbeuf E2
Saint-Pierre-le-Viger E1
Saint-Romain-de-Colbosc D2
Saint-Saëns E2
Saint-Valery-en-Caux E1
Saint-Wandrille D2
Sainte-Croix-sur-Buchy E2
Sassetot-le-Mauconduit D1
Sept-Meules F1
Sommery E2
Sotteville-sur-Mer E1
Sotteville-le-Val E2
Tancarville D2
Tôtes E2
Tourville-les-Ifs D1
Tourville-sur-Arques E1
Le Trait E2
Le Tréport E1
Val-de-la-Haye E2
Valmont D1
Varengeville-sur-Mer E1
Veules-les-Roses E1
Veulettes-sur-Mer D1
Villequiers D2
Yainville D2
Yerville E2
Yport D1
Yvetot E2

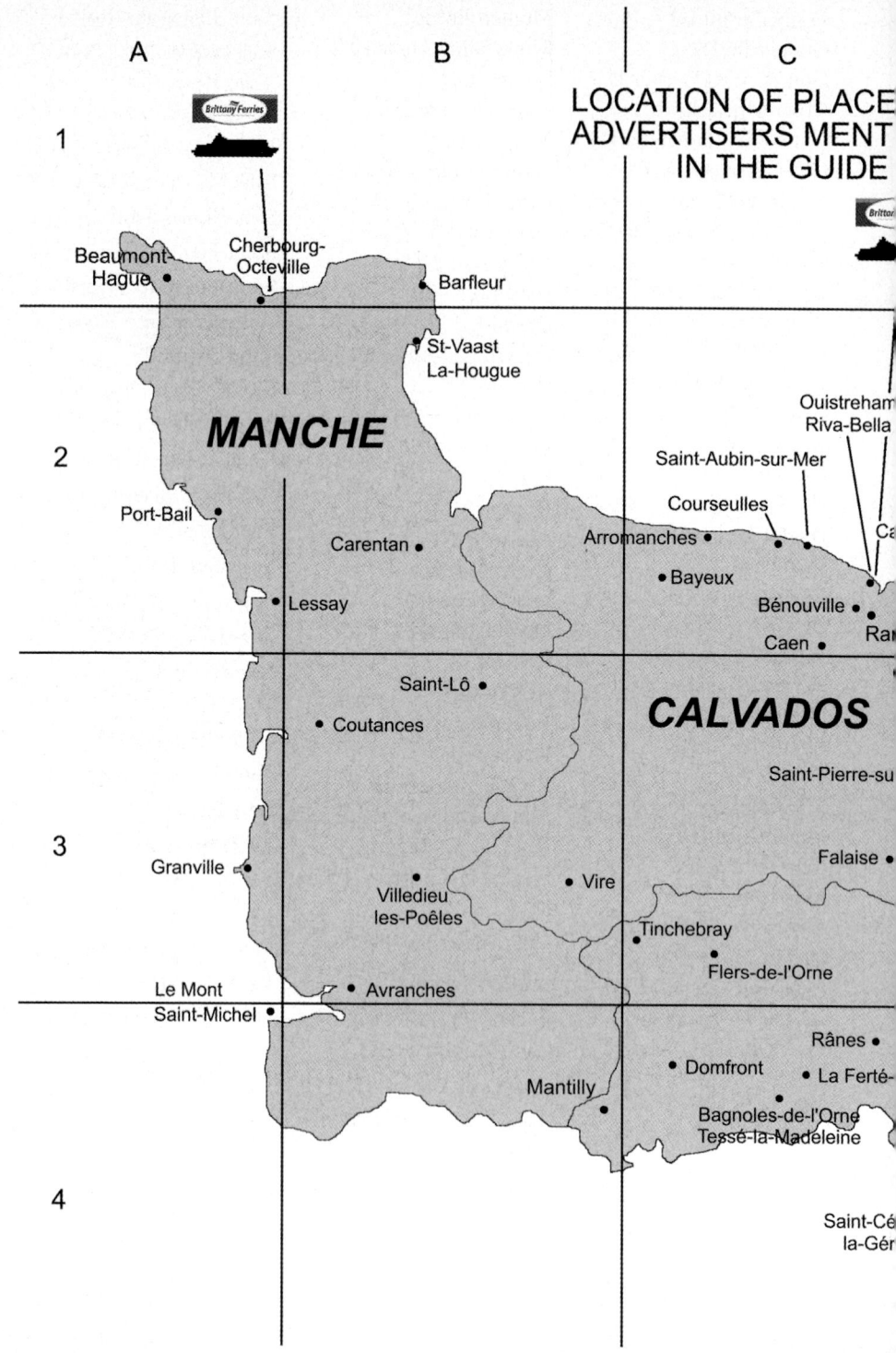

LOCATION OF PLACE
ADVERTISERS MENT
IN THE GUIDE

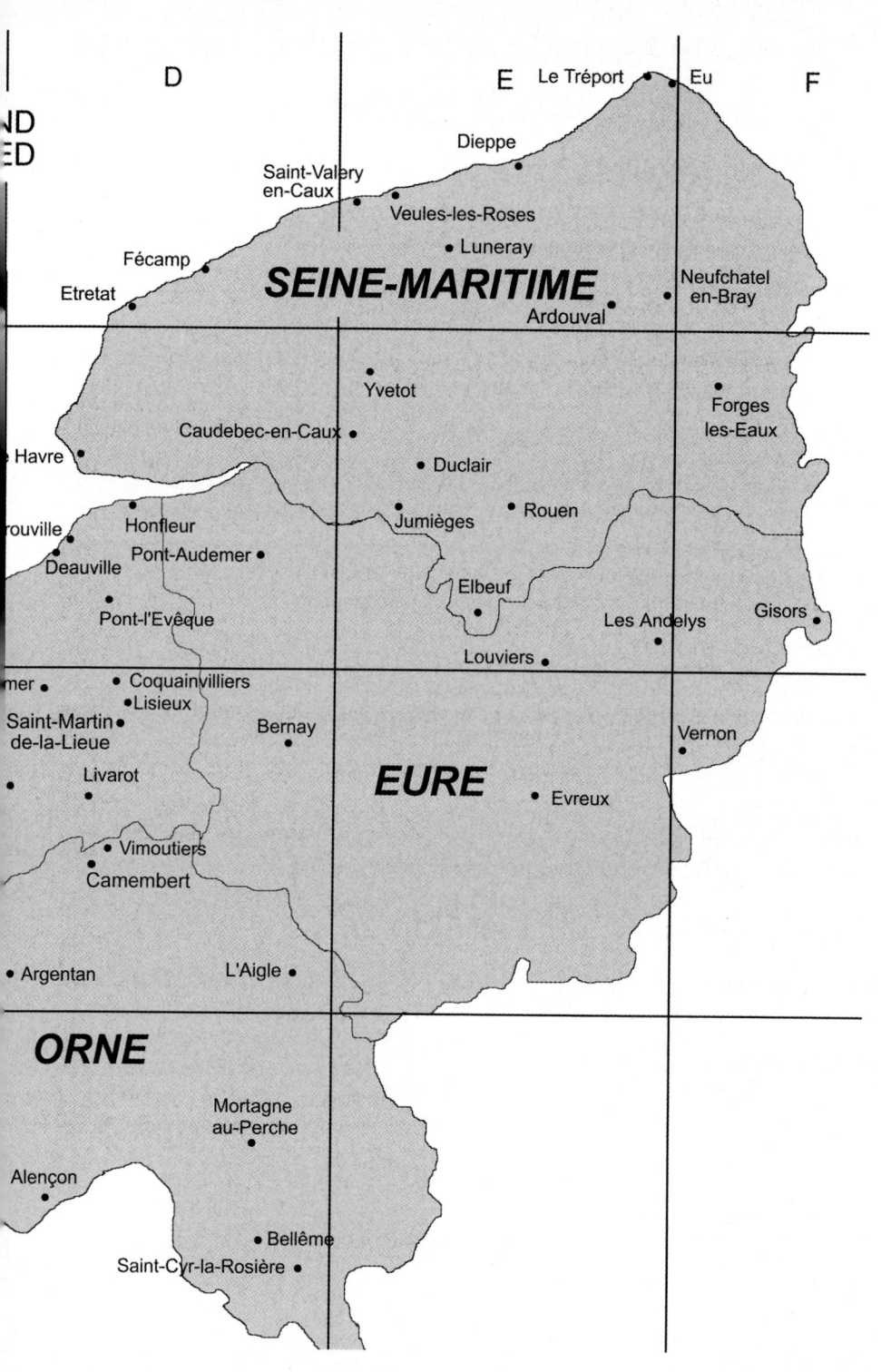

LIST OF ADVERTISERS MENTIONED IN THE GUIDE

AREA OF MANCHE

Comité départemental du Tourisme de la Manche   **p. 86-87 ; 390-391**   **B3**
Saint-Lô
Tel 0800 028 6572 or (33) 2 33 05 98 70 - Fax (33) 2 33 56 07 03
Internet : www.manchetourisme.com - E-mail : manchetourisme@cg50.fr

Ville d'Avranches   **p. 83 ; 395**   **B3**
Tel (33) 2 33 58 00 22 - Internet : www.ville.avranches.fr

Musée du Meuble   **p. 85 ; 387**   **B3**
9, rue du Reculé - Villedieu -les-Poêles - Tel (33) 2 33 61 11 78

Le Village Enchanté   **p. 95 ; 226**   **B3**
Bellefontaine
Tel (33) 2 33 59 01 93 - Fax (33) 2 33 69 52 60
Internet : www.village-enchante.fr - E-mail : village-enchante@wanadoo.fr

Cité de la Mer   **p. 75 ; 393**   **A1**
Cherbourg-Octeville
Tel (33) 825 33 50 50 - Internet : www.citedelamer.com

District de La Hague   **3ᵉ de couv ; 392 A1**
Beaumont - Tel (33) 2 33 52 74 94

Luciver (Observatory-planetarium at Cap de la Hague)   **p. 77**   **A1**
Beaumont
Tel (33) 2 33 78 13 00 - Internet : www.ludiver.com

Brittany Ferries   **p. 72 ; 398**   **A1**
Cherbourg-Octeville
Tel 0870 908 9699 - Internet : www.britannyferries.com

AREA OF CALVADOS

Halle aux Vins   **p. 254 ; 277**   **D2**
10, quai de la Touques - Deauville - Tel/Fax (33) 2 31 98 33 85

Halle aux Vins   **p. 254 ; 277**   **D2**
6, rue du Bouloir - Honfleur - Tel (33) 2 31 89 11 60

Ville de Lisieux   **p. 109 ; 388**   **D2**
Tel (33) 2 31 48 18 10

Musée du Débarquement - Ranville   **p. 65 ; 389**   **C2**
Tel (33) 2 31 78 19 44 - Fax (33) 2 31 78 19 42

Musée du Débarquement - Arromanches   **p. 65 ; 389**   **C2**
Tel (33) 2 31 22 34 31 - Fax (33) 2 31 92 68 83
Internet : www.normandy1944.com

Ville de Caen   **3ᵉ de couv ; 396**   **C2**
Tel (33) 2 31 27 14 14 - Internet : www.ville-caen.fr

Connaissance des Jardins   **p. 374**   **C2**
26, avenue de Thiès - Caen - Tel/Fax (33) 2 31 08 27 21
E.mail : connaissance-des-jardins@wanadoo.fr

Domaine Saint-Hippolyte   **p. 109 ; 388**   **D3**
Saint-Martin-de-la-Lieue - Tel (33) 2 31 31 30 68

Espace Boulard - Coquainvilliers   **p. 108 ; 387**   **D3**
Tel (33) 2 31 48 24 01 - Fax (33) 2 31 62 21 22
Internet : www.espace-boulard.com
E-mail : info@espace-boulard.com

Le Relais Côté Jardin   **p. 48 ; 134**   **D2**
20, rue des Buttes - Honfleur
Tel (33) 2 31 89 98 52 or (33) 2 31 98 75 26 - fax (33) 2 31 98 75 21
Internet : www.lerelaiscotejardin.com

Brittany Ferries   **p. 72 ; 398**   **C2**
Ouistreham-Riva-Bella
Tel 0870 908 9699 - Internet : www.britannyferries.com

Landy Valette   **p. 58 ; 417**   **C2**
(Communication and marketing specialists)
Telex 170 268 - Fax (33) 2 31 72 80 03
E-mail : valette.landy@wanadoo.fr

AREA OF ORNE

Ville d'Argentan   **p. 117 ; 394**   **D3**
Tel (33) 2 33 67 12 48.

Office du Tourisme du Pays d'Alençon   **p. 122 ; 385**   **D4**
Place de la Magdeleine - Alençon
Tel (33) 2 33 80 66 33 - Fax (33) 2 33 80 66 32
Internet : www.paysdalencontourisme.com
E-mail : alençon.tourisme@wanadoo.fr

Distillerie Fourmond-Lemorton   **p. 264 ; 274**   **D4**
'Le Douët Gasnier' - Mantilly - Tel/Fax (33) 2 33 38 71 63

Ecomusée du Perche　　　　　　　　　　　　　　p. 120 ; 394　　　**D4**
　　Prieuré de Sainte-Gauburge - Saint-Cyr-la-Rosière
　　Tel (33) 2 33 73 48 04.

Commune de Saint-Céneri-la-Gérei　　　　　　　p. 195 ; 231'　　**C4**

Conseil Général de l'Orne - Alençon　　　　2ᵉ de couv ; 397　　**D2**
　　Tel (33) 2 33 81 60 00 - Internet : www.cg61.fr

Syndicat d'Economie Mixte d'Alençon　　　　　p. 133' ; 385　　**D4**
　　Hôtel de Ville d'Alençon - Place Foch
　　Tel (33) 2 33 32 40 00 - Fax (33) 2 33 32 40 66
　　E-mail : joel.mercier@ville-alencon.fr

AREA OF EURE

Ville des Andelys　　　　　　　　　　　　　　p. 128 ; 386　　**E2**
　　Tel (33) 2 32 54 04 16 - Internet : www.villeandelys.fr

Ville d'Evreux　　　　　　　　　　　　　　　　p. 127 ; 386　　**E3**
　　Tel (33) 2 32 31 82 60

AREA OF SEINE-MARITIME

Ville du Tréport　　　　　　　　　　　　　　　p. 71 ; 386　　**E1**
　　Tel (33) 2 35 86 05 69 - Fax (33) 2 35 86 73 96
　　Internet : www.ville-le-treport.fr - E-mail : officetourismeletreport@wanadoo.fr

Site des V1 du Val-Ygot - Ardouval　　　　　　p. 71　　　　**E1**

Royal Garden　　　　　　　　　　　　　　　　p. 36 ; 384　　**E1**
　　Rue du Marquis de Radiolles - Luneray - Tel (33) 2 35 04 56 32

Editions Bertout　　　　　　　　　　　　　　　p. 329　　　　**E1**
　　6, rue Gutenberg - Luneray - Tel (33) 2 35 04 69 68

IMPRIMERIE NOUVELLE NORMANDIE
76190 Yvetot - France
Dépôt légal : 2ᵉᵐᵉ trimestre 2003
Printed in France